World Studies
for Christian Schools

World Studies

for Christian Schools®

SECOND EDITION

Terri Koontz, B.S.
Mark Sidwell, Ph.D.
S. M. Bunker, M.A.

Bob Jones University Press
Greenville, South Carolina 29614

WORLD STUDIES for Christian Schools® Second Edition

Terri Koontz, B.S.
Mark Sidwell, Ph.D.
S. M. Bunker, M.A.

Produced in cooperation with the Bob Jones University Department of History of the College of Arts and Science, the School of Religion, and Bob Jones Junior High.

for Christian Schools is a registered
trademark of Bob Jones University Press.

© 1998, 2000 Bob Jones University Press
Greenville, South Carolina 29614
First edition © 1985 Bob Jones University Press

ISBN 1-59166-431-4

15 14 13 12 11 10 9 8 7 6 5 4 3 2

Contents

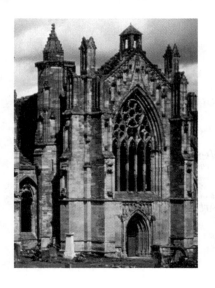

List of Settings Maps

Pronunciation Guide

The pronunciation key used in this text is designed to give readers a self-evident, acceptable pronunciation for a word as they read it from the page. For more nearly accurate pronunciations, consult a good dictionary.

Syllables with primary stress appear in LARGE CAPITAL letters. Syllables with secondary stress and one-syllable words appear in SMALL CAPITAL letters; for example, *Afghanistan* appears as (af GAN uh STAN). Where two or more words appear together, hyphens separate the syllables within each word; for example, the *Rub al Khali* appears as (ROOB ohl KHAH-lee).

Symbol	Example	Symbol	Example
g	get = GET	th	thin = THIN
j	gentle = JEN tul	*th*	then = *TH*EN
s	cent = SENT	zh	lesion = LEE zhun
a	cat = KAT	i-e	might = MITE
ah	cot = KAHT	eye	icy = EYE see
ar	car = KAR	oh	slow = SLOH
aw	all = AWL	ou	loud = LOUD
a-e	cape = KAPE	oy	toil = TOYL
ay	paint = PAYNT	u	some = SUM
e	jet = JET	uh	abet = uh BET
ee	fiend = FEEND	oo	crew = CROO
i	swim = SWIM	*oo*	push = P*OO*SH

As You Like It *by William Shakespeare (Bob Jones University Classic Players)*

Suddenly all is quiet. The flurried activity of the last few hours comes to an end. The months of preparation draw to a close. But this is not an end; it is a beginning. Tonight is opening night. You wait, breathless, for the director to signal the stagehands. Your lines race through your head. Attempting to calm yourself, you smooth your costume, breathe deeply, and take your opening stance. The director signals. The curtain rises. You are now onstage to the delight of your audience and yourself.

If you have ever had a part in a school play or program, you remember the excitement of the occasion. For weeks, or even months, you learned your lines. Your costume was made and pressed. The stage crew worked hard to build props for each scene. The director led you through many practices to help you do your part just right. When performance time came, everyone hoped for a successful production.

What goes into making a play? First, a play has roles—different characters whose actions tell the play's story. Each character has his own personality and actions. Second, a play requires a place to happen—a stage. The stage may be in a clump of trees in your back yard or in an elegant European opera house. It is usually set with scenery and props that add to the action of the play. Third, a drama follows a script that gives the plot of the play. These three elements make a drama a complete production.

The Drama of World Studies

The elements of *world studies* are similar to those in a play. In world studies the roles are played both by individuals and groups of people. Their lives and actions make up their culture. **Culture,** or way of life, is the first element of world studies. The second element is **geography,** through which we learn about the stage, or the earth. The great variety of the earth's landscapes and resources affects the world's cultures. The third element, the script, is history. **History** is the record of how people have lived and what they have done on the earth. Culture, geography, and history are the three elements of world studies.

Plays also have directors to guide the actors and to keep order. In world studies we recognize God as the director of the world's people. In a play the actors are responsible to follow the director's instructions. The person who most closely follows these instructions will have played his role the best. In the drama of world studies, you are under God's direction. The better you follow His instructions, the better you will live your life.

Shared culture fades the lines of ethnic diversity.

Culture

Culture means way of life. You share the same culture with many other people around you because they live in much the same way that you do. They may not get up in the morning at the same time you do or dress in the same brand of clothes that you wear. Nevertheless, your family, friends, fellow church members, neighbors in your community, and even many of your fellow countrymen have similar activities, interests, and opportunities. Thus, you have a shared culture—a shared way of life—with them.

For example, many Americans enjoy watching and playing baseball, a distinctively Ameri-can activity. Most Americans claim some form of Christianity as their religion. Americans also expect to elect their governmental leaders and to buy and sell goods and services in local businesses. These features are part of the basic American culture.

People living in other countries often have much different cultures. They speak different languages and play different games. They may be ruled by a powerful dictator. They may have to raise most of the food they eat. Their children may not be able to attend school. The different experiences of these people set their cultures apart from yours.

You will be able to understand other cultures by comparing them with your own culture. As you compare specific activities of your way of life with those of others, you will see differences and similarities. To help you in this study, we will divide culture into six areas.

1. Government

Every group of people has some form of government, or way of ruling itself. For example, a government may be ruled by an all-powerful king, a committee of ten members, or a pure democracy in which each citizen votes on every issue. As we study different cultures, ask yourself, "How do these people govern themselves? What is their form of government?"

2. Economics

Every group of people has used the earth's resources to make or grow goods to use or sell. Bartering for a sweet potato crop in a South American street market or purchasing a complex computer by special order from a Japanese company are both examples of economic activities. "What do these people produce? How and what do they buy and sell?" are the economic questions you should ask about each group of people.

3. Religion

Every group of people has some religious beliefs and some form of worship. They may bow to idols, follow a man's teaching, or obey the truth of Scripture. To find out about religion, ask, "What and how do they worship? What are their beliefs?"

4. Society

Every group of people has families and communities that make up its society. A society may tend to have large families or small families, several social classes or none. In this area you will also find information about daily life and customs. Ask the questions "What are their families and communities like? What are some of their daily activities?"

5. Thought and Learning

Every group of people forms ideas and has some way of teaching its members. This area includes achievements in speaking, writing, mathematics, science, and thought. It also includes their methods of education. The questions to ask are "What do they think about? How do they learn?"

6. Arts and Crafts

Every group of people has arts and crafts. Art includes painting, sculpture, architecture, and music. Crafts are handmade items used as decoration, household items, or tools. Pottery, fabrics, and jewelry are some examples of crafts. As you study each group, ask yourself, "What are their arts and crafts?"

Because God created and controls our world, we can see His handiwork reflected in various cultures. God established government and laws because fallen man needs to be restrained. God filled the earth with resources to meet man's physical needs. God created man in His own image and likeness. Man's need to worship shows his spiritual nature, and his need for fellowship shows his social nature. His ability to think is a gift of God, and so is his ability to appreciate beauty.

A people's culture is influenced by their knowledge of God and what they do with that knowledge. Those people who respond well to a knowledge of God and follow biblical principles in their way of life will receive blessing. Those people who reject a knowledge of God and do not live by biblical principles will be judged. God has promised to bless or judge, although in His wisdom and mercy He may delay that action. (See Ps. 103:8-9 and Prov. 14:34.)

No culture is better than the individuals who create it. Your individual culture contributes to your community's culture and your country's culture. Think about your way of life. What is your culture? A Christian's way of life should follow the teachings of Scripture and measure up to God's standards. As you study cultures, see how closely they follow God's standards. By doing this you will also see where you meet or fall short of God's standard. Then you will know what areas of your life need improvement in order to live as God expects you to live.

As you study other cultures, you will learn how to share the gospel with other people because you will better understand their way of life. The Scriptures command Christians to tell the gospel to all people. The more you know about other people, the better your witness will be.

This view of earth from space reveals more of God's wondrous power.

Geography

Geography is the study of the earth, where people live. God created the earth to be a perfect home for mankind. He filled it with all the resources man needs and made it beautiful for man to enjoy. As the psalmist said, "O Lord, how manifold are thy works! in wisdom hast thou made them all: the earth is full of thy riches" (Ps. 104:24). God commanded Adam to subdue the earth, and today we still have the responsibility to be good stewards of God's creation.

Throughout *WORLD STUDIES for Christian Schools* you will find Settings pages like the ones on the next page. These pages contain up-to-date information on the location, climate, topography, natural resources, and economy and shows the connection between the country's geography and its culture. This material provides a quick reference source for you. Page vii lists all the Settings pages in *WORLD STUDIES*.

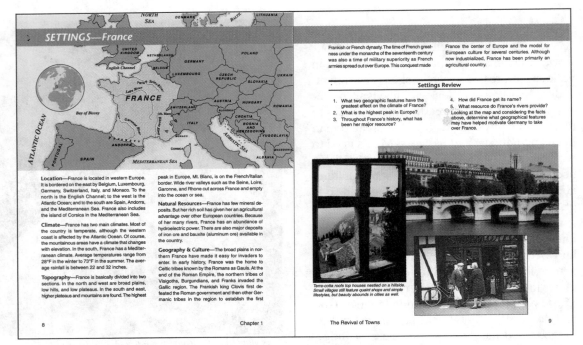

Take a few minutes now to look carefully at this sample.

1. Location

The first section helps you locate the region you are about to study. The small map drawn from the hemisphere map shows you how the country fits into the larger global area. A brief paragraph describes other regions or bodies of water surrounding the area.

2. Climate

The second section of the Settings page describes the climate of the area. The normal weather conditions that a region has throughout the year make up its climate. Weather includes both temperature and precipitation (rain and snowfall). The box will describe the climate based on the climate map on pages 608-9. The climate map divides climate into five basic categories.

3. Topography

In the third section of Settings you will find out about the region's topography (tuh POG ruh fee). Topography means the land features of a region. It also includes a list of major landforms such as mountains, rivers, and plains.

4. Natural Resources and Economy

This section lists the natural resources found in the region, such as minerals, fossil fuels, animal life, and vegetation, such as forests. It also highlights the most important factor in that nation's economy.

5. Geography & Culture

This section discusses how the geography of an area has influenced the culture of the people who live there. For example, if an area is mountainous, are its people isolated, protected, or hindered by the mountains? Reading this section carefully will help you understand more about how the people live and why they live that way.

History

The third element of world studies is history. Like a play script, history supplies the reader with a story to follow. History is the record of past activities and events in the lives of the earth's people. As a play script is divided into sections called acts, history can be divided into time periods. A major theme or idea characterizes the culture in each time period. In *WORLD STUDIES* we have divided history into four acts. Each act contains one theme, which is discussed in the introduction to the act.

UNIT	TIME FRAME
ACT ONE: Changes	1100-1400
ACT TWO: Challenges	1400-1800
ACT THREE: Conquests	1800-1900
ACT FOUR: Conflicts	1900-present

God is the director of history. He has a divine plan in history, which we can discover in part. Only He knows all the future, but we can understand much of the present and the future by what we learn of the past. History presents a series of different cultures from which have come today's cultures. By learning about the lives of these people in the past, you will better understand the lives of people today, including your own.

Throughout history individuals and groups of people have obeyed or disobeyed God. We, as they, are individuals who are responsible for our actions. Either you will submit to God's plan for you and receive eternal life and blessing, or you will ignore His plan and come under certain judgment. Joshua's command to the children of Israel in Joshua 24:15, "Choose you this day whom ye will serve," still applies today. What choice will you make?

The three elements of *WORLD STUDIES for Christian Schools* are culture, geography, and history. Within each act you will study different geographical regions. Each chapter discusses the culture of a people living in a particular place and time period.

As you begin this course of study, ask yourself, "How does my culture fit in? Is the Lord pleased with my culture?"

The Earliest People

In the Beginning

The study of the world begins with the creation of the first people—Adam and Eve. Their story is recorded in the most accurate source of ancient history, the Bible. God made Adam and Eve sinless and put them in a perfect place, the Garden of Eden. Because God created them and the earth perfect, their culture was perfect. God governed them perfectly. All their needs were supplied from the garden. They worshiped God freely and enjoyed His fellowship. They also enjoyed each other's company. Their intelligence was shown by Adam's naming of all the animals that God created. Of course, they enjoyed the beauty of God's creation that surrounded them.

This perfect culture did not last. Adam and Eve made a wrong choice. They decided not to follow God and not to live by His instructions. When they listened to Satan and ate the forbidden fruit, they sinned and were no longer perfect. From then on all men were sinners; as a result, no culture could be perfect.

Because Adam and Eve sinned by disobeying God, God had to judge them. He placed them and the earth under a curse. From that time on, people have needed laws and governments to restrain their wicked ways. They have had to work hard to provide for their needs. Many people have refused to worship the true God but have instead bowed down to idols or to other men. Problems have arisen among people in families and communities, causing quarrels and fights. People have used their intelligence to devise wickedness rather than to please God. Art has reflected not only beauty but also ugliness and sin.

With His judgment, however, God also promised blessing. He promised a way of salvation from sin through His Son, the Lord Jesus Christ. A person can accept God's way of salvation through faith in His Son. Or he can reject God's way and attempt to work out his own salvation. In every culture you study, you will see people accepting either God's way or man's way. But the Bible tells us that God's way alone brings salvation; Jesus said, "I am the way, the truth, and the life: no man cometh unto the Father, but by me" (John 14:6).

The Generations After Adam

In the early chapters of Genesis, Scripture records the events in the lives of people who lived after Adam. Scripture tells us of the earliest civilizations on earth. **Civilization** is characterized by advanced culture. The word *civilization* comes from the Latin word meaning "city." Marks of civilization include permanent towns and cities as well as specialized labor and a written language. Scripture tells us that Cain built a city. His descendants specialized as herdsmen, metalsmiths, and musicians (Gen. 4:17-22). These early people became highly civilized. They also became very sinful.

The people's wickedness grieved the Lord. "And the Lord said, I will destroy man whom I have created from the face of the earth; both man, and beast, and the creeping thing, and the fowls of the air; for it repenteth me that I have made them" (Gen. 6:7). God sent destruction on the earth in the form of a flood. Every living thing on the earth was destroyed—everything except Noah and all those with him in the ark. God saved the one family that had found grace in His sight and that had honored Him and had

chosen to do His will when no one else had. God blessed Noah for his faithfulness and obedience. After the Flood, God promised never to destroy the earth again by a flood. He told Noah and his family to "be fruitful, and multiply, and replenish the earth" (Gen. 9:1).

God's plan was for people to travel over the earth and to inhabit it. But man had another plan. Genesis 11:1-9 describes how the people of the earth came together in the land of Shinar. They built a tower to honor themselves. Because they had not followed God's instructions, He punished their disobedience. He confused their language and scattered the people all over the earth.

And so began the drama of civilization. Confused and displaced, small bands of people came together in groups and formed new cultures in new lands. As time passed, some forgot their common heritage in God, and their cultures became more and more diverse. In Act One we join the drama already in progress as Europe, locked for five hundred years in the Dark Ages, slowly emerges from its cell of ignorance.

ACT ONE

CHANGES

1100 TO 1650

The curtain of history opens to reveal a crisp, clear morning on November 25, 1095. Nobles and peasants have gathered at the town of Clermont in southern France to hear a speech by Pope Urban II, leader of the Roman Catholic Church. Soon the pope's powerful words ring out in the cool air.

> Dearest brethren, I, Urban, supreme pontiff and by the permission of God prelate [bishop] of the whole world, have come in this time of urgent necessity to you, the servants of God in these regions. You must hasten to carry aid to your brethren dwelling in the East, who need your help for which they have often entreated. For the Turks . . . have attacked them. They have seized more and more of the lands of the Christians. If you allow them to continue much longer they will conquer God's faithful people much more extensively. Let nothing delay those who are going to go. Let them settle their affairs, collect money, and when winter has ended and spring has come, zealously undertake the journey under the guidance of the Lord.

With one voice, the people shout, "God wills it!" Their fight would be a holy war—a crusade.

By the spring of 1096, an army of knights, foot soldiers, and other followers are ready to set out for Asia Minor and the Holy Land. For Europeans who have seen little of the world except the country around their manor homes, travel will open a desire for products of the Byzantine Empire, the fine craftsmanship of the Muslims, and the exotic goods of the Far East and Africa. They will find new reward in discovering the knowledge of the Greeks and Romans. But conflict will not end, because Europe itself will be in turmoil as the Reformation challenges the Roman Catholic Church.

By the time the curtain draws closed on this act, Europe will be out of the darkness of the early Middle Ages. They will be threatened by a new enemy—the Mongols. They will have met people they had thought existed only in stories. They will develop skills that will prepare them to explore new lands.

CHAPTER 1

Castles dominated Europe's landscape during the middle part of the Middle Ages, but from the beginning of the Crusades to about 1500 (the late Middle Ages) a change occurred. Although many people continued to live on castle lands, more and more people moved to towns. These new townspeople came from many places for many reasons and started new towns or settled in old ones. Towns grew to dominate the land.

One reason for the growth of towns was Europe's population growth. Improved farming methods meant that farmers could produce more and better crops to feed more people. Better methods in crop production meant that the castle lords needed fewer people to run the castle lands. Many people, no longer needed by their lord, moved to towns.

Another reason for the growth of towns was the growth of trade. Along the trade routes reopened by the crusaders came exotic, desirable goods from the East. Towns became centers of trade for these goods.

Finally, towns became a place of opportunity. Poor farmers and craftsmen struck out on their own in towns, and soon merchants and craftsmen challenged the power of the castle lords.

The growth of towns signaled a change in economics and politics that would continue beyond the Middle Ages into the modern world. Slowly the rigidness of class divisions would break down, and the ability to work to improve financially and politically would become a reality. These changes would affect not only local regions but also most of Europe and later, the New World.

A.D. 900 - A.D. 1300

European Dark Ages 476-1095

900

The Revival of Towns

Crusades 1095-1291

| 1000 | 1100 | 1200 | 1300 |

Byzantine Empire 476-1453

Romanesque Architectural Style 1000-1200

Gothic Architectural Style 1200-1500

How a Town Was Formed

Beginning of a Town

The drawing below shows the beginnings of a town: the town's first people and the place they chose to build their town. These weary traders traveled many miles in a normal season of trade. At the start of the season, they bought their goods far in the East and then set out for the West. Travel was dangerous and hard on the few remaining Roman roads of Europe, and often traders had only paths to follow. They could travel only in seasons of good weather. Rather than travel all over Europe to sell their goods, the traders wanted a permanent place in which to sell and also to live during the off-season. The right spot had to be a protected place near a fortress, such as a castle. Because the traders also needed transportation, the site had to be near a river or a major road. The traders in the illustration have found such a place. After obtaining the lord's permission, they will begin to build homes and shops.

Three slender things that best support the world: the slender stream of milk from the cow's dug [udder] into the pail; the slender blade of green corn upon the ground; the slender thread over the hand of a skilled woman.

Three sounds of increase: the lowing of a cow in milk; the din of a smithy [forge]; the swish of a plough.

This excerpt from *The Triads of Ireland* (ninth century) reveals the main income and lifestyle of the Middle Ages. With the increase of towns and movement away from small farms, how would this proverb be affected? What made these sounds pleasant to the medieval farmer and landowner? What would be pleasant sounds to medieval town and city dwellers? If you were asked what three things best support our modern world, what would they be? What would three sounds of increase be?

The Young Town

Once the traders settled permanently, others joined them. Peasant families sometimes bought their freedom from the lord of their castle lands. The second son of a noble knew he would inherit no land. His father's land would go to the first son. A man in his position might decide that the town would be an adventurous place to live. Butchers, bakers, smiths, carpenters, and other craftsmen came to the town to provide their skills for the people. The Roman Catholic Church sent priests to minister to the people of the growing towns. And, of course, more traders came to sell their wares. Some traders stayed and settled in one town, while others moved on to markets in other towns. All who came built houses or workshops, adding to the size of the town.

The Bulging Town

To protect themselves, the first townspeople built walls around their homes and shops. But as the towns continued to grow, the space

inside the walls became too small. Newcomers added more and more stories to existing buildings, making them dangerously high. The town began to bulge at its seams; the time had come to expand. The old walls might come down as new walls went up or the old walls might remain and the town be built outside them, but the town would continue to grow and fill the extra space.

The Chartered Town

The receiving of its charter was an important event in the town's history. The leading men of the town spent much time talking with the lord who owned the land on which the town sat. The lord finally agreed to give the town a charter. The **town charter** was a legal document listing the privileges of the townspeople. This freed the people from many feudal duties and manorial payments. The people still paid taxes to the lord, but they governed themselves. Every year the townspeople celebrated this day with parades and games. The town had grown greatly since the first two traders settled it. The people had worked hard, and at last the town was truly their own.

Section Review

1. Who were the first people to settle in the towns?
2. What other people came to live in the towns?
3. How did towns change to hold more people?
4. What event did the townspeople celebrate every year?
5. List two reasons people moved to towns.

One sentence from the paragraph above says, "The lord finally agreed to give town a charter." What word implies that he did not want to give the town a charter? Give your opinion as to why the lord would not have wanted to give a charter to the town.

Cloves are used to flavor stews and baked goods.

Why Spices?

Using spices in cooking may seem commonplace to you. Just look in your cupboard at home and see the variety of powdered, crushed, or whole seeds and plants that are used in your favorite foods. Now imagine that you are transported to a serf's home in the 1100s. It is winter. The only thing to eat is food that can be dried or stored in barrels. There is coarsely ground grain made into hard brown bread, as well as onions, garlic, beans or peas, and meat. Unfortunately, the meat is dried, pickled, or salted and may be rancid or have insects on it. Your mother seasons your dinner with onions or garlic, and that is not enough to cover the spoiled taste or smell of the meat. Surely you begin to see that, even if the food was not spoiled, spices like ginger, cloves, oregano, and black pepper added zest and variety to otherwise dreary dishes.

Europeans also used spices for other purposes. They cleaned their teeth with sage—the medieval tooth paste. Medieval doctors applied mint to cuts or garlic to dog bites. Cinnamon was mixed into a paste, rolled into a ball, and carried to protect against colds. Spices also made sweet smelling perfumes, a must in an age when people rarely took baths and perfumes served as deodorants. Some people even believed spices had magical powers. Superstitious peasants carried garlic cloves to ward off vampires and werewolves!

Spices such as cinnamon, ginger, and nutmeg come from various plants not grown in Europe. Medieval Europeans could not go to the local grocery store to buy them. Instead they had

The yellow stigma of the crocus is used to make saffron.

to buy them from traders, who bought them in the Middle East, India, and China. Since travel was so difficult and the distance so great, merchants charged high prices for these spices. Pepper sold for sixty dollars a pound, a fortune in medieval times.

The value of spices can be understood better by understanding not only the treacherous journey of the early traders but also the difficulty of harvesting the spices. Many spices are rare and complicated to harvest. Saffron, still the world's most expensive spice, is the dried stigma of a certain crocus flower. There are three stigma on each crocus and it takes 225,000 stigmas to yield one pound of saffron spice. Cinnamon is the dried inner bark of a tree. Cloves are the dried buds of a flower.

Unripe pepper berries are dried for black pepper.

When you eat dinner tonight, consider the spices that went into it. Is it any wonder that people were willing to pay high prices and risk their lives to get the spices they loved?

Location—France is located in western Europe. It is bordered on the east by Belgium, Luxembourg, Germany, Switzerland, Italy, and Monaco. To the north is the English Channel; to the west is the Atlantic Ocean; and to the south are Spain, Andorra, and the Mediterranean Sea. France also includes the island of Corsica in the Mediterranean Sea.

Climate—France has two main climates. Most of the country is temperate, although the western coast is affected by the Atlantic Ocean. Of course, the mountainous areas have a climate that changes with elevation. In the south, France has a Mediterranean climate. Average temperatures range from 28°F in the winter to 73°F in the summer. The average rainfall is between 22 and 32 inches.

Topography—France is basically divided into two sections. In the north and west are broad plains, low hills, and low plateaus. In the south and east, higher plateaus and mountains are found. The high-est peak in Europe, Mt. Blanc, is on the French/Italian border. Wide river valleys such as the Seine, Loire, Garonne, and Rhone cut across France and empty into the ocean or sea.

Natural Resources—France has few mineral deposits. But her rich soil has given her an agricultural advantage over other European countries. Because of her many rivers, France has an abundance of hydroelectric power. There are also major deposits of iron ore and bauxite (aluminum ore) available in the country.

Geography & Culture—The broad plains in northern France have made it easy for invaders to enter. In early history, France was the home to Celtic tribes known by the Romans as Gauls. At the end of the Roman Empire, the northern tribes of Visigoths, Burgundians, and Franks invaded the Gallic region. The Frankish king Clovis first defeated the Roman government and then other Germanic tribes in the region to establish the first

Frankish or French dynasty. The time of French greatness under the monarchs of the seventeenth century was also a time of military superiority as French armies spread out over Europe. This conquest made France the center of Europe and the model for European culture for several centuries. Although now industrialized, France has been primarily an agricultural country.

Settings Review

1. What two geographic features have the greatest effect on the climate of France?
2. What is the highest peak in Europe?
3. Throughout France's history, what has been her major resource?

4. How did France get its name?
5. What resource do France's rivers provide?

Looking at the map and considering the facts above, determine what geographical features may have helped motivate Germany to take over France.

Terra-cotta roofs top houses nestled on a hillside. Small villages still feature quaint shops and simple lifestyles, but beauty abounds in cities as well.

The Revival of Towns

Towns and Trade

The life of the town depended on one thing: trade. For hundreds of years since the fall of Rome in A.D. 476, trade had nearly stopped in Europe. Poorly maintained roads and the danger of warfare and bandits kept traders off the roads. Instead of depending on goods brought by traders, manors tried to be self-sufficient. When the people needed an item they did not grow or make, they traded for it by **barter.** In a barter economy a person trades goods rather than money for goods or services. During the early Middle Ages, few people used money in buying and selling.

However, during the later Middle Ages, trade revived, and the towns were the centers of this trade. People also began to use money again.

Foreign Trade

Often new towns grew up around temporary markets and **fairs.** In older towns, markets became important once again as traders returned. In either case, much of the merchandise traded came from distant lands. The Crusaders, who had brought back goods from the East, had sparked this foreign trade.

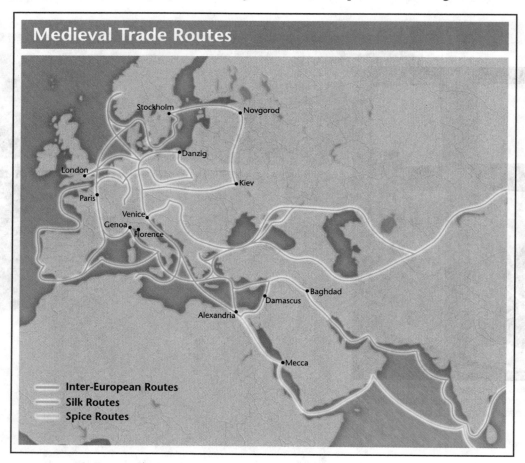

Medieval Trade Routes

Stockholm
Novgorod
Danzig
London
Kiev
Paris
Venice
Genoa
Florence
Baghdad
Damascus
Alexandria
Mecca

=== Inter-European Routes
=== Silk Routes
=== Spice Routes

At a typical town market or fair, whether it was held weekly or yearly, one could find many unusual goods. From the Far East came fragrant spices and soft, colorful silks, which only the wealthy could buy. Although many people could not afford silk, they could afford dyes brought by traders. Using these dyes, local craftsmen or housewives dyed their cloth to match the rich colors of silk. These strange goods from faraway places made medieval markets fascinating places to visit. They helped to open the eyes of Europeans to the lands of the rest of the world.

Local Trade

Local trade soon became as vital to the town as foreign trade. Local peasants brought their extra produce to the town market, where they traded it for the goods of craftsmen or merchants. The farmers often returned home with better tools to further increase their harvests. On the other hand, the craftsmen and merchants needed the farmers' produce because they did not farm. These men spent their time making or transporting goods for the farmers, nobles, and other townspeople. From these beginnings grew the complex economic systems of today.

Money and Banking

As trade increased, bartering became too difficult. To simplify trade, people began to use money again. Instead of goods for goods, they received money for selling an item and paid money when buying another item. Problems arose, however, because every town had its own kind of money. Merchants traveling from town to town had to use many different kinds of money. To handle these problems, some men became **moneychangers.** Moneychangers knew the values of different kinds and sizes of coins. At the market they exchanged money from other towns for local coins.

From the use of money and work of moneychangers grew **banks.** The word *bank* comes from the Italian word *banca* (BAHNK uh), meaning "bench." Moneychangers and early bankers sat on benches, and people referred to doing banking business as "going to the bench."

Banks soon became more than just places of exchanging money. As banking grew, bankers began to lend money to merchants for business and trading ventures. With this extra money, a merchant could expand his business. Banks also issued **letters of credit** to wealthy merchants. To obtain a letter of credit, a merchant first left an amount of money with the banker, who gave him a letter of credit equal to that amount. Thus, the merchant could travel without having to carry large sums of money. When he arrived at his destination, the banker in that town accepted the other bank's letter of credit and gave the merchant his money. This system of letters of credit was a forerunner of our modern checking-account system.

Section Review

1. What replaced bartering for goods?
2. Why does our word for *bank* come from the Italian word for *bench?*
3. Why did the farmer need local craftsmen?
4. Why did craftsmen and merchants need local farmers?

Jack raises chickens for eggs. He trades his eggs with merchants for goods he needs. Sometimes people do not want his eggs and sometimes he has more eggs than he needs to trade for goods he wants. What would happen if people bought Jack's eggs for money instead of barter?

Towns and Industry

When a town grew, the diversity of its population grew as well. More services and products became available, and as a result, a need for order and control of those services and products arose. In the history of early European towns, groups of men and women who worked in the same industry joined together to control their product.

Merchant and Craft Guilds

Two groups of people made up the industry of medieval towns: merchants and craftsmen. The merchants bought and sold goods, while the craftsmen manufactured goods. In the later Middle Ages merchants and craftsmen organized themselves into **guilds** (GILDZ). Merchant guilds included all the merchants selling one product. Craft guilds included all the craftsmen who made the same product. No merchant or craftsmen could sell or make his product in the town unless he belonged to a guild. The guilds had rules about membership and production. They set standards for quality, quantity, and price. The guilds worked to protect their members and their customers by regulating industry.

Learning a Trade

Anyone who wanted to learn a certain trade did so according to craft guild rules. He had to go through three stages. In the first stage, the young boy, called an **apprentice,** went to live and work in the home and shop of a master craftsman who was a guild member. There he learned his master's trade, whether it was making shoes, weaving cloth, or baking bread. He also served his master and mistress by doing other chores. The apprentice was successful if he did his job well and faithfully.

The apprentice served under the master for two to ten years, depending on the difficulty of the trade and how fast the boy learned. After his apprenticeship, he became a **journeyman.** A journeyman hired himself out to work for other masters, sometimes wandering from town to town seeking work. The name *journeyman* comes from French words meaning "a day's work." A journeyman usually hired himself out for only short periods.

When the journeyman excelled at his trade, he came before the craft guild of his town to be tested. As part of the test, he presented his **masterpiece,** the best piece of work he had ever done. The members of the guild examined it carefully, and if it were truly a "masterpiece," they gave him the title of **master** and allowed him to join the guild. As a guild member, he could open his own shop and

teach others his trade. Because the guild's standards were high, a craftsman had to do his best to meet them. Even after he joined the guild, his work had to meet guild standards. By following high standards, guild members produced high-quality workmanship. These craftsmen are a good example to us of being "not slothful in business" (Rom. 12:11).

Section Review

1. What two types of businessmen lived in medieval towns?
2. What organizations controlled medieval industry?
3. List the three stages in learning a trade.

Use the three stages of learning a trade to describe what stage each of the following is in: *(a)* a junior lawyer, *(b)* one of the men on a landscape crew who is doing extra jobs after work, (c) the chief architect of an architectural firm, *(d)* a student teacher, *(e)* an intern in a hospital.

Living in a Town

Unlike manor life, life in the town was rarely dull. All day long the streets, markets, and workshops bustled with activity. Peddlers selling their wares cried out "Fish! Fresh fish!" "Old clothes! Rags!" "Vegetables! Beans! Peas!" Children played in the streets and ran errands for their mothers or masters. Animals wandered about, searching for food or a place to nap. At street corners businessmen met to discuss the latest news or the latest product from the East. Shoppers and shopkeepers haggled over prices, while servants giggled and gossiped their way home from the well. Not until evening did the noise of the town quiet down.

Daily Life

Guilds were more than mere business organizations. They also became centers of much of the town's social life. To pass the time, guild members gathered in their guild halls to visit, play games such as chess, or have meetings. On special days the guilds celebrated with banquets and pageants.

The guilds also looked after their members. If a member was sick and unable to work, the guild saw that his family had food to eat. When a member became too old to work, the guild helped provide for his needs.

Although the townspeople worked hard to make their lives and towns better, they also enjoyed the relaxation of holidays. Parades, banquets, and sports events made holiday celebrations noisy and colorful. Often the guilds made parade floats, which were judged and awarded prizes. Horseracing, boxing, bullfighting, jousting, and boat racing also highlighted holidays.

After a busy day of work or celebration, the townspeople returned to their homes. Their homes were usually small; many families had only one or two rooms with little furniture. Many craftsmen made their homes behind or over their shops. Some wealthier families had larger homes with several rooms.

Because the space inside the town walls was limited, the townspeople added upper stories to existing buildings rather than live outside the walls. These extra stories hung out over the narrow streets, making the streets even darker. Some people built their homes on bridges in the town or on the town wall, or even in the moat. Newcomers quickly filled any empty space in the growing medieval town.

Although rarely dull, life in the town was not always pleasant or safe. A constant danger

Open-air markets help make big cities seem smaller and more friendly.

was fire. Most buildings were made of wood, and a stray spark could start a fire that could quickly consume a large part of the town. Disease was another problem because of the towns' crowded conditions, narrow streets, and poor sanitation. Epidemics killed many people. In the mid-fourteenth century, the dreaded **Black Death** (the bubonic plague) swept across Europe. One-quarter to one-half of Europe's population died from the Black Death.

Religious Life

The Roman Church played an important role in medieval European towns. Most townspeople of the late Middle Ages followed the teachings of the Roman Church. Every town had its own church and priest, and the people faithfully attended the services. In many ways most townspeople improved their lives economically and socially, but they were still lost in sin and living in spiritual darkness.

The needs of the townspeople and traders differed from those of people living on the manor. To meet these new needs, the church sent out a new order (rank) of clergy. These men were called **friars** (FRY urz), from the Latin word *frater* (FRAH tare), meaning "brother." The friars did not live in remote monasteries or minister in a single church but lived in monasteries in or near the towns. They

Not only were the houses close together, but the streets were filled with refuse thrown from upstairs windows. A wise pedestrian walked close to the sides of the street.

preached and taught, and they cared for the poor and sick. Two orders begun at this time were the Dominicans (duh MIN ih kunz) and the Franciscans (fran SIS kunz). These orders still exist today.

The friars had a great burden to help other people. They also believed that they would receive special rewards for their labors, including earning salvation. The Bible teaches that Christians are to help others. Their labors are not to earn salvation, however (for salvation is by faith, not works), but to be a testimony of God's love and grace. The Epistle of James tells us that one way a Christian shows his faith in God is through works to others (James 2:14-17).

Section Review

1. Besides work, what did the guilds provide for the people?
2. What two dangers were especially great in medieval towns?
3. What religion did most medieval townspeople follow?
4. What new order of clergy did the Roman Catholic Church send out?
5. How did these orders differ from other clergy?

How has modern city design reduced the risk of the two dangers in question two above?

Wagon level · Hay Storage · Cattle · Threshing Floor · Cattle · GAMBREL

Steep Roof · Side Stalls

Dutch Barn

Shaker Round Barn

FORE BAY

Wisconsin Swedish

Pennsylvania German

Architecture Reflects Reality

If you live or have traveled in a farming area, you have seen barns. When you look at older barns in America, you can often tell what country the early owner of that property came from. In the same way, you can identify the era and location in which ancient buildings were constructed by identifying their historical architectural styles.

Classical Greek architecture has several identifying characteristics. One is the post-and-lintel structure—horizontal blocks resting on walls or columns. Straight lines are another characteristic. In Greek architecture there are no arches or curves. Greek temples, unlike Roman ones, had dark interiors and were never domed. The most important part of the temple to the Greeks was the outside, since only a few priests could actually enter the dark interior—the domain of the god.

Classic Roman architecture is evidenced by a more open style. The clean Greek uniformity of columns was expanded with the addition of the arch, which allowed buildings to be taller than a single story and to support the weight of concrete,

a recent Roman development. With concrete the Romans were no longer limited to bricks and block and other square objects from which to build. Now they could pour concrete directly into a mold . . . and so the dome was introduced. The Roman dome was shallow, like an upside-down saucer. As engineering and building materials improved, later domes were higher, more like upside-down bowls. Roman architecture also reflected a new interest in the interior of the temple. Once plain, now the interior became a thing of beauty, designed not just to honor the gods but for the enjoyment of all. Small windows along the walls and a hole in the dome allowed light in from the outside, reducing the need for smoky torches.

With the growth of towns came the need for larger, more central churches. Coming out of the Dark Ages, architects needed new models for their work, so they looked to their Roman heritage. But even though they modeled after Roman works, they developed the unique style we call Romanesque.

The Cathedral

As towns grew and prospered, the people decided to construct new **cathedrals.** They wanted new places to worship, and they wanted to show other towns their wealth and confidence. They also wanted to thank God for the blessings of town life. In short, the cathedral was the symbol of the town's spirit. All over Europe, townspeople tore down small churches or added on to ones already standing. Often this rebuilding took over a hundred years.

Throughout the early Middle Ages, the architectural style was called **Romanesque** (ROH muh NESK) because it used many elements of Roman style. The Romanesque style used rounded vaults (made from putting several arches together) for roofs. Thick stone walls, similar to those found in castles, were required to support these heavy roofs. Like the castles, Romanesque cathedrals had only small windows, which let in little light. To brighten the interior, the builders painted the walls and hung colorful tapestries. Candles and torches added some light. Even so, the Romanesque churches remained dark and cold.

The Gothic Style

With the growth of towns, a new architectural style, called **Gothic,** developed. Compared to the older, heavier Romanesque style, the Gothic style was light and airy. Gothic architects discovered ways to make roofs higher, walls thinner, and windows bigger.

Small windows and thick walls made Romanesque church interiors dark and forbidding.

Barrel vault ceilings distributed the weight of the roof down the sides of the arches so that walls could be thinner.

Instead of rounded vaults for the roof, they used pointed arches. To add support to the outside walls, they built **flying buttresses,** props attached to the wall (see illustration). This extra support allowed walls to be thinner, and the thinner walls allowed for more windows. Instead of being cold and dark, Gothic cathedrals rose warm and bright. These beautiful cathedrals reflected the people's enthusiasm for their new way of life.

The church building had always been the tallest one in the medieval village or town. Gothic cathedrals could be built taller and taller. Many towns competed against one another to have the tallest church with the highest tower. Sometimes this competition led to disastrous results. An ambitious architect who tried to put a high ceiling

on walls that were too thin might see the whole thing collapse. To the townspeople and to us today, this situation is a vivid example of how pride causes destruction (Prov. 16:18).

To add to the cathedral's beauty, the builders covered it inside and out with decoration. Carvings, sculptures, paintings, and tapestries of biblical scenes filled nearly every empty space. Craftsmen and artisans from near and far worked hard to finish the cathedral. A special characteristic of Gothic cathedrals was the **stained glass** windows that covered the walls and colored the light that filtered through them into the church. Patient craftsmen spent many weeks making the colored glass and then fitting it into patterns held together by lead. Because the stained glass windows were costly to make, wealthy nobles or businessmen often donated them to their local cathedrals.

New support methods, such as the flying buttress at the left, gave Gothic architects new options for design. Some cathedrals took more than one hundred years to build. During that time the original design was often changed and expanded.

Chapter 1

Beautiful designs of stained glass colored the sunlight that poured into the Gothic cathedrals.

When finished, the cathedral was truly the town's most special building. Generations of local craftsmen and laborers had worked on it. All the townspeople had given money for it and watched its progress. From then on, the cathedral served as their place of worship, and the square in front of it became the center of town life. Meetings and markets took place in the square. On holidays it was the place of parades and plays. And every day the church bells rang from the tower to remind the people of the time, warn them of danger, and announce good or bad news.

Section Review

1. What type of architecture replaced Romanesque architecture?
2. List three qualities of this new architecture.
3. What material was used to hold the pieces of a stained glass window together?

4. How did the new cathedral symbolize the town's spirit?

If you had to design a cathedral, what Bible stories would you portray in the stained glass windows to have the greatest impact on the people?

Summary

As peace returned to Europe during the Crusades and travelers returned from the East with unusual goods, trade revived in Europe. A result of this trade was the building of towns. Old towns and new towns alike began to grow as people left the manors to enjoy town life. The towns existed for trade, both foreign and local. As trade increased, so did the use of money and banking. Within the towns, all business was controlled by guilds of merchants and craftsmen. The guilds also provided much of the towns' social life. The Roman Church continued to play an important role in the lives of the townspeople through the ministries of friars. The townspeople built huge Gothic cathedrals that showed their enthusiasm and wealth to others. Many of these cathedrals still stand in Europe today, a reminder of this age of towns in the late Middle Ages.

People, Places, and Terms to Know

town charter	letters of credit	master	Romanesque
barter	guilds	Black Death	Gothic
fairs	apprentice	friars	flying buttresses
moneychangers	journeyman	cathedral	stained glass
banks	masterpiece		

Review Questions

Completion

Complete the following comparisons.

1. As castles dominated during the middle centuries of the Middle Ages, so (a) _____ dominated during the (b) _____ centuries of the Middle Ages.

2. In early medieval trade the people used (a) _____ to obtain goods, while in the late Middle Ages they used (b) _____ to obtain goods.

Matching

Match each item to its meaning.

3. moneychangers

4. town charter

5. Black Death

6. guild

7. friars

(a) the bubonic plague

(b) order of clergy

(c) organization that set standards

(d) a legal document granting privileges

(e) the earliest bankers

Short Answer

For each of the following pairs of items, write a sentence or two explaining the connection between them.

8. bank / letters of credit

9. merchants / craftsmen

10. apprentice / journeyman

Application

11. On your paper draw two columns. Label one Romanesque and the other Gothic. By writing words or phrases under each heading, compare Romanesque churches with Gothic churches. Include at least three entries in each column.

12. Look at the drawing on this page; then tell if it is a Romanesque or Gothic church.

Show the Steps

On a separate sheet of paper, draw a sequence of pictures showing the steps in one of the processes listed below. Draw at least one picture for each step listed and write a caption beneath it. You may choose to write two or three sentences about each step instead of drawing a picture.

I. **Growth of a Town**
   Traders build house near a castle
   Craftsmen build shops and homes
   Walls built around the town
   Town grows outside the walls

II. **Trading Goods**
   On a trade route
   Setting up a shop
   Bartering trade
   Money trade

III. **Becoming a Master**
   Apprenticing
   Working as a journeyman
   Presenting the masterpiece

IV. **Building a Cathedral**
   Laying the foundation
   Building walls with flying buttresses
   Raising the roof
   The first church service

Think About It!

Guilds were an important part of the industry of early towns. How did they help early production? What did they do to discourage production? Imagine that you are a town craftsman. Write a two-paragraph essay on why you like or dislike the guild that controls your craft and how that guild affects your daily life as well as your business.

CHAPTER 2

Prior to the Crusades, Europeans knew little about classical Greek and Roman writings. In their travels, however, crusaders found that Byzantine and Islamic scholars had preserved these ancient writings. Some Europeans recognized the value of these manuscripts. The search was on. Wealthy men sent scholars to find manuscripts in libraries and monasteries. Then they had other scholars copy and translate them. Soon these Greek manuscripts began changing the way of life in Europe. The translated manuscripts contained knowledge that helped bring Europe into the modern age.

The works of Greek and Roman philosophers, doctors, poets, dramatists, and mathematicians, which had been forgotten in Europe for centuries, once more came to light. Europeans eagerly read the rediscovered writings and began to pattern their thinking and works after them. Inspired by classical ideas, Europeans over the next few centuries produced some of the world's finest art and literature. Beginning shortly before 1400 and continuing into the 1600s, this period in the later Middle Ages is known as the **Renaissance** (REN ih SAHNS), from the French word meaning "rebirth." The name reminds us that this period began with a rebirth of interest in classical Greece and Rome. To Europeans long ignorant of classical accomplishments, the Renaissance brought new life after years of medieval darkness.

A.D. 1300 - A.D. 1600

Gothic Architectural Style 1200-1500

1300

Byzantine Empire 476-1453

The Renaissance

Great Schism
1378-1415

Leonardo da Vinci
1452-1519

1400   1500   1600

Michelangelo 1475-1564

Renaissance 1350-1616

Shakespeare
1564-1616

First
Gutenberg
Bible 1456

Medieval vs. Renaissance

Although the transition was slow, there was a definite change in people's attitudes and actions during the Renaissance. With the growth of towns and trade and the discovery of lost Greek and Roman writings, people had much to be excited about.

A New Way of Thinking

Renaissance people thought of the world differently from the way medieval people had. During the Middle Ages, people had looked at the world as a place of toil and sadness. They often lived only for the hope of one day going to heaven. They thought that they could earn salvation by following the teachings of the Roman Church. They saw this life as one filled with evil and pain, one which held little happiness for the average man or woman.

With the growth of trade and towns in the later Middle Ages, this attitude began to change. Increased wealth provided some people with more free time. They began to look at life around them and to realize that this life offered many good and enjoyable things. They still believed in heaven and followed the Roman Church's teachings. But they also knew that God had created man as a special creature, above the animals, with particular talents and abilities. They used these talents to study and appreciate the beauty of God's creation. To them, the world became a bright and exciting place to live.

The Renaissance Man

A man who lived up to the Renaissance attitude of life was called a **Renaissance man.** He was interested and talented in a wide variety of fields. To him all of life was open to study and mastery. A Renaissance man was a writer, poet, painter, musician, architect, inventor, and more. He applied his learning to deal with people in any situation and to solve problems successfully.

In many ways the Renaissance man reflected Paul's statement in I Corinthians 9:22—"I am made all things to all men, that I might by all means save some." Although we do not know how many Renaissance men were actually converted, they are a good example to Christians in that they used their talents, or

Portrait of a Young Man, *by Agnolo di Cosimo di Mariano, shows the confidence of Europeans during the Renaissance. The young man is holding a book, which is the basis of Renaissance learning and achievement.*

God-given gifts. Christians should develop their talents and use them to serve and glorify God. They should have a wide variety of interests so that they can witness to people with many different interests. The Renaissance man, however, did not always have this goal for his studying. He often desired knowledge and talents to glorify himself, not to serve God.

A New Emphasis

Although Renaissance men studied nature, their favorite subject was man. They recognized that humans have abilities animals do not have. For example, human beings can think, reason, speak, read, write, and create art. Renaissance men believed that these gifts showed the glory of man, God's finest creation. This emphasis on man and his abilities is called **humanism.**

As Renaissance ideas spread, some people took humanism too far. They emphasized man's ability over God's power and served themselves with their talents rather than God. They forgot that man is a sinner who falls short of God's glory (Rom. 3:23). In their selfish pride these Renaissance people replaced God with man. Their pride resulted in much sin, corruption, greed, and immorality; and it eventually led to their destruction (Prov. 16:18). Although man reached new artistic and intellectual heights during the Renaissance, he ended at a spiritual low. But God in His love and mercy sent a revival of His truth during the Reformation (see Chapter 3). In any age, He is "not willing that any should perish, but that all should come to repentance" (II Pet. 3:9).

Section Review

1. Give one difference between the Middle Ages and the Renaissance.
2. What was the ideal Renaissance person called?
3. How does a Christian's use of his talents differ from a Renaissance person's?
4. What philosophy characterized the Renaissance?
5. What problem resulted from this philosophy?

How can Christians avoid becoming self-dependent and prideful when their lives are going well?

Behave!

"Stand up straight." "Don't talk with your mouth full!" "Don't forget to say 'please' and 'thank you.'" Have your parents ever said these things to you? Well, you are not alone. Concerned adults have been instructing young people in good manners and etiquette for centuries. Some things have changed, but others have stayed the same. In his *Book of Nurture,* Hugh Rhodes, a medieval gentleman, gave these instructions for beginning the day.

> Brush them and sponge thy clothes too
> that thou that day shalt wear.
> In comely sort cast up your bed,
> lose you none of your gear.
> Make clean your shoes, and comb your head
> and your clothes button or lace,
> And see at no time you forget
> to wash your hands and face.

Here are some more words of wisdom written to the nephew of Giovanni della Casa in his *Book of Manners.* This text was published in 1558; does it sound appropriate for today?

> Refrain as far as possible from making noises which grate upon the ear, such as grinding or sucking your teeth.

> Wit should be like the nibble of a sheep rather than the bite of a dog, for if it were to bite like a dog it would not be witty but insulting.

> A man should never boast of his birth, his honors or his wealth, and still less of his brains.

> And when thou hast blown thy nose, use not to open thy handkerchief, . . . as if thou hadst pearls and rubies fallen from thy brains.

What are some manners that we observe today? What behaviors show that we are well-mannered? What behaviors reflect badly on the Lord? How do our manners affect our testimony?

"I have the finest brain in all of Italy. Just look at its size, its color, its folds! Isn't it a wondrous thing?"

Education in the Renaissance

This detail from The School of Athens *by Raphael portrays Aristotle and Plato as teacher and student.*

You may remember from earlier studies that few people during the Middle Ages went to school. Usually only men training for the priesthood or the sons of wealthy nobles had the need or means for an education. Even kings did not always know how to read and write; most people did not. For those who did get an education, teachers taught Latin grammar, speech, law, medicine, and theology.

An Expanded Range of Study

During the Renaissance, education changed. If a person was to sharpen his abilities, he needed an education. To study the world around him, he needed to know how to read, write, and reason. Many students hired private teachers, and most towns started academies that taught both Latin and Greek. Usually only boys went to the academies, but often girls had tutors at home. All students spent hours reading the classical writers. In the towns, wealthy men collected large libraries of manuscripts brought from the East.

The subjects taught in the Renaissance differed from those of the Middle Ages. Known as the **humanities,** these subjects covered human interests and experiences. Literature, philosophy, art, history, grammar, and speech were all taught. Renaissance teachers encouraged their students to invent, explore, and discover. They also expected students to appreciate and create beauty through art. They believed that any area of study helped a student better understand his world. The goal of Renaissance education was to make the student a well-rounded person, educated and interested in many fields.

A Comfortable Language to Read

During the European Middle Ages, scholars usually wrote in Latin. Most people, however, did not understand Latin. Beginning shortly before and continuing into the Renaissance, some writers stopped using Latin and used their native languages. A native language is one spoken by the people, such as Italian, German, or English. It is called a **vernacular** language. For the uneducated person who knew no Latin, vernacular writing opened up new subjects of interest. Even if he could not read, he could understand when someone read to him.

The use of the vernacular also helped combine people into nations. The Roman Empire broke down national divisions and made all people Roman subjects. They came under the control of an enormous empire and were governed by decisions made far away in Rome. When the empire fell and the Dark Ages descended, life on manors narrowed people's view. They thought of themselves as belonging to a particular lord and his manor. Many never went beyond the border of the manor property and knew little of the outside world. With the revival of towns, people heard more of the world around them. Traders came from distant lands and brought a vision of people and things that had not even entered into the common man's imagination before. In the Renaissance, as learning blossomed so did people's awareness of their common heritage. Vernacular writing helped divide Europe into **ethnic** groups (people with a common heritage) and give people a national spirit.

Writers to the Newly Educated

Although Renaissance writers still used Latin, more and more wrote in the vernacular. The following paragraphs note some famous Renaissance writers.

Dante: An early vernacular writer was Italy's Dante Alighieri (DAHN-tay ah-lee-GYAY-ree) (1265-1321). Dante's best-known work is *The Divine Comedy.* In this long poem Dante records his imaginary visit to the world beyond the grave. He begins in hell, moves to purgatory, and ends in heaven. In the poem he meets several ancient writers and heroes. He also points out the corruption in the Roman Church by showing some popes in hell with the worst sinners. *The Divine Comedy* is the greatest work of early Italian literature. Dante's successful use of the vernacular encouraged other writers to use it too.

Chaucer: Englishman Geoffrey Chaucer (JEF-ree CHAW-sur) (1341?-1400) was another vernacular writer. In his *Canterbury Tales,* Chaucer put together several stories told by the members of an imaginary group going on a pilgrimage (a journey to a

The Divine Comedy *begins with the Roman poet Virgil leading Dante toward the realm of the damned.*

sacred place). The stories reflect English life during the Middle Ages. Chaucer's use of the vernacular encouraged the development of modern English.

Petrarch: Another important Italian writer of the Renaissance was Petrarch (PEH trark) (1304-74). Writing in both Latin and Italian, Petrarch spread the ideas of Renaissance humanism and is known as the Father of Humanism. He urged people to develop their gifts. In praise of beauty and love, some of the most beautiful poetry of all time came from Petrarch's pen.

Shakespeare: More familiar to English-speaking students is William Shakespeare (1564-1616), the greatest English writer of the Renaissance. Shakespeare lived at the time the King James translation of the Bible was made. The language he uses is similar to that found in the King James Version.

Shakespeare wrote many poems but is best known for his plays. *Romeo and Juliet, Hamlet,* and *Julius Caesar* are three of his more than thirty plays. In the plays, Shakespeare showed the full range of human personality with both its strengths and its weaknesses.

Petrarch

From slapstick comedy to light-hearted romance to pitiful tragedy, his plays reveal man's limitations and abilities. It is no wonder they are still enjoyed today.

Section Review

1. What subjects did a student study during the Renaissance?

2. What was the goal of Renaissance education?

3. What is another name for a native language?

4. List four writers of the Renaissance who used their native languages in their literature.

5. Why are Shakespeare's plays still produced today?

Do you think vernacular writing helped to promote learning? How?

CHARACTERIZATIONS

Who Was William Shakespeare?

You had probably heard of William Shakespeare before you read this chapter, but you may have no idea why there is so much interest in this late-Renaissance playwright and poet. When you read that within approximately twenty-five years Shakespeare authored thirty-seven plays, most of which are still performed today, and 154 sonnets (fourteen-line poems), you can begin to understand the enthusiasm over this man and the timelessness of his legacy.

There is little factual information available about William Shakespeare. We do know that he was born in 1564 to John Shakespeare, a prosperous member of the Stratford-on-Avon community. As a child of a city leader, William was able to attend the local grammar school. Evidence of his education is easily seen in the references to Latin literary works found in his plays. We know that he was married to Anne Hathaway, a woman

five or six years older than he, and that they had three children, but little else is known about Shakespeare's personal life. By 1592 he had become an actor and was becoming well-known as a playwright. At his death in 1616, Shakespeare had never published his plays. The plays were compiled and published several years after his death when friends realized that other people were publishing modified copies of the plays.

Because of lack of information and Shakespeare's seeming unwillingness to take credit for his work, there has been occasional controversy about the authorship of the plays. Theories have surfaced suggesting that other authors of Shakespeare's time were the true writers and that Shakespeare stole the credit. One of the most unusual suggestions was that Queen Elizabeth wrote the plays under the pseudonym (false name) William Shakespeare! These theories, however, are based on little foundation and can be discounted. There is evidence that Shakespeare's contemporaries commended him, and after his death, even his rival Ben Jonson said of his work,

Triumph, my Britain, thou hast one to show
    To whom all scenes of Europe homage owe.
He was not of an age, but for all time!

Test your creative abilities. Read Shakespeare's Sonnet 18 and then try to write a sonnet of your own. Shakespeare's Sonnet 18 is a fourteen-line poem in which the first twelve lines rhyme every other line and the last two lines rhyme with each other.

Shall I compare thee to a summer's day?
    Thou art more lovely and more temperate:
Rough winds do shake the darling buds of May,
    And summer's lease hath all too short a date:
Sometime too hot the eye of heaven shines
    And often is his gold complexion dimmed;
And every fair from fair sometimes declines,
    By chance or nature's changing course untrimmed;
But thy eternal summer shall not fade,
    Nor lose possession of that fair thou ow'st;
Nor shall death brag thou wander'st in his shade,
    When in eternal lines to time thou grow'st:
So long as men can breathe, or eyes can see,
    So long lives this, and this gives life to thee.

Productions of Shakespeare's plays are still popular today. In this scene from Hamlet, *Hamlet accuses Guildenstern of "playing him like a flute." (Bob Jones University Classic Players)*

The Church and the Renaissance

The Roman Catholic Church had dominated the spiritual life of the Middle Ages. During the Renaissance the church changed. It became more and more tied with politics and power struggles. Men looked to the church less for eternal peace and more for worldly gain.

The Church and the Arts

The Roman Catholic Church was interested in the revival of education and the arts. Popes and other church officials helped support artists and writers and eagerly purchased rare manuscripts of works by ancient authors. The Catholic Church used the greatest painters, sculptors, and architects of the day to design and decorate churches and monuments. Works such as the Sistine Chapel, with its lavish art and design, would not exist if it had not been for the support of the church. The church's patronage of Renaissance artists is revealed by the enormous amount of religious art that was produced during the Renaissance.

Domes, inlaid ceilings, sculptures, portraits, and ornate carvings all speak of the wealth of the Roman Catholic Church during the Renaissance.

St. Peter's Basilica in Vatican City, the largest Christian church in the world, features a dome designed by Michelangelo.

Torture Tools of the Inquisition

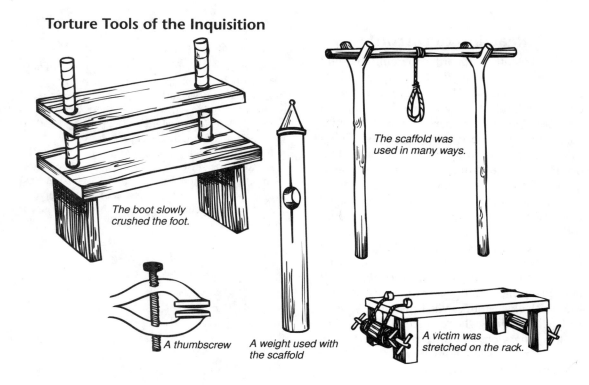

The boot slowly crushed the foot.

The scaffold was used in many ways.

A thumbscrew

A weight used with the scaffold

A victim was stretched on the rack.

The Decline of the Clergy

But this revival of arts was not matched by a revival of religion. Corruption in the clergy was common, with few high church officials holding to their spiritual vows. This is not surprising, since most came into office by appointment rather than by spiritual calling.

The **Vatican,** the pope's residence, changed from a place of piety to a place of parties featuring enormous banquets and immoral after-dinner entertainment. This expensive lifestyle plus the building and decorating of lavish cathedrals forced the church to seek new ways to raise money. Their methods prompted a young German monk to question the church and stir up the Reformation, which will be discussed in the next chapter.

One event that jarred the Roman Church was the **Papal Schism** or **Great Schism.** From 1378 to the end of the Council of Constance in 1418, the church fought over which of two men should be pope. Each man claimed to have God-given authority and was supported by a different political region. In a time when the church was supposed to be the final and infallible authority in the lives of the people, this squabbling shook the faith of many followers.

But the popes who held office after the healing of the schism were often worldly men more interested in art, culture, and pleasure than in the affairs of God. One of these popes, Leo X, was described by a Catholic historian as a man "who would have made an excellent Pope if he had only been a little religious." Leo himself is supposed to have said to his brother, "God has given us the papacy; let us enjoy it."

Reaction to Discord

In this state of disorder the church could not afford to have its doctrines or decisions questioned. Those who disagreed with the church or held other doctrines were labeled **heretics.** The height of persecution for heretics was the time of the **Inquisition.** The Inquisition was a church-appointed tribunal that originated in the thirteenth century to suppress heresy. During the Inquisition heretics were tortured until they confessed. Stretched on the rack, burned with iron pokers, or crushed by rocks, many heretics finally repented and accepted the doctrines of the church. Many were put to death even after repenting. Those who refused to give in to their torturers were burned at the stake, hanged, or beheaded. Many Blacks, Moors (Muslims), and Jews as well as Christians who rejected Roman Catholic teaching were put to death for heresy. In 1506 four thousand Jews were killed in one night in Lisbon, Portugal. As time went on, the Inquisition became the excuse that any tyrant used to rid his country of unwanted dissenters and minorities, including the handicapped and the mentally ill.

Section Review

1. What is the residence of the pope called?
2. What were two reasons that the church needed more money?
3. Why did the Great Schism shake the faith of the Roman Church's followers?
4. What was the purpose of the Inquisition?

How is the Great Schism an example of the mistake that is made by putting faith in people or institutions instead of in God?

Books! Books! Books!

Renaissance scholars wrote many books. They had much to say about the knowledge being rediscovered almost daily. Yet these writers faced a serious problem: how to get their writings to readers. Manuscripts were still copied by hand, a slow and costly method. They were copied onto parchment, a specially prepared sheepskin or goatskin. Careless scribes, some of whom could not read, at times entered errors into a manuscript as they copied. Unless these problems were solved, the budding intellectual life of the Renaissance might die.

Johannes Gutenberg (1400-1468)

The Gutenberg Bible featured printed pages decorated with handpainted illustrations.

Paper, you may remember from earlier studies, gets its name from the papyrus plant that the ancient Egyptians had pounded into paper. The early Chinese also had paper originally made of the pulp of plant fibers and tree bark and later pounded from cotton rags, linen, and even rope. During the Renaissance this technology was available in the West. By the end of the 1200s, Europe had its first paper mill that used cotton or linen fibers. Having paper was wonderful, but an efficient method for printing on it was still needed.

This efficient method, already used in China for four hundred years, was developed in Europe by a German inventor named **Johannes Gutenberg** (yo-HAHN-us GOOT-un-BURG) (1400-1468). In the mid-fifteenth century Gutenberg invented a movable-type printing press. The Chinese had difficulty using movable type because their language had so many characters. However, movable-type printing proved to be more suited for European languages (Latin, German, French, and so on), which have only a few letters. Gutenberg made individual metal carvings, called types, of each letter. These could be easily rearranged to form each page of a book.

Pages were printed one at a time.

The printing process had several steps. First a typesetter "composed the type"; that is, he set the letters together side by side in their proper order. Next the printer took the set type, placed it securely in the press, and carefully coated it with ink. Then he lowered the press, bringing the freshly inked type against paper. After applying pressure, he raised the press, took out the newly printed page, placed a new sheet of paper in the press, and repeated the process. This went on until the printer had as many copies of the material as he needed. Gutenberg's system allowed printers to make many clear copies both quickly and cheaply. The price of books dropped, more people bought them, and reading increased. Writers continued to write, now knowing their ideas would surely be read.

In 1456 Gutenberg printed his first volume—the Bible. Indeed, the movable-type printing press allowed people in all countries to publish the Scriptures. The lower price and larger number of printed Bibles helped spread the Word of God to all people, rich and poor. Today, however, Gutenberg's Bibles are very expensive because they are rare and famous. (Approximately fifty still exist.) Original Gutenberg Bibles have sold for thousands of dollars. But we can buy a newly printed Bible for just a few dollars today, thanks to the work of Johannes Gutenberg.

The terms uppercase *and* lowercase *come from the printer's type box. Capital letters were stored in the upper case while small letters were stored in the lower case.*

Location—Italy is in southern Europe. It is a long boot-shaped peninsula which is bordered on the east, south, and west by the Adriatic, Ionian, and Tyrrhenian Seas (each part of the Mediterranean Sea). In the north, Italy borders France, Switzerland, Austria, and Slovenia. Included as part of Italy are the large islands of Sardinia and Sicily as well as a number of smaller islands.

Climate—Italy has a mediterranean climate except in the northeast where the climate is humid subtropical. Variation in the climate due to high elevation does occur in the Alps in the north. The average temperature ranges from 33° to 70°F. Rainfall averages about thirty-five inches.

Topography—Italy is divided into three parts. In the north is a broad plain bordered by the Alps. The rest of the peninsula has as its backbone the rugged Apennine range. There are broad lowlands on the west coast. Italy's islands are mountainous.

Natural Resources—Though Italy has small quantities of several different minerals, its only important ones are sulfur and mercury. In the northern plains some natural gas has been discovered. Italy has abundant hydroelectric power produced by streams and small rivers. It also has rich soil in the northern plains.

Geography & Culture—While it would seem that the Alps in the north should have protected Italy from invasions, they have not because there are several mountain passes through which numerous conquerors have come. However, because of Italy's high-cliffed coastline in the south, few invaders have taken the country from the sea. Italy is surrounded by water; consequently, early in its history its people learned to conquer the sea. When challenged by others who sailed the Mediterranean, Italians eventually conquered them too. Italy's early history, its central location in the Mediterranean Sea, and its people's practical nature made it one of the first countries to establish a vast empire. During the Renaissance, Italian cities distinguished themselves as major trading ports and crossroads. Italy is currently distinguished worldwide as the home of Vatican City, the 108.5-acre domain of the pope and hierarchy of the Roman Catholic Church. Although located in the city of Rome, Vatican City is an independent country.

Settings Review

1. What mountain range runs along the length of Italy like a backbone?

2. Name Italy's two important mineral resources.

3. What two large islands are part of Italy?

4. What mountain range lies along Italy's northern border?

5. What country is within Italy's borders?

Greece, Italy, and Spain have all been world powers at one time. What geographical advantages do they share? How did these advantages help them establish power?

Italy has a rich history as evidenced in the ancient ruins of the Roman Colosseum and the canaled streets of Venice.

Renaissance Painting

The three paintings on this page show the same subject: the Madonna and child (Mary and Jesus). The first one is a Russian icon, which was influenced by Byzantine art. The second comes from a medieval Gothic church. The third was painted during the Renaissance. You can see that each one is different, but you may not be able to tell why. By taking a closer look, we will find out how the Renaissance artists made their paintings look different.

New Rules Influenced Painting

Perhaps the first thing you notice is that the people in the Renaissance painting look real, whereas the others look flat. Renaissance artists had begun to study the structure of humans, animals, and plants. The artists learned about **anatomy**—how bones and muscles work together. Using this information, they could make their subjects appear more real. Because medieval artists knew little about anatomy and did not want to glorify man too highly, their people and animals were often not only flat but also distorted.

The Renaissance artist also added dimension to his figures by **shading.** You can see that some parts of the faces, bodies, and clothes are darker. This shading makes these areas seem farther away. The Renaissance artist painted nearer areas lighter and farther areas darker to make objects and figures appear rounded. The gradually changing colors in the folds of cloth show this technique especially well.

In the Renaissance painting, the background seems to be far away. The Renaissance artist gave depth to his background by painting far-away objects smaller than nearby objects. The ability to give depth to paintings was the result of the new study of **perspective.** The artist could figure out mathematically what size objects should be and at what angle they should be placed to give the appearance of reality. A Renaissance artist had to be a good mathematician

These paintings show the great contrast in style from Byzantine to Renaissance.

Novgorod School, Our Lady of Tihvin, *Bob Jones University Collection*

Niccolo di Pietro Gerini, Virgin and Child with Saints, *Bob Jones University Collection*

Master of San Filippo, Madonna and Child with Infant St. John and Angels, *Bob Jones University Collection*

Da Vinci studied people and faces. The face on this statue, called The Equestrian, *shows the rider's intensity.*

as well as a painter. In contrast, most medieval and Byzantine paintings had no backgrounds at all, or they had backgrounds that were flat and distorted.

The Renaissance artist used anatomy, shading, and perspective to make his works lifelike. The more he studied man and his surroundings, the better he was able to portray the world beautifully and accurately.

The Artists

Although most Renaissance men and women had an interest in art, only a few were great artists. These individuals used their talents in the arts to create beauty. In the Middle Ages artists had been generally unknown by name because they produced their work through a guild and many times in apprenticeship to a master. Individual creativity did not matter because medieval artists were seen as

no different from any other craftsmen. They were simply doing their job. During the Renaissance, however, artists were looked upon as creative geniuses with a special gift. Individual artists became known and praised by name.

The revival of trade and increase in wealth during the late Middle Ages helped Renaissance artists. Wealthy nobles and merchants supported artists in their schooling and work. Called **patrons,** these wealthy men paid artists to produce art to decorate their homes and to record their doings. These men loved beauty and provided for those who could create it. Many paintings from this period are of patrons and their families. Had it not been for these people, much Renaissance art might never have been done.

The most well known Renaissance artist was probably also the leading Renaissance man. **Leonardo da Vinci** (LEE-uh-NAR-doh duh VIN-chee) spent his life in several different Italian cities, where he worked for different patrons. Da Vinci's interests and talents covered a wide range of fields. You have

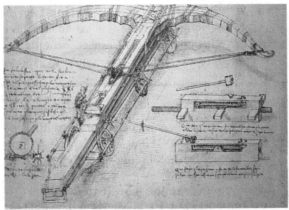

A giant catapult is one of the many inventions in da Vinci's notebooks. His notebooks are filled with writing that can be read only in a mirror as shown in his signature above.

God's hand touches Adam's and brings life to His creation in Michelangelo's painting on the ceiling of the Sistine Chapel.

David's face seems to show that he knows that God has given him the victory over Goliath.

probably seen a photograph of his painting *Mona Lisa*, which many critics consider his best work. He also developed his talents as an architect, sculptor, poet, and mathematician. He experimented with inventions ranging from a machine gun to a helicopter. To record his work, he made careful drawings and notes in several notebooks. Always interested in understanding and recording life around him, he left much information for future generations to study. Inventors today still study Leonardo's notebooks.

Another important artist of the Renaissance was also Italian: Michelangelo Buonarroti, better known as simply **Michelangelo** (MY kul AN juh loh). A sensitive man, he filled his art with emotion and power, whether it was sculpture, painting, or poetry. At times

Michelangelo worked for popes, decorating different buildings in Rome. Although he considered himself to be first a sculptor, his paintings display the great talent he had in that area as well. His most extensive work is the ceiling of the **Sistine (SIS TEEN) Chapel** in Rome. Nearly every day for four years he climbed scaffolding on which he lay to paint the ceiling. The result of his patient determination is a ceiling filled with powerful figures taken mainly from Old Testament stories.

Section Review

1. How did Renaissance paintings differ from medieval paintings?
2. What three techniques did Renaissance painters use?
3. Why was individual creativity more important to Renaissance artists than to medieval artists?
4. What two factors of late medieval life helped Renaissance artists?
5. What were wealthy men who supported artists called?

What qualities of Leonardo da Vinci's life classify him as an example of a Renaissance man?

Other Renaissance Arts

The Renaissance was an age of many types of artists. Although we may be more familiar with Renaissance painters, sculptors, architects, and musicians also used their skills to focus on man and his abilities. Their works reflect the spirit of the age.

Arts to Please the Eye

Sculpture

The sculptures of the Renaissance remind us of the sculpture of the Greeks and Romans. The statues are lifelike, powerful, and beautiful. The new knowledge of anatomy helped sculptors in forming human figures. Working with stone or bronze, they tried to make their figures as realistic as possible.

As a sculptor Michelangelo created figures that seem almost alive. In the closeup of the statue of *David* on the previous page, you can sense David's courage and resolve as he faces Goliath. Michelangelo's fourteen-foot-tall David stands relaxed and ready for the battle before him.

Much medieval sculpture was relief sculpture. That is, it was attached to a flat surface, such as the wall of a cathedral or castle, and could not be viewed from all sides. However many Renaissance sculptors preferred to make freestanding statues. They followed the principles of classical art: balance, harmony, and realism. Some sculptors even imitated the works of Greek and Roman masters. One artist did such a good job that an antique dealer at that time sold one of his works as an antique.

Even in relief sculpture, Renaissance works differ from medieval works. By rounding the figures, showing anatomy, and following the rules of perspective, the artist brought flat sculpture to life.

Architecture

Renaissance architecture rejected most of the Gothic style. Architects came to believe that pointed arches, tall towers, and flying buttresses were neither graceful nor beautiful. Instead, they wanted to return to the architectural style of the Greeks and Romans. Rounded arches, columns, and domes characterized Renaissance architecture. The principles of balance and harmony also influenced Renaissance architects. The soaring towers and ornate decoration of the Gothic cathedrals were judged old-fashioned. In contrast, Renaissance churches and palaces sat solidly balanced on the ground.

Every panel of Ghiberti's chapel doors tells a Bible story from either the Old or New Testament.

During the Renaissance, music had to be painstakingly copied by hand.

Music to Delight the Ear

Music had provided an important source of entertainment during the Middle Ages. Wandering musicians visited castles and towns to perform for the people. Writing, singing, and playing songs were important accomplishments for both young women and men in feudal society. Songs of love and bravery entertained knights and ladies, while townspeople sang songs about work and town life.

Vocal Music

Music was also used as a tool for worship. Monks sang or chanted Scripture at **offices** (services) eight times a day for worship and prayer. Priests, boys' choirs, and the congregation sang as a part of mass. This church music was usually responsive, with a line sung by the priest or choir and then a response sung by the congregation. Since almost everyone in medieval Europe was Catholic, these songs were very familiar to the people.

Because a musical notation, or note, system was not developed until the eleventh century, medieval music had to be taught by memory and was not very consistent. Church music and entertaining songs had many variations as each geographical region added its own changes.

During the Renaissance, music remained important. Renaissance musicians changed both musical forms and instruments. Medieval music, especially church music, had grown confusing. Each voice part might have a different text and might even be in a different language. The Renaissance composers unified the text and also began to clarify the harmonies.

Instrumental Music

Instrumental music became more important during the Renaissance. Towns often had their own bands and other musical groups. Kings' courts, wealthy merchants' households, and even poorer families' celebrations included

Choir boys are still used today to lead processionals in the Roman Catholic Church and other denominations.

Some Renaissance instruments looked very similar to their modern counterparts.

instrumental groups. Today many Renaissance instruments are unknown, but a few we know as forerunners of modern instruments. For example, the oboe comes from the shawm, a reed instrument with a piercing sound. The sackbut was the ancestor of our trombone. The different flutes of the age influenced our modern flute. And of course, the viols, in various sizes and tones, are related to the string family of modern orchestras. Some instruments have changed very little since the Renaissance—recorders, bagpipes, and lutes are still used today. These instruments, plus percussion instruments, added much noise to parties and parades.

Section Review

1. Why were artists important in the Renaissance?
2. What style of sculpting did Renaissance sculptors imitate?
3. How did Renaissance churches differ from Gothic cathedrals?
4. What development allowed songs and hymns to be more consistent?

In what ways does the use of music in church help? In what ways can it hurt?

Summary

As the Middle Ages came to an end and the modern age began, the Renaissance occurred in Europe. The Renaissance was a period of rebirth of interest in the writings and art of classical Greece and Rome. The Renaissance began with the recovery of manuscripts from the East. It continued with a flowering of learning and art. This age emphasized man's abilities and talents, often without giving glory or service to God, man's Creator. This emphasis on man is known as humanism. Although the people of the Renaissance made many advances, they were still lost in sin. The emphasis on man sometimes led them into many sins of the flesh and away from the grace of God. Into this world God sent a period of revival during which His Word was rediscovered and preached abroad.

People, Places, and Things to Know

Renaissance	*The Divine Comedy*	Papal Schism	perspective
Renaissance man	Chaucer	(Great Schism)	patrons
humanism	*Canterbury Tales*	heretics	Leonardo da Vinci
humanities	Petrarch	Inquisition	Mona Lisa
vernacular	Shakespeare	Johannes Gutenberg	Michelangelo
ethnic	*Romeo and Juliet*	anatomy	Sistine Chapel
Dante	Vatican	shading	*David*
			offices

Review Questions

Comparisons

On your paper draw two columns. Label one *Medieval Art* and the other *Renaissance Art.* From the list below, write the items in the correct columns.

balanced   freestanding statues

perspective   relief statues

realistic   flat

no backgrounds

Multiple Choice

Choose the correct answer(s) for each of the following.

1. Renaissance architecture contained all of the following features except
   - (a) rounded arches.
   - (b) columns.
   - (c) flying buttresses.
   - (d) domes.

2. Renaissance men tried to be all of these except a
   - (a) writer.
   - (b) farmer.
   - (c) musician.
   - (d) architect.
   - (e) painter.

3. Which of these men wrote in the vernacular?
   - (a) Dante
   - (b) Chaucer
   - (c) Petrarch
   - (d) Shakespeare

Definitions

Define or explain each of these terms in one or two phrases.

4. patron
5. vernacular
6. perspective
7. Renaissance

Connections

For each of the following pairs of items, write a sentence or two explaining the connection between them.

8. Sistine Chapel / Michelangelo
9. notebooks / Leonardo da Vinci
10. movable type / revival of learning

Masters and Their Pieces

Match each of the following masters at the left with the correct piece of art or work of literature.

11. Shakespeare
12. Michelangelo
13. Chaucer
14. Dante
15. Da Vinci

(a) *Canterbury Tales*
(b) *Mona Lisa*
(c) *The Divine Comedy*
(d) *David*
(e) *Romeo and Juliet*

Think About It!

Renaissance humanists believed that individuals should develop and use their talents to the fullest. Christians today should have the same goal for the talents and abilities that God has given them. Review the text material describing the humanists' view. Then read Romans 12 and Matthew 25:14-30. What should be the difference between your goals for your talents as a Christian and the humanists' goals? Write a two-paragraph essay listing the talents that you believe God has given you. Describe how you can use your talents to glorify God, and tell how you can improve those talents.

CHAPTER 3

The monk wearily pulled himself up from the last step. Looking back, he saw the twenty-eight steps of the staircase below him. He had crawled up them, kneeling at each one and repeating a prayer. He hoped his prayers would release his grandfather from purgatory. The Roman Church said they would, but he could not help thinking to himself, "I wonder whether it's really true?"

The monk was **Martin Luther.** He had traveled to Rome from Germany with another monk on business for his monastery. To a Roman Catholic, Rome was a sacred city where one received blessings for visiting shrines and churches. A devout priest, Luther desired the blessing and the hope of eternal life promised by the church. He spent his days in Rome hurrying from one church to another; he wanted to visit them all. At each one he prayed, and sometimes he said the mass.

At the time of Luther's visit in 1510, the Renaissance was at its height in Rome. Michelangelo lay on his scaffolding while he painted the ceiling of the Sistine Chapel. The foundation for the great church of St. Peter, which was to have the largest dome since the Pantheon, was just being laid. Yet Martin Luther little noticed these works of men's hands. He looked only for peace and blessing for himself and his family.

However, Luther found little peace and spirituality among Rome's clergy. Instead he saw their corruption and lack of interest. Few cared for the things of God, and many wondered why Luther cared so much. The religious Luther was laughed at and scorned by those who were more concerned about the things of this world than the things of God.

A.D. 1400 - A.D. 1650

John Huss Martyred 1415

Great Schism
1378-1415

Gothic Architectural Style 1200-1500

1400	1450

Byzantine Empire 476-1453

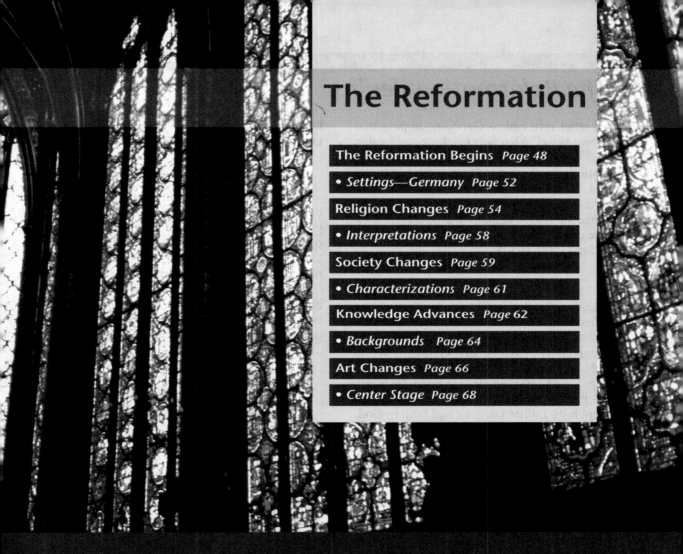

The Reformation

Ninety-five
Theses Posted
1517

England Separates from
Roman Catholic Church 1534

Reformation 1500-1650

1500   1550   1600   1650

Baroque Style 1550-1750

Renaissance 1350-1616

The Reformation Begins

Luther returned to Germany, hoping that his own belief in Rome's teaching gave value to his works. But the sights of Rome and the questions they had raised remained in Luther's mind. Little did he know that when he found the answers, he would upset all of Europe and change the course of history. This change took place during the period known as the **Reformation** (1500-1650).

Luther Finds Peace

Luther lived a good life. As a monk, he studied the Scriptures and writings of church scholars. He was appointed to teach Bible at the university in Wittenberg, Germany. While teaching there, Luther continued his search for the peace of forgiven sin. He knew he was a sinner and that a righteous God could not accept him. Luther knew he had faith in God. What part did his faithful performance of the sacraments have in his salvation? Did they make him more acceptable to God? Luther asked these questions and continued to seek peace.

During his studies Luther finally found the answer to his needs. While studying the book of Romans, he came to understand the meaning of Romans 1:17—"The just shall live by faith." He realized fully that justification, or the meeting of God's demands for justice, is by faith and not by works. Salvation is a free gift of God that cannot be earned. Forgiveness and peace are God's gifts, which the Roman Church could not promise as rewards for works. Luther now received the full assurance that he had long sought. The peace of God comes to a person who understands that his salvation is by faith alone in the Lord Jesus Christ as his Savior from sin. Luther joined Christians of all the ages and rejoiced with Paul: "Therefore being justified by faith, we have peace with God through our Lord Jesus Christ" (Rom. 5:1).

Luther Speaks Out

Luther stayed at the university in Wittenberg and taught his students about the love and grace of God. Luther also continued his study of Scripture. He had not yet left the Roman Church, for he hoped to find and encourage more believers within the church.

Gradually, however, Luther grew angry about corrupt church practices. Finally, he spoke out about one in particular, the selling of indulgences. According to the Roman Church,

AETHERNA IPSE SVAE MENTIS SIMVLACHRA LVTHERVS
EXPRIMIT AT VVLTVS CERA LVCAE OCCIDVOS
·M·D·X·X·

An etching of Martin Luther made in 1520

When a coin rings in the bowl, a soul flies immediately to heaven. That is what Johann Tetzel told the people buying indulgences.

the pope could grant **indulgences,** which were replacements for **penance.** In the sacrament of penance, the church member confessed his sins to the priest, who then assigned him works to do to help him atone for his sins. The earliest indulgences were granted for doing good works, such as giving money or going on a crusade. But by the time of the Renaissance, indulgences were bought and sold outright. The church sold them to raise money.

In 1517, indulgence sellers came to Germany. The pope had sent them to raise money for the building of **St. Peter's Basilica** in Rome. To raise enough money, the sellers abused even the church's purpose for indulgences. They claimed that indulgences had more power than the church had stated. For example, the sellers claimed that indulgences could release the dead from purgatory. Ignorant people eagerly bought them to help their dead loved ones. They also bought them to cover future, deliberate sins; they thought they

Luther responded to indulgence sales by posting ninety-five arguments against them.

The Reformation

The base of this monument features a relief sculpture of Luther before the Diet of Worms. Luther stands to the right of center with his hand over his heart.

could sin and not be punished. But Scripture tells us, "Be sure your sin will find you out" (Num. 32:23).

On October 31, 1517, Luther spoke out against the abuses of indulgence sellers. He posted a list on the Wittenberg church door, the place where town announcements were posted. The list had ninety-five theses, or statements for debate, on the subject of indulgences. Luther had written them in Latin and expected them to be read only by other scholars and churchmen. However, the people of Germany were tired of paying to build an Italian church. Some of them also knew that indulgences did not give the inner peace they sought. Soon Luther's **Ninety-five Theses** were translated into German, printed in great numbers, and sent all over Germany. Without really knowing what he had done, Luther had sparked the movement that grew into the Reformation.

Luther Receives Judgment

In the four years after Luther posted his Ninety-five Theses, he debated monks, wrote

tracts, and kept teaching in Wittenberg. However, church leaders in Rome began to see the trouble he was causing and demanded that he **recant** (take back what he had said). Luther refused, and the pope responded with an order of **excommunication,** which expelled him from the church and withheld the sacraments from him. To a Roman Catholic, excommunication meant the removal of the means of salvation. Yet Luther trusted God, not the church.

Luther was excommunicated in January of 1521. In April of that year he was brought to trial by the emperor for his beliefs. This trial occurred at the **Diet of Worms,** an official assembly of the emperor and German princes meeting in the city of Worms. When commanded again to recant, he refused. In a clear, bold speech, he told the Diet:

Unless I am shown by Scripture and reason that I am wrong, I cannot recant. Here I stand; I can do nothing else. God help me. Amen.

Before the most powerful political and religious leaders of his day, Luther stood strong in his belief in God and the Bible. His faith in

God made him strong. His love of God made him obedient. Luther followed in the footsteps of Peter, who had told the leaders of his day, "We ought to obey God rather than men" (Acts 5:29).

After the Diet of Worms, the emperor declared Luther an **outlaw.** From then on his life was no longer protected by the law; anyone could kill or harm him at any time without fear of punishment. However, God was not yet finished with Luther. God protected Luther while he spent the next twenty-five years writing and teaching about God's truth. God protects His servants until He calls them home.

Every part of European life felt the touch of the Reformation. Many changes that had begun during the Renaissance continued in the Reformation era. These changes marked the beginning of the modern age, and many of them still influence our lives today.

Section Review

1. For what was Luther searching that the Roman Church could not give him? What verse finally gave him the answer?

2. Against what abuse by the Roman Church did Luther speak out?

3. What two things caused the Ninety-five Theses to be spread throughout Germany?

4. Where was Luther brought to trial?

5. How did he respond to his judges?

6. What two judgments were placed on Luther in 1521?

Find another verse besides the one in the text that gives principles for Christians to follow in their attitude toward government. Explain it in your own words.

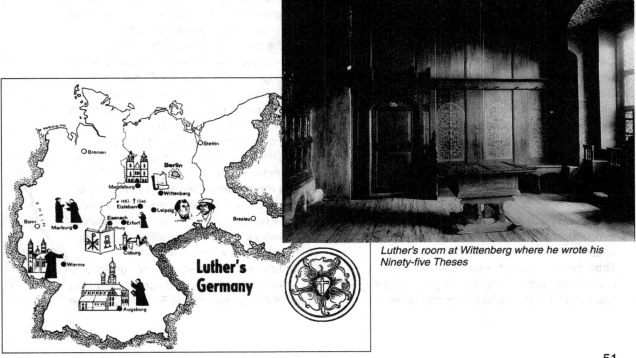

Luther's room at Wittenberg where he wrote his Ninety-five Theses

Luther's Germany

Location—Germany is located in central Europe between France and Poland. It is also bordered by Luxembourg, Belgium, the Netherlands, Denmark, the Czech Republic, Austria, and Switzerland.

Climate—The climate is mostly marine west coast due to the effect of the Baltic and North Seas that border it in the north. In the east, the climate is classified as humid continental. The winds from the sea blow warmer than the land temperature in the winter and cooler than the land temperature in the summer. In the summer the temperature across Germany averages 65°F with cities such as Berlin reaching as high as 74°F. In the winter, temperatures are quite cold in the mountains; but on average across the nation, temperatures do not dip below 30°F. Rainfall averages about thirty-one inches annually.

Topography—Along the coastline, Germany is low and flat, and most of Germany's agriculture takes place on these plains. German farms are small and produce only approximately two-thirds of the food needed by the nation. Because of this lack of production, Germany is one of the world's largest importers of agricultural products. The rest of the country features high plateaus, hills, and mountains. Two well-known features of German topography are the Black Forest and the Bavarian Alps. The Black Forest has been the scene of many fairy tales and legends. The Alps are a favorite vacation spot. Germany has a number of rivers that have acted as highways through the ages. The most important of these rivers are the Rhine, the Weser, and the Elbe.

Natural Resources—Germany's resources of coal and iron have helped to make her a leading industrial nation. Germany has the fourth largest coal reserve in the world as well as large deposits of lead, iron ore, zinc, and potash.

Geography & Culture—Germany's geography has influenced its history and thus its culture. Lying north of the Alps and the Rhine and Danube

Rivers, Germany was outside the northern boundary of the Roman Empire. The tribes that lived there did not unify, and Germany remained a land of separate kingdoms until 1871. Its culture was markedly different from that of the Roman Empire. In 962, Otto I was crowned emperor in Rome, drawing the ties of attachment from the Catholic Church to what would be called the Holy Roman Empire. These ties were not loosened until the stirring of the Reformation. Today Germany's main religion is Lutheranism. The darkest days in Germany's history came from the horrible events that surrounded the dictatorship of Adolf Hitler. World War II left Germany divided into two countries, but East Germany and West Germany were reunited in 1990.

Settings Review

1. What are the three most important rivers in Germany?
2. What natural boundaries kept Germany from becoming a Roman territory?
3. What region became the setting for many legends and stories?
4. What caused Germany to divide?
5. In what year were East Germany and West Germany reunited?

How do you think Germany's natural resources help it in industry and manufacturing?

Scenic towns, castles on hilltops, and villagers in native costumes disguise the fact that Germany is a major industrial force in the modern world.

Religion Changes

Undoubtedly, the most important changes of the Reformation were in religion. Before the Reformation most Europeans followed the teaching of the Roman Church. Some reformers, such as John Wycliffe (WIK lif) in England and John Huss in Bohemia (boh HEE mee uh), had lived before Luther's time. However, not until Luther was the time ripe for the Reformation to occur.

Doctrines Develop

Luther and other reformers of this era opposed the Church of Rome and taught the truth of Scripture. They condemned the Roman Catholic Church for adding tradition to God's Word. Using Scripture alone, the Reformers taught three key doctrines.

1. *The Authority of Scripture.* Luther pointed out that Scripture and tradition often conflicted. God's Word is inspired, while man's traditions are not. Scripture alone is the only reliable authority in spiritual matters (II Tim. 3:16).

2. *Justification by Faith.* As Luther read the Bible, he learned that salvation cannot be earned but is a free gift received by faith. The sacraments of the Roman Church had no power to save. The reformers taught God's truth that a person is saved by faith in Christ's blood (Titus 3:5; Eph. 2:8-9).

3. *The Priesthood of the Believer.* The Renaissance emphasis on the individual helped the reformers state this third doctrine. Luther emphasized that people had to come to God as individuals. At salvation, the individual was made a priest (I Pet. 2:9; Rev. 1:6). The Roman Church taught that priests stood between individuals and God.

John Calvin led the Reformation movement in France and later in Switzerland.

The Reformers proclaimed the truth of I Timothy 2:5—"For there is one God, and one mediator between God and men, the man Christ Jesus."

Each of these three doctrines conflicted with Roman teaching. Because the Reformers based their doctrines on Scripture, they showed how Rome had left the truth of Scripture. With the truth clearly revealed, people began to choose sides.

People Protest

The people who chose to follow Scripture and leave the Roman Catholic Church were called **Protestants.** They received this name when they protested an attempt by Roman Catholic princes in Germany to stop the Reformation. Although their protest did not change the princes' attitude, it did strengthen the Reformation movement. The Protestant movement grew as other people learned of God's truth. The example of these first Protestants still encourages true Christians to practice their heritage of protesting sin and attacks on God's Word.

While Luther worked in Germany, other reformers preached in other parts of Europe. One group of Protestants became known as the **"Reformed" church.** They agreed with Luther on important doctrines, such as justification and opposition to Rome. They differed, however, over certain practices. Luther believed he could follow Roman Church practices as long as they were not forbidden in Scripture. On the other hand, the Reformed Christians said that they should follow only those practices directly commanded in Scripture. As a result, Reformed church services were much plainer and simpler than Lutheran ones.

Men Lead

John Calvin

The most important Reformed leader was **John Calvin** of Geneva, Switzerland. Sometimes Reformed Christians are called simply **"Calvinists,"** after their leader. Calvin was fervent in his study of God's Word, and some called him "the Theologian" (one who studies God's nature and Word). Perhaps his greatest contribution to the Christian church was his writing. Calvin organized and explained the great doctrines of the Reformation and wrote commentaries (books of his observations and explanations) on all but three New Testament books.

Calvinists emphasize that God is sovereign, that He completely rules the universe as He wills, and that He knows who will be saved. Many critics of Calvinism argue that evangelism is useless if those who are to be saved *will* be saved, regardless of man's actions. Calvin answered this criticism when he said, "For as we do not know who belongs to the number of the predestined or who does not belong, we ought to be so minded as to wish that all men be saved. So shall it come about that we try to make everyone we meet a sharer

in our peace." Reformed preachers spread these teachings across Europe.

John Knox

The Reformed Protestants in Scotland were led by **John Knox.** A long-standing feud between Catholic France and Protestant England for control over Scotland was reawakened by the Reformation. As the battle between Protestantism and Catholicism progressed, power changed hands frequently. Knox spent many months as a galley slave as well as time in exile to pay for his Protestant viewpoint. During a return visit to his native land, Knox's preaching strengthened the Protestant movement. Several Protestant noblemen banded together to form a group called the Lords of the Congregation. When the group had gained more power, they invited Knox back to Scotland permanently.

Fiery Scotsman John Knox challenged government and church officials in his stand for God's Word.

During 1560 and 1561, the Scottish Parliament accepted the Reformed confession of faith drawn up by Knox and others. One of Knox's most memorable fights was with Mary, Queen of Scots. In his book *History of the Reformation in Scotland,* he records his five "conversations" with the Roman Catholic queen. In one of these conversations, Mary questioned Knox's right to rebuke the queen openly. Knox was aware of his lack of status and yet felt his responsibility before God to speak of sins in the church and in the state. In response to Mary's questioning, Knox said, "As touching nature I am a worm of this earth, and yet a subject of this commonwealth; but as touching the office wherein it has pleased God to place me [head of the Reformed church in Scotland], I am a watchman, both over the realm and the Kirk [Church] of God. . . . For that reason I am bound in conscience to blow the trumpet publicly."

Knox had several meetings with Queen Mary. Eventually Mary fled to England, and Scotland became a Protestant country.

Mary's sinful lifestyle finally caused her to lose favor with even her Catholic supporters, and she was forced to abdicate the throne. This left Knox unopposed in establishing the Protestant church in Scotland. The Presbyterian Church was the result of Knox's labors.

French Reformers

Reformed Protestants in France were called **Huguenots** (HYOO guh NAHTS). Although there was not one specific French leader who dominated the French Calvinist movement, it still received much persecution from the Catholic monarchy. One of the most infamous events in French history was the Massacre of St. Bartholomew's Day in 1572. On this day the anti-Protestant population of Paris rose up and slaughtered thousands of Huguenots—men, women and children.

England Reforms

The Reformation occurred differently in England. Instead of a reformer leading the fight against Rome, King **Henry VIII** first broke with the pope. His reasons were more political than religious, but his son, **Edward VI,** and daughter **Elizabeth I** strengthened the Protestant cause as well. They established the **Church of England** (or Anglican Church) as the official church, headed by the monarch. In England, the Protestant church was often used to accomplish political goals rather than to answer the needs of a spiritually dead people. However, England's break with the pope did open the way for future revivals in that land.

Catholicism Reacts

The Reformation began because many Catholics were dissatisfied with the Catholic Church. When the reformers began to speak out about problems in Catholic doctrine and practice, they did so with a desire to reform the Catholic Church itself. In the early stages of the Reformation, many Catholics and reformers desired unity. With the goal of bringing the two sides back together, Emperor Charles V sent a request to the pope for a conference on reuniting Catholicism and Protestantism. The pope sent Cardinal **Gaspar Contarini** as his representative to a meeting with Luther's good friend and fellow reformer **Philipp Melanchthon.** Contarini was a sincerely pious man who himself had come to an understanding of justification by faith. In an attempt to bring unity, the two men produced a statement on justification by faith that in the end pleased no one. Protestants accused Melanchthon of being too Catholic, and Catholics accused Contarini of being too Protestant.

As the Reformation spread throughout Europe, Roman Catholics grew more dissatisfied with their church. Many members of the Roman clergy were corrupt and lazy. The Protestants' attacks on the church caused church members to demand changes. In response to these demands, a meeting of high church officials was called. Known as the **Council of Trent,** it met several times over nearly twenty years.

The council wrote a statement of Roman Catholic beliefs and practices. This statement was the first time all Roman Catholic beliefs

The Council of Trent met to discuss reforms needed in the Catholic Church.

and practices were put into writing. The council members confirmed the authority of both Scripture and tradition. They stated justification by faith *and* works as a Roman doctrine. They also set down the doctrine of a human priesthood standing between God and individuals. The church made no attempt to change its doctrines. However, the council did order corrupt practices to stop, removed corrupt clergy, and set stricter standards of discipline. Although the corruption was reduced, the doctrinal problems remained. Many of Rome's doctrines still blinded people to God's truth.

Section Review

1. On what did the reformers base their beliefs?
2. How did the Protestants receive their name?
3. Who was the leader of the Reformed Christians? the Presbyterian Church?
4. Which English monarchs aided the Protestant cause in England?

5. What two men attempted to bring the Catholics and Protestants back together?
6. Why was the Council of Trent called and what was its result?

How did each of the three key doctrines of the reformers differ from the doctrines of the Roman Catholic Church?

INTERPRETATIONS

Communication Through Cartoons

The printing press proved a great tool for the Reformers. They published sermons, tracts, and books for everyone to read. One problem remained, however: what about people who could not read? In response to this need, the reformers, as well as the Roman Church, began producing cartoons to communicate their cause. These cartoons are the forerunners of political cartoons.

You have probably seen political cartoons in your local newspaper. These cartoons express an opinion, usually by making fun of some famous person or event. The cartoons of the Reformation were usually not "funny." Instead they simply attacked the opposing position, sometimes viciously. Here are two examples of Reformation cartoons. The first is a Roman Catholic cartoon attacking Luther, entitled "The Devil Playing Luther as a Pair of Bagpipes." This drawing intends to show that Luther's words and actions were directly inspired by Satan by showing Luther as merely an instrument "played" by Satan. The

bagpipes supposedly represent the droning tone of voice used by preachers of that time.

A pro-Luther artist drew a cartoon entitled "The German Hercules." This cartoon shows Luther as the German equivalent of the Greek mythological hero Hercules. Luther has Hercules' symbols, such as a great war club and the lion's skin worn as a sign of power. But whereas Hercules triumphed over creatures such as the fierce, three-headed dog Cerberus (SUR bur us), the artist shows Luther defeating the great scholars of the Roman Church. The idea, of course, is that Luther has single-handedly overcome the whole Roman Church by proclaiming justification by faith alone. The pope himself is in the drawing, dangling helplessly from Luther's nose. The Devil is shown fleeing in the background.

Political cartoons continued to flourish. One of the most famous American political cartoonists was Thomas Nast. His cartoons helped reduce political corruption in New York City in the late 1800s. Just as in earlier cartoons, Nast's cartoons relied on easily recognized characters so that even a person who could not read could understand the message.

Political cartoons eventually found their place on the editorial pages of newspapers. They continue to be biased and make their point by being extreme in their attack on a subject. The art has changed, and the intent is now usually more humorous. Still the underlying goal of the political cartoon remains the same: to stimulate thinking and to inspire change by expressing an opinion or by defending or attacking a certain position.

Society Changes

Besides emphasizing right doctrine, the reformers also emphasized right family relationships. Luther knew families were a gift from God. Although he remained single for several years after breaking with Rome, Luther encouraged other former monks and nuns to marry. In 1525, he decided to marry too in order to set an example for other Protestant families and to rear children to serve the Lord. He chose Katherine von Bora, a former nun, whom he affectionately called Katie. They had six children, three sons and three daughters. They also reared several orphans, boarded students, and played host to guests and relatives. The Luther household often held as many as twenty-five people.

Christian Families

From the Scripture Luther formed definite ideas about families. A faithful, loving, and obedient wife was a blessing second only to the Word of God for the Christian man. Parents should love and discipline their children to teach them to obey authority—whether it be God's, a parent's, or the government's. Proverbs 22:6 states, "Train up a child in the way he should go: and when he is old, he will not depart from it." Bringing up children to honor and serve the Lord is a Christian parent's God-given responsibility. Luther knew that what a child learned at home greatly influenced his moral and spiritual life.

> Sermons very little edify children, who learn little thereby; it is more needful they be taught and well instructed in schools, and at home, and that they be heard and examined what they have learned; this way profits much; 'tis very wearisome, but very necessary.
>
> (Martin Luther—*Table Talks*, #266)

Luther's family set an example for other Christian families. The Luther home was a happy, busy place. Mealtimes with children and students were usually times of talking. The students so admired their teacher that they

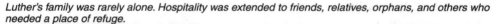

Luther's family was rarely alone. Hospitality was extended to friends, relatives, orphans, and others who needed a place of refuge.

often brought paper and pens to the table to take notes. On special occasions, Luther wrote pageants and songs for his household. His children especially enjoyed the Christmas carols he wrote for them.

Christians in the Community

Luther and other reformers emphasized the role of Christians in society. They taught their followers that God desired servants who worked not for their own glory but for God's glory (I Cor. 10:31). Christians are responsible to God for how they use their talents and abilities. Unlike the Renaissance humanists, the reformers said that a person should dedicate his talents to God, not to himself.

The reformers also encouraged Christians to work hard in their occupations. Any consecrated Christian worker, whether shoemaker, carpenter, or farmer, is as much God's servant as a clergyman. The reformers did not agree with the Roman Church, which said only clergy were doing God's service. They taught that everything a believer did was service to God. Christians are to be a testimony of God's grace as they go about their daily tasks.

Political Changes

The Reformation brought not only religious and social changes to Europe but also political changes. Many nobles did not like the power that the pope and the Roman Church had in their lands. They saw Protestantism as a way to free themselves from the church's influence. For 130 years after Luther posted his Ninety-five Theses, Roman Catholics and Protestants fought one another in the so-called **Wars of Religion.**

These wars resulted in the freeing of northern Europe from the domination of the pope. Kings and princes gained the right and power to rule their people. They now had the authority to decide whether their people would follow Protestant or Roman Catholic teaching. Whichever church the noble chose received support from state taxes. Everyone in that town had to join the church in that area. Any people who did not want that choice either moved to a different town or suffered persecution. Although the reformers had shown individuals the way of peace through Christ's blood, they had not brought peace to Europe. Peace will not come until the Prince of Peace rules on earth.

Section Review

1. Why did Luther finally decide to marry?
2. What should a Christian do with his talents?
3. In what way did the reformers differ from the Roman Church regarding service to God?
4. Why did European princes fight the Wars of Religion?
5. Name one result of the Wars of Religion.

   Why do rules or laws fail to make a school or city good? What is required for true goodness?

Luther's Life and Family

Luther preached against the Catholic Church's insistence that ministers of the gospel remain single. After hearing his preaching, many nuns wrote for help to escape their convents. Luther helped nine nuns leave one convent. On April 4, 1524, a friend of Luther helped the nuns sneak over the wall and then hid them in barrels on a wagon until they were out of the city. One of these nuns was Katherine von Bora.

After making diligent efforts to find good husbands for the nuns whose families would not receive them, Luther was left to find a husband for Katherine von Bora. One suitor refused her in October of 1524, and when Luther arranged for another match, Katie showed that she had a mind of her own by not only rejecting that match but also saying that she would accept only Luther or another pastor named Amsdorf as her suitor.

Luther endured much teasing about getting married. He responded with, "I shall not take a wife; not because I am by nature averse to matrimony—for I am neither wood nor stone,—but I am disinclined to it, because I am every day expecting death as inflicted upon a heretic. I do not wish to obstruct God's work in me, nor rely upon my own heart for comfort."

At first Luther did not care for Katherine and "supposed she was proud and haughty." That feeling changed, though, and Katherine and Luther were married on June 13, 1525. Luther later said, "And thank God, it hath turned out well; for I have a pious and faithful wife, to whom one may safely commit his heart."

The Luthers' marriage was blessed with six children. On June 6, 1526, Luther wrote, "I am a happy husband, and may God continue to send me happiness, for from the most precious woman, my best of wives, I have received, by the blessing of God, a little son, John Luther, and, by God's wonderful grace, I have become a father."

The firstborn was followed by a daughter, Elizabeth. Elizabeth died at eight months, and the following letter, written by Luther, reveals his sorrow—"My little daughter Elizabeth is taken from me, and hath left me with a bleeding and almost womanly heart, so sad am I on her account. I never thought the heart of a father was so tender toward his children. Pray the Lord for me."

A third child, Magdalene, was born in 1529. She also died young. Luther's words at the coffin of his thirteen-year-old daughter show his father's heart and the Christian's hope: "Darling Lena, you will rise and shine like a star, yea, like the sun. I am happy in spirit, but the flesh grieves me beyond measure. I have sent a saint to heaven."

After Magdalene came Martin, then Paul, and finally Margaret. Each child helped to fill the Luther home with joy. It was for his children that Luther wrote the Small Catechism—a book giving the fundamentals of Lutheran beliefs.

Knowledge Advances

Luther was well educated. Before becoming a monk, he had studied to be a lawyer. He knew Latin, Greek, and Hebrew and had read many ancient manuscripts. This knowledge especially helped him read and understand Scripture in the original languages. He encouraged Christians to study hard and use their knowledge to serve the Lord and understand Him better. All his life Luther studied and taught others.

Luther and Education

Although Luther read Scripture in the original languages, he knew that most people did not know Greek or Hebrew. The Roman Church used a Latin translation of the Bible, but few commoners knew Latin. To bring God's Word to the people, Luther decided to translate and publish the Bible in the vernacular. In 1534 he finished the complete Bible in German, translated from the Hebrew and Greek. Now the Germans could read and understand Scripture

in their own language. Many German Christians today still use Luther's translation.

Luther used the vernacular for most of his writings. Following his example, other reformers also wrote in their native languages. The Reformation, along with the Renaissance, encouraged reading and education as well as the development of the modern languages used today. With more books and pamphlets available in the language they understood, people began to learn to read. Education using the vernacular (rather than Latin and Greek) increased, and more people were able to receive an education.

New Interest in Science

The interest in learning about the world continued in the Reformation era. Many new ideas, methods, and inventions were added to the scientific knowledge of this time. People questioned how and why things worked. They experimented, observed, and reached conclusions. Several of their methods are similar to those used by scientists today. This period marks the beginning of the modern age of science.

An area in which several discoveries occurred was astronomy. In 1543 **Copernicus** (koh PUR nuh kus) presented his view that the earth revolved around the sun, not the sun around the earth. We accept this truth today, but the men of Copernicus's day laughed at him and condemned him for being foolish. Copernicus used mathematics to reach his conclusions. Another astronomer, **Galileo Galilei** (GAL-uh-LEE-oh GAL-uh-LAY-ee), used the newly invented telescope for his observations. His results supported Copernicus's ideas. Although scientific data supported these views, most people held on to their former beliefs about the earth. Years passed before people accepted scientific views.

Other Advances

Advances also came in medicine. Rejecting superstitious remedies, scientists began to investigate the body and treat its diseases. One scientist stated that the body is mostly chemicals and should be treated with chemicals. Your doctor follows this practice when he prescribes medicine for you. Other scientists studied anatomy. By learning the positions of bones, muscles, and organs, they were able to give better diagnoses and treatment. The Englishman **William Harvey** discovered that blood is pumped by the heart, travels through the body in blood vessels, and returns to the heart in the circulatory system. This information seems commonplace to us today. But during the 1600s it greatly improved the care of the sick and opened the door of modern medical research.

The interest in business and science encouraged improvements in mathematics. Two improvements that occurred around the time of the Reformation were the more common use of Arabic numerals and the use of the decimal point. Prior to this time, mathematic equations were written in standard form (every number word written out), making equations enormous and difficult to read. The use of the decimal point made problems with fractions, which had once taken hours, easy and quick to figure. These changes in mathematics aided people in the early modern age and still help us today.

Section Review

1. What truth did Copernicus state in his day?
2. How did Galileo support Copernicus's theory?
3. List three advances in medicine during the Reformation era.
4. How did the use of decimals improve mathematics?

Explain why you think it was so hard for people to accept Copernicus's findings even after Galileo supported them.

The telescope invented by Galileo gave further evidence that Copernicus's view of the solar system was accurate.

Medicine or Myth?

Medicine during the late Renaissance followed the same course that medicine had for hundreds of years—guesses, myths, and quackery. Because they had few ways of analyzing the functions of the body, early doctors were really in the dark as to how to treat illness. When a plague (epidemic) broke out, they knew how to do little else but attempt to ease the pain of the victim while the disease ran its course. One of the fundamental mistakes they made was in the area of hygiene. Because they thought the air carried the disease, which it sometimes did, or that sickness was caused by "flying venom," they would cover their mouths or burn aromatic leaves but then fail to wash their hands after attending an afflicted friend or family member. When William Harvey practiced medicine in 1618, only a few of his friends were doing dissections and experiments on animals to find out *how* the body worked. Very few of his fellow physicians believed Harvey's suggestion that the blood was pumped in a circular flow by the heart. Most people thought he was a quack. Slowly they accepted his findings.

With the development of the microscope by Leeuwenhoek and Hooke, scientists began to see that small organisms actually carried disease, and therefore physicians looked for more sound methods of treatment.

Note the following strange remedies:

If an adder (snake) strike a man, wash a black snail in holy water, and give to the sick to drink.

If a man eat wolfsbane (a poisonous plant), let him stand upon his head, let someone strike him with many scarifications on the shanks; then the venom departs out through the incisions.

"Quick! More snails!" Renaissance cures seem strange to us, but early doctors sometimes found the basis for later cures. However, today doctors use antivenin, not snails, to cure snake bites.

In his medical book *Rosa Angelica,* John Gaddesen tells how he treated smallpox in the son of Edward II by putting him in a room draped with red because "reds cure red." It was commonly thought that red rashes, fevers, and other red diseases could be treated by having the patient look at the color red.

Some treatments that we would consider strange did work. Occasionally wounds that today would require stitches were held together using beetles with pincers. The edges of the wound were held together, and a large beetle with pincers was brought to the wound. The angry beetle would pinch the edges together. When its pincers were in place, the beetle's head would be severed from its body and remain pinched onto the wound until it healed. Spider webs were used to help wounds clot faster. The web formed a base on which the blood cells could collect and coagulate.

As doctors and scientists learned more about the inner workings of the body, many previously accepted medical methods were discontinued. One method that doctors stopped using was leeching. When someone was sick or perhaps just as a precaution, doctors prescribed that bad blood be removed. To remove the bad blood, the doctor attached leeches to the patient. When the leech was full, the job was finished. But when someone was sick, further weakening by blood loss sometimes proved fatal. (Medicinal leeches average ten to twelve centimeters in length and can expand quite a bit.) With advanced science and medicine, leeching was put aside until recently, when medical professionals began occasionally using leeches on patients who had severed fingers and hands reattached. One of the greatest discomforts of reattachment occurs immediately after surgery before the small capillaries reroute. The blood pools under the skin and causes throbbing pain. (If you have ever gotten your finger pinched in a door and had blood pool under your fingernail, you can begin to know how much reattachment hurts and throbs.) Doctors have found that using leeches to drain away the excess blood greatly relieves the pain.

Doctors are looking into other remedies that were used in the past to see if they have any medical value. The result for us may be better healing that does not require eating snails or poisonous plants.

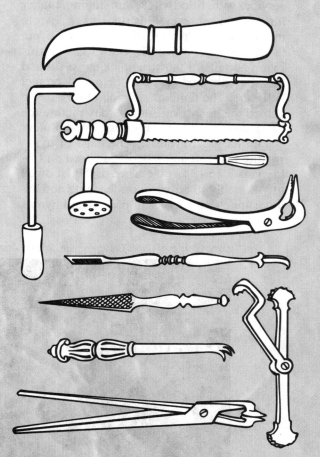

These Renaissance doctor's instruments look more like something you would find in your father's tool chest.

Art Changes

Music in the Church

The reformer Martin Luther enjoyed music and believed that it helped people worship and praise God. He encouraged Christians to sing in church, at home, or at work. Unlike services in the Roman Church, where congregational singing was discouraged, Luther's services were filled with hymn singing. Luther himself played several instruments and wrote many songs and hymns. His best-known hymn is "A Mighty Fortress Is Our God." In this hymn he tells of the struggle against sin and the strength God gives to help and protect believers. The familiar sight of a lord's castle helped the people of Luther's day picture the Lord God as a "Mighty Fortress." With Luther began the great Protestant heritage of hymn writing and singing, a heritage based on Colossians 3:16—"Let the word of Christ dwell in you richly in all wisdom; teaching and admonishing one another in psalms and hymns

St. Jerome as a Cardinal, *by El Greco, typifies mannerist style.*

and spiritual songs, singing with grace in your hearts to the Lord."

Mannerism in Painting

The painting of the early Reformation era reflected the spirit of that age. Uncertainty and turmoil resulted from the attacks on the Roman

Luca Giordano, Christ Cleansing the Temple, *The Bob Jones University Collection*

The Latin inscription on this harpsichord says "to the glory of God alone."

Church and the Protestants' break with Rome. The style called **mannerism** contrasted the warmth and confidence of the Renaissance style with coldness and distortion. Mannerists used confined space, showed movement, and used contorted figures. Some artists, such as El Greco, showed distortion in exaggerated long, thin figures. To a Europe torn by religious and political strife, the mannerist style mirrored conflict and uncertainty.

The Baroque Style

Beginning around 1600, a new style began to appear in Europe. The **baroque** (buh ROKE) style looked back to both the Gothic and Renaissance styles. Rejecting the coldness of mannerism, baroque artists celebrated life as they showed the energy and vitality of this age of change. Round, bold flourishes, great movement, open spaces, and attention to detail all characterize the baroque style.

The baroque style affected all of the arts. Painting, architecture, sculpture, and music of the seventeenth century show a baroque influence. Many churches and palaces were built in the baroque style, and these structures displayed the wealth and majesty of their owners. The interiors of such buildings were covered with baroque paintings. In some instances it is hard to tell where architecture ends and painting begins.

Music also changed greatly during the baroque period. For the first time, several instruments familiar to us today were used. String instruments (which had their beginning in the Middle Ages) took the shape and sound we recognize today. Two favorite baroque instruments were the organ and the harpsichord, the forerunner of the piano. Composers wrote music to fit these different instruments. They also combined several instruments to form small chamber groups or larger orchestras.

The music itself changed as well. Composers began to use the octave (eight-note) scales we use today. They used harmony and added musical decorations such as trills. They also invented standard musical forms still used today. One example is the concerto, in which a solo instrument plays a duet with a larger instrumental group.

Johann Sebastian Bach is one of the most well-known baroque composers.

Renaissance Women in Art?

You may think that the only historic women in art are the ones *in* the pictures, but that is not the case. Pliny the Elder tells of Greek and Roman female artists, and there is evidence of women doing manuscript illustrations in the Middle Ages. However, prior to the Renaissance, few artists, male or female, took personal credit for their art. Famous late-Renaissance female artists did not have shops on every street, but here are two who deserve some attention.

Sofonisba Anguissola (ang GWEE so la) was born in 1532 to a wealthy noble family. Her father took humanist philosophy to heart and trained his daughters in music and art. When Sofonisba's father recognized her special ability, he wrote to ask Michelangelo to critique her drawing and painting. After having received Sofonisba's drawing of a smiling girl, Michelangelo wrote back and said that a true challenge was to draw a crying child. She accepted the challenge and created her drawing entitled *Boy Being Pinched by a Crayfish*.

At age twenty-seven, Sofonisba Anguissola was invited to paint for King Philip II of Spain. Her example as the first professional woman painter became an inspiration to women who would follow in her footsteps.

Artemesia Gentileschi (jane tee LES kee) was a painter who followed in her father's footsteps. Her father, Orazio, was a painter himself and a friend of a more famous painter, Caravaggio (CAR ah VA jo). Both painters of the late Renaissance, Gentileschi and Caravaggio were affected by the realism of the Renaissance and the tension of mannerism. Caravaggio's use of chiaroscuro (kee ahr uh SKOOR oh) is especially notable and helped him create what became the baroque style. (Chiaroscuro is the high contrast of light and dark in a painting.)

The influence of Caravaggio is evident in Artemesia's work in chiaroscuro and in strong color, but her work tends to have greater emotion. Many of her paintings appear to have caught the event in photographic style at the moment of highest intensity. In the 1625 painting *Judith and Maidservant with the Head of Holofernes* (below), there is a feeling of suspense and quiet as the two women have committed the crime and now must flee the enemy camp. (This story is from the Apocrypha, a collection of nonbiblical Jewish writings.) Artemesia is especially known for her portrayal of female biblical characters.

Artemesia painted during the baroque era. As artistic fashion changed in one location, she maintained the demand for her paintings by moving to France and later England rather than change her style.

Courtesy of the Detroit Institute of Arts

The baroque era lasted until the middle 1700s. The two most important baroque composers lived near the end of this era. **Johann Sebastian Bach** (BAHKH) was born in Germany. Bach composed pieces for organ, harpsichord, and chamber groups. He worked for many years as the choirmaster and organist for the Protestant church in Leipzig, Germany. There he wrote weekly services of music. With words taken from Scripture, his choral works express the Reformation thought and spirit of devotion to God. Another great baroque composer was **George Frederick Handel** (HAN dul). Although born in Germany, he spent most of his life in England. His best-known work is the oratorio ***Messiah,*** which combines vocalists and instrumentalists. This masterpiece of baroque style and expression remains a vivid account of Christ's life. The goal of baroque composers was to glorify God, show majesty, and express human feelings such as sorrow, pain, joy, or heroism.

Section Review

1. Why did Luther encourage Christians to sing?
2. What style of art expressed the turmoil of the early Reformation?
3. What style of art celebrated the energy and life of the later Reformation?
4. What two composers best captured the spirit of the baroque era?

How does singing hymns or spiritual songs help us in our walk with the Lord? Give an example of a hymn or spiritual song you like, and tell how it has helped you.

Summary

The Reformation began when Martin Luther spoke out against the Roman Catholic Church. Luther had found forgiveness for his sin through Christ's blood. Gradually he concluded that Roman Church doctrine did not agree with Scripture. Luther was excommunicated and, after the Diet of Worms, outlawed. He spent the rest of his life teaching others about Christ. The Reformation spread to other countries in Europe, where other reformers led the movement. The Reformation sparked many changes in European life and is usually considered the beginning of the modern age. Changes occurred in science, math, education, the arts, and governments. Even so, the most important change brought by the Reformation was the availability of the Scriptures. Individual hearts were transformed as they accepted the teachings of Scripture and were saved by faith in Christ.

CHAPTER REVIEW

People, Places, and Things to Know

Martin Luther
Reformation
indulgences
penance
St. Peter's Basilica
Ninety-five Theses
recant
excommunication
Diet of Worms

outlaw
Protestants
Reformed church
John Calvin
Calvinists
John Knox
Huguenots
Henry VIII
Edward VI

Elizabeth I
Church of England
Anglican Church
Gaspar Contarini
Philipp Melanchthon
Council of Trent
Wars of Religion
Copernicus
Galileo Galilei

William Harvey
mannerism
baroque
Johann Sebastian
Bach
George Frederick
Handel
Messiah

Review Questions

Charting

Copy the chart below onto your paper; then complete it.

Man	Country	Name of Church
1. Martin Luther		
2.	Switzerland	
3.		Presbyterian
4. Edward VI		

Short Answer

Answer the following questions with one word or phrase. When you have finished, the first letter of each answer will spell the word that means "to take back what one has said."

5. What term is given to the historical period from 1500-1650?

6. What did the pope do to Luther when he refused to give up his ideas?

7. Which reformer taught that God knows who will be saved?

8. What Protestant doctrine threw out the authority of Roman Catholic Church tradition?

9. What did Luther post on the Wittenberg church door?

10. Where was the council held that put Roman Catholic Church doctrine in writing for the first time?

Matching

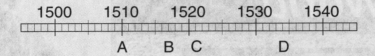

Match these events in Luther's life to the time line.

11. finished translating the German Bible
12. attended the Diet of Worms
13. posted his Ninety-five Theses
14. visited Rome

Connections

For each of the following pairs of items, write a sentence or two explaining the connection between them.

15. indulgences / St. Peter's Basilica
16. Protestants / Huguenots
17. justification by faith / priesthood of believers

Matching

Match these items.

18. Copernicus
19. Galileo
20. Harvey
21. mannerism
22. Bach
23. Handel

(a) *Messiah*
(b) earth revolved around the sun
(c) telescope
(d) baroque organ music
(e) circulation of the blood
(f) used distortion

Think About It!

Martin Luther, John Calvin, and John Knox were willing to stand firm for their beliefs and make a difference. How do these men evidence the working of God? What principles in their victories and defeats can you use in your own walk with the Lord?

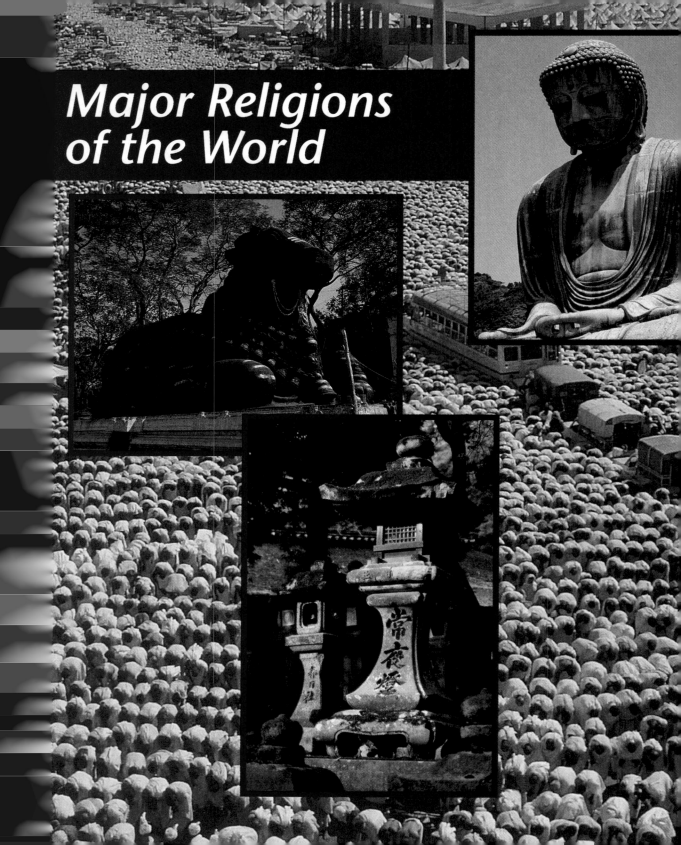

Major Religions of the World

Hinduism

A Hindu woman pours her prayer into the sacred Ganges River.

Hinduism (HIN doo iz um) is the main religion of India. In fact it is more than just a religion. The beliefs and practices of Hinduism influence the whole Indian way of life.

Hinduism is polytheistic. The Hindus worship thousands of gods, although they consider three gods to be more important than the others. According to Hindu teaching, Brahma (BRAH muh) is the Creator, Shiva (SHEE vuh) is the Destroyer, and Vishnu (VISH noo) is the Preserver. Hindus believe that these three gods, plus the other thousands they worship, are only different forms of the World Soul. In fact, everything in the world—plants, animals, gods—is part of the World Soul.

Hinduism also teaches that people are part of the World Soul. But while a person is on earth, his soul is separated from the World Soul. The Hindu's goal in life is to reunite his soul with the World Soul. This reunion is his

form of salvation. All life to the Hindus is a cycle. They believe that one is born from the World Soul into a body. Eventually the person will return to the World Soul.

By following Hindu practices, the Hindu hopes to be good enough to obtain salvation. Rarely, however, can a person achieve his goal in one lifetime. Because of this problem, Hinduism teaches that a person is reborn several times into different bodies, both human and animal. This process of several rebirths is called reincarnation. In each new body he works to earn release from the cycle of reincarnation. Reincarnation adds many steps to the cycle of Indian life: after passing through several bodies, the soul finally returns to the World Soul.

In John 3:7 Jesus says, "Ye must be born again." When a person is saved by Christ, he is born again and receives eternal life. This new birth is a spiritual rebirth that occurs only once. In contrast, Hinduism teaches many physical rebirths in which the soul receives a new body.

Hindus believe that by doing good works they will reunite with the World Soul. Therefore, they faithfully pray and go to their temples to offer sacrifices and give money. Some Hindus even believe they can earn reunification by starving themselves or inflicting pain on themselves. They believe that harming their bodies in this way will make their souls purer.

The number of hands on the Hindu god Kali symbolizes her power.

Hinduism does not concern itself only with man's relationship to the gods but also with man's relationship to other men. Everything is part of the World Soul to Hinduism. Therefore, groups are more important than individuals. A basic social group in India throughout its history has been the caste.

Every Hindu belongs to a caste (KAST), one of the divisions of Hindu society. These castes come in a particular order. The Hindus believe that the higher a person is in the caste system, the closer he is to reuniting with the World Soul. Every Hindu hopes that his next rebirth will put him in a higher caste.

Traditionally, there are four main varnas (groups of castes) in Hindu society. Within these varnas are hundreds of castes. The highest varna is the priestly one. A member of this varna is said to reunite immediately with the World Soul when he dies. Next in importance is the varna of rulers and warriors. Merchants and traders make up the third varna, and servants belong to the lowest varna. Some Indians are completely outside the caste system. They are called untouchables, or outcastes. Untouchables include any non-Hindu, anyone who works with dead flesh, and anyone expelled from his own caste.

The caste determines many of a Hindu's activities in life. Each caste has rules governing its members. The caste rules dictate where one lives, what one wears, whom one marries, with whom one can eat, and what one's occupation is. In order to be reborn into a higher caste, a Hindu has to accept his present caste and keep all the caste rules. A Hindu who does more or less than his caste demands is unlikely to be reborn on a higher level. In recent years, Indian governments have tried to modify the caste system, but it remains a major influence in the lives of Hindus.

Buddhism

A Buddhist temple framed against the backdrop of Mount Fuji in Japan

Near the end of the sixth century B.C. there lived a man in India who disagreed with Hinduism. He particularly rejected the idea that only members of the highest caste were ready to reunite with the World Soul. This rejection of Hinduism started Siddhartha Gautama (GAW-tuh-muh) on a journey that would not end until he had gone beyond Hinduism to found his own religion.

Gautama was the son of a ruler and therefore a member of a high caste. He had great wealth and a loving family, but still he felt unsatisfied. Furthermore, he saw illness, pain, and death outside the walls of his palace. Finally, at age twenty-nine, Gautama left his home to seek peace not only for himself but also for all of those he saw suffering around

him. For several years he tried living as a hermit, meditating deeply while nearly starving himself to death. But this self-discipline brought no satisfaction. Then one day while meditating under a tree, Gautama became "enlightened" about the meaning of life. He became known as *Buddha*, which means "Enlightened One."

Buddha stated his enlightenment—his new view of life—in Four Noble Truths:

1. All life is suffering.
2. Man's desire for pleasure, possessions, and power is the cause of that suffering.
3. To remove suffering, man must overcome his desires.
4. By doing good works, man can overcome his desires and his suffering.

As guidelines for how to do good works, Buddha offered as part of the Fourth Noble Truth what is called the Eightfold Path.

1. Right Understanding—Recognize the truth of the Four Noble Truths.
2. Right Thought—Resolve to embrace good thoughts and to shun evil ones, such as hatred.
3. Right Speech—Direct one's words toward peace and truth instead of lying or slander.
4. Right Action—Live in a moral manner and shun sins such as murder, stealing, and sexual immorality.
5. Right Livelihood—Work in an occupation that brings no harm to anyone else.
6. Right Effort—Stifle evil desires and strengthen good ones.
7. Right Awareness—Think through choices carefully and do not give in to desires.
8. Right Meditation—Practice meditation, the concentration on what is true and good.

Buddha said that a person did not have to be a priest or follow the priest's instructions and religious rituals. Rather he must be good and kind in order to be happy. If one is kind to others, behaves well, and meditates on good things, he will not have to continue in his reincarnation process. A person does not have to accept his caste, live by his caste's rules, and hope to enter a higher caste at death. Buddha taught that a person could work and achieve salvation by his own efforts.

Buddhism never became popular in India, probably because Buddha rejected some Hindu teaching. The religion spread, however, to other Asian lands. It went to China and from there to Japan and eventually to all of Southeast Asia. Different forms of Buddhism developed. Two competing forms are Mahayana ("greater vehicle") Buddhism and Hinayana ("lesser vehicle") Buddhism. The "vehicles" refer to the way of salvation. As Buddhists describe it, imagine that one's house is on fire and that all of one's family and possessions must be gathered into a wagon to be saved. The stricter Hinayana "wagon," with its rules and high standards, can carry fewer people to safety. The larger vehicle of the more tolerant, less demanding Mahayana version can carry more.

A popular form that developed in Japan is Zen Buddhism. This form places special emphasis on the importance of meditation. A Zen Buddhist will usually meditate by concentrating on solving an unsolvable question, such as "What is the sound of one hand clapping?" This form of Buddhism has become one of the best-known forms in North America and Europe.

Images of Buddha vary according to the country in which they are worshiped. This Buddha is located in Sri Lanka.

Islam

No matter where they are, Muslim men take off their shoes, kneel on their prayer mats, and face Mecca to pray.

Muhammad, the founder of Islam, was born in Mecca in the Arabian peninsula in A.D. 570. Muhammad claimed to have had visions of an angel who came from Allah, an Arab god. Muhammad said that he had become Allah's messenger, or prophet, to take Allah's message to the world. He proclaimed that Allah was the only god and that all must worship Allah alone. In the year 632 Muhammad and his followers made the city of Mecca their center of operations. Mecca in Arabia is the holy city of Islam. It is the site of the Kaaba (KAH buh), a shrine that is sacred to the Muslims. From Arabia, Muhammad's religion grew in power and numbers, spreading far and wide.

Muhammad taught his followers that all people must convert to Islam. Rather than sending out missionaries to teach people about Allah, Muhammad and later leaders sent out armies to force people to Allah. Muhammad named these battles of conquest *jihad* (jih HAHD), meaning "striving." Muslim horsemen and infantry set out from Mecca to conquer the world for Allah. Within a hundred years after Muhammad's death, the Islamic empire stretched from Spain to India. Today Muslims are strongest in the Middle East, but they are also numerous in Asia and Africa.

The Muslims brought new social customs and ideas on family life to their converts. They frown upon drinking wine, eating pork, and gambling. They also teach that women should be kept apart from men. Beginning at age twelve, women veil their faces and are rarely seen in public.

Muslims follow the Koran (kuh RAN), the sacred book of Islamic teaching. They believe that the Koran is the word of Allah that came through Muhammad's visions of the angel. Islam has five basic beliefs known as the Five Pillars. The Koran teaches that a Muslim must submit to Allah by keeping the Five Pillars. According to the Koran, a Muslim who faithfully practices all Five Pillars and does good to others will enter heaven. The Five Pillars are as follows.

Belief—To become a Muslim one must only repeat the Islamic statement of belief: "There is no god but Allah and Muhammad is his prophet." Islam is a monotheistic religion that teaches that Allah is the only god. Muhammad said that other prophets had come before him—Adam, Noah, Abraham, Moses, and Jesus—but he was the last one and had the true message of God. He taught that Jesus Christ was just a man and not the Son of God.

Prayer—"Allah is most great. I testify that there is no god but Allah. I testify that Muhammad is the Messenger of Allah. Come to prayer. Come to security. Allah is most great." Five times a day Muslims hear this call to prayer. At dawn, noon, mid-afternoon, evening, and bedtime, a faithful Muslim removes his shoes and stands on a prayer rug facing toward Mecca. While reciting memorized prayers, he stands, sits, kneels, and bows. A Muslim follows this prayer ritual no matter where he is. Sometimes he goes to a mosque (MAHSK), a Muslim house of worship, to pray.

Alms giving—Alms giving is giving to the poor. Muslims must give a certain amount of their income to help the poor. They give either money or products from their fields and flocks as alms. Usually the government collects and gives out the alms. Today Muslims give their alms by paying a religious tax.

Fasting—Muslims fast during the month of Ramadan (RAM uh DAHN), the month in which Muhammad had his first vision. For the twenty-eight days of this month, Muslims must not eat, drink, or smoke between dawn and sunset. Once the sun sets, however, life returns to normal. Muslims visit their friends and family, attend religious instruction in the mosques, and, of course, eat. When the sun rises, the fast is once more in effect.

Pilgrimage—A Muslim must make a pilgrimage to Mecca once during his lifetime if he is able. The time for pilgrimage is two months after Ramadan. Thousands of Muslims visit Mecca. The pilgrimage is the highlight of a Muslim's life, and a pilgrim receives great respect from other Muslims.

Pages from the Koran

Conclusion

The Woman at the Well *by François de Troy (The Bob Jones University Collection)*

As a Christian considers the teachings of other religions—such as Hinduism, Buddhism, and Islam—he may note that some points are correct. He can agree with Buddhism that a person should not murder or steal, and he can agree with Islam that people should give to the poor. Many of the beliefs and practices of Islam, as well as many of the stories in the Koran, are similar to those of Christianity and the Bible. But a Christian must judge everything by the teachings of Scripture. The Bible reveals how other religions of the world are desperately wrong on some essential facts.

Hinduism, Buddhism, and Islam teach that a person can do enough good works to save himself. The Bible teaches that salvation is not by good works but by God's grace: "Not by works of righteousness which we have done, but according to his mercy he saved us" (Titus 3:5). There is only one answer to life's unhappiness and only one way of salvation. Scripture tells us that Jesus Christ is both that answer and "the way, the truth, and the life" (John 14:6). There is no salvation apart from Him: "He that hath the Son hath life; and he that hath not the Son of God hath not life" (I John 5:12).

Part of the problem is how these religions view man's nature. They believe that people are perfectly capable of obeying God's commands. Followers of these religions do not recognize the fact that everyone is born a sinner. Because the human heart is "desperately wicked" (Jer. 17:9), it is impossible for people to live good lives simply by following a man's teachings. The only real power for living a good life comes from the indwelling Holy Spirit, who enters a person's life when Christ becomes his Savior.

Basically, all non-Christian religions teach salvation by good works, that a person *earns* his salvation. The Christian, however, knows that salvation is a *gift* that comes from God alone: "For God so loved the world, that he gave his only begotten Son, that whosoever believeth in him should not perish, but have everlasting life" (John 3:16).

CHAPTER 4

Short, stocky, and unimpressive, yet invaluable to its owner. This phrase describes the small horse of the northeast Asian plains. Bred by the people of the plains, the Mongols, these horses were their prized possessions. Astride them, the Mongols burst out of their homeland to conquer land and people to the east, south, and west. The horses proved their courage, strength, and stamina over and over in battle and on the march. With their horses' help, the Mongols built the largest empire in history. Although ugly and often stubborn, the Mongol horse was the key to this Mongol success.

This horse was only pony-sized. It stood thirteen or fourteen hands high. (A hand equals about four inches, so the horse was about four and a half feet high at the shoulder.) Big-boned and heavy-muscled, it would not have won a prize for beauty or grace. Yet its compact body could live on one watering a day and the scarce grasses of the barren Asian plateau. Through driving blizzards and burning desert heat, these horses went on even with their riders asleep or unconscious. Their size also helped them to cover long distances quickly. They could cover the empire in record time.

The Mongol's horse was not beautiful, but it was loyal. It was not large, but it was dependable. To its owner, the horse's character meant more than appearance; usefulness meant more than size. The same principle applies to Christians. A Christian's size and appearance do not matter to God. He looks inside a person—at his heart and character—and uses him accordingly. First Samuel 16:7 says, "For the Lord seeth not as man seeth; for man looketh on the outward appearance, but the Lord looketh on the heart." God has made and prepared each of His children for a special purpose.

A.D. 1200 - A.D. 1400

Genghis Khan Leads
the Mongols 1206-27

1200

The Mongol Empires

Marco Polo Serves
Kublai Khan 1275-92

Gothic Architectural Style 1200-1500

1300

1400

Byzantine Empire 476-1453

Yuan Dynasty in China 1279-1368

Kublai Khan
1260-94

Renaissance 1350-1616

ngols Conquer
sia 1237-1240

The Rise of the Mongols

The Mongols were nomads who lived in tribes on the Mongolian plateau north of China. These warlike tribes fought constantly among themselves over grazing lands. However, in 1162 a Mongol boy was born who would someday unite these fighting tribes. By 1206 that day had come, and this young leader received the title **Genghis Khan** (JENG-gis KAHN), which means "Universal Ruler." As his first task, Genghis Khan began making the Mongol tribes into a strong, efficient army. His goal was to conquer the world. When he died in 1227, his empire reached from western Russia to eastern Korea. Although he had not conquered the world, he did rule one of the largest empires ever created.

The Government of Genghis Khan

Genghis Khan organized his government by dividing the Mongols into groups, some having one thousand soldiers and some having ten thousand soldiers plus their families. Genghis chose trusted friends to lead each group. Working through these leaders, Genghis directed the groups' activities both in battle and at times of peace. In this form of government, a person's loyalty to his leader was supreme. For example, a soldier who gave loyalty to the leader of another group was punished by death. Genghis admired loyalty and believed it was one of the greatest character qualities a man could have.

Genghis also knew the importance of law. He wrote a law code called the **Great Yasa,** which dealt with every area of life. It included military rules, criminal law, tax regulations, court procedures, and moral laws. The punishment for several crimes—including horse stealing—was death. Other penalties included beatings and fines. Every Mongol, even the khan, was under the laws of the Great Yasa. Genghis used this strict and detailed law to govern his people and to direct their activities toward military conquest.

Genghis Khan

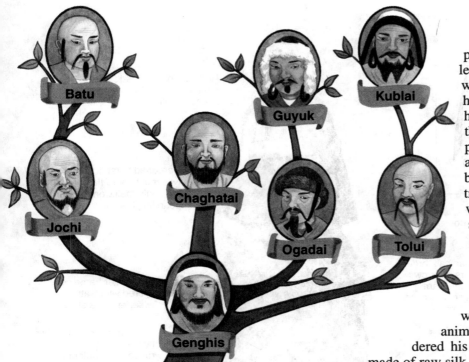

Genghis Khan's sons and grandsons eventually broke the Mongol Empire into pieces.

The Military Leadership of Genghis Khan

The Mongols were born warriors. Whether fighting other tribes or hunting animals, warfare was the Mongol way of life. Genghis Khan organized this power into a strong, disciplined army. The success of the Mongol army shows the military genius of Genghis Khan.

Genghis harnessed the Mongols' horsemanship skills in building his mighty army. Trained as the ultimate fighting cavalry, the Mongolian horde took the West by storm. Fast, ruthless, and lethal, the Mongols swooped down on their targets with predictable results—death to all who stood in their way. The Mongol archer was suited to battle. Trained to ride at the age of two or three, the archer soon

perfected his ability and learned to string his bow while riding and to shoot his arrows when all the horse's hooves were off the ground so that no hoof pounding would affect his aim. The Mongols rode into battle at top speed on their trusty horses and fought with arrows, lances, and swords. Through training and discipline, Genghis encouraged his horsemen to excel.

To protect themselves, Mongol horsemen wore stiff armor made from animal hides. Genghis also ordered his soldiers to wear a shirt made of raw silk because arrows could not easily penetrate the silk. Of course, if a man was shot, he was still hurt. But then his fellow soldiers gently pulled the shirt to pop the arrow out of the wound. Protected from the arrow point by the silk, the wound stayed cleaner and usually healed quickly.

Genghis's military genius was challenged when the Mongols started fighting settled people instead of other nomads. His major problem was the walled towns. Surrounded by moats and thick, stone walls, the towns seemed unconquerable barriers for the nomads of the open plains. Their usual direct attacks proved fruitless. Unwilling to give up, Genghis tried several methods, some old, some new. One method was **siege warfare,** a tactic used against towns and cities since the days of ancient empires. For days, weeks, and months, Mongol soldiers sent arrows over the walls and kept food out until finally the townspeople gave up. There is also evidence that the Mongols shot incendiary (fire-producing) balls

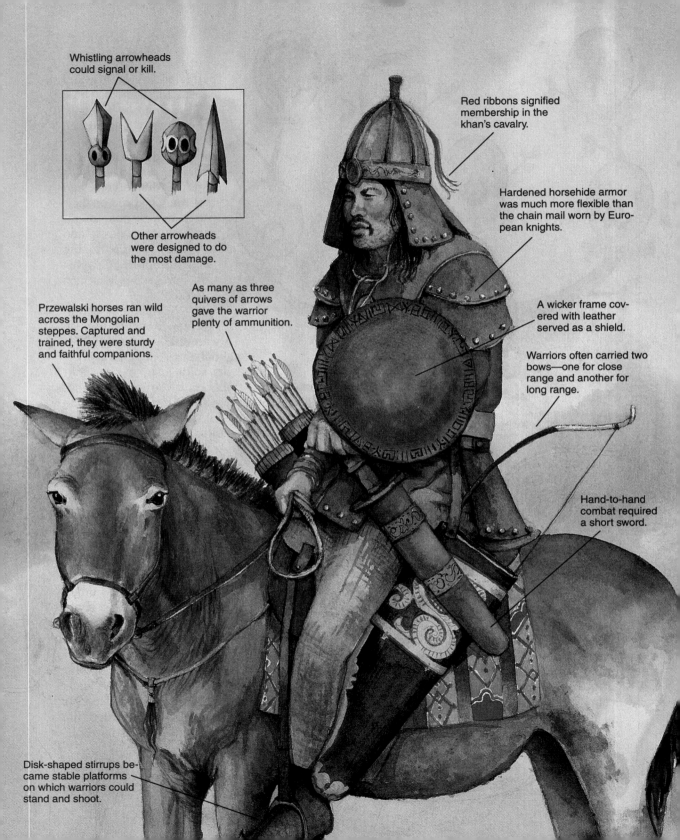

Whistling arrowheads could signal or kill.

Other arrowheads were designed to do the most damage.

Red ribbons signified membership in the khan's cavalry.

Hardened horsehide armor was much more flexible than the chain mail worn by European knights.

As many as three quivers of arrows gave the warrior plenty of ammunition.

Przewalski horses ran wild across the Mongolian steppes. Captured and trained, they were sturdy and faithful companions.

A wicker frame covered with leather served as a shield.

Warriors often carried two bows—one for close range and another for long range.

Hand-to-hand combat required a short sword.

Disk-shaped stirrups became stable platforms on which warriors could stand and shoot.

into the cities. They also fired gunpowder-filled bamboo rockets into cities and into the ranks of the opposition. These made noise and confusion but did little actual damage.

Besides the siege, Genghis often used the **pretend retreat.** Pretending to be beaten, the Mongol soldiers retreated, leaving their camp empty. Soon the townspeople, believing the Mongols had left, came out to plunder the camp. Just at that moment, however, the Mongols swiftly returned from their nearby hiding place. The unprepared people fell to the Mongol attack and lost their lives and town.

The fierce Mongols killed and destroyed wherever they went. As stories of Mongol cruelty spread, the very name *Mongol* struck fear in the hearts of their enemies. Often the Mongols massacred whole cities and piled the skulls of their victims in huge pyramids. They destroyed many towns completely—after looting them, of course. Often needlessly cruel, Genghis Khan and his Mongols extended their empire of terror across Asia and into Europe.

Once he had conquered other lands and peoples, Genghis needed to keep his empire in order. To keep in touch with every part of this empire, he organized a system of postal riders that crossed the empire. These horsemen were known as "**arrow riders**" because of their swift travel. Their bodies bandaged

Arrow riders carried a special medallion to identify them as the khan's officials.

and greased against the weather and the wear of riding, the arrow riders ate and slept on horseback, never stopping until they reached their destination. Bells attached to the horses warned people of the approach of the arrow rider so that no one would get in his way or hinder his progress. Orders, messages, and reports between the khan's headquarters and his leaders and spies traveled through this system.

Section Review

1. What was at the center of Mongol life?
2. Who united the Mongols and built a great empire? In what century?
3. What laws did he use to rule his people?
4. What skill did Mongol horsemen perfect?
5. What piece of protection did Genghis Khan add to his soldiers' equipment?
6. Name two types of attacks Mongols used against towns.
7. Name one way Genghis Khan kept in touch with his empire.

Why is communication vital to keep a large empire together? What areas can you think of where communication is vital today?

Location—Situated in the center of Asia, the Central Asian region includes Tibet, Qinghai, and Xinjiang of western China and the former Communist Soviet Union nations of Kazakhstan, Kyrgyzstan, Mongolia, Tajikistan, Turkmenistan, and Uzbekistan.

Climate—Most of Central Asia has steppe climate with subarctic areas in the north and highland and desert in the south and west. The area has short, hot summers and long, cold winters. In the capital of Mongolia, Ulan Bator, temperatures vary from -57° to 96°F. The climate is dry and receives only four to eighteen inches of rain per year. Mongolia is known for its clear, sunny days—about 240 a year.

Topography—Much of Central Asia is several thousand feet above sea level. It is an area of deserts, high mountains and plateaus, and grassy plains. The Tibetan plateau, sometimes called the Rooftop of the World, is enclosed by the Himalaya and Kunlun Mountains and averages between thirteen thousand and sixteen thousand feet above sea level. Other mountain ranges cross the area such as the Altai Mountains, which lie along the Mongolian border, and the Tien Shan, which run east and west in Kyrgyzstan and Xinjiang. Each of these mountain ranges is equal to or higher than the United States's Rocky Mountain range with high peaks above twenty thousand feet. Desert areas also abound in Central Asia. The Gobi Desert in Mongolia and the Taklimakan Desert of western China are wastelands.

Natural Resources—This region has one of the poorest soils in all of Asia. Since the soil is so poor, most Central Asians depend on the natural grassy plains to feed their herds of livestock. Although it has decreased some since the mid-1900s, raising livestock is still the mainstay of the economy. Deposits of coal, copper, gold, iron, and petroleum are located in the former USSR holdings, but these resources have not been fully developed.

Geography & Culture—Central Asia's geography explains why for many years there was no large nation in the region but rather several small warring tribes. The fact that Genghis Khan was able to bring these factions together is amazing and required great skill. Because of its rugged topography and harsh climate, Central Asia has not suffered from would-be conquerors. Mongolia has served as a buffer zone between the USSR and China. Through the years, Central Asia has been influenced by Chinese, Indian, and Russian cultures. The main religion in Central Asia is Islam. Lamaism, a form of Buddhism, is followed in Mongolia, Tibet, and Qinghai.

Settings Review

1. What are two factors of the Central Asian climate and topography that might have helped produce strong, rugged people? Explain your answer.

2. What is the main occupation of the people?

3. Using the information in the topography section, name two areas that you would expect to have a sparse population.

What things have prevented the Mongol people from having a more economically successful life?

Crisscrossed by several moutain ranges, Central Asia is home to isolated communities that use livestock for transportation and as beasts of burden. The yak, with its thick coat, is indispensible in this cold region.

The Life of the Mongols

The region of the world in which the Mongols lived was inhospitable. Little rain, great changes in temperature, and desertlike terrain caused the Mongols to move about constantly to find the best pasture areas for their flocks. The nomadic Mongols lived not in towns but in camps that could be easily moved. A camp where a general lived was called an **ordu.** The people of the ordu kept busy, for there was always work to be done—clothes to make, carts to build, food to cook, and children to look after.

Making Homes in the Ordu

The Mongols were called the "People of the Felt Tents" because they lived in round tents called **yurts.** The round shape kept the yurt standing in the strong winds of the open plains. The Mongols made their yurts with frames of light wood covered with layers of heavy **felt.** In the winter they added more layers of felt for warmth. The Mongols used the fur and wool of their animals to make the heavy felt, which they waterproofed by greasing. The outer layer of felt on the yurt was whitened with a coat of lime. This white coating helped to reflect the hot summer sun and keep the tents cool inside.

The doorway of the yurt was draped with heavy felt. The women painted or embroidered designs of birds, animals, vines, and trees across the felt. These designs made each tent unique. In warm weather the people pulled aside the felt to leave the doorway open to breezes.

Regardless of their size, all the yurts were movable. When it was time to move, the Mongols took down the smaller tents and laid them on carts. The larger yurts (about thirty feet wide) were not taken apart but were put directly on carts. Sometimes as many as twenty oxen were needed to pull these carts.

When setting up a new campsite, the Mongols always faced their doorways to the south to keep out the prevailing winds from the northeast. As one entered a yurt, the eastern, or right-hand, side was reserved for the women. They kept their cooking utensils and food there. The western, or left-hand, side was for men and visitors. In the center of the roof was the smoke hole, underneath which sat the family's hearth. The head of the family had his couch behind the hearth, facing the doorway. The larger yurts had couches for wives and sons also, but in most yurts only the master

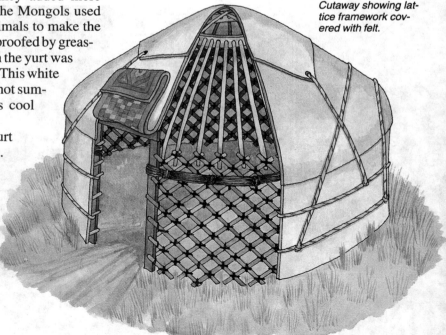

Cutaway showing lattice framework covered with felt.

Many Mongols have adopted Western-style dress but still live in traditional yurt dwellings.

had a couch. On the inside walls were idols, dried meats, cooking vessels, bows, quivers, and arrows, all hung from hooks made from goat horns. Felt, skins, or rugs were laid over dried grass to cover the floor.

Living in the Ordu

The women did most of the work in the ordu. They set up and took down the tents and made the felt to cover them. When the ordu moved, the women drove the ox carts carrying the families' belongings. Clothing their families from hats to shoes meant hours of sewing skins and felt. The women also cared for the ordu's flocks of sheep and herds of goats and cattle. Mealtime was especially busy for the women, for the Mongols were big eaters. They loved meat, whether from their own flocks or from animals caught on the hunt. However, two jobs the women did not have were washing the dishes and washing the clothes—the

Mongols did not believe in doing these chores. Women caught washing clothes were sometimes beaten by the other women.

To the Mongols the most beautiful women were heavy and had small noses. Wealthy women wore huge headdresses that looked similar to an upside-down boot. The headdress was made of bone and feathers. Its decoration and size helped to show the woman's rank in the clan. Most men had several wives, whom they bought from the girls' parents. Even so, husbands often valued their horses more than their wives. As bad as these conditions sound, Mongol women did have more freedom than most Muslim or Chinese women. Their opinions were often heeded, and they were allowed to ride with the men. Many women could handle a bow as well as the men.

The horse was at the center of Mongol life. Before children could walk, they learned to ride. Most Mongols probably spent more of their lives in the saddle than out. Traveling the

Asian plains, the Mongol and his horse were one as they warred, hunted, and made their yearly nomadic moves. The Mongols also kept extra horses to have fresh mounts on long journeys or in battle. The number of horses a man owned was a sign of his wealth and power.

The men spent much of their time hunting or fighting. Genghis ordered them to hunt during the winter months, not only to supply the people with food but also to keep the men in top fighting condition. When not fighting or hunting, the men did some of the heavier work in the ordu. They built carts and the wooden frames for the yurts. They also made and repaired weapons, saddles, and harnesses. The men also had the important responsibility of caring for the horses. They captured, herded, trained, and milked them. Interestingly, the most common Mongol drink, **kumiss,** was made from mare's milk.

Leisure time in the ordu was spent in storytelling and music. One of the oldest instruments used by the Mongol people is the *khil-khuur.* The *khil-khuur* is a long, narrow, stringed instrument played with a bow. Traditionally, the *khil-khuur* is decorated with a horse's head.

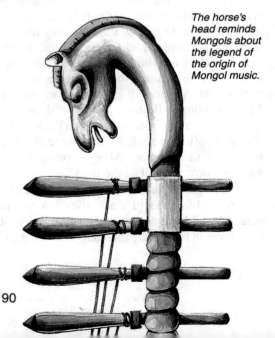

The horse's head reminds Mongols about the legend of the origin of Mongol music.

Instinctively the families drew closer to the central fire as the north wind howled against the sides of the yurt. The mothers talked soothingly to their restless children. One of the men lightly stroked the strings of a *khil-khuur.* Sensing the uneasiness in the tent, Bakti began to speak in a low tone.

Listen all as I tell how the people [Mongolians] got the *khil-khuur* and music. It is said that in the far north is a sacred mountain, Jasaktu Ul. The mountain is protected by swarms of poisonous insects and is ruled by a mighty lion. In the valleys of Jasaktu Ul once lived the *Erdenin naiman mori*, the eight precious horses. Seven of these stallions were sleek and smooth but the eighth was thin and woeful looking. It hung its head, and its ribs stuck out like the uncovered staves of a yurt. Wonder of wonders! Beneath its ugliness, the eighth horse was the swiftest and most enduring of all.

In that time each night twenty-eight stars fell from the sky, and when they touched the earth, they became warriors dressed in golden armor. Twenty of them came mounted on horseback, but the other eight owned the *Erdenin naiman mori*. Throughout the night the riders galloped across the steppes. The riders brought beauty and vitality wherever their horses trod. Each night, just before dawn, the riders came back to Jasaktu Ul to ascend into the sky and shine as morning stars. When the sun rose, they disappeared.

One night a young shepherdess saw the riders and fell in love with their leader, who rode on the thin horse. The star-prince returned her love. Instead of riding with his brothers on the steppe, he stayed with the shepherdess far from the mountain. Each morning his horse, Jönung Khara Mori, ran harder and faster than any of the other "precious horses" to reach the mountain before dawn. So much did the shepherdess and star-prince love each other that each day it became harder and harder for them to part before morning. Jönung Khara Mori became thinner and thinner, and yet, wonder of wonders, he remained as swift.

The shepherdess desired to follow her star-prince each morning, but Jönung Khara Mori was so fast and light of hoof that he vanished with his rider like a gust of wind. The shepherdess's longing to see where her loved one lived was so strong that one evening, when the prince did not see, she went to the wondrous horse to discover the secret of its speed. As she stroked its side, how astonished she was to find that a set of wings was folded behind each leg. Here was her way of discovery. Quickly she cut off each wing hoping that by this she could follow her love and be with him forever. The next morning the maiden secretly prepared her horse for travel. She said farewell to her prince, but her glory was turned to screams of anguish as once again Jönung Khara Mori left as a gust of wind, taking her prince with him.

As the star-prince rode toward the sacred mountain that morning he began to feel his horse tire beneath him. How could this be! The fleet-footed Jönung Khara Mori slowed and then collapsed. The star-prince looked around and saw that he was in a desert far from the mountain and far from his love. He stroked his wondrous horse and began to cry. As the star-prince cried, a miracle occurred. The dead horse, Jönung Khara Mori, was transformed. His head became small and his neck grew long and thin. His mane and tail became sounding strings. Jönung became the first *khil-khuur*.

At that moment the sun rose over the horizon and the star-prince's brothers disappeared from the sky. Moved by the beauty of the hour and the melancholy of the moment, the prince touched the strings, and upon his lips words were born which became the first Mongol song. He sang of the horse, the stars, and his love, and that is why to this day the people play the *khil-khuur* and sing of horses, love, and unreachable stars.

The delicate sound of the *khil-khuur* followed the smoke up through the hole in the yurt roof. The visiting families softly drifted out of the yurt carrying their drowsing children with them. With the sleeplessness of old age, Bakti was left to stir the fire's dying embers.

Making Felt

Have you ever noticed the difference between felt and a common fabric such as cotton? What do you think that difference is? If you look closely, you will see that cotton fabric has a regular criss-cross, in-and-out pattern like a basket weave, but felt looks like a helter-skelter jumble of threads.

That is the difference. Most fabrics are woven for strength and smoothness. They require carding to straighten the fibers, spinning to turn the fibers into long threads and weaving to make fabric. Felt is a much more practical fabric for a nomadic people, since all but one of these steps is left out and the only tool needed is a carding comb.

Carding makes the wool fibers lie in the same direction.

normal woven fabric

felt

To make felt you need the following:

- wool (you also can use poodle hair)
- mild dish soap
- two dog brushes or carding combs
- towels

The first step in felting is combing the fibers in one direction or carding. Place a wad of wool on one brush and place the other brush on top and pull the two brushes away from each other as if you are combing the brushes. Always pull the wool the same direction. In a few minutes you should see the hairs all lying one way. Peel this layer off the brush and set it aside. Repeat this step until you have three or four equal amounts carded. Next, lay these combed pieces on top of one another with each layer going a different direction. Now saturate the wool by pouring warm water over it. You may want to do this in a large cooking pan such as a jelly roll pan. While the wool is wet, squirt a generous amount of dish soap over the surface and begin *gently* working the wool with your fingertips. The wool will stiffen and begin to feel like a single piece of material as the fibers intertwine and the wool shrinks.

After carding, lay the wool in perpendicular layers.

Once the wool is soapy, gently rub the entire surface with your fingertips.

Wrap the wool in a towel and roll it back and forth under the palms of your hands.

and begin to feel like a single piece of material as the fibers intertwine and the wool shrinks.

As this intertwining continues, roll the wool piece up in a towel and roll the towel back and forth under the palms of your hands to further condense the fibers and compact the material. Unroll, rinse, and reroll the felt in a dry towel. Unroll again and set the piece out to dry.

The final piece of felt will be a flat sheet. However, the interesting feature of felt is that it can be shaped or even sewn before it dries. You may want to shape your felt over your hand to make a miniature hat. When it dries, the felt will retain its shape. Felt was one of the earliest fabrics made by man. Today people use felt for hat-making, insulating, sound-proofing, and cushioning.

Mongols roll the new felt up in an old piece, wrap it in leather, and drag it behind a running horse.

Trading in the Mongol Empire

The Mongols manufactured nothing beyond the items they needed for daily living, such as felt, harnesses, and carts. Because they did not stay in one place for a whole growing season, they rarely grew crops. Only by trading did the Mongols obtain goods other than necessities. Even before Genghis Khan built his empire, the wealthier Mongols traded fur and hides for Chinese silk and cotton.

As the empire grew, trade grew also. When the Mongols conquered China (1279), their empire reached from the Caspian Sea to the Pacific Ocean. They reopened trade along the ancient silk routes, which had been closed since the days of the Roman and Han Empires. After nearly a thousand years, the West had direct contact with the cultures of the Far East. While the later crusaders were traveling to Jerusalem to fight the Muslims, Mongol traders brought exotic goods from the Far East into Middle Eastern markets.

This traveling back and forth to prosperous cities and towns gave the Mongols a desire for the goods they saw there. After a time the Mongols settled into towns and gave up their nomadic ways. Once settled, the Mongols began to lose their zeal for conquest. Genghis's grandson, Kublai Khan, stopped living in a

yurt, built a palace, and settled in northern China.

After about a hundred years of peaceful trade, the Muslims in the Middle East closed the East-West trade routes and began to attack Constantinople. Europeans, acquainted with the goods of the Far East, still wanted them. With the land routes closed, however, they had to find a different way to the East. When they turned to the sea in search of new routes, the age of exploration began.

Section Review

1. What was a general's camp called?
2. How did Mongol men keep in fighting shape during the off-season?
3. What two jobs were not done by anyone in the ordu?
4. Which direction did the yurt face, and why?
5. How do you think its round shape helped the yurt on the plains?
6. How did trade with the West affect the Mongols?
7. How did the closing of Eastern trade affect the Europeans?

When you examine the Mongol lifestyle and climate, can you think of any reasons that the women would be so angry when someone washed clothes or did dishes?

The Religion of the Mongols

The Mongol religion did little to encourage a better way of life. The polytheistic Mongols believed that good and evil spirits controlled the world. They also believed in a supreme god, who ruled all the spirits. They called him **Tengri** (TENG gree), meaning "the great god of heaven." The Mongols lived in fear of the spirits and hoped for blessing from them.

Every yurt had small idols made of felt. The wives and daughters of the nobles made these idols at sewing parties. The Mongols believed that these idols protected their family members and animals. Before every meal they spread food and drink on the idols' lips. They also prayed to them. They believed that these idols had power to bless them, but the Bible condemns idolaters (Exod. 20:4-5). They have "changed the glory of the uncorruptible God into an image made like to corruptible man" (Rom. 1:23).

The Mongols believed that certain men, called **shamans** (SHAH muns), had power over the spirits. The shamans were the priests of the traditional Mongol religion, which is called **shamanism** (SHAH muh NIZ um). The shamans were medicine men and witch doctors who used a special language when performing their magical rituals. The Mongols always consulted their shamans before making big decisions and then followed their advice. The shamans led the Mongols in their religion of evil and spiritual darkness. These lost people did not know the salvation that comes only through Jesus Christ (John 3:16).

Other Religions Come to the Mongols

The later empire of the Mongols included people of many religions, including Christians.

The most important Christian group in the Mongol Empire was the Nestorian Church, sometimes called the Church of the East. These Christians were named for Nestorius, bishop of Constantinople (died c. 451). He had been accused of a false teaching concerning Christ. **Nestorians** claimed that neither they nor their namesake held that false teaching, but their churches remained separate from the Roman Catholic Church and Eastern Orthodox Church. During the Middle Ages, perhaps as many as one-fourth of the Christians in the world were Nestorians.

The Nestorian Church first arose in Persia and soon spread eastward into Mongolian territory. Some of the groups we call "Nestorian" may have actually existed before Nestorius's time. Many of them point to the story that the apostle Thomas went to India to preach the gospel. They say Thomas founded their churches on his missionary journey. Nestorian missionaries traveled as far as Arabia, India, and China. It is said to be a Nestorian Christian who taught Muhammad, founder of Islam, what he knew about Christianity.

Led by a missionary named Alopen, the Nestorians conducted the first mission work in China long before Mongolian control there. As a witness to the Christian faith, the Nestorians in China erected a monument in 781. Rediscovered in 1623, part of this monument reads as follows:

"One Person of our Trinity, the Messiah, who is the Luminous Lord of the Universe, folding up Himself and concealing His true Majesty, appeared upon earth as a man. Angels proclaimed the Glad Tidings. A virgin gave birth to the Holy One. . . . A bright star announced the blessed event. Persians saw the splendour and came forth with their tribute."

When Italian Marco Polo traveled to China from Europe in the 1300s, he found Nestorian churches all along the route.

But the Nestorians often suffered persecution. The Muslims sometimes tolerated them and sometimes tried to force them to convert. Muslim rulers often made Christians wear distinctive clothes, such as a yellow patch, marking them as Christians. They made laws that Christians had to wear special haircuts and ride horses sidesaddle so that Muslims could identify them. Once a group of Muslims hung a Nestorian bishop upside down, naked, and filled his mouth with ashes. They then beat him saying, "Abandon your faith; turn Muslim and you will be saved."

The Mongols were often friendly to the Nestorians at first. Some Mongol leaders converted to Nestorian Christianity. Christians served as officials in the courts of Mongol rulers. Members of the family of Genghis Khan even married Nestorian Christians. But as more Mongols converted to Islam, persecution grew. The final blow was persecution of Christians by Tamerlane. His severe treatment of the Nestorians reduced them in numbers to small pockets of Christians living in remote areas of the Middle East.

Today some scattered descendants of the Nestorian churches still exist. They can be found in the Middle East, in India, and—through immigration—in the United States.

The Nestorian monument gives silent witness to early Christians in China.

Section Review

1. What type of religion did the early Mongols follow?
2. Why is idol worship wrong?
3. What were the priests of Mongol religion called?
4. What important Christian group grew up in the Mongolian Empire?
5. According to legend, who founded the Christian churches in India, Persia, and China?

How much power do you think shamans had over the people? Why?

The Empire After Genghis Khan

Before Genghis Khan died in 1227, he had encouraged his sons to rule the empire together. Soon after his death, however, their rivalries split the empire into several independent provinces ruled outwardly by one of Genghis's descendants who was chosen as khan; there would never be another Mongol empire as solid as Genghis Khan's. Under the descendants of Genghis, Mongol rule was felt in many places in Asia for the next few hundred years. The maps and brief descriptions that follow provide an overview of Mongol history after Genghis Khan.

Kublai Khan in China

In 1279 Genghis's grandson, **Kublai Khan,** achieved his grandfather's dream of defeating China. After defeating the ruling Chinese dynasty, Kublai established the **Yuan dynasty.** The Yuan was China's first foreign dynasty.

The story of Kublai Khan's legendary lifestyle in China was told by Marco Polo. Five hundred years later that story inspired Samuel Coleridge to write *Kubla Khan.* The following is a portion of that poem.

> In Xanadu did Kubla Khan
> A stately pleasure dome decree,
> Where Alph, the sacred river, ran
> Through caverns measureless to man
> Down to a sunless sea.

Although Kublai tolerated the Chinese, he staffed the government mostly with Mongols and other non-Chinese. Nevertheless the Yuan dynasty promoted Chinese culture without adding anything really Mongolian. The Mongols brought very little change to China. By 1368, Mongol rule had fallen to a native Chinese dynasty.

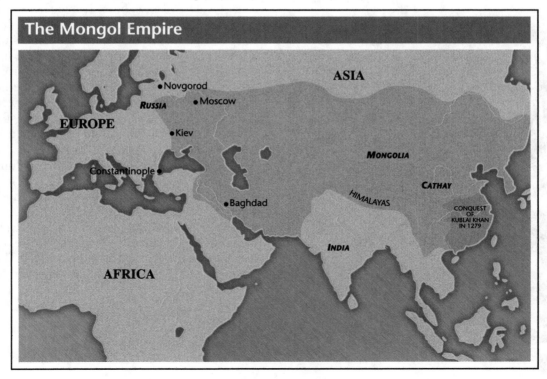

The Mongol Empire

This statue commemorates the raising of the American flag on the Pacific island of Iwo Jima.

Battles in the Pacific

Under Kublai Khan, Genghis Khan's grandson, the Mongols swept through China until stopped by the sea. After Kublai Khan conquered China, he looked across the sea to Japan. The islands of Japan seemed easy targets, so Kublai determined to conquer them.

But conquering an island from the sea was not as easy as Kublai Khan supposed, and his ships and men suffered defeat. The defeat was a result of strategic problems and the weather, as well as the determination of people willing to sacrifice all to defend their land.

Similar problems occurred during World War II in the Pacific Theater. The weather was less of a problem for huge ships, but the strategic difficulty for the Allies and the sacrifice of the Japanese to defend their holding was almost overwhelming. Allied troops found great difficulty and opposition as they tried to capture the tiny islands leading to victory over Japan.

First, strategic problems occurred. How do you get men onto shore when there is empty beach between them and possible cover from weapon fire? The logical solution is to destroy all the cover farther inland so that the enemy cannot hide close to shore. Kublai Khan did not have the technology to accomplish this task, so hundreds of men were lost coming on shore. The Allies in World War II did have the technology. Three days of bombardment from offshore reduced the southeast side of the island of Iwo Jima to barren rock. This allowed troops to come on shore, but they were still pressed by the waiting Japanese men and weapons bunkered farther inland.

The eight-square-mile island of Iwo Jima took over a month to capture. The Allies lost more than six thousand men and had thousands of casualties. They successfully dealt with the strategic problems, but the determination of the Japanese to maintain control of the island almost caused an Allied defeat. The Japanese sacrificed twenty thousand men to defend the island.

In some history books you may see Mongols called *Tatars,* while in others you may see them called **Tartars**. Which is right?

The original name for these people is *Tatar,* coming from a Manchurian word meaning "archer" or "nomad." However, as the Mongols approached Europe, tales of their horrible deeds preceded them. Because the name *Tatar* was much like an ancient Greek name for hell, *Tartarus,* Europeans linked the two together into *Tartar.* (This word for hell occurs once in the Greek Bible, in II Peter 2:4.) This name portrayed the Mongols as being as evil and cruel as demons from hell.

Today, one reminder we have of the Tartars (or Tatars, as the case may be) is the tartar sauce we eat on fish.

Golden Horde in Russia

Genghis's grandson Batu Khan, with the help of one of Genghis's most honored generals, conquered much of Russia. Although his first aggressive press across Europe was halted by the death of Genghis, Batu continued to expand the area of conquest for many years while maintaining a loose alliance with the main Mongol empire. In 1243 Batu and his descendants settled down on the Volga River and established their rule in Moscow. The Russians called them the **Golden Horde** because their greased yurts shone in the sun. (The word *horde* comes from *ordu.*)

The Mongols greatly influenced the history of Russia. The Mongol conquest cut off Russia from the discoveries and inventions of the Renaissance and the West for over a century. The adoption of Islam by the Golden Horde in the early fourteenth century also left its mark on Russian culture. By 1500 Mongol power was broken, and Moscow became the

Onion-topped domes in Russia reveal the early Islamic influence brought by the Mongols.

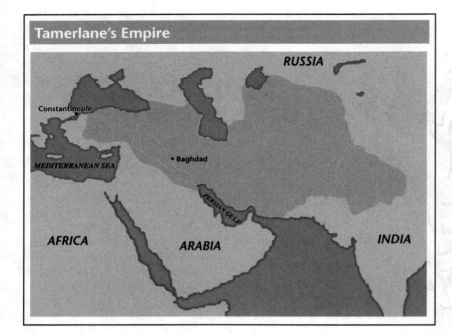

Tamerlane's Empire

Mughul Dynasty in India

The last Mongol empire was the small **Mughul** (MOO gul) **dynasty** in India. The Mughuls brought an era of peace and artistic achievement to India. The most famous Mughul ruler was **Akbar** (AHK bar), a wise and generous leader. He extended his empire over all except southern India. The Mughuls were a peaceful people, far different from their Mongol ancestors. Under the Mughuls, some of India's greatest architecture was built, including the **Taj Mahal** (TAHZH muh-HAHL). After Akbar's death the Mughuls had few strong leaders. Their empire slowly declined until the British finally took over India in the nineteenth century.

capital of native Russian rule. However, not until the time of Peter the Great in the 1700s did Russia again open up to the West. Even today one can see the influence of the East in Russian life.

Tamerlane in Central Asia

During the second half of the fourteenth century, another Mongol leader came to power in central Asia. Only five feet eight inches tall, Timur stood taller than most Mongols, but as the result of an accident in his youth, Timur was lame. Thus, he was called Timur the Lame, or **Tamerlane** (TAM ur LANE). Despite his handicap, Tamerlane became a powerful conqueror. Through cruelty much worse than that of the earlier Mongols, he extended his empire from Turkey to India. More interested in the spoils of battle than building a well-ruled empire, Tamerlane did not plan for the future. His empire fell soon after his death.

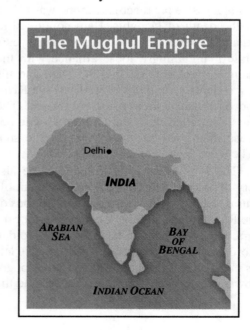

The Mughul Empire

Shah Jahan built the Taj Mahal to honor his wife. When she died before its completion it became a shrine to her memory.

Section Review

1. What was the name of the Mongol dynasty in China?

2. What was Tamerlane's main interest during his reign in the Middle East?

3. What great architectural piece was built during Akbar's reign?

When you consider how big the Mongol Empire was, why don't we see more of Mongol culture in Europe and Asia today?

Summary

From their homeland on the Mongolian plains of east Asia, the Mongols built a huge empire in the thirteenth century. Under the leadership of Genghis Khan, the Mongols joined together and swept out of Mongolia on their horses to conquer people throughout Asia and Europe. Their empire was one of the largest in history. The Mongols were a simple, although fierce, people. They lived in tents called yurts and moved frequently. Their lives centered on warfare, and their activities promoted victory. After Genghis Khan died, his descendants could not keep the empire united. For the next few hundred years, Mongol influence continued in several different empires in Asia. These empires included the Yuan dynasty in China, the Golden Horde in Russia, Tamerlane's empire in central Asia, and the Mughuls in India.

People, Places, and Terms to Know

Genghis Khan	yurts	shamanism	Golden Horde
Great Yasa	felt	Nestorians	Tamerlane
siege warfare	kumiss	Kublai Khan	Mughul dynasty
pretend retreat	Tengri	Yuan dynasty	Akbar
arrow riders	shaman	Tartar	Taj Mahal
ordu			

Review Questions

Short Answer

Answer each of the following questions about the Mongols with a one-word answer.

1. What was their main means of transportation?
2. What were their camps called?
3. What were their tents called?
4. What were their tents made of?
5. What was their religion called?

Multiple Choice

Choose the answer(s) that will make the sentence correct.

6. The god of the Mongols was
   - (a) Dagon.
   - (b) Genghis Khan.
   - (c) Tengri.
   - (d) Temuchin.

7. When trying to conquer a town, the Mongols would
   - (a) besiege it for a month or so.
   - (b) bombard it with cannons.
   - (c) pretend to retreat in order to draw the people out.
   - (d) storm it with battering rams.

8. When in camp, the Mongols placed the doors of their tents facing
   - (a) north.
   - (b) south.
   - (c) east.
   - (d) west.

Fill in the Blank

Fill in the correct words to complete the comparisons in the following statements.

9. In India the Mongol dynasty was called _____ while in China it was called _____.

10. The Europeans called the Mongols _____, but in Russia they were called the _____ _____.

Who Am I?

Identify the speaker in the following statements from the list below. You will use each answer more than once.

Genghis Khan   Kublai Khan   Tamerlane   Akbar

11. I brought peace to India.

12. I made an unsuccessful attempt to conquer Japan.

13. Cruelty was a key word in my conquering.

14. Although my empire was small, it was peaceful.

15. I wrote a law code called the Great Yasa.

16. I extended Mongol control into Turkey and India.

17. I was the most famous Mughul leader.

18. I created one of the largest empires in the history of the world.

19. I was able to establish the Yuan dynasty in China.

20. Under my leadership the silk routes were reopened.

Think About It!

Choose one of the following quotations and write a paragraph agreeing or disagreeing with the author. Then write another paragraph discussing how law affects a nation and what is required of government to enforce the laws it establishes. What character trait in people makes law easy to enforce?

"Law is order, and good law is good order." —Aristotle

"Any government is free to the people under it where the laws rule and the people are a party to the laws." —William Penn, *Frame of Government*, 1682

CHAPTER 5

"Now, children, this strange red beast had an enormous appetite, and all the animals helped to feed it. The monkey threw it coconuts, which it devoured with a crackling snap. The elephant brought it hay and dry branches. Still the beast's tongue searched for more to fill its growing belly.

"The animals decided that the monkey should have the job of feeding the glowing red ball. The monkey thought, 'I will take it into the forest to eat rather than bring wood and hay here.' So the monkey cut a long vine, threw it to the beast (who caught it in his mouth), and started off into the forest.

"The beast followed the monkey, stopping here and there to eat. He ate everything in sight—a bush, a tree, dry grass—and all the while he nibbled on the vine the monkey held.

"The monkey grew scared as his hungry charge ate closer and closer to his hand. Faster and faster he raced through the forest. Finally he came to the fishing village near the sea. With only a tiny piece of his leash left, the monkey dropped into the water and let the red beast go. Falling at the water's edge, the beast began to drink. As he gulped the water, he slowly grew smaller. Finally his tongue disappeared, and the huge animal crumbled into a pile of red, glowing bones.

"The men from the village came and picked up the beast's remains and brought them to the village. There they set them in a special place—inside a circle of three stones, the three stones that still form the traditional hearth in every home.

"Now children, the animals did not know how to handle the gift of the red beast, but men took the gift and tamed it, and that is how we got fire."

A.D. 1000 - A.D. 1700

European Dark Ages 476-1095	
Empire of Ghana 500-1100(?)	
1000	1100

The Traditions of Africa

Genghis Khan
Leads the Mongols
1206-27

Mali Empire 1230-1400(?)

Empire of Songhai
1470-1600(?)

Kingdom of Benin 1200-1700(?)

1200   1300   1400   1500   1600   1700

Byzantine Empire 476-1453

Reformation 1500-1650

Renaissance 1350-1616

Yuan Dynasty in
China 1279-1368

Slave Trade
Begins 1510

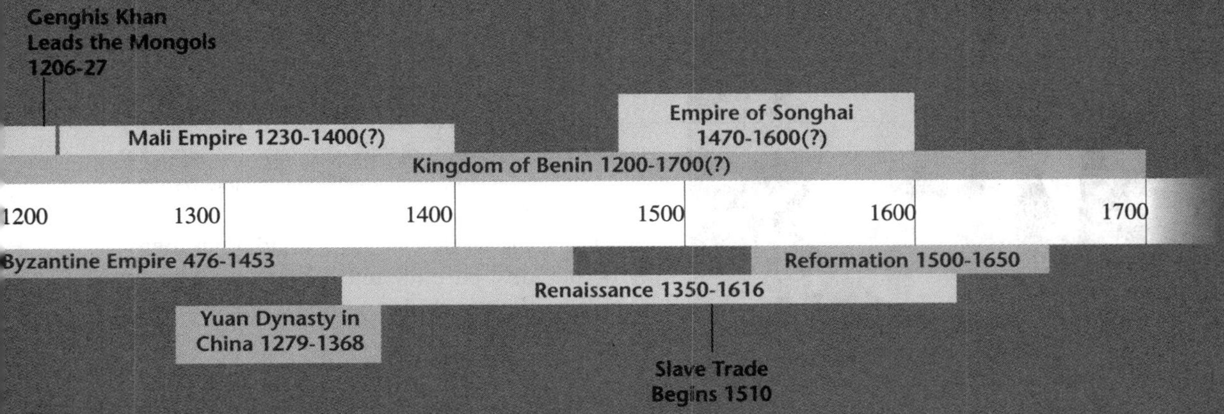

Traditional African Culture

The children had sat wide-eyed around the evening fire as the old storyteller had told them again the story of the gift of fire. The entire time a drummer had beat out a constant rhythm. Occasionally the older children and adults had joined the storyteller with singing choruses.

For generations storytellers told and retold this story on the continent of Africa. The children of Africa learned about their history and culture by listening to their elders tell stories.

The tribal chief spent much of his day giving advice, making decisions, and telling stories of the past.

The elders handed down the traditions of African life from one generation to the next. These traditions characterized African culture. In this chapter we will learn about traditional Africa up to 1650.

The Family and Society

The family was the most important element of traditional African culture. An African's family affected every area of his life. The family provided a person not only with a history and traditions but also with guidance throughout his life. The family leader decided where its members lived and how they earned their living. Family leaders also told them how to behave and what to believe. Other Africans judged a person according to his position in a family, not individually.

The Africans believed that children were important and that a man should have several wives to rear many children. Usually Africans did not marry for love. The parents of the children arranged the marriage for money and political benefit. The primary purpose of marriage was to rear children to carry on family traditions and to increase family honor and wealth.

A man with several wives had children who were either brothers and sisters or half brothers and half sisters. Sometimes rivalry to gain the father's favor occurred among the wives and their children. Keeping peace at home was a difficult job for the husband. Usually each wife had a hut in the family compound. Daughters and sons lived in separate huts as well. This arrangement helped to prevent many quarrels.

The typical African family had other members besides parents and children. African families often included grandparents, uncles,

Hut arrangement helps preserve the peace in large families. The diagram represents one kind of compound arrangement.

Within the diagram:
young children's hut
husband's hut
older girls' hut
guest hut and entrance
older boys' hut
wife's hut

aunts, and cousins. When a young woman married, she left her family group to join her husband's family group. These groups tended to live together. Sometimes a whole community consisted of people belonging to the same family.

The largest family group in Africa was the clan. A **clan** included everyone who could trace his ancestry to a common relative. The clan gave the individual his history and culture. In Africa single families belonged to clans and lived under the authority of the clan elder or chief. The clan, not families and individuals, owned and controlled the land used by the clan members. The chief decided where the clan lived, divided the land, and determined its use. A small clan might live together in a single community, while larger clans lived in several communities. On important occasions the whole clan met together to celebrate.

African society continued one level beyond families and clans: tribes. A **tribe** was two or more clans living together; they shared a common language, beliefs, and customs. Some tribes were small, while others had thousands of members. Africa's traditional clans and tribes formed the basis for later African states and kingdoms, and from these came several modern African nations.

Traditional Dwellings

Many African people today have never lived in a hut. They wear Western clothes and do not dance around with spears and masks except at cultural celebration times. Typically, early people in all areas of the world lived in hutlike houses. The climate, lifestyle of the inhabitants, and availability of materials determined the style and permanence of the dwelling. There was not a "typical" African home.

Because of the climate, geography, and economics, African tribes in sub-Saharan West Africa and East Africa did not mingle much and therefore developed different methods for building houses. Generally traditional African peoples construct their homes on a plan similar to that of the people of India. Families live together in compounds of several houses. Each house is only a room for the husband or a wife and young child. Families come together in one place in the compound to cook and eat food.

This compound system has taken many forms. In areas of East Africa where people had permanent farms or lived in cities, the people constructed homes of stones and mortar with clay spread over the surface. These buildings were much more Middle Eastern in appearance, with flat roofs and interior courtyards. The builders used the family compound arrangement and included small buildings to hold grain or livestock. In the more forested regions of West Africa, few people lived in the same location very long. West Africans needed to move often to more fertile soil and to better hunting areas. The houses in this area are more temporary hutlike structures of sticks, leaves, and grass. Even these temporary homes varied greatly. Each tribe was isolated within the tropical forests and therefore developed its own construction techniques.

African houses are built with stick frames or baked clay bricks, depending on what materials are available.

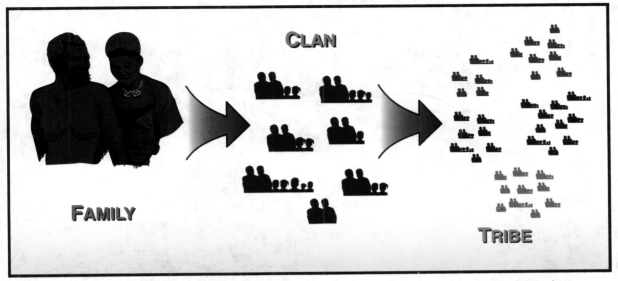

CLAN

FAMILY

TRIBE

Much of African family life focused on clan and tribal connections. Tribal loyalties are still important to many regions.

Oral History

Before the nineteenth century, most Africans did not have written languages, so they could not write—or read—books about their history. Instead, the people learned the history of their clan and tribe from storytellers. The **storytellers,** called *griots* in western Africa, memorized the long ancestry of their people. They knew stories or folktales about important and heroic family members as well as bad ones. Children grew up learning these stories around family and clan fires. When a child came to the age of initiation (usually in the early teen or preteen years), he heard his family's whole history. From these **oral histories,** which some Africans can still recite today, we know much about African history and culture.

Section Review

1. What was the most important element in African society?
2. Who belonged to a clan? to a tribe?
3. What determined the type of home used in particular areas?
4. Many African homes were constructed using a design similar to what other country's design?
5. Why are West African homes built of less-permanent materials?
6. How did children learn about their family history and culture?

New homes being built reflect changes in society. Ask your parents what homes were like when they grew up. From what you know, how are home designs changing today?

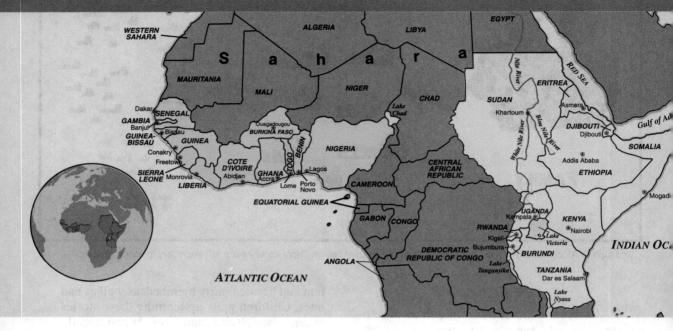

Location
Stretching along the Sahara Desert in the north to below the equator in the south, from the Atlantic Ocean in the west to the Indian Ocean in the east is a region sometimes referred to as sub-Saharan Africa. It is made up of three separate regions and many African nations. Two of those regions are West Africa and East Africa. West Africa includes Senegal, Burkina Faso, Gambia, Guinea-Bissau, Guinea, Sierra Leone, Liberia, Côte d'Ivoire, Ghana, Togo, Benin, and Nigeria. East Africa includes Sudan, Eritrea, Ethiopia, Djibouti, Somalia, Uganda, Kenya, Rwanda, Burundi, and Tanzania. Each region is about two-thirds the size of the United States.

Climate
The climate varies from the desert region of the Sahara to the steppe region and then the tropical savanna. Humid tropical areas are located in the forests of the west coast. Temperatures average between 77° and 99°F, except in the highlands of Ethiopia and in the wastes of the Sahara.

Topography
As in much of Africa, a narrow coastal plain rises sharply to an inland plateau. In the east there are mountain ranges. While there are many rivers draining this area, most are not navigable because of rapids and waterfalls.

Natural Resources
There are many natural resources that are only now beginning to be maximized. Among these are oil, iron ore, bauxite, and manganese. Much of Africa has infertile soil, making large-scale agricultural efforts difficult. Many of the people in these regions have small farms to feed their families. Tourism related to the wild animal parks is important in Kenya.

Geography & Culture
The Sahara Desert has kept this part of Africa separate from European

culture. Muslim traders made early contact with Africa but penetrated only the northern fringe of the expansive interior. The climate and topography kept it from European exploration until the nineteenth century. When Europeans did enter in the late nineteenth century, it was to exploit the areas of conquest.

Settings Review

1. Which river is described in each of the following statements?

   a. It flows through the Sudan region into the Atlantic Ocean.

   b. It is the great river that flows north to the Mediterranean Sea.

   c. It flows through the heart of tropical Africa into the Atlantic Ocean.

2. Name the three bodies of water that surround Africa.

3. What desert would a person cross to get from Egypt to Timbuktu?

   North America has high mountains, big rivers, and varied weather. Explain briefly how differences in North American and African topography have affected the development of the two continents.

Africa is a continent, not a country. It includes many different types of people and geography that varies from rain forest to savannah to desert.

Traditional African Religion

Togo women must care for their dead babies' spirits by caring for the babies' idols.

The family was at the heart of traditional African religion. Knowing that the High God was a spirit, Africans also believed that those who left this life continued to live in spirit. Thus the family included not only living members but also those dead and unborn. Like the Chinese, Africans believed that their dead ancestors influenced their present lives. They also believed that their actions affected their yet unborn children. Africans looked at their families as a continuous line from generation to generation. The present generation's duty was to preserve the traditions of their parents and pass them on to their children. Religious traditions were the most important traditions in African society.

Africans believed that when the High God left he left both spirits and humans in the world to run its affairs. This left most Africans living in fear of vengeful spirits. These many spirits, not the Creator God, were the object of African worship. Africans believed that some spirits lived in trees, rocks, rivers, or mountains, while others simply lived in the air. This belief is called **animism.** They also believed that some spirits lived in humans; people inhabited by spirits were called witches. By praying and sacrificing to these spirits, the Africans hoped to receive blessings. They treated the spirits of ancestors the same as these other spirits. They believed that all spirits had power to affect a person's life. The biggest effect these spirits had on the people of Africa was to keep them bound in sin and lost in its darkness. "For we wrestle not against flesh and blood, but against

Almost all Africans believed in a High God. They learned that he was a spiritual being who walked with man until something caused the High God to separate himself from the people. The Dinka tribe of Ghana told the story that the High God walked with man until a selfish woman made him angry and he left man's company. The Sudanese told the story that a woman was so noisy that the High God went into heaven to get away from her. Africans saw the High God as kind but generally unconcerned with the affairs of men. As missionaries go to the African people, they need to show that God is indeed concerned with the affairs of men—so concerned that He would send His Son to die for the sins of mankind. "For God so loved the world, that he gave his only begotten Son, that whosoever believeth in him should not perish, but have everlasting life" (John 3:16).

principalities, against powers, against the rulers of the darkness of this world, against spiritual wickedness in high places" (Eph. 6:12).

African religious leaders in every community promoted this hopeless religion. These leaders were **witch doctors,** who, much like the shamans of Mongolia, used magic and superstition in dealing with the people. The people believed that the witch doctor knew both the cause of and the cure for their troubles. When they went to the witch doctor for help, he performed a magical ceremony. The people believed that his magical powers showed him the details of the problem. In reality, he often knew the cause beforehand because he had seen the person's actions or heard a report that explained the problem. However, the people accepted his knowledge as a magical ability and lived in fear of his power.

After the ceremony, the witch doctor informed the person of the cause of his problem—whether it was an irritated ancestor or a local enemy. Then he told him to stop his bad behavior. Finally, he prescribed a ritual of prayers and sacrifices. The person believed that these works would end his problems and bring him blessing. Before leaving, the person paid the witch doctor with goods or produce for his services.

This witch doctor is reverenced and feared in his tribe. He uses masks, herbs, and fetishes to call on spirits, heal the sick, and prophesy the future.

CENTER STAGE

Ethiopian Orthodox priests from Lalibela swing rattles, sing, and dance in celebration of a holy day. Above is St. Stephen's Church in Addis Ababa .

Focus on Ethiopia

West African kingdoms were not the only African kingdoms to carry on trade with other cultures. As the Egyptian kingdom moved up the Nile, it encountered Kush. In the eighth century B.C. a Kushite king conquered Egypt and established the capital of Upper Egypt in the Kush city of Napata. Napata maintained its position of power for one hundred years until the Assyrians took over. The kingdom of Kush was little affected by these power changes. In the fighting with the Assyrians, however, they did see the use of iron weapons for the first time. The new awareness of iron and iron smelting would spread across Africa in the next five hundred years.

Below Kush was another ancient kingdom known as **Aksum** (Axum). In the first century A.D., Aksum and the nearby Red Sea port city of Adulis were important trading centers for the Greeks. The Greeks gave Aksum (and all the territory below it) the name *Ethiopia*, which comes from the Greek word meaning "burnt face."

Ethiopian legend states that the queen of Sheba and King Solomon had a child, Menelik, from whom all Ethiopian rulers are descended. The Ethiopians even use the imperial title "The Conquering Lion of the Tribe of Judah." Legend also said that the *Tabot,* a wooden box on the altar at the Cathedral at Aksum, contained the original Ark of the Covenant.

In the mid-fourth century A.D. in the court at Aksum, a slave, later known as St. Frumentius, rose in favor with the king and introduced Christianity to the people. When King Ezana accepted Christianity, the head of the Coptic Church in Egypt (an offshoot of the Roman Catholic and the Eastern Orthodox Churches) ordained **Frumentius** as bishop of the Ethiopian church. Slowly over the next two hundred years a great number of the population were converted to Christianity. When the Muslims conquered Egypt during the 1200s, ties to the Egyptian church were cut, and Ethiopia struggled to defend itself from the onslaught of the Muslims. During this period, Ethiopian Christianity developed its own unique way of worship, incorporating drums and dancing into its services. It was also during this time that unique structures for worship were built in Lalibela.

Ethiopia's official church has been the Ethiopian Orthodox Church for many years. The current population, however, is almost equally divided between the Muslim religion and Ethiopian Orthodoxy. About 20 percent of the population practice other religions, including traditional African beliefs. Many Ethiopian Jews have now emigrated to Israel.

This priest beats on his drum to announce the arrival of the Ark of the Covenant to an epiphany celebration.

Early Ethiopian Kingdoms

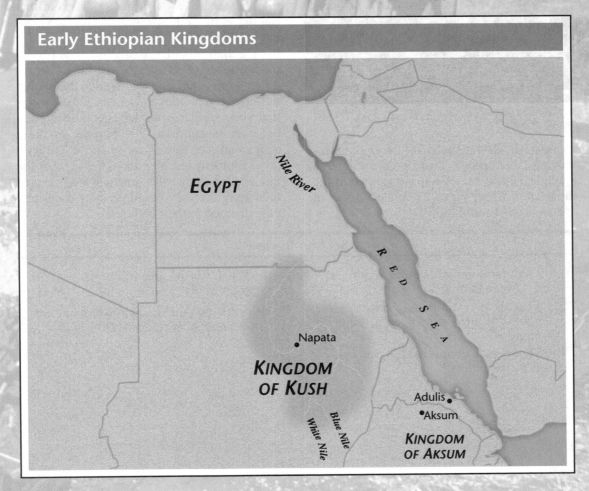

EGYPT

Nile River

RED SEA

Napata

KINGDOM OF KUSH

Blue Nile

White Nile

Adulis

Aksum

KINGDOM OF AKSUM

This Tuareg nomad girl has her face painted to ward off demon influences.

African religion had many ceremonies involving large groups. These groups might be a single village or several villages from the same clan. Ceremonies celebrated different events, such as initiation for boys and girls.

The witch doctor led the people in the rituals performed for the celebration. Almost every group ceremony included music, both vocal and instrumental. Many parts of these ceremonies—from rituals to dances—promoted magic and **demonism** (demon worship), holding Africa in spiritual darkness.

Animism and demonism, like all false religions, base salvation on works and cannot give blessing or eternal life (Eph. 2:8-9). The strong influence of magic and demonism on African religion continues to make much of African life unhappy and savage. Satan's strong hold on these people keeps them worshiping him rather than the true God. Lions are a very real danger to the Africans' bodies, but that roaring lion, the Devil, is a much greater enemy to their souls (I Pet. 5:8).

Through folktales, children learned religious beliefs as well as family histories. Storytellers sang songs and told stories that taught religious ceremonies and rituals. Other stories that were similar to fables encouraged good behavior in children. The purpose of these songs and stories was to make the children good adults by teaching them the ways of the family. Once they had learned the traditions of their religion, they could practice them and pass them on to their children.

Section Review

1. What traditions were most important in African families?

2. What are two traditional African religions? What is worshiped in these religions?

3. What person controlled religion in each community?

4. What was the greatest threat to Africans' souls?

   Why do you think many modern cultures are losing family traditions?

The Arts of Traditional Africa

These Togo musicians are dressed in traditional costumes of fur and beads to celebrate a holiday.

Instrumentalists played drums, rattles, horns, bells, and gongs. Different tribes had different types of instruments. One tribe had drums that could be played at different pitches. By changing the pitch, the drummer could imitate his language and make his drum "talk." Using **"talking drums,"** members of this tribe communicated rapidly between villages spread miles apart.

Many arts are represented in traditional Africa. Music and dance have accompanied events of life for centuries. Sculpture recorded history and aided religious practice. Although much early African architecture did not last, the architecture that remains reveals excellent craftsmanship and design. Each art form tells something about the people who created it.

Music

Little of African life passed without singing. From cutting down trees to burying their dead, Africans sang about everything. Music accompanied work, religious ceremonies, community events, and recreation. Usually professional singers or storytellers led the music while everyone else joined in for the choruses.

Dance

Where there was music in Africa, there was usually dance. Dancing often accompanied religious ceremonies. Every ceremony had its specific dances to be performed. Some religious ceremonial dances even had demon possession as their purpose. In a traditional

Drums keep the beat while people gather together to sing traditional songs.

dance of the Kalahari Bushmen in South Africa, the women remain seated while the men dance themselves into a trancelike state. In this state the men go from person to person supposedly pulling disease or illness out and throwing it to waiting dead ancestors and spirits.

Dance also accompanied many of the events of life. Africans danced for celebrations, such as a child passing into adulthood, marriage, victory over an enemy, or a successful hunt. Often professional dancers led the dances.

Women and men danced separately in most cases. Often one group danced while the other group encircled them, keeping the beat with foot stomping and chanting or singing.

Sculpture

Another important African art was sculpture. In many cultures, artists sculpted stylized figures from a single piece of wood, chiseled them in stone, or cast them in metal to represent political or religious powers. Craftsmen made sculptures of chiefs and clan leaders. They also made figurines as charms for the people to ward off bad spirits or bring good luck. Other sculptures honored spirits and dead ancestors. Africans believed that these statues had spiritual powers. But Scripture tells us, "The idols of the heathen are silver and gold, the work of men's hands. They have mouths, but they speak not; eyes have they, but they see not; they have ears, but they hear not; neither is there any breath in their mouths" (Ps. 135:15-17).

African craftsmen also made **masks** worn by witch doctors and dancers in religious ceremonies. The masks portrayed faces of spirits or animals. Often they were frightening faces with deformed features. Sometimes craftsmen painted them with bright colors, and sometimes they left them plain. Each mask had a special purpose, and during the ceremony the person wearing the mask "became" the spirit or animal that the mask represented.

Craftsmen sculpted for their rulers cups and stools with intricate designs or stylized figures not only to look beautiful but also to please the spirits. In **Benin,** the oba (king) commissioned artists to make **bronze plaques** commemorating the life of the people. The oba decorated his palace with these plaques. Although there is no written record of this southern Nigerian empire, these plaques provide a record of important events and of the daily life of these ancient people.

Masks, once used in worship, reveal the skill and craftsmanship of their carver.

Architecture

Because there were few large African cities and because the building materials used in them were not strong, there is little significant architecture from ancient sub-Saharan Africa. Many cities were a walled collection of clay brick compounds with a central palace and government buildings of the same materials. Once an empire fell and a city was no longer used, the buildings quickly fell into ruin because of weather damage.

However, Portuguese explorer and missionary Francisco Alvares made a marvelous find in 1520 in Ethiopia. In the isolated village of **Lalibela,** Alvares found a Christian community. These Christians were part of the Ethiopian (or Abyssinian) church, which is connected to the Coptic Church of Egypt. The Ethiopian churches and worship were similar in many ways to that of Roman Catholicism and Eastern Orthodoxy.

Legend tells that King Lalibela received a command from God to build churches. In the city of Lasta (later called Lalibela), workers carved ten churches in solid rock during the 1200s. The largest of these churches, the **Church of the Redeemer of the World,** is one hundred feet long by seventy-five feet wide. The architecture is a combination of Byzantine, Greek, and Roman. Some scholars speculated that portions of the architecture came from as far away as Persia and China.

Carved in solid rock, the roof of the Church of St. George is level with the surrounding hilltop.

The interior walls of these churches feature murals depicting biblical stories and Ethiopian history.

Perhaps the most striking of the churches is the **Church of St. George.** This church was built inside a hill. Workers dug a forty-foot-deep trench around a solid block of lava rock. This block was then carved and hollowed out to form the church. The church is in the middle of a square pit in the hill. The top of the church is level with the top of the hill. The entrance is a narrow trench cut into the side of the hill.

Unlike the European craftsmen of this period who were building churches from materials that could be moved and changed to correct errors in architecture, the carvers of the Lalibela churches had to be completely accurate. One error or miscalculation could have ruined the whole building.

Section Review

1. For what purposes did the Africans use music?
2. What was the purpose of masks in Africa?
3. Why did little of African architecture last?

4. Where did a Portuguese explorer find a Christian community?
5. What is unique about the churches he found there?

Why was much of African art functional (useful) rather than merely aesthetic (just to look at)?

Nomads Around the World

Nomadic people have been found on every continent. The term **nomad** refers to people who change locations to survive. The people of Israel started out as nomads until the Lord brought them to the Promised Land. In the Middle Ages, traders traveled from the Silk Road to the European fairs and back in a consistent nomadic cycle. American Plains Indians followed the buffalo and antelope on their seasonal migration. Gypsy bands early in the twentieth century still traveled in their house-wagons selling goods, doing odd jobs, and trading horses. Today, Africa's Masai people, Arabia's Bedouins, Mongolia's Tatars, and Norway's Lapps all move to provide for the needs of their herds. North Africa's Tuareg traders move across the Sahara on annual migrations for trade, and India's Lohars move to practice their metalwork.

People are nomadic for various reasons. Most nomads are husbandmen herding their livestock from pasture to pasture. These people change location based on the weather. Other nomads are traders and craftsmen traveling to exchange goods or to practice their craft where needed. Even with these differences, there are factors that are common to all nomads.

Nomadic herdsmen may take their herds across vast stretches of terrain to find adequate grazing.

Nomads who follow herds usually live in portable dwellings with minimal furnishings. From the previous chapter you are aware of the Mongol yurt. Look at the drawings of the Indian tepee and the Bedouin tent. How are the yurt, tepee, and tent similar? In what ways do they vary? What environmental conditions have affected their design?

Nomads who trade or practice crafts usually have wagons in which they travel. Why do you think they do not use tentlike structures? How is a wagon more suited for carrying goods? Why would it be difficult for nomads who follow flocks to use wheeled vehicles?

Another common characteristic of nomadic people is their lack of education. How do you think their lifestyle makes getting an education difficult? Do you think there is a place for nomadic life in today's world?

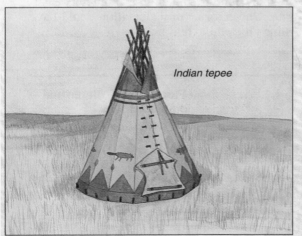

Indian tepee

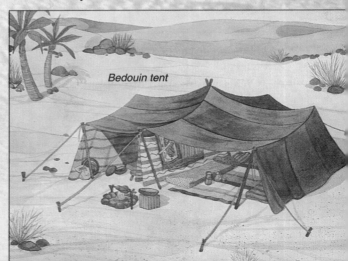

Bedouin tent

Making a Living

Many Africans spent their lives simply finding or growing enough food to live on each day. In the interior of Africa, most tribes hunted game and gathered fruits and nuts. In the northern and eastern regions, the people did more farming and herding, but African soil is not generally fertile. Without proper care it wears out quickly and produces poorly. Because of this problem, African farmers moved often to find fertile soil and to find pasture and water for their animals. Tribes that hunted and gathered their food moved whenever their supply of game and fruits ran low. The large African continent provided space for all this movement. After several years of lying **fallow,** or dormant, the soil became fertile again and the tribes could return to previous settlements.

Communities that raised their food involved every member in the work of farming. After the community had found an area to farm, the chief decided who farmed what land. Then with musical accompaniment, men, women, and children cleared the land and planted it. They grew millet (a grain), rice, and sorghum. The women also tended smaller vegetable gardens. During the growing season, the children sat on raised stands or in trees out in the fields to shoo away birds. The men spent these months hunting game to add meat to their families' diets. At harvest everyone helped to bring in the crop.

This Nigerian girl carries water in a calabash gourd much the way her ancestors have done for centuries.

Herders spent their lives looking after livestock—cattle, sheep, goats. During times of drought they searched out new areas of water and green pasture for their animals. To obtain grain and vegetables from local farmers, they traded their animals for produce.

All African communities had craftsmen who made goods for the people. Village people needed iron tools, weapons, dishes, storage containers, and baskets. Of course, each community had craftsmen who made masks and figurines for the people. These craftsmen traded their wares for food from the farmers and herders. The Africans generally did not use money in their trade but exchanged goods by barter.

Section Review

1. List four ways Africans obtained food.
2. Why did African communities move often?
3. What job did the children have during growing season?
4. How did Africans exchange goods and produce?

Compare African life to medieval European life. In what ways was African life similar to medieval European life? How was it different?

Large blocks of salt are pried up in rectangles that will be loaded onto camels and carried to market.

"They may be called 'the ships of the desert,' but they sure are hard to steer."

Salt

Salt seems to be such an insignificant item today. Of course, salt is in almost every processed food that we buy and is essential to many foods (yeast breads, for one), but as far as value is concerned, a 26-ounce container of salt can be purchased for around a penny an ounce. That is fairly inexpensive for an essential seasoning. Next time you are at the grocery store, look at the prices of other spices. Cinnamon is a common spice, but it can cost over three dollars for only a few ounces!

You may remember, however, that at one time salt was an important trade item. Everyone needed salt. In ancient Rome, the Latin word *salārium*, from which we get our word *salary*, referred to the money given to Roman soldiers to buy salt. Salt was a crucial item for preserving foods. It continued as an important preserving item until refrigeration became available in the early 1900s.

Salt was one of the main items in the trans-Saharan trade system in Africa; gold was the other one. Why were two such different items traded back and forth? Gold was plentiful in West Africa; salt was not. Europeans wanted gold for their crowns, jewelry, coins, and such; western Africa had gold in abundance. Kings' dogs had gold chains and food dishes!

One area of early salt production was the northern Mali oasis town of Taghaza. For over five hundred years, trade caravans have traveled from the north and the south to trade salt and other goods there. Taghaza has salt deposits that are quarried (cut or dug directly from the earth). Two-hundred-pound slabs were cut and loaded two to a camel. In other locations in the Sahara Desert and at Lake Chad in Chad, the salt is produced by evaporation pits just as it has been for centuries. Water from springs is poured into small pits in the sand. The spring water absorbs the natural salt in the sand. When it evaporates, it leaves behind blocks of salt. In the twentieth century, modern methods of salt extraction became available; but in Africa caravans still come, pack animals or vehicles are loaded, and the precious salt is redirected to areas of need.

African Kingdoms and Empires

Although traditional African culture continued into the modern age, other cultures have influenced it. This happened especially when Africans came into contact with Asians and Europeans. Some of the earliest contact took place in the kingdoms and empires of western Africa.

Western African Kingdoms

The states of western Africa began around the year 500. Starting as small states headed by a clan or tribal chief, these tribal kingdoms conquered other states and clans, thus growing into empires. The largest and most important empires of the region followed one another: **Ghana** (GAH nuh), **Mali** (MAH lee), and **Songhai** (SONG HYE). This final kingdom lasted into the seventeenth century.

These kingdoms grew large and powerful because of their position on trade routes. Caravan routes crossing the Sahara Desert ended along the northern Niger River. But merchants from North Africa desired the goods of interior Africa: gold, ebony, ivory, spices, hides, iron, and slaves. In exchange, the merchants brought salt, cloth, jewelry, and manufactured goods, which were not readily available in the interior. Because Ghana, Mali, and Songhai controlled the region between northern Africa and the interior, they acted as middlemen. They obtained gold and other goods from the interior to trade for goods from North Africa. They took these goods to the interior and traded for more gold and other goods. From this trade these kingdoms gained wealth. As their wealth grew, they no longer depended on the soil for their living. Unlike most African tribes, these kingdoms remained in the same location for centuries and established permanent settlements.

Many merchants who traveled the Saharan trade routes were Muslims. They had converted during the Islamic conquest of North Africa. These African Muslims controlled many of the trade routes. When they came to trade in these kingdoms, they brought not only their goods but also their religion. Because of the Muslims' avid witness, many people of these ancient kingdoms converted to Islam. Wherever they went, the Muslims enthusiastically spread their false religion. How much more fervent Christians should be in spreading the truth of the gospel.

In addition to their beliefs, the Muslims brought other gifts to the Africans. First they brought a written language. Islamic scholars traveling in Africa taught the people to read and write Arabic. The same scholars recorded what they saw in Africa and gave us the first written history of the continent. Slowly the ability to read and write changed the culture of Africa, which had known only oral recording of history and tradition.

Although some African rulers converted to Islam, they still practiced many traditional African rituals. Sadly, those who accepted Islam were as lost as those who followed traditional African religions. Islam does not teach the true way of salvation by the Lord Jesus Christ (John 14:6). Africans had the witness of nature and their consciences to show them the true God (Rom. 1:20; 2:15). However, not until the coming of European missionaries in the nineteenth century did many Africans hear the gospel for the first time.

East African Kingdoms

Trading cities grew up along the coast, where Africans from the interior brought gold, ivory, and precious stones. Many of these

"From Here to Timbuktu"

When someone wants to describe something as being far away, he may say, "It's as far as from here to Timbuktu." Most people think Timbuktu is a fictional place, much like Never-Never Land. Actually **Timbuktu** is a real city and still exists today. Hundreds of years ago Timbuktu was an important trade center in Africa.

Timbuktu is located in western Africa near the Niger River, at the southern edge of the great Sahara. From about the year 1100 Timbuktu became a leading city of the African kingdom of Mali. Trade caravans crossed the desert to buy and sell goods in Timbuktu. Merchants from as far away as Egypt and Italy traded in fabrics, salt, ivory, spices, ostrich feathers, and, most important, gold and slaves.

The great Mali ruler **Mansa Musa** (1312-37) transformed the city into a center for the arts and learning as well. He built a great Islamic mosque and encouraged the founding of schools and libraries. So many scholars came to Timbuktu that books soon became an item of trade almost as important as gold and slaves. At its height, Timbuktu had over twenty-five thousand inhabitants, a large number for medieval times. (By comparison, Rome at that time had a population of seventeen thousand.) A merchant from Florence, Benedetto Dei, visited in 1470 and found a prosperous city with ornate mosques and the rich and the poor dwelling together. In the sixth century, Leo Africanus, a Moor (a Muslim of North African and Berber descent), told of a splendid city with many scholars and a dazzling court life. Such prosperity did not last, however. Warfare disrupted trade and stopped the flow of wealth into the city. By 1828 French explorers found the city in ruins from constant raids by rival tribes. Today Timbuktu is only a small town in the nation of Mali and is visited mostly by a few tourists who are fascinated by the name Timbuktu.

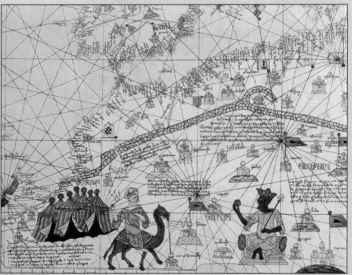

On a medieval map, Timbuktu was about as far as Europeans could travel into Western Africa.

goods arrived at the coastal cities on the heads of porters who had walked hundreds of miles across the continent. Merchants from Arabia, India, and even China sailed to these cities to trade. Eventually these goods from Africa went to markets throughout Asia. The language of these cities reflects the meeting of many cultures. The people spoke **Swahili** (swah HEE lee), a mixture of Arabic, Persian, Portuguese, Indian (Hindi), and Bantu (a native African language).

Another reflection of the meeting of cultures in these east coast cities was the highly developed system of trade and government. When later explorers arrived, they were greatly impressed by the wealth and advancement of the area. The goods that they wanted to exchange were not interesting or necessary to the Africans. As in the Sudan kingdoms, this development was encouraged by outside influences, such as trade and Islam.

In Africa, two distinct cultures coexisted. The centers of trade on the east and west coasts and in northern Africa were mixtures of many cultures. Evidences of this mix occurred in language and development. In contrast, the people of Africa's interior, so long isolated from the outside world, held on to their traditional culture. The interior region remained unknown and mysterious to the outside world until Europeans penetrated it in the nineteenth century.

Section Review

1. In what part of Africa did large trading kingdoms grow up?
2. How were these kingdoms able to stay settled in permanent locations?
3. What religion did traders bring to these kingdoms? What other area of Africa came under that religion's influence?
4. What was probably the most important gift brought by the Muslims to Africa?
5. How does Swahili reflect a mixing of cultures?

Does education have a positive effect on nations? Explain your answer.

Summary

Tradition guided every part of African culture. Families followed the traditions passed down to them and passed them on to their children. Because Africans had no written language, they passed on their traditions orally. African families combined into clans, which included all families having a common ancestor. Clans with common cultures grouped together in tribes. Based on the worship of spirits, African religion used much magic and demonism. The arts in Africa promoted this worship through singing, dancing, and sculpting idols. Most African tribes moved often. They needed to find new sources of food, whether that meant new farmland or new herds of animals to hunt. In the Sudan and along the east coast, permanent cities and kingdoms grew up. These settlements relied on trade for their prosperity.

CHAPTER REVIEW

People, Places, and Terms to Know

clan	Frumentius	Church of the	Ghana
tribe	demonism	Redeemer of the	Mali
storytellers	"talking drums"	World	Songhai
oral histories	masks	Church of St. George	Timbuktu
animism	Benin	nomad	Mansa Musa
witch doctors	bronze plaques	fallow	Swahili
Aksum	Lalibela		

Review Questions

Completion

Complete the following statements about Africa.

1. In Africa clans were made up of many (a) _____ groups. A group of clans formed a (b) _____.

2. Traditional African homes were built of (a) _____, (b) _____, (c) _____, and (d) _____.

3. Little is known about early African history because it was handed down (a) _____. After (b) _____ traders entered the Sudan, scholars gave the world the first (c) _____ record of African history.

4. The three great kingdoms in the Sudan were (a) _____, (b) _____, and (c) _____.

Matching

Match each of these terms to its meaning.

5. witch doctor
6. "talking drums"
7. Swahili
8. masks

(a) worn in religious ceremonies
(b) a mixture of languages
(c) religious leader
(d) sent messages from village to village

Fill in the Blank

Choose words from the list below to fill in the blanks correctly.

language	folktales
chief	traditions
tribe	ancestor
beliefs	customs
clan	

9. African children learned the history and traditions of their land by listening to _____ told by elders.

10. Many Africans believed that the purpose of children was to carry on family _____.

11. Tribes shared the same _____, _____, and _____.

12. The _____ was the largest family group in African society.

13. All the members of a clan could trace their ancestry to a common _____.

14. The clan was ruled by the oldest male clan member, who was called the _____.

15. A _____ was more than one clan living together.

Think About It!

How do a country's natural resources affect its ability to compete in a world market? What problems does Africa face that are due to its location and natural condition?

Does America face similar problems? Would America have gotten the international status it enjoys if it were faced with the same problems native to Africa? What other factors affected Africa's development?

NOVA ANGLIA
MARILAND
VIRGINIA
FLORIDA
CVBA
TERRAFIRMA
POPAIANA
PERV
AMAZONES

CHALLENGES

Entering Act Two, we take a step back in time to the late 1400s. We see the effects of the Renaissance as the Europeans took up the challenge of exploring the lands that had only been imagined before this time.

Europeans are now traveling to the Americas, the Pacific, and the Far East. There they cultivate the land and establish colonies and trading centers. As a result they often conquer native kingdoms and destroy native cultures; but with this devastation they also bring technology, new ideas, and education. Most important, by opening these lands, the Europeans allow Christians in later years to bring to these lost people the gospel of Christ's love.

Not all of the players in this act are willing participants. Some of the characters come into the scene because of outside pressures. The Puritans and Pilgrims arrive in North America to avoid the persecution that came as a backlash from the Reformation. Black Africans arrive in North and South America as a result of the slave trade. Even willing participants face extreme difficulty during exploration and colonization.

The next five chapters deal with the early contacts Europeans made with people in new lands as well as the effect those contacts had on Europe. Because of the push to explore and settle, Europe makes many advances. Improved transportation, communications, industry, farming, education, and living standards put Europe in a position of world leadership. New ideas and technology shake the foundations of science, religion, and politics. Challenges abound for explorers, settlers, governments, inventors, and philosophers, especially those who are Christians.

CHAPTER 6

Marco Polo had journeyed to the Far East (1271-95), a land of mystery to thirteenth-century Europe. Describing the capital of Kublai Khan's China, Marco excited his medieval readers' minds.

The multitude of inhabitants, and the number of houses in the city, as also in the suburbs without the city, is greater than the mind can comprehend. To this city everything that is most rare and valuable in all parts of the world finds its way; and more especially does this apply to India, which furnishes precious stones, pearls, and various drugs and spices. From the provinces of Cathay itself, as well as from the other provinces of the empire . . . the quantity of merchandise sold there exceeds also the traffic of any other place; for no fewer than a thousand carriages and pack-horses, loaded with raw silk, make their daily entry; and gold tissues [a rich cloth] and silks of various kinds are manufactured to an immense extent.

The Europeans were amazed by what they read. A land of gold, silks, and spices? A land where the people burn black stones instead of wood for heat and use money made of paper? Incredible! And yet for the first time, they had true information about the land of China, the land they called Cathay (ka THAY). No longer a total mystery, Cathay became the object of European desire.

With their appetite for foreign lands and goods whetted, Europeans spent the next several hundred years finding ways to get there. In this chapter you will study the age of exploration.

A.D. **1200** - A.D. **1600**

1200

Marco Polo journeys to China 1271-1295

The Age of Exploration

Cortes Arrives in
Tenochtitlán 1519

Columbus's First
Voyage 1492

Pizarro Overthrows
the Inca Empire 1532

Drake Circumnavigates
the World 1577-1580

Mali Empire 1230-1400

Empire of Songhai 1470-1600(?)

Renaissance 1350-1616

1400

1500

1600

Kingdom of Benin 1200-1700(?)

Prince Henry the
Navigator 1394-1460

Reformation 1500-1650

Francis Xavier Arrives in Japan 1549

Magellan Circumnavigates
the World 1519-1522

Bartolomeu Dias
Rounds Africa 1487

Da Gama sails to
India 1497

Sailing Uncharted Seas

Imagine that the leader of a nation is offering money to finance an expedition to find a new planet beyond the solar system. Unfortunately the expedition can pack only enough supplies to reach Pluto, and no one knows exactly where or if the planet is beyond there. To complicate matters further, everyone believes that a terrible void exists beyond the solar system and strange aliens wait to devour anyone who trespasses in outer space. Along with the emotion of excitement, anyone who accepts the challenge will probably feel fear.

What you imagine in the story above is probably close to what the crews of the early ocean expeditions felt. Ocean expeditions were a daunting task fit for only a few of the bravest of crews.

This brass astrolabe, made in 1304 by an Arabian astronomer, is similar to those used by early explorers.

"Go as Far as You Can, and Try to Bring News of These People"

With these words, **Prince Henry** of Portugal sent out sailors and ships to explore the coast of Africa in the fifteenth century. For a long time, Arabs and Italians had controlled the land routes to the East and had charged high prices to the rest of Europe. To compete with these traders, the Portuguese decided to find a sea route to India and China. However, for these men the sea contained many unknown dangers: stories of sea monsters, deadly heat at the equator, and violent storms filled the minds of sailors. Despite these dangers, some men, supported by their kings, set out to find and explore distant lands. The hope of adventure, fame, and wealth was too strong for them to stay away.

Prince Henry the Navigator challenged the Portuguese to lead the nations in exploration.

The wheelhouse of a modern vessel includes new technological equipment to help today's sailor navigate across the high seas.

Prince Henry of Portugal, who was called Prince Henry the Navigator, knew that men needed training before sailing the open seas. To provide such training, Prince Henry set up a school for navigation. Portuguese sea captains learned how to use new methods and instruments. Much of this new knowledge of navigation resulted from Renaissance learning.

New Tools for Exploration

As Renaissance scholars learned more about their world, they provided the explorers with new inventions. Other navigational information came to Europe through Arabia. The Arabs had used this information as they navigated across desert wastes, but the Europeans put it to use on water.

The sailor's most useful instrument was the **compass,** which allowed him to set a course and follow its direction faithfully. The origin of the compass is debated, but the Chinese record the use of the compass at the earliest date, A.D. 1100. Twelfth-century compasses were nothing more than a needle that had been stroked with magnetite and placed on a chip of wood floating in water. Even this rough compass gave the sailor a reference point other than his own sense of direction. He knew whether he was on or off course by the compass reading. The compass was of great value for sailing on the open sea with no landmarks. By the fifteenth century, compasses were of an improved design with the needle spinning on a pin over a base on which several points of direction had been marked. As vital as this instrument was to the early navigator, so is the Word of God vital to the Christian and provides the reference point by which he can check the course of his life and actions.

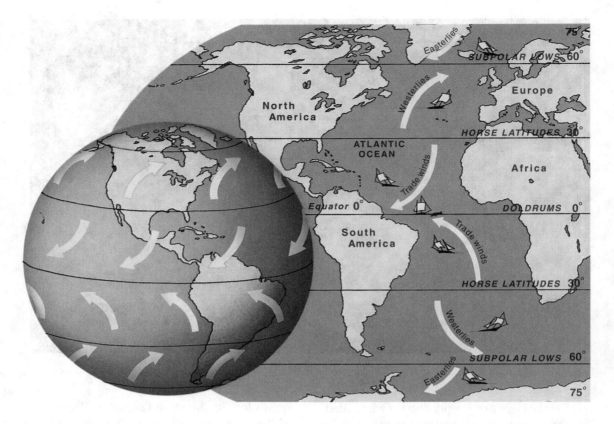

Another helpful instrument was the **astrolabe** (AS truh LAYB). Sailors used the astrolabe to measure the angle between the sun or a star and the horizon at a specific time of day or night. From this measure the sailor could find his latitude. However, on a tossing ship the angle was often hard to measure. Also, with only an hourglass to keep time, the captain rarely knew the exact time of his reading. Astrolabes were later replaced with the quadrant and then with the modern sextant.

Most early seamen navigated by **dead reckoning.** They decided what they thought their location was, estimated how fast they were traveling, looked at the map, and aimed for a certain compass heading that they thought would get them to their goal. Another similar method, except that it involved the astrolabe, was to sail latitudes. In this method the captain would sail north or south from his starting point until he got to the latitude he wanted and then would sail east or west along that latitude until he came to land.

Fortunately, good mariners knew the sea. They knew the winds, birds, and fish that helped pinpoint their ship's location or at least showed how near they were to land. Perhaps the most important discovery these early navigators made was the wind routes. The knowledge that winds blew a certain direction in specific locations helped the explorers reach their destinations more quickly or at least avoid areas of contrary winds.

Winds that were especially important to the early explorers and later settlers were the **trade winds.** These belts of consistent winds blow from east to west. They start around 30° north in the Northern Hemisphere and 30° south in the Southern Hemisphere. From that beginning they blow toward the equator. These fast-moving, favorable winds blew the explorers across the Atlantic Ocean.

Two areas that the travelers had to beware of were the doldrums and the horse latitudes. The **doldrums** are an area of calm or light fluctuating winds along the equator. Equally difficult were the **horse latitudes,** which lie around 30-35° N where the trade winds and the prevailing westerlies meet. (See wind chart.) Soon maps not only showed land locations but also charted wind directions.

Another factor that helped the travelers with their explorations was a new type of ship designed by the Portuguese. Called a **caravel,** this ship was sturdy enough for ocean travel and large enough to bring back a good cargo. The caravel usually had three masts and used both square and triangular sails to power and direct the ship. The caravel offered few comforts. Only the head officers had beds; the other sailors slept wherever they found room. On long voyages food and water often spoiled or ran out. The hardships of a long trip killed numbers of sailors. When supplies ran low, the captain tried to maintain morale or else risked mutiny by his crew.

Once trained and supplied with ships and instruments, Portuguese explorers set out to find a way to India by sailing around Africa. As crews sailed farther south along the coast, they proved that the equator's heat would not kill them and that strange monsters did not live there. Growing braver, they continued south hoping to find India just around the corner.

Section Review

1. Whose writings helped spark Europeans' curiosity about the Far East?

2. What man from what nation took the early lead in training and sending out explorers?

3. From what two sources did captains obtain navigational methods and instruments? What instruments did they obtain?

4. What navigational method involves estimating sailing speed and location to choose compass heading?

5. What is the area of light winds around the equator called?

Write a short paragraph that compares (shows similarities) and contrasts (shows differences) desert navigation and ocean navigation.

ANALYSIS

LATEENERS

carvel-built hull

Advances in Sailing

Today the United States regularly sends astronauts into space on the space shuttles. The technology required for these flights advanced by leaps and bounds in the 1960s. With today's advanced technology, we may look down our noses at changes in sailing vessels before the age of exploration, but for that time, the new sailing ships were just like the shuttles of today. Used to sailing close to the coastlines of known land, explorers were now considering venturing into the great unknown seas, an "outer space" with many dangers both real and imagined. Attempting these sailing expeditions required new ships. The ships that navigated well on the coastal waters of Northern Europe and the Mediterranean had to be refitted to the new task of sailing the open ocean. The ship style eventually used was a combination of the best features of the twelfth-century Mediterranean ships called lateeners (la TEEN er; taken from the word *latin*) and the Northern European knarrs (NARS). Both lateeners and knarrs used a single sail, but that sail and the overall construction of the two ships were quite different.

The Mediterranean lateener sailed with a triangular sail. This triangular sail could catch even the smallest amount of wind to take the ship out of port and made the ship easy to maneuver. This characteristic was ideal for the port-hopping done in that highly populated area. The Northern European knarr, on the other hand, had a square sail. For sailing great distances on the open sea, this sail could hold more wind and could outrun a lateener ship. However, it took far more wind to pull the knarr out of port.

The lateener steered with two oars mounted on either side at the back of the ship. The knarr

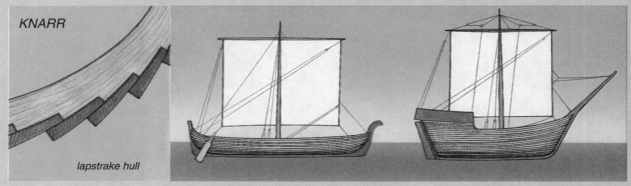

KNARR

lapstrake hull

used a single steering board positioned at the back of the ship on the right side.

Another major difference between the ships was the construction of the hull. The lateener was carvel-built. A skeleton frame was made, and then boards were laid side by side down to the keel. Any gaps were filled with caulk to seal them. Although lateeners were prone to leak, the over-riding advantage of this frame building was that the lateener could be built to any size. In contrast, the knarr was built using lapstrake construction. In this construction the planks were overlapped

Advances came in both ships before a combination design resulted. Thirteenth-century lateener ships became deeper, added a sail, and cut down to one steering oar. The knarr was replaced by the cog. The cog still used one square sail but was deeper and had a straight sternpost with the rudder set on it. The rudder replaced the steering board of the knarr.

The ship that Columbus sailed was a carrack. Blending the good qualities of the knarr and the lateener, it was an advanced sailing vessel for its time. It was deep enough to have a main deck with two higher decks at the aft (rear)—the quarter-deck and the poop deck—and a single higher deck called the forecastle at the front. It sailed with a large square sail, three smaller square sails, and at least one smaller lateen sail. It was carvel-built with a rudder (steering board) straight up the back.

Columbus's ships were tiny compared to the vessels that would carry trade across the sea to America in the early to middle 1800s. Because speed became the most important factor, those later ships were built longer, deeper, and with more sails. The fastest sailing vessel before the age of the steamboat was the clipper ship that was used for trade in the mid-1800s.

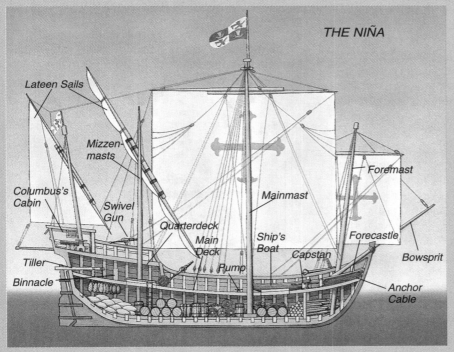

THE NIÑA

Lateen Sails
Mizzen-masts
Columbus's Cabin
Swivel Gun
Quarterdeck
Main Deck
Tiller
Binnacle
Pump
Ship's Boat
Mainmast
Capstan
Foremast
Forecastle
Bowsprit
Anchor Cable

and riveted together. The knarr was very water-tight, but when a ship was over one hundred feet long, problems with joining the boards became overwhelming.

New Regions and Routes

The Europeans were accustomed to the overland route they used to reach the East. Exploring for new routes by sea brought Europe in contact with new people in the lands which were familiar to them and eventually into contact with new worlds in unfamiliar seas.

To the East by Sailing South

In 1487 the Portuguese explorer **Bartolomeu Dias** (DEE us) finally turned the corner that would open sea trade with India. Caught in a bad storm, Dias's ships rounded the tip of Africa without realizing it. When Dias did become aware of what he had done, he turned back and saw land. After such a nerve-wracking trip, Dias named this point of land the **Cape of Storms.** The Portuguese had proved that they could reach the East by sailing south around Africa.

Ten years later, in 1497, the first Portuguese ship landed in India. After rounding the **Cape of Good Hope** (the Cape of Storms renamed by King John II), **Vasco da Gama** (VAHS-ko duh GAHM-uh) and his crew sailed up the east coast of Africa and crossed the Indian Ocean to the port of Calicut. Along the African coast they stopped in the trading cities and met both African and Arab traders. Landing in Mughul India, da Gama and his men were surprised to find an advanced people. The logbook from one of da Gama's ships contained descriptions of India. The following selection shows that the wealth and splendor of the local king's court greatly impressed the Portuguese sailors.

> The king was in a small court, reclining upon a couch covered with a cloth of green velvet, above which was a good mattress, and upon this again a sheet of cotton stuff, very white and fine, more so than any linen.

The cushions were after the same fashion. In his left hand the king held a very large golden cup (spittoon), having a capacity of half an almude (eight pints). At its mouth this cup was two palmas (sixteen inches) wide, and apparently it was massive. On the right side of the king stood a basin of gold, so large that a man might just encircle it with his arms; this contained the herbs. There were likewise many silver jugs. The canopy above the couch was all gilt.

When they tried to trade, the Portuguese were surprised that the Indians rejected the items they had brought. Their cloth, honey, and oil interested few Indians. Eventually, the Portuguese sold enough of their goods to buy spices to return home.

Portuguese seamen sailed farther and farther out from Sagres, establishing bases all along the African coast.

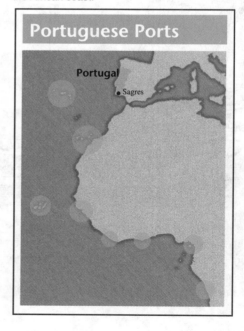

Portuguese Ports

Portugal
• Sagres

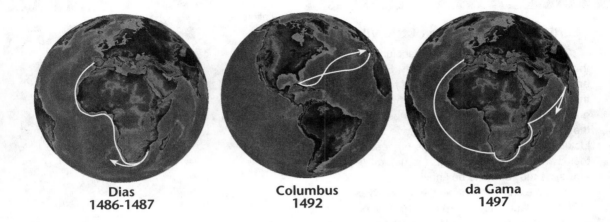

Dias
1486-1487

Columbus
1492

da Gama
1497

To the East by Sailing West

The Portuguese monarchs sent their ships to the East by sailing south, but another Portuguese explorer believed he could get to the East by sailing west. His ideas were scoffed at in his own country, but after several meetings, **Christopher Columbus** finally convinced **King Ferdinand** and **Queen Isabella** of Spain that his plan could work. By sailing west, he hoped to discover a shorter route to China and the Indies (the islands near China, now known as Indonesia). In August 1492 he set sail with three ships. In October he landed on an island in what he thought were the Indies. He describes his discovery in a letter to his royal supporters:

> This island and all the others are very fertile to a limitless degree, and this island is extremely so. In it there are many harbors on the coast of the sea, beyond comparison with others which I know in Christendom, and many rivers, good and large, which is marvelous.

The sierras and mountains, and plains and arable lands and pastures, are so lovely and rich for planting and sowing, for breeding cattle of every kind, for building towns and villages. The harbors of the sea here are such as cannot be believed to exist unless they had been seen, and so with the rivers, many and great, and good waters, the majority of which contain gold. In this island there are many and great mines of gold and of other metals.

Although Columbus was right about sailing west to get east, he did not sail far enough. Thinking he had landed in the Indies, he called the natives "Indians." In reality he had landed in the Caribbean. The nearby mainland was not China but the Americas. Neither the Caribbean islands nor North America yielded the precious metals and spices the Europeans found in Middle and South America. Nevertheless, in later centuries North America became a land of hope and freedom for millions.

Earlier Explorers: Men of the Viks

Toward the end of the first millennium A.D., the people of Scandinavia—Norway, Sweden, and Denmark—were running out of room in their countries. With pasturelands limited to the grassy areas lining the fjords, all sons other than the firstborn, who inherited family land, had to look to other areas if they wanted homesteads of their own. The men of the viks (fjords), or **Vikings,** as they came to be known, began to explore. Some came to inhabited areas such as Ireland, England, France, Spain, and Italy, burning and pillaging as they went. Others settled peaceably within some of those lands. Still others discovered new lands to possess for themselves.

One land that the Vikings inhabited and established trade routes to was Iceland. Because of warm ocean air and geothermic forces, Iceland was a fertile and easily inhabited area. The Vikings might have been content to stay in Iceland, but one Icelander, **Erik the Red,** was sentenced to banishment by the Icelandic government. In seeking a place to inhabit during his banishment, Erik discovered a new land. After choosing the best location for himself, Erik named this barren sheet of glacial ice *Greenland* to draw settlers over whom he could be leader. When his banishment was over, Erik went back to Iceland and enlisted one thousand people to come back to Greenland to settle. The year was A.D. 986.

Among these settlers was a man named Herjulf. Herjulf's son Bjarni was a trader on the seas between Iceland, Ireland, and Scandinavia. On his next return trip to Iceland, Bjarni discovered that his father had gone west to Greenland. Not wanting to miss the opportunity to see his father, Bjarni set off. Instead of finding Greenland right away, Bjarni realized that he had been blown far southwest of his destination. When he and his men sighted land, it was green and heavily wooded,

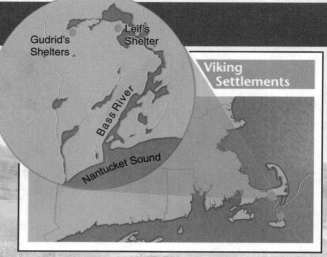

Were Leif's settlements in Massachusetts? Archaeologists have found possible evidence of Viking settlement at the sites shown above.

not at all like the descriptions of Greenland Bjarni had heard. Sailing north up this coastline, Bjarni found another land that was high, mountainous, and glacial. Thinking it might be Greenland, he and his men sailed along its coastline until they realized it was a small island. Correcting their navigation again, they began to sail northeast and four days later sailed into harbor in Greenland. Bjarni had sighted what we now identify as Nova Scotia, New Brunswick, and Labrador. Knowledge of this other land would send Erik's son, **Leif Erikson,** to explore for himself by 1003.

Greenland had been able to support its settlers for many years, but the inhospitable climate did not allow rapid growth of trees. The settlers began noticing the shortage of wood. This shortage, combined with the slow trade with Iceland, made the people talk about seeking new lands. Leif had heard about Bjarni's discoveries to the west and decided to see for himself. With thirty-five men, Leif set off for the other lands to the west. He would name these land *Helluland* (Flat Rock Land), *Markland* (Forest Land), and *Vinland* (Land of Vines or Wineland) respectively. Possible evidence of Leif's settlement has been found on the peninsula of Cape Cod up the Bass River from Nantucket Sound.

Leif and his men spent the winter in Vinland and in the summer returned to Greenland. Although Leif never gave up claim to the buildings that he and his men built, he did give permission to his brother Thorvald to use them. Thorvald and twenty-five men went to Vinland. They spent the winter in Leif's shelters and then explored the coastline northwards up to present-day Maine. It was there that they met their first **skraelings** (shriekers or war-whoopers)—Native Americans. The meeting was unfortunate. Thorvald was killed. His men spent another winter in Leif's dwellings and then sailed back to Greenland.

The next sailing to Vinland was with the purpose of settlement. Leif's sister, Gudrid, sailed with her husband and at least sixty men, five women, and livestock. The settlement lasted for only three years because of the continual onslaught from the skraelings. This was the last Viking attempt to settle Vinland, although there are records of other Viking explorers coming to look for wealth. The next settlers in the New World would come about five hundred years later seeking a place of refuge from religious persecution.

These sod houses are replicas of those originally built by Vikings on this site in L'Anse aux Meadows on the island of Newfoundland, Canada. Some scholars believe this is the landing site described by Leif Erikson.

The Age of Exploration

All Around the World

Da Gama had sailed east. Columbus had sailed west. Why not sail around the entire world? This challenge was taken up by **Ferdinand Magellan** (FUR-duh-nand muh-JEL-un). Sailing from Spain, Magellan and his crew began by sailing west. They rounded the tip of South America and crossed the Pacific Ocean. Unfortunately Magellan was killed in the East Indies (present-day Indonesia). His crew, however, continued and completed the trip back to Spain. The voyage took three years, but they proved Columbus right: it was possible to reach the East by sailing west.

Another adventurous explorer was **Sir Francis Drake.** Sent out by Queen Elizabeth of England, Drake spent nearly three years sailing the world and exploring new lands. On returning, he published a report of his voyage. He told of seeing new lands and peoples and enjoying God's gifts in nature. He also reported times of hardship in their crossings. Winds, storms, heat, and lack of fresh water plagued their voyage. On entering the Pacific, Drake did not find the sea as peaceful as Magellan had. (Magellan had named the sea *Pacific,* from the Latin word for "peace.") You can almost hear the wind howling and feel the ship roll under you as you read the following record of these awful days aboard ship.

> The winds were such as if the bowels of the earth had set all at libertie; or as if all the clouds under heaven had beene called together, to lay their force upon that one place: The seas, which by nature and of themselves are heavie, and of a weightie substance, were rowled up from the depths, to water the exceeding tops of high and loftie mountaines. Our anchors, as false friends in such a danger, gave over their holdfast, and as if it had beene with horror of the thing, did shrinke downe to hide themselves in this miserable storm; committing the distressed ship and helpless men to the uncertain and rowling seas, which tossed them, like a ball in a racket. . . . For truly, it was more likely that the mountaines should have beene rent in sunder, from the top to the bottome, and cast headlong into the sea, by these unnatural winds; than that we, by any helpe or cunning of man, should free the life of any one amongst us.

Voyages Around the World

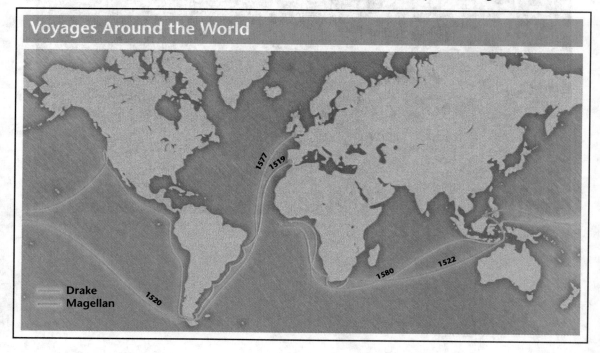

Drake
Magellan

1577 1519 1580 1522 1520

Drake's Own Account

Part of Drake's account reminds us of what the psalmist said in Psalm 107:23-24: "They that go down to the sea in ships, that do business in great waters; these see the works of the Lord, and his wonders in the deep." Such is this report of Drake's ships crossing the Atlantic. The selection below appears in the original type style. All *s*'s in words look similar to *f*'s today. The *s*'s at ends of words look like modern *s*'s. Also, *u*'s look like *v*'s. So put on your sleuth's (flevth's) hat and use these clues to read Drake's account.

During which long paffage on the vaft gulph, where nothing but fea beneath vs and aire aboue vs was to be feene, as our eies did behold the wonderfull workes of God in his creatures, which he hath made innumerable both fmall and great beafts, in the great and wide seas: fo did our mouthes tafte, and our natures feed on, the goodneffe thereof in fuch fulneffe at all times, and in the contemplation of his excellence, in beholding the variety profitable and glorious works of his hands to waite vpon vs, not alone for the reliefe of our neceffities, but alfo to giue vs delight in euery place, as if he had commanded and enioyned the moft and order of his prouidence, with a particular taft of his fatherly care ouer vs all the while.

were by his holy Angles still guiding and conducting us, that more then the affright and amaze of this estate, we received no part of damage in all the things that belonged unto us.

Notwithstanding the same God of mercy which delivered Jonas out of the Whale's belly, and heareth all those that call upon him faithfully, in their distresse; looked downe from heaven, beheld our tears, and heard our humble petitions, joined with holy vowes. Even God (whom not the winds and seas alone, but even the devils themselves and powers of hell obey) did so wonderfully free us, and make our way open before us, as it

Drake and his crew finally arrived safely in the East Indies. There they rested, traded, made friends, and repaired their ships. Finally leaving this pleasant place, they arrived home "safely with joyful minds and thankful hearts to God." Most explorers recognized God's hand in Creation—even if they were not Christians. As they traveled the globe seeing new places and meeting new people, they saw the variety of His work.

Section Review

1. Who was the first European explorer to sail around the tip of Africa?

2. How did Columbus's plan for getting to the East differ from other plans?

3. Why are Native Americans also called Indians?

4. Who was the first European explorer to reach India by sailing around Africa?

5. Who was the first European to attempt to circumnavigate the globe?

6. For what country did Sir Francis Drake sail? To whom did Drake attribute his crew's safety?

Why do you think each country needed its own route and stopping places to get to other lands?

As sea routes to the East opened up, other Europeans began to travel to foreign lands. Many were traders hoping to gain wealth for themselves and their countries. Others were government officials desiring to establish political control of new areas. Still others were missionaries, mostly from the Roman Catholic Church, who sought to convert Hindus, Buddhists, and others to Roman Catholicism. For most of these lands, Protestant missionaries with the pure gospel would not arrive for several centuries.

In Africa

As we saw in Chapter 5, explorers were surprised to find many cities and empires that were comparable to European standards. With the press to find the western route to China and the inhospitable nature of the African inland, however, African exploration was set aside for a time. Unfortunately, attention did come back to Africa for the slave trade.

To understand the slave trade, we have to examine the first colonies in the New World. If you were going to establish a colony in a strange land, whom would you want to take along with you as colonists? It is easy to imagine ships bringing farmers and craftsmen to the New World, but many of the first colonists in the New World were neither. Instead, the first settlers were either soldiers or aristocrats looking for a "get rich quick" scheme or a way to have property or just adventure. Were these people used to hard work? To growing their own food? To living on their own? No. So immediately the rich looked to the native people to meet their needs. But the natives were not always cooperative, and so many natives died of abuse and disease that the aristocratic settlers were hard-pressed to find

replacements. This lack of workers created a need which, regrettably, the slave trade filled.

Directly across the Atlantic Ocean was an answer to the need. Africans had been enslaved by each other through the years, so the concept was not new even to them. The slavers landed along the coast and let their African contacts know their need for slaves with the promise of cloth and beads as payment. Slaves were soon pouring out of Africa, destined for the sugar cane fields, rice fields, haciendas, and plantations of the Indies, South America, and, later, the North American colonies. In their greed, the slave traders and slave owners were like the wicked Israelites "which oppress the poor, which crush the needy, which say . . . Bring, and let us drink"(Amos 4:1).

Aristocratic explorers chose slaves to do the manual labor that they were unwilling to do for themselves.

In Japan

When the Europeans first arrived in the sixteenth century, Japan was not at peace. Many strong families were fighting wars among themselves. During this period several monks traveled to Japan to convert the people. They also observed and reported Japanese culture for readers at home in Europe. One monk, **Francis Xavier** (FRAN-sis ZAY-vee-ur), described the people of Japan, the "Country at War."

> The people are all white, courteous and highly civilized, so much so that they surpass all the other known races of the world. They are naturally very intelligent, although they have no knowledge of sciences, because they are the most warlike and bellicose race yet discovered on the earth. From the age of fifteen onwards, all youths and men, rich and poor, in all walks of life, wear a sword and dagger at their side. Moreover, every man, whether a gentleman or common fellow, has such complete control over his sons, servants, and others of his household, that he can kill any of them on the smallest pretext at any time he likes, and seize their land or goods. They think nothing more of killing a man than they do an animal; so that they will kill a man not only on the smallest excuse but merely to try the edge of their swords. Similarly many men kill themselves by cutting their intestines with a dagger.

Xavier reported accurately. The "Country at War" was a land where murder and suicide were accepted. The leader of a family, the

Shogun, with samurai as their loyal knights, were the Eastern equivalent of medieval lords.

landholder, had complete control over all family members. Family loyalty had replaced loyalty to the government. Thus the central government grew ever weaker.

Japanese heroes of this age were the **samurai** (SAM uh RYE) warriors. Similar to the knights of Europe, these soldiers wore armor and rode horses. However, their armor was lighter and more flexible than that worn by knights. It was made from small pieces of lacquered iron sewn together by silk cord. This strong armor protected the samurai from his enemy.

The samurai's most important weapon was his sword. Made by a special process, the steel blade was flexible yet hard enough to hold a sharp edge. This sword could slice a man in two with a single blow. A prized sword was passed on through generations as a family treasure. Sometimes a samurai used his sword or a smaller dagger to kill himself by **seppuku** (SEP oo koo). In the seppuku ceremony the samurai killed himself by cutting out his intestines. These people thought it more honorable

These ornate samurai swords were vital to their owner.

to die by their own swords than by their ene-mies'. But the Bible teaches that suicide, which is murder, is wrong. In Genesis 9:6 God tells us, "Whoso sheddeth man's blood, by man shall his blood be shed: for in the image of God made he man."

The Europeans remained in Japan for about one century. During that time strong leaders called **shoguns** (SHOH gunz) united the coun-try and brought peace through strict laws. Fearing foreign influence, the shoguns began to persecute Roman Catholic clergy and con-verts. Finally one shogun ordered all foreign-ers out of Japan. By 1650 Japan closed its doors, an act that kept Japan isolated for two hundred years.

Section Review

1. List three groups of people who trav-eled to foreign lands.
2. Why did the European settlers need la-borers? Name two things that attracted the Europeans to Africa for slaves.
3. Why was Japan called the "Country at War" during this time?
4. Who were the heroes of Japanese society?
5. What government leader ordered for-eigners out of Japan?

Go back and reread Francis Xavier's account of Japan. Why do you think the Japanese held such low regard for life?

Exploring the Western Hemisphere

Columbus always believed that America was China, a land of gold. America was not China, but later explorers also believed that America was a land of gold. Spain sent out several men to find this gold, conquer the people, and convert them to Roman Catholi-cism. Called **conquistadors** (kon KEES tuh DORZ), Spanish for "conquerors," these men kept records of any dealings with wealthy South American Indians.

In Middle America

In the region of modern Mexico, the con-quistador **Hernando Cortés** (ayr-NAHN-doh kor-TEZ) discovered the **Aztecs.** In 1519 he arrived in the Aztec capital, **Tenochtitlán** (modern Mexico City), where an amazing sight greeted him: the city sat in the middle of a lake. To build the city there, the Aztecs had first made floating islands from mounds of water plants and put them in the middle of the lake. When these had rooted, the Aztecs filled the roots with soil and built on them. The finished city had many islands, be-tween which the Aztecs traveled in boats. Several long bridges and cause-ways connected the islands of Tenoch-titlán to each other and to the mainland.

In a letter back to his king, Cortés described his first entrance into the

Hernando Cortés

Because Cortes coveted the wealth of Tenochtitlán, he stirred up a rebellion among some discontented people and overthrew Montezuma. He then set himself up as leader.

city, where he met the Aztec ruler **Montezuma.**

We were received by that lord, Montezuma, with about two hundred chiefs, all barefooted, and dressed in a kind of livery, very rich, according to their custom, and some more so than others. They approached in two processions near the walls of the street, which is very broad, and straight, and beautiful, and very uniform from one end to the other, . . . and having, on both sides, very large houses.

Cortés was not disappointed in his search for wealth because the Aztecs had gold. On telling Montezuma that his king needed gold, Cortés was overwhelmed with the Aztec response. The chiefs brought

not only in valuables, but also in bars and sheets of gold besides all the jewels of gold, and silver, and the feather work, and the stones, and the many other things of value which I assigned and allotted to Your Sacred Majesty. Let not what I say appear fabulous to Your Majesty, because, in truth, all the things created on land, as well as in the sea, of which Montezuma had ever heard, were

imitated in gold, most naturally, as well as in silver, and in precious stones, and feather work, with such perfection that they seemed almost real.

Although the Aztecs had material wealth, they were spiritually poor. Writing of Aztec religion, Cortés described the temple where they offered human hearts to idols. The Aztecs believed these hearts, cut from living people, appeased their war god. But the war god demanded many hearts, and the Aztecs spent much time in war, capturing other people to have hearts to sacrifice. These people thought they could appease their gods with human blood. The Bible teaches that only Christ's blood can satisfy God's wrath against sin. "The blood of Jesus Christ his Son cleanseth us from all sin" (I John 1:7).

Despite the honor and gifts he received, Cortés eventually massacred most of the Aztecs because they refused his leadership. With guns and armor and horses, the Spanish had a definite advantage over the Aztecs. In 1521, during a four-month siege, he destroyed Tenochtitlán. On this site he built a fine city,

Early Kingdoms of the New World

Gulf of Mexico
TOLTEC
OLMEC
MAYA
AZTEC
ATLANTIC OCEAN
PACIFIC OCEAN
INCA

INTERPRETATIONS

Indigenous People of Central America

The Aztecs of Mexico and the Incas of Peru were not the only Indian civilizations in Central and South America. Actually they are the more recent of a long succession of civilizations that crossed the land.

Prior to the Aztecs, at least three other peoples inhabited and influenced the area—the **Olmecs,** the **Toltecs,** and the **Mayas.** From their architecture, it appears that the Toltecs borrowed from the Olmecs. Although its origin is disputed, the Toltec city Teotihuacán came to the height of its influence in the fifth century. The Toltec capital would later move, but the city of Teotihuacán is a marvel to archeologists.

Teotihuacán may have been the spiritual center of the area. Covering eight acres, Teotihuacán rivaled ancient Rome in size and planning. At its peak, the city's population reached an estimated 150,000 to 200,000 inhabitants. The city was planned with two main avenues which intersect at right angles. The feature that stands out in the center of town is the Pyramid of the Sun. An impressive monument to draw the attention of all worshipers, the pyramid's stepped design is similar to the ziggurats of ancient Sumer. Its height of 240 feet would easily hold the Statue of Liberty, just the lady and her torch (151 feet), inside.

No one knows why the city was abandoned. Some archeologists speculate that the city became too big to support itself with food from the surrounding area. Others suggest that, faced with being overrun by the Aztecs, the people left to relocate somewhere southeast.

The Mayas (MAH yuz) lived in what is today a portion of Central America that includes Guatemala and the Yucatan Peninsula. Unlike the Aztecs and Incas, the Mayas did not have one strong central government. Instead, Mayan civilization—

Mexico City. Over the temple of the Aztecs, Cortés built a Roman Catholic cathedral. He thought he could force people to accept the God of the Christians. But only those who come willingly to Christ through the preaching of the gospel can truly know God. The apostle Paul said, "It pleased God by the foolishness of preaching to save them that believe" (I Cor. 1:21). Jesus did not use a sword to force men to come to Him. "Come unto me, all ye that labour and are heavy laden," He said, "and I will give you rest" (Matt. 11:28).

like that of the Greeks—consisted of many independent city-states. Each city-state had its own ruler and government. In the middle of many of these cities stood large pyramids similar to the ones in Egypt. The Mayan pyramids, however, were not always burial places for kings. Usually they served as temples. Mayan religion was cruel and involved human sacrifice. Archaeologists have found large graves containing the remaining artifacts of men and women whom the Mayas slaughtered to please their gods.

The height of Mayan culture lasted from A.D. 300 to 800. Intellectually, the Mayas outshone the Aztecs and Incas. They developed a calendar as accurate as the one we use today. The Mayas also had a form of writing far superior to any other system found in the New World. They were accomplished mathematicians and astronomers as well. For example, they predicted eclipses of the sun and moon with impressive regularity. For easier numbering and counting, the Mayas also introduced the concept of zero.

The different Mayan city-states often fought with one another. As a result, they proved unable to unite in resistance against other enemies, especially the Aztecs, who took many Mayan cities. The Mayas grew weaker and weaker. The Spanish conquistadors who came in 1540 had little trouble capturing the remaining Mayan territory and establishing Spanish rule.

Enormous stone pyramids, intricate carvings, and elaborate ceremonial wear remind us of the wealth of the early civilizations of Middle America.

The Age of Exploration

Map of Middle America showing:

- UNITED STATES
- Gulf of California
- MEXICO
- Mexico City
- Gulf of Mexico
- ATLANTIC OCEAN
- THE BAHAMAS
- Havana
- CUBA
- DOMINICAN REPUBLIC
- Gulf of Honduras
- JAMAICA
- Port-au-Prince
- San Juan
- Kingston
- HAITI
- Santo Domingo
- PUERTO RICO
- GREATER ANTILLES
- Belmopan
- BELIZE
- HONDURAS
- CARIBBEAN SEA
- LESSER ANTILLES
- Guatemala City
- Tegucigalpa
- GUATEMALA
- EL SALVADOR
- San Salvador
- Managua
- NICARAGUA
- Lake Nicaragua
- COSTA RICA
- Panama Canal
- Panama City
- San Jose
- PANAMA
- PACIFIC OCEAN

Location—Middle America is composed of three regions: Mexico, Central America, and the islands of the Caribbean Sea. The funnel-shaped mainland connects North and South America. It includes Mexico and the seven countries of Central America: Belize, Costa Rica, El Salvador, Guatemala, Honduras, Nicaragua, and Panama. The Pacific Ocean lies to the west, and the Gulf of Mexico and the Caribbean Sea lie to the east. The islands in the Caribbean are divided into three island groups: to the north, the Bahamas; in the center, the Greater Antilles; to the south, the Lesser Antilles.

Climate—The climate of the mainland differs greatly from north to south starting with desert and steppe climates in the north and ending with the tropical savannah and tropical climates of the south. Most of the region, including the islands, is very warm, cooling down only in the highland climate of the mountains. Hurricanes often develop in the Caribbean Sea.

Topography—Much of mainland Central America is a mountainous plateau bordered by narrow coastal plains. There is a broad band of tropical rain forest on the Caribbean coast from Guatemala to Panama. The islands have volcanic mountains, fertile coastlands, and sandy beaches.

Natural Resources—The most important resource in Central America is the fertile land, which along with the tropical climate allows this region to produce crops from nine to twelve months of the year. Central America exports almost 10 percent of the world's coffee and bananas. The islands' leading crop is sugar cane. Tourism is also very important to the island economy.

Geography & Culture—The Mayas and other people inhabited Central America for several thousand years before the Europeans discovered the New World; however, European influence affected this region greatly. Today the economic, cultural, and ethnic mix is so great that the region is faced with many conflicts.

The islands are very diverse. Languages spoken in the islands include English, Spanish, French, and Dutch. The majority of people populating islands such as Jamaica and Haiti are descendants of slaves brought from Africa to work on plantations.

At the end of the slave trade, a labor shortage brought to the islands a large immigration of Asians and East Indians looking for work. The tourist trade further complicates the problems. Wealthy American and European tourists come to cities where beautiful strips of resorts are bordered by poverty-stricken slums.

Mainland Central America was greatly influenced by its Spanish conquerors. Spanish is the main language spoken, except in Belize where English is the official language. Most cities are based on Spanish design.

Today Central America is still a vital link between the two American continents. The opening of the Panama Canal in 1914 made this region an important transportation link between the Atlantic and Pacific Oceans. The island countries are a study in contrast as they try to establish a balance between many cultural influences.

Settings Review

1. What two factors together allow the region to be so agriculturally rich?
2. Besides agriculture, what other factor is important to island economy?
3. What weather event often develops in the Caribbean Sea?
4. What important transportation link lies in Central America?

How do you think the diversity of the island people could help them to develop as countries and could help them relate to tourists?

Diversity. That word holds the key to understanding the culture, foods, and lifestyles of Middle America.

Francisco Pizarro crossed the Andes to find the isolated empire of the Incas.

In South America

A few years after Cortés conquered the Aztecs, another Spanish conquistador entered the South American region now known as Peru. **Francisco Pizarro** (frahn-SIS-koh pih-ZAHR-oh) discovered the wealthy Inca Indians in the Andes (AN deez) Mountains of western South America. Their empire stretched twenty-five hundred miles in the mountains. The Incas were skillful builders. They constructed two major highways running the length of the empire. Long bridges crossed steep valleys and ravines. Every day messengers and travelers walked these roads.

The Incas' greatest natural resource was land; however, most of it was on steep mountainsides. To use this land for farming, the Incas learned to terrace it. They used irrigation and fertilizers to make it more productive. On this land they grew corn and white potatoes—

two foods unknown to Europeans. The Incas also grew some other grains and vegetables. In areas having soil too poor to farm, the Incas raised llamas and alpacas.

The Inca capital was at **Cuzco** (KOO skoh) in southern Peru. Pizarro marveled at the well-

The rubble of Machu Picchu remains as evidence of a once rich and thriving Incan empire.

built buildings covered with sheets of gold. Cuzco was the center of the Inca religion. The Incas worshiped the sun god, and the golden buildings that reflected the sun's rays reminded the people of their sun god. The Incas did not offer human sacrifice to the sun god. Instead they gave him offerings of food and riches.

As the center of government, Cuzco was always busy. Messengers from all over the empire came to Cuzco. Men bringing tribute of food and other goods arrived daily. Pizarro and his men were awestruck at the Incan wealth. One of his party described the goods to be found in the markets or on the people of Cuzco:

> There were many other plumes of divers colours for the purpose of making clothing with which the Lords and Ladies bedight themselves at the time of the festivals. There were also mantles made with very delicate little spangles of mother-of-pearl, gold and silver in such wise as to cause astonishment at the dexterity of the work, for the whole was so covered with these spangles that nothing of the closely woven network [which formed the basis of the garment] was

A member of the camel family, the alpaca is native to the Andes Mountain. Its fine wool was used for Incan royalty alone.

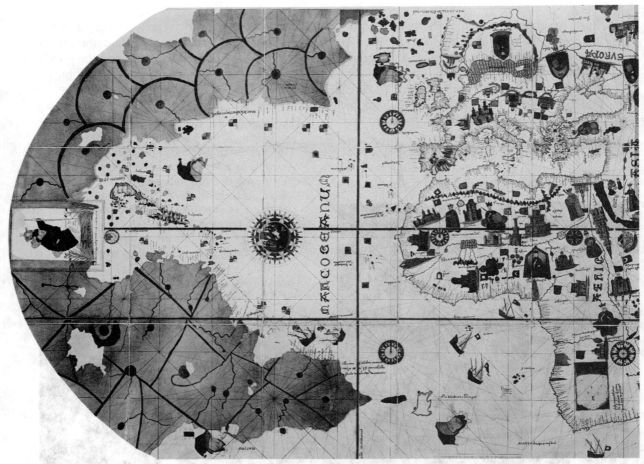

In this ancient map Europe and Africa are easily recognized, but can you find the outline of North and South America? Why do you think the map ends in a semicircle with no defined outline?

visible. These garments were likewise for the Ladies. There were many stores of small bars of copper [from] the mines, of sacks and ropes, of wooden vessels, of plates of gold and silver . . . , although the Indians did not esteem it greatly according to what I understood later, for had they done so, they would have hidden it better.

The hidden treasures, we are told, were even more breathtaking to the Spaniards. They had found the gold they searched for but were not satisfied. Greedily they demanded more and more. When the Incas resisted, the Spanish fought against them. Finally they killed the Inca emperor, and Pizarro made himself emperor. The mighty Inca empire fell because of greed. As in Mexico, the Spanish in Peru established the Catholic religion. Today much of South America follows Roman Catholic traditions. Many South Americans remain lost in sin.

1. What were the conquerors of South America called?

2. What people did Cortés find in the region of modern Mexico?

3. Why did the Aztecs spend so much time at war?

4. Where did the Incas live? Who conquered them?

5. How were the Incas reminded of their religion?

6. Why did the Spanish destroy the Incan empire?

Why do you think it may have been difficult for the Aztecs and the Incas to accept the religion of the Spanish?

Summary

The Age of Exploration began as the Middle Ages drew to a close. The writings of Marco Polo's stay in China encouraged the Europeans to find ways to China. They began by seeking sea routes to the East. Using methods and instruments invented by Renaissance scholars and Muslim astronomers, they set out. Some explorers went east, while others went west. They did find sea routes to the East and also discovered the continents of North and South America. They recorded many of their adventures in letters or diaries that we may read today. They tell of the voyages they took and the lands they found. From them we learn about Japan during the age of the shoguns. We also learn about the Aztecs and Incas of South America. These explorers opened the world for total exploration.

People, Places, and Terms to Know

Prince Henry	Cape of Storms	skraelings	Aztecs
compass	Cape of Good Hope	Ferdinand Magellan	Tenochtitlán
astrolabe	Vasco da Gama	Sir Francis Drake	Montezuma
dead reckoning	Christopher Columbus	Francis Xavier	Olmecs
trade winds	King Ferdinand	samurai	Toltecs
doldrums	Queen Isabella	seppuku	Mayas
horse latitudes	Vikings	shoguns	Francisco Pizarro
caravel	Erik the Red	conquistadors	Cuzco
Bartolomeu Dias	Leif Erikson	Hernando Cortés	

Review Questions

Completion
Complete the following statements.

1. Early Portuguese explorers sailing in (a) _____ used a (b) _____ to find direction and an (c) _____ to find the latitude.

2. The (a) _____ Hernando Cortés conquered the (b) _____ in Mexico, and (c) _____ conquered the (d) _____ in Peru.

Identification
Identify the following.

3. Bartolomeu Dias

4. Francis Xavier

5. seppuku

6. Tenochtitlán

Jumbles
Below are the names of explorers with the letters jumbled. Find the name of each explorer and then tell why he is remembered.

7. KARED

8. MAAGAD

9. MOULSCUB

10. GALLEMNA

Matching
Match the following items.

11. King Ferdinand

12. Montezuma

13. shogun

14. Prince Henry

(a) Portuguese ruler

(b) Japanese ruler

(c) Aztec ruler

(d) Spanish ruler

From Here to There

On a separate sheet of paper, fill in the blanks in each of the following statements.

15. Ferdinand and Isabella sent Columbus from _____ to find China by sailing _____ (direction).

16. From _____ Dias sailed around _____.

17. Vasco da Gama was the first one from _____ to sail to _____.

18. Cortés discovered the _____ in the area that is now _____.

19. Xavier wrote to _____ about the land of _____.

20. The Inca empire stretched along the _____ in _____.

21. Sailing for _____, Drake traveled around the world.

22. Columbus thought he had landed in _____ but was really in _____.

Think About It!

As you think about the explorers that you have studied in this chapter, what common characteristics do you see? (Try to think of at least three things.) How are some of these characteristics present in scientists, inventors, astronauts, and missionaries? Can you think of some specific people who are not usually thought of as explorers but who display some of the same characteristics?

CHAPTER 7

A piece of land ninety-five hundred miles long, up to thirty-three hundred miles wide, spanning latitudes from 72° N to 56° S was not what Columbus expected to find when he sailed west from Europe in 1492. He hoped to discover a faster route to the Far East. Instead he encountered two continents then unknown to the European world. Columbus refused to believe that he had not reached the East Indies, but future explorations proved that the two major landmasses he discovered in the Western Hemisphere were previously undiscovered lands.

In writing to Europeans about this discovery, a sixteenth-century scholar described the land as *Orbe Novo* (OR-beh NOH-voh), which in Latin means "New World." To Europeans living on a crowded, cultivated continent, the Americas *were* a New World: over sixteen million square miles of almost uninhabited, undeveloped countryside. With climates ranging from arctic cold to equatorial heat and with topography including mountains, plains, deserts, and jungles, the New World appealed to almost any taste. A wealth of resources in precious metals, land, wood, and wildlife beckoned many to make the Americas their home. The people who came to the New World brought their old cultures with them. They also created new cultures to suit the New World.

This chapter and the next are dedicated to what the settlers found and what they made of their New World. The Spanish and the Portuguese were the first to come in great numbers, and soon they were establishing themselves all around the Middle and South American lands.

A.D. 1400 - A.D. 1850

Pedro Cabral Discovers Brazil 1500

1400 | 1500

Renaissance 1350-1616

Treaty of
Tordesillas 1494

Developing Latin America

Portuguese Settle
in Brazil 1530

Empire of Songhai 1470-1600(?)
Reformation 1500-1650
Kingdom of Benin 1200-1700(?)

South American
Independence 1816-22

| 1600 | 1700 | 1800 |

Spanish Slave
Trading Begins 1528

Settling South America

South America was settled by people from the **Iberian Peninsula** in Europe—that is, from Spain and Portugal. Because these two countries are Latin in origin, the area they settled, South and Central America, is often referred to as **Latin America.** Once the boundaries dividing their holdings were set, the Spanish and Portuguese rarely conflicted. Their similar cultures enabled them to establish a single Latin American culture and to avoid many of the conflicts that the French and British would have in North America.

Settlement and the Line of Demarcation

In the previous chapter, you read that the Portuguese were the leaders in the race to find a sea route to China. Through the influence of Prince Henry, Portuguese sailors were charting new waters. They went south around Africa and soon monopolized that route to the trade in the East. Because the Portuguese controlled this route, the Spanish were left to find another way. Then the New World was discovered.

The Spanish wanted just as great a monopoly over the New World as the Portuguese had over the Eastern trade route. They laid claim to and colonized many lands. At first they were frustrated by the lack of a direct route to China and the fact that the first Indians they met were poor. Spanish satisfaction improved, however, when the Portuguese also met with limited success in their trade with China. Spanish enthusiasm rallied completely when they found Indian tribes with gold in Mexico and Panama. This enthusiasm and the search for riches pushed the Spanish onward to Peru, Ecuador, Bolivia, Chile, Argentina, and eventually Venezuela.

In an effort to establish their early claims, Queen Isabella and King Ferdinand of Spain called upon Pope Alexander VI (who happened to be Spanish) to decide which country could explore and lay claim to certain areas. The line the pope decided on was called the **Line of Demarcation.** Everything to the east of the line could be claimed by Portugal; everything to the west, by Spain. The Portuguese complained about the line, however, because as they explored Africa, they often had to sail far to the west before catching favorable winds to take them southeast. With the line in its first position, the Portuguese would often risk sailing into Spanish waters.

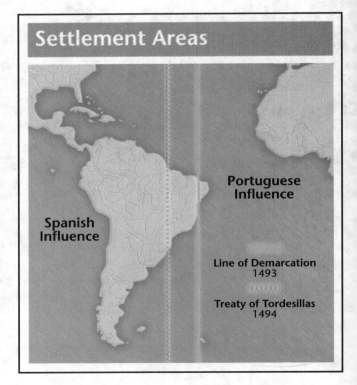

Settlement Areas

Spanish Influence

Portuguese Influence

Line of Demarcation 1493

Treaty of Tordesillas 1494

King Ferdinand and Queen Isabella of Spain

In a final agreement between the two countries, the line was moved in 1494 by the **Treaty of Tordesillas** (tor de SEE yah). The new line was set at 370 leagues west of the Cape Verde Islands. The Portuguese did not realize what they were getting when the Line of Demarcation was changed. In 1494, the Spanish were still exploring the islands of the Caribbean and the southern coast of North America. No one yet knew of the existence of Brazil.

Not until 1500 was the "island of Brazil" discovered. Pedro Cabral was blown off course as he sailed west to catch good winds to Africa. To his surprise, the ships came to land—Brazil. Cabral and his men planted a stone cross to claim the land for Portugal. The friendly local Indians looked on without realizing the effect that meeting would have.

For years the effect from the discovery was only slight. The Portuguese were busy in Africa and India and saw little in Brazil that would meet their need for trade goods. They did continue exploring the coastline and occasionally dropped off a *degredado* (an undesirable citizen or convict). The *degredado* was left on shore with the supposition that if the Indians were friendly, he would learn the language and the people. This would prepare the land for further contact. If the Indians were not friendly, then as far as the Portuguese were concerned nothing had been lost.

Many times the Indians did prove friendly, and the former *degredado* was brought into Indian society. There were later reports of settlements started by these men and their Indian wives and children long before Portuguese colonies were established.

Conflicts over Settlements

Although conflict was rare between Spain and Portugal, it did occur as their territories drew closer together. The major area of conflict was around the Rio de la Plata in present-day Uruguay. Brazil claimed the land down to the river, but before the Portuguese were able to settle the area, the Spanish settled the town of Montevideo on the Brazilian side of the river. Spain agreed to give up the land but later took the settlements of Colonia and the coastal Rio Grande. With these two settlements in Spanish control, the Spanish also claimed the rights to the land between them. After a decade of land control passing from Spanish to Portuguese hands, the conflict was eventually ended in 1777 by the Treaty of San Ildefonso.

The Portuguese and Spanish also had to deal with trespasses by the French, Dutch, and English. The French did much exploring of the Brazilian coast from 1503 to 1509. Their explorations made the Portuguese nervous enough to send a fleet of ships to rid their shores of the unwanted explorers and settlers. The Portuguese soon wearied of the effort, though, and in 1604 the French were able to establish a foothold in what would later be known as French Guiana.

The two other countries that went by the name Guiana were tossed back and forth by the Dutch and English. Oddly enough, in 1581 the Dutch settled what later became British Guiana, and the British settled the area that later became Dutch Guiana. (The Dutch lost their original territory to the English after several battles, and the English traded Guiana to the Dutch for New York.) Later the names of both areas changed. British Guiana became Guyana, and Dutch Guiana became Suriname.

Section Review

1. What is another name for the part of the New World controlled by Spain and Portugal?
2. What line determined where Spain and Portugal could settle?
3. Who set this line?
4. Why did the Portuguese complain about the line's location?
5. How was the issue resolved?
6. Why do you think Portugal gave up its northern holding (the Guianas) so easily?

Ruling Distant Settlements

The problem Spain and Portugal faced when they tried to rule these distant settlements directly was enormous, similar to the dilemma faced by the Roman and Mongol Empires. The traveling necessary for the Romans and Mongols to communicate and regulate their empires was done on well-planned roads and routes. The Spanish and Portuguese, however, were separated from their colonies by hundreds of miles of ocean. To add to the difficulty, the ocean was ever changing and often undependable.

Attempts at Direct Rule

In spite of the distance, early Spanish and Portuguese rule in Latin America was strict. The rulers of Spain and Portugal had absolute power in their lands and so exercised the same authority in the new settlements. This governing method worked fairly efficiently at first, but as the settlement populations grew, more problems occurred which required more immediate decisions. It became very difficult for the settlers to wait for directives from the king.

Unfortunately, the Spanish and Portuguese governed with too much control, and they made the mistake of ignoring the **creoles** (KREE olz) (people of pure Spanish or Portuguese descent born in the Americas). At first, the king gave all governing duties to those who were born in the **mother country** (controlling European country). The creoles had no right to rule even though they were direct descendants of noble families from the mother country. This disregard eventually led to revolt.

Difficulties arose not only in long distance governing but also in managing the production of goods. The mother country determined the price, quantity, and types of goods that could be produced and sold. It highly taxed goods being **exported** (taken outside the country) and charged high prices for goods being **imported** (brought into the country). This practice greatly restricted personal as well as national economic growth.

Portuguese Rule in the New World

The government system used by the Portuguese was not very effective in the early colonies. It actually did not give Portugal enough power. At first, the colonial land was divided into twelve captaincies, which were ruled (literally owned) by nobles who were given the title *donatarios* (doh nah TAH ree ohs). Their rule was a hereditary rule to be passed down to their children. They had total control of the land given to them and determined how the land would be divided among colonists. Their job was to colonize, defend, and tax their captaincy and to send excess revenues to Portugal.

There were some checks on the power of the donatario. Church officials brought the complaints of the colonists before the donatarios and, if unheeded, to Portugal. Many bitter battles occurred between the government and the church.

In 1549, King John of Portugal bought the captaincy of Bahia from its donatario to bring it into greater Portuguese control. He appointed a governor-general in place of the donatario. Eventually Portugal regained control of all of Brazil.

The first governor-general of Brazil was **Thomé de Souza.** De Souza, with the Jesuit priest Manuel da Nobrega, established São Salvador (now Salvador) as the capital of the Royal Captaincy of Bahia. At the same time that de Souza was appointed, the king appointed a commissioner-general of finances, a chief justice, and a captain-major for defense.

De Souza helped to unify Brazil and regulate colonial government. Unfortunately the governor-generals that followed de Souza were not all honorable men. Some of de Souza's successors did great damage to the colony. One of the problems with administrators in the colonies was the lack of moral character. Most officials were appointed for a short term and used the time to make as many financial gains for themselves as possible before going back to Portugal. The fact that government officials were poorly paid (and subject to sin) led to corruption on an enormous scale. In spite of the corruption, however, the tiny country of Portugal was able to administrate a colony eighty times its size for three hundred years.

Many areas of South America lack modern facilities. This Colombian woman washes clothes in a wooden trough.

Spanish Authority in the New World

All laws and policies for the Spanish colonies came directly from Spain, including religious and economic policies. One-fifth of all gold and silver mined in the colonies went to Spain. In 1524 Spain established the **Council of the Indies** to oversee its colonies. The king appointed a **viceroy** (*vice*= in place of; *roy*= king) to rule each colony. Early viceroys appeared to have a great deal of power to deal with the problems that affected the colonies, since messages relayed to Spain sometimes took months to be answered; however, the viceroys were actually controlled by the council.

The Council of the Indies directed colonial affairs from Spain while the viceroys lived in Mexico. The Spanish soon realized that the land expanse was too great to be governed by distant viceroys alone. Each territory was then divided into *audiencias* (ow *TH*YEN see ahs). Each *audiencia* was administered by a Spanish lawyer who presided over a court. This court communicated with the viceroy and judged local matters. Later the *audiencias* were further divided into provinces and municipalities.

The old and the new meet on this modern city street where a university student waits at a crosswalk near the overloaded bicycle of a street peddler.

Most government positions were held by Spaniards born in Spain, *peninsulares*. Creoles had only a small role in government, even though some had great wealth and owned much land. Many Roman Catholic clergy also held positions in the government.

Section Review

1. What was one of the biggest difficulties that the Iberians faced in communicating with their colonies?

2. What mistake did the Iberians make when they chose leaders for the New World colonies?

3. Who was the first governor-general of Bahia?

4. Define the words *creole* and *peninsulare*.

5. What organization did Spain establish to oversee its colonies?

Do you think that the Iberians were wise to appoint people to office who were directly from the Iberian Peninsula? Explain your answer.

The Faces of South America

contain Uruguay, Paraguay, and Argentina. Brazil, being the largest country, stands alone.

Climate—The climate in most of South America is some variety of tropical—humid tropical and tropical savanna in the north to humid subtropical in the southeast. A narrow band along the west coast beginning in Ecuador and proceeding almost to South America's southern tip is dry, with desert, highland, and steppe climates represented. In the far south of Chile, mediterranean and marine west coast conditions prevail. Rainfall varies from zero inches in the desert area to eighty inches in the mountains. Temperatures also vary greatly. The average in the mountains is 59°, while temperatures in the Tropics climb above 100°.

Topography—South America's topography is as varied as its climate. The lowlands in the east rise until they meet the **Andes Mountains** along the western coast. The Andes range is the longest uninterrupted mountain barrier in the world. The second longest river in the world, the **Amazon River,** flows through the lowlands. In northern Chile lies a region called the Atacama Desert. Many parts of the desert have never recorded rain. The **Pampas** of the River Plate region is known for its fertile grasslands.

Location—South America is attached to Central America at the boundary of Panama. The long continent extends from the Caribbean Sea almost to Antarctica, separating the Atlantic and Pacific Oceans. South America can be divided into four regions. The Caribbean Republics include Colombia, Venezuela, Guyana, Suriname, and French Guiana. The Andean Republics consist of Bolivia, Chile, Ecuador, and Peru. The River Plate Republics

Natural Resources—The soil in Argentina's Pampas is among the richest in the world. Brazil's soil is just right for growing coffee. Many minerals have been found, but few have been mined. Among those mined are iron, manganese, gold, and gemstones. The tropical forests have valuable trees, such as mahogany, ebony, and rubber. Oil is also a resource in some areas. In the Atacama Desert large deposits of sodium nitrate were mined for fertilizer and explosives. This area also contains the world's largest reserves of copper ore.

Geography & Culture—South America's position made it a natural area for settlement by the nations looking for a western route to the East. Because Portugal and Spain were the first nations to seek this route, it was they who took possession of South America. Their language and culture have greatly influenced the culture of South America. The land itself has affected the culture. In the jungle area around the Amazon River, little has changed. Tribal people still occupy their villages, living in traditional huts. In the southern regions where the great plains of the Pampas are, cattle are raised on large ranches. In central Chile, mediterranean climate and vegetation lends itself to higher population and tourism. In the Andes Mountains, remote Indian groups retain much of their ancient culture.

Settings Review

1. What are the four regions of South America?

2. What major mountain range runs down the western coast of South America?

3. What natural resource is found in the Atacama Desert of Chile?

4. What is the name for the plains area of the River Plate region?

Looking at the map of South America, why do you think some Indian tribes were able to remain unaffected by the Europeans for hundreds of years after their arrival?

High mountains separate the western coastline of Chile from the Pampas and tropical rain forests of the east.

Pirates of the Caribbean

Pirates were the curse of the Caribbean Sea, especially to the Spanish navy that dominated those seas. Although the English had defeated the Spanish Armada (fleet) in 1588 and by that victory broke the Spanish control of the oceans, the Spanish still controlled the Caribbean. In the 1700s the English used some of the most notorious pirates as agents of their government. By wearing down the Spanish navy and export, the English hoped to gain more territory in the New World and end the Spanish monopoly over New World trade. They accomplished their goal but created a new problem.

Sir Henry Morgan was one well-known pirate who was encouraged by the English government and commissioned by the governor of the English colony of Jamaica. He worked for the government, but he kept the profits. As time went on, Morgan stopped working for the government and began working solely for personal profit. He and other pirates soon began attacking any trading vessel, even if it was English.

Morgan and his cohorts called themselves the Brethren. They wore coarse shirts, knee-length trousers, felt hats, and untanned leather belts upon which hung powder flasks, butcher's knives, and blunderbusses (short muskets). They lived by their guns under a curious "pirate law" in which each man had the right to vote on all issues, from choosing a captain to choosing the next ship to plunder.

The pirates had little trouble recruiting new members. Seamen in true naval service often lived under conditions much more severe than did the pirates. Naval men were subject to cruel punishment by their superiors, meager food supplies, and low wages. The pirates offered equality, good food (when it was available), and the opportunity to become rich by the day's standard.

to Spain

Havana

Cuba

New Providence

Jamaica

Kingston

to Veracruz

to Spain

N

Cartagena

Portobelo

✠ *Possible Locations of Treasure*

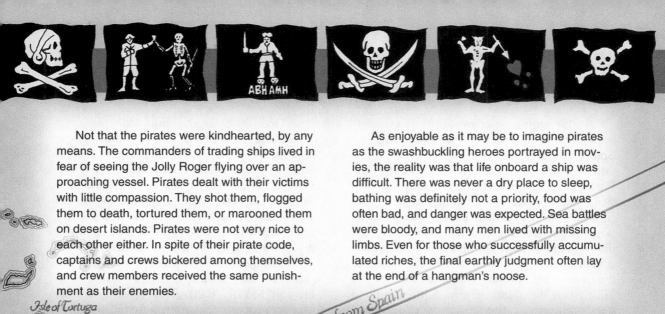

Not that the pirates were kindhearted, by any means. The commanders of trading ships lived in fear of seeing the Jolly Roger flying over an approaching vessel. Pirates dealt with their victims with little compassion. They shot them, flogged them to death, tortured them, or marooned them on desert islands. Pirates were not very nice to each other either. In spite of their pirate code, captains and crews bickered among themselves, and crew members received the same punishment as their enemies.

As enjoyable as it may be to imagine pirates as the swashbuckling heroes portrayed in movies, the reality was that life onboard a ship was difficult. There was never a dry place to sleep, bathing was definitely not a priority, food was often bad, and danger was expected. Sea battles were bloody, and many men lived with missing limbs. Even for those who successfully accumulated riches, the final earthly judgment often lay at the end of a hangman's noose.

169

Developing the Colonies

At the beginning of exploration, possessing and controlling an area *was* the goal. The Spanish royalty saw the New World as a fountain of resources for the mother country. The Portuguese, with their attention directed toward their African trade route, at first paid little attention to Brazil except to ensure its possession. But the Spanish, driven by the discovery and desire for precious metals, continued to explore farther and farther into the continent. The previous chapter told of the efforts of Cortés and Pizarro. Settlement and development of the colonies progressed slowly but surely after early discoveries.

Dealing with the Native Population

The Spanish government never officially approved of enslaving the native South Americans. They initially sent the explorers as ambassadors from the Spanish ruler to the Indian empires. The explorers, and later settlers, were given permission to enslave only Indians who were cannibals or who attacked the Spanish. Reports soon came from South America that several Indian groups were cannibals and totally hostile (whether they actually were or not).

The Catholic Church was very influential in relations with the Indian population. The church sent friars and priests to colonies and outposts for the purpose of evangelization. While they evangelized, the priests promoted education and European culture. This influence made the Indians adapt more readily as the colonies grew. Once the Spanish conquered an area, the Indians were moved into settlements. These settlements featured a church, government buildings, and shops surrounded with well-planned blocks of houses. In this way the Catholic Church and the Spanish government could keep a watchful eye on the new inhabitants, who would have to move in and out of the center of town for trade and business.

When the Spanish wanted to reward a conquistador, they awarded him an *encomienda* (en coh MYEN dah). This reward was an estate or property that often included an Indian labor force. With this ready-made labor force, the former conquistadors, now landowners, were able to farm, mine, or manufacture goods for trade or sale.

Many conquistadors were merciless in their treatment of the Indians. As a result of mistreatment, uprisings, and disease, the native Indian population suffered greatly. Intermarriage also thinned the bloodlines until there

The Catholic Church and religion are still central to most South American communities.

were very few full-blooded native Indians in many parts of South America.

The church sometimes negotiated in defense of the Indians over labor situations and ill-treatment. One man who saw the unfair treatment of the Indians and spoke out against it was the Dominican friar **Bartolomé de Las Casas.** Through his efforts, the **New Laws of 1542** were passed. Those laws set up a government system in which courts were established to protect the Indians and **mestizos** (mes TEE sohs) (people with Indian and Spanish parents) from some of the abuses that they suffered. The laws also prohibited the enslaving of the Indians and outlawed the passing on of the *encomiendas* to later generations.

Unfortunately, when the landowners of Peru revolted against this law, the first viceroy was killed. The new viceroy decided it might not be a good political move to enforce the laws so strictly. Eventually the king backed down on his first decree and allowed the *encomiendas* to be passed down to future generations. The establishment of haciendas (HA see EN dahs; see page 178) changed the conditions of the Indian laborers. On the haciendas, they were able to work on the land of their ancestors, keep some of the produce or receive a small salary, and pass their houses and positions on to their children.

Controlling the Church

The Catholic Church had great control over the Spanish and Indian population of South America. Because of its protecting power, the church received more loyalty from the Indians than the Indians gave to the Iberians.

One arm of the church, the **Jesuits,** also called the Society of Jesus, especially fell into disfavor with the Spanish and Portuguese governments. The disfavor came largely in re-

Bartolomé de Las Casas pleaded for the humane treatment of the native population of Latin America.

sponse to increased Jesuit control over trade and the Indians.

The Jesuits established missions shortly after initial settlement in the New World. In those missions the priests worked toward converting the Indians. They learned the Indians' language and taught them to read and write. Sadly, as time went on, Jesuit control over the Indians became very similar to the Spanish and Portuguese control over the Indians. The Jesuits did speak out against abuse of the Indians and for Indian rights but at the same time used them as workers at the mission facilities. This made the secular landowners angry.

Some Jesuits with their Indian helpers eventually controlled large tracts of land and the agricultural production on it. They operated sugar mills and slaughter houses. Because the church was not subject to taxation and received tithes, it was often able to monopolize an industry. The regular tradesmen could not compete. Jealousy over profits and power brought about the expulsion of the Jesuit Order from the New World. The Jesuits were expelled by the Portuguese in 1759 and by the Spanish in 1767.

The expulsion of the Jesuits may have expanded the economic market for the rest of the people in the land, but it took away a vital connection between the people and government. The Indians connected the priests with the government. With the priests gone, the Indian mission land and buildings fell into disrepair, and many Indians went back to their former way of life. The expulsion also served to undermine the educational system that the order had set up. With their teachers gone, the schools and universities that were just becoming established suffered setbacks from which they would not recover until after independence.

Bringing Black Slaves into Latin America

In Brazil and the Caribbean Islands, the Indian population was so reduced by disease that shipments of African slaves were used in place of Indian labor. The replacement of Indian slaves by African slaves was almost complete by 1620. Interestingly, many of the early conquis-

tadors brought their own black slaves with them from Spain. The slaves brought from the Iberian Peninsula were already firmly ingrained in Latin culture, and the Indians readily saw them as "black white men." One black Spanish slave, Juan Valiente, came to Chile with the conquistador Pedro de Valdivia, founder of Santiago, Chile. After their conquest, Juan received his own *encomienda,* including a native labor force.

Although the Indians were defined by law as equals of the Spanish, at first the black slaves brought from Spain often helped direct Indian laborers. Eventually, as slaves were brought from Africa and as Indians and mestizos were used as free laborers (not forced), the balance shifted, and the blacks were held in very low esteem.

Developing Natural Resources

Refined silver and sugar were the two major exports of colonial Latin America. Slaves were most often used in mines in Peru and on sugar plantations in Brazil and the Caribbean. In the mines, Indians often worked as free laborers. As time went on, Indians provided the skilled labor and supervision, and slaves

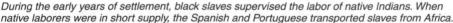

During the early years of settlement, black slaves supervised the labor of native Indians. When native laborers were in short supply, the Spanish and Portuguese transported slaves from Africa.

Peter Paul Rubens painted this sensitive study of two African slaves.

Coffee beans are picked, roasted, ground, and brewed to produce the hot drink enjoyed by millions.

provided the general hard labor force—diggers and loaders.

After early attempts to settle inland were discouraged by poor soil and competition from North American exports, the Dutch discovered the rich soils on the coastline of Dutch Guiana. Accustomed to reclaiming land below sea level, the Dutch used sea walls and dike systems to retrieve land from the sea and establish sugar plantations. The British used the same methods to establish their plantations in British Guiana.

One of the most important resources of South America was the land itself. Its development came with the natural influx of immigrants. Overcrowding in Europe and the lack of available land made people willing to start over in a new location where they could make a place for themselves and their children.

Today, Brazil and Colombia produce the most coffee in the world, but coffee is not native to South America. Originally from Arabia, coffee plants were taken by the Dutch to Java (Indonesia). The Dutch then gave plants to botanical gardens throughout Europe. In 1723, an enterprising (and dishonest) young officer stole a plant from a French botanical garden to bring with him to the Caribbean island of Martinique, where he was sure it would do well. It flourished. The plant was transported to Brazil in 1727, and the rest, as they say, is history.

Section Review

1. How did the Catholic Church help prepare the Indians for colonial life?
2. Who spoke out against enslaving the Indians? What was the result of his work?
3. Why did the Spanish bring Africans to South America?
4. What were the two main exports of colonial Latin America?

How do you think the Jesuits justified their use of the Indians? Was it right?

The Trouble with Transports

The Spanish discovered some wonderful new foods when they came to the New World. Foods such as corn and potatoes and cocoa delighted the Europeans. As the Europeans settled in the New World, they brought cows, horses, and sugar cane with them. The consequences of transporting these items affected both the New and Old Worlds for centuries.

One consequence was the Great Famine in Ireland. The potato became a staple (necessary part) of the Irish diet when the people found that the potato was more resistant to humidity and temperature changes than many of their common grains. Unfortunately, the Irish understood very little about crop disease and hybridization when the potato was introduced. The entire Irish potato crop came from only a handful of original plants. Due to this lack of variation in genetic material, almost all of the potato plants were susceptible to the blight that struck from 1845-48. By then the Irish were so dependent on the crop that more than 750,000 people died from the effects of what was called the Great Famine.

Other effects of transported goods were deforestation and the slave trade. Sugar cane was not native to the Caribbean or South America. To grow sugar cane, vast areas were deforested. To harvest sugar cane, hundreds of thousands of slaves were bought and taken to the New World.

Today we still transport items intentionally and accidentally from their native areas. Many times we must deal with the consequences. Sometimes the transport results in something good. Take the zebra mussel, for instance. Stuck to the hulls of ships, it traveled up the St. Lawrence River all the way to the Great Lakes. There it multiplied quickly and overwhelmed the native mussel population. Fortunately, it worked out well for the

Kudzu vines cover trees and power lines, creating weird shapes and killing the trees..

Great Lakes. The zebra mussels are filter feeders, and they successfully filter the water and increase its cleanliness. The once highly polluted Great Lakes have benefited from these stowaways. Unfortunately, not all transports are beneficial.

Anyone who has traveled in the southeastern United States has seen the kudzu plant. Its heart-shaped leaves and interwoven vines cover anything that is standing still, including trees and power lines. This overwhelming transport from Asia came to the United States as an ornamental porch vine. In the 1930s southern farmers began to plant it for erosion control and later as cattle feed. Kudzu has become a huge nuisance and in many areas is out of control.

Can you think of transports in your area? Are they harmful or beneficial? What can be done to prevent the problem?

Living in the Colonies

The people who came from the Iberian Peninsula to the New World faced many changes in lifestyle. Although the European world at the time was not extremely advanced according to today's standards, the colonists still faced a shock when they came to a world where there were unusual animals, strange foods, foreign people, and few roads. The people who came had to adapt to their new situation. Since most of the settlers were from the Iberian Peninsula, they brought their Iberian culture and architecture to the New World.

Living in the City

Much of South America's development occurred around the cities. The central portion of the city became the hub of trade and society. The wealthy built their homes and businesses around the center of town.

These homes were easily distinguished from those of the lower classes. Usually two-story in design, the house of the wealthy was set up for business on the first floor (with rooms for workers and servants) while the second floor was used for family apartments. The whole house opened onto an interior courtyard. The kitchen was usually a separate building at the back of the house. Not only was the house itself a beautiful structure with decorative moldings and carved shutters, but the furnishings inside were elegant as well. Imported Spanish goods were intermingled with oriental silk draperies and New World silver.

The arts played an important role in bringing civility to New Spain and Brazil. Decorative statues, religious works, and portraits were very popular. Drama and music transported from Europe helped to bring civility to the rough surroundings. As more and more children were born in the colonies, the arts helped to connect them to their Iberian heritage.

Beyond the wealth of the central city were the *barrios,* or neighborhoods, of the poor. These were the homes of the free blacks, In-

The ornate balconies of the rich hung out over the street. Window screens could be shut for privacy or opened to allow the people below to catch a glimpse of the rich and famous.

dians, and mestizos. Here apartments were the choice housing. A family often lived in a one-room apartment divided into two rooms by a blanket, but these accommodations were better than the shacks which were the next choice.

Social or economic status played a part in the poor *barrios* just as it did in the wealth of the central city. New immigrants from Spain, poorer Spanish people, and Indian artisans formed the top level. On the next level were gardeners, laborers, porters, and merchants. Unskilled or temporary Indian laborers and blacks were left to the bottom level.

City life held more opportunity for distraction than rural life did. In the city, the rich could attend plays, banquets, and concerts. They entertained with lavish parties to display

Even today the poor often live in ramshackle homes on the fringes of wealthy neighborhoods.

their goods or show the latest imports. The arrival of a new bishop or a new wealthy immigrant from Europe could provide gossip for weeks.

The poor in the city also had many diversions. Cock fights, where roosters were made to fight to the death while onlookers bet on the outcome, were a common source of entertainment for the men. Religious holidays with parades and prayers provided a break from work as well. Not unlike today, the poor also enjoyed watching the spectacle of the wealthy Spanish parading by in their new clothes and fine carriages.

Living in the Country

The settlement of the Latin American countryside took a different course from that of North America. The Latin Americans did not settle on individual family farms because the government did not promote private ownership of land. Wealthy men owned most of the land, from which they made huge country estates, called **haciendas** (HAH see EN dahs). The poorer people worked on these estates for low wages and had little hope of ever owning their own land. The landowners also forced the native Indians to work on the haciendas and later imported millions of African slaves for the same purpose.

Many of these men cared little for developing their land or using it wisely. As long as they gained wealth from their sugar cane, coffee, cacao (seed from which cocoa is made), rice, cotton, wheat, or cattle, they were content. This attitude kept the workers in poverty and the land undeveloped. Many Latin American nations remain agricultural, supplying important products for the rest of the world. Industrial development is still needed in these countries today.

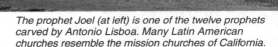

The prophet Joel (at left) is one of the twelve prophets carved by Antonio Lisboa. Many Latin American churches resemble the mission churches of California.

Arts in the Colonies

Because the colonies were established almost solely by the Iberians, it is not surprising that much of the art and architecture followed Iberian heritage. Many of the Indian cultures had individual art and architectural styles, but these were not used by the Iberians in their homes. Much of the notable art and architecture is found in the South American Catholic churches.

One of the most famous South American artists was Brazilian. **Antonio Lisboa** (1738-1814), also known as O Aleijadinho (the Little Cripple), was afflicted with a debilitating disease, possibly leprosy. He worked for many years with disfigurement and eventually lost the use of his hands. It is said that his servant had to tie the chisel and hammer to Lisboa's wrists so that he could continue to sculpt. His best-known works are the statues of twelve prophets outside of the Sanctuary of Bom Jesus at Congonhas do Campo. These huge statues are carved from soapstone in a style similar to that of the Mannerists. The statues are not soft images of perfect people but rather are angular and realistic. The legs on the statue of Hosea are twisted at odd angles that some believe reflect the deformity of Lisboa himself.

Section Review

1. What function did the first floor in the home of the wealthy city dweller have?

2. In what kind of housing did the poor dwell?

3. What were two entertainment activities of the rich? the poor?

4. Why was Antonio Lisboa called "the Little Cripple"?

Why do you think the rich liked to live in the center of town?

Life on a Hacienda

Just as medieval serfs knew only about their manor and had little hope of ever leaving it, so too were the peons (PEE ahnz) (people who were held in servitude to work off a debt) who lived on a South American hacienda. The hacendado (HAH sen DAH thoh) (the owner) was like the lord of the medieval manor. He had complete control over life on the hacienda and provided homes, land, necessities, and protection for the peons. He was also their ruler and judge. In return they, like medieval serfs, worked for him. Many peons thought of the people on the hacienda as a large family and the hacendado as their father. However, these "families" were not always happy, for the hacendado usually kept the peons in debt and unable to buy freedom.

A hacienda often covered hundreds of square miles of land. This land usually contained a number of villages. People living in these villages had to pay the hacendado rent for their homes, land, and grazing rights. But because they had no money, they paid by working for the hacendado.

The hacienda was self-sufficient; that is, it produced everything—food, clothes, dishes, furniture, and tools—that the people needed. Little, if anything, was purchased from the outside. People could obtain anything they needed from the hacienda store. However, no money changed hands. Again, the people worked to pay for the goods. In this way, most of those living on the hacienda were always in debt. Whatever the hacienda produced—grain, fruit, sugar, meat, coffee—was sold for the owner's profit. Many hacendados did not even bother to live on the hacienda. Instead they placed a manager in charge and built themselves luxurious mansions in one of the major cities.

Though few in number, the hacendados owned almost half the land in South America. As a result, they had great influence on their national governments. In many of the political struggles in the nineteenth and twentieth centuries, the people fought to overthrow the power of the hacendados. Today, for the most part, the haciendas have disappeared.

Quiet pools and cooling shade trees grace the entrance to this hacendado's home.

Becoming Independent

Independence came to Latin America through numerous revolutions in the nineteenth century. The creoles had grown to resent their lack of power in the government. They saw an opportunity to gain control while the Iberian nations fought in Europe.

Discontentment in the Spanish Colonies

Part of the colonies' discontentment with Spanish rule was over the mother country's control. Until the 1700s, the Spanish colonies were allowed to trade only with Spain. They could not trade with each other even for necessary goods. The Spanish were not interested in controlling just physical goods. They tried to control even the hearing or sharing of new ideas among colonies. The Spanish government had no desire for their subjects to accept the teachings of English and French philosophers, whose views eventually helped revolutionary ideas take hold in America and France. They wanted to keep the colonies totally separate from European influence. But that tight control only made the colonists want more information and freedom. The people secretly passed the European philosophies and discontentment by word of mouth and in written form from person to person. This quiet network of information spread seeds of revolution. (Chapter 9 will deal more with these revolutionary ideas.)

Another problem in the Spanish colonies was extreme classism (prejudice based on economic and racial distinctions). The divisions between Spanish born in Spain, creoles, mestizos, and Indians were distinct. There was no place in government or high society for anyone of less than pure Spanish blood unless he was wealthy. Classism caused great discontent, es-

Simón Bolívar's efforts to free South America from Spanish control have made him a hero.

pecially among the wealthy creoles and the mestizos. Unfortunately this same classism later made it difficult for the colonists to fight together against the Spanish.

Men Who Made a Difference

With the frustrations mentioned above, it is easy to imagine why many people were ready for someone to lead them to freedom and independence. Two men are best known as leaders in the Spanish colonies' struggle for independence, **Simón Bolívar** (boh LEE vahr) and **José de San Martín** (hoh-ZAY day SAN mahr-TEEN). They are still regarded as great heroes in Latin America today.

Born in 1783 in Caracas, Venezuela, Simón Bolívar was the fourth child of Juan Vicente and Doña María Bolívar. Both his parents had died by the time Bolívar was nine. Bolívar and his brother and sisters were left in the care of his uncle, Carlos Palacio.

As a boy, Bolívar learned Latin, Greek, Spanish, and French from a tutor named Simón Rodríguez. Rodríguez exposed him to the teachings of several eighteenth-century philosophers. Bolívar was influenced by Rousseau and Voltaire, who believed that freedom was the source of men's happiness. This philosophy stirred the spirit of independence in Bolívar's heart.

In 1799 his Uncle Carlos sent him to Spain to complete his education. During his time in Europe, Bolívar assembled several dissidents who gathered in the home of General Francisco de Miranda, a fellow Venezuelan. Miranda thought Bolívar was young and ungovernable, so when Bolívar returned home in 1807, convinced that the South American colonies were ready for independence, General Miranda gave him only a minor military position despite Bolívar's arguments for a position with rebel forces. Ordered not to raise his own army, he disobeyed and with a small army caused much damage to the Spanish forces in Venezuela.

In 1810 Miranda continued to set Bolívar aside. He sent Bolívar, now twenty-seven years old, to England as an ambassador. Bolívar studied the British system of government and compared it with the French and Spanish forms. Although Bolívar questioned Miranda's judgment in sending him to Europe, this European experience helped Bolívar when he later wrote constitutions for the emerging nations. Over the next few years, Bolívar's military position improved.

Under General Bolívar's direction, patriots pushed the Spaniards out of Venezuela from the south, east, and west. Bolívar's men followed him through plains, deserts, swamps, and rivers. Several times during the course of the fighting, Bolívar took his men through the Cordillera Mérida in the Andes, which rises to sixteen thousand feet in some places.

In 1816 the final move to independence began with Venezuela and then Colombia. Bolívar decided that the only way to free Venezuela was to free the entire continent of foreign rule. His greatest victories came in 1819 at the battle of Boyacá, Colombia, and in 1821 at the battle for Carabobo, Venezuela, with faithful general Antonio José de Sucre's military support. With the exception of a few Spanish holdouts, the entire northern portion of South America was independent. In 1822 Sucre went on to free Ecuador from Spanish dominion. At that time Bolívar wrote to San Martín and offered to help with the struggle for independence in Peru.

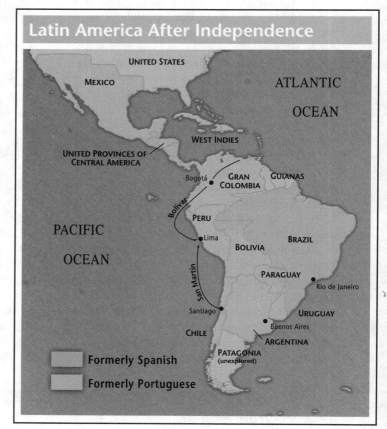

Latin America After Independence

CHARACTERIZATIONS

Cowboys of Argentina

Like the cowboys of the western United States, the **gauchos** of Argentina have become a symbol of rugged independence.

Working with his horse, a lasso, *boleodoros,* and a knife, the early gaucho roamed the Pampas, slaughtering wild cattle whose hides he sold on the black market. Basically outlaws, the gauchos did not become respectable until they fought with San Martín for Argentine independence. Eventually, many gauchos worked as hired men for *hacendados* and spent their lives guiding huge herds of cattle over the Pampas. Ever independent, they chose whom they worked for and roamed from place to place. In those days the Pampas were unfenced, so the gauchos drove their herds across vast stretches of prairie unhindered.

In cooperation with his horse, the gaucho would use his lasso to encircle the neck or leg of a wild horse or stray cow. He sometimes used his *boleodoro* for the same task. A *boleodoro* is made of three golf-ball-sized stones wrapped with rawhide and attached to three rawhide cords. The cords are then joined. When thrown, the *boleodoro* spins. When it comes in contact with the legs of a cow or a horse, it wraps around them and trips the animal. When the rhea (a large South American flightless bird) was plentiful, the *boleodoro* was used in its capture.

Much like the traditional American cowboy, the gaucho has a traditional outfit that consists of a wide-brimmed hat, a collared shirt, and baggy pants called *bombachas,* which are tucked into leather boots. A colorful sash or a wide leather belt decorated with silver coins or buckles goes around his waist, and round silver spurs decorate his boots. When working, a gaucho also wears a wide leather apron.

Today the way of the gaucho is fading. Fenced pastures, trucks, roads, and automation are changing the gaucho into a more stationary ranch hand and farmer instead of the independent individual of the past. Traditional dress is left for festival days, when sentimental songs remind the gaucho of his glorious past.

While Bolívar was fighting for independence in the north, Buenos Aires, Argentina, declared its independence from Spanish control in 1810, and that independence quickly spread across the country. The Argentine government chose José de San Martín to take independence to Peru.

San Martín was born to a prominent Argentine family in 1778. At age nine he crossed the ocean to study in Spain and went on to serve in the Spanish army. In 1812 San Martín resigned from the army to return to Argentina and help in the independence movement.

San Martín chose as his troops the gauchos of Argentina. (See Characterizations, page 181.) Although the gauchos were unruly, they made faithful fighting companions and fought ferociously for independence.

Unlike Bolívar, who rushed into battle, San Martín studied the strategies of his heroes, Napoleon and the Duke of Wellington (see Chapter 11) as he made decisions about the best methods of attack against the Spanish. He decided that instead of attacking the Spanish in Peru as commissioned, he would go with his troops across the Andes Mountains and free Chile first. In 1817 the troops crossed the Andes and slowly forced the Spanish from one city after another. With Chile free, San Martín turned to Peru.

In August of 1820, San Martín packed troops onto ships and set sail for Pisco, Peru. It was in Peru that San Martín received Bolívar's offer of help. In a pincer-like movement, Bolívar's troops came down from the north and San Martín's troops came up from the south. Independence had come to Peru.

During this final campaign, Bolívar, now called "the Liberator," fell gravely ill with tuberculosis. In the following years the Liberator maintained South American control in Peru and Gran Colombia (Columbia and Venezuela),

wrote constitutions for the emerging nations, and nursed his deteriorating health.

When Bolívar received the news of General Sucre's assassination in June 1830, his health declined even further. Six months later, the man who had helped Bolivia, Colombia, Ecuador, Chile, Peru, and Venezuela achieve independence was dead at the age of forty-seven.

After obtaining independence, the Spanish colonies in South America faced many problems in governing themselves. The wealthy landowners took over the governments and continued many Spanish policies. The only difference in their rule was that the wealth went to them rather than to Spain. The common people still had no say in government. They were no better off under these leaders than they had been under the Spanish. These weak governments were often overthrown by other strong men, called *caudillos* (KAW DEEL yohs). Generally military leaders, the *caudillos* rarely encouraged republican government but ruled as dictators. As powerful leaders fought to gain power, civil wars and revolts occurred regularly in most of these new nations. Even today some of these countries continue to have unstable governments.

Independence in Brazil

Brazil gained its independence at the same time as the other Latin American nations but without violence. There were early stirrings of revolution in Brazil supported by upper-class society: doctors, lawyers, clergy, and the military. Its named leader was a young dental worker nicknamed Tiradentes, or Toothpuller. The revolutionary plans were discovered early, and Tiradentes was tried and executed in 1789. Although hindered for the present, Brazil's people were still set for independence.

Oddly, independence came as a result of Portugal's capture by Napoleon of France. In 1807, the Portuguese royalty fled to Brazil and declared it the center of the Portuguese empire. King João (John) then adopted economic reforms to make Brazil a proper environment for the monarchy. King João repealed an earlier factory ban, introduced a trade treaty with England, established a printing press, and declared Brazil to be equal to instead of a colony of Portugal. All these things helped Brazil towards independence.

In 1820, Portugal demanded that King João return. He left his son Pedro as regent of Brazil. In 1822, when Pedro was to return to Portugal, he refused. On September 7, 1822,

Pedro I of Brazil

Pedro shouted "Independence or death!" and tore the symbol of Portugal from his military uniform. He was crowned emperor of independent Brazil as **Pedro I.**

Section Review

1. What were two things that made the colonists dissatisfied with Spanish rule?
2. What two men were great heroes of Spanish independence?
3. What was Simón Bolívar's nickname?
4. What European event affected Brazil's move for independence?

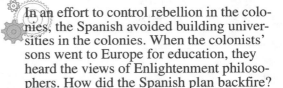 In an effort to control rebellion in the colonies, the Spanish avoided building universities in the colonies. When the colonists' sons went to Europe for education, they heard the views of Enlightenment philosophers. How did the Spanish plan backfire?

Summary

When the Iberians first came to South America, they found the wealth of the Incas. They set up tightly controlled colonies with little consideration of the native people or the children of the original settlers. Spain tried to limit the interaction of its colonists with each other and other European countries. Portugal also maintained a firm grip on its holdings. Despite all these controls, the events and philosophies in Europe still made their way to the colonies and had an effect. Unintentionally, one element of Iberian rule, severe classism, almost prevented the colonists from uniting to achieve independence. When independence was finally achieved, the colonists found themselves ill prepared to take over. The class discrimination that was a trait of Iberian control continues to hinder the growth of some South American nations.

CHAPTER REVIEW

People, Places, and Terms to Know

Iberian Peninsula	imported	Amazon River	haciendas
Latin America	*donatarios*	Pampas	Antonio Lisboa
Line of Demarcation	Thomé de Souza	Bartolomé de Las	Simón Bolívar
Treaty of Tordesillas	Council of the Indies	Casas	José de San Martín
creoles	viceroys	New Laws of 1542	gauchos
mother country	*peninsulares*	Mestizos	*caudillos*
exported	Andes Mountains	Jesuits	Pedro I

Review Questions

Matching

Match each term to its definition.

1. viceroys
2. governor-generals
3. *caudillos*
4. haciendas

(a) Brazilian colonial rulers
(b) large country estates
(c) Spanish colonial rulers
(d) military leaders

5. creoles
6. mestizos
7. gauchos
8. *peninsulares*

(a) colonists born in Spain
(b) South American cowboys
(c) Spaniards born in the colonies
(d) persons with Spanish and Indian heritage

Completion

Complete the following sentences using the choices provided.

Council of the Indies
encomienda
Bartolomé de Las Casas

Treaty of Tordesillas
Thomé de Souza

9. _____ wrote an essay that caused the Spanish to change their policies toward the Indians.
10. The _____ watched over the activities of the viceroys.
11. The _____ gave the Portuguese a foothold in South America.
12. The _____ was a land payment that the Spanish government gave to conquistadors.
13. The first governor-general of Bahia was _____.

Connections

For the following pairs of items, write a sentence or two showing their connection.

14. gauchos / San Martín
15. New Laws of 1542 / Bartolomé de Las Casas
16. Iberian Peninsula / Latin America
17. creoles / *peninsulares*

Multiple Choice

Choose the letter of the answer that correctly finishes the statement.

18. The Jesuits were
    (a) part of the Spanish government.
    (b) military rulers.
    (c) the Society of Monks.
    (d) an arm of the Catholic Church.

19. The general called "the Liberator" was
    (a) Simón Bolívar.
    (b) Bartolomé de Las Casas.
    (c) Thomé de Souza.
    (d) José de San Martín.

20. The gauchos lived in
    (a) the Andean Republics.
    (b) the River Plate Republics.
    (c) Brazil.
    (d) the Caribbean Republics.

Think About It!

Much of early South American life revolved around classism (partiality based on social or economic class). Some people think that the United States is a classless society. Do you think that is true? Explain your answer. Find a verse in the Bible that deals with classism and explain what the verse means.

CHAPTER 8

When the Spanish came home from the New World with great riches, many other countries were envious. With very little effort, the Spanish had conquered South and Central American nations and had reaped the "golden" benefits. It was only a matter of time before all the wealthy European nations were in a race for the unclaimed lands and the treasures they held. Since the Spanish centered their interest in South and Central America, the North was left for the other European countries.

The great riches that the North American settlers found were not in gold and silver but in far more lasting goods. North America was a continent with rich natural resources, a varied climate, and much wildlife. North America was not just for conquering but also for inhabiting. Soon people from all across Europe came to start a new life in a New World.

North America was initially divided among several countries. Spain, not content with its already massive conquests, came into North America by Mexico and the Caribbean Islands. France began exploring in Canada. The English, Swedes, and Dutch wrangled over the coast of what would one day be the United States. The Native Americans soon were squeezed off their ancestral lands by the steady stream of settlers. Because each group had the goal of claiming or keeping as much land as it could, conflict was inevitable. The results of the conflicts would shape centuries to come.

A.D. 1500 - A.D. 1900

Jacques Cartier
Explores Canada 1534

Reformation 1500-1650

1500

Renaissance 1350-1616

St. Augustine
Founded 1535

Ponce de León Lands
in Florida 1513

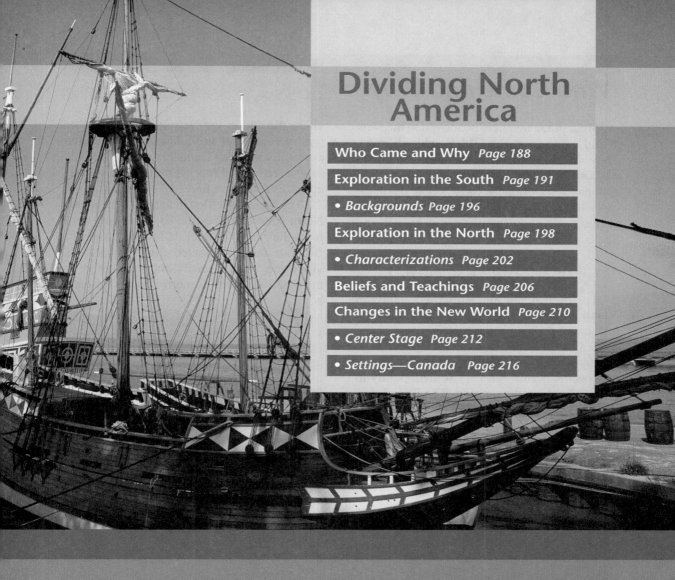

Dividing North America

Quebec Act 1774

South American Independence 1816-22

Revolutionary War Begins 1776-81

British North America Act 1867

First British Colonies Established 1607-30

Slave Trade in North America 1651-1865

1700

1800

1900

California Missions Established 1769-1823

French and Indian War Ends September 18, 1759

Brazil Declares Independence December 1, 1822

Who Came and Why

Most of the people who moved to the New World came from the **Old World**—Europe. They were English, French, Portuguese, Spanish, Dutch, German, Italian, and many other nationalities. During the early period of American settlement up to 1780, the greatest number of Europeans came from England, France, and Spain.

Where Did They Settle?

The French and English settled mainly in **North America.** The English settled the land that today makes up the eastern coast of the United States. They also claimed portions of present-day Canada. The French explored much of North America, but they settled mainly in the eastern Canadian region. The French and English were not always on good terms in either the Old or the New World. Often their rivalry broke out in violence. This problem especially affected Canadian culture and history; even today French-English rivalry characterizes Canadian life.

The Spanish settled in the southern area of North America. They did so by moving north from their early conquests in Latin America. Because they dominated the Caribbean Islands, the Spanish easily hopped over to the mainland of North America into Florida as well.

Why Did They Come to the New World?

Europeans left the Old World for the New for several reasons. One reason was the desire for wealth. Spain had discovered that South

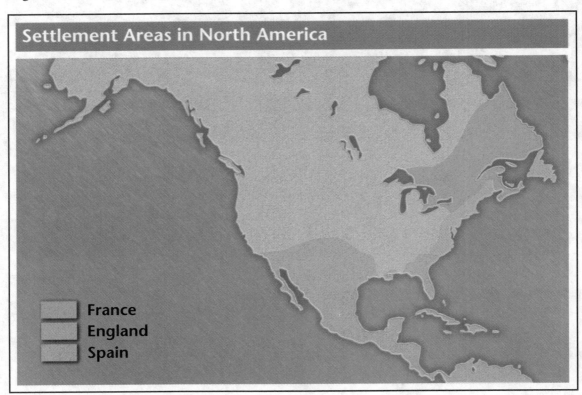

Settlement Areas in North America

France
England
Spain

Plentiful wildlife and pristine wilderness invited Europeans to explore.

and Central America were rich with deposits of silver and gold. All looked to North America for the same promised riches. Although there was less silver and gold in North America, furs provided a source of wealth, especially in Canada and the northern United States.

Another reason people came to the New World was to make a new life. Europe was very overcrowded. Farmland was scarce, and jobs were not always available. People saw the Americas as a land of plenty where they could own land and establish their own farms and communities. The New World gave these people the opportunity for a life they never could have had in the Old World.

Still others came for adventure. Explorers, hunters, and traders traveled to the Americas to discover what this new land had to offer. They came into an unknown region, lived off the land, and met new peoples, all for adventure. To these men we owe a great debt for their original descriptions and early mapping of the continents, which later opened the way for settlement.

Religion was another important reason that men and women came to the Americas. As we will see with the Pilgrims, the New World promised freedom of worship. After the Protestant Reformation, persecuted Christians came to the New World to worship freely and to share their faith with both the Indians and the settlers. Reforms in the Catholic Church, as a result of the Protestant Reformation, sparked a new Catholic missionary effort. The Franciscan and Jesuit orders were among the leaders of this effort. Out of a sincere desire to carry their teachings to the Indians, priests accompanied almost every French and Spanish expedition. These Catholic missionaries showed genuine zeal by their willingness to be martyred for their faith. Because of their zeal and labor, Latin America is still strongly Roman Catholic.

Many millions came to the Americas for a reason other than wealth, land, adventure, or

Not only were slaves taken from their native lands, but once purchased, they were often resold. Families were broken apart and lives were changed forever.

religion. In fact, these men, women, and children did not even come on their own; they were brought. They were black slaves from Africa. Beginning in the seventeenth century and continuing until the nineteenth, the **slave trade** brought nearly fifteen million Africans to North and South America. The majority went to Brazil and the Caribbean to work the large estates.

Many also came to the southern United States to work on rice and tobacco plantations. From its beginning in the mid-1600s until the mid-1700s, slavery grew so much that in the South blacks outnumbered whites almost two to one. White plantation owners were so outnumbered that they lived in constant fear of rebellion. This fear caused them to react harshly toward anything that looked like rebellion. It also caused many white owners to place great restrictions on slave behavior. Slavery became a major issue in the Americas, greatly contributing to the Civil War (1861-65) in the United States. By 1888 the practice of slavery was outlawed entirely in all the Americas.

Section Review

1. From what three countries did most early settlers come?
2. List five reasons that settlers came to the New World.
3. Why is Latin America still strongly Catholic?
4. Where did the slaves work in North America?

If a new world were discovered today, do you think that people would settle there for the same reasons that they came to America? Would you go there? Why?

Exploration and Settlement in the South

Because Spanish exploration began in the Caribbean and Gulf of Mexico, the Spanish established their settlements in southern North America. Explorers did travel farther north, but the difficulties that they faced there caused them to give up further exploration or settlement inland.

The Spanish Expeditions

During the 1500s Spain dominated the exploration of North America. The Spanish quest for gold in South and Central America had met with such success that they wanted to be the first into North America too. They became frustrated, though, when several expeditions mapped land and met Indians but found no gold.

After having traveled on Columbus's second journey, **Juan Ponce de León** (PONS duh LEE-ohn) set sail from Puerto Rico at his own expense to discover new islands. He also wanted to find the Fountain of Youth, whose legendary waters miraculously re-stored strength and youth. Ponce de León arrived off the coast of North America between Daytona Beach and Cape Canaveral on March 28, 1513, the day after Easter. He named the new land *Pascua florida* (Easter Flower), in honor of the Easter season. No one welcomed him on Florida's shores, however. The Indians had already met Spanish slave traders. Before Ponce de León's men could settle on shore, the Indians drove them away. The Spaniards decided to follow the shore south around the tip of Florida. As they neared the island of Sanibel in the Gulf of Mexico (near Fort Myers), they were attacked by eighty canoes full of Indians armed with bows and arrows. Ponce de León had had enough. While traveling around Florida, he had gone ashore long enough to taste every inlet and stream that he could reach. He did not find the Fountain of Youth, but he did find several Indians who would have liked him to die young. De León gave up the exploration and went back to Puerto Rico.

Ponce de León was hounded by natives wherever he tried to land his ship.

The next attempt to explore Florida came in 1528 by **Pánfilo de Narváez** (nar VAH ayz). Narváez received a royal charter from the Spanish king to explore and govern Florida (which to the Spanish meant all the lands north of Mexico). In April Narváez landed near Tampa, Florida, with 260 men and forty horses. In the first village that Narváez reached, he saw the Indians making coffins out of wooden boxes that had washed ashore from a Spanish ship. In his anger over "misuse" of Spanish goods, Narváez ordered his men to burn the boxes, bodies and all. This action did not make the Indians fond of him and his men. After that, the Indians harassed the Spanish wherever they went.

One man on Narváez's expedition wrote that the men were surprised to find that the Indian bows were too big for the Spanish to pull. He told how the arrows flew with such force that they pierced trees the size of a man's thigh. He also praised the Indians' skill with this weapon. Because of that skill, many men were killed or wounded as arrows found their mark between the joints in the Spanish armor.

During his time in Florida, Narváez and his men were under constant attack and had great difficulty finding food. They finally decided to build boats and go over water to Mexico (already in Spanish possession). In September 1528, Narváez and his remaining 242 men set sail in five longboats that they had constructed. They traveled along the coastline past the mouth of the Mississippi River, where they encountered rough waters and the boats capsized. Narváez died and only eighty other men survived.

One of the survivors was **Cabeza de Vaca** (kah-BAY-zuh duh VAH-kuh). Washed ashore on an island, de Vaca and three other men were given food and cared for by the Indians. The Cahoques Indians made servants of de Vaca and his friends.

During his eight years with the Indians, de Vaca saw them from a different viewpoint than most Spaniards of his time. He saw the Indians as human beings. De Vaca marveled at the way they fished with the bow and arrow by standing still in the water, waiting to feel a swirl of movement that meant a fish was nearby. He appreciated their affection for one another and the sorrow of a village at the death of one of

Cabeza de Vaca's feelings toward the Native Americans changed when he lived with them for several years.

Chapter 8

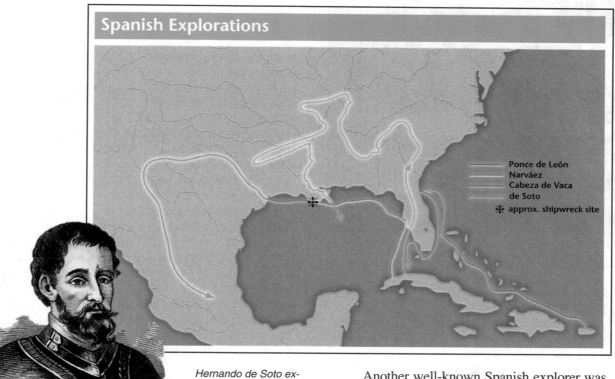

Spanish Explorations

Ponce de León
Narváez
Cabeza de Vaca
de Soto
✳ approx. shipwreck site

Hernando de Soto explored much of the southeastern United States.

their children. De Vaca recognized for the first time that each tribe was different and had different customs.

As time went on, de Vaca was given more freedom and became known as a medicine man. He traveled as a merchant and healer from tribe to tribe and learned that each tribe spoke a different language. He also found that the Indians fought with each other and not with just the white man. Sadly, as de Vaca traveled west through Texas, he began to hear stories of villages burned and Indians hanged by the "Christian" white men. Cabeza de Vaca's heart was changed toward the Indians and Spanish exploration. He eventually traveled to Mexico and then returned to Spain. Once there, he published the story of his adventures in the New World.

Another well-known Spanish explorer was **Hernando de Soto** (di SO-toh), former captain under the command of Francisco Pizarro. (See Chapter 6.) De Soto landed near Tampa Bay in 1539. He came prepared to stay; he brought with him 570 men, 243 horses, pigs, attack dogs, and equipment to make anything the explorers might need. Early in the expedition, de Soto found one of the survivors of Narváez's expedition living in an Indian village. This man traveled with de Soto as an interpreter.

De Soto was not very popular with the Indians. He made it a habit to enslave Indians to carry equipment for the Spanish, and he regularly stole Indian grain reserves. When de Soto asked about gold, the Indians always pointed him to the next village. This was an effective way to get rid of the unwelcome Spanish, but it did not get rid of the diseases they carried. After de Soto and his men passed, epidemics of European diseases plagued the

The flags of four nations have flown over St. Augustine. The Spanish fortress Castillo de San Marcos was built in 1672.

Indians and greatly reduced the Florida Indian population.

De Soto traveled north through Florida and then into Alabama, northern Mississippi, and Arkansas. He finally came to the Mississippi River in 1542. It took a total of three years for de Soto's expedition to travel from Florida across Texas to Vera Cruz, Mexico. Of the original number, 312 men survived, but de Soto was not among them.

Spanish Settlements

The Spanish finally did establish themselves in North America. They took territory in Texas, Arizona, New Mexico, Nevada, California, and Florida. The French almost beat them in actually settling Florida by establishing an early outpost there. To stop them, Phillip II of Spain sent **Pedro Menéndez de Avilés** to settle Florida. Menéndez took with him six hundred men. These men were not only soldiers but also laborers, craftsmen, and merchants. Many of them brought their wives and families. In 1535 Menéndez and these settlers founded **St. Augustine,** the oldest continuously inhabited city in the United States. Menéndez chased the French from their set-

tlement and established Spanish dominance in Florida for the next three hundred years.

Spanish settlements in Texas and the West took much longer to establish. In 1597 **Juan de Oñate** began an expedition into New Mexico following earlier expeditions. His purpose was to "pacify" (subdue) the Indians and convert them to Catholicism. He was also on the lookout for gold and silver.

In 1598 Oñate established a temporary settlement at present-day Española. The representatives that he sent out encountered many Indians. Oñate's men also encountered buffalo. They were impressed by the massive animals and tried to take a herd back to Española. To their surprise the animals could not be herded like normal cattle. Instead of returning with buffalo, the Spaniards lost four horses and had another forty injured by the shaggy beasts with the slashing horns.

The Spanish also claimed California, but they did not actually settle there until 1769. Prior to that time, it was generally accepted that California was an island. Most explorers thought that the Gulf of Mexico went farther

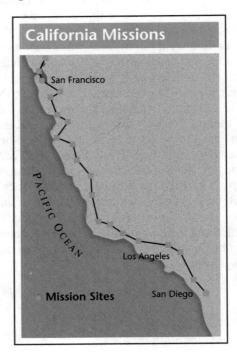

California Missions

San Francisco

PACIFIC OCEAN

Los Angeles

San Diego

■ **Mission Sites**

north and ended in a narrow strait that went back out to the Atlantic Ocean.

The path of exploration to California was so treacherous that the Spanish made little attempt to explore the coastline or interior until word came of a threat to Spanish control—the English were exploring California north of present-day San Francisco. With that news came an immediate press to find the best harbors and land routes to connect the Spanish holdings in New Mexico with the Pacific coast. Eventually the Spanish established twenty-one **missions,** beginning with San Diego in the south (established in 1769) and ending with Sonoma just north of San Francisco (1823). The missions were placed about a day's journey apart. Although many of the friars in control of the missions were good men, the mission system promoted servitude of the Indian population. The Indians' work at the missions benefited the church and the Spanish government more than it benefited the Indians themselves.

The Catholic Church and governors were often in conflict in the Spanish settlements. They sometimes struggled more for power than for souls. Many priests were genuinely concerned for the Indians and told them of a Savior's love and forgiveness. However, the contrast between the preaching and the actual behavior of most of the Spanish "Christians" made many Indians accept religion outwardly but retain their old religion in private. It should remind us that we need to live our faith con-

This mission in San Diego was the first of twenty-one missions established by the Spanish in California.

sistently so that those who do not know the Lord will see Him in us. First Peter 2:12 says, "Having your conversation [manner of life] honest among the Gentiles: that, whereas they speak against you as evildoers, they may by your good works, which they shall behold, glorify God in the day of visitation."

The Spanish were able to establish the first permanent settlements in North America. They explored and claimed much territory. As you will learn in Chapter 9, war in Europe affected Spain's ability to maintain so much territory in the New World. As more settlers came to America, Spain was unable to divide either its finances or its attention between the New World and Spain's domestic (internal) troubles. Its conquests in North America were overrun by the determined settlers of the budding American nation.

Section Review

1. Why did Ponce de León name the land he explored *Florida?*

2. How did de Vaca end up living with the Indians?

3. Who used a survivor of Narváez's mission to interpret for his own expedition?

4. What city is the oldest continuously inhabited city in America?

5. How many mission towns did the Spanish establish in California? Where and when was the first mission established?

How do your actions affect the way people think about God?

From Fins to Fur

Before the governments of France or England considered settling in the New World, men eagerly came to the coastline of Newfoundland to catch cod. Years of fishing the coastal waters of England and France had depleted the fish stock. When fishermen began coming to the New World, they found the fishing easy. Fishing along the shores of Newfoundland from April to June, fleets returned home with full holds to make their owners rich.

The English and French used two different methods for processing and packing the fish to take home. The French used a wet method. Onboard ships anchored on the Grand Banks, men line-fished, bringing in one cod at a time. They then passed the fish to men standing at tables nearby. Those men cleaned and split the fish before throwing them into the hold to be packed in thick layers of salt. The interesting part of this method was the way the fishermen kept warm. To keep dry and comfortable, the fishermen and cleaners all stood inside barrels while wearing heavy leather aprons that they draped over the top of the barrel. To further protect them from the

Beaver were easy to find by their stick dams and lodges.

cold ocean spray, the men fished behind wind screens while they stood inside their barrels.

The English fishermen lacked the extensive salt supplies of the French. Their processing area was known as a dry fishery. (The fish *and* the men stayed dry.) In the dry process the English landed on shore and set up drying sheds. When the fishermen came in from fishing each day, they gutted and split the fish, then lightly salted them and laid them out to dry on the open-air racks in the sheds. The inconvenience of this method was that it sometimes took months to dry the fish, depending on the weather. (If it was a damp summer, the fish took longer to dry.) The English were always in a race against time and weather to get home before autumn.

Because their method depended on these shore-based fisheries, the English were especially hostile when settlers finally came to the shores of Newfoundland. The fishermen burned the settlers' homes, crops, and mills. The government

The English left fish to dry on drying racks for weeks.

Chapter 8

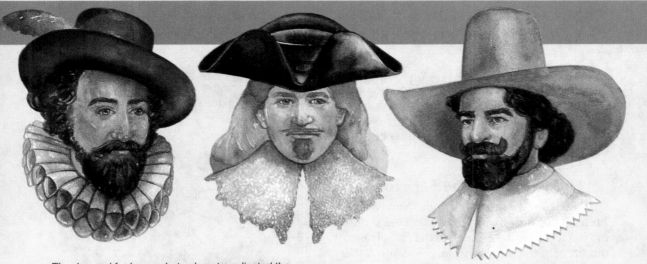

The demand for beaver hats almost eradicated the beaver population in North America.

finally prohibited the settlement of areas within six miles of shore.

With the coming of more and more settlers, a peace was eventually made with the fisheries, and settlements were raised along the shore by 1677.

The French and English came not only to fish but also to trade for furs. Early visitors to the shores of the New World met Indians wearing animal skin blankets. The fur on these skins was soft and thick and ideal for felting. The Europeans wanted felt hats; the Indians wanted metal tools; so fur trading in the New World began.

Beaver was the favored fur for hats. At that time in North America, there were an estimated sixty million beavers. Only the soft inner fur was used for felting. The prime time for collecting the beaver's fur was winter when this inner fur was thickest. It was also a prime time to hunt, since the beaver stayed close to its lodge in the winter and was easy to trap. The fur trade profited the European traders more than the Indians. The traders made enormous profits on the furs they

collected. The Indians got the tools and pots and beads that they wanted, but it cost them their way of life and their land.

New World Fisheries

NEWFOUNDLAND

ENGLAND

FRANCE

Exploration and Settlement in the North

With reports of Spanish successes in the New World, the French and English soon began looking for ways to establish colonies. They concentrated their efforts in the North. The winters there were treacherous, but the rewards were great.

The French in the Far North

Soon after the discovery of the New World, French fishermen fished for cod off the shores of Newfoundland. As much as the fish pleased the French, the king of France was not to be outdone by the Spanish in the discovery of riches. If there was gold and silver in the South, there could be gold and silver in the North. Besides, the French had also heard from the Indians of a waterway that could lead to Cathay (China). In 1534 the French king commissioned **Jacques Cartier** (kar TYAY) to find "isles and countries where, it is

Jacques Cartier opened the St. Lawrence River to French exploration.

Communities of Iroquois Indians lived in the region claimed by the French.

said, there must be great quantities of gold and other riches."

Cartier made several trips to the New World. On his first trip he came into the Gulf of St. Lawrence. Cartier and his men sailed into Gaspé Bay at the top of New Brunswick. There they met an Iroquois Indian fishing party headed by Chief Donnaconna of the Iroquois nation. The Indians were not hostile, but they became very suspicious when they saw the Europeans set on the beach a thirty-foot cross bearing the French coat of arms. With hand signs, Donnaconna protested the Frenchmen's right to the land, but Cartier told him that the cross was only a guidepost for other explorers. Cartier took two of Donnaconna's sons back to France with him to teach them the French language. This provided him with interpreters for his next voyage.

Early French Exploration

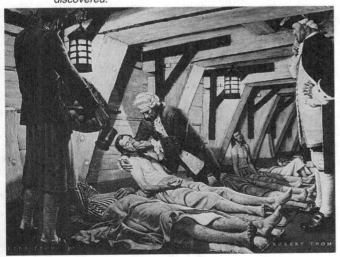

Quebec

Montreal

Lake Champlain

St. Lawrence R.

Lake Ontario

Lake Erie

On Cartier's second voyage, Donnaconna's two sons led him straight up the St. Lawrence until the river narrowed suddenly. There on a rock outcropping was the Indian settlement called Stadacona. Donnaconna welcomed his sons and Cartier to the village but discouraged Cartier from traveling any farther upstream. (Donnaconna wanted to control the French trade with other Indians.) Cartier persisted and sailed upstream until he came to another Indian

Scurvy killed hundreds of seamen before its cure was discovered.

village. The French eventually settled that area and called it **Montreal.**

Returning downriver, Cartier and his men wintered near Stadacona. The harsh winter surprised them. Everything was coated with ice. The ice on the river was twelve feet thick. Soon Cartier and his men began to suffer from a strange disease that would centuries later be diagnosed as a vitamin deficiency called **scurvy.** Their gums swelled and their teeth fell out. Their joints became swollen and sore. Twenty-five of his men died. The fate of the expedition seemed hopeless until Cartier saw one of the Indians, who had been just as sick as they, walking around healthy. Cartier asked about this miraculous recovery. The Indians shared their cure with Cartier. They prescribed a brew of the vitamin C-rich needles and bark of the white cedar tree to cure the disease. Sadly, Cartier did not at that time record the cure, and later settlers dying from scurvy did not find Indians who were as interested in sharing.

Another major French explorer was **Samuel de Champlain.** He is best known for discovering two of the Great Lakes (Ontario and Huron) and Lake Champlain, but Champlain's greatest legacy may have been his love for the French frontier. Because of his love, he was given the title **Father of New France.**

In 1608 Champlain and thirty men established the **Habitation** where the St. Lawrence River narrows. (The narrowing was called a

The Father of New France

199

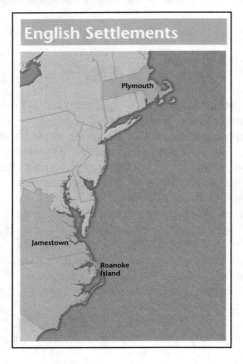

English Settlements

Plymouth

Jamestown

Roanoke Island

Sir Walter Raleigh brought potatoes and tobacco to Europe from the New World.

kébec by the Algonquin Indians and would later be the site of Quebec City.) During his time in America, Champlain helped establish the *coureurs de bois* (messengers of the woods). These young men were fur traders who lived with and learned the culture and language of the Indians. Agents of France, the *coureurs* helped Champlain form the French alliance with the Algonquin and Huron tribes.

Champlain was orderly and disciplined in directing his settlement. An excellent leader, he brought unity to the Indians and French and encouraged hard work among those at the Habitation. With his unique perspective, Champlain made the French king aware of the agricultural wealth of the New World. He encouraged the king to obligate new settlers to come ready to till the soil so that the colony could be self-supporting.

Champlain's colony experienced some very hard times—including Indian attack, scurvy, and an English takeover. But before his death in 1635, Champlain saw his small colony rooted firmly in the soil of Canada.

A New World for the English

With the Spanish already in control in the South and the French hanging on to trade and settlement along the St. Lawrence, a few enterprising Englishmen began to settle what was left—the land that today makes up the eastern coast of the United States. They also claimed portions of present-day Canada.

When the English, under the funding of **Sir Walter Raleigh,** made their first attempt to settle in 1587, they chose as their site **Roanoke, North Carolina.** The first colonists sailed back to England after a year. A second set of colonists came as the first set left. When a supply ship returned to the colony a year later, there were no colonists to be found. The word *Croatoan* carved in a tree was the only clue to the disappearance of what we now call the **"Lost Colony."**

When the Virginia Company made an attempt at settlement, its ships wound their way up the Chesapeake Bay until they came to an island in the James River. They chose as their landing area one of the most heavily populated Indian regions along the eastern coast. Everywhere they stopped was settled with Indians already. If the Indians did not want the small island on the James River, the settlers should have suspected something.

The settlement called **Jamestown** was years in the making. Advertised as paradise by its investors, Jamestown was a shock to the 104 original settlers—especially to the 54 gentlemen settlers who did not expect to do much work. Of the 575 settlers who came to Jamestown from 1607 to 1610, all but 60 died of disease, starvation, and Indian attacks.

John Smith helped the settlers make some progress from 1608 to 1609. He brought discipline to the group and told the men to work or they would not get to eat. His help was cut short when he was hurt in a gunpowder explosion and forced to return to England in October. The winter of 1609-10 was known as the "starving time." It was the worst year for the colony. When a ship arrived the next spring, all of the colonists were ready to leave. They changed their plans only when they met Lord De La Warr coming up the Chesapeake Bay with supplies and 150 new colonists.

Jamestown's recovery began in 1611. Through the influence of Acting Governor **Sir Thomas Dale,** Jamestown began to improve economically. Dale set himself to the task of bringing discipline to the colony. He established a high penalty for many unacceptable behaviors such as stealing and swearing. He required colonists to attend church services twice a day. Dale required everyone to work many hours a day. With all this seemingly harsh discipline, Dale also began to reward the colonists by giving three acres of land to every settler who had paid his obligation to the chartering company. When people had their own land, production increased. Once unable to feed themselves from common ground (ground owned by the colony and farmed together), now each settler raised as much corn alone as had been raised by several men together.

When colonist **John Rolfe** married **Pocahontas**, the Indian chief's daughter, the threat from Indian attack was removed. Working in peace, the settlers continued to flourish. Besides making a marriage alliance with the Indians, John Rolfe also helped the colony when he introduced tobacco as a **cash crop** (a crop which could be sold for cash or supplies).

In 1614 the colonists shipped the first barrels of tobacco to England, thus establishing a basis for trade that would continue for years to come.

Buildings in Jamestown, such as this church and this settler's home, have been restored.

CHARACTERIZATIONS

Eliza Lucas Pinckney

When settlers came to the New World, they wanted not only to live off the land by **subsistence farming** (producing what you need to live) but also to produce a cash crop. One young woman named Eliza Lucas (now known by her married name, Pinckney) became influential in providing a new cash crop for the Carolinas. Eliza is known not only for this contribution but also for her character.

Eliza came to South Carolina with her family around 1737. In 1739 when Eliza was sixteen, her father was recalled to service in the English navy. Because of her mother's poor health, Eliza was left in control of the family plantation. In a letter to a friend, Eliza tells a little of what she thinks of this responsibility. Notice her attitude.

I have the business of 3 plantations to transact which requires much writing and more business and fatigue of other sorts than you can imagine, but least you should imagine it too burthensom [burdensome] to a girl at my early time of life, give mee leave to assure you I think myself happy that I can be useful to so good a father.

Indigo had to be harvested while the leaves were still green. The process of extracting the dye required strict attention to detail.

Indigofera *is a member of the pea family.*

How would you like to be left to take care of your family's house, bills, grocery shopping, and six-hundred-acre farm? If you think that Eliza could be so happy because she was rich and everyone took care of her, look at the schedule she set up for herself. She wrote the following to answer a friend's question about what Eliza did with her day.

In general then I rise at five o'Clock in the morning, read till seven—then take a walk in the garden or fields, see that the Servants are at their respective business, then to breakfast. The first hour after breakfast is spent in musick, the next is constantly employed in recolecting something I have learned, least for want of practise it should be quite lost, such as french and shorthand. After that, I devote the rest of the time till I dress for dinner to our little polly, and two black girls who I teach to read, and if I have my papa's approbation (my mama's I have got) I intend for school mistress's for the rest of the Negroe children. Another scheme you see, but to proceed, the first hour after dinner, as the first after breakfast, at musick, the rest of the afternoon in needle work till candle light, and from that time to bed time read or write. . . .

In spite of her busy schedule, Eliza looked for ways to improve her father's property. Having an interest in plants and agriculture, Eliza asked her father to send her seeds from some plants in the West Indies. One of these plants was indigo.

The indigo plant provided a blue dye essential in a time before synthetic dyes. No one had tried to grow the plant in the colonies before. Eliza saw it as an opportunity for a cash crop for people who lived too far inland to grow rice. After two bad years, the indigo finally began to flourish. Eliza oversaw the entire project, from the growing of the plants to the final lumps of indigo dye. The process was very difficult, but eventually it was perfected.

Eliza dedicated her whole crop in 1744 to making seed. (Once it went to seed, it could not be harvested for dye.) Eliza did not hoard this seed for herself, but unselfishly gave it as gifts to other planters in the area. For thirty years, indigo was the chief crop of the inland planters. Just before the American Revolution, the annual export was 1,107,630 pounds of indigo dye! Eliza's determination, discipline, and unselfishness had allowed her to bring success to the southern colonies.

But English settlers did not come to the New World for financial gain only. While Jamestown was struggling, another little group of settlers came to America at Plymouth, Massachusetts, in 1620. These families came looking for a haven from persecution and a place to rear godly children. They were the **Pilgrims.**

Commissioned by the Virginia Company, the Pilgrims received more freedom than they expected when they landed in Massachusetts, many miles outside Virginia Company land. As they established their colony, they began by organizing a legal system, judging criminals by jury, and starting a free market system (where prices are set by individuals, not the government).

The Pilgrim colony had less difficulty with Indians than some of the other colonies for two reasons. The first reason was that the Indian tribes in the area had been decimated by a plague in 1616-17. As the Pilgrims explored, they saw that the plague had been so bad that the Indians had not even been able to bury their dead. Skeletons lay everywhere in deserted Indian villages.

The second reason was the Pilgrims' Christlike behavior in dealing with them. Although they saw the sin in some Indian practices, they respected the Indians as humans. They shared the gospel with the Indians and made alliances with them when the opportunity arose.

The governor of Plymouth, William Bradford, chronicled the events of the colony in his work *History of Plymouth Plantation*. He honestly and openly recorded the events, telling the good and the bad. Toward the end of his life he wrote with discouragement that many of their children's children had forsaken the church. Though the Pilgrims had taken their children out of a bad environment, they forgot the important biblical principle found in Mark 7:20-23.

> And he [Jesus] said, That which cometh out of the man, that defileth the man.
> For from within, out of the heart of men, proceed evil thoughts, adulteries, fornications, murders, thefts, covetousness, wickedness, deceit, lasciviousness, an evil eye, blasphemy, pride, foolishness:
> All these evil things come from within, and defile the man.

After a treacherous voyage, the Pilgrims thanked God for His protection.

One religion dominated French and Spanish colonies—Roman Catholicism. The English colonies were known for religious freedom.

Did you find the principle? It is that evil is within our hearts and comes from inside even if external conditions are good. Even though the Pilgrim parents were godly and the children were away from worldly influence, many of the Pilgrim children did not have a personal relationship with the Lord. Thus, they were quickly caught up in materialism and desires of the flesh. The experiences of the Plymouth colony remind us that we cannot rest in the righteousness of our parents or pastor but must concentrate on our own personal walk with God.

The English settlements differed from French and Spanish settlements in three important ways. The English colonists came under private investors, not government sponsorship. The English colonists came to live with their families. Most English colonists who came were Protestants. However, the English settlements were similar to the French and Spanish in that they found, instead of Eden, a hostile and unfamiliar environment, filled with dangers, challenges, and adventures.

Section Review

1. Why did France want Cartier to explore?
2. What Indian tribe did Cartier encounter?
3. What is a *coureur du bois?*
4. What did Champlain discover?
5. What happened to the first English attempt to colonize North America?
6. What man helped Jamestown recover after its first few years? How?
7. Who was the governor of Plymouth?
8. What did he write to chronicle the events of the colony?

Could the exploration and settlement of the New World have been handled in a better way? How?

Beliefs and Teachings

When Columbus made his voyage to the New World, he asked King Ferdinand and Queen Isabella to set it aside for Roman Catholics only.

> And I say that Your Highnesses ought not to consent that any foreigner does business or sets foot here, except Christian Catholics, since this was the end and the beginning of the enterprise, that it should be for the enhancement and glory of the Christian religion, nor should anyone who is not a good Christian come to these parts. *(Journal of the First Voyage)*

But God ordained that people of other religions would come into the New World. Their religions would affect every area of life in this new land.

Religion in the New World

To the people who moved to the New World for religious reasons, their beliefs were very important. The second oldest English settlement in North America was made by the Pilgrims at Plymouth (1620). They sought a place to worship freely. The **Puritans,** who settled **Massachusetts Bay Colony** (1630), also desired to worship the Lord as they saw fit. The Puritans were Anglicans who disagreed with certain church practices. They came to America to set up a community based on scriptural principles. They considered their settlement a "city that is set on an hill" (Matt. 5:14), a light shining in darkness. They wanted to show others the truth of God. The experiment succeeded for a while. But the second-generation Puritans did not know the hardships and persecutions their parents had suffered in England. These people knew only peace and prosperity. Many trusted their form of godliness for salvation rather than Christ's blood. Christians today must beware of the danger of "having a form of godliness, but denying the power thereof" (II Tim. 3:5).

In general the English colonies offered the greatest religious freedom. Although freedom was limited and some groups suffered persecution, the principle of religious freedom was gradually accepted. Eventually Presbyterians, Anglicans, Baptists, and Roman Catholics were allowed to practice their religions freely.

In the parts of Canada ruled by France, there was no religious freedom. The Roman Catholic Church controlled the religious life of the settlements. When English Protestants moved into Canada, problems arose. Religious and cultural differences between the French and English are still a major source of difficulty for the Canadians.

Like French Canada, the Spanish colonies in America had no religious freedom. The Spanish did not even allow Protestants in their lands in the New World because the Roman Catholic Church was the religion supported by the government. As the Roman Church became established in southern North America and Latin America, it grew wealthy. It received land and money from wealthy members who died or wanted to give gifts to the church as a work toward earning salvation. However, this wealth caused much corruption in the church. Some churchmen were truly concerned about religious matters and converting the Indians to Roman Catholicism, but many gave in to the temptations of luxurious living that surrounded them.

LOOKING AT FIRSTHAND ACCOUNTS

Coming to a New Land

William Bradford kept a journal of the Pilgrims' venture to America. The following selection is from Bradford's *History of Plymouth Plantation.* It tells about the Pilgrims' first glimpse of America. Many of the same impressions probably went through the minds of other new settlers in other locations.

But here I cannot but stay and make a pause, and stand half amazed at this poor people's present condition; and so I think will the reader, too, when he well considers the same. Being thus passed the vast ocean, and a sea of troubles before in their preparation . . . , they had now no friends to welcome them nor inns to entertain or refresh their weather-beaten bodies; no houses or much less towns to repair to, to seek succor. It is recorded in scripture, as a mercy to the Apostle and his shipwrecked company, that the barbarians shewed them no small kindness in refreshing them, but these savage barbarians, when they met with them (as after will appear), were readier to fill their sides full of arrows than otherwise. And for the season it was winter, and they that know the winters of that country know them to be sharp and violent, and subject to cruel and fierce storms, dangerous to travel to known places, much more to search an unknown coast. Besides, what could they see but a hideous and desolate wilderness, full of wild beasts and wild men—and what multitudes there might be of them they knew not. Neither could they, as it were, go up to the top of Pisgah to view from this wilderness a more goodly country to feed their hopes; for which way soever they turned their eyes (save upward to the heavens) they could have little solace or content in respect of any outward objects. For summer being done, all things stand upon them with a weather-beaten face, and the whole country, full of woods and thickets, represented a wild and savage hue. . . . What could now sustain them but the Spirit of God and His grace? May not and ought not the children of these fathers rightly say: "Our fathers were Englishmen which came over this great ocean and were ready to perish in this wilderness; but they cried unto the Lord, and He heard their voice and looked on their adversity."

William Bradford

Log cabins served as schoolhouses for early settlers. A priority in English colonies, education enabled common people to read their Bibles as well as improve their position in life.

Education in the New World

The people who came to the New World brought with them the ideas of the Old World. The settlers used this knowledge to shape their culture in the New World.

In the English North American colonies, education was considered important. The settlers in Massachusetts believed that education was necessary for reading Scripture, learning of God, and understanding His will. Before there was a school building, parents taught their children at home. The parents recognized their God-given responsibility to teach their children (Deut. 6:7; Prov. 22:6). As towns and villages grew, one of the first buildings the settlers set up was the school. Then they hired a teacher. These schools were often simple one-room buildings with one teacher. For six to eight years, boys attended school and learned the basics of reading, writing, speaking, and mathematics.

After finishing this schooling, a boy who had studied hard and had done well might be able to attend one of the new colleges. Most of the early colleges in the English colonies were founded to promote biblical learning and to train preachers to minister to the people. Harvard, William and Mary, Yale, Princeton, Rutgers, and Dartmouth were just some of the schools founded to prepare young men to serve the Lord. The students studied Latin, Greek, Hebrew, theology, writing, and speech. Not many years passed, however, before these schools left Bible teaching to concentrate on other subjects.

In the colonies where the Roman Catholic Church was strong, less emphasis was put on education. In French Canada, only the wealthy pursued education. The sons of wealthy men received a basic education in the colonies and often traveled to Europe to study in the universities. Because the Roman Church did not encourage Bible reading, they felt it unnecessary to teach the poorer people to read or write. Although the church set up some schools, few people had the time or money to attend. The colonial leaders saw little reason to educate the people, for they were simply farmers with little need for learning. This lack of education proved to be a great problem later when the colonies gained independence. Because the people were uneducated, they were unready to handle the responsibilities of governing.

Section Review

1. How did the English colonies' views on religious freedom differ from the views of the Spanish and French?
2. What was the major religion of Canada?
3. What caused corruption among the Roman Catholic clergy?
4. How did religious belief affect education in the colonies?
5. What was the purpose of education in the English North American colonies?
6. For what reason were many early American colleges founded?

7. Why was education less important in the Catholic colonies?

Why did religious beliefs have an effect on the colonies and their government?

Yale is the second oldest college in the United States. Here it is shown in 1805 and today.

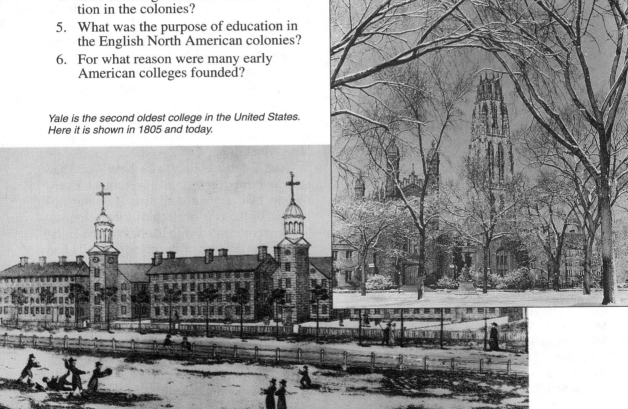

Changes in the New World

Many miles of unexplored land faced the first settlers of the New World. Exploring and settling this vast amount of territory took much of the energy of the American people until the twentieth century. The early settlers began the task of learning about their new home.

Restored Williamsburg, Virginia, features townspeople in historic costume.

Exploration and Colonization

Whichever European nation first explored a new territory usually claimed that land as its own. The largest landholders were France and England. France claimed territory stretching from eastern Canada south to the Gulf of Mexico, including the Great Lakes and the Mississippi River. The English claimed the land along the east coast of North America west to the Appalachian Mountains. Although the English king gave some colonies grants for land extending from sea to sea, east to west, these grants often overlapped French holdings. As settlement progressed, these claims led to French-English conflicts.

Ruling the Colonies

By the mid-1700s, the English colonies between the Atlantic coast and the Appalachian Mountains contained over one million people. In contrast, only about seventy thousand settlers lived in the French territory stretching from Canada down the Mississippi River to Louisiana. Fewer than eight thousand European people called the Spanish territories in the West and in Florida home. What made the British territory so successful?

In their new lands, European nations established colonies, which they controlled. The amount and type of control differed from colony to colony. In general, England gave its colonies more freedom for self-rule, while France kept a tighter hold on its colonies. This freedom allowed English colonies to expand at a greater rate.

Each English colony in the New World had some control over its own government. Every colony had a governor, usually either appointed by the king or elected by the colonists. The governor ruled with the help of the legislature. The citizens of the colony usually had the privilege of electing members of the legislature, although citizenship was limited to free, white men who owned some property or paid taxes. The legislature obtained rights and privileges from the king and colonial governor by withholding money from them. The English colonists' heritage of self-rule prepared them well for independence. They were ready to run and maintain a stable government.

In contrast to the English colonists, the French colonists had little say in their government. The settlement of the New World took place during the reigns of absolute kings. The French king believed he should have absolute rule over his Canadian colonies as well as over his country. He appointed governors who ruled Canada without a legislature. The king also controlled the colonies' trade and taxation.

Canada's wealth supported the king's court in France rather than developing the land of Canada. The French Canadians had no heritage of self-rule. When France lost Canada to England in 1763 (as a result of the French and Indian War), the French and English colonists differed over how to rule. These differences added to the delay of Canadian independence until the nineteenth century.

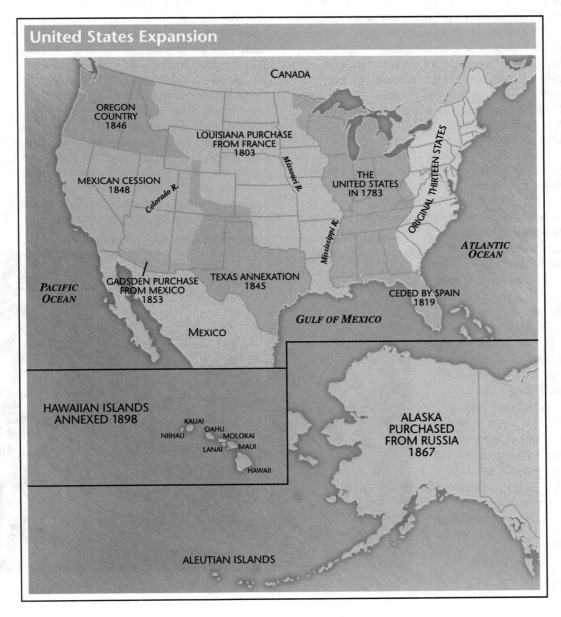

United States Expansion

CANADA

OREGON COUNTRY 1846

LOUISIANA PURCHASE FROM FRANCE 1803

Missouri R.

THE UNITED STATES IN 1783

ORIGINAL THIRTEEN STATES

MEXICAN CESSION 1848

Colorado R.

PACIFIC OCEAN

GADSDEN PURCHASE FROM MEXICO 1853

TEXAS ANNEXATION 1845

Mississippi R.

ATLANTIC OCEAN

CEDED BY SPAIN 1819

GULF OF MEXICO

MEXICO

HAWAIIAN ISLANDS ANNEXED 1898

KAUAI
OAHU
NIIHAU MOLOKAI
LANAI MAUI
HAWAII

ALASKA PURCHASED FROM RUSSIA 1867

ALEUTIAN ISLANDS

CENTER STAGE

Battle on the Plains of Abraham

During the French and Indian War, France slowly lost control of its forts in what is now the United States. By 1759, with all its forts on the Great Lakes and Lake Champlain fallen into British hands, New France was left with Louisiana and a little territory in the St. Lawrence River Valley. Now the British waited in the waters below Quebec.

Months before, Marquis de Montcalm, leader of the French troops, had requested that France send reinforcements; but France was too occupied with her own battles in Europe. Montcalm called in men (ages twelve to eighty) and troops from the surrounding area and amassed a defending force of 16,200 men. Strengthened and fortified, they waited.

British General James Wolfe arrived in June 1759 with 13,500 sailors, 8,500 soldiers, and 168 ships. By July the English ships had begun bombarding Quebec, but Wolfe knew that he needed to land troops if he was to take over the city. How could he get his troops up the steep cliffs that surrounded Quebec?

In July, Wolfe tried to take Beauport Flats, but the flats were defended. He lost 200 men. In another effort, Wolfe landed 2,000 men across the river from the flats, but the French and Indians attacked. Wolfe lost another 443 men. In September he tried a site twelve miles upstream. If he did not take the city soon, ice would close up the river, and he would be forced to retreat. Then the advantage he had hoped for came to light. As he returned from the failed mission upstream, Wolfe saw a small dry streambed that went from the river to the heights above just two miles from the city.

On September 12, Wolfe ordered his men to divert attention with maneuvers against Beauport Flats. At 4:00 A.M. an advance guard of twenty-four men clambered up the streambed and overpowered thirty French guards asleep in their tents. Now the British could march up the streambed in a double column. When dawn broke, British troops were on the Plains of Abraham. Marquis de Montcalm refused to believe that the British were "where they have no right to be" until he saw them with his own eyes.

Montcalm could have sent word for troops at Cap Rouge to come and cut off the British with a pincer movement (an attack from both sides). Or he could have stayed within the city walls and waited for winter to seal the British fate. Instead he ordered the French army to assemble.

The Death of General Wolfe *by Henry Bryan Hall (Library of Congress)*

After weeks of frustration, the British scaled the cliffs to reach the Plains of Abraham where the Battle of Quebec took place.

When the two armies had marched within forty yards of one another, Wolfe ordered his men to fire. The shots thundered. They reloaded and fired again. Before they fired again, the smoke cleared, and the British saw that the French line was riddled with holes. Wolfe gave the order to charge. His wrist was already bound with a handkerchief to stanch the blood from a bullet wound. As they advanced, Wolfe was hit again in the stomach. Still he advanced. Then he was struck in the chest. As the dying thirty-two-year-old Wolfe was carried from the field, he heard with satisfaction that the French were on the run.

Marquis de Montcalm tried to rally his troops as they fled, but he was struck by the bullet that would cause his death. When he was buried a few days later, a nun wrote that, with Montcalm, New France was laid in the tomb.

The city did not immediately surrender. As Wolfe's replacement, General Townsend considered leaving Quebec for the winter; the garrison commander of Quebec finally surrendered the besieged city. The date was September 18, 1759. By spring, the French and Indian War was ended.

The United States Constitution is the basis for most of the world's written constitutions.

Independence in the Colonies

Between 1776 and 1903 most of the colonies of North America gained independence from their mother countries. The story of how the thirteen English colonies in North America became the **United States of America** is probably familiar to you. The colonists' success in the **Revolutionary War** finally brought them complete freedom from English rule in 1783. The temporary legislature of the new nation wrote a constitution, which the new states approved. After the states ratified (voted to accept) the Constitution, they elected men to serve in the new **Congress,** the nation's legislature.

The **Constitution** is the most important document of U.S. history. The Constitution outlines the pattern of government. It sets down limits of power on both the government and the citizens and guarantees certain rights for the people. The United States has a representative government in which the citizens elect leaders to office. Each citizen has the responsibility to be aware of issues, to have an opinion on them, and to vote accordingly when given the opportunity. Elected officials have the responsibility to rule wisely and to uphold the laws of the land.

The type of government set up by the United States recognized a biblical view of man and attempted to restrain his sinful nature. Both the government and the people are kept in check by this form of government. No one part of the government—whether it be president, legislature, or court—should have too much power. Each branch of government checks the other. The government then checks the people by passing and enforcing laws. Most important, the people check the government by electing those who run it. For over two hundred years this system has successfully

The Canadian Parliament buildings are located in Ottawa, Canada.

provided a stable government for the United States.

From 1763 to 1867 Canada prepared for and achieved self-rule, or independence in domestic matters. When Great Britain obtained Canada in 1763, the majority of the population was French. Because the French did not have experience in running their government, they were not given self-rule. Instead, the British king and Parliament controlled the colony. The British government protected the French way of life by passing the **Quebec Act** in 1774. This act guaranteed the continuance of French law and custom in the French part of Canada (mainly Quebec), including the special position of the Roman Catholic Church. The Quebec Act greatly influenced French Canadian reaction to the Revolutionary War. Because relations with Britain were so good and treatment of the French was fair, the Canadians refused to join the colonies in a bid for independence. Instead, Canada became a haven for Loyalists fleeing America. Many Loyalists made their home in Nova Scotia.

As more Britons came to Canada, they wanted independence, but there were advantages to British rule. Under Britain, Canada did not have to maintain an army or navy; Britain was committed to Canadian defense. Canada also had a ready market for all its products; Britain bought and resold Canadian goods around the world. Britain also supplied Canada with all its trade needs.

But by the end of the 1830s, these advantages were not enough. Riots and rebellion broke out in Montreal and Toronto. Britain sent the earl of Durham to Canada to assess the situation. After five months of observing and listening to complaints, he presented the **Durham Report** to the British government. In this report the earl analyzed the problems and suggested that Britain relax control of Canada. The British government tried hard to satisfy both the French and British. Finally, in 1867 the **British North America Act** made Canada a self-ruling dominion. On July 1, 1867, the new nation was proclaimed "One Dominion under the Name of Canada," a name which comes from Psalm 72:8: "He shall have dominion also from sea to sea." Although Canada ruled itself in domestic matters, it was still under Britain's control. Canada set up its own representative government similar to those of the United States and Great Britain.

Britain's control over its foreign holdings continued to weaken until finally in 1931 several former British holdings were declared independent and equal. At that time Canada continued its association with Britain as a member of the **British Commonwealth of Nations,** a group of nations who swear allegiance to Britain.

The Canadian seal includes the fleur-de-lis of France, the lions of England and Scotland, and the harp of Ireland.

SETTINGS—Canada

Location—Canada is the second largest country in the world. (Russia is the largest.) Canada includes all of mainland North America between the United States border and the Arctic Ocean as well as the Arctic Islands (not including Greenland). Canada's eastern border is the Atlantic Ocean, and its western border is the Pacific Ocean and Alaska.

Climate—Weather patterns in Canada generally move from west to east. Temperatures vary when warm air surges north from the United States or when polar air pushes down from the Arctic. Along the border of the United States, Canada's climate tends to be similar regionally to the United States, but colder due to the higher latitudes.

Canada's coastal regions are greatly affected by the ocean. While two-thirds of tundra and subartic Canada is trapped in below 0°F weather

in January, the marine west coast climate of the Pacific coast province of British Columbia stays above freezing due to the mild ocean winds. The coastal regions in the east and west both tend to have much higher precipitation as well.

Topography—Canada's general topography is an extension of United States topography. One distinctive feature is the Arctic Islands and surrounding mainland area. This area is treeless tundra that is too cold and dry for large plant growth. All but a thin top layer of soil is permanently frozen. Many Arctic animals live in these tundra areas, including caribou, musk oxen, lemmings, polar bears, and ptarmigans.

Another feature is the huge inland Hudson Bay. Although Hudson Bay is surrounded by tundra along its eastern and western coasts, its southern lowlands are covered with scrubby forests and swamps. This area also has huge deposits of peat (decayed vegetable matter), which is harvested and sold as a soil enrichment product.

Natural Resources—Canada has abundant natural resources. Fish along its coastal waters have been used for centuries for food and income. Hydroelectric power is abundant because of Canada's many rivers. Forests of the west are used in the lumbering industry. Besides these renewable resources, Canada has metal ores and oil deposits.

Geography & Culture—Canada's vast land holdings have helped it establish a productive industrial economy. Nevertheless, due to the harsh northern climate, most of the population lies in the Plains region (north of Montana and North Dakota) and along the United States/Canada border.

Canada is a federation divided into ten provinces and two territories. However, another division exists due to language conflicts. Because the French originally settled the St. Lawrence River area, more than 80 percent of the population of Quebec speaks French. Protective of its distinct heritage, French-speaking Quebec has often come into conflict with the rest of English-speaking Canada.

Settings Review

1. What three oceans border Canada?
2. Why does British Columbia have a milder climate than the rest of Canada?
3. What product is harvested around Hudson Bay?
4. List three of Canada's natural resources.
5. Why do most people in the province of Quebec speak French?

From what you have read so far of Canadian history and the information above, do you think that the French-speaking Canadians should be allowed to separate from the rest of Canada? Explain your answer.

Canada is a land of contrasts. A Scotch-Irish bagpiper plays a tune in front of an Inuit totem pole.

Handbills advertising the new Transcontinental Railroad

Settlement and Economic Growth

Both before and after independence, a major challenge facing the people of the Americas was cultivating their vast territories. The land stretching from sea to sea held great resources of fertile soil, minerals, and wildlife. Throughout the Americas, tapping this wealth was a major goal.

Following the Revolutionary War, Americans started moving west across the Appalachian Mountains into the Great Plains. Until 1890 the United States had a still unsettled frontier region. The frontier offered land and opportunity for millions of immigrants. Throughout the nineteenth century many families traveled west in covered wagons. At first they stopped and settled in the Midwest; later settlers continued for months across the plains to the Rocky Mountains and beyond to the California coast. They obtained land cheaply from the government and set up homesteads, which eventually grew into farms. Often the nearest neighbors were miles away, and there was little chance for fellowship. Children were taught at home between their farm chores. Prairie life was hard and lonely for the early settlers.

As more and more people went west, towns and villages developed. With the completion of the **Transcontinental Railroad** (1869), travel to the West was easier, and even more people moved there. When enough people lived in a region, the territory was admitted to the Union as a new state. The goods of the western plains—grain, cattle, pigs, and sheep—were transported quickly back East, while manufactured goods were shipped out by rail in return. As industry in the East grew, agriculture in the West provided food for the growing nation. By the beginning of the twentieth century, the United States was a productive and optimistic nation, the leading nation in the Americas.

The Union Pacific and Central Pacific railroads met at Promontory Point, Utah, to form the Transcontinental Railroad.

In many ways the settlement of Canada was similar to that of the United States. The vast land areas of the western region were opened up for settlement with the completion of the **Canadian Pacific Railroad** (1885), linking the east and west coasts. The government offered land cheaply to Canadians and immigrants. Life in Canada was hard, especially in the harsh winters, but the fertile soil produced abundant harvests for the families who settled there. For most of the nineteenth century, Canada remained an agricultural nation, supplying great amounts of food to Great Britain and Europe. Canadian industry was located mostly in the East, as it was in the United States.

Section Review

1. What land claims led to conflicts between the English and French?
2. Which colonies had more self-rule than the others?
3. How did absolutism affect rule in the colonies?
4. Which colonists were better prepared for independence?
5. What document defines the type of government in the United States? What type of government is it?
6. What act (a) affected French Canadian response to the Revolutionary War? (b) established Canada as a dominion?
7. What one factor made it easy for immigrants in the United States and Canada to get farmland?
8. What railroads connected the East and West in the United States and Canada?

How do transportation and communication unite a nation?

Summary

In 1492 Columbus discovered the New World. Over the next few centuries, the continent of North America became home for millions of people. The continent began as colonies of European nations. North America was mostly controlled by France and Britain. The people came to the New World for many reasons: wealth, fame, adventure, political freedom, and religious freedom. In the eighteenth and nineteenth centuries, all the colonies became independent of their mother nations. They had to build their own governments. In the United States and Canada, the people set up representative governments. These governments have proved stable. Canada and the United States settled their lands and prospered from new agriculture and industry.

CHAPTER REVIEW

People, Places, and Terms to Know

Old World
North America
slave trade
Juan Ponce de León
Pánfilo de Narváez
Cabeza de Vaca
Hernando de Soto
Pedro Menéndez de
   Avilés
St. Augustine
Juan de Oñate
missions
Jacques Cartier

Montreal
scurvy
Samuel de Champlain
Father of New France
habitation
coureurs du bois
Sir Walter Raleigh
Roanoke, North
   Carolina
"Lost Colony"
Jamestown
John Smith
Sir Thomas Dale

John Rolfe
Pocahontas
cash crop
subsistence farming
Pilgrims
Puritans
Massachusetts Bay
   Colony
United States of
   America
Revolutionary War
Congress
Constitution

Quebec Act
Durham Report
British North America
   Act
British Commonwealth
   of Nations
Transcontinental
   Railroad
Canadian Pacific
   Railroad

Review Questions

Ordering
Which came first, (a) or (b)?

1. (a) St. Augustine
2. (a) Massachusetts Bay Colony
3. (a) Quebec Act
4. (a) Canadian Pacific Railroad

(b) Jamestown
(b) Plymouth settlement
(b) British North America Act
(b) Transcontinental Railroad

Listing
For each of the following questions, list at least three items.

5. What did de Vaca discover about the Indians?

6. Why did people come to the New World?

7. Which European nations established the largest colonies in the early years of New World colonization?

Short Answer
For each of the following pairs of items, write a sentence or two explaining the connection between them.

8. Narváez / de Vaca

9. Pilgrims / Puritans

10. Revolutionary War / Quebec Act

Living in the New World

The following statements describe life in the New World. Match each description of the New World with the land where the speaker probably lived. Some sentences may have more than one answer.

    (a) French colonies

    (b) Spanish colonies

    (c) English colonies

11. I lived under the rule of the Spanish king.

12. I was a slave imported to work on a rice plantation.

13. I spent much time fur trapping.

14. My family moved westward in covered wagons.

15. I fought in a war to gain independence from England.

16. I spoke French.

17. I attended school in a one-room schoolhouse.

18. The landowner on whose farm I worked did not feel that I needed to attend school.

19. Because of our education, we were well prepared for self-rule.

20. We did not have enough people in the New World to possess our land.

Think About It!

The United States fought a revolution to gain its independence from England within 150 years of its first colony. Canada did not gain independence from European control for almost four hundred years after Cartier first came to Canada. Canada had riots and revolts but never had a war. What are some advantages or disadvantages to each situation?

How did having a war add to the United States's patriotism? What were the advantages of Canada's having the protection of England?

CHAPTER 9

"Hurry, Babette! Everything must be perfect. And we must not be late!" The pretty young duchess scolded her maid. Dashing about the chamber to gather things for her mistress, Babette sighed inwardly but worked faster.

"One more ribbon to tie, Mademoiselle. Then you shall be the most beautiful belle at the ball. His Majesty, the king, will be enchanted." Babette deftly tied the pink silk into a fashionable bow and made final adjustments to her lady's costume. "Ah, there you are, a picture beyond words."

Striking a stately pose, the duchess examined herself in the mirrors that lined the room. Her powdered wig shone pure white on her head. (The metal frame underneath kept it secure.) Her silk and satin skirts fell gracefully from her tiny waist. Every lace and ribbon was in its proper place. Nothing must be amiss at the ball or the duchess would be the subject of the other ladies' gossip. She dreaded that thought and checked everything once more.

"We are ready, Babette. My cape, please."

A.D. 1600 - A.D. 1900

1600

Louis XV

Isaac Newton
Discovers Gravity 1665

English Bill
of Rights 1688

The Age of
Absolutism

James Watt Develops the Steam Engine 1775

Catherine the Great
Rules Russia 1762-96

Maria Theresa Rules
Austria 1740-80

Peter the Great Rules
Russia 1682-1725

Napoleon Becomes First Consul in France 1800

John Wesley 1703-1791

Age of Reason 1600-1800

1700   1800   1900

Frederick the Great
Rules Prussia 1740-86

Isaac Watts Writes "Hymns
and Spiritual Songs" 1707

The French Revolution Begins 1789

Mozart Tours Europe as Child
Prodigy at Six Years Old 1762

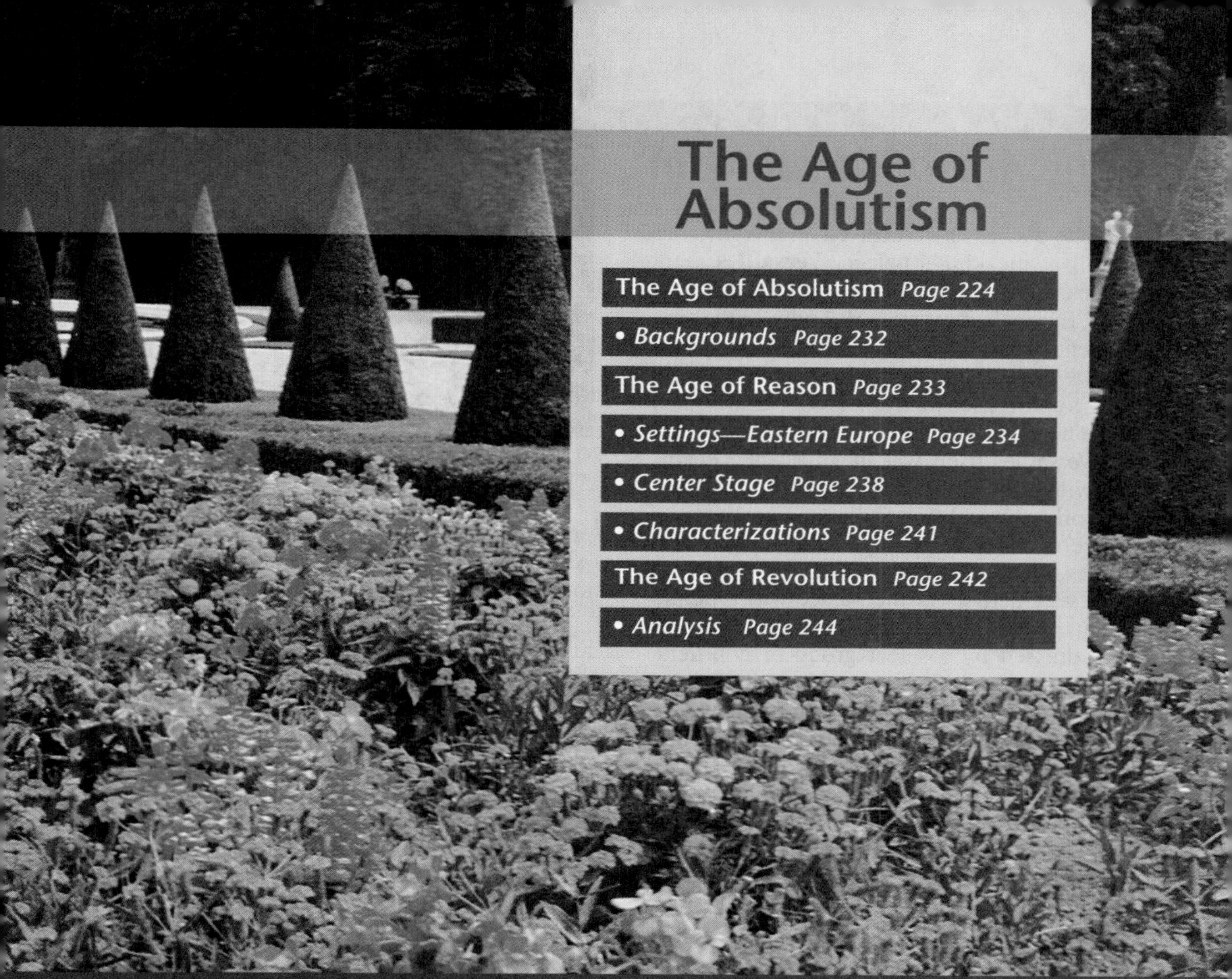

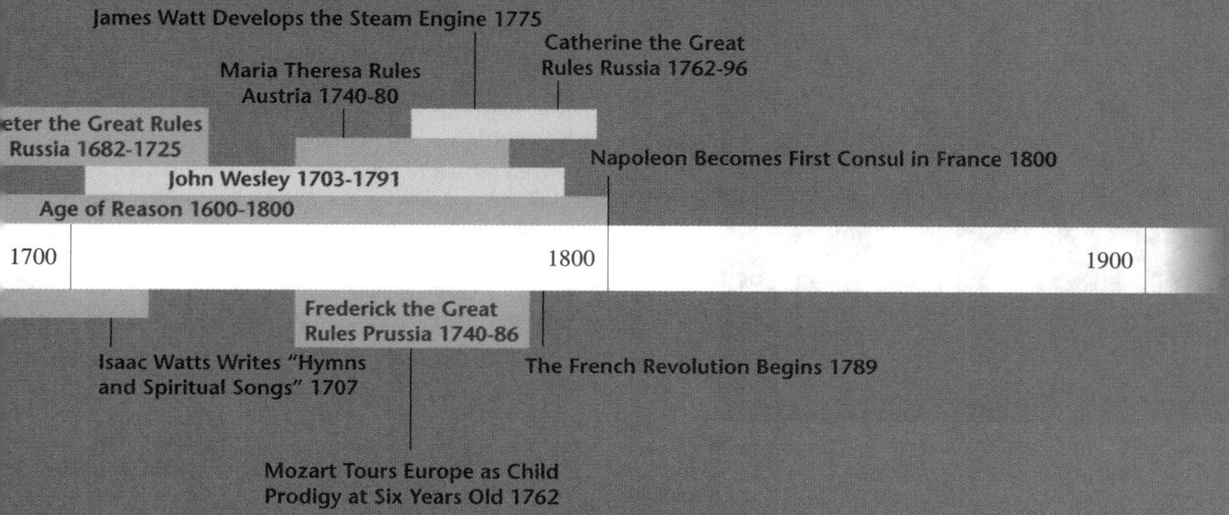

The Age of Absolutism

The duchess had received an invitation to a ball at the king's palace, **Versailles**. Versailles was the home of France's king, **Louis XIV,** Europe's most powerful ruler of the seventeenth century. An invitation to Versailles was a great honor. **Courtiers** (nobles at the king's court) tried many means, often devious, to be noticed by the king at Versailles.

Versailles itself was magnificent. Gleaming with gold, silver, precious jewels, and fine artwork, the palace displayed the extravagance of the baroque style. Louis used Versailles to show off his power and wealth.

Every activity at the palace was a public event, beginning in the morning, when Louis was dressed by a select group of courtiers. These same men attended to his undressing at night. As many as two thousand nobles at a time stayed at Versailles and sought for any

Ornate carvings gilded with gold give a hint of the wealth represented by the palace at Versailles.

privilege that would bring them near the king. After gaining the king's attention, they hoped to receive favors from him.

Every evening at Versailles, servants lit hundreds of candles and scurried about making final preparations. At the stated time, men and women, dressed in their finest clothes, arrived in coaches. The guests accompanied the king as he played games, watched plays, gambled, and listened to concerts. In these activities, as in every activity at Versailles, the courtiers followed a strict code of etiquette. Louis stated these rules and knew of any violations. How, when, and where one stood, sat, and spoke were all matters regulated by Louis. An improper action often resulted in one's being excluded from Versailles. Courtiers spent much time discussing the proper etiquette and fashion. These vain people depended on Louis's approval for their happiness.

Late that night the duchess returned to her lodging.

"Mademoiselle, did you enjoy yourself?" Babette asked as she helped her mistress with her dress.

"Oh, Babette. It was superb! So much glitter and laughter! But now I must sleep, for His Majesty has extended another invitation for tomorrow."

Portrait of Two Young Girls *by Alexis-Simon Belle shows children dressed as miniature adults.*

Chapter 9

Louis XIV (1643-1715) was an **absolute ruler,** one who holds complete, or absolute, power over his people. This type of rule is called **absolutism.** An absolute ruler directs all the activities in his kingdom, from major state decisions to everyday details, even what type of uniforms his servants should wear. In return, every activity of his subjects is expected to glorify the absolute ruler. He believes that what he does is good for his people and that they should try to please and imitate him. From the description of life at Versailles, you can see that Louis XIV was an absolute ruler.

Louis XIV Rules France

Louis was the strongest absolute ruler in Europe during this period, which is known as the *Age of Absolutism.* His rule set the example for later kings and emperors. A phrase that well describes Louis's attitude (and which he may even have said) is "I am the state." This means that he and his people were one. Louis made all the decisions, and the people praised him. He was known as the **Sun King.** Everything in France—and Europe—revolved around him. Nothing took place in government or society without his

Louis XIV--The Sun King

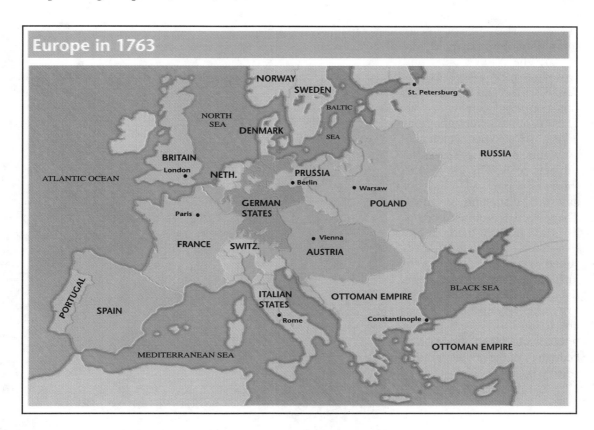

influence touching it, just as the sun's rays touch everything on earth.

Louis's decisions and policies grew out of his absolute power. In the area of economics he believed that all wealth gained from the colonies belonged to and benefited the state, not individuals. In the area of foreign policy he often waged war, both to show his army's power and to conquer others. In the area of religion he forced Frenchmen to follow Roman Catholicism, the religion he practiced. He thought it wrong to allow more than one religion in an absolutist country. Louis's encouragement of the arts and learning earned this era in French history the title "The Great Century."

Under Louis XIV, France prospered. He was a strong leader whom the people liked. Nevertheless, absolute power caused problems in France. The king and his nobles spent huge sums of money but paid few, if any, taxes, leaving the middle class and peasants to carry a large tax burden. Near the end of his reign, Louis suffered defeats in war. These problems stemmed from his desire for power, which outgrew his desire to serve his subjects well. The kings who followed Louis XIV did not have his leadership abilities. They lived frivolous, corrupt lives and ignored their people. Eventually their behavior resulted in the end of absolutism in France. The fall of absolutism illustrates the message of Proverbs: "When the righteous are in authority, the people rejoice: but when the wicked beareth rule, the people mourn" (Proverbs 29:2).

A Modern Exodus: Revocation of the Edict of Nantes

The Reformation brought true Christianity to France. Frenchmen who converted to Protestantism were called Huguenots. Although most of France remained Roman Catholic, in 1598 the French king issued the **Edict of Nantes** (NAHNT). This edict guaranteed the Huguenots the right to practice their faith freely and without interference.

Louis XIV disliked the Edict of Nantes. Being an absolute ruler, Louis thought that there should be one king, one nation, and one church—and that church must be the Roman Catholic Church. The king allowed Roman Catholics to persecute Protestants despite the Edict. He hoped the Huguenots would convert to Roman Catholicism. Finally, in 1685 King Louis revoked, or withdrew, the Edict of Nantes altogether.

The Catholic Church influenced French politics but did not promote godliness. Today Notre Dame Cathedral is a well-known landmark.

The government decreed that no one could practice any religion except Roman Catholicism. Anyone caught participating in a Protestant service could be executed. As a result, many Huguenots died for their faith. Some, however, gave up their faith and became Roman Catholics. Others, refusing to abandon their religion, said with Peter and the other apostles that they must obey God and not men (Acts 5:29). With sadness, these Huguenots left their homes and possessions and departed from France.

Louis XIV was horrified at the loss of the Huguenots. He had thought they would convert rather than leave. The Huguenots were among the finest workers in the nation. Many bankers, weavers, and merchants were Huguenots. France could not afford to lose such men, so Louis had all the borders closed and forbade anyone to leave the country without his permission. Determined to preserve their faith, the Protestants found ways to escape. Some hid in barrels aboard ships sailing from France. Others disguised themselves as peasants and sneaked out of the country. In all, probably more than two hundred thousand Huguenots fled.

Protestant countries in Europe welcomed the Huguenots. They were glad to have such talented, hard-working subjects. Over a third of the Huguenots went to the Netherlands. From there many went to the Dutch colony at the Cape of Good Hope. The ruler of Brandenburg in Germany (later called Prussia) set up stations to aid the Huguenots on their way. He paid to establish settlements for them in his territory. Many went to England and from there to the American colonies—especially Virginia and the Carolinas.

These immigrants proved extremely valuable to their new home countries. They served with distinction and valor in the army and proved to be diligent, obedient citizens. Most notably, they

Many Huguenots were killed before they could flee the country.

brought secrets of French manufacturing with them. For example, the French had made a large profit from silk production, but the Huguenots introduced the process to the rest of Europe. The loss to France proved a great gain to the Protestant nations of Europe.

Absolutism in Other Kingdoms

Louis XIV set the example of absolutist rule for other European monarchs. During and after his reign, the other courts of Europe began to look and act much like Versailles. The following section describes some of these absolute rulers.

Peter the Great of Russia

Maria Theresa, queen of Austria

Austria

In 1740 **Maria Theresa** (1740-80) came to the throne of Austria. During her reign she remodeled the royal palace outside Vienna (the Austrian capital) to look much like Versailles. Vienna itself became an important center for the arts, especially music. Maria Theresa added support to her absolute power by tightening her hold on the government and by improving conditions for the peasants. Her foreign affairs policies included sending troops to fight in the wars of Europe and taking territory from Poland.

Russia

When **Peter the Great** (1682-1725) came to the throne, Russia was a backward country. During his reign Peter worked to make his power absolute and to modernize Russia. As a young **czar** (ZAHR; the Russian title for "emperor"), he traveled in western Europe. The goal of his trip was to learn several trades and to meet other monarchs. Back in Russia he put these Western methods and ideas into practice. To increase his power, he eliminated much local government and centered it in himself. He also conquered land from Sweden and built **St. Petersburg** on the Baltic Sea.

Catherine the Great, who ruled after Peter, (1762-96), increased the power of the throne even more. She also increased Russian territory, adding land in the west and south, including part of Poland. During Catherine's reign, Russia became a strong power in Europe.

Frederick II, the Great

Prussia

The kingdom of **Prussia** was the beginning of modern-day Germany. The most powerful king of Prussia was **Frederick the Great** (1740-86). Continuing the policies of his father and grandfather, he made Prussia a strong European kingdom. He built up the army and used it to add territory to Prussia. Frederick also encouraged the arts and learning; he himself played the flute and studied science. His court in Berlin attracted many artists and writers as well as Prussian nobles.

England

England was an exception to the movement toward absolutism. For many centuries the English legislative body, **Parliament,** had been gaining power from the king. This process began in 1215, when King John signed the **Magna Carta** (MAG-nuh KAHR-tuh), which guaranteed the nobles certain rights and limited the king's power. During the seventeenth century, King Charles I tried to take away those rights and rule as an absolute king. His actions resulted in a civil war between his supporters and Parliament's supporters (1642-48). The king's forces lost the war, and the king was executed. Parliament again limited the king's power. However, two more kings tried to take power from Parliament. Finally, many questions about the king's power were settled with the **English Bill of Rights.** This bill was

The nobles of England forced King John to sign the Magna Carta, which gave many new rights to the nobility.

William III and Mary were given the privilege to rule by the English Parliament, but Parliament still retained much power.

accepted in 1688 before the new monarchs **William and Mary** could take the throne. It gave several rights to Parliament and the people. While the nations of Europe headed toward increasing absolute rule, England moved toward a government of limited monarchy and freedom for the people.

Section Review

1. Who was the most important political figure in Europe during this time?

2. Why were other absolutist kings in France less successful?

3. Which monarch made her capital a center for the arts?

4. Which monarch toured Europe and learned trades to teach his people?

5. Under what English king did a civil war occur?

6. Which English monarchs accepted limits to their power?

Why do you think the extravagant living of the aristocrats fanned the fires of revolution?

Men's periwigs covered shaved heads.

Men as well as women painted, patched, and rouged their faces.

Women's wigs were built on wire and muslin frames. Sometimes they were so tall that they brushed against chandelier candles and caught fire.

Panniers, stiffened with cane, made women's hips fashionably wide.

The walking stick became a necessary fashion accessory.

Lace in abundance was a must for ladies and gentlemen.

Men hung leather purses from their belts.

Fans held in front of the face hid bad teeth or blew away bad breath.

Man's suit and accessories
3000£

Woman's dress and accessories
1500£

Taking the Grand Tour

During the 1700s it became popular for young Englishmen to complete their education by taking a Grand Tour of the Continent (continental Europe). France was at the height of style and sophistication, so young men went there to throw off their coarse behavior and put on the polish that set them apart as the aristocracy of England.

Under the watchful eye of his tutor and cared for by his valet, the young man set off. The first step in the tour was to cross the English Channel to Calais, France. For many young men this was a test in itself since seasickness was often the result of the turbulent crossing. In Paris, all outward traces of the backward Englishman were erased as he was fitted for a totally French wardrobe. Dressed like a Frenchman, he was now ready to be introduced to French society. After his introduction in France, the tourist went on to Dijon, Lyons, and finally Marseilles.

The next step of his tour presented problems. He now had to go on to Italy. He had two routes to choose from—the overland route by sedan chair through narrow mountain passes or the water route out onto the Mediterranean with the risk of piracy. His destination was Rome, with stops in Genoa and Florence. In Rome his tutor would keep a close eye on him to make sure he was not adversely affected by the Catholic doctrines that surrounded him. Although his parents wanted to expand his education, they also wanted to make sure he returned to England as an Anglican.

Most Grand Tours ended in Italy, but some travelers chose to continue their tour by traveling into Prussia and Austria. This portion of the journey was difficult because the living conditions were less than desirable. The Austrian court, with its emphasis on music, was worth the inconvenience though.

When the tour ended, the now polished and presentable young man was ready to take his place in English society, whether or not the tour truly increased his education. The practice of the Grand Tour continued through the 1800s and later. It extended then to the wealthy American youth and actually became a symbol of that wealth. If you read books from or based in the 1800s, you may see a reference to the "Grand Tour."

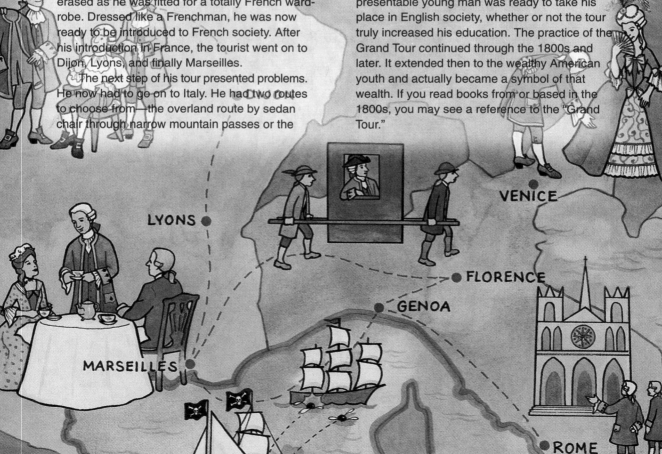

The Age of Reason

Sapere Aude! These Latin words mean "dare to know," a phrase that well describes the seventeenth and eighteenth centuries in Europe. Called the **Age of Reason,** this period saw men daring to learn about many things. They used their minds to study the world around them. They based their study on reason, the ability to think clearly and logically. God created man with a mind that could reason. He wanted people to love Him with their minds as well as their souls and hearts (Matt. 22:37). Christians should use their minds to serve God. However, reason can be overemphasized. During the Age of Reason, many people came to believe that reason could replace faith. Although many good things came out of the Age of Reason, the emphasis on man's ability often turned people away from the Lord God.

An early microscope

Reason and the Sciences

In Chapter 3 you learned about Copernicus and Galileo and the discoveries they made in astronomy (see p. 62). In the Age of Reason, another scientist, **Sir Isaac Newton,** added to that knowledge by stating the **laws of gravity and motion.** According to these laws, gravity keeps the planets in their orbits.

Scientific laws are statements that describe occurrences in nature and that have no known exceptions. The discovery of laws in nature greatly affected scientific thought and research. Aware that occurrences in nature followed orderly patterns, scientists used reason and stated more laws. These laws helped scientists better understand and predict occurrences in nature.

Scientists looked for laws in the heavens as well as in life on earth. Using **microscopes,** scientists looked at objects close up. They learned about living tissue through the discovery of individual cells and tiny organisms. The microscopes that you use in your science classroom are improvements on the ones invented by scientists of the Age of Reason. Microscopes were not limited to classrooms or laboratories, however. In the eighteenth century it was the height of fashion to have a microscope in one's drawing room. Men, women, and children alike were interested in learning more about living things.

The systematic study of nature encouraged scientists to classify their observations. The plant and animal classification systems that we still use today began at this time. To determine correct classifications, scientists spent many years collecting, naming, and recording thousands of different species.

Location—Eastern Europe is bordered in the west by Germany and in the east by Russia. The northern border of Eastern Europe is the Baltic Sea and a detached portion of Russia called Kaliningrad. The southern border includes Austria, Slovenia, Croatia, Yugoslavia, and Romania. The countries included in Eastern Europe are Poland, the Czech Republic, Slovakia, Hungary, Moldova, Ukraine, Belarus, Lithuania, Latvia, and Estonia.

Climate—The marine west coast (temperate) climate dominates the western part of this region but yields to the humid continental climate to the east. Rainfall varies from 20 to 25 inches per year. Temperatures range from 28°-32°F in the winter to 66°-73°F in the summer. The temperatures and rainfall amounts vary more in the mountainous regions.

Topography—The topography of this region is best described as a series of plains and mountains. The north begins as a marshy plain and turns into rich farmland farther south. In the north central area, plains give way to hills rising to the Carpathian Mountains. On the southern side of the mountains, the Great Hungarian Plain exists as a result of the Danube River and its tributaries.

Natural Resources—Fertile soils exist in the hill region of Poland and in the plains of the Danube. In the mountains, rich veins of iron ore and coal help local industry.

Geography & Culture—Eastern Europe has gone through many changes in the past fifty years. The region was a crossing ground for forces in World Wars I and II. Boundaries changed many times, and Poland was tossed from German control to Russian domination. With the breakup of the

Soviet Union, the area has once again changed internally and externally. Two new countries formed from what used to be the nation of Czechoslovakia. Poland, the Czech Republic, and Slovakia have also come out from the influence of the former Soviet Union and are now turning to western Europe for trade and alliances. Eastern Europe is sometimes known as the "Shatter Belt" of Europe. Strong nationalism has allowed each country to retain its individualism despite external pressures.

Settings Review

1. What mountain range runs through Eastern Europe?
2. What river drains the Great Hungarian Plain?
3. What natural resources are found in the mountains?

Why has this region been so influenced by war in Europe?

Although overrun by other countries in the past, Eastern Europe has a rich heritage of its own seen in its cities, castles, and costumed villagers celebrating Palm Sunday.

The neoclassical symmetry, columns, and domes of Versailles and the U.S. Capitol building stand in contrast to the baroque style of Versailles's interior.

Reason and the Arts

The interest in finding order in nature affected the art of the Age of Reason. Scorning the wild exuberance of the baroque style, artists emphasized restraint. Much about their new style reminds us of the art of Greece and Rome, the classical style. The art of the Age of Reason so resembled Greek and Roman art that it is called **neoclassical,** meaning "new classical." Like earlier classical styles, eighteenth-century neoclassicism emphasized balance, order, harmony, and simplicity.

In architecture, neoclassicism gradually replaced the baroque style. The palace of Versailles displays a mixture of baroque and classical styles. Baroque paintings, sculpture, and furnishings fill the interior, but the exterior is neoclassical. The architects used columns and geometric shapes in designing the palace. These elements of classical style appear in many buildings built in the United States during the same period in history. Government buildings in the United States typically follow the neoclassical style.

In music the neoclassical period produced some of the world's finest composers and works. Louis XIV loved music, and he had musicians playing all day long at Versailles. His court composers wrote new music almost daily. The other courts of Europe copied Louis. Maria Theresa made Vienna the center of European classical music. **Franz Joseph Haydn** (HY dun) (1732-1809) and **Wolfgang Amadeus Mozart** (MOHT sahrt) (1756-91), the two leading classical composers, both performed at her court.

Franz Joseph Haydn began his career as a choirboy and ended as a court composer.

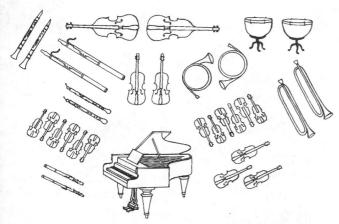

This diagram shows the instruments and arrangement of the orchestras used by classical composers.

Order and restraint characterize classical music. Baroque music had grown more and more intricate until it was almost overbearing. Classical composers used clear, simple melodies and harmonies, which were a relief to many European ears. Composers also wrote their works for more instruments, increasing the size of the orchestra. These larger groups played concerts before large audiences in public halls. Music also came into more homes with the invention of the piano and the simplification of the note system. Times of singing around the piano or listening to informal recitals filled many evenings with enjoyment and relaxation.

Neoclassical Art but Classical Music

You may find it confusing that composers of the neoclassical era are usually called simply writers of "classical music." This label is even more confusing since we often use the phrase "classical music" to describe other styles of formal music, such as baroque music.

The problem arises because *neoclassical* means "new classical." In art, architecture, and literature, the neoclassic artists and writers were copying the "classical" styles of Greece and Rome. These works were in the "new classical" style.

But musicians of this era had no idea of what Greek and Roman music sounded like. They could not therefore duplicate older styles. Composers had to settle for writing music with the qualities of neoclassical art and literature—order, balance, and restraint. This kind of music from the 1700s is called "classical" music.

There *is* a kind of neoclassical music. That term is used for some twentieth-century composers such as Heitor Villa-Lobos. (See p. 594.) These modern musicians took their inspiration from the classical composers of the Age of Reason, so *they* were the followers of a "new classical" style.

So while artists in the Age of Reason painted neoclassical canvases, composers scored classical symphonies. It's a classic example of confusing historical terms.

In a time when the other arts were imitating Rome, musicians were developing their own classic style.

Reason, Religion, and Enlightenment

During this time of absolutism in government and reason in science, a new philosophy began to change Europe and spread from there to the New World. Using reasoning, a group of men called *philosophes* (the French word for "philosopher") began to examine values as well as religious and social beliefs. Some of the most well known philosophers were Francis Bacon and John Locke from England, René Descartes (day KART) and Voltaire (vole TEHR) from France, and Immanuel Kant from Germany. They decided that knowledge and truth about anything could be discovered only by using reason. This period is called the Enlightenment.

Although the Enlightenment introduced many political and social changes that were important to democratic societies, it also brought a basic

French philosopher and writer Voltaire

Diderot catalogued the new scientific knowledge in his work Encyclopedie.

undermining of religion. The Enlightenment sought to teach knowledge separate from God, the church, or any moral base. Knowledge came not from the application of God's Word, philosophers believed, but from the use of reasoning, science, and logic. They believed that God established certain laws of nature, but after that He took His hands off and allowed the world to function alone. Beyond Creation, Enlightenment philosophy left no room for miracles or the unexplained.

The Enlightenment encouraged men and women to be confident in their abilities and potential. Immanuel Kant's *sapere aude* was a call to confidence. It taught that man could know everything that reason could figure out. "Trust in yourself and your intellect!" cried the *philosophes.* The philosophers taught that man could reach a state of perfection on earth—that man has within himself all he needs to know to deal with the questions of life. The Enlightenment gave the people of the age the same promise Satan gave Eve in the Garden of Eden: "Your eyes shall be opened, and *ye shall be as gods*" (Gen. 3:5).

Reason and Religion

During the Age of Reason, God allowed people to discover much about His creation and His work in nature. However, many of these people did not submit to the authority of God's Word about man's sin and his need of forgiveness and salvation. They refused to accept God's invitation to know Him personally. Rather, they said that God had created the universe and then stepped back. They claimed that God was no longer personally concerned with His creation. The universe ran according to scientific laws, ordered by God and understandable by man. The people who followed these beliefs called themselves **deists** (DEE ists), from the Latin word meaning "god."

Deism

The deists taught that miracles were impossible. God could not interfere with the laws He had set in motion at Creation, they said. They also taught that there was no need for worship because God was not a personal God and could not receive worship.

The most dangerous deistic belief was that one could find truth through reason rather than through Scripture. However, the Bible says that *God* is truth (John 14:6) and that *His Word* is truth (II Tim. 2:15; John 17:17). We find truth in His Word as we learn about Him. The deists thought they were wise because they used their minds, but "professing themselves to be wise, they became fools" (Rom. 1:22). Many deists later became atheists (people who believe there is no God). These "wise" men of the Age of Reason became fools when they

denied God. "The fool hath said in his heart, There is no God" (Ps. 14:1).

Methodist Revival

The deists challenged God's truth and power, but God had prepared a man to meet these challenges. In 1703 **John Wesley** was born in England. Although he grew up in a loving and religious home, he did not accept Christ as Savior until he was thirty-five. From then until his death in 1791, Wesley faithfully preached the gospel. Traveling on horseback, he rode throughout England and preached several times a day. People came from all over to hear him. His message of God's love and personal salvation through the Lord Jesus Christ spoke

Charles Wesley, like his brother, was a faithful preacher of the gospel. He also wrote several hymns.

to many hearts. Hundreds of people came to know Christ as their Savior under Wesley's preaching.

Wesley and his followers were called **Methodists.** After his death, his followers withdrew from the Church of England and formed the Methodist Church. Wesley wrote many books on Scripture and the Christian life. John Wesley's brother **Charles Wesley** contributed to this revival with the many hymns he wrote. His hymns tell of God's love and salvation through His Son. Today Christians still sing Wesley's hymns, such as "Love Divine, All Loves Excelling," "O for a Thousand Tongues to Sing," and perhaps most familiar, "Hark, the Herald Angels Sing."

Section Review

1. Who made an important discovery about gravity?

2. How did the scientists of the Age of Reason help our study of plants and animals today?

3. What artistic style reflects reason?

4. Name two important composers of this period.

5. What instrument brought more music into the home?

6. What is the most dangerous teaching of deism?

7. Who rode throughout England on horseback to preach the gospel?

Remembering past chapters and events, why do you think that so much music from this classical period has been preserved to this day?

John Wesley spent much of his time on horseback ministering to groups of believers across the countryside of England.

CHARACTERIZATIONS

Isaac Watts

When Isaac Watts was born in 1674, his father was in prison for being a Nonconformist preacher. At that time in England, a man who did not preach in accordance with the views of the leaders of the Church of England could expect to serve time in prison. The government so despised the Dissenters that it required only two people to accuse someone of dissenting, and those two people shared a cash reward for informing! Do you remember another group of people in this time period whose disagreement with the Church of England affected America?

Young Isaac grew up in this atmosphere of persecution. Dissenting Christians met in back-alley rooms, fields, and barns to hide from would-be informers. Dissenters were fined for serving communion or for preaching anywhere if five or more people were present. If there was ever a time when churches needed inspiring and encouraging hymns, it was during this time.

Young Isaac showed an interest in rhyming at an early age. When he was six, he presented his mother an acrostic for his name. (See illustration.) When he was in his early twenties, Isaac saw a need in the church. He told his father that the psalms that were sung in the church were rough and difficult. His father challenged him to write something better. Isaac Watts began writing hymns. Academically and spiritually prepared for the task, Watts produced hymns for which he is now famous.

Watts also saw a need for children to have hymns that suited their age, songs that they could sing as they went about their day. Because of this need, in 1720 he wrote *Divine and Moral Songs, for the Use of Children*. These songs addressed problems of youth at that time (and still today!) with titles such as *Against Evil Company* and *Against Pride in Clothes*.

Watts's early interest in words and rhyming served him well in his later days of hymn writing.

Watts lived a long and full life preaching the gospel, teaching, and writing books and hymns. In the spiritually dark beginning of the Age of Reason, Watts's songs and hymns inspired the faithful to stand for Christ.

Am I a soldier of the cross,
A follower of the Lamb?
And shall I fear to own His cause,
Or blush to speak His name?
Sure I must fight if I would reign;
Increase my courage, Lord!
I'll bear the toil, endure the pain,
Supported by Thy Word.

The Age of Revolution

Agricultural Revolution

The work of scientists eventually affected farmers during this period. The earliest examples of this influence appeared in Great Britain. (Other European farmers felt few changes until the nineteenth century.) British landowners began to apply scientific principles to farming. Improvements included crop rotation, fertilization, and newly invented machinery. Farmers were able to grow more in less space. Better methods of animal breeding and care increased milk and meat production. These advancements marked the beginning of modern, scientific farming.

Bigger harvests meant more food, which in turn meant increased population. For example, in Great Britain from 1750 to 1800, the population grew by 2.5 million people (from 6.5 million to 9 million). As another result of scientific farming, wealthy landowners chose to use their land for more profitable purposes than growing food. In Britain many landowners began to raise sheep. The sheep's wool provided raw materials for the new textile factories. However, raising sheep required fewer workers than crop farming did. Many peasant farmers had to leave the country to find work in towns.

Industrial Revolution

Industry as well as agriculture felt the hand of science in the eighteenth century. The changes in manufacturing were so great that this century, together with the nineteenth century, is called the **Industrial Revolution.** As with farming, these changes started in Great Britain. Britain had a stable government and the large supplies of labor and coal needed for

New farming techniques allowed farmers to reap more abundant harvests, which in turn fed more people.

industry. In the nineteenth century the Industrial Revolution came to Europe.

The Industrial Revolution began in textiles. Several inventions appeared early in the eighteenth century. The most important invention was the **steam engine,** especially once it was improved by the Scot **James Watt.** Power from the steam engine replaced human or animal power in textile machines. Producing thread and cloth on spinning wheels and hand looms took hours, while the same results required only a few minutes on steam-powered machines.

Before steam engines, spinning wheels and hand looms had been owned and used by individuals. They kept them in their homes or shops. Often farmers' wives did spinning and weaving at home to earn extra money. Even in the towns, craftsmen worked in their shops. However, with the coming of steam power, individual labor was no longer practical. Farmers and craftsmen could not afford to purchase expensive machines. The solution was to place several machines in one building, a factory. Usually a wealthy person built and equipped a factory and then hired laborers. Many of these laborers were peasant farmers no longer needed in the country. They came to the factories to find jobs. Around the factories older towns grew larger, or new towns began.

Although many people found job opportunities, living in a factory town was usually not pleasant. Crowded, dark, and dirty, factory towns were built quickly and cheaply. Often several families crowded into a tiny apartment. Working different shifts, family members would take turns sleeping during their off hours. Rarely was a family together at one time. Men, women, and children worked long shifts. Twelve-, fourteen-, or even eighteen-hour workdays were common, and the pay was hardly enough to feed the family. Unsafe and unsanitary workplaces caused many accidents and illnesses among workers. Some bosses were cruel to their workers, pushing them to work harder and even beating them. Many young workers died because of these circumstances. Even though these conditions seem harsh to us today, they were an improvement over what many people had known. The factory jobs provided an income for many poor people who might have starved otherwise.

The Industrial Revolution began in Britain, the same country where John Wesley did most of his preaching. He often went to factories, arriving before sunrise to preach before the day shift began. He also preached during meal breaks. Many of these poor factory workers found the riches of salvation in Christ. Their new lives in Christ and the hope of heaven's glory taught them to be content with their present hard lives. They learned to rest in God and His promises, saying with the psalmist, "My flesh and my heart faileth: but God is the strength of my heart, and my portion for ever" (Ps. 73:26).

John Wesley's messages to factory workers brought hope to their weary hearts.

Putting Steam to Work

The potential power of steam was discovered around A.D. 100 by a Greek named Hero, but the application of that power would not occur until many centuries later. James Watt usually gets the credit for inventing the steam engine, but what he actually did was improve on a style already in use.

In 1698 Thomas Savery, a military engineer, developed and patented a steam-driven pump for pumping water out of mine shafts. That pump and the improvement developed by Thomas New-comen in 1712 allowed up to 120 gallons of water per minute to be pumped from a mine shaft, but there was one drawback to those steam engines—fuel consumption.

In the method used by Newcomen, steam was forced into a cylinder. As the cylinder filled, a piston was raised (see figure 1), which in turn lowered the pump plunger. To continue pumping, Newcomen cooled the cylinder with cold water. This action condensed the steam, created a vacuum, and drew the piston down. This in turn pulled the pump plunger up and sucked up the water.

This cooling process made the cylinder need much more steam because it had to not only fill the cylinder but also reheat it. This required enormous

(fig. 1) The Newcomen engine pumped water quickly but used too much fuel to be practical.

amounts of fuel. The pump required so much fuel, in fact, that it could be used only in mines where coal was readily available. Pumping water was a good idea, but industry needed a way to operate machinery without storing enormous amounts of fuel. This is where James Watt's improvement caused a revolution.

Watt devised a way to separate the steam cylinder from the condenser so that the steam cylinder could remain hot. His improved engine used 75 percent less fuel than the earlier versions. He patented his engine in 1769. Industry could now

(fig. 2) Watt's improved double-action engine

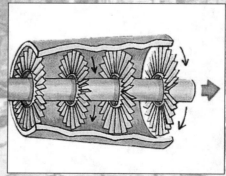

(fig. 3) The steam turbine

The practical steam engine revolutionized industry. Factories could produce goods more efficiently than a single family working in their home, thus contributing to the end of many cottage industries and forcing people into the cities for employment.

use the engine without having huge fuel supplies on hand.

Later, Watt developed a way to use steam to push on one side of the piston and then the other using a double-action principle. (See figure 2.) Now the steam could remain hot enough to go through one, two, three, or four cylinders, pushing the pistons in turn.

Today's steam engines are very different from their predecessors. The steam is superheated (up to 1200° F), put under high pressure (3500 pounds per square inch), and shot through huge tubes containing large turbines. (See figure 3.) Steam turbine engines are used to power ocean liners, industrial equipment, and electric generators.

The Age of Absolutism

Wesley's ministry touched wealthy people as well as poor people. Once saved, they saw the need to "do good unto all men" (Gal. 6:10) and began several organizations to help the poor. For example, **Robert Raikes** opened the first Sunday school in 1780. At a time when there were no public schools to teach the children of workers, his Sunday school met all day, teaching children reading, writing, and the Word of God.

The desire to help the workers reached even the government. Several members of Parliament drafted bills for regulation of working conditions. The process of passing bills in Parliament moves slowly, however, and not all workers were content to wait for Parliament. In some towns they formed groups and staged riots. Police and factory owners put these riots down, usually harshly. Although the riots may have sped up Parliament, the Bible teaches us that workers are to obey their masters whether they are kind or mean (I Pet. 2:18). Although one must obey God before man, God has put employers in positions of authority. This authority is to be obeyed unless it contradicts God's commands.

Napoleon in His Study, 1810-11 by Jacques Louis David

The French Revolution

The revolutions in agriculture and industry did not arrive on the Continent of Europe until the nineteenth century. At the end of the eighteenth century, the Continent had its first revolution of another sort—a political revolution. The **French Revolution** began in 1789. By the time it ended, absolutism was gone in France. In the nineteenth century, political revolutions occurred in other European nations, replacing absolutism with other forms of rule.

France was the center of thought and learning during the Age of Reason. Thinkers stated ideas that said all men have certain natural rights. Even the government cannot abuse these rights, they said. After Louis XIV died, absolute rule grew increasingly harsh for the people. Finally, under **Louis XVI** (1774-92), the French people revolted against the king. Romans 13:1-2 tells us that governments are established by God and should therefore be obeyed. God will

During the French Revolution, hundreds of condemned French aristocrats lost their heads at the guillotine.

judge wicked rulers; the people need not do it.

The French revolutionaries set up a new government based on man's natural rights. As the revolution continued, it grew out of control. The early leaders had wanted only to remove the absolute monarchs, Louis XVI and Marie Antoinette (AN twuh NET). Later leaders took the revolution further and demanded that everyone follow their orders. These leaders ruled only for the sake of power. Yet they too lost their power, and by 1804 a new dictator, **Napoleon** (nuh POH lee un), ruled France.

Section Review

1. Where did the agricultural revolution begin?

2. List three improvements in farming and two effects of scientific farming.

3. What invention began the Industrial Revolution?

4. How did the factory system come about? Describe the conditions in early factories.

5. How did the Wesleyan revivals affect the Industrial Revolution?

6. What new ruler finally came to power after the French Revolution?

How do you think that the revolutions (agricultural, industrial, and political) were a result of the ages of absolutism, enlightenment, and reason?

Summary

Several movements occurred in Europe between 1650 and 1800. In politics this was the Age of Absolutism. Absolute kings ruled their kingdoms completely. They expected total obedience, and their subjects usually obliged. Louis XIV was the leading absolute monarch. In thought and learning, this period was the Age of Reason. People used their minds to solve problems clearly and logically. In science many new discoveries were made. Scientists also stated laws that described occurrences in nature. Reason affected the arts with the revival of classicism. In religion, reason led to deism, a teaching that said God is not personal and man need not have a personal relationship with Him. The truth of God answered these deists through the preaching of John Wesley and the Methodist revival. These years were also an age of revolutions. Changes in farming increased production. The Industrial Revolution began at this time. It brought steam-powered machinery to factories. Revolution also came to lands ruled by absolute kings. The French Revolution was the first; other revolutions occurred in the 1800s.

CHAPTER REVIEW

People, Places, and Things to Know

Versailles	St. Petersburg	laws of gravity and	Methodists
Louis XIV	Catherine the Great	motion	Charles Wesley
courtiers	Prussia	microscopes	Industrial Revolution
absolute ruler	Frederick the Great	neoclassical	steam engine
absolutism	Parliament	Franz Joseph Haydn	James Watt
Sun King	Magna Carta	Wolfgang Amadeus	Robert Raikes
Edict of Nantes	English Bill of Rights	Mozart	French Revolution
Maria Theresa	William and Mary	deists	Louis XVI
Peter the Great	Age of Reason	John Wesley	Napoleon
czar	Sir Isaac Newton		

Matching
Match these rulers to their nations.

1. Louis XIV
2. Charles I
3. Frederick the Great
4. John
5. Peter the Great
6. William and Mary
7. Louis XVI
8. Catherine the Great
9. Maria Theresa
10. Napoleon

(a) Austria
(b) England
(c) France
(d) Prussia
(e) Russia

Short Answer
During whose reign did each of these events occur?

11. The start of the French Revolution
12. Magna Carta signed
13. English Civil War fought
14. Versailles built
15. Russia westernized
16. Palace at Vienna remodeled to look like Versailles

Matching

Match these men to their accomplishments.

17. James Watt
18. Isaac Newton
19. Robert Raikes
20. Franz Haydn
21. Charles Wesley

(a) wrote hymns
(b) composed classical music
(c) discovered the laws of gravity and motion
(d) started Sunday schools
(e) improved the steam engine

Multiple Choice

Choose the *best* answer to make the sentence correct.

22. _____ was characterized by restraint, balance, and simplicity.

    (a) Absolutism   (c) Neoclassicism

    (b) Methodism   (d) Deism

23. _____ brought revival to England.

    (a) Absolutism   (c) Reason

    (b) Revolution   (d) Methodism

24. _____ taught that God created the world but did not take care of it.

    (a) Methodism   (c) Reason

    (b) Deism   (d) Neoclassicism

25. _____ was based on clear, logical thinking.

    (a) Revolution   (c) Neoclassicism

    (b) Reason   (d) Absolutism

Think About It!

After talking to the rich young ruler in Luke 18:18-23, Jesus went on to say in verses 24-25, "How hardly shall they that have riches enter into the kingdom of God! For it is easier for a camel to go through a needle's eye, than for a rich man to enter into the kingdom of God." Looking at the Industrial Revolution and the Methodist revival in this chapter, do these verses apply? Explain your answer.

Fulfilling the Great Commission

The Christian call to missions began when Jesus told His disciples, "All power is given unto me in heaven and in earth. Go ye therefore, and teach all nations, baptizing them in the name of the Father, and of the Son, and of the Holy Ghost: teaching them to observe all things whatsoever I have commanded you: and, lo, I am with you alway, even unto the end of the world" (Matt. 28:18-20). The following pages provide a brief overview of the history of missions, from the days of the New Testament to the present. Although the missionaries, being human, displayed weaknesses and sometimes failed, the story of missions has been marked by triumph. The history of missions demonstrates the blessing of God on His Word—as Haydn's oratorio *Creation* says, "In all the lands resounds the word, never unperceived, ever understood."

Early Mission Work

After healing a lame man at Lystra, Paul and Silas attempt to prevent sacrifices from being offered to them. (Giovanni Coli and Filippo Gherardi, *Sacrifice at Lystra, The Bob Jones University Collection*)

Jesus told His disciples, "Ye shall be witnesses unto me both in Jerusalem, and in all Judea, and in Samaria, and unto the uttermost part of the earth" (Acts 1:8). Bible interpreters have often cited this verse as an outline of the book of Acts—the spread of the gospel in Jerusalem (1-7), in Judea and Samaria (8-12), and then to "the uttermost part of the earth" (13-28). The first two waves of expansion—in Jerusalem and in Judea and Samaria—covered the whole of Palestine. The third wave was the real beginning of foreign missions, and the leader in that movement was the apostle Paul.

Christ changed Saul of Tarsus, fierce persecutor of the church, into Paul, apostle to the Gentiles and zealous missionary for the gospel. Paul made three great evangelistic sweeps of the Mediterranean world, popularly known as his "missionary journeys" (Acts 13:1–21:8). He preached the gospel throughout Asia Minor, across the Mediterranean, and in Europe.

His mission work was interrupted for four or five years by his imprisonment by the Romans. But afterwards Paul was released for a time, during which he visited Macedonia (I Tim. 1:3), Troas (II Tim. 4:13), Crete (Titus 1:5), and other areas. A tradition, perhaps based on Romans 15:24 and 28, says he even visited Spain. Tradition says Paul was then arrested again and beheaded by order of the emperor Nero.

Paul's death marked the end of that first great surge to carry the gospel to "the uttermost part of the earth." Only a few years after the close of the New Testament, around A.D. 110, Pliny the Younger, the Roman governor of Bithynia (today northern Turkey) wrote to the emperor Trajan, "This contagious superstition [Christianity] is not confined to the cities but has spread throughout the villages and countryside." The first-century Christians had indeed "turned the world upside down" (Acts 17:6).

The close of the New Testament hardly marked the close of missionary activity. Christianity continued to spread not only throughout the Roman Empire but also beyond the empire's bounds into other regions. Several men figure prominently in the earliest "foreign missions." Gregory the Illuminator (c. 240-332) earned the title "Apostle of Armenia" by his work in that land. His success in winning King Tiridates II to Christianity made Armenia the first nation to accept Christianity as its official religion.

The earliest major center of missionary work in Europe was in Ireland. The father of this work was Patrick (c. 390–c. 461). Born in Britain, Patrick spent most of his life in Ireland preaching the gospel and establishing churches. Building on Patrick's pioneer work was the Irish monk Columba (521-97). On the tiny Scottish island of Iona, he established a mo-

Columba, Irish missionary of the sixth century

nastic community that became a leading center of mission work to the peoples of Scotland, England, and eastern France.

A good example of a zealous missionary in the Middle Ages was Boniface (680-754), the "Apostle to the Germans." Boniface labored among the barbarian tribes in what is now Germany. He confronted these people with a blunt bravery that won their respect. Typical of his character is his most famous act. He cut down a sacred oak dedicated to the Thunder God, Thor, and used the planks to construct a chapel. He was martyred while trying to establish a new work among the Frisians in what is now the Netherlands.

Mission work also took place farther east. Two of the most important missionaries for what is known today as the Eastern Orthodox Church were the brothers Cyril (826-69) and Methodius (c. 815-85), Greek missionaries to the Slavs of Central Europe. Unlike western Catholics who maintained Latin in their services, the brothers worked in the common language of the people. Their translation work in the Slavic language proved enormously beneficial to the Eastern church in reaching other Slavic lands, notably Russia.

Mission work dwindled as the Middle Ages progressed. Meanwhile Islam arose in Arabia and spread across Asia Minor, North Africa, and into Spain, thus encircling Europe. The main European reaction to Muslim expansion was the Crusades, a series of "holy wars" to recapture territory—particularly Palestine—from the Muslims. A few Christians, however, saw Muslim lands as mission fields. The most famous of these was Raymond Lull (1232-1315). He encouraged the study of Arabic and the establishment of monasteries for the training of would-be missionaries to the Muslims. Lull himself eventually went to North Africa and saw a little success before he was stoned by a Muslim mob.

Missions in the Modern Church

The Reformation and the Age of Reason

The modern period of church history begins with the Reformation and the division between Protestantism and Catholicism. Roman Catholics were quicker to take up work in foreign fields. A major force in Catholic missions was the Jesuits, a monastic order begun during the Reformation to oppose Protestantism. Francis Xavier (1506-52), the most famous Jesuit missionary, was instrumental in spreading Catholicism to India and Japan. In Latin America and French-controlled North America, the Jesuits conducted works among the Indians.

Two of the more controversial examples of Jesuit mission work were Robert de Nobili (1577-1656), missionary to India, and Matteo Ricci (1552-1610), missionary to China. These men both built thriving works by adapting Catholicism to these foreign cultures. They argued that they could blend Christianity with the Hindu culture of India and the Confucian culture of China without harming the essence of Christianity. Their methods proved too extreme for the church, however, and the pope condemned their practices.

Protestant mission work was a little slower in starting. New England Puritan John Eliot (1604-90) conducted a successful work among the Indians in Massachusetts in the 1600s. During the so-called Age of Reason (1648-1789), religious revivals sparked an interest in missions. The most important leaders in early Protestant missions were the Moravians, a small but influential denomination based in Germany. They conducted mission work in

David Zeisberger, Moravian missionary to the Indians

Greenland, among the slaves in the Caribbean, and among the American Indians. Their brave and selfless work helped prepare the way for the greater missionary expansion in the nineteenth century.

The Great Century

Historian of missions Kenneth Scott Latourette has aptly called the nineteenth century "the Great Century" of Christian missions. That period saw an explosion of mission work across the globe. The era began in 1793 when the Father of Modern Missions, William Carey (1761-1834), arrived in India.

Carey was a shoemaker and pastor of a small Baptist church in England. He was inspired by Isaiah 54:2-3, "Enlarge the place of thy tent, and let them stretch forth the curtains of thine habitations: spare not, lengthen thy cords, and strengthen thy stakes; for thou shalt break forth on the right hand and on the left; and thy seed

shall inherit the Gentiles, and make the desolate cities to be inhabited." Burdened by the thought of the multitudes who were perishing without the gospel, he challenged his fellow pastors in a famous missionary sermon: "Expect great things from God; attempt great things for God." Carey did not present them with a task he was unwilling to do himself. He went to India, where he translated the Bible and preached the gospel.

Carey was obviously not the first Protestant missionary. However, he was the pioneer to capture the attention of the Christian world. He held up before the church its responsibility to carry the gospel to the lost. Furthermore, Carey inspired the organized support of mission work through the founding of the Baptist Missionary Society. Finally, he had a broad vision for missions. Carey aimed to evangelize a whole country, not a few individuals. Through his translation work, he sought to

William Carey

Adoniram Judson

ernment once threw him into prison, where he nearly died. Judson buried his first wife and some of his children in Burma. His second wife died while returning from Burma to try to recover her health. But through the efforts of Judson and missionaries he inspired, thousands of lost souls throughout Asia found salvation in Jesus Christ.

The nineteenth century was also the era of imperialism. European powers scrambled to build empires by establishing colonies in Africa and Asia. Imperialism itself was a mixed blessing for the people who were colonized. Some of the imperialistic nations exploited the lands they colonized; Belgium's hideous treatment of the Congo is a painful example. Often forgotten, however, are the blessings brought by foreign powers such as roads and modern hospitals. Even so, the European powers were usually more interested in profit and prestige than the benefit of the native peoples.

Critics of European colonization often accuse missionaries of using the gospel as a cover for planting foreign flags in other lands. Actually, missionaries and imperialists were sometimes at odds. The opposition of the British East India Company, for instance, forced Carey to work in Danish-controlled India and pushed Adoniram Judson out of India altogether and into Burma. The relationship between imperialism and missions at its best is perhaps represented by David Livingstone (1813-73). He staunchly opposed the cruelest form of imperial exploitation—the slave trade. British expansion, thought Livingstone, would end the slave trade and open new lands to the gospel.

However, it is certainly true that some missionaries stressed "civilizing" converts in order to "evangelize" them. Such missionaries saw the advance of European culture as the advance of civilization and, hence, of Christianity. But not all Christians thought this way.

provide the means for reaching all of India with the gospel. He set the pattern for the missionaries of the Great Century.

Shortly after Carey went to India, Americans joined the worldwide effort in missions. The first great American missions movement resulted from the Second Great Awakening, a revival that swept the United States in the early 1800s. One young man touched by this revival became the first notable American missionary. Adoniram Judson (1788-1850), a Baptist like Carey, performed an important work in Burma. He diligently translated the Bible and preached to the Burmese people. But there was a great cost. The Burmese gov-

Many evangelical missionaries cared only for evangelism of the lost. One of the most famous evangelistic missionary efforts of the late 1800s and early 1900s was the Student Volunteer Movement (SVM). Taking as its motto "The evangelization of the world in this generation," the SVM challenged Christians to go to "the regions beyond" with the gospel. In its history, the SVM is credited with sending more then twenty thousand missionaries to the field. Probably the most famous student volunteer was C. T. Studd (1862-1931), a renowned English cricket player who forsook fame to go to the field. Studd served in China, India, and Africa.

In the later nineteenth century, a new kind of mission board developed—the "faith mission." Originally, denominations would collect money from their member churches and then send it to the missionaries on the field. Many notable missionaries served under denominational boards, such as Southern Baptist Lottie Moon (1840-1912) and Canadian Presbyterian Jonathan Goforth (1859-1936), both of whom labored in China. Faith missions, however, are independent mission boards that have no guaranteed income; missionaries ask for funds directly from individual Christians or supporting churches. "But the concept of living entirely by faith went far beyond the matter of finances," notes historian Ruth Tucker. "The missions were born out of faith, often at great risks."

The pioneer of faith missions was J. Hudson Taylor (1832-1905) and his China Inland Mission, founded in 1865. Taylor combined a zeal for the gospel with a love for the Chinese people. Others followed his lead in founding faith missions. Such mission work was

John and Betty Stam, missionary martyrs in China

not easy and not always safe. For example, thirty-five missionaries of the Christian and Missionary Alliance and their children lost their lives in the Boxer Rebellion in China in 1900. Missionary service in the nineteenth century was a sacrifice—as true Christian service often is.

The Twentieth Century

The fading of the nineteenth century into the twentieth saw the eventual collapse of imperialism. The elimination of European dominance in Africa and Asia resulted in a loss of protection for missionaries on the field. In fact, resentment of European and American influence often made missionaries targets. John and Betty Stam, missionaries to China in the 1930s, were captured and executed by Chinese Communists in 1934. In 1981 left-wing terrorists in Colombia kidnapped and murdered missionary translator Chet Bitterman.

An obvious characteristic of twentieth-century missions has been a shift from British to American domination of mission work. This change was seen particularly after World War II when America emerged as the leader of the free world against Communism. There was a tremendous surge in foreign missions after World War II, as American involvement abroad reawakened missionary vision in the United States.

Another characteristic is increased professionalism. Students in missionary programs now take courses in cultural anthropology and linguistics, as well as traditional Bible and theology courses. Professionalism has also created a desire for specialization. Some earlier missionaries specialized in medical missions or translation work. New technology in the twentieth century allowed missionaries to branch into other fields, such as broadcasting or missionary aviation.

The twentieth century also saw an increased dependence on native, or national, workers. With many fields closing to foreigners, western missionaries have needed to turn over evangelistic work to citizens of these lands. Even where the fields remain open, many missionaries realize how much more easily a native of a particular culture can reach his own people with the gospel.

With the coming of the twenty-first century, the outlook for Christian missions is uncertain. The retirement of many of the missionaries who went to the field after World War II created problems for many mission boards because replacements were slow to volunteer. Many countries closed their borders to missionaries and mission work. Nevertheless, the spread of the gospel continues, for God has placed His omnipotent promise behind the preaching of His message of salvation.

> For as the rain cometh down, and the snow from heaven, and returneth not thither, but watereth the earth, and maketh it bring forth and bud, that it may give seed to the sower, and bread to the eater: so shall my word be that goeth forth out of my mouth: it shall not return unto me void, but it shall accomplish that which I please, and it shall prosper in the thing whereto I sent it (Isa. 55:10-11).

Mission work in the twentieth century has increasingly made use of modern technology, such as radio broadcasting and missionary aviation.

CHAPTER 10

When Columbus began a new age of exploration in 1492, mapmakers did not refer to "Antarctica" on their charts. Instead they labeled the mythical land at the southern pole the *Terra Australis Incognita* (Latin for "unknown southern land"). The cartographers had support for their idea of an unknown land in the writings of second-century Greek astronomer Ptolemy, who proposed that there must be a land in the Southern Hemisphere equal in size or mass to Europe and Asia or else the world would topple over. The Europeans pictured a huge continent, probably as large as Asia, overflowing with riches, treasures, and perhaps even unknown civilizations. Believing this wealth existed, each European country sought to be the first to find the "unknown southern land."

The places to begin looking were at the southern tips of Africa and South America. The Spanish and Dutch seemed to have the advantage, since they each had a colony in one of those regions (the Dutch in South Africa and the Spanish in Argentina). But when the English colonies began to revolt in North America, thus putting England in danger of losing one of its major sources of goods and trade, England's motive for exploration far outweighed the Spanish and Dutch advantage. Vast areas of the Pacific lay unexplored, ready for any willing adventurer. Who knew where the mysterious land might jut north into the Pacific Ocean?

Soon ships from Europe traversed the Pacific. Their hopes for a great southern continent of riches were dashed, but their exploration was not fruitless. Explorers found new people on island paradises, discovered the large continent of Australia, and completed the map of the world by proving that the great unknown land that Ptolemy predicted did not exist.

A.D. 1550 - A.D. 1950

Voyages of Mendaña
and Quirós 1567-95

Reformation 1500-1650

| 1550 | 1600 | 16 |

Renaissance 1300-1616

Tasman Explo
Australia's Coast 1642

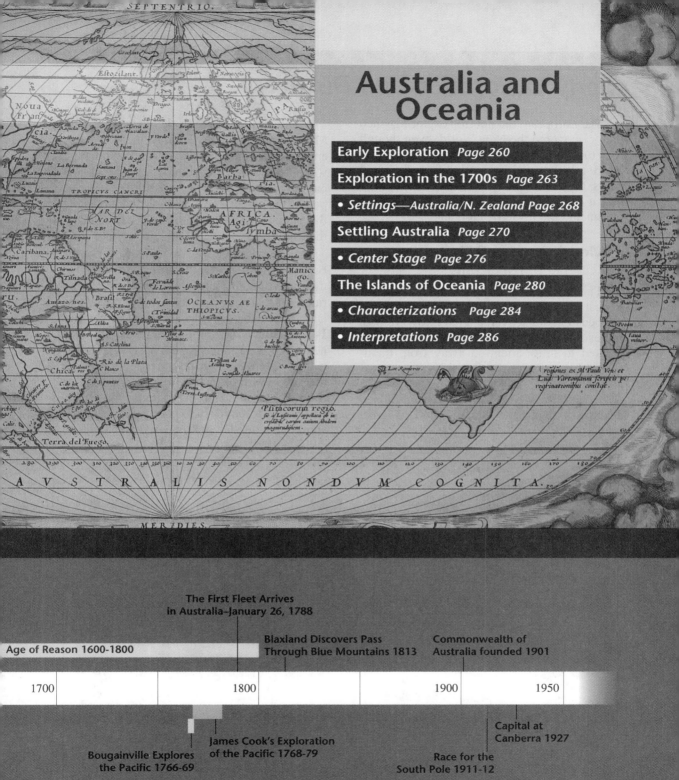

Australia and Oceania

The First Fleet Arrives
in Australia–January 26, 1788

Age of Reason 1600-1800

Blaxland Discovers Pass
Through Blue Mountains 1813

Commonwealth of
Australia founded 1901

1700   1800   1900   1950

Bougainville Explores
the Pacific 1766-69

James Cook's Exploration
of the Pacific 1768-79

Race for the
South Pole 1911-12

Capital at
Canberra 1927

Early Exploration and Discovery

The Europeans did not stop exploring when they discovered the New World, even though for a time they directed their efforts toward the interior of the continents. Within one hundred years of Columbus's discovery, Europeans began directing their attention to the Pacific Ocean and the mysteries it held.

Mendaña and Quirós Explore for Spain

The Incas told their Spanish conquerors of a great Incan king who had traveled west over the ocean and discovered a land flowing with riches. Whether it was true or the Incas just wanted to draw attention away from themselves for a while, the Spanish interest was aroused.

In 1567 the viceroy of Peru commissioned an expedition into the Pacific to find this great land.

The first expedition, led by **Alvaro de Mendaña,** included two ships, the *Los Reyes* and the *Todos Santos*. Discontentment ran high when Mendaña, the viceroy's nephew, was chosen to captain this voyage. Little faith was put in the twenty-five-year-old captain, and the captain and crewmen relied instead on their navigator, Hernán Gallego.

Mendaña sailed for two and a half months before he came to land. The island at which they arrived at first appeared fruitful, and hopes ran high that they had found the fabled Inca land. They named the island chain the **Solomon Islands** after King Solomon of the Bible, since he was known for his great riches. After an initial friendly welcome and a few days of peace, the situation took a turn for the worse. The Spanish, rather than trying to trade with the natives, used force to try to get food. They fired shots and wounded or killed several islanders.

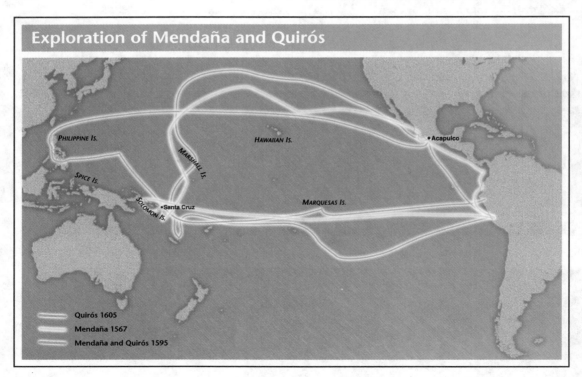

Exploration of Mendaña and Quirós

PHILIPPINE IS.

SPICE IS.

SOLOMON IS.

• Santa Cruz

MARSHALL IS.

HAWAIIAN IS.

MARQUESAS IS.

• Acapulco

Quirós 1605
Mendaña 1567
Mendaña and Quirós 1595

The natives no longer welcomed the men from the big ships to their shores.

When a ten-man landing party tried to go ashore after that incident, they were ambushed. Only one man escaped to swim back to the ship. The next day reinforcements rowed toward shore to save the missing men, only to see angry natives on shore yelling and waving dismembered arms and legs. Mendaña decided that it would be best to go on to explore other islands. With food and water running low, the expedition returned to Peru. The Solomon Islands that they discovered were not seen by Europeans for another hundred years.

However, Mendaña was not put off by this failure, and by 1595, he and a young navigator named **Pedro Fernández de Quirós** were ready to lead another expedition. This time the expedition had four ships and carried settlers, including women and children. Among the passengers was Mendaña's own wife, Doña Isabel, and her three brothers. Doña Isabel and her brothers were pampered aristocrats that brought their own supplies of water and Peruvian oil and wine.

The expedition charted a course for the Solomon Islands but miscalculated. Instead they came to a new set of islands that they named the **Marquesas,** after the current viceroy of Lima. The friendly islanders came out to greet Mendaña's ships. When Mendaña invited them to come aboard, the natives began stealing. The frightened and frustrated crewmen shot and wounded several Marquesans. Unfortunately, the Spaniards continued dealing harshly with the islanders. Within the two weeks that it took to resupply the ship, they killed two hundred natives.

With the ships well supplied, Mendaña and Quirós decided to continue their pursuit of the Solomons. But the ill-fated expedition once again missed its mark. On the next island they encountered, Mendaña tried to speak to the

natives in a language he remembered from the Solomon Islands. They did not understand him. Realizing his mistake, Mendaña named the new island **Santa Cruz.**

Mendaña decided that this island would be a perfect place for a settlement. Settlers came ashore and in high spirits began building a fort. But fever broke out, and soon several settlers died, including Mendaña. With the expedition in jeopardy, Quirós took over. He left the island when food stores were so low that each day each person was rationed a half pound of flour mixed with salt water and baked. Doña Isabel and her brothers, however, still had a plentiful supply of animals, oil, water, and wine.

Quirós began to search for the Solomon Islands once again. He dared not look for long, though, because his ships were wearing out. Ship worms were eating through their hulls, rope was rotting on the masts, and the sails were a tattered mess. The Solomons were within four days sailing, but Quirós did not know that. He sailed two days and then headed northwest for the Philippines, where the Spanish already had an established colony.

After three grueling months, the one remaining ship of the expedition limped into Manila Bay. The Spanish Coast Guard came out to meet them. The authorities were shocked when they saw almost one hundred men, women, and children starving to death while two of Doña Isabel's pigs lounged on the deck. After receiving a harsh scolding, Doña Isabel reluctantly agreed to have the pigs immediately slaughtered to feed the starving travelers.

When Quirós got back to Peru, he began requesting support for another expedition. After ten years of pleading, he set

Dutch explorer Abel Tasman and his family

sail with three ships heading toward Santa Cruz. But Quirós was ill. He complained of headaches and constantly changed his mind over where he thought the ships should go. On this expedition, the Spanish encountered some new islands, and one of the ships sailed between New Guinea and Australia without ever realizing the significance of what it had done. Quirós's illness got worse, and his navigator eventually took control of the ship.

The height of Spanish control of the seas had ended, and Spain could not afford to continue sending expeditions on fruitless missions. Soon the Dutch took over the task of exploration.

Abel Tasman Represents the Dutch

The Dutch authorities in Batavia, the chief Dutch base of the East Indies, called on one of their best captains, **Abel Tasman** (1603-59), to search for the unknown southern land. In 1642 Tasman took two ships and began his

voyage. He started in southern India and sailed east. This way, Tasman thought, he could not miss the huge landmass that he believed lay before him.

Tasman sailed on, vainly looking for the unknown land. He went south of Australia and landed on the island now named for him: **Tasmania.** The Dutch sailors found signs of life on the island but could never catch sight of the shy natives.

Tasman soon realized that this island was not the continent that he sought, so he sailed even farther east. He crossed a large stretch of water (now called the Tasman Sea) and discovered another set of islands that we now call **New Zealand.** Tasman and his men made contact with the natives there and discovered that they were not friendly. The tall, fierce **Maoris,** as they are called, resisted the Dutch attempts to land. Once they attacked a group of sailors exploring one of the bays. The natives killed four Dutchmen and drove the others back to the main ships. Tasman named this place "Murderer's Bay."

In a second expedition in 1644, Tasman mapped out parts of the western coastline of Australia. Even though the west coastline looked uninviting, the Dutch knew that in a land that was obviously sizable there might be better places for settlement. At the time, however, the Dutch had neither the manpower nor the money to explore and colonize. To avoid drawing attention to the area, the Dutch East India company suppressed many of Tasman's findings. They claimed the land they found and named it **New Holland.** Tasman retired in 1652, having never found the mythical "unknown southern land." But he had discovered two new and important islands: Tasmania and New Zealand.

Section Review

1. Who was commissioned by the viceroy of Peru to find the land of riches in the Pacific?

2. Why did the Spanish run into so many problems with the natives?

3. Who took over the expedition when Mendaña died?

4. What two islands did Abel Tasman discover? What country did he represent?

How did the rigid Spanish class system that was discussed in Chapter 9 evidence itself in the expeditions of Mendaña and Quirós?

Exploration and Discovery in the 1700s

During the sixteenth and seventeenth centuries, the English and the French stayed busy developing territory in the American colonies. However, when changes occurred in their colonies in the 1700s, the French and British once again turned their thoughts and resources to exploration. Several French and British explorers sailed the Pacific during the 1700s, but this section highlights only one man from each country.

The French Send Bougainville

In the midst of his training to become a lawyer, **Louis Antoine de Bougainville** (BOO gun vil) became bored with his studies and decided on the excitement of a military career. In 1756 military leaders appointed Bougainville as aide to General Montcalm in Canada.

Louis Antoine de Bougainville

The bougainvillea, named by Philibert Commerson in honor of his captain

After the loss of Quebec to the British (see p. 196, Chapter 8), Bougainville returned to France. But life in France bored him, and soon he was seeking a new adventure.

Hoping to regain power and respect for France after the loss of her New World colonies, Bougainville organized an expedition to settle the Falkland Islands off the coast of Argentina. (See page 588, Chapter 20.) With thirteen Acadians (French colonists from Nova Scotia), Bougainville set sail for the Falklands in the fall of 1763. By February of 1764 the colony had constructed an earthen fort and had begun plowing. The effort was short-lived, however, not because of the harsh climate, but because of the political furor raised over French possession of the islands. The English had previously claimed the Falklands and immediately sent a naval detachment to enforce their claim. The Spanish claimed the Falklands as part of South America. The French government commanded Bougainville, who had already returned to France, to go back to the Falklands, close the settlement, and give the title of the islands over to the Spanish (France's way of getting back at the British for recent losses). Bougainville asked permission to continue sailing toward the South Pacific once his task was finished. The French government agreed and commissioned Bougainville to search for *Terra Australis Incognita*.

Accompanying Bougainville were two scientists. **Philibert Commerson,** a naturalist, was brought along to describe and classify the animals and plants discovered. **Antoine Véron,** an astronomer, would try to work out new ways of determining longitude. Their contributions to the voyage were perhaps the most significant. Bougainville's idea of taking a naturalist and an astronomer became the custom for other explorers.

On his way to the Falklands, Bougainville's ship, the *Boudeuse,* proved very unseaworthy. Once he had reclaimed the Acadians, Bougainville returned to Rio de Janeiro to refit his ship. In the months of waiting for Spanish cooperation, Commerson took time to study the local plants. He discovered a beautiful and unusual-looking vine which he named *bougainvillea* after his captain. When the expedition returned to Europe, this unusual plant became a favorite with gardeners.

On his journey across the Pacific, Bougainville revisited and claimed for France several islands, including **Tahiti** (which had already been discovered by a British captain named Wallis). These eighteenth-century explorers thought of Tahiti as an unspoiled tropical paradise. Philosophers of the Enlightenment used the stories about Tahiti to further their belief that man was born unspoiled and that the effects of society corrupted him. The philosophers did not take into account the many "perfect" islands whose inhabitants practiced cannibalism or the fact that the Tahitians were in constant tribal warfare and performed human sacrifices.

Islands that looked like the Garden of Eden held natives that were sometimes very hostile to foreigners.

The Adventures of Captain Cook

The best-known explorer of the Pacific was the English captain **James Cook.** His fame is especially amazing since he came from a working-class background with little formal education. He rose in rank during a time when the wealthy and well educated were usually the only men put in high-ranking positions such as captain.

Indeed, Cook was probably the best sailor and finest explorer of his time. His mission for the British was to discover the real truth about the "unknown southern land" and claim land for England. In three voyages he crisscrossed the Pacific. First, Cook sailed around Australia. Then he sailed north between Alaska and Russia, vainly trying to find a passage above northern Canada. Finally, he sailed south of the Pacific islands until massive icebergs and

An early, and not too flattering, portrait of Captain James Cook

The philosophers compared Tahiti to the Garden of Eden for its perfection, but they failed to take the comparison further to see the sin. If Adam and Eve sinned in the perfect environment of Eden, then how could the Tahitians be perfect? Romans 5:12 reminds us that Adam's sin passed to all people. "Wherefore, as by one man sin entered into the world, and death by sin; and so death passed upon all men, for that all have sinned."

From Tahiti, Bougainville continued to sail west to the Solomon Islands, the largest of which bears his name. Having failed to sight Australia, Bougainville traveled on to Java and then around the Cape of Good Hope back to France.

One sidelight of Bougainville's trip around the world was the discovery that the cabin boy who helped Commerson was actually a woman. **Jeanne Baret** had the interesting distinction of being the first European woman to circumnavigate the world.

A mistake in judgment in dealing with the Hawaiian islanders caused normally good relations to go bad. Captain Cook was killed in the fighting.

fierce snowstorms forced him back into more temperate waters. Cook became the first man to sail completely around Antarctica, although he never actually saw that continent. In the end, Cook proved conclusively that there was no great "southern land."

During Cook's voyages, danger was always present. Once while sailing along the Great Barrier Reef off the coast of Australia, Cook's ship grounded on a reef. The captain ordered his men to lighten the ship, hoping that the tides would lift it off the reef. When the ship broke free, a large piece of coral broke off as well, plugging the hole until the ship could be repaired.

In his travels, Captain Cook discovered many islands in the Pacific, notably the Ha-

waiian Islands. One thing that set Cook apart from other explorers was his fair and generous treatment of the natives. Many times Cook noted in his diaries good characteristics and abilities that he saw in the natives. He treated the natives with respect, tried to make friends, and avoided violence whenever possible. He became the first white man to make peaceful contact with the Maoris of New Zealand.

One method that Captain Cook used in dealing with the natives, however, finally backfired on him. Whenever natives stole an item from the English ships or camps, Cook would capture a chief or another important person. Then he would announce that the captive would not be freed until the thief returned the stolen items. The method worked well—until the last time Cook tried it. In 1779, while the British were in Hawaii, some natives stole some tools and a canoe. Cook responded by trying to take an old chief hostage. A mob of angry natives attacked Cook and his men. The men escaped, but Cook did not. The furious natives beat Cook to death with their war clubs. The greatest explorer of the Pacific came to a violent end on one of the very islands he had discovered.

Section Review

1. Why did Bougainville organize an expedition to explore the Falkland Islands?
2. Who was the first European woman to sail around the world?
3. What island did the Enlightenment philosophers think proved their theories?
4. Who is the most famous explorer of the Pacific?

Captain Cook had great success with the island natives. Often he was welcomed back to the islands that he visited. Write one biblical principle that we can learn from his treatment of the natives. (Support your answer with Scripture.)

Sauerkraut and the Exploration of the Pacific

Not everybody likes sauerkraut. This German cabbage dish tastes sour, looks stringy, and smells strong. Others enjoy its sharp flavor. Still, whether you like sauerkraut or not, you would not think it important to the exploration of the Pacific Ocean—but it was!

Captain James Cook was one of the greatest explorers in history, and he owes a small part of his success to sauerkraut. You may remember from previous chapters that early sailors often suffered from scurvy. Doctors discovered that a lack of vitamin C (which can be found in oranges, lemons, and cabbages) causes scurvy. Some doctors in the British navy gave sailors lime juice to fight scurvy, so British sailors became known as "limeys."

Captain Cook, however, used sauerkraut (which he called "sour krout") to fight scurvy. His men did not like sauerkraut any more than some of you may. To persuade his men, Cook had his officers eat large amounts of sauerkraut at meals and loudly proclaim how delicious it was. Eventually the men learned to eat the strange food, and few of them ever came down with scurvy.

Most kids feel the same about sauerkraut as Captain Cook's men did.

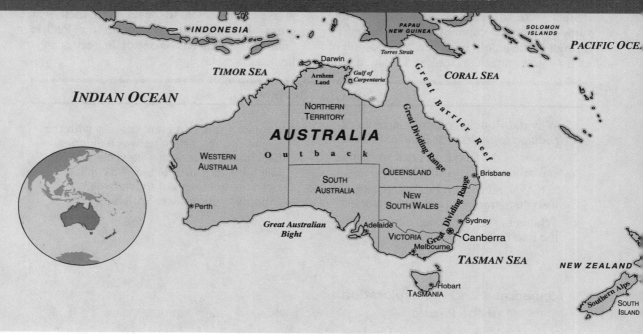

Location—Australia and New Zealand lie in the Southern Hemisphere. They are bordered on the west by the Indian Ocean, on the east by the Pacific Ocean, and on the south by Antarctica. Their closest neighbors are Indonesia and Papua New Guinea in the north.

Climate—The climate varies from dry in central and western Australia to temperate in the far southwest, on the east coast, and in New Zealand. Northern Australia is tropical. Temperatures average from 55°F to 83°F. Rainfall averages between 10 inches and 59 inches.

Topography—Australia lacks any major relief features in terms of world geography; however, the **Great Dividing Range** is similar to the Appalachian Mountains in the United States. Beyond them to the west are the Central Lowlands followed by the Western Plateau. The area west of the mountains is sometimes called the **Outback.** Off Australia's eastern shore is a unique feature called the **Great Barrier Reef.** It is a 1,250-mile series of coral reefs that stretch from Torres Straits south along Queensland. The reef is 10 to 200 miles off the coastline of Australia. It is known for the unusual marine life it supports. New Zealand consists of two mountainous islands—the **North Island** and the **South Island.** The South Island's snowcapped mountains are sometimes called the **Southern Alps** because of their ten- and eleven-thousand-foot peaks.

Natural Resources—Australia has enormous mineral resources, such as gold, coal, iron ore, bauxite, and oil. Some precious stones, such as fire opals and sapphires, are also mined. It features a wide variety of unusual animal life. New Zealand has rich forests and coastal plains, hydroelectric power, and geothermal power as well as natural gas and coal.

Geography & Culture—Although far from Britain, Australia and New Zealand are very British in culture. These lands were settled mostly by Englishmen, and because the native culture was primitive, the English became dominant. Both lands are agricultural. Much of Australia's land is well suited for raising sheep and cattle, which are major occupations there. About half of New Zealand is pastureland. These lands have become independent and self-sufficient because they are so far away from many other industrial nations.

Settings Review

1. What is the low range of mountains in Australia called?
2. What is the Great Barrier Reef known for?
3. Why are the mountains of New Zealand called the Southern Alps?
4. Which European country's culture dominates Australia and New Zealand?

Australia and New Zealand were very self-sufficient colonies. Name two ways that this self-sufficiency helped them when they became independent. Explain your answers.

Australia has crocodiles, open plains, and snow-capped mountains as well as cosmopolitan cities such as the capital, Canberra.

Australia and Oceania

Settling Australia

The Olgas are one of the many sacred places of the Aborigines.

Which European first saw the coast of Australia may never be known. Certainly the Portuguese may have seen Cape York Peninsula when they passed through the Torres Straits in 1606. The Dutch many times followed Australia's coastline as they explored the region for more trade goods. Captain Cook and his men landed in Botany Bay on August 23, 1770, and then surveyed the entire eastern coastline. All of these countries looked at Australia as ready to be claimed and used by any able-bodied Europeans who might settle there. But people were already there. Australia was inhabited by a poor but proud group of indigenous people whom the Europeans called **Aborigines.**

The Original Australians

When Captain Cook landed in Botany Bay, he met a group of native people who had no name for themselves. The general term *aborigine* was applied to these indigenous Australians. The word *aborigine* comes from Latin:

ab=from; *origine*=the beginning or origin. The name stayed, and the natives of Australia became known as Aborigines.

The Aborigines were one of the most isolated groups of people in the world. They were separated not only from other countries but also within Australia. The inhospitable coastline of the west and north was anything but inviting. This hostile front helped prevent earlier European or Asian contact. Australia's rugged and dry terrain also separated groups of Aborigines from each other. In a continent the size of the United States, the small population of the Aborigines was spread far and wide. Some historians estimate that only 750,000 Aborigines (roughly the population of San Francisco) lived in Australia before the Europeans came.

Aborigine men dressed in traditional costumes for a tribal festival

This Aborigine man looks as if he stepped out of Australia's past.

The Aborigines followed a lifestyle similar to most hunter-gatherer tribes. The men spent time hunting and worshiping the tribal gods in secret rituals. The women gathered staple (basic) foods early in the day and spent the rest of the day preparing dinner, relaxing, and caring for the children. Much of Aborigine life was unstressful.

Although the Aborigines were often involved in tribal conflict, they were very rarely hostile to the early settlers. The Aborigines became hostile after the English settlement was well established and began pushing into Aboriginal territory and hunting grounds. By then it was too late for the Aborigines to resist the superior weaponry of the English. Over the next centuries, the natives lost more and more of their land and rights.

England Claims New South Wales

The Dutch had claimed an area called New Holland in northern Australia, but that did not mean that they could claim all of Australia. Just as different European countries made claims all around North America, so claiming land in Australia was a first-come-first-served proposition. When the *Endeavour* sailed into the green-rimmed harbor of Botany Bay, Captain Cook claimed the land he saw for England and called it **New South Wales.**

Because the American Declaration of Independence cut off British use of the prison colony of Georgia, the English decided to settle their claim in Australia and rid themselves of the overflow of British prisons and poorhouses. The **First Fleet** left harbor in Portsmouth, England, in May of 1787 bound for Australia. The fleet included six ships for transporting people, three ships for supplies, and two warships. Of the 1,138 people in the fleet, 821 were convicts.

The restored houses of Old Sydney reveal the early settlers' meager way of life.

Arthur Phillips, captain of the First Fleet and first governor of New South Wales

After traveling for eight months, the Fleet's captain, **Arthur Phillips** (later the colony's governor), sighted Australia. He had traveled ahead expecting to prepare a small settlement before the other ships arrived. Much to his surprise, the other nine ships of the Fleet arrived two days later. By this time, he had realized that Botany Bay was too shallow and exposed to the open ocean to provide protection for the Fleet. After informing his officers of the trouble, Phillips took a short excursion to the north and found **Port Jackson** (sighted and mapped but not explored by Cook). This deep harbor included many protected coves. Phillips chose to settle in **Sydney Cove**, a beautiful, deep, sand-fringed harbor

with a freshwater stream at its tip. The day the Fleet arrived was January 26, 1788. Now that date is celebrated as **Australia Day.**

But a good cove was not enough to ensure a good colony. As they started to settle, Phillips realized that his men and the convicts were not skilled laborers. The plentiful eucalyptus and gum trees that they expected to use for building materials were impossibly hard and ruined their axes. Even when the trees could be cut, it took as many as twelve men all day to dig out one stump. The settlers finally resorted to building houses from cabbage tree panels covered with wattle and daub (sticks and mud plaster).

Soon Phillips saw that the settlement faced another problem. On the long voyage he had kept his crew and human cargo healthy, but much of the transported grain and flour was ruined. Without flour and grain there would be no bread for a long time. Also, many settlers showed signs of scurvy. They had to begin

English convicts leave for Botany Bay to begin serving their sentences.

Chapter 10

Cabbage palm trees were used to make thatch-roofed wattle-and-daub houses when the settlers found that other trees, such as the eucalyptus tree, took all day to chop down.

eating native plants to ensure their health even though they were not sure which plants were edible.

At first the settlers did not worry too much about short supplies. Phillips carefully rationed the remaining flour while they waited for the supply ship that was supposed to come within the first year. Unknown to the colonists and to England, the supply ship sank after it hit an iceberg. It would be two years before the colony heard from England. By that time the colony appeared doomed.

Always expecting a ship to come, Governor Phillips stationed an outpost at Botany Bay to look for ships (since that was where the British expected the settlement to be). Finally the news came that an English ship had been sighted. Excitement ran through the settlement. Imagine their disappointment when the ship turned out to be another transport ship with over two hundred convicts and few supplies. Fortunately, a well-stocked supply ship was close behind. The famine ended, and the colony was never so close to disaster again.

Although they were thousands of miles away from England, these Australian shepherds lived in conditions very similar to their English counterparts.

Expansion and Establishment

For several years the colonists stayed near the coast. The Great Dividing Range, with its sheer rock faces and giant chasms, effectively trapped the colonists along the ocean, but it did not hinder their settlement. Many convicts finished serving their prison terms and went on to be profitable members of the colony.

One colonist, John Ruse, was the first settler to live entirely off his own land. He and his wife, a former convict, set up a farm north of Sydney on the Parramatta River. Using crop rotation and fertilizer, they achieved such success that for a while Parramatta was a rival to Sydney. After his success, other colonists moved from Sydney and began farming along the Parramatta River. Their greatest problem

was thievery by the convict laborers that they received with their land grants.

A great change occurred in the colony with the crossing of the Great Dividing Range and the opening of the interior of Australia. Just when it seemed that ranchers on the coastal side of the mountains were running out of grazing area for their cattle and sheep, three men decided to attempt to cross the seemingly impassable Blue Mountains.

In May 1813, twenty-five years after the colony was planted, **Gregory Blaxland** and two companions started out from Blaxland's farm at the foothills of the mountains. After three weeks, the exploration party looked down from a cliff edge and saw a stream sparkling in the center of a valley. Further exploration by colony surveyors found a way to the western plains, thus enabling exploration and colonization of the Outback.

In 1836, explorers traveled southwest from Sydney around the coast and founded a new colony at Perth called **South Australia.** In 1851 sheep farmers in search of more pasture traveled south overland and discovered a river that they named the Murray. At the mouth of the Murray, they founded the town of Melbourne and called the colony **Victoria.**

Many people were granted land by England, but others chose to just wander off and explore until they found an area they liked. They built homes and staked out land for their fields and animals, but because they had no land grant, they were considered *squatters* by the government. Eventually there were so many squatters north of Sydney that the government designated another colony called **Queensland.**

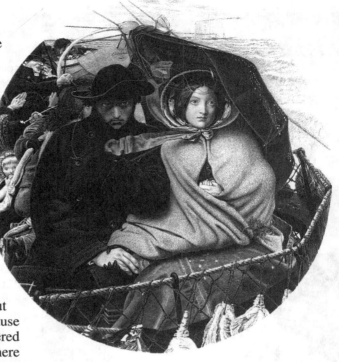

Two pensive emigrants take a last look at England as they head to a new life in Australia. This painting by Ford Madox Brown is titled The Last of England.

Australian History

Western Australia 1829

New South Wales 1788

Van Dieman's Land 1825

South Australia 1836

Victoria 1854

Northern Territory
part of South Australia 1863-1911

Western Australia

Queensland 1859

South Australia

New South Wales
Australian Capitol terr. 1911

Victoria

Tasmania
renamed in 1855

Aboriginal Art

Throughout their history, Aborigines have used art to reflect their religious beliefs. Aborigines believe that their culture and environment is the result of the *jugurrba* or Dreaming. During the Dreaming, spirit beings took the forms of men and animals and created the land and animals. Wherever the spirits touched and created, they supposedly left some of their essence. The Aborigines believe that the spirits' essence caused life to spring up. The Aborigines still call on the spirits of animals and places to ensure good weather or hunting and so on. Rock painting, body painting, and painting on the interior of bark huts have been integral to the process of appeasing or calling on spirits.

Since the 1960s the art world has become interested in Aboriginal bark painting. This interest has generated a market for the artwork, and Aborigines are producing more art to sell than ever before.

One of the selling points of bark art is that it is produced using all-natural materials. The canvas used by the Aborigines is the bark of the stringy bark tree. First, the bark is stripped from the tree. It is then heated over fire, and the outer rough bark is removed. The inner side is then smoothed by rubbing. Finally, the bark is pressed with weights to take out the natural curve and cause it to lie flat.

Not only the canvas is natural but also the paints and brushes. The paints that the artists use are made from natural clays held together with egg, orchid juice, or wax. Because the colors come from clay, they tend to be earthen tones, such as yellow, red, and brown. The artists add white from kaolin, also a type of clay, and black from coal to this palette. The brushes are made from sticks and twigs with feathers or palm leaves bound to the tips. Sometimes an artist chews a stick end, and the chewed tip becomes the brush. For very fine detail, artists use a stick with a few animal hairs attached to the end. Using this brush is very time consuming since it holds only a little paint at a time.

Aboriginal paintings are not landscapes or realistic works. The main topics for art are stylized drawings of animals and people, and shapes and designs that represent forces of nature. One of the interesting elements of Aboriginal art is the use of a technique called X-ray painting. In this technique, the artist shows not only the shape of

This bark painting shows the Aboriginal technique of X-ray painting.

the animal but the internal organs or skeletal structure as well.

With the modern emphasis on diverse cultures, Aboriginal art has become very popular. People cling to things that show ethnic heritage. The spiritual element of oneness between man and his environment appeals to many people who are seeking God in nature, but Christians know that although nature reveals God's creative power, it is not God. The Bible tells us in Psalm 19:1, "The heavens declare the glory of God; and the firmament sheweth his handywork." Romans 1:21-23, 25 tells that when people reject God and make nature their god, their spiritual hearts are darkened to the truth. "Because that, when they knew God, they glorified him not as God, neither were thankful; but became vain in their imaginations, and their foolish heart was darkened. Professing themselves to be wise, they became fools, and changed the glory of the uncorruptible God into an image made like to corruptible man, and to birds, and fourfooted beasts, and creeping things. . . . Who changed the truth of God into a lie, and worshipped and served the creature more than the Creator, who is blessed for ever. Amen."

Aborigine women use the handle end of the paint brush to complete this intricate painting.

In worship, Aborigines use their hands as a stencil over which they spray red ocher paint.

Grazing dominates most of Australia's land. Sheep and cattle far outnumber people.

A New Nation

All of the colonies were under the rule of England during the New South Wales gold rush of 1851. Around that time the convict transports to the east coast stopped, and with the rush of gold-hungry immigrants, the percentage of free citizens to convicts changed dramatically. In 1850 the population of the colonies was about 400,000 people; by 1860 it had skyrocketed to 1,100,000 people.

These new colonists wanted more freedom to govern themselves. In 1856 England granted self-government to all the colonies except **Western Australia** (whose few inhabitants were convicts and Aborigines). England still protected the colonies and intervened in foreign affairs.

Finally, in 1901, after intense negotiations, Australia became the **Commonwealth of Australia,** made up of six states—Queensland, New South Wales, Victoria, Tasmania, South Australia, Western Australia—and two federal territories. Instead of each colony governing itself independently, the Commonwealth would now have a single federal capital. By 1927 the government buildings in the new capital of **Canberra** were ready for use. Canberra is similar to Washington, D.C., in the United States. It is the seat of government but is not part of any state.

Modern Concerns

Australia currently faces many conflicts in its economy, social policy, and ecology. Before World War II, Australia's main trade partner was England. From early in its history, Australia set up what geographers call **import-substitution industries** (industries designed to meet the needs of the country, not for export) and then imported from England only goods that it could not produce. However, in the last two decades, Pacific traders such as Taiwan, Japan, and Hong Kong have offered such inexpensive products that it no longer benefits Australia to produce items in the country when it can purchase imported items at a cheaper price. It has also become more economical for Australia to trade with its close Asian neighbors instead of distant England, further loosening its ties with Europe. Australia continues to try to balance trade at home and abroad.

Another area of concern is civil rights for Aborigines. For years, Australia limited immigration to only whites to avoid addressing Aboriginal issues, but in 1973 Australia changed it policy and opened immigration to all people regardless of race. With this change came the need for new policies toward the native Aborigines as well. Aborigines have been given more say in government decisions and were even able to block further development of their ancestral lands in the Northern Territory. The platinum and gold deposits near Kakadu National Park (Aboriginal lands) have not been exploited, in honor of sacred Aboriginal lands nearby.

Decisions concerning the environment and conservation also face Australia. Especially as their economy faces challenges, Australians are looking for new ways to make money. Tourism on the Great Barrier Reef brings in revenue, but some ecologists blame tourists for damage to the reef as well as increased pollution. Logging efforts in the south and on Tasmania are being challenged as the question of destroying ancient forests and the effect on the local ecology are discussed. Australia faces many changes as it balances these issues in the twenty-first century.

Section Review

1. What did Captain Cook name the native Australians? Why?

2. What kept the Aborigines isolated from one another?

3. Where did Phillips start the first colony?

4. What kept the colony from expanding west?

5. What is the name for industries that meet the needs of the nation but do not produce goods for exports?

Why do you think it is important that the capital of Australia not be a part of any state?

Bright colors flash on the sails of boats in Brisbane's harbor and on the red, white, and blue costumes of the participants in the Commonwealth Games.

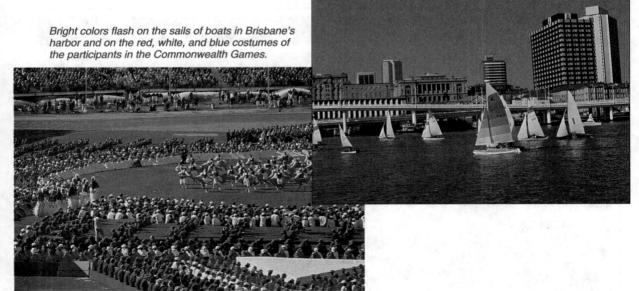

The Islands of Oceania

During the exploration of the Pacific in the 1700s and 1800s, many of the Pacific islands were discovered and claimed by Europeans. Many of the island people of the Pacific had developed inter-island trade and travel years before the Europeans arrived and did not need to be discovered or want to be claimed. The Europeans, though, found that these island paradises offered supply stops for their trade ships traveling from the Orient.

Low island

Defining the Islands

The islands of Oceania lie east of the Philippines and south of Japan. If all the islands were combined, they would be only the size of Texas. The largest island is New Guinea, and half of it is claimed by Indonesia. The population of all the islands combined is less than the population of the city of Los Angeles, California. Many of the islands are still territories of other countries, but a few have achieved independence.

Two types of islands dot the Pacific—**high islands** and **low islands.** The high islands are composed of volcanos and volcanic debris; the low islands are composed of coral remains. The composition of each island greatly affects the lifestyle of the inhabitants.

High islands tend to be better for people and agriculture. The high altitude of volcanic mountains allows the islands to capture moisture from the warm ocean breezes. As the air travels across the island, it rises over the mountain, cools, and then releases its moisture in rain or snow. Consistent moisture makes

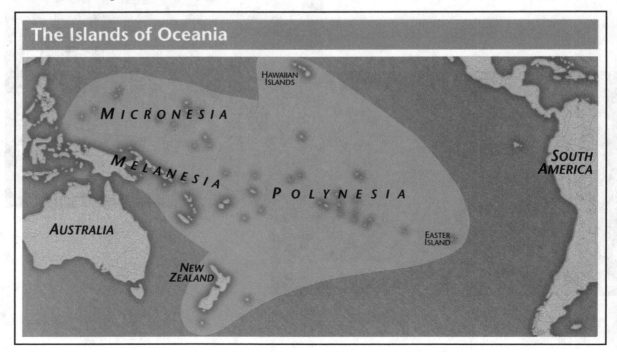

The Islands of Oceania

HAWAIIAN ISLANDS

MICRONESIA

MELANESIA

POLYNESIA

SOUTH AMERICA

AUSTRALIA

EASTER ISLAND

NEW ZEALAND

growing crops easier, and mountain streams provide plentiful drinking water. High island soil is the fertile volcanic soil that makes plants more productive, and that steady agricultural supply provides a more stable economy for the people. When explorers were cruising around the Pacific, they were much more likely to find needed supplies on high islands.

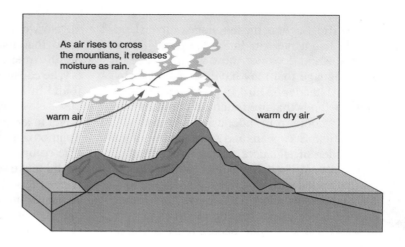

As air rises to cross the mountains, it releases moisture as rain.

warm air

warm dry air

Low islands, on the other hand, tend to be drier. Fresh water is not readily available for people or agriculture. People living on the islands are more dependent on using native coconut palms and fishing as a means of living. Low islands are also more susceptible to damage from tropical storms and high waves.

Another way of defining the Pacific islands is by the groupings of **Melanesia, Micronesia,** and **Polynesia.** Melanesia is so named

High island

because of the dark-skinned, dark-haired people who live in the region. It includes Papua New Guinea, the Solomon Islands, and Fiji. Micronesia is north of Melanesia and east of the Philippines. It is defined by island size (*micro* means "small"). Most of Micronesia's more than two thousand islands are small and low. Some are less than one square mile in size. Polynesia lies within the great triangle formed by the Hawaiian Islands, Easter Island, and New Zealand. It is called Polynesia because of the many (*poly-*) islands in the region.

Discovery and Colonization

Scientists have theorized that the islands of the Pacific were originally colonized from the west. They believe that Indonesians and Asians made their way to New Guinea first and then "island hopped" their way across the Pacific.

Archaeologists and anthropologists (people who study the origin and development of man) came to this conclusion by studying a number of characteristics of the islands. First, the archeaological record of New Guinea shows earlier civilizations than the other islands in the Pacific. Second, the language of the island people has a base in Indonesian and Asian language and does not show the influence of any language that may have been spoken by original islanders. Third, of plants and animals on the islands that are found other places, the majority come from Indonesia and Asia.

At first, Europeans and Americans scoffed at the idea of islanders sailing over miles of empty ocean. Then they began finding islanders that traded with far-off islands. These modern islanders were not only able to get to other islands, sometimes crossing as much as five hundred miles of open ocean, but they were able to accurately sail into the small space between two islands, even in stormy weather and cloudy skies. Seeing these navigational skills made later scientists agree that the Pacific islander could have even traveled two thousand miles to Easter Island, which is near South America.

Heyerdahl traveled from Peru to the island of Tuamoto in the Pacific.

Norwegian explorer **Thor Heyerdahl** theorized that the first Polynesians came from South America, not Asia. To support his theory, he constructed a reed boat similar to those found in Peru. In the *Kon Tiki* expedition in 1947, Heyerdahl proved that it was possible to travel in a reed boat from Peru to the island of Tuamoto in the Pacific. Although the scientific community rejected Heyerdahl's claims, he did make some interesting associations between the architecture and culture of Northern Africa, South America, and the Pacific Islands. Whether it was Asians or South Americans that came to the Pacific first, both cultures influenced the Polynesian islands.

Kon Tiki

Marshall Islanders' Wickerwork Ocean Charts

Sailors everywhere learn to identify characteristics of the winds and waters in which they sail. Knowing these characteristics helps sailors navigate across open waters. The Marshall Islanders of Micronesia developed an unusual way to navigate among the thousands of low islands in the region.

Instead of making star charts or maps, as many cultures did, the islanders designed complex wicker charts. These charts show the patterns of the ocean swells (waves) that occur near different islands. The islands themselves are marked with small shells.

Using this method, the islanders could pass down the knowledge of the seas from generation to generation. The charts could also be taken to sea to be used as ready maps of the trackless ocean.

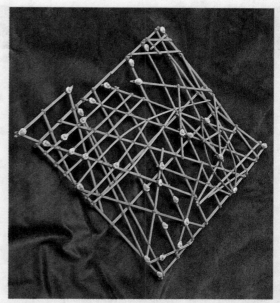

Of the many islands claimed by European countries, only a few were heavily colonized. As in other colonial endeavors, colonization was in some ways beneficial but in other ways harmful. The harms most often discussed are the diseases that ravaged many of the islands and the destruction of the native culture. Smallpox wiped out large portions of the native population on some islands. Not having been exposed to this common European disease, the natives had no immunity against it. Europeans changed the cultures of the native islanders. They brought new religions, new clothes, new trade goods, and new customs. Some of the islanders longed for the old ways, but many more embraced the new ways.

James Chalmers— Missionary to New Guinea

When Reverend Gilbert Meikle had finished reading the missionary letter, he looked around the room and said, "I wonder if there is a boy here this afternoon who will become a missionary, and by and by bring the gospel to cannibals like these?" James Chalmers immediately responded in his heart, "Yes, God helping me, I will."

For the next several years, James strayed far from the church and the influence of Sunday school. He led his peers in adventures and fights. But this all changed in 1859, when friends convinced him to attend special meetings held by two preachers from Northern Ireland. After that meeting, eighteen-year-old James Chalmers wrote, "I was pierced through and through from the conviction of sin, and felt lost beyond all hope of salvation. On the Monday Mr. Meikle came to my help, and led me kindly to promises and to light . . . I felt that God was speaking to me in His Word, and I believed unto salvation."

Then Chalmers renewed his boyhood vow to be a missionary. He applied to the London Missionary Society and was accepted. Soon he and his new wife, Jane, were on their way to the mission field. On May 20, 1867, the Chalmerses sighted the mountains of Rarotonga, one of the Cook Islands, where they would begin their missionary endeavors.

Chalmers was surprised to find that an extensive missionary work had already been accomplished there in Rarotonga. He longed for a "pioneering" work but steadfastly dedicated himself to the continued smooth operation of a well-established mission station.

Another surprise for Chalmers was the name the islanders gave him. They were unable to pronounce the name *Chalmers.* For the thirty-five

years of his ministry, the natives came as close as they could to the pronunciation of Chalmers with the name "Tamate."

An important aspect of Chalmers's missionary method began on Rarotonga: he encouraged self-government and independence from European influence once a native work was well established. He wrote: "So long as the native churches have foreign pastors, so long will they remain weak and dependent." He reported that the "out-stations under the charge of native pastors contrast very favorably with the stations under the care of European missionaries."

James Chalmers' dedication allowed him to have an effective ministry with the islanders of the Pacific.

In 1877, after repeated requests to be assigned to a new field, Chalmers received instructions to move on to Papua New Guinea. Chalmers became to New Guinea what Livingstone was to Africa. (See Chapter 14, page 396.) He found the people "a very fine race physically, but living in the wildest barbarism." Tribal disputes were settled by bloodshed, and victorious tribes celebrated with cannibal feasts. Chalmers also saw that the Papuans were industrious in the cultivation of the soil. There were talented craftsmen among them in woodwork and pottery. Parents were affectionate with their children, and children, in turn, cared for sick or aging parents.

Upon arrival in New Guinea, Chalmers handed out presents—leather belts, beads, red cloth—to the suspicious natives to convince them that the missionaries were coming peaceably. The village chief offered the Chalmerses the hospitality of his hut, complete with household decorations of human skulls, other bones, and blood-stained weapons.

"Tamate" warily accepted the welcome and watched carefully. One day when he was leaving the village, he saw a group of armed and yelling natives surrounding the partly-built mission house. Tamate rushed back and was confronted by a native warrior brandishing a stone club. The missionary looked at him coolly and demanded the reason for the attack. The warrior responded that the villagers wanted "tomahawks, knives, iron, beads" and that if these were not supplied, the missionaries would be killed. Tamate replied calmly that he did not give presents to armed people. Again and again the threat was repeated, but Tamate refused. The natives eventually retreated to the bush to discuss the situation, and the missionaries spent a watchful, uneasy night. The next morning, a man without war paint approached Tamate and apologized. Tamate received him cordially. "Now you are unarmed and clean, we are glad to make friends with you," and he gave the native a present. Tamate, by his refusal to be cowed by threats, won the respect of the natives and eventually won their loyalty and friendship.

Both Chalmerses worked tirelessly to make the mission a spiritual success, he by conducting services and she by teaching. Those who accepted Christ were carefully nurtured in the faith. Tamate baptized only those who demonstrated a genuine transformation and a growing knowledge of the Word of God.

James "Tamate" Chalmers outlived two wives in New Guinea. His last years were spent visiting existing mission stations. In his last year he was much encouraged by the arrival of a dedicated young helper, Oliver Tomkins. Together they planned an expedition to a region where the natives were reputed to be fierce and unapproachable, even by Papuan standards. No white man had ever seen them. On April 4, 1901, the mission steamship landed off the shore of the village of Dopima. After an initial meeting with the natives on the ship, Tamate promised to come ashore in the morning. The next day both Tomkins and Tamate went ashore, saying they would return shortly. When the natives later appeared on shore without the two men, the captain suspected that they were dead. He sailed away to tell the governor. British investigators later found out that the missionaries had been clubbed, beheaded, and eaten.

The news of Chalmers's murder made headlines all over the world. Those who had worked closely with him were shocked and grieved about his death but felt strongly that he would have wished to die as he did—engaged in service to the natives of New Guinea. As an old friend wrote: "Hitherto God had preserved him; now he allowed the blow to fall, and His faithful servant to be called up home."

Two great explorers, Peary and Amundsen, meet after their discoveries of the North and South Poles.

The Last Frontier

Have you ever seen a race like the Indianapolis 500? Or perhaps you prefer the exciting track races of the summer Olympics. In 1911 the world witnessed a different sort of race. Two men led two different expeditions to accomplish what no man had ever done before—reach the South Pole.

Norwegian Roald Amundsen (1872-1928) led the first team. He had wanted to be an explorer since he was fifteen. Even at that age he began to toughen himself by sleeping with his window open in midwinter. By the age of thirty, Amundsen had become a noted explorer. He wanted to be the first man to go to the North Pole and spent three years preparing to go there. Then, just as his expedition was ready to leave, word came that Admiral Peary was claiming to have reached the Pole already. Without hesitation, Amundsen announced that he would instead try to reach the South Pole.

Robert Scott (1868-1912) led the other team. He was quite different from Amundsen. Scott was primarily a sailor, not an explorer. He served loyally in the British navy and in 1901 led a British scientific expedition to Antarctica. This trip was so successful that the British government chose Scott to lead an expedition to the Pole in 1910.

The two expeditions differed in more than leadership. Amundsen concentrated only on the drive for the Pole. Scott, on the other hand, planned a full-scale scientific expedition. Amundsen relied on dog teams for transportation, while Scott preferred motorized sledges, Siberian ponies, and manpower. Both groups reached Antarctica early in 1911. Amundsen set out for the Pole on October 19, 1911. Scott left four days later.

Amundsen covered twenty-five miles a day, but Scott encountered all sorts of problems. The motorized sledges broke down and had to be abandoned. Then the Siberian ponies died. Scott and his men had to pull the sleds themselves. The heavy loads exhausted them, but the sturdy British explorers pressed on. On January 16, 1912, they approached the Pole with high hopes. Then one of Scott's men spotted something ahead—the remains of a camp. Amundsen had already been to the Pole. In fact, the Norwegian had arrived at the South Pole on December 14 and was nearly back to his base when Scott finally reached the Pole.

Disappointed, Scott and his men prepared to return. Then the weather worsened. One man lapsed into a coma and died. Another, named Oates, became so hobbled by frostbite that he slowed the party down even more. One day Oates deliberately left the tent and went out into a blizzard, probably hoping that his sacrifice would save the others. He died in vain, however. Scott and the remaining two men managed to return to within 150 miles of their base, but a fierce blizzard forced them to stop. They died there.

Months later, other explorers found the bodies, still in their sleeping bags. The freezing cold had preserved Scott's notes, photographs, and samples. Amundsen returned to civilization as the "winner" of the race, the discoverer of the South Pole. Scott died in Antarctica, but he was not a failure. The notes, records, and samples he took provided valuable information about Antarctica. In different ways, both Amundsen and Scott contributed to the exploration of the last unknown continent.

Today the South Pole is home to several permanent research stations, and seven countries claim territory in the region. You may wonder why anyone would want to claim such a harsh, barren territory. The fact is that Antarctica and the neighboring seas contain raw materials, such as oil and minerals, and the seas contain a plentiful fish and whale population. The ice itself may have value someday as a source of fresh water.

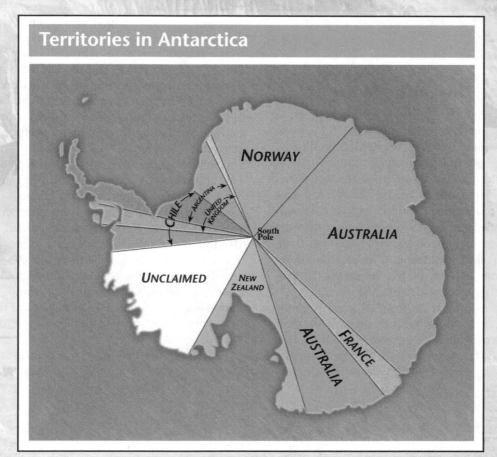

Territories in Antarctica

A World War II plane occupies a watery grave at the bottom of the Pacific Ocean.

The Pacific Today

For years the Pacific islands continued to function as trade and supply bases for Europe and America. But after the Japanese attacked Pearl Harbor in Hawaii on December 7, 1941, the world directed its attention to the Pacific. During World War II, Japanese or Allied troops suddenly occupied hundreds of islands. Small islands became home to hundreds of foreign troops working their way to the enemies' frontlines. Today, in the island jungles and coral reefs, remnants of the war linger in the form of rusting planes and sunken ships.

The memorial at Pearl Harbor reminds visitors of the thousands of men who lost their lives there as their ships sunk beneath them in the harbor. On the island of Saipan in the Marianas, two cliffs bear witness to the unnecessary loss of life in the islands. Suicide Cliff and Banzai Cliff are memorials to the hundreds of Japanese soldiers and civilians who threw themselves to their death on the rocks below rather than be captured by the Americans. The Japanese government had told the people that the Americans were merciless and would torture and kill them. As the men, women, and children jumped over the cliffs, American military personnel in boats below pleaded with them to stop.

But fifty years have helped to dim the memories of war, and new conflicts have arisen. Some island groups remain as territories of New Zealand, France, and the United States. They are dependent on the industries and economies set up by their supporting nations. Other island groups have proclaimed independence and are struggling to establish working governments.

Some islands must learn to deal with tourism and the stress it puts on local resources. When businesses buy land on islands, they usually bring skilled labor from other countries to build hotels and resorts rather than take the time to train the locals. They use precious water supplies and pollute the ocean. Only a small amount of the money coming onto the island is available to improve the island. The natives support themselves as maids and waiters, or they produce native crafts to sell to the tourists.

Although the Pacific island countries occupy only a small amount of land, they control vast amounts of ocean. A decision made in the 1950s by the United Nations Conference on the Law of the Sea (UNCLOS) determined that every country that has coastline on an ocean has a twelve-mile territorial sea and a two hundred-mile **Exclusive Economic Zone** (**EEZ**). Since the islands are surrounded by the sea, they have 212 miles of territory around them which they control. Small islands can require large countries to pay for the right to fish in their waters. This power may someday change the economy of the Pacific.

Section Review

1. Which type of island, low or high, is best for agriculture?

2. Which type of island has problems with drinking water? Why?

3. Name the island group that is defined by (a) the color of the people, (b) the size of the islands, (c) the number of islands.

4. The creation of what zone gave the islands more control of their waters?

Look at the map of islands on page 280. What conflict between islands might occur over the EEZ of each island? How do you think this conflict could be solved?

Summary

When the explorers set out for *Terra Australis Incognita*, they expected to find a massive continent of great riches. Instead, they found several small islands and one island continent nestled in the vast Pacific Ocean. They used the paradise they found to suit their needs, and many native cultures were all but swallowed up by European influence. Australia and Oceania continue to change as they find their places in the world. Australia, once a prison colony, adjusted to life as an independent commonwealth by slowly breaking its ties with England and realigning itself with the nations of the Pacific. Oceania grapples with new problems, trying to balance independence, industry, and tourism. Once a forgotten corner of the world, the Pacific countries must continue to meet the challenges of a changing world.

People, Places, and Things to Know

Alvaro de Mendaña
Solomon Islands
Pedro Fernández de
  Quirós
Marquesas
Santa Cruz
Abel Tasman
Tasmania
New Zealand
Maoris
New Holland
Louis Antoine de
  Bougainville

Philibert Commerson
Antoine Véron
Tahiti
Jeanne Baret
James Cook
Great Dividing Range
Outback
Great Barrier Reef
North Island
South Island
Southern Alps
Aborigines
New South Wales

First Fleet
Arthur Phillips
Port Jackson
Sydney Cove
Australia Day
Gregory Blaxland
South Australia
Victoria
Queensland
Western Australia
Commonwealth of
  Australia
Canberra

import-substitution
  industries
high islands
low islands
Melanesia
Micronesia
Polynesia
Thor Heyerdahl
Exclusive Economic
  Zone (EEZ)

Review Questions

Matching

Match each captain with the information about him. Some captains will have two answers.

1. Mendaña

2. Cook

3. Quirós

4. Tasman

5. Bougainville

(a) first woman to circumnavigate the world sailed on his ship

(b) known as the greatest sailor and explorer

(c) discovered a small island southeast of Australia

(d) tried to establish a colony on Santa Cruz

(e) was known for his fair treatment of the natives

(f) had a flower named in his honor

(g) rationed food while the former captain's wife ate well

Fill in the Blank

Put the correct answer in the blank.

6. The original people of Australia are called _____.

7. Coral islands are called _____ islands.

8. The First Fleet settled in _____ Cove.

9. The _____ _____ Range separates the coastline of Australia from the Outback.

10. A _____ _____ brought new immigrants into Australia by the thousands.

Multiple Choice

Choose the letter of the answer that correctly finishes the statement.

11. The Maoris drove Abel Tasman away from

   (a) Australia.   (c) New Zealand.

   (b) Tasmania.   (d) Tahiti.

12. James Cook prevented scurvy on ship by having his crew eat

   (a) limes.   (c) Brussels sprouts.

   (b) sauerkraut.   (d) lettuce.

13. The first Australian territory claimed by the English was

   (a) New South Wales.   (c) New Holland.

   (b) Queensland.   (d) Victoria.

14. The Pacific island group that is composed of small islands is

   (a) Melanesia.   (c) Polynesia.

   (b) Micronesia.   (d) Indonesia.

15. The world focused attention on the islands of the Pacific during

   (a) the Maori wars.   (c) World War I.

   (b) the Korean War.   (d) World War II.

Essay

Write a short paragraph explaining which type of island, high or low, you would like to live on and why.

Think About It!

Do you think that developed countries such as the United States should help underdeveloped island nations? Explain your answer.

CONQUESTS

1800 TO 1900

The challenges and accomplishments of Act Two will greatly affect the events of the nineteenth century played out in this act. European countries have lost some colonies but are still convinced that colonization is an important way to extend their influence and trading power. Colonization efforts in this century turn to more familiar territories—India, China, and Africa.

This act reveals the nineteenth century as a century of conquest over lands and people, natural laws, and energy. In this century Britain shines as a world leader in industrialism, imperialism, and missions.

New players come to the stage as the old rule of the aristocrats gives way to the rule of anyone who can rise from poverty to wealth. A new, powerful middle class awakens, looking for new things to buy and places to go. Britons, and Europeans in general, look increasingly to their exotic colonies to fill these needs.

This act uncovers internal friction in Europe over ideas and philosophies such as Marxism and evolution. It also displays struggles over the exploitation and division of India, China, and Africa as imperialism takes hold in Europe. By the end of this act, the stage will be set for conflicts on an unprecedented scale.

But as that main plot weaves its way through the century, other events show a greater hand directing history. Missionary efforts flourish as young men and women go out to all the world, taking the gospel to people who have never heard of Christ's great sacrifice.

CHAPTER 11

The Great Exhibition of the Works of Industry of All Nations opened in London on May 1, 1851. People came from around the world to visit the **Great Exhibition.** It was housed in a huge iron-and-glass structure called the **Crystal Palace,** built in London's Hyde Park. Nearly three hundred thousand panes of glass, held in place by more than five thousand iron columns and girders, enclosed the Crystal Palace's nearly one million square feet of floor space. Running the width of the building was a central vault high enough to cover the park's ancient elms. Inside, flowers and trees, fountains, and statues surrounded the exhibits. Joseph Paxton's design was a success.

On May 1, 1851, everything was ready for the opening except one finishing touch: the arrival of the queen. Promptly at noon **Queen Victoria,** dressed in pink brocade and wearing diamonds, arrived with her husband, **Prince Albert,** and two of their children. The excited crowd cheered their arrival. The people loved their queen and her family. She so characterized this age that it is often called the **Victorian Age.** Trumpet fanfares, speeches, dedicatory prayers, and a thousand-voice choir singing Handel's "Hallelujah Chorus" highlighted the day's opening ceremonies. For the next six months, more than six million people viewed the displays of over thirteen thousand exhibitors.

In addition to displaying the world's manufactured items, the Great Exhibition also underscored Great Britain's position in the world. She was the unchallenged leader in industry and commerce. Her factories produced the most advanced products available, while her ships ruled the sea routes of the world. In areas besides industry Britain was also first. The activities and culture of Britain influenced and characterized Europe in the nineteenth century.

A.D. 1750 - A.D. 1900

The First F
Arrive
Australia 1

U.S. Revolutionary
War 1776-81

1750

Age of Reason 1600-1800

European Transformation

Congress of Vienna
1814-15

Greece and Belgium
Gain Independence 1831

Darwin Proposes Evolution
in His *Origin of Species* 1859

Telegraph Cable Between
the U.S. and Europe 1866

Karl Marx Writes *Das Kapital* 1867

800   1850   1900

Napoleon Defeated
at Waterloo 1815

Italy and Germany
Are Formed 1871

Great Exhibition 1851

Napoleon Becomes First
Consul in France 1799

*Communist
Manifesto 1848*

Bell Invents the Telephone 1875

The Rise of the Middle Class

The elevator, invented by Elisha Graves Otis, was one of many inventions demonstrated at the Great Exhibition.

Queen Victoria left her name and her values on a generation of Britishers and much of the world.

The nineteenth century saw the growth, both in numbers and importance, of the middle class. A class of merchants and manufacturers had existed in Europe since the late Middle Ages. However, during the Industrial Age this middle class gained new wealth and power in Europe, ranking next to nobles and land-owners. Many members of the middle class had their start as poorer businessmen who had used new technology to make their businesses more efficient and productive. Through hard work and creativity, they had improved their businesses and gained wealth.

The Great Exhibition was a tribute to this new middle class, especially Britain's middle class. Many of the goods displayed had been made by the middle class and for the middle class. Whether they were new gadgets for the home or intricate machines for the factory, these goods symbolized the twofold focus of middle-class life: home and business.

Middle-Class Houses

Members of the middle class generally lived in the cities. They owned or rented large homes in the better sections of town. Often these houses were highly decorated, as if to show off the extent of their owners' newly gained wealth. The interior of these houses also showed the new wealth of the middle class. The main rule of Victorian decorating was to fill every bit of space. Heavy wooden furniture, covered with curves and carvings, had been turned out by machine rather than handcrafted. Bushy plants and feathers filled every corner, while ribbons, pictures, and fans hung on the papered walls. The wallpaper was also made by machine, not hand painted. The parlor had overstuffed furniture of heavy brocade, and ruffled pillows lay everywhere.

Other new items equipped the middle-class home. One was the special piece of furniture called a *whatnot*—a set of shelves just to hold knickknacks. Another was the piano, which up until this time had been in only a few homes. Now many middle-class homes had an upright piano, and evenings spent playing and singing were common. The coal that provided the power for new factories also heated houses in the nineteenth century. Rooms which had previously been heated by wood now used coal in newly invented coal stoves placed in each fireplace.

Middle-Class Lifestyles

Every middle-class family had servants—butlers, maids, grooms, washerwomen, and cooks. The lady of the house directed their activities. They kept busy cleaning and taking care of those large households. Their jobs became somewhat easier as new inventions entered the home. Iron stoves and wringer-style washers made cooking and laundering easier.

A very important servant in the house was the **governess.** Her job was to supervise the family's children. She saw to their discipline and early education. Often girls received all their education from their governess or a tutor, but boys usually went away to boarding school before their teen years, and then some went on to college. Boys were sent to school not to become scholars but only to become reasonably well educated. The most important part of school was meeting other young men of their social class and developing character. The boys who attended school together would be the men who later did business together.

Governesses were a Victorian addition to middle-class homes.

SETTINGS—England

Location—England is the name of part of the United Kingdom located in the southern portion of Great Britain. The United Kingdom is located off the northwestern corner of Europe. England's borders include the Irish Sea and Wales in the west, Scotland in the north, the North Sea in the east, and the English Channel in the south.

Climate—All of Great Britain has a marine west coast climate. It is greatly affected by the water that surrounds it. Although it is only 360 miles from the southernmost part to the northern border, England has great variety in its weather. When snows blanket the mountain ranges of the north, palm trees still grow well in the south. The North Atlantic current of the Gulf Stream brings moist, warm air to the country and with it the constant potential for rain.

Topography—England is divided into three regions. The Pennines are a mountain range that runs from the Scottish border to the center of England. England's highest peak, Scafell Pike (3,210 ft.), is located west of the Pennines in the Cumbrian Mountains. Another feature of this area is the Lake District, which was immortalized by the Lake Poets of the 1800s. Fifteen beautiful lakes nestle down among the mountains. The next area is the Midlands. This is the fertile farmland of the country. The third region is the Southwest Peninsula. Another interesting topographical feature is the famous white chalk cliffs of Dover which line the coast of the Straits of Dover.

Natural Resources—The most important natural resource in England's early history was its fertile soil. Coal and iron ore deposits exist near the Pennines. Access to the rest of the world by water has been especially important to trade throughout the British Isles.

Geography & Culture—England's green, fertile land attracted settlers to its shores. Evidence of human occupation of the island goes back to thousands of years before Christ. England came to the attention of the Romans during the Roman Empire and later to the Scandinavian Vikings.

The fact that England is an island has added to its appeal. Water access has made England a prime trading center for centuries. With the defeat of the Spanish Armada in 1588, England claimed control of the seas.

England's separation from the rest of Europe has allowed it to take a different path politically and culturally from much of the rest of Europe.

Settings Review

1. What geographical feature has a great impact on England's weather?
2. What mountain range runs through northern England?
3. What district was written about by a set of poets?
4. What are two features of England that attracted settlers to its shores?

Look at a world map for other countries that are geographically separate from their neighboring countries. Choose one of those countries and look in the encyclopedia to see whether its geographic isolation has caused that country to develop differently from the countries around it.

Although England is a relatively small country, its fertile land has allowed it to become a major force in world history.

Middle-Class Optimism

The middle class was a group of people filled with optimism. They looked around them and saw how much life had changed during their century. They watched fast trains, steamships, iron stoves, and running water grow from being special to being commonplace. They saw improvements in living and working conditions, education, and health. These people overflowed with belief in their way of life, their culture. They desired to share their culture with others in the world whom they viewed as unfortunate and uncivilized.

Poverty in the Midst of Prosperity

In Mark 14:7 Jesus makes a sobering observation that is hard for many to accept: "For ye have the poor with you always." Chapter 9 described the poverty that many people in Europe suffered during the Industrial Revolution. In the 1800s the poor suffered in many of the same ways that they had a century earlier—families were crowded into one room, people lived in the streets, children worked long hours in dangerous conditions.

Poverty and its suffering have always existed. It should not surprise us, then, that in the era of Victorian optimism among the middle classes there was still great misery among the lower classes. But Jesus went on to say, "And whensoever ye will ye may do them good." Victorians took these words to heart. Many in the upper class believed that they were responsible to help change the conditions of the poor. There were some wealthy Englishmen with such a heart for the poor that they were willing to share their wealth to help relieve some of their suffering. What resulted was not a free handout but low-cost housing that met needs previously disregarded.

Rows of flats (apartment houses) built by rich men who charged nominal rentals sprang up to help provide the housing needs of the working class. They provided multiple bedrooms as well as a living area, indoor plumbing, and gas lighting. Low-cost houses that resembled the row houses of many cities in the United States today were also built. Working people could own a home with upstairs bedrooms, a kitchen, and two parlors. They even had a patch of yard to call their own.

Other philanthropists (wealthy people who give their resources to benefit humanity) such as **W. H. Lever**, founder of Lever Brothers,

London's streets teemed with poor people looking for a way to earn a living. This young girl is selling scarves.

Philanthropists set up factory towns such as New Lanark in Manchester, England, to meet the social and physical needs of their workers.

took his factory and workers out of the city and built the town of **Port Sunlight.** This model town included two styles of houses with three or four bedrooms in each. Every house had a back yard, but Lever insisted that the company maintain the front yard so that the entire town would be well kept. He also included in his town an art gallery and public gardens.

Through the efforts of these good people, conditions changed for some of the poor of England. As the middle class grew wealthier, the benefits spread to the lower classes in the form of jobs. The middle class could now afford to buy services and hire help, thus employing the lower classes and improving their conditions in this age of optimism.

Section Review

1. What jobs did the middle class hold?
2. What principle guided their tastes?
3. What musical instrument became a part of many middle-class homes?
4. What servant became especially important to middle-class children?
5. What attitude characterized the middle class?

6. Name the philanthropist who developed a model town. What was the town called?

Many wealthy people saw the poverty around them but did nothing to ease it. They knew what needed to be done but did not do it. Are we like that today? What are at least three things we know to do from God's Word but fail to do? How can we get the power to accomplish those things?

Balancing Power

In Chapter 9 you saw the power of the absolute rulers and the aristocracy of the eighteenth century. This system continued into the nineteenth century, but not without disruption. Revolutions in the United States and France challenged the rights of monarchy. The rise of the middle class encouraged the common man to demand more control of his destiny. Extreme contrast in wealth caused discontentment. Conflict in government caused unrest in much of Europe.

Parliamentary Government in Great Britain

One reason for Great Britain's strength in the nineteenth century was its stable government. Because England was ruled by a representative body, Parliament, and not an absolute king, the British people were more content than other Europeans. At the beginning of the century, few people had the right to vote. However, beginning in 1832, Parliament passed laws giving the right to vote to more and more people. These laws decreased the power of the king and upper class and increased that of the middle and lower classes. Britain's parliamentary government is much like the representative government of the United States. Changes can be made gradually and legally. Because the British followed this procedure, they escaped the disruptive revolts that plagued the rest of Europe.

By the end of the century, most men in Britain were permitted to vote. (Women did not get the vote until the twentieth century.) Because Parliament was elected by the people, it passed laws that the people wanted. Throughout the nineteenth century, the British Parliament often voted to aid the working poor. It passed laws to help women and children

working in the mines and factories. It also tried to improve living conditions in the new industrial cities. By recognizing and responding to the need for changes and making them gradually, the British maintained governmental stability. This in turn encouraged business prosperity. This heritage of stability and prosperity made Queen Victoria's era one of greatness.

Disruption on the Continent

The power of the French king was broken by the French Revolution. The revolution went through four phases as it attempted to reorganize its government. When the third attempt at reorganization was overthrown by the army, conditions were right for **Napoleon Bonaparte** to come to power. In 1799, with the help of a

A romantic vision of Napoleon at Waterloo before his defeat

Citizens wore the tricolors of France to display their nationalism and loyalty to the new government.

faced three problems: (1) redrawing boundaries, (2) punishing France, and (3) putting kings back on their thrones. Their goal was to restore peace and security to Europe.

The leaders at the Congress feared the ideas spread by Napoleon's armies throughout Europe. France had been the home of ideas about man's natural rights. These ideas emphasized that all men had certain natural rights to freedom. The French expressed these ideas with the phrase "Liberty, Equality, Fraternity." Accepting these ideas, people demanded more liberty from their leaders. They also wanted equality of representation in government. Finally, the French promoted the idea of nationalism. **Nationalism** is intense devotion and loyalty to one's own people (or nationality). People who shared a common language and culture but lived under the rule of another country desired freedom to rule themselves. As hard as the Congress tried to restrain these ideas, it could not. Soon revolts broke out all over Europe.

new constitution, he gave himself the title First Consul. In 1804 Napoleon proclaimed himself emperor of France, but his vision went far beyond France's boundaries. By 1812 he and his mighty armies had conquered much of Europe, making him the master of the continent. But his mastery was short-lived. By 1815 Napoleon was defeated and sent into exile. (See p. 304.)

With Napoleon gone, the leaders of Europe faced the problem of putting the Continent back together. For two years these leaders came together for meetings, called the **Congress of Vienna** (1814-15). **Prince Metternich** (MET ur nik) of Austria was the leading statesman at the Congress, and his ideas were very influential. The Congress

Leading statesmen met at the Congress of Vienna to put Europe back together after Napoleon was defeated.

Napoleon at Waterloo

You may have heard of someone "meeting his Waterloo." A person using this expression usually means that someone has suffered a major setback, a final defeat. The expression comes from the Battle of Waterloo, perhaps the most famous battle of all history. There France's emperor Napoleon met his final defeat.

In June of 1815, Napoleon's situation was desperate. Nearly every other country in Europe had allied itself against him. Napoleon decided that only a quick, decisive victory could save his throne. He quickly raised an army and marched north into Belgium. Opposing him were a Prussian army and a British army under the Duke of Wellington.

Napoleon knew his army was outnumbered by these combined forces. Therefore, he decided to try to divide the enemy forces, concentrate on one part and defeat it, and then turn and crush the rest. A large French force launched a surprise attack against the Prussians, sending them reeling away from the British. Napoleon assumed that he had shattered the Prussian forces and could now ignore them. This was a great mistake, for the Prussians were daunted but not destroyed.

Nonetheless, the French turned to crush the British. Wellington took up a strong defensive position near the Belgian village of Waterloo. He knew that his best chance lay in holding off the French until the Prussians could come to his aid. Napoleon was overconfident. He delayed the beginning of the attack for several hours, waiting for the ground to dry from recent thunderstorms. When he finally attacked, his maneuvers were not subtle; instead, he charged head-on into the British lines. He believed that the British would surely collapse in the face of a fierce attack.

The British held on, however. They bravely beat back attack after attack. As evening approached, the supposedly defeated Prussian army entered the eastern end of the battlefield. Caught between two armies, the French army collapsed and fell into a confused retreat. At Waterloo Napoleon lost not only a battle but also the war and his throne.

Nationalism and Revolution

The revolts came in three waves. The first wave hit in the 1820s. Most of these revolts were crushed, but in 1829 **Greece** gained its independence from the Ottoman Empire after ten years of fighting. Starting in 1830, a second wave of revolts occurred. In 1831 **Belgium** became independent from the Netherlands, but the Poles and Hungarians were crushed when they fought for independence. The last wave came in 1848. By this time, Europe's rulers knew they had to make changes or continue to risk revolt. The second half of the century was marked by a gradual movement away from absolutism.

Nationalism also encouraged the formation of two other nations during this century—**Italy** and **Germany.** For centuries these areas had been made up of many individual states, some ruled independently and some ruled by empires such as Austria. After years of trying, Italy and Germany were born in 1871.

CHARGED WITH ROMANCE

The Romantic movement produced many great poets. One of the most outstanding was Alfred, Lord Tennyson (TEN ih sun). An Englishman, he was proclaimed Britain's poet laureate (LOR ee it), the official poet of the king and queen.

In the following poem, Tennyson is telling the story of the Light Brigade that made a charge against the Russians in the Crimean War. The job of the Light Brigade was to retake guns at the end of a valley flanked by the enemy. Unfortunately, a badly worded command sent the brigade charging straight into the enemy's guns.

Look ahead to page 316 and read the paragraphs that deal with the Romantic movement. As you read the poem below, what Romantic themes do you see in it? What is your reaction to the poem? Do you think that was the reaction that Tennyson wanted?

The Charge of the Light Brigade

Half a league, half a league,
Half a league onward,
All in the valley of Death
Rode the six hundred.
"Forward, the Light Brigade!
Charge for the guns!" he said.
Into the valley of Death
Rode the six hundred.

"Forward, the Light Brigade!"
Was there a man dismayed?
Not tho' the soldier knew
Someone had blundered.
Theirs not to make reply,
Theirs not to reason why,
Theirs but to do and die.
Into the valley of Death
Rode the six hundred.

Cannon to the right of them,
Cannon to the left of them,
Cannon in front of them
Volleyed and thundered;
Stormed at with shot and shell,
Boldly they rode and well,
Into the jaws of Death,
Into the mouth of Hell
Rode the six hundred.

Flashed all their sabres bare,
Flashed as they turned in air
Sabring the gunners there,
Charging an army, while
All the world wondered.
Plunged in the battery-smoke
Right thro' the line they broke;
Cossack and Russian
Reeled from the sabre-stroke
Shattered and sundered.
Then they rode back, but not,
Not the six hundred.

Cannon to the right of them,
Cannon to the left of them,
Cannon in front of them
Volleyed and thundered;
Stormed at with shot and shell,
While horse and hero fell,
They that had fought so well
Came thro' the jaws of Death,
Back from the mouth of Hell,
All that was left of them,
Left of the six hundred.

When can their glory fade?
O the wild charge they made!
All the world wondered.
Honor the charge they made!
Honor the Light Brigade,
Noble six hundred!

Imperialism

The rulers of Europe were not concerned just with events on the continent during the nineteenth century. They were also interested in building empires, a movement called **imperialism.** The Americas, India, China, and Africa all contained areas that the European nations desired to control. Their motives were several. First they needed raw materials and markets to support their growing industries. Next they desired to share European culture with others whom they viewed as less civilized. This motive included the spreading of Christianity to lost people. A third reason was to appear powerful before other European nations. Unless a nation had colonies, it was considered weak. Toward the end of the century, the race for colonies reached a furious pace and was one of the major causes of World War I (1914-18). In later chapters we will look at how European nations treated their colonies.

New Countries in the 1800s

NETHERLANDS
BELGIUM
GERMANY
POLAND
FRANCE
SWITZ.
AUSTRIA
ITALY
GREECE

Section Review

1. What type of government did Great Britain have?

2. What problems did the workers in the new cities have? How did Parliament help them?

3. What group tried to restore Europe to pre-Napoleonic conditions?

4. Although Napoleon was defeated, what ideas did he spread through Europe? What did this French influence promote in Europe?

5. Give two examples of unsuccessful nationalism.

6. Name two nations that gained independence in Europe in the 1800s.

In this chapter we see many revolutions occurring. Is revolting against government a proper response for a Christian? Support your answer with Scripture.

The Age of Industrialism

The Industrial Revolution began in the eighteenth century and was fully underway by the mid-nineteenth century. At the Great Exhibition many exhibits showed the results of new industries. Undoubtedly, Great Britain was the leader in manufacturing. But slowly the other nations of Europe, the United States, and Japan caught up.

Technology and Invention

The nineteenth century was the heyday of inventors, both European and American. Using new technologies and simple guesswork, they all had the same goal in mind: discover something new. The "new" might be an entirely new object or an improved version of an old one. From this attitude of discovery came such important inventions as the **steam locomotive,** electrical generators, the telephone, and the automobile.

The new inventions dramatically changed almost every aspect of life—especially transportation. The steam locomotive and iron rails improved land travel. Now, instead of walking or riding in bumpy carriages on dirt roads, people could travel on steam-powered trains. Some of these trains sped along at almost sixty miles per hour. In sea travel, steam engines replaced sails on ocean-going vessels. Gradually iron, which made the ship move faster and last longer, replaced wood in ships' hulls.

New inventions also affected communication. The **telegraph** allowed people to send messages quickly over great distances by wire instead of relying on the slower delivery by foot or horse. In 1866 an undersea telegraph cable was laid between Europe and North

New inventions such as the camera and the motor car brought change to the world.

Alexander Graham Bell's telephone brought instant communication to people miles apart.

meager and unappealing. With the advent of the telephone and typewriter, women took a new place in the work force in offices and other businesses. People began to accept the idea of single women working outside the home.

As expected, technology especially affected the factories. Machines that made goods more quickly and efficiently were constantly being invented and improved. New processes for casting iron and smelting steel made these two metals much easier to produce. As a result, these metals became basic to many manufactured goods. Cast iron was used for everything from textile looms to garden fountains, while steel became as common in the kitchen as in the factory.

America. Near the end of the nineteenth century an American inventor named **Alexander Graham Bell** invented the **telephone.** Technological advances in printed communications resulted in larger printing presses run by steam engines. These presses turned out newspapers and books faster and more economically than before.

Two other important inventions for publishing, writing, and business were the **typewriter** and the camera. The typewriter produced easily readable, consistent text for business forms and correspondence. The science of **photography** added a new dimension to publishing. It also allowed families and historians to chronicle the events of life more accurately.

Two of the inventions mentioned above, the typewriter and the telephone, changed women's lives especially. Before this time, women worked outside the home only if they were poor or if their families were unable to support them. The jobs available to them were

The invention of the camera allowed this young girl to keep a visual record of her first telephone call.

Steel

In the mid-1800s men on both continents and England were racing to produce inexpensive steel. Prior to this time, cast iron, wrought iron, and brick were the building materials of choice, but their usage was limited. The inexpensive production of steel changed architecture, transportation, and daily life in the late 1800s.

With new means such as the Bessemer converter and the open-hearth method, steel producers could quickly separate the impurities in iron into a slag that was poured off and gases that blew away. The product of these processes was a material that could be poured, rolled, and shaped into many forms that were stronger than the iron from which they came.

The great strength of steel allowed the Firth of Forth Bridge to be built. For the first time a bridge spanned 1,710 feet between piers. Previously iron had spanned only 500-600 feet between piers and brickwork only about 300 feet. The Eiffel Tower, built for the Paris Exposition in 1889, was a miracle in technology, not only because of its maze of steel beams and wires but also because it was outfitted with electric lights.

Steel transformed transportation. Railroad tracks were smoother and engines finer. By the late 1800s France had nearly eleven thousand miles of railway. Trains traveled an amazing fifty miles an hour to rush the French from town to coast. In the late 1800s motor cars came on the scene, allowing personal mobility for the wealthy and soon for many more.

In daily life, steel was used for common household implements such as knives, but its most significant impact was as a sheathing for the transatlantic cable that allowed messages to be sent back and forth from continent to continent. The main copper wires in the cable were first surrounded by insulation and lastly surrounded by ten steel wires that were each insulated and protected by hemp. The steel wires formed a protection against the sea and the rocks.

The easy production of steel was one of the technological advances that revolutionized life in the 1800s and continues to allow comfort and facility in our lives today. Practically every building, every machine, and every vehicle that you use today contains steel components.

The open hearth method of steel production

The Firth of Forth

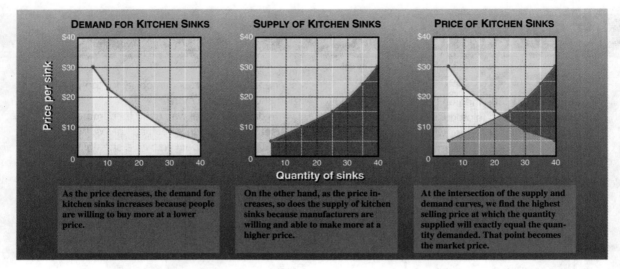

DEMAND FOR KITCHEN SINKS

As the price decreases, the demand for kitchen sinks increases because people are willing to buy more at a lower price.

SUPPLY OF KITCHEN SINKS

On the other hand, as the price increases, so does the supply of kitchen sinks because manufacturers are willing and able to make more at a higher price.

PRICE OF KITCHEN SINKS

At the intersection of the supply and demand curves, we find the highest selling price at which the quantity supplied will exactly equal the quantity demanded. That point becomes the market price.

Managing Industrialism

Two major problems faced the early industrialists: production and marketing. **Production** includes designing or inventing new products. It also includes building machinery to produce them and finding raw materials. **Marketing** includes setting prices for the products and advertising them. The businessman must also find markets for his products and transport them there.

One answer to the problems of production and marketing was **capitalism.** In capitalism, all property (factory buildings and equipment) is owned privately by a businessman or group of businessmen. This property is known as *capital,* hence the name *capitalism.* Capitalism thrives on competition: businessmen trying to outdo each other with newer, better, or less expensive products.

In marketing, capitalism relies on **supply and demand.** Supply and demand deals with how much there is of a product and how many people want it or need it. The product's price depends on how much of a product is in supply as well as customers' demands for that product. The diagrams above show this principle at work.

Capitalism works best when there is **free trade,** trade between or within countries without taxes on goods. Great Britain led the free-trade movement by trading freely with her colonies. Britain's leadership in sea trade encouraged other nations to practice free trade. Gradually throughout the nineteenth century, more countries followed the principle of free trade.

Capitalism also discourages government interference. However, man's sinful, greedy nature often leads to unethical or unsafe practices in production and marketing. By the end of the century many governments passed regulations to protect owners, workers, and consumers.

Labor: Problems and Responses

In Chapter 9 you read about the working conditions and living conditions of factory workers. As industrialism grew, these problems worsened. They contributed to many of the revolts of the nineteenth century. The people desired better working environments and living conditions as well as political freedom. In some countries, such as Great Britain, governments passed bills in an attempt to improve the workers' lives. In many European countries, though, governments often did not respond to the workers' needs, and the workers did not wait for the slow process of lawmaking.

Because it seemed unlikely that some governments would ever change, many workers turned to the ideas of the socialists. **Socialism** is opposed to capitalism. The socialists encourage governmental control. They say that the government—not individuals—should own all business property. Socialists also believe that government can use this power for the good of society. The name *socialist* came from this emphasis on society or social good. According to this philosophy, workers benefit by sharing equally in the profits rather than by earning according to their labor.

One problem with this belief is best shown by illustration. A man who produced twenty pairs of shoes in a day was paid the same amount as a man who produced only ten pairs. The man who produced twenty pairs of shoes received no recognition or increased pay for his greater effort. Do you think he will want to continue producing twenty shoes a day?

Another problem of socialism is that it assumes government is capable of determining what should be produced. It is far from clear in socialist writings, however, how government is supposed to know how to make such decisions. Socialism ignores the limitations of human knowledge and assumes that government is not susceptible to the same evil excesses of which it accuses businessmen.

A socialist government is involved with society as well as with business. It seeks to provide services, such as welfare, housing, education, and health care. Heavy taxation pays for these programs. As one man said, "Taxation for social benefit is like getting a blood transfusion from your right arm to your left arm, and losing half the blood in the

process." Although people receive many material benefits in a socialistic system, individual worth, achievement, and responsibility are valued little. Also, the resulting economic burden on the nation can be disastrous.

Karl Marx (1818-83) developed a philosophy called **Marxism.**

> "Philosophers have only sought to *interpret* the real world in various ways; the real point is to *change* society." Karl Marx

As the quotation above reveals, Marx wanted to change society. He felt that society's main problem was that the rich controlled the means of producing goods. Karl Marx wrote two books about his philosophy that have been used as guidebooks for other leaders: the *Communist Manifesto,* written with Friedrich Engels, and *Das Kapital* (DAHS kah-pee-TAHL). In these books Marx envisioned his philosophy helping the evolution of government to result in the perfect society—**Communism.** In Communism all people would share in labor and in the goods that resulted from that labor.

Marx promoted revolution as a means of overthrowing governments that oppressed the working class. Marx's philosophy was used by later Communist leaders to urge workers to rebel against their employers and rulers. Because the governments of Europe gradually responded to the needs of workers and made some reforms, Communism did not take over in Europe entirely. Only in Russia were the Communists successful in overthrowing the government (see pp. 448-49).

With a socialist economic system meeting the needs of the people and no private ownership of goods, Marx believed that people should be perfectly content. Unfortunately, Marx did not consider man's sin nature. In the early Christian communities of the New Testament, a type of communism was used. Acts 4:32-35 says,

Hunger and poverty sometimes motivated people to follow socialist revolutions. German expressionist artist Käthe Kollwitz caught this mood in her print Uprising, 1899. (Courtesy of Emery Bopp)

And the multitude of them that believed were of one heart and of one soul: neither said any of them that ought of the things which he possessed was his own; but they had all things common.

And with great power gave the apostles witness of the resurrection of the Lord Jesus: and great grace was upon them all.

Neither was there any among them that lacked: for as many as were possessors of lands or houses sold them, and brought the prices of the things that were sold,

And laid them down at the apostles' feet: and distribution was made unto every man according as he had need.

Even in this Christian community where "great grace" was upon them, problems arose. Shortly after these verses, the pride and lies of Ananias and Sapphira were revealed (Acts 5:1-10) and the murmuring over the neglect of the widows began (Acts 6:1). There is little possibility of Marx's vision of Communism becoming a reality in this sinful world.

Section Review

1. What nation led industry in the nineteenth century?
2. List three inventions of this period.
3. What two problems faced nineteenth-century businessmen?
4. What two factors influence the setting of a price in capitalism? What type of trade makes capitalism work best?

5. How did many governments of Europe handle labor problems?
6. To what did workers turn when the governments did not respond quickly?

List four things that would hinder Communism from working in a society. Explain the effect of each item on your list.

Belief and Expression

Accidents in the lab don't always bring disaster.

Science and Evolution

The amazing achievements of science caused many people to look at science as the answer to all their problems. To them, scientifically "proving" something gave it a stamp of approval. Science is a useful tool; however, an undue emphasis on science is dangerous because a person may hold the results of science above the truth of Scripture.

This danger became reality with the work of **Charles Darwin.** Darwin struck at the root of Christian belief and biblical teaching with his theory of evolution. **Evolution** denied Creation by God's direct act. Evolutionists said that all creatures, including man, evolved from nonliving elements. They stated that simple life forms came from these basic elements; then the less complex animals evolved, and finally man appeared. According to Darwin, this process took hundreds of millions of years with improvements coming gradually as creatures adapted to their changing environments. With his theory, Darwin denied Scripture on two counts: first, he denied divine Creation (Gen. 1:1); second, by saying man evolved, he denied man's special creation after God's likeness and image (Gen. 1:26). Evolution was and is today a direct attack on God's sovereignty and power.

Charles Darwin

Science obviously held an important place at the Great Exhibition in 1851. The exhibits showed new scientific discoveries. Scientists of this century carried on the work begun in the Age of Reason. Many inventions at the Exhibition were the result of scientific study put to work on specific problems. But sometimes new inventions were merely side benefits of scientific research. An example of this was the development of synthetic dyes. While trying to find a new medicine, a young researcher accidentally discovered a substance that dyed cloth purple. Purple had always been the color of royalty and wealth because it was expensive to make from natural substances. With the discovery of the synthetic purple, which was cheap and easy to use, nearly everyone could afford purple cloth. Mauve (MOHV), a shade of purple, became so fashionable that the 1890s were called the "Mauve Decade."

Charles Haddon Spurgeon

Science and Religion

The emphasis on science which had begun during the Age of Reason in the 1700s continued to greatly influence people's religious beliefs and actions. The ideas of evolution and the questioning of the power and existence of God shook the faith of many. Unbelieving theologians used scientific methods and principles to attack God's Word. They denied the inspiration of Scripture. Believers who were not fully grounded in the Word and unbelievers who had no foundation in Christ were often misled by the claims of "scholars" who questioned and denied Scripture. Many ideas of these nineteenth-century theologians are still alive today. Christians must study the Bible and become firmly rooted in the truth of Scripture so that they can use "the sword of the Spirit, which is the word of God" (Eph. 6:17) against these attacks.

The people who accepted Darwin's ideas believed that, with the proper external influences, man could still be made better. They believed the **social gospel,** which taught that people could be improved by changing their living conditions rather than by converting their souls. However, *true* improvement comes only from God's power and starts at salvation. Second Corinthians 5:17 tells us, "Therefore if any man be in Christ, he is a new creature: old things are passed away; behold, all things are become new." Despite the attempts at reform in the nineteenth century, poverty, disease, and crime remained. Once again this evidence shows the failure of man to permanently improve his external conditions without first improving his heart.

As in any age, the only true answer to society's problems is Christ. During the 1800s several revivals swept England and America. The preaching of **Charles H. Spurgeon** and **Dwight L. Moody** brought many people to the Savior. These new Christians wanted to help others by teaching them of Christ. Improved transportation allowed many to go to the mission fields of China, India, and Africa. (See "Fulfilling the Great Commission," on p. 250.)

Other believers stayed in Europe to establish ministries at home. These Christians helped people by pointing them to Christ's saving blood. The **Salvation Army,** the Young Men's Christian Association (YMCA), and the Young Women's Christian Association (YWCA) were started to meet both physical and spiritual needs. Orphanages, schools, hospitals, and Sunday schools provided for the poor and needy. The dedicated Christian men and women who ran these ministries touched many lives as they spread the love of God to those in need. Their works showed their faith by combining the Bible's commands to "preach the gospel" (Mark 16:15) and to "do good unto all men" (Gal. 6:10).

Christian Orphanages: The Work of Thomas Barnardo and George Mueller

The plight of orphans in Victorian England was severe. Even orphanages built expressly to help such children were often managed by cruel, unconcerned people. Many Englishmen called attention to this unhappy situation and demanded changes. Christians especially felt compassion toward the orphans and tried to help them. They took seriously the word of Psalm 82:3, "Defend the poor and fatherless: do justice to the afflicted and needy."

One Christian man, Dr. Thomas Barnardo (1845-1905), devoted his life to building orphan-

George Mueller

Unwanted and orphaned children were everywhere in England.

ages. Converted as a result of the Irish Revival of 1859, Dr. Barnardo wanted to be a medical missionary to China. However, health problems prevented his going. Instead, he became interested in the needs of orphans. In 1867 he opened his first home for them. Making his motto "no destitute child ever refused admission," Dr. Barnardo eventually helped over ten thousand orphans in his homes.

Perhaps even better known than Dr. Barnardo was George Mueller (1805-1898). Born in Prussia, Mueller was converted at the age of twenty and came to England to prepare for the mission field. While living in the city of Bristol, he became concerned about the orphans there. Believing himself to be led of God, Mueller built an orphanage. Mueller ran his home on faith. He had no governmental or even church funding. He simply prayed for God to supply his needs, and the Lord always did. Often, Mueller would go to bed not knowing where the next day's food would come from. Yet God graciously rewarded his faith and supplied his needs. As a result of God's faithful provision, thousands of orphans benefited from the work of George Mueller.

The Hay Wain *by John Constable*

Changes in the Arts

The nineteenth century was an age of change, and the arts were no exception. Several styles of art appeared in the nineteenth century. **Romanticism** dominated the first half of the century. Several themes characterize romanticism: a desire to imitate the past, especially the medieval time with its higher call to chivalry; an emphasis on the mysterious and the supernatural; a love of freedom; nationalism; and nature. These themes also reflect the political ideas of the time. Romantic themes appeared in nineteenth-century literature as well, such as Sir Walter Scott's medieval story *Ivanhoe.*

Romantic paintings often are peaceful scenes of rural life or landscapes. Some artists also painted scenes from the revolutions. In music, composers reacted to the orderly, classical style by changing to the full, emotion-filled romantic style. **Ludwig van Beethoven** (BAY-TOH-vun) is perhaps the best-known composer of this age. He mixed classical and romantic elements in his works. The romantic composers **Johannes Brahms** and **Frédéric Chopin** (shoh PAN) used folksongs in their works, showing the influence of nationalism. This century was also the height of opera, a combination of music, drama, and literature. The leading opera composer, **Giuseppe Verdi,** lived at this time.

By midcentury, romanticism lost popularity to a new style: **realism.** Realism reacted against romanticism's dreamlike quality by emphasizing, as its name suggests, how life really is. In writing and painting, realists pictured everyday life in realistic detail. For example, the novelist **Charles Dickens** used realistic elements in his stories of working-class Englishmen. His books did much to publicize the horrible conditions of the lower classes. The new science of photography influenced realistic painters. They often tried to copy the precision of photographs.

By the end of the century a third style called **impressionism** (im PRESH uh NIZ um) emerged, continuing into the twentieth century. Impressionism differed from both romanticism and realism. The impressionists sought to capture the impression a scene made on one's mind. New scientific discoveries showed that the mind perceived images through light and color. Impressionist painters were less concerned with their subject matter than with

A Boat on the Shore *by Gustave Courbet (Metropolitan Museum of Art)*

Two Views of London

Early Victorian author Jane Austen often showed London as a city where the rich rented homes in the winter so that they could be part of the round of social events held by the social elite. She said very little about the plight of the poor.

Dickens presented quite a different view of London in many of his books. His perspective dwells on the trials of the poor across England but especially in London. In the following excerpt from *Dombey and Son,* Chapter 33, Dickens gives us a glimpse of people who are migrating to London from the country.

She often looked with compassion, at such a time, upon the stragglers who came wandering into London, by the great highway hard by, and who, footsore and weary, and gazing fearfully at the huge town before them, as if foreboding that their misery there would be but as a drop of water in the sea, or as a grain of sea-sand on the shore, went shrinking on, cowering before the angry weather, and looking as if the very elements rejected them. Day after day, such travellers crept past, but always, as she thought in one direction—always towards the town. Swallowed up in one phase or other of its immensity, towards which they seemed impelled by a desperate fascination, they never returned. Food for the hospitals, the churchyards, the prisons, the rivers, fever, madness, vice, and death—they passed on to the monster, roaring in the distance, and were lost.

High hopes for a new life were often dashed by the reality of a dirty, bustling city filled with many people and few jobs.

the technical aspects of their work, especially light and color. By observing scenes at various hours, they saw how changes in light caused changes in color. They recorded these effects of light on their canvases. Each impressionistic painting captures a scene at a particular moment and often seems to lack purpose or substance. For these reasons impressionistic art was at first rejected by art critics.

In music, impressionism was displayed in shimmering music with no standard form. A leading impressionistic composer was **Claude Debussy** (duh BYOO see). Debussy rejected the emotionalism and form of the romantic composers. Instead of producing a connected work that builds emotion, the impressionist composer uses unconnected musical phrases to create a temporary mood. Debussy is so identified with the impressionist form that some argue that he is the only true impressionist composer.

Claude Debussy was the inventor of impressionistic music.

House of Parliament—
Sun Breaking Through
the Fog, *Claude Monet*

Section Review

1. How did many people look at science in the nineteenth century?
2. What most dangerous result of science came in this age?
3. In what two ways did Darwin deny Scripture?
4. What did the social gospel teach? What is really the only answer to man's problems?
5. How did the romantic composers react against classicism? Who was the best-known early romantic composer?
6. What two elements of painting did impressionistic artists concentrate on?

What are three things in this section that were affected by science? Why does science have such a strong effect on so many areas of life?

Summary

Throughout the nineteenth century a growing middle class glowed with optimism. This optimism carried them to all corners of the world, where they shared their culture with others. The nineteenth century was Britain's great century. Britain led the world in manufacturing, trade, empire building, and society. The nineteenth century on the Continent was confronted by the ideas spread by Napoleon. One result of this confrontation was the formation of new nations—Greece, Belgium, Germany, and Italy. In industry and trade, the opposing systems of capitalism and socialism conflicted. Governments and businessmen learned to improve living conditions and working conditions at least slightly or face the threat of riots, revolts, and even Communism. In thought and religion, science became even more important. Darwin proposed his theory of evolution, while scholars attacked God's Word by using so-called "scientific" methods. But God sent revival through godly preachers, and many believers reached out to help those around them and give them the gospel. Many went to foreign mission fields. In art, three styles dominated the 1800s: romanticism, realism, and impressionism. These styles reflected the spirit of the age.

CHAPTER REVIEW

People, Places, and Things to Know

Great Exhibition
Crystal Palace
Queen Victoria
Prince Albert
Victorian Age
governess
W. H. Lever
Port Sunlight
Napoleon Bonaparte
Congress of Vienna
Prince Metternich
nationalism

Greece
Belgium
Italy
Germany
imperialism
steam locomotive
telegraph
Alexander Graham
  Bell
telephone
typewriter
photography

production
marketing
capitalism
supply and demand
free trade
socialism
Karl Marx
Marxism
Communism
Charles Darwin
evolution
social gospel

Charles H. Spurgeon
Dwight L. Moody
Salvation Army
romanticism
Ludwig van Beethoven
Johannes Brahms
Frédéric Chopin
Giuseppe Verdi
realism
Charles Dickens
impressionism
Claude Debussy

Review Questions

Completion

Choose the appropriate word to complete these statements.

1. The nineteenth century was an age of (change, stagnation).

2. The nineteenth-century middle class was (optimistic, pessimistic).

3. The nineteenth century was a time of (peace, revolution)

Fill in the Blanks

Complete the statements by filling in the correct terms.

4. In the nineteenth century, carriages were replaced by (a) _____, sailing ships by (b) _____.

5. During most of the nineteenth century, the ruler of Great Britain was (a) _____, and her husband was (b) _____. During her reign the (c) _____, showing Great Britain as the leading industrial power, was held.

Matching

Match the following statements to the nineteenth-century movement each describes.

6. attempt to gain foreign territory
7. property is owned by the government
8. creatures came from nonliving elements
9. art style showing everyday life
10. extreme loyalty to one's own people
11. property is owned by individuals
12. all people share labor and goods
13. art style emphasizing nature and freedom
14. art style that captures the impression of a scene

(a) capitalism
(b) Communism
(c) evolution
(d) imperialism
(e) impressionism
(f) nationalism
(g) realism
(h) romanticism
(i) socialism

Connections

For each of the following pairs of items, write a sentence or two explaining the connection between them.

15. Italy / Germany
16. Spurgeon / Moody
17. Salvation Army / YMCA

Multiple Choice

Choose the man who is connected to each movement.

18. evolution: Napoleon, Darwin, Marx, Metternich
19. realism: Chopin, Darwin, Dickens, Verdi
20. romanticism: Beethoven, Haydn, Debussy, Bach
21. Communism: Darwin, Lever, Marx, Spurgeon

Think About It!

This chapter has shown some of the changes that occurred in Europe during the 1800s. Those changes were reflected by the three art styles: romanticism, realism, and impressionism. Write a one-paragraph essay that explains how art reflects the spirit of an era. Compare the three styles while telling what you know about the time.

CHAPTER 12

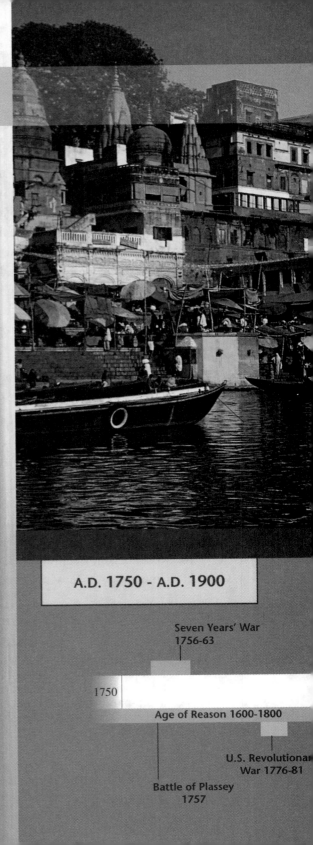

The flow of Indian history has been periodically interrupted by invaders. The Aryans disrupted Indian life around 1500 B.C. A thousand years later, the Persians conquered them. Although Alexander the Great did not conquer India, he did threaten its borders in the fourth century B.C. Another thousand years passed before the coming of the Muslim Arabs. The Mongol Tamerlane invaded India around 1400, and the Mughuls (also of Mongol heritage) came to rule India in 1500. At the same time, Europeans landed in India. These new invaders were traders. The first one was the Portuguese Vasco da Gama. (See Chapter 6.)

After hesitant first encounters, the Portuguese established fortified factories along the western coast of India. The supreme sea power of the Portuguese, and eventually the Spanish, allowed them to monopolize European trade in India throughout the sixteenth century. But when the Spanish Armada was destroyed in 1588, the opportunity came for other European nations to establish control—first the Dutch, then the English, and finally the French.

A.D. 1750 - A.D. 1900

Seven Years' War
1756-63

1750

Age of Reason 1600-1800

U.S. Revolutionar
War 1776-81

Battle of Plassey
1757

Raj India

Telegraph System
Starts in India 1853

Charter Act 1814

Sepoy Mutiny
1857

Carey's Mission Work in
India 1794-1834

British Raj Begins 1868

00

1850

1900

Great Century of Christian Missions 1800-1900

Queen Victoria's Reign 1838-1901

Expanding English Control

The English came to trade and ended up ruling the country. They helped develop India by bringing Western culture and technology. The British contributed much to the people of India yet did not understand or appreciate native Indian culture. Throughout the years of their rule, occasional conflicts flared up because of these cultural differences. Eventually British rule ended when the Indians gained their independence in 1947.

The East India Company

The growth of English control in India was gradual, taking over 250 years. The first Englishmen to come to India were not even officials of the government. They represented the **East India Company,** a company chartered by Queen Elizabeth I in 1600. The company's main purpose was trade. The traders desired the cotton, silks, spices, drugs, and other goods from India as well as a place to sell English goods. When they finally arrived in India in 1608 with a letter from James I, the Indians were not impressed. For the next eleven years, the English tried to "impress" the Mughul emperors with their power by using well-armed ships to bombard ports and rival ships. Finally, in 1619, the Mughuls allowed the English to set up trading stations in Surat. Within a hundred years, the company had centers at **Bombay, Madras,** and **Calcutta.**

The India trade was profitable, and the company's business grew. A major problem, however, was the French, who also had trading posts in India. The French, who had made political agreements with several Indian princes, tried to harm British trade. In 1756 French and British rivalry erupted. The Seven Years' War broke out between these two nations in Europe and India. In the **Battle of Plassey** (PLAHS ee) in 1757, the British defeated a leading Indian prince. With only three thousand men, British commander **Robert Clive** (KLIVE) routed a disorganized Indian force of eighty thousand. The victory at Plassey broke

Prior to England's involvement, India was ruled by several princes who lived richly on the taxes of the people.

France's strength in India. Within three years the French were completely defeated.

For the next hundred years, British trade with India grew. The East India Company opened more markets and added more territory to its holdings. The company's official reasons for annexing lands and exerting control over India were twofold. One was to protect its trade and employees from Indian violence. A second reason was to provide stable governments for the Indian frontiers, especially in the north. Many frontier areas had weak or lawless governments that hampered company trade and safety.

Although these reasons may be true in part, another major motive for the company's

Robert Clive used his victory at Plassey to influence British investors. As a result, he became wealthy at a young age.

action was greed. The British traders desired to increase their company's income. In opportunistic moves they annexed one territory after another as weak Indian princes and warring Indian factions proved unable to control their lands and people. With the annexing of these lands came the monetary tribute normally paid to the prince. Indian silver poured into company coffers and eventually into England.

While their motives may not have been philanthropic, the East India Company did nothing to really harm life for the common people. The princes of the land did not care for the people. The people had no say in their government. In essence, the people just exchanged one absolute ruler for another.

The Black Hole of Calcutta

When war broke out between France and England in 1756, some Indian rulers tried to take advantage of the situation. One such leader seized the British-controlled city of Calcutta. Most of the British citizens escaped, but others could not make it out in time. The story reported to the British by the surviving British commander, John Holwell, was that the Indian commander ordered all the British prisoners to be placed in the city's fortress, in a cell called "the Black Hole."

The cell measured only about eighteen feet by fourteen feet—about the size of a large bedroom. Holwell said that 146 people, including one woman and about a dozen wounded officers, were crowded into the room. In the hot, humid climate of India with only one small window for air, many prisoners suffocated overnight. Only twenty-three survived the ordeal. Holwell himself lived only by staying near the window and sucking his shirt sleeve to relieve his thirst.

The incident horrified the British, who later recaptured Calcutta and drove the French completely out of India. The British used this atrocity to help justify their takeover of India.

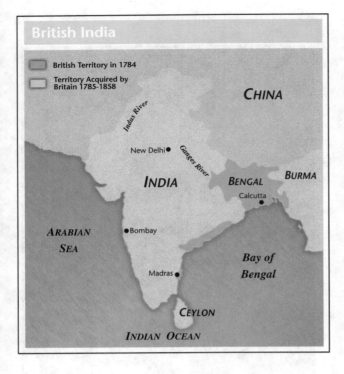

British India

British Territory in 1784

Territory Acquired by Britain 1785-1858

CHINA

Indus River

Ganges River

New Delhi

INDIA

BENGAL

BURMA

Calcutta

ARABIAN SEA

Bombay

Bay of Bengal

Madras

CEYLON

INDIAN OCEAN

The British Government Takes Over

In 1858 the British government took final control of affairs in India. During the late 1700s and early 1800s, the government had been exerting more and more control over the activities of the East India Company. In 1814 the **Charter Act** gave the crown control over all that the company possessed. The final takeover came in response to an uprising of Indian soldiers, called **sepoys** (SEE POYZ).

The **Sepoy Mutiny** (1857-58) was the result of the Indians' fear and discontent about some of the changes the British were making in traditional Indian life. There was much worry within the ranks that the British were conspiring with the missionaries. The sepoys thought that the missionaries wanted to make them unclean so that they would be more willing to convert.

Each new incident seemed to support that belief. The British passed a **General Enlistment Act,** requiring troops to serve anywhere the British deemed necessary, even across the sea in Burma, where they would be forced to mingle with other castes. However, the match that ignited the fear and resentment came in the form of a new type of rifle. At that time, ammunition cartridges had to be opened before they were used. Usually the soldiers bit them open. The problems arose because the cartridges for the new rifle required greasing, and the sepoys believed that they were greased with either pork or beef fat. The Hindu soldiers were offended because the cow was sacred to them; the Muslim soldiers were offended because pork was considered unclean. Therefore, both factions of Indian soldiers were insulted by the new cartridges.

When they were commanded to load weapons, regiment after regiment of sepoys refused, and the British stripped them of their uniforms and pensions. The sepoys' once proud loyalty to the British was gone, and only hatred was left.

On Saturday, May 9, 1857, the mutiny became war in Meerut, India. Eighty-five sepoys there refused to use the weapons and were imprisoned. The next day they were freed by other rebellious soldiers, and the violence of the Sepoy Mutiny had begun. In the days that followed, both the Indians and the British massacred many innocent people.

Within a year the mutiny was stopped. Six months later Queen Victoria proclaimed India under control of the British crown rather than the East India Company. In the proclamation, the British government for the first time recognized the rights of a native people to have a voice in their own government. The document also committed the British government to protect the rights and beliefs of the Indian people and disclaimed any desire to extend British holdings in India.

Queen Victoria appointed a **viceroy** to rule India. The viceroy lived in splendor typical of past Indian emperors. He rode about the capital on a bejeweled elephant with many servants following. Official British rule is called the **British Raj** (RAHJ), from the Sanskrit word *raj,* meaning "ruler." Twenty years after the Sepoy Mutiny, the remaining independent princes pledged loyalty to the queen. In a grand ceremony Queen Victoria was proclaimed **Empress of India.** India was now part of the British Empire.

Queen Victoria, Empress of India, catches up on correspondence while attended by an Indian servant.

Section Review

1. What first brought the English to India?

2. What major problem faced the English in India? How was the problem resolved?

3. Why did the East India Company take over land?

4. In what year did the British government take control of India? What caused the takeover?

5. What was British rule in India called?

What might have been different in India if the British had tried to adapt to the Indian culture rather than assume British cultural superiority?

The Sepoy Mutiny allowed England to take control of India and weaken the East India Company's influence.

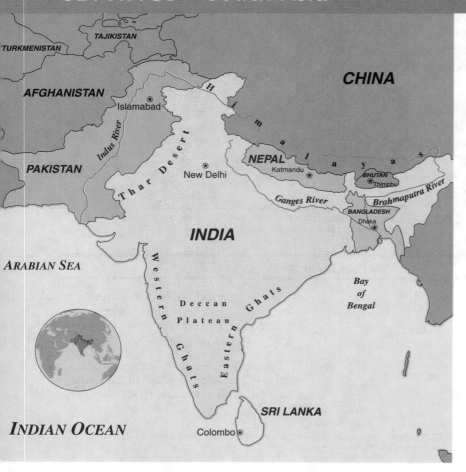

climate similar to the Middle East. There is also a portion of steppe climate in the center of the lower peninsula. Two features of the South Asian climate especially affect the people. One is the monsoons. These shifting winds are responsible for bringing most of the area's rain, so when they are absent or late, great drought and famine result. Cyclones, called hurricanes in America, are also a yearly event and sometimes cause great destruction. In the extreme north of India and Pakistan, the climate is affected by the mountains.

Topography—South Asia is a land of high mountains and plateaus with fertile plains tucked between. The Himalaya Mountains stretch across the far north of the region. Two other ranges, called the Western and Eastern Ghats, run up the flanks of the Indian peninsula. Between the Ghats is the Deccan Plateau. Fertile plains run beside the Ganges, Brahmaputra, and Indus Rivers. To the east of the Indus River is the Thar Desert.

Location—This area is sometimes called the Indian subcontinent. It includes Pakistan, India, Nepal, Bhutan, Bangladesh (BAHNG gluh DESH), and the island of Sri Lanka (sree LAHNG-kuh), formerly known as Ceylon. The Arabian Sea lies to the west and the Bay of Bengal to the east.

Climate—The climate of the area can be divided into three basic types—tropical, dry, and temperate. The northeast ranges from tropical to subtropical (temperate). Moving west the moisture and elevation change, causing a steppe and desert

Natural Resources—The natural resource most used by the people is the fertile land. Most of South Asia's inhabitants are farmers. They rank first in the world's production of cashews, millet, peanuts, sesame seeds, and tea. Great reserves of ores and natural gas are available to the people of South Asia, yet these resources remain mostly underdeveloped. Hydroelectric power is also an underdeveloped resource that South Asians are hoping to utilize in the future. Many people of the region raise cattle and sheep. The cattle are raised for their milk or as beasts of burden in Hindu areas.

Geography & Culture—The Indus and Ganges River valleys provided the first homes for the ancient civilization of South Asia. The rivers supplied water, fish, and transportation. Although the Himalaya Mountains prevented invasion from the north, foreigners did come through the passes in the northwest to invade South Asia regularly throughout its history. Because desert and rough terrain lie south of the river valleys, invaders rarely penetrated farther south. The final invasion, the one that changed the area's history most, was the invasion by the Europeans from the waters of the Arabian Sea.

Settings Review

1. What countries are included in South Asia?
2. What climate feature brings yearly rains?
3. What mountain ranges run down the sides of the Indian peninsula?
4. What land feature prevented general invasion from the north?

Why are the resources of South Asia underdeveloped? What are some changes that could result from greater development of those resources?

A bustling city scene stands in sharp contrast to work elephants being ridden along a country road. India struggles with poverty and a high percentage of illiteracy.

Establishing British Rule

Even though the British were in control of India's government, changes in India did not occur immediately. The mutual distrust between the Indians and British continued. The segregation that resulted further complicated communication between the two cultures.

Problems

The British faced many problems in ruling India. The country was much larger than the British Isles and had several million inhabitants. These millions spoke over a hundred different languages and followed several different religions. The few thousand British officials in India often misunderstood their Indian subjects. Many had little desire to learn about Indian culture or even have much contact with the Indians. When their wives and children began joining them in India, the British officials cut themselves off from the Indians more and more and lived separate lives. Most white *sahibs* (SAH ibz; meaning "master" in Hindi) chose to have Indians as servants rather than as friends.

In an effort to avoid more strife, Queen Victoria announced "that none be in anywise favoured, none molested or disquieted, by reason of their religious faith or observances, but that all shall alike enjoy the equal and impartial protection of the law; and we do strictly charge and enjoin all those who may be in authority under us that they abstain from all interference with the religious belief or worship of any of our subjects on pain of our highest displeasure." This declaration greatly curtailed missionary activity and social efforts to protect women and children and outcastes.

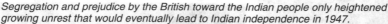
Segregation and prejudice by the British toward the Indian people only heightened growing unrest that would eventually lead to Indian independence in 1947.

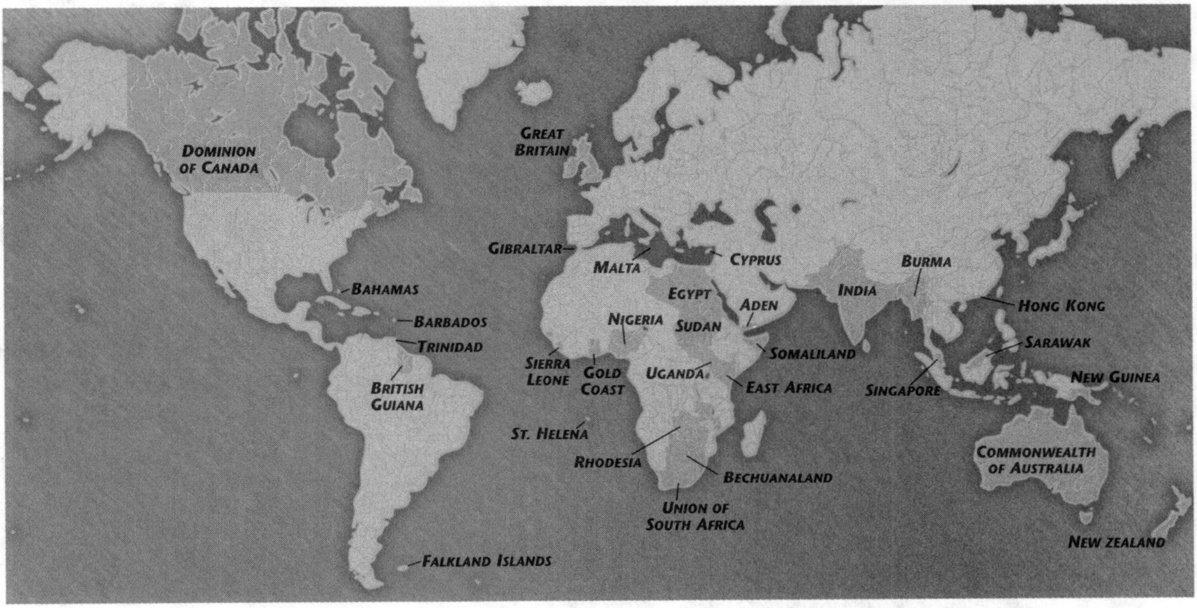

Opportunities

Despite its problems, India presented many opportunities for Britain. First it gave Britain economic advantages. India played a key role in the prosperity of the **British Empire,** which covered one-quarter of the globe in the nineteenth century. India's problems also gave the British an opportunity to help another people. They could apply the new learning and technology of Europe to an underdeveloped land. Agriculture, industry, transportation, and education improved under British rule. Most important, India presented a huge mission field. With the new policy of noninterference, the missionaries' focus changed to a less direct form of evangelism—meeting health and educational needs as a means to witness. The millions of Indians who worshiped false gods needed to hear the gospel. British missionaries eagerly took up Christ's Great Commission: "Go ye into all the world, and preach the gospel to every creature" (Mark 16:15).

Section Review

1. What attitude did the British have toward the Indians?
2. What does the word *sahib* mean?
3. List two things that the British gained from controlling India.
4. List three things that India gained through British control.

   Describe both the cause and effect of Queen Victoria's edict (see page 330). In other words, why did she say it, and what resulted from it?

The Congress or Gandhi hat became popular in the 20th century.

The *safa* is a large, loose turban worn by farmers and herdsmen.

The *kumkum* adorns the forehead as a beauty mark. In the Hindu religion it sometimes signifies a married woman whose husband is still living.

The *choli* is a short waisted shirt worn under the *sari*.

Jewelry decorates for beauty and proclaims wealth.

Tight turban, long fitted jacket with sash and *shalwai* pants identify this man as a member of the upper class Muslim community in 19th-century India.

The *sari* is a single piece of fabric wrapped and draped to form a skirt and head covering. The highly decorated silk fabric used for this *sari* reveals that its wearer is from the upper class.

Effects on Indian Culture

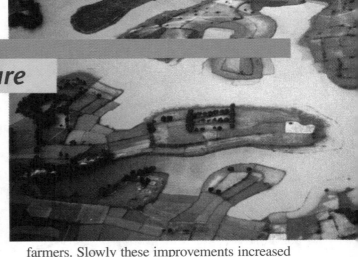

British rule changed the Indian way of life. Some changes started on paper and took years to complete. Others occurred immediately. In the following sections we will look at the changes the British made in India and how these affected that country. The Indians did not always think these changes were improvements. The changes often seemed to threaten parts of traditional Indian culture and to ignore India's own heritage. Nevertheless, these changes eventually helped to make India a self-governing power in the modern world.

Agriculture

Over two-thirds of India's people were farmers. They used primitive farming methods, much like those used in Europe during the Middle Ages. These methods plus unpredictable **monsoons** (winds that bring rain during one season) made famine a constant threat. Despite these problems, the British did much to improve farming in India. They brought better equipment, fertilizer, new ideas in farm management, and agricultural research to Indian

Although there are large cities in India, the majority of Indian people live in the country and are farmers.

farmers. Slowly these improvements increased the amount of land farmed and food produced.

The biggest farming improvement the British made was in building miles of irrigation canals. These canals brought water to dry areas, easing times of drought. Even with improved irrigation, though, famine remained a problem in India, as it still is today. To help people in times of famine, the British began an emergency relief plan. They moved food cross-country on railroads to the areas of worst famine. Although many were saved from starvation, in years of bad famine millions still died.

The British improved Indian farming not only to help the Indians but also to acquire India's agricultural products for trade. Indian cotton and jute supplied Britain's factories, and Indian spices filled Britain's shops. The British also developed the important tea industry of India, providing jobs for many Indians on large tea plantations. Soon India became a major supplier of this drink, which the British Empire made famous in both the Old and New Worlds. The British also brought the first rubber trees to the island of Ceylon (now Sri Lanka). The plant grew well, and Ceylon became a major rubber exporter. Thus the British not only helped India's food farming but also improved her production of other goods for export.

"Take some more tea," the March Hare said to Alice, very earnestly.

Tea Time!

Once upon a time, long ago in ancient China, the servants of the Emperor Shen Nung were boiling water to purify it for drinking. A few leaves from a nearby bush fluttered into the water, turning it brown. The emperor tasted the brew and pronounced it delicious. And so, the legend states, tea was discovered.

Actually, we have no idea when or how tea was discovered, but it did originate in China. Tea drinking spread to Europe during the age of exploration. Traders carried back shiploads of tea from China. Tea was extremely expensive; only the rich could afford it at first. Gradually prices dropped, and by the eighteenth century tea had become the most popular drink in England. Enterprising businessmen opened "tea shops" all over England. Nobles, scholars, businessmen, and common people gathered in these shops for refreshment and companionship.

Tea rapidly became an important part of English life. Englishmen began to drink tea with all their meals. In fact, supper became "tea time"—a light meal often consisting of nothing more than tea and a pastry. Shops offered a variety of teas. One could buy strong teas, mild teas, scented teas, or spiced teas. Ladies bought elaborate tea sets of silver or china with which to serve their tea. Methods for brewing a perfect cup of tea were tried and refined. Only water remained a more popular beverage than tea. (The English drank their tea hot. Iced tea is an American invention—the result of a heat wave during the World's Fair of 1904 in St. Louis.)

One problem confronted the English tea merchants. China had a monopoly on tea production. This meant that all merchants had to buy tea from China at whatever price the Chinese asked. Then in the 1800s, someone discovered wild tea bushes growing in India. The English quickly took advantage of this discovery and built huge tea plantations. Today India and the nearby island of Sri Lanka produce most of the tea drunk in the West.

Tea must be hand-picked leaf by leaf.

Flag from 1900 representing the Importers of Indian Textiles

Industry

In Chapter 11 you learned that Britain was in the middle of the Age of Industrialism during the 1800s. In India the British found many of the raw materials their factories needed, especially cotton and jute. India also provided Britain with markets for her manufactured goods, such as woolens, clothing, and hardware. At first the British were content to obtain India's agricultural goods and sell British manufactured goods there. Not until the end of the nineteenth century did the British start industry to produce goods in India.

At that time in some of the larger Indian cities, British businessmen set up factories.

Cotton mills, jute factories, and even some iron- and steelworks were built. They employed many Indians. The factories had some of the best British-made machinery and modern management. Although these factories were only the start of an industrial economy, they helped prepare India to enter the twentieth century.

Transportation and Communication

Perhaps the most important improvement the British made to India was the railroad system. Private companies and the British government laid several thousand miles of track and by 1900 had lines to most areas of India. Railroads made travel faster and more pleasant than walking or riding in oxcarts on dusty roads. The railroad also made the transportation of goods to market easier so that cotton and tea grown far inland could be shipped quickly to coastal ports. Likewise, goods brought into the country by boat could be sent inland to new markets. The railroad

Overcrowded trains transport travelers from the country to the city. If you have to sit on the roof, bring your own chair.

also played a major role in famine relief as supplies moved quickly to areas of need.

Although the railroad seemed one of the best British gifts to India, not all Indians liked it. Many complained that it disrupted family and village life by allowing family members to travel far away. Many more Indians complained that trains made them break the rules of their caste. The caste system taught that different castes should not mix. In a train car, however, it was impossible for them not to mix; the trains could not run a car for every different caste and subcaste. Nevertheless, many Indians rode the trains. They traveled in search of work or on visits to relatives or to make religious pilgrimages.

The British also improved communications in India. They set up a telegraph system that sent news quickly around the land. They also reorganized the postal system so that both government and personal mail moved faster. Although most Indians could not read or write,

they did send letters. Whenever an Indian wanted to send a letter, he went to the **bazaar** (marketplace) and hired a letter-writer. This man knew how to write several languages, and for a fee he wrote down the sender's dictated letter. The sender then stamped the letter and mailed it through the new postal system.

Education

Before the coming of the British, few Indians had any formal schooling. Only those from the higher castes who could afford private teachers or schools received an education, and rarely were girls taught to read or write. The British government and missionaries set up schools to educate more Indians. In the cities and towns, grade schools taught grammar, mathematics, and science in the language of the people. They also taught English, because English was the official language of the government. Even with these new schools,

Letter-writers either wrote or read letters for paying customers anxious to hear from friends in other cities and villages.

There was no place for a widow in Hindu society.

Social Change

As British families and missionaries settled in India, they were shocked at the religious practices they saw. Many Hindu and Muslim practices show little regard for a person and his freedom. Gradually the British were able to outlaw certain abuses. Several laws especially helped the position of women, who were often considered of less worth than their husbands' livestock. One such law made **suttee** (suh TEE), or widow-burning, illegal. Because a woman was not allowed to remarry when her husband died, a higher caste woman might join her husband's burning body on the funeral pyre. Even though outlawed, the Hindu tradition of *suttee* was still followed by some women.

The British also helped widows by changing the law forbidding them to remarry. Widowhood was a great problem in India because a girl was often engaged in childhood. Even if her fiancé died before the wedding day, the girl was still considered a widow and forbidden

few Indian children were able to attend. Many of them needed to work to support their families. Others did not have the desire to learn. India remains to this day a highly illiterate country.

Some boys completed their grade-school classes and then went on to study at British universities in India. These educated Indians were called **babus** (BAH booz). A *babu* had an education similar to that of any young Englishman graduating from a British university. Because they knew English, *babus* usually held minor offices in the government of India or were lawyers for their people.

One problem with the British educational system in India was that it ignored India's native culture. The rich **Sanskrit** (ancient Indian language) literature and the accomplishments in mathematics and science of the Indian Golden Age were not taught. The British tried to replace Indian culture with their own culture. This effort eventually led to conflict between these two cultures.

This girl paints a prayer in sand in front of her home to honor a Hindu deity.

An elephant salute honors the Prince of Wales during a trip to India in 1876. There was little mingling of the British and Indians.

ever to marry. She was confined to widow's quarters (separate rooms in the house) for the rest of her life. With the law changed, a widow could remarry. She might still lose her caste position if she remarried, but she was pro-

tected under the law. Although some Indians complained that the British were changing traditional Indian life, the British did much to help thousands of hopeless Indian women.

Section Review

1. What problems in farming faced the Indians?

2. What was the best farming improvement the British brought to India?

3. How did the British help in time of famine?

4. List three industries the British built in India.

5. Why was the railroad important in India? List two reasons that the Indians did not like the railroad.

6. What language did the British use in the Indian educational system? Why did this cause conflict between the two cultures?

7. List two laws that helped Indian women.

What were some of the pros and cons of the changes which the British brought to India? Were the changes good or bad, or were the changes a mixture of both? Explain your answer.

RUDYARD KIPLING: SON OF INDIA

"Oh East is East, and West is West, and never the twain shall meet," wrote **Rudyard Kipling** (1865-1936). Yet in a sense East did meet West in the life of Kipling himself. Kipling was Western, being not only a British citizen but also a staunch defender against critics of the British Empire. But Kipling was also Eastern. He was born in Bombay, India, while his father was working there as an art teacher. Kipling spent the first six years of life in India, learning the native language thoroughly. Although his family moved back to Britain, Kipling later returned to India and worked there as a newspaper reporter from 1882 to 1889.

During this second period in India, Kipling began writing the stories and poems that earned him wealth and fame. Though he eventually returned to Britain, Kipling still made India the central theme of his work. His finest works, *Kim, The Jungle Book, The Light That Failed*, and others, are set in India. He understood Indian culture better than most Britons. He showed deep respect and sympathy for both the British soldiers in India and the native Indian people. His poem "Gunga Din," for example, tells how an Indian water boy saves the life of a British soldier at the cost of his own life. Kipling also believed that British rule was in the best interest of India, although he realized—as others did not—that such rule could not last forever.

In his poem "The White Man's Burden" he reveals his belief that British imperialism was a duty and an opportunity to help out those "less fortunate" countries and peoples. To properly carry out the duty required patience, sacrifice, and maturity. Yet Kipling also expressed the sense of superiority that native peoples resented in Europeans. Who, they wanted to know, asked the white man to take up this burden?

Rudyard Kipling

The White Man's Burden

Take up the White Man's burden—
Send forth the best ye breed—
Go bind your sons to exile
To serve your captives' need;
To wait in heavy harness,
On fluttered folk and wild—
Your new-caught, sullen peoples,
Half-devil and half-child.

Take up the White Man's burden—
In patience to abide,
To veil the threat of terror
And check the show of pride;
By open speech and simple,
An hundred times made plain,
To seek another's profit,
And work another's gain.

. . . .

Take up the White Man's burden—
Ye dare not stoop to less—
Nor call too loud on Freedom
To cloak your weariness;
By all ye cry or whisper,
By all ye leave or do,
The silent, sullen peoples
Shall weigh your Gods and you.

Take up the White Man's burden—
Have done with childish days—
The lightly proffered laurel,
The easy, ungrudged praise.
Comes now, to search your manhood
Through all the thankless years,
Cold, edged with dear-bought wisdom,
The judgment of your peers!

Missionaries to India

All India is full of holy men stammering gospels in strange tongues; shaken and consumed in the fires of their own zeal; dreamers, babblers, and visionaries; as it has been from the beginning and will continue to the end.

—Rudyard Kipling, *Kim*

India under the British was still a land of many religions. Hinduism, Buddhism, Islam, and many variations of these bound the people in their sin. Their superstitions kept them in fear and ruled their daily actions. To these millions of lost people, Christian missionaries came with the burden of the truth of the gospel and the love of the Lord Jesus Christ. India presented a great field of opportunity for service to God, and in the early nineteenth century British Christians began the harvest.

Shiva, worshiped by Hindus as destroyer and restorer of worlds, is one of thousands of Hindu gods.

Early Missionary Endeavors

The first British missionaries, however, were not allowed into British territory because the East India Company did not want to disrupt

A statue of the god Nandi decorated for a festival

relations with the Indians. They thought that the missionaries' message would anger the Indians and harm their trade. These men thought more of their own material gain than the spiritual condition of their neighbors. Proverbs 15:27 tells us, "He that is greedy of gain troubleth his own house." These men brought trouble to their neighbors as well as to themselves. Their greed kept the Indians from hearing the gospel message. Yet Christian missionaries willingly gave up all hope of gain to witness to the Indians. In the end these dedicated servants of God gained the riches of God's blessing, a much more valuable possession than material riches. As Proverbs 13:7 says, "There is that maketh himself rich, yet hath nothing: there is that maketh himself poor, yet hath great riches."

slow indeed. Carey and his coworkers saw Indians come to Christ, and many more heard the Word in their own language.

In 1813 the British government ordered the East India Company to allow missionaries into its territory. Now other British missionaries traveled to India. Like the Careys, they also found India a hard mission field. The bonds of caste and superstition held the people. The tropical heat and humidity were hard on the Europeans. Yet the missionaries worked faithfully, and slowly they reaped fruit for their labors. The poorer people often responded first to the truth of the gospel. They had no satisfaction from their caste and desired the freedom and peace of which the missionaries talked. The missionaries often concentrated their work among the poorer people. Sometimes they set up schools to teach the gospel along with reading and writing. The missionaries also witnessed faithfully to higher-caste Indians and eventually saw some of these come to the Lord.

William Carey labored for the Lord in India for forty years. He translated the Bible into Bengali and other Indian languages.

Christian Indians such as these suffer persecution from Muslims and Hindus.

Even after being turned away by the company, one man, **William Carey,** was still convinced that God had called him to India. For forty years (1794-1834) this missionary to India labored with the people. He taught the natives the truths of God's Word and also translated the Scripture into the languages of India. Another missionary, **William Ward**, who worked with Carey was a printer by trade. He set the type and printed copies of the new translations. Without the help of this dedicated printer, the work in India would have been

Raj India

Pandita Ramabai—A Woman of Faith

Hindu women had little hope of heaven. The Brahman priest said that a woman's hope lay in being a good wife to her husband so that she could serve him in heaven or in doing so much good during her current life that she would be born as a man in the next life. Missionaries had the gospel message for these hopeless hearts but had great difficulty getting that message to them. So it was that the Lord raised up Pandita Ramabai (RAH mah bye) to minister to the women of India.

Pandita did not quickly come to Christ. Born in the home of a prominent and open-minded Brahman, Pandita Ramabai had more freedom than many Indian women. Her father taught her

Pandita Ramabai

and her mother to read Sanskrit writing. It was through her reading of the Hindu holy writings that she became dissatisfied with her religion and its hopelessness. She then began to study Christianity in India and later in England. Intellectually, Pandita decided that it was the best religion and that she should be baptized as a Christian. Ramabai later said,

It was nobody's fault that I had not found Christ. He must have been preached to me from the beginning. My mind at that time had been too dull to grasp the teaching of the Holy Scriptures. The open Bible had been before me, but I had given much of my time to the study of other books about the Bible, and had not studied the Bible itself as I should have done. Hence my ignorance of many important doctrines taught in it. I gave up the study of other books about the Bible and took to reading the Bible regularly. I came to know, after eight years from the time of my baptism, that I had found the Christian religion, but I had not found Christ, who is the Life of the religion and "the Light of every man that cometh into the world." One thing I knew by this time, that I needed Christ, and not merely His religion.

Pandita and two workers with some of the children that she rescued during times of famine

Chapter 12

Pandita saw her people as slaves to false religions.

Shortly after her true conversion, Pandita Ramabai started a faith mission for the girls and widows of India. In the spirit of George Mueller and Hudson Taylor, whose biographies she had read, Pandita and her helpers started a school and prayed for their needs to be met each day. When a great famine swept over India, Pandita went into the refugee camps and rescued widows and girls from certain death or abuse. Soon she had over a thousand women and girls at the mission. Providing for this many people during a time of great famine could have caused Pandita worry, but she said in her autobiography,

> I am spared all trouble and care, casting my burden upon the Lord. There are over 1,500 people living here; we are not rich, nor great, but we are happy, getting our daily bread directly from the loving hands of our Heavenly Father, having not a *pice* [a piece of money] over and above our daily necessities, having no banking account anywhere, no endowment or income from any earthly source, but depending altogether on our Father God; we have nothing to fear from anybody, nothing to lose, and nothing to regret. The Lord is our *inexhaustible treasure.*

Daily Pandita Ramabai and her helpers taught the women to read and write, showed them basic cleanliness, and encouraged them to learn a trade. But the most important thing the women learned was salvation through Jesus Christ. Several thousand Indian women came to Christ through Pandita Ramabai's ministry. Many of the women trained in her school became "Bible-women" who also took the gospel to the women of India.

Pandita saw the needs of her people and prayed that God would help others to see as well. She pleads with those who hear her story, "Dear brother and sister, whoever may happen to read this testimony, may you realize your responsibility to give the Gospel of Jesus Christ to my people in this land, and pray for them that they may each and all be cleansed from their filthiness and from all their idols, that they may find the true way of salvation."

Men, women, and children listen eagerly to a message from the gospel.

Ministering to the Women of India

A very fruitful field in India was in women's work. Most Indian women were not allowed to associate with any man outside their immediate family members. Thus, male missionaries could have no contact with them, but a woman could. The first woman missionary to India was **Hannah Marshman.** She went to the field with her husband, one of Carey's partners. After arriving in India, she became burdened for the women and saw the opportunity she had to work with them. She opened schools for poor Indian children and also for young women. Often the girls converted under her teaching went out to tell other women about Christ.

As the century went on, more single women came to the field. They were burdened for the many higher-caste wives and widows who were confined to their husbands' houses. Missionaries who came as teachers and nurses gained entrance to these women's quarters.

They taught these lonely, lost women about the love of Christ. They brought divine healing to their souls as well as physical care to their bodies. Many Indian women came to know the love and joy of salvation because these missionaries took them the message.

The Great Century

The nineteenth century is often called the **"Great Century of Christian Missions."** Prompted by the revivals begun in England under John Wesley and George Whitefield, British Christians formed missionary societies to send missionaries to foreign fields. The **Baptist Missionary Society** sent out Carey and his partners. Many other societies from both Europe and America sent missionaries. Dedicated to the Lord and burdened to win others, these men and women went out motivated by Acts 1:8, "And ye shall be witnesses unto me both in Jerusalem, and in all Judaea, and in Samaria, and unto the uttermost part of the earth."

Millions in India have never heard the gospel of Christ. Will you take the message to them?

Section Review

1. What religions did the people of India follow?
2. Why did the East India Company not allow missionaries into its territory?
3. Who was the first missionary to India?
4. How did Mrs. Marshman work with Indian women?

5. What did Christians do to prove that the nineteenth century was the "Great Century of Christian Missions"?

What do you think was different about the people or the era that caused so many to be interested in missions? What changes would have to occur in our world today to cause more missionaries to be sent out across the world? How could you make a difference?

Summary

India was an important part of the British Empire. The English first came to India around 1600 to trade under the leadership of the East India Company. For 250 years the East India Company increased its power in India. However, trouble arose between the British and the Indians, and in 1858 the British government took control of the country, which became a part of the empire. The British Raj ruled India for nearly a hundred years. During that time the British tried to help the Indians. They improved farming by teaching new methods, bringing new machinery, and building canals. They also brought some industry to India. To unite the country, the British built railroads and telegraph lines to all parts of the land. They increased education for more people, teaching mostly Western subjects, and also wrote laws to protect the people. The greatest contribution the British made to India was spreading the gospel. Many dedicated missionaries traveled to India and spent their lives telling the Indians about Christ. Despite these accomplishments, the British ignored India's long and fruitful heritage. They did not understand traditional Indian culture and often offended their Indian subjects. These two ways of life eventually clashed, and the Indians later gained their independence in 1947.

CHAPTER REVIEW

People, Places, and Terms to Know

East India Company
Bombay
Madras
Calcutta
Battle of Plassey
Robert Clive
Charter Act
sepoys

Sepoy Mutiny
General
    Enlistment Act
viceroy
British Raj
Empress of India
sahibs

British Empire
monsoons
bazaar
babus
Sanskrit
suttee
Rudyard Kipling

William Carey
William Ward
Hannah Marshman
"Great Century of
    Christian Missions"
Baptist Missionary
    Society

Review Questions

Map Analysis

Look at the map on page 326 and answer the following questions.

1. On which river is Calcutta located?
2. Which East India Company port is located on the Arabian Sea?
3. Near which East India Company port is Ceylon located?
4. Which Indian river flows into the Arabian Sea?

Completion

Complete the following statements.

5. In 1600 (a) _____, the English queen, granted a charter to the (b) _____ to trade in India.

6. For years England competed with (a) _____ for territory and trade until the Battle of (b) _____ gave England victory in India.

7. The East India Company expanded its territory until a group of Indian soldiers, called (a) _____, rose against them in the (b) _____.

8. The British government took control of India in the year (a) _____ and established official British rule called the (b) _____.

Multiple Choice

Choose all the correct answers for each of the following questions.

9. Some of the problems the British faced in ruling India were
   - (a) its size.
   - (b) its languages.
   - (c) its poverty.
   - (d) its religions.

10. Britain made agricultural improvements in India. These included
    - (a) irrigation canals.
    - (b) introduction of fertilizer.
    - (c) improvement of the tea industry.
    - (d) redistribution of farmland.

11. India supplied Britain with certain raw materials. Among these were
    - (a) wool.
    - (b) cotton.
    - (c) timber.
    - (d) jute.

Definition

Define or explain each of these terms.

12. sepoys
13. viceroy
14. British Raj

Matching

Match these items.

15. Robert Clive
16. Victoria
17. William Carey
18. *babu*

   - (a) missionary to India
   - (b) educated Indian
   - (c) Battle of Plassey
   - (d) Empress of India

Think About It!

Remember that many of the chapters you are studying overlap chronologically. Add to the following list of major events in the history of British India at least seven other events from the past five chapters. Put these events in the proper order of occurrence. Use a separate sheet of paper and place them on a time line.

Battle of Plassey

William Carey in India

Beginning of British Raj

Completion of India's railroad

Sepoy Mutiny

Indian independence

CHAPTER 13

Sunday morning, August 23, 1868. The small mission station stood strangely silent. Smoke from smoldering piles of debris hung heavily in the summer air, already hot and humid hours before daybreak. As Hudson Taylor entered the house, he saw more destruction—broken furniture, burned books, ruined medical equipment and supplies, pieces of toys, and torn clothing. Leaving the house, he searched diligently until he found his wife and family. Injured and weary, they were with other missionaries at a neighbor's house. Hudson brought them home and waited. At dawn, the Chinese from the town returned and began to loot the station once more.

Unable to allow them to continue, Hudson climbed onto a broken chair and began to speak:

We were a party of strangers; we came from a distance to seek your good. Had we meant evil, should we have come unarmed? Or in such small numbers? Or with our women and children? Without provocation you have broken open our dwelling, plundered our property, wounded our persons, and tried to burn down our premises. And now you are back in your greed of plunder to do us more mischief.

We are defenseless. We cannot withstand you. If we could, we would not. We are here for good, not for evil. . . . If you abuse us or kill us, we will not retaliate. But high Heaven will avenge. Our God, in whom we trust, is able to protect us and punish you, if you offend against Him.

Hudson Taylor had come to China with a deep love for the millions of Chinese who had never heard the gospel. Under his ministry many Chinese found true salvation in the Lord Jesus Christ. However, many opposed him and his message.

A.D. **1500** - A.D. **1900**

1500		160
	Ming Dynasty 1386-1644	

China and the West

Treaty of Kanagawa 1854

Sino-Japan War Begins 1894

Robert Morrison Arrives in China 1807

Queen Victoria's Reign 1838-1901

Great Century of Christian Missions 1800-1900

Age of Reason 1600-1800

1700

1800

1900

Manchu Dynasty 1644-1911

Opium War 1839-42

Hudson Taylor Arrives in China 1853

Boxer Rebellion 1899-1900

Taiping Rebellion 1851-64

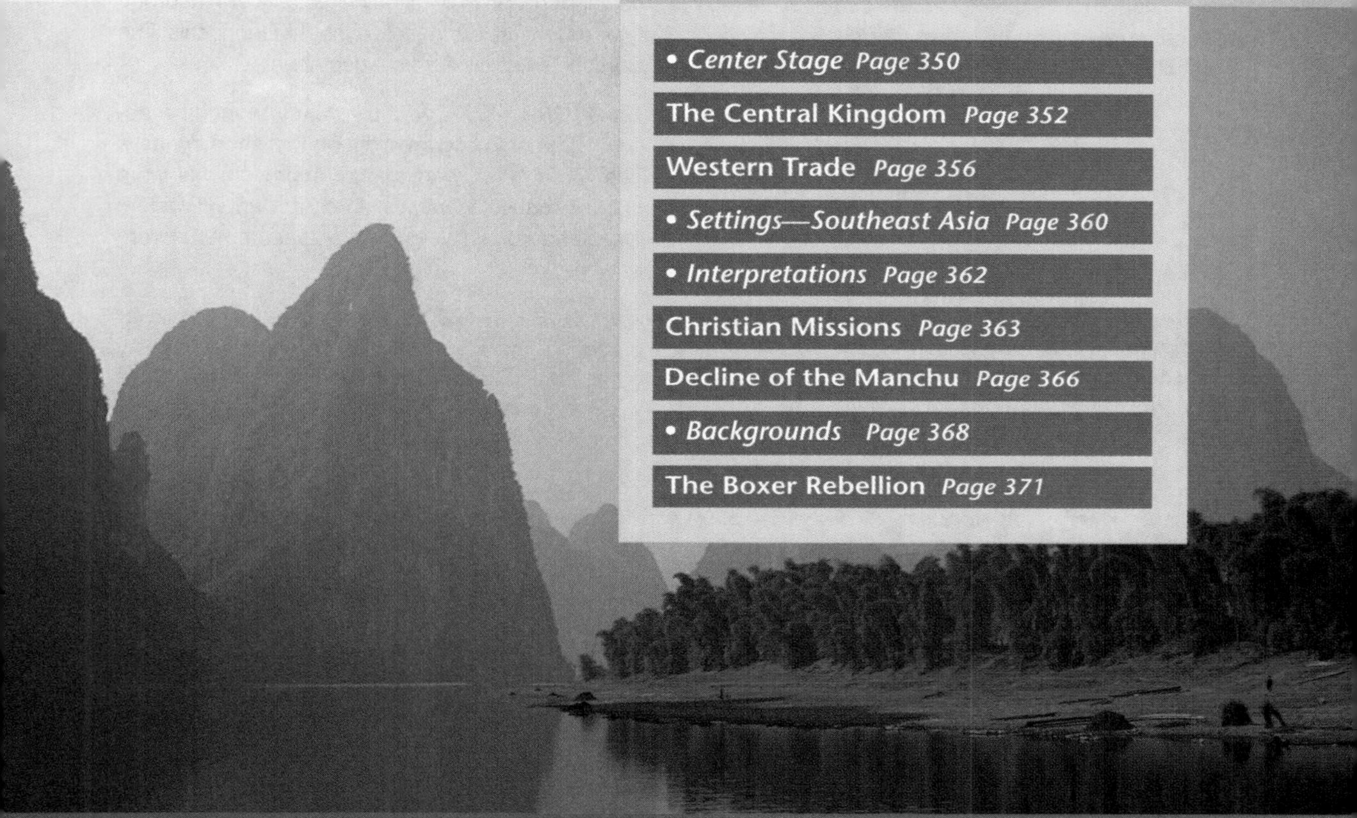

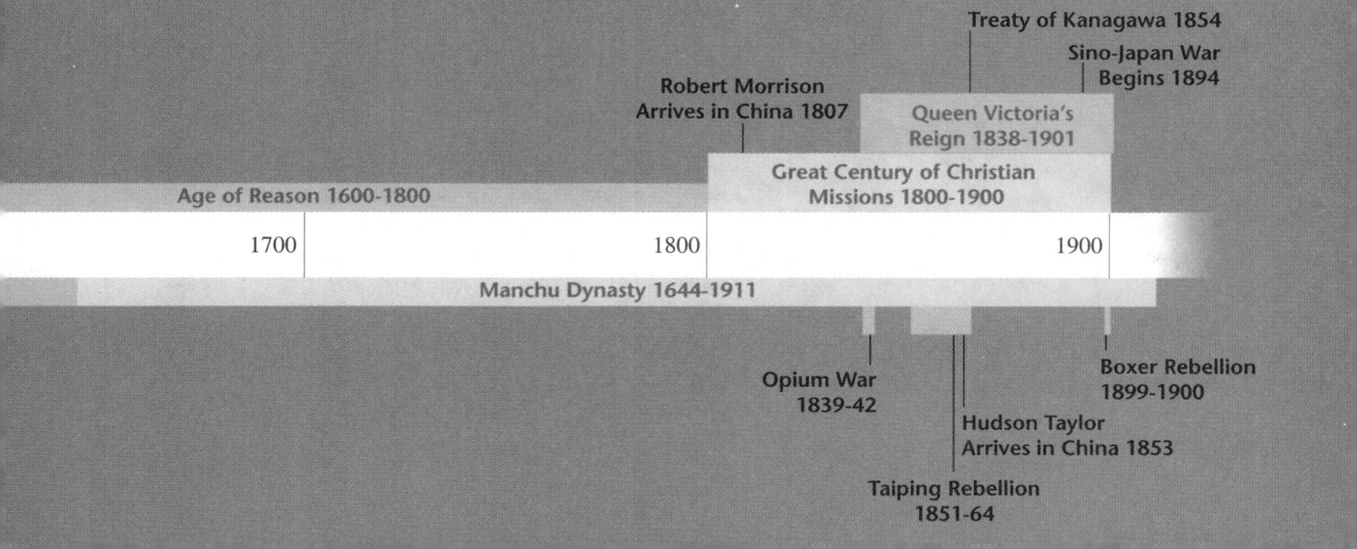

CENTER STAGE

A Time Line of China's Past China has an ancient history that helps explain the people's feeling of superiority. China's history encompasses the rise and fall of several other empires. As you read the following time line, try to remember other empires that occurred during the same periods.

Chinese Dynasties

Xia, 2200-1766 B.C.—This legendary, ancient dynasty domesticated animals and wove silk.

Shang, 1766-1122 B.C.—This dynasty saw the widespread use of oracle bones. During this dynasty the Chinese also perfected the wheel for use on chariots and made bronze vessels.

Empress Dowager Tz'u-hsi ruled during the Manchu dynasty.

Chou (Zhou), 1122-221 B.C.—Iron casting was developed, and multiplication tables were recorded for the first time during this dynasty. During this time Confucius established his doctrines.

Chin (Qin), 221-206 B.C.—Many wonderful accomplishments occurred during this short dynasty. The Great Wall was begun. Improvements were made in roads and canals. A uniform writing system and standardized weights and measurements were established.

Han, 202 B.C.–A.D. 220—Four years of civil war preceded the Han dynasty. During this dynasty great technological developments occurred. Steel was manufactured, and the seismograph was invented.

Four centuries of war divided China into smaller kingdoms and dynasties. China was once again united in the Tang dynasty.

Tang, A.D. 618-906—The Tang dynasty claimed land stretching from Mongolia to Vietnam and from Korea to Iran. Great Chinese poets wrote, and craftsmen produced fine porcelain. A period of political division occurred between the Tang and Song dynasties.

Song (Sung), 960-1279—Movable type improved Chinese printing. The compass was invented but was used for fortunetelling. Paper money was developed but caused economic disaster.

Yuan (Mongol), 1279-1368—Kublai Khan came from the north and within a year conquered the Chinese. The Mongols adapted to the Chinese lifestyle.

Ming, 1368-1644—Rebels overthrew the weakened Mongol dynasty. Porcelain of this dynasty is famous. The Great Wall was extended, and the Imperial Palace was built.

Manchu (Qing), 1644-1911—Chinese influence spread throughout the East. The Opium Wars, Taiping Rebellion, and Boxer Rebellion weakened the empire. European nations carved out holdings in the East. Empress Dowager Tz'u-hsi retained control of the dynasty and prevented the modernization of China.

(The next two entries will be discussed in greater detail in Chapter 17.)

Republic of China, 1911-1949—Revolutionary forces under the influence of Dr. Sun Yat-sen over-threw the Manchus. The Kuomintang party tried to unite China. Chiang Kai-shek took over the party after Sun Yat-sen died.

Communist China, 1949-present—The Communists, under Mao Zedong, defeated opposition forces. The Kuomintang government fled to Taiwan, where it established the Nationalist regime. The People's Republic of China established its capital in Peking, later called Beijing.

Geography helped isolate China from other cultures. In its thousands of years of history it has been ruled by foreigners only twice.

China and the West

The Central Kingdom

Historically, the Chinese called their land *Chung Kuo,* the **Central Kingdom.** For two thousand years China has existed as the central nation and great power in Asia. Its borders have changed, and one dynasty has overthrown another, but China has remained. Other empires that traded with the Chinese have come and gone. The Babylonians, the Persians, the Greeks, the Romans, all great at one time, have fallen, but China has carried on as a central power among the other Asian nations.

Reclaiming Chinese Rule

Chapter 4 introduced China during a time when it was ruled by a foreign power—the Mongols. Their rule was called the Yuan dynasty. The Chinese found it bearable only because Kublai Khan set up his palaces in China and relied on Chinese advisors. The Yuan dynasty did little to disrupt the flow of Chinese life. However, the relaxed life that the Mongols lived in China weakened their nomadic warrior ways. After a little over one hundred years, defiant Chinese forces overthrew the Mongols and established a new dynasty called the **Ming dynasty** (1386-1644).

The Ming dynasty reestablished native Chinese rule. In reaction to foreign rule, the new dynasty looked down on all foreigners, including European traders. Instead the Ming directed their attention to the internal problems and needs of China. This helped the dynasty establish an era of peace and prosperity.

The Ming concentrated on the arts, reconstruction, and exploration. Craftsmen perfected **porcelain** production, which helped to continue the demand for exports. The Ming took time to fix broken portions of the Great Wall and to extend it even further. They repaired roads and bridges and built the **Imperial City** in their capital city Peking (later called Beijing). They also began sending out **junks** (sailing vessels) to explore Southeast Asia and the Red Sea. But while the Ming directed their attention to the south and east, foreign invaders slowly took control of the Imperial City.

The Manchu Dynasty

In 1644 the **Manchu dynasty** took power from the failing Ming dynasty. The Manchus came from **Manchuria,** the region northeast of China. The Manchus came into China to help the Ming government defeat a group of rebels. Once invited into the country, however, the Manchus slowly took power from the weak Ming rulers. They established the second foreign dynasty to rule in Chinese history. The Manchu, or Qing, dynasty

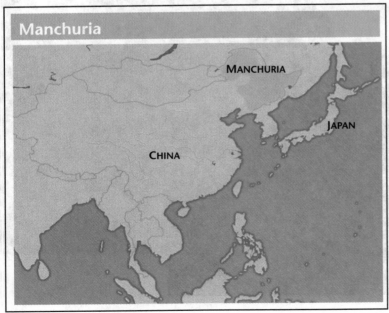

Manchuria

MANCHURIA

JAPAN

CHINA

Chapter 13

ruled China from 1644 to 1911, when dynasty rule ended in China.

The Manchu rulers worked hard to build a good relationship with the people of their newly conquered empire. They knew that to stay in power and have a successful government, they needed the support of the people. The Manchus tried to become "Chinese" rather than making the Chinese become Manchurian. The Manchus allowed the Chinese to have a part in the government. At the higher levels of government, a Chinese and a Manchu often shared the same office. At the local level almost all government officials were Chinese.

Actually the Manchu government differed little from earlier dynastic governments. The emperor still held supreme power and could order any policy throughout the empire. Scholars received positions in government by doing well on civil service exams. Many Chinese scholars held important positions at the imperial court in Peking. Each level of government was responsible to the next higher level so that local governors had little control over their own affairs. In this way the Manchus successfully governed their Chinese

A Chinese junk

subjects for nearly two centuries before discontent with their rule broke out.

Chinese Superiority

Throughout their history the Chinese have had an attitude of superiority toward all other countries in the world. They called themselves the Central Kingdom because they considered themselves to be the center of the world. In many ways China truly was superior to other countries. For example, during the Dark Ages in Europe, China had a period of great achievement under the Tang and Sung dynasties. The Chinese invented printing, papermaking, gunpowder, and the compass. Before Europe entered the modern age, China was the most technologically advanced region in the world.

The Manchus continued to promote this attitude of superiority. They especially tried to keep China from having any contact with the West through trade. China closed all but one or two ports to Western trade during the eighteenth century.

However, this policy turned out to be a double-edged sword. It not only kept the West from receiving quantities of desirable Chinese

This selection from a Chinese book on Europe gives an account of the Chinese opinion of Europeans.

In ancient times [Europe's] people hunted for a living, ate meat, and wore skins. Their customs were barbaric, and their spirit was wild and free. But during our own Shang period (2000 B.C.), Greece and other countries gradually came under the influence of the Orient. For the first time they began to till fields and manufacture products, build cities, and dig lakes. They began to do all kinds of things. Before long, writing and civilization began to flourish. Thus they became beautiful like the countries of the East.

(*From* Hsiao-fang hu-chai yü-ti ts'ung-ch'ao, *compiled by Wang Hsi-ch'i, published in 1891.*)

Macartney's refusal to kowtow was not appreciated by the emperor.

Macartney's Mission to China

In 1793 Great Britain decided to break through China's resistance to foreign trade. King George III sent a group to China led by Lord Macartney. Supposedly Macartney went to honor the Chinese emperor on his eighty-third birthday. In reality he planned to use this opportunity to negotiate a trade agreement with China.

Macartney came bearing numerous gifts to flatter the emperor. (The British government spent over seventy-five thousand pounds on the enterprise.) To the delight of Macartney, the Chinese welcomed him and his party warmly. The British were dismayed a bit, however, when the Chinese treated their gifts as "tribute," as though the British were submitting to the emperor as vassals. When meeting the emperor himself, Macartney created a stir when he refused to perform the customary kowtow. The emperor, however, allowed Macartney to bow as he would to his own king—kneeling on one knee.

Although Macartney was well treated and the Chinese proved gracious hosts, the mission failed. The Chinese emperor refused to recognize the group as anything more than tribute-bearers come to honor him on his birthday. The Chinese flatly denied any trade privileges. The emperor sent a letter to King George saying, "The Celestial Empire possesses all things in prolific abundance and lacks no product within its borders. There is therefore no need to import the manufactures of outside barbarians in exchange for our own products."

Then with condescending tone, he added, "It behooves you, O King, to respect my sentiments and to display even greater devotion and loyalty in future, so that, by perpetual submission to our Throne, you may secure peace and prosperity for your country thereafter."

goods but also kept the Chinese from receiving the new inventions and learning of the West. While the Western world moved rapidly into the modern age, the Chinese refused to change their traditional culture. Their pride in their traditional culture blinded them to the valuable achievements of other people. As individuals we must not let pride in our own abilities blind us to the wisdom and ability of others around us.

China's attitude of superiority was especially seen in its dealings with foreign ambassadors. When an ambassador from another land, whether it were Mongolia or Britain, came with a request, the Chinese official who greeted him demanded humble honor. This honor was given in the form of a **tribute**, usually money or goods, and the performance of the **kowtow.** The kowtow was performed by kneeling down and bowing one's forehead to the ground in a show of humility. The Chinese considered all foreigners "Outer Barbarians" and the tribute and kowtow only appropriate.

To those peoples living around China and having subordinate cultures, the kowtow was not offensive. Many of these areas owed their safety to China's good pleasure. However, to Europeans this practice was unthinkable, for they thought their own culture superior to the Chinese and regarded the Chinese as the barbarians. These two cultures were bound to clash, and as one might expect, it came in the area of trade.

Section Review

1. On which Chinese dynasty does this chapter focus?
2. What dynasty lost power at the beginning of this period?
3. How did the Manchurians successfully rule the Chinese?

4. What name for China showed her people's attitude of superiority?
5. How did the Chinese hurt themselves by their superior attitude?

Do you think that the British were right to refuse to kowtow? Explain your answer.

Fine fabrics, especially silks, have drawn traders to the East for centuries.

Challenges to China: Western Trade

Ever since the Crusades, when Europeans were introduced to the luxuries of the Far East, they had wanted more. Explorers set out to find routes to these far-off lands. Nations set up trading companies to do business with the explorers. China, or Cathay, was one of the richest sources of these goods. Silks, spices, porcelain, and tea were in great demand in both European palaces and humble households. Following both land and sea routes, Europeans made long and hazardous journeys to the rich trading centers of the Central Kingdom.

Restrictions to Trade

Little did the early traders expect the first obstacle they met once safely in China: the Chinese did not really care to trade with them.

The beauty of the opium poppy masks the sorrow that addiction to opium and heroin causes.

The goods of the West—woolens, metals, and some machinery—had little appeal to the Chinese. They considered themselves well supplied with all their daily needs and desires. The Chinese saw no need to grant the foreigners unlimited trading rights. In fact, they looked at trade as a privilege that could be taken away at any time.

During the eighteenth century, foreign traders were mostly limited to the port of **Canton**, the foreign trading center. The British controlled most of this trade. Their merchants lived in a specific section of the town and traded only through authorized Chinese agents. These agents set prices as high as they liked and could refuse to trade at any time. They also collected the high taxes on goods. Some of this money never showed up in the imperial treasury but stayed in the agents' pockets.

Beginning of the Opium Trade

The British merchants knew how to improve their unfavorable trading relationship with China—they simply needed to find a product the Chinese wanted. They found that product growing in India: **opium.** Opium is an addictive narcotic drug. Although sometimes used to treat disease, opium is also used as a drug that changes the user's state of mind. Usually this change brings about a false feeling of happiness and peace. Opium users desire this feeling because they believe they are escaping from their problems. However, this feeling is only temporary and solves no problems. Once the drug has worn off, the person still has his problems. Opium, or any other narcotic drug, is not the source of peace or answer to one's problems. The Bible tells us that salvation through Christ is the only source of peace. "And the peace of God, which passeth all understanding, shall keep your hearts and minds through Christ Jesus" (Phil. 4:7). The Christian does not need drugs to deal with his problems and should not use them for this purpose. As Philippians 4:7 promises, Christ will keep the believer's heart *and* mind.

Opium had been used in China for several centuries before the British came, mostly to treat illness. When the British began importing large amounts of the drug, the Chinese began to use opium for its narcotic (mind-changing) effect. As more people became addicted to opium, the demand for it grew. To meet the demand, the British imported more and more opium. By selling this drug, the British slowly began to make more profit on their exports to China than they spent on their imports of Chinese luxury goods. From the mid-1700s to the mid-1800s, the exporting of opium by Britain to China skyrocketed. The British went from bringing in about four hundred chests (one hundred kilograms or approximately forty-five pounds each) in 1736 to thirty thousand chests in 1850.

Negotiations between Europeans and Chinese officials did little to open trade to the West.

Chinese Response to the Opium Trade

As the opium trade grew, the Chinese government took action to stop it. Opium addiction produced many problems, especially idleness and poor production. These twin problems produced much poverty among the Chinese people. Another problem was that the Chinese people were spending more money on drugs than they were receiving from trade. This imbalance was draining China's silver reserves. (For a time the Chinese government discussed planting their own opium in China

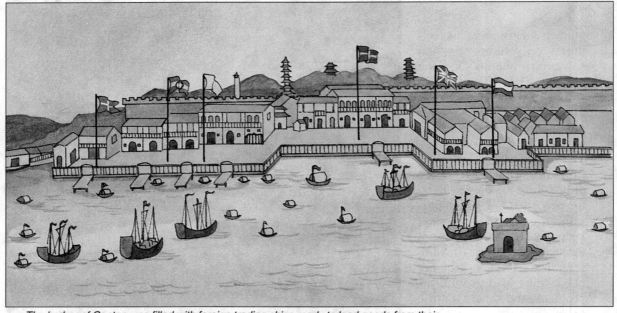

The harbor of Canton was filled with foreign trading ships ready to load goods from their respective trading houses. What foreign countries are represented by the flags?

to keep the money in the country.) The emperor ordered all opium sales to stop and made it illegal to import. However, the greed of both British and Chinese merchants caused them to keep up the trade, usually by smuggling the drug in along the coast.

Finally, the Chinese emperor appointed **Lin Tse-hsü** as his High Commissioner. Lin Tse-hsü took a message of prohibition and enforcement to the British. On March 10, 1839, Lin came to Canton to confront British traders with a question: "How dare you bring your country's vile opium into China, cheating and harming our people?" Then he made two demands. First, the British traders were to hand over all their unsold opium. Second, the British were to stop the import of opium into China. "If you continue, the opium will be confiscated, and those involved will be decapitated," said Lin.

Lin Tse-hsü gave the British two weeks to comply with the proclamation. The British

had heard proclamations before and assumed that Lin was as corrupt as other politicians had been. Imagine their surprise when Lin ordered all transport to and from Canton to stop and ordered Chinese troops to surround the thirteen foreign factories (trade houses) in Canton. He then ordered all of the Chinese workers out of the factory and forbade the sale of food to those inside. The British trading houses became prisons.

At this point, Captain Charles Elliot, the English Superintendent of Trade, made a decision that affected British/Chinese negotiations later. Rather than tell the British merchants to turn their opium supply over to the Chinese directly, Elliot had them turn it over to him. This made the opium property of the British government. Then Elliot gave Lin access to the opium.

With the opium now in Lin's hands, Elliot once again expected Lin to be as corrupt as his predecessors. Lin surprised the British once more by having two huge pools dug. He then had the water salted, the opium poured in, and lime added. This decomposed the opium. When the twenty-three day process was over, Lin had channels opened from the pools to the ocean and let the tide carry the residue out to sea.

Feeling that he had achieved a victory over the British, Lin presented a document for Captain Elliot to sign. It was an agreement that the British would honor Chinese regulations. Elliot refused to sign. He sent a letter to England and waited for a response.

The response came in the summer. The British blockaded (blocked trade from entering the harbor of) Canton and then went north to capture the city of Tinghai. The Emperor, angry with Lin for the situation, appointed a new negotiator, Ch'i-shan. When Ch'i-shan went onboard a British ship and saw the weapons, he quickly realized that the Chinese were outgunned. To prevent a total takeover, Ch'i-shan suggested that the Emperor adopt a policy of appeasement (to satisfy or calm) toward the British.

The Chinese offered to return to their former trading policy and to pay the British a small sum of money for their inconvenience. But the British saw the opportunity for gaining much more control in China. Since Captain Elliot had had all the opium turned over to the British government, the British now demanded to be paid for the "British" opium that had been destroyed. They also insisted that they be given the city of Hong Kong and access to other ports of trade.

The Chinese refused, and war broke out. Called the **Opium War,** the fighting lasted three years (1839-42). British military power proved superior, and the Chinese were defeated. The peace treaty, the **Treaty of Nanking,** signed at the end of the war ended hostility and gave in to the British demands.

A second opium war a few years later resulted in more open ports. At that time inland China was also opened for the first time to both trade and travel by foreigners. Through these wars the Western nations forced China to open. Although the Europeans obtained the trade rights they desired, they did not encourage good relations between China and the West. Resentment against the foreigners grew and led to many problems in China.

Section Review

1. What goods of the Far East did Europeans want? Why did the Chinese refuse to grant unlimited trading?

2. What European nation controlled much of the China trade?

3. How did Chinese agents cheat the European traders?

4. What trade item did the English introduce to solve their trade problem?

5. What wars were caused by the British "solution"?

How did the Chinese feel about foreign powers before the British came to China? List at least three ways that the British increased the Chinese hatred of foreigners.

SETTINGS—Southeast Asia

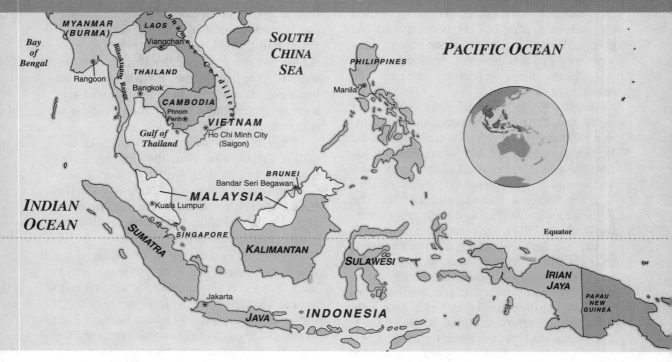

Location—The majority of the region called Southeast Asia lies between the tropic of Cancer and the equator. The region is bordered by China in the north, the Bay of Bengal and the Indian Ocean in the west and south, and the Pacific Ocean in the east. Southeast Asia includes Myanmar, Thailand, Laos, Vietnam, Cambodia, Malaysia, Singapore, the islands of Indonesia, and the Philippines.

Climate—Unlike most regions of its size, Southeast Asia has a fairly uniform climate. The region's climate is tropical. Rain forest (tropical wet) climate occurs in all the islands and up both coasts of the mainland. Savanna (tropical wet and dry) climate occurs between the **cordilleras** (parallel mountain ranges). Rain occurs an average of two hundred days per year, and the region receives approximately eighty inches of rain per year. Areas of humid subtropical climate are found in the north along with the highland climate in the higher elevations.

Topography—Thailand's long peninsula and the islands of Southeast Asia are known as the Malay Peninsula and the Malay **Archipelago** (a large cluster of islands). The Malay Archipelago is part of the **"Ring of Fire"**—the area in the Pacific known for volcanic and seismic (earthquake) activity. The Annamese Cordillera, Bilauktaung Range, and Arakan Range divide the fertile regions of the mainland. Few of the mountains in these ranges reach over ten thousand feet.

Natural Resources—Southeast Asia supplies most of the world's teakwood. Teakwood is a very hard, dense wood used for building ships and furniture. Mahogany, rubber, and ebony trees are also abundant. The rivers of the mainland and Malay Archipelago are used in hydroelectric production. The region also has deposits of coal, oil, and tin.

Geography & Culture—The Chinese greatly affected the eastern mainland of Southeast Asia, especially Vietnam. The Chinese brought information about fertilizers and other rice-growing techniques to the area. Rice farms in Vietnam are very productive. However, plowing is still done with water buffalo, and planting is done by hand.

Traders from the Arabian Peninsula came to the Malay Peninsula and Archipelago. Their contact brought not only trade but also the religion of Islam, which has become dominant in the region. Buddhism and Hinduism were brought to Southeast Asia from China and India.

Much of the region was divided by imperial powers in the eighteenth and nineteenth centuries. Imperialists introduced new technology, products, and ethnic diversity. Since the breakup of imperialist control, Southeast Asia has had to deal with self-government and ethnic conflict.

Settings Review

1. What type of climate is most widespread in Southeast Asia?
2. What is a term used for parallel mountain ranges?
3. What is an archipelago?
4. What Pacific area of high volcanic and earthquake activity is the Malay Peninsula a part of?

Remembering what you read about climate and rainfall in Southeast Asia, give one practical reason that Southeast Asian farmers would prefer to plant by hand and use water buffalos.

Volcanic mountains, religious shrines, and close families reflect some of the countries and cultures in Southeast Asia.

INTERPRETATIONS

British Control of Hong Kong

When the British and Chinese sealed the Treaty of Nanking, Hong Kong became the first portion of China owned by the British Empire. By 1860 further treaties gave England possession of Kowloon Peninsula, but Britain needed more mainland territory to keep Hong Kong self-sufficient. In 1898 Britain signed a ninety-nine-year lease with China for the New Territories. It is the end of this lease that has caused upheaval for Hong Kong.

Britain leased the New Territories to help support the growing population in Hong Kong. The empty island that Captain Elliot declared would be free of tariffs (trade taxes) soon became filled with more people than Hong Kong's resources could support. If you have ever been to Los Angeles, California, you know how crowded that city is. Hong Kong and its surrounding territories have almost one hundred fewer square miles than Los Angeles but have twice as many people. Today, Hong Kong must pipe water from mainland China, buy all its food from other countries, and import all its raw materials for industry.

Despite these seeming handicaps, Hong Kong

- ranks in the top ten countries for average household income.
- is the world's busiest container port.
- operates one of the world's largest gold bullion markets.
- has two of the world's top ten billionaires.

Seeing these statistics should help you understand why England would want to retain control of Hong Kong and why China would want the territory back.

In 1982 China and England began negotiations to discuss the ending of the ninety-nine-year lease. The **Sino-British Joint Declaration**

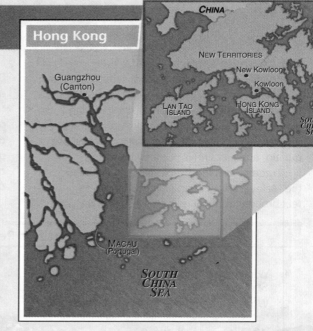

(*Sino* is another word for China) signed in 1984 stated that England would give up all control of Hong Kong, Kowloon, and the New Territories with the guarantee that China would allow Hong Kong to retain control of its own government and economy for the next fifty years. This policy is called "one country, two systems."

Much to China's dismay, Britain boosted Hong Kong's democracy during the thirteen years before 1997 to prepare it for self-rule. Britain turned more and more power over to the Hong Kong people by adding more natives of Hong Kong to the Legislative Council (the governing body of Hong Kong). China argued that the new government was not part of the agreement and vowed to replace the Legislative Council in 1997.

The impact of the Chinese takeover of Hong Kong will be closely analyzed over the next several years. It will also affect the return of Macau (a Portuguese holding) to Chinese control in 1999 and further attempts by China to control Taiwan.

Challenges to China: Christian Missions

The treaties made after the Opium Wars encouraged both Western traders and Western missionaries to come to China. Few missionaries had come before that time. The earliest was **Robert Morrison,** who arrived in China in 1807. Although he worked for many years, he saw few converts. The strong power of Confucianism, Taoism, Buddhism, and ancestor worship bound many Chinese in their sins.

Hudson Taylor used new methods to bring the gospel to the Chinese people.

Morrison's greatest contribution to Chinese missions was a Chinese translation of the Bible and several books on Chinese language and grammar. His faithful work in this difficult language helped later missionaries learn Chinese.

Soon other missionaries came to China, sent out by the same missionary societies that had sent men and women to India. These missionaries usually settled in the ports opened up by the treaties. They lived in special sections of the towns reserved for foreigners. From there they preached, taught, and gave medical care to many Chinese. They aided the Chinese during times of famine and treated many opium addicts. The missionaries also ministered to the many foreign traders and their families in China.

Hudson Taylor

One young English missionary came to China from England with a great burden for the Chinese people. After a six-month ocean voyage, **Hudson Taylor** settled in at the mission compound in 1853. Taylor spent many hours learning to speak and read Chinese. He also accompanied other missionaries on preaching tours. As he went out among the Chinese people, Taylor became aware that the people immediately rejected him because of his European clothing. He did not want the Chinese to reject Christianity simply because they thought it was a Western idea. He began to pray for wisdom to know how to reach the people. After reading I Corinthians 9:22 where Paul says he was "made all things to all men," Hudson Taylor decided to give up his Western attire to look more Chinese. He wrote the following letter to his sister Amelia about the results of his decision.

Hai-Yen City, August 28, 1855

My Dear Amelia—By way of surprise I mean to write you a letter—for I know you have never received one before from a man with a long tail and a shaven head! But lest your head should be bewildered with conjectures, I had better tell you at once that on Thursday last at 11 P.M. I resigned my locks to the barber, dyed my hair a good black, and in the morning had a proper *queue* [long braided pigtail] plaited in with my own, and a quantity of heavy silk to lengthen it out according to Chinese custom. Then, in Chinese dress, I set out with Dr. Parker, accompanying him about a hundred miles on his way to Ning-po. This journey we made an occasion for evangelistic work, and now that I am returning alone I hope to have even better facilities for book-distribution and preaching.

But I have not commenced the recital of my tribulations, and as there is some doubt as to whether they will all go into a single letter, the sooner I begin the better.

First, then, it is a very sore thing to have one's head shaved for the first time, especially if the skin is irritable with prickly heat. And I can assure you that the subsequent application of hair-dye for five or six hours does not do much to soothe the irritation. But when it comes to combing out the remaining hair which has been allowed to grow longer than usual, the climax is reached! But there are no gains without pains, and certainly if suffering for a thing makes it dearer, I shall regard my *queue* when I attain one with no small amount of pride and affection.

Secondly, . . . you no longer wonder that many Chinese in the employ of Europeans wear foreign shoes and stockings as soon as they can get them. For native socks are made of calico and of course are not elastic . . . and average toes decidedly object to be squeezed out of shape, nor do one's heels appreciate their low position in perfectly flat-soled heels. Next come the breeches— but oh, what unheard-of garments! Mine are two feet too wide for me around the waist, which amplitude is laid in a fold in front, and kept in place by a strong girdle.

The legs are short not coming much below the knee, and wide in proportion with the waist measurement. Tucked into the long, white socks, they have a bloomer-like fulness capable, as Dr. Parker remarked, of storing a fortnight's provisions! No shirt is worn. But a white washing-jacket, with sleeves as wide as ladies affected twenty years ago, supplies its place. And over all goes a heavy silk gown of some rich or delicate colour, with sleeves equally wide and reaching some twelve or fifteen inches beyond the tips of one's fingers—folded back of course when the hands are in use. Unfortunately no cap or hat is used at this season of the year, except on state occasions, which is trying as the sun is awfully hot.

Wednesday, August 29

While still with Dr. Parker on the way to Hwang-chow Bay I was frequently recognized as a foreigner, because of having to speak to him in English, but to-day in going about Hai-yen City, no one even guessed that such a being was near. It was not until I began to distribute books and see patients that I became known. Then of course my men were asked where I came from, and the news soon spread. Dressed in this way one is not so much respected at first sight as one might be in foreign clothing. But a little medical work soon puts that all right, and it is evidently to be one's chief help for the interior. Women and children, it seems to me, manifest more readiness to come for medical aid now than they did before . . . and in this way, too, I think the native costume will be of service

Taylor knew that his decision would be unpopular with the other missionaries. They would not agree with him. Yet he knew God had led him in making the decision. He wrote in his journal at this time, "And why should a foreign aspect be given to Christianity? . . . It is not the denationalization but the Christianization of these people we seek."

As he thought of "a million a month dying without God," Taylor's burden soon turned to China's interior, where most Europeans did not go. Acting on faith that God would supply his needs, Taylor began the **China Inland Mission** (C.I.M.) with a handful of dedicated men and women. Most C.I.M. missionaries followed Taylor's example of wearing Chinese clothing, eating with chopsticks, and using Chinese manners.

Many Chinese Christians today meet in house churches to avoid persecution.

Opposition to Missions

The Chinese did not always kindly receive Hudson Taylor and the other missionaries. The incident told about at the beginning of this chapter shows the opposition they sometimes faced. Against these threats, the missionaries tried to show the Chinese that they loved them and that God loved them even more. Often their testimony in returning good for evil won them a hearing and then converts among the people. However, opposition to them and to God's Word continued.

Section Review

1. Who was the first Christian missionary to China?

2. What was his greatest accomplishment there?

3. How did Hudson Taylor's method of reaching the Chinese differ from the methods of other missionaries?

4. How did the missionaries respond to the hatred manifested by some Chinese?

Why do you think that Hudson Taylor's decision to dress like the Chinese made such an impact on his ministry?

The Decline of the Manchu Dynasty

Throughout the nineteenth century, the Manchu rulers were losing power in China. Several conditions in China showed that the Manchus were coming to the end of their dynastic cycle and that a change in government would soon take place. Had the Manchus accepted the changing times and worked with the new conditions, their fall might have been stopped. However, they were unwilling to change and clung to the old traditions of their culture. They believed their way to be superior to any other way.

Weakness Inside China

Throughout China the people rebelled and revolted to show their discontent with the Manchu government. The heavy taxation and government corruption especially angered the people. Another major problem was famine. China's population had grown greatly during this time, but the amount of farmland had not increased. Sometimes crops did not produce enough for a peasant to pay taxes and feed his family. Hungry and angry peasants often willingly joined leaders in rebelling against the government.

One rebellious uprising was initiated by a frustrated student, **Hung Hsiu-chuan.** Hung was a gifted student and desired to go into government service. He studied hard and could have passed any government exam except that, along with the test, the officials in charge expected to be bribed. Hung, whose poor family was loyal to the old Ming dynasty, saw his failure directly attached to the corrupt Manchu dynasty.

Shortly after Hung realized that his dream to become a government scholar would not come true, he became seriously ill. In a delirious (hallucinating) fever, Hung saw himself in the "Thirty-third Heaven." There he was met by a man called the Venerable in Years (*venerable* means "revered" or "respected"). The Venerable in Years gave Hung a sword and told him to exterminate the demon-worshipers who had rebelled against the Venerable in Years. With the help of the Venerable in Years's son, Hung saw himself doing battle against demon forces. When the battle was over, the Venerable in Years told Hung to return to earth and be encouraged, "for you are my son."

When Hung recovered from his fever, he was a new man with a purpose. He felt called to relieve the people's distress—the oppression

Historically, wealthy aristocratic families lived off the taxes of poor farmers. Undependable annual rains made famine a regular event but affected the farmers the most.

Chapter 13

Charles Gordon received the Yellow Riding Jacket of the Imperial Army in honor of his leadership during the Taiping Rebellion.

cult, God was the Father, Christ was the Son and Elder Brother, and Hung was the Younger Brother. He renamed the New Testament the Former Testament and called his own "revelations" the New Testament.

Encouraged by the weakness that was evident in Manchurian dealings with the British during the first Opium War and frustrated by government response to the famine of 1849-50, people began to flock to Hung's new religion and cause. By 1851 Hung had a ten-thousand-man army that was discontent and desired revenge on the Manchurians. The rebels cut off their pigtails and wore their hair loose in open rebellion to the Manchu.

The **Taiping** (ty PING) **Rebellion** lasted from 1851 to 1864. It has been estimated that in the prolonged fighting twenty to thirty million people lost their lives. Finally, corruption of the rebellion's leadership caused dissatisfaction with the Taiping cause. Hung committed suicide in June 1864, before his besieged capital, Nanking, fell into Imperial Army control.

Another character in the sequence of events surrounding the Taiping Rebellion was **Charles Gordon**, also known as "Chinese Gordon." A British officer, Gordon was given command of the "Ever Victorious Army" of the Manchus. Gordon's discipline and strategy helped lead the army to victory over the rebels.

Gordon made a good impression on the Chinese. Commander Li of the Imperial Army wrote in his diary of Gordon, "[He is] a direct blessing from Heaven. . . . He is superior in manner and bearing to any of the foreigners I have come into contact with and does not show outwardly that conceit which makes most of them repugnant in my sight." For his leadership, Empress Tz'u-hsi awarded Gordon the Yellow Riding Jacket, the highest order of the empire.

of the Manchus. Shortly after this change, Hung came in contact with a Chinese Christian who shared with Hung a Chinese Bible. Hung began reading the Old Testament and believed it confirmed his vision. He felt that he had met with God and that God had chosen him for a son.

Hung wanted to know more about the Christian religion. The missionaries he met saw the falsehood in Hung's vision. When they pointed it out, Hung left them and produced his own doctrines. He formed a cult called the God Worshipper's Society. In Hung's

The Opening of Japan

On July 8, 1853, the Japanese people near the city of Yedo (modern Tokyo) were busy about their daily tasks. Fishing boats bobbed up and down off the coast as their crews hauled in catches of fish, crabs, oysters, and other seafoods. Life in Japan had changed little in the past two hundred years. In the 1600s, the ruler of Japan, the shogun, had decreed that no foreigners would be allowed into Japan and that no Japanese could leave the islands.

That morning, however, the course of Japanese history changed dramatically. On the horizon appeared several huge, black ships. They drew near to the harbor, then stopped and anchored off the coast. When Japanese officials sailed out to investigate, they found that the vessels were American warships. The commander, Commodore Matthew Perry, informed the shogun that he had been sent by the government of the United States to open trade relations with Japan. He would return the next year, Perry said, for the Japanese answer.

Perry did return as promised—with an even larger fleet. Some Japanese officials urged the shogun to drive out these "barbarians" and pre-serve Japan's isolation. Others realized that resistance would be difficult, if not impossible. Some even welcomed the Americans eagerly and greeted the opening of trade with the rest of the world. Faced with the American show of strength, the shogun gave in. By the Treaty of Kanagawa (1854) the United States received the desired trading privileges, and two hundred years of Japanese isolation came to an end. Unlike China, Japan accepted many Western ways. Soon the Japanese adopted Western styles in government, war, industry—even in fashion and diet. Within a few years Japan had become the most prosperous and powerful nation in Asia. It even joined the ranks of the Europeans in laying claim to portions of China. Perry's mission had an additional effect: Christian missionaries entered Japan and carried the gospel to many lost people who had never heard of Christ.

Japanese boats paddle out to investigate the black ships anchored in the harbor.

Pressures from Outside China

As foreign nations saw the Manchu dynasty weakening, they decided to take advantage of China. As you read in the Backgrounds page (p. 368), when Japan ended its years of isolation from the West, it began to modernize in many ways. One of the ways it modernized was in its military machinery and techniques. This gave Japan an advantage over China when Japan decided to seize control of Korea.

For years Korea had been under moderate Chinese control. In 1876 Japan forced a treaty of independence on Korea. China immediately began to maneuver to retain control. When a Korean secret society rebelled against the pro-Chinese king, he called for China to send troops to help. The Japanese also sent troops, and in 1894 the **Sino-Japan War** began. The result of this war was the resounding defeat of Chinese land and sea forces and humiliation for the Manchu government. In the peace agreement, Korea was left to Japa-

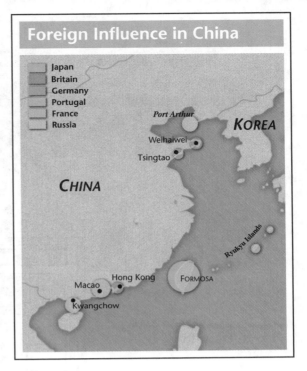

Foreign Influence in China

Japan
Britain
Germany
Portugal
France
Russia

Port Arthur
KOREA
Weihaiwei
Tsingtao
CHINA
Ryukyu Islands
Macao Hong Kong FORMOSA
Kwangchow

nese influence, and Japan received Taiwan as well as other territories. Fearing that Japan would seek control of more Chinese territory, European countries with interest in China sought ways to claim territory for themselves and establish **spheres of influence** in China.

Like children eyeing a huge melon, each nation demanded a "slice" of China. Britain, France, Germany, and Russia all chose areas they wished to control. The desire to establish such spheres of influence led to rivalry not only with China but also among the negotiators. The weak Manchu government had little say in these decisions except to give away land. It seemed that China would be carved up and given to the Europeans, but the tensions displayed in China would soon erupt on a larger scale with the outbreak of World War I.

The actions of these nations plus the weaknesses of the Manchu rulers increased the people's resentment toward foreigners and their own discontent with the government. The pot of Chinese unrest was beginning to boil.

Uncle Sam holds back European powers in order to encourage free trade.

The Forbidden City inside Peking was a stronghold of safety and privacy for Chinese emperors.

Section Review

1. What attitude kept the Manchus from successfully addressing their problems?
2. Name three things that contributed to the Chinese people's discontent.
3. What was the rebellion against the Manchu government called?
4. What British officer helped lead the Chinese army to victory?
5. What did European countries try to establish for themselves in China?

The foreign governments did not take much territory compared to China's overall size, but they did take ports and trade centers. Why did this lost territory cause so much bitterness in the Chinese?

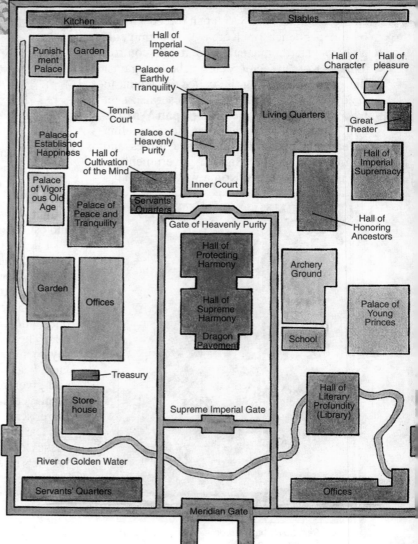

The Boxer Rebellion

In 1899 the pot of unrest boiled over when the **Boxer Rebellion** broke out. The Boxers were members of a secret society officially named the *Society of Righteous and Harmonious Fists*. The Europeans nicknamed the organization Boxers because the martial arts they practiced looked like shadowboxing. The society was anti-Manchu in the beginning, but they saw alliance with the Imperial government as a way to achieve their goals. They took on the slogan "Support the Qing [Manchu dynasty] and exterminate foreigners." Impressed by the society's claim of mystical powers and immunity to foreign weapons, Empress Dowager Tz'u-hsi encouraged the Imperial government not to attempt to restrain the movement.

Attacks on Foreigners

In the early months of 1900, the Boxers began by attacking missionaries and other foreigners in northern China. Many missionaries were aware of their danger but feared that leaving the mission would be more dangerous than staying. No missionaries were safe in areas where the Boxers were present, and many missionaries were killed. About 250 foreigners died in the attacks.

Canadian missionary **Jonathan Goforth** and his wife and children, along with other missionary families, began their escape on June 28, 1900, from Chang Te. They faced a journey of about twenty-four days through territory overrun with Boxers.

The Chinese Christians at their mission urged them to go. They knew that the Boxers had a special hatred for Chinese converts to Christianity. (They believed these Christians had denied traditional Chinese culture and

The Boxers killed many Christian missionaries in their attempt to rid China of foreign influence.

heritage.) However, the Chinese Christians also knew that they could blend into their villages or hide in the countryside as the foreigners could not.

But He Passing Through the Midst of Them Went on His Way

Rosalind Goforth recalls the missionaries' flight from China in her book, *How I Know God Answers Prayer.* Several times along their journey, angry villagers gathered around their carts and shouted and threw things at them. One of the worst of these events came on July 8.

> After prayer we all got on our carts, and one by one passed out into the densely crowded street. As we approached the city gate we could see that the road was black with crowds awaiting us. I had just remarked to my husband on how well we were getting through the crowds, when our carts passed through the gates. My husband turned pale as he pointed to a group of several hundred men, fully armed, awaiting us. They waited till all the carts had passed through the gate, then hurled down upon us a shower of stones, at the same time rushing forward and maiming or killing some of the animals. Mr. Goforth jumped down from our cart and cried to them, "Take everything, but don't kill." His only answer was a blow. The confusion that followed was so great it would be impossible to describe the escape of each one in detail. . . . But I must give the details of Mr. Goforth's experience.

> One man struck him a blow on the neck with a great sword wielded with two hands. "Somehow" the blunt edge of the sword struck his neck; the blow left a wide mark almost around his neck, but did no further harm. Had the sharp edge struck his neck he would certainly have been beheaded!

His thick helmet was cut almost to pieces, one blow cutting through the leather lining *just over the temple,* but without even scratching the skin!

Again he was felled to the ground, with a fearful sword cut, which entered the bone of the skull behind and almost cleft it in two. As he fell he seemed to hear distinctly a voice saying, "Fear not, they are praying for you." Rising from this blow, he was again struck down by a club. As he was falling almost unconscious to the ground he saw a horse coming at full speed toward him; when he became conscious again he found the horse had tripped and fallen (on level ground) so near that its tail almost touched him. The animal, kicking furiously, had served as a barrier between him and his assailants. While dazed and not knowing what to do, a man came up as if to strike but whispered, "Leave the carts." By that time the onlookers began to rush forward to get the loot, but the attacking party felt the things were theirs, so desisted in their attack upon us in order to secure their booty.

At that point the missionaries slipped through the crowd to safety. This was only one incident on the missionaries' trip to the sea and safety. Many times along the way God used Chinese Christians and miraculous intervention to spare their lives. Within two years after their terrifying flight, the Goforths returned to China and their mission. The Boxer Rebellion was the first of many persecutions that the Chinese Christians would experience.

The Goforths and other missionaries experienced a miracle of God's love and protection in their lives. Yet the truth is that God was just as concerned for those missionaries who died; they were just as much under His love and protection, but God chose to glorify Himself in their deaths rather than in their deliverance.

Hebrews 11:32-35a illustrates this point. The writer speaks of those who were triumphant in victory in this world.

And what shall I more say? for the time would fail me to tell of Gedeon, and of Barak, and of Samson, and of Jephthae; of David also and Samuel, and of the prophets: who through faith subdued kingdoms, wrought righteousness, obtained promises, stopped the mouths of lions, quenched the violence of fire, escaped the edge of the sword, out of weakness were made strong, waxed valiant in fight, turned to flight the armies of the aliens. Women received their dead raised to life again.

But in 11:35b-38 the epistle goes on to describe those who were triumphant in death.

And others were tortured, not accepting deliverance; that they might obtain a better resurrection: and others had trial of cruel mockings and scourgings, yea, moreover of bonds and imprisonment: they were stoned, they were sawn asunder, were tempted, were slain with the sword: they wandered about in sheepskins and goatskins; being destitute, afflicted, tormented; (of whom the world was not worthy:) they wandered in deserts, and in mountains, and in dens and caves of the earth.

It is always difficult to understand why good people suffer. One of the ways that God works in lives is by teaching His children to trust Him. God in His sovereignty works out His will.

This copy of a painting by Sgt. John Clymer shows marines fighting Chinese Boxers outside the Peking Legation Quarter. (National Archives)

Foreign Governments Respond

To protect their citizens in China, foreign nations sent in troops. The troops were occupied mainly with trying to retake Peking. On June 20, 1900, the Boxers had attacked the **Legation Quarter** (embassies) of the main foreign powers. The legations were located just inside the wall of the Imperial City. From June 20 to August 14, hundreds of foreigners and thousands of Chinese Christians were held under siege by the Boxers. By the time international troops broke through the siege, hundreds of captives were dead, many were injured, and all were undernourished.

After defeating the Boxers at Peking, the Europeans demanded apologies and money payments from the Chinese government. Too weak politically to argue, the Manchus agreed. The Russians, Germans, Japanese, English, Americans, and French each won concessions. The Chinese paid indemnities (reimbursements) that totaled approximately sixty-five million dollars to the foreign governments. The United States gave its share of the money to a special fund that Chinese students could use for education in America. Using this money, thousands of Chinese were educated in the United States over a period of almost fifty years. The Communist takeover of China ended this arrangement.

Hardly ten years after the end of the Boxer Rebellion, the Manchu dynasty fell to a new Chinese government. (See Chapter 17.) The new government was not a dynasty headed by an emperor, but a republic headed by a president. The Manchus had tried hard to preserve ancient Chinese culture. However, their inability to deal with the problems of a changing world resulted in much of that traditional culture being destroyed. Even with their new government, the Chinese did not have peace. Within forty years China would be controlled by a Communist government.

Section Review

1. What group led a rebellion against foreigners?
2. Why did the rebels especially hate the Chinese Christians?
3. What city did the Boxers beseige?
4. What did the United States do with its share of the indemnity?
5. What type of government finally came to China in the twentieth century?

In Rosalind Goforth's account of their flight, find at least two incidents that show God's miraculous protection of Mr. Goforth. Then find two Scripture verses in which God promises protection to His children.

Summary

For centuries the Chinese were confident in their superiority. Their power and dominance in the East were undisputed. In 1644 the Manchu dynasty came to power in China, and the Chinese world was shaken. For the next two hundred fifty years, China faced the challenges of the modern Western world. Holding on to their attitude of superiority, the Chinese refused to recognize the abilities of other nations. To Europeans this attitude was highly offensive. They made every effort to break down China's obstinate position. The Europeans desired China's luxury goods. Having no goods of their own worthy of Chinese purchase, the Europeans began trading in opium. Thousands of Chinese became addicted to this drug. Although the Chinese outlawed its import, the Europeans still brought it to China. Finally war broke out. As a result of the Opium Wars, more ports and inland China were opened for trade and travel. In response to these openings, traders and missionaries poured into China. The Christian missionaries tried to show the Chinese God's love and salvation through Jesus Christ. Despite their efforts, antiforeign feelings grew until the Boxer Rebellion broke out in 1899. The rebellion was finally put down by European forces. Internal and external pressures weakened the Manchu government so much that it fell in 1911.

People, Places, and Things to Know

Central Kingdom	kowtow	"Ring of Fire"	Taiping Rebellion
Ming dynasty	Canton	Sino-British Joint	Charles Gordon
porcelain	opium	Declaration	Sino-Japan War
Imperial City	Lin Tze-hsü	Robert Morrison	spheres of influence
junks	Opium War	Hudson Taylor	Boxer Rebellion
Manchu dynasty	Treaty of Nanking	China Inland Mission	Jonathan Goforth
Manchuria	cordilleras	Hung Hsiu-chuan	Legation Quarter
tribute	archipelago		

Review Questions

Matching

Match these missionaries with the statement(s) that apply to them.

Robert Morrison   Hudson Taylor   Jonathan Goforth

1. Translated the Bible into Chinese

2. Successfully escaped the Boxers

3. Wore Chinese dress and adopted Chinese customs

4. Started the China Inland Mission

5. One of the earliest missionaries to China

6. Wrote books on the Chinese language and grammar

Short Answer

Write a one- or two-sentence explanation of the following terms.

7. Manchu dynasty

8. spheres of influence

9. Taiping Rebellion

10. Treaty of Nanking

Connections

For each of the following pairs of items, write a sentence or two explaining the connection between them.

11. kowtow / tribute

12. silk / porcelain

Short Answer

Answer the following questions about the first Opium War.

13. When did the war occur, and what two nations fought in it?

14. What was the cause of the war?

15. What was one result of the war?

Think About It!

The British ignored the Chinese rejection of trade and imported opium to get around the rejection. Sometimes, as Christians, we try to maneuver around the authority over us when they reject our requests. Talk to your parents about how to appeal to authority and how to handle rejection. Write out three Scripture verses that deal with authority. Explain one of them in a paragraph.

CHAPTER 14

The natives of Ujiji . . . hurry up by the hundreds to ask what it all means, this fusillading [shooting], shouting, and blowing of horns, and flag-flying. There are Yambos (How do you do's) shouted out to me by the dozen; and delighted Arabs have run up breathlessly to shake my hand, and ask anxiously where I came from. But I have no patience with them; the expedition goes far too slow; I should like to settle the vexed question by one personal view. Where is he? Has he fled? Suddenly a man, a black man at my elbow, shouts in English, "How do you do, sir?"—"Hallo! who . . . are you?"—"I am the servant of Dr. Livingstone," he says; but, before I can ask any more questions, he is running like a madman towards the town.

We have at last entered the town. The expedition comes to a halt; the journey is ended for a time; but I alone have a few more steps to make. There is a group of the most respectable Arabs; and, as I come nearer, I see the white face of an old man among them. He has a cap with a gold band around it; his dress is a short jacket of red blanket-cloth; and his pants—well, I didn't observe. I am shaking hands with him. We raise our hats; and I say, "Dr. Livingstone, I presume?" and he says, "Yes. Finis coronat opus." [Latin for "The end crowns the work."]

With these famous words, Henry M. Stanley met David Livingstone deep in the heart of Africa. Livingstone had spent over thirty years in Africa as a missionary, explorer, and representative of the British government. Like other Europeans who traveled in Africa in the nineteenth century, Livingstone gave the world much of its knowledge of Africa's interior.

A.D. 1750 - A.D. 1950

1750	180

Age of Reason 1600-1800

Slave Trade Outlawed
in Great Britain 1772

Colonial Africa

The Berlin Act 1884

Boxer Rebellion
1899-1900

...very Abolished in the
British Empire 1833

David Livingstone in
Africa 1840-73

British Control of the Suez Canal 1875-1956

1850   1900   1950

Robert Moffat in South Africa 1817-70

Queen Victoria's Reign 1838-1901

Great Trek Begins 1836

Union of
South Africa
1909

Liberia Founded 1821

Boer War 1899-1902

Africans Enslaved

In Chapter 6 we learned about the first explorers who sailed around Africa. Although their goal was to find routes to the East, they set up a few trading ports along the African coast. They traded European goods for the wealth of Africa-gold, spices, ivory, and ebony. However, what they desired most was slaves, black Africans captured and sold into bondage by other Africans. For centuries Africans had taken captives in war and made them slaves. These slaves were bought and sold throughout the continent. The Europeans discovered that they could also buy slaves for yards of cloth, pieces of gold, or colored glass beads. From these beginnings grew what was to become a horrible worldwide trade in human beings, the **slave trade.**

Growth of the Slave Trade

Before 1600 only about two thousand slaves were taken from Africa each year. One hundred eighty years later this figure had climbed to over seventy thousand slaves per year. The major reason for this growth was the settlement of the Americas. Throughout South America, the Caribbean, and North America, large plantations were built. These plantations needed laborers. Most of the native Indian population had been killed or forced to move when the settlers came. Europeans did not want to do heavy work in the hot, tropical climate. They felt that they were unsuited to it since they were from more moderate climates. When Indians were no longer available, Africans seemed the best solution to many Europeans.

This diagram shows how slaves were to be placed into slave ships. In these horrible conditions, many slaves died before they reached their destination.

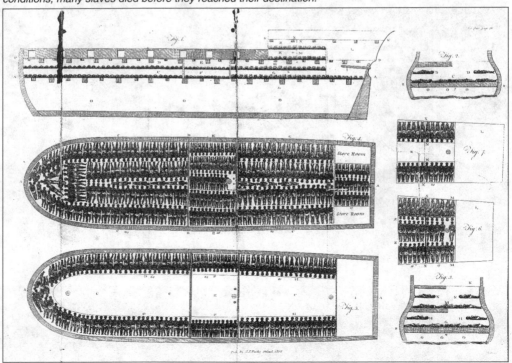

After all, they said, Africans were used to the hot climate and hard work. With this as one excuse, the Europeans lulled themselves into believing that the slave trade was a respectable alternative to working the fields and mines themselves.

European slavers (mostly from Britain, France, and Portugal) anchored their ships off the western coast of Africa to pick up their human cargoes. African traders brought slaves from the interior to the coast. Held captive by chains, ropes, or yokes, slaves had often been forced to walk many miles to the coast. After the harsh treatment on the land journey, their sea voyage was no better. The traders crammed the slaves into their ships, which had decks too low to stand between and were often too crowded to move in. Each slave was chained to the ship to prevent his escape. For two months they lived—or died—in these hot, filthy quarters. At times they were allowed fresh air and exercise above deck, but in poor weather they were kept below with no fresh air. It is no wonder that many of these men, women, and children died before reaching their new home.

Opposition to the Slave Trade

As the eighteenth century wore on, more Europeans became aware of the atrocities of the slave trade. They began to speak out against this trade that caused so much human suffering. Much of this opposition resulted from the Wesleyan revivals in England. As people accepted the gospel, they became concerned about the conditions of these human beings. The movement to help other people, which characterized Europe at this time, began to reach out to Africa.

Attempts to end slavery began in Great Britain. This movement to abolish slavery is called **abolition.** Many heated debates oc-

President James Monroe and the American Colonization Society devised a plan for starting a free African state called Liberia.

curred in Parliament between those who profited from the slave trade and those who saw it as a wicked practice. Many British had grown wealthy from the slave trade. Their greed kept them from admitting the evils of slave trading. Finally in 1772 slavery in Great Britain was outlawed. In 1807 Parliament outlawed the slave trade and in 1833 abolished slavery in the British Empire. Other nations followed Britain's lead in abolishing slavery and the slave trade. The slavery that had existed for centuries and whose evils had been magnified under European trade was by those same hands removed. By 1880 the slave trade was officially ended throughout the world.

Founding Liberia

Americans would finally resolve the issue of slavery at the end of the Civil War in 1865. But in 1816, United States president James Monroe and the American Colonization Society had a goal of finding a homeland for freed slaves. The plan was to start a country where

Shops and stalls line the bustling streets of Liberia's coastal capital, Monrovia.

the former slaves would be not only free but also self-ruled. To meet their goal, the society purchased land along the west coast of Africa. This land, **Liberia,** would become home to thousands of resettled slaves.

The history of Liberia began in 1821 when a shipload of freed black slaves from the United States landed on Providence Island off the coast of West Africa. Early settlement was difficult. Most of the first 114 settlers died from disease. The next group of settlers fared better and established a permanent settlement. About 6,000 freed slaves were eventually resettled in Liberia. Those early settlers established Monrovia, which in 1847 became the capital of the independent Republic of Liberia. (The name *Liberia* comes from the Latin word for "free," and Monrovia was named in honor

of President Monroe.) Liberia was the only black African republic in Africa for over one hundred years. (It is the second oldest independent black African republic. Haiti is the first.)

There are two main groups of people living in Liberia: the Americo-Liberians, whose ancestors came from America, and the tribal people, whose ancestors were African. Even today many of Liberia's government officials and their other leaders come from the Americo-Liberian group; however, a revolt in 1980 brought the indigenous Africans into power. Most Americo-Liberians live in Monrovia or other coastal cities, speak English (the official language), and have a westernized culture. Most of the tribal people (over 90 percent of the population) live in rural areas.

About sixteen different tribes are represented in Liberia, each with its own language, customs, and religion. Although roads and schools are bringing gradual change, most tribes preserve the traditional ways of life. It is not unusual for extended families to live together, even in the urban areas. A relatively small number of Europeans, Americans, and Asians live in the country as well. They often serve as businessmen, teachers, and engineers, but they cannot become citizens or own land. Black ancestry is a requirement of Liberian citizenship, and only citizens may own land. This policy was instituted to ensure that Africans would retain control of the republic that was established especially for them.

Section Review

1. When did Europeans begin the slave trade?
2. In what country did the movement to help the slaves begin?
3. Why did some people want to continue the slave trade?
4. By what year did the slave trade officially end?
5. Where did the United States resettle freed slaves?

The former slaves who went to Liberia had either been born in America or been in America for several years. The area in which they settled was not only already claimed by indigenous tribes but was also wilderness. There were British and French colonies on either side of the region. Review this information and the section on Liberia. In a paragraph or two, discuss the advantages and disadvantages possible settlers would have had to consider before deciding to immigrate.

Looking over Monrovia from a hilltop above the city

Discovering the Source of the Nile

The ancient Egyptians knew where the Nile ended, but they did not know where it began. Finding "the source of the Nile" was not simply a matter of following the river upstream. Difficult obstacles such as swift cataracts (falls or rapids), rugged mountains, and dense jungles hampered would-be explorers. The Romans were halted by one of these obstacles when the emperor Nero sent an expedition southward to find the source of the Nile. The expedition was stopped when it confronted a huge, impassable swamp in the Sudan region. Around the same time, a Greek explorer said that he had found the source of the Nile. The river began, he said, from two lakes near a mountain range called the "Mountains of the Moon" (now the Ruwenzori Mountains).

Stories like those of the Greek explorer spurred further interest in the river. Little by little, explorers

Sir Richard Burton dressed in costume to blend in with the native people as he traveled.

learned more about the Nile. They discovered that two great rivers joined to form the Nile. Explorers found the smaller of these two rivers, called the Blue Nile (because of its clearer waters), easier to explore. In the 1600s a Spanish missionary first discovered the source of the Blue Nile in the highlands of Ethiopia. The larger branch, called the White Nile, proved more difficult. The rough, dense jungle of mountainous central Africa hid its source.

British explorer Sir Richard Burton (1821-90) was in the front rank of men who risked their lives to discover the secrets of unknown lands. Burton, although rather eccentric all his life, was a man of great intelligence. He also had a natural talent for languages and had learned six before he was eighteen years old. At the age of twenty-one he made his first trip to an exotic land, arriving in India as an army officer. His keen mind soon earned him a position in British Intelligence. On his assignments Burton often disguised himself as an Indian, using walnut juice to stain his face. His fluency in Indian languages further disguised his identity. He later did the same type of undercover work in Arabia and

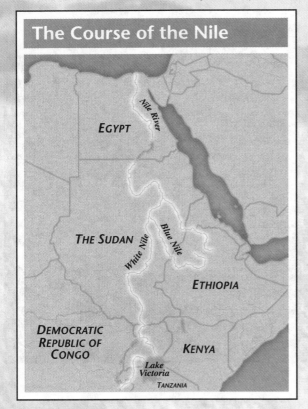

The Course of the Nile

EGYPT

Nile River

THE SUDAN

White Nile

Blue Nile

ETHIOPIA

DEMOCRATIC REPUBLIC OF CONGO

KENYA

Lake Victoria

TANZANIA

Chapter 14

Africa. But Burton had one great goal shared by explorers for centuries—to find the source of the Nile River.

In 1855, with a fellow officer named John Speke, Burton made his first attempt to penetrate the African interior. Turned back by a native ambush, the two did not try again until 1858. Striking inland from Zanzibar, the explorers constantly faced obstacles that ranged from malaria to hills so steep that pack animals died trying to climb them. At last they reached the shores of Lake Tanganyika, then pressed on to find an even larger lake. By this time, both men were terribly ill but determined to continue their search. Burton finally had to stop and wait while Speke, who recovered more quickly, pushed on to discover **Lake Victoria.** He was convinced that he had found the source of the Nile. Burton, however, wanted more proof; the two men quarreled and eventually separated.

Speke returned to England first. He had agreed to wait until Burton arrived to publicize their findings, but Burton reached England to find that Speke had already reported that he "saw that old father Nile without any doubt rises in [Lake] Victoria." (He named the lake "Victoria" in honor of the queen of England.) Speke took full credit for their discoveries. After years of quarreling in print and in person, the two men agreed to meet in a public debate to settle the issue. As he waited for the debate to begin, Burton was informed that Speke had died of a gunshot wound on a hunting trip the day before. Although officials concluded that Speke had shot himself accidentally, some historians believe that he committed suicide, driven by guilt over his injustice to Burton so many years before.

Burton and Speke were only partly right in claiming to have found the Nile's source. Although Lake Victoria is the greatest source of the Nile, it is not the most distant. It took later explorers to find that a river called the Kagera flows into the lake. That river is fed by another river, the **Ruvironza,** that flows north from Burundi. The Ruvironza River is now considered to be the farthest source of the Nile. Starting from the Ruvironza, the Nile measures 4,145 miles long, making it the longest river in the world.

This bust of John Speke is done in Roman style except for the Scottish plaid on the toga.

Africa Explored

Much of Europe's knowledge of Africa came from brave explorers of the continent. Fascinated by the secrets of Africa, these men and women set out on long, hard trips to discover what lay beyond the coastline.

The Delight and Danger of Exploration

The explorers invaded Africa from all sides in many different manners. Some rode south across the burning Sahara on camels. Others traveled as far as they could by canoe or steamship up rivers and streams. They were curious to know where the mighty rivers—the Nile, Niger, Zambezi, and Congo—flowed. They wanted to study the deserts and jungles

and to meet the people of Africa. Some desired fame or wealth. Some desired to hunt big game. Some desired to share the gospel with the millions of lost Africans. All the explorers desired the thrill of discovery, of seeing something first. And all of them desired adventure, which they found abundant in Africa.

Explorers faced many hardships on their way to adventure. There were no roads for them to take and often not even trails. The

Adventure and discovery for explorers included the wild animals of Africa.

Alexandrine Tinné

Not all the explorers of Africa were men. Alexandrine Tinné (1839-69), a Dutch woman, explored both the Nile and Sahara regions of Africa. She used her large inheritance to satisfy her own curiosity about the "dark continent." Miss Tinné was a beautiful, intelligent woman. She knew several languages and was an accomplished horsewoman as well. Above all, she possessed the combined qualities of courage and tenacity.

Accompanied by her mother and several scientists, Miss Tinné first traveled down the Nile in 1863. The expedition proved successful in acquiring scientific information, but Miss Tinné's mother and two of the scientists died. Undaunted, she prepared another expedition across the Sahara. On the journey, she took two large iron tanks of water. The Muslim natives in the party, thinking that the tanks contained gold, attacked Miss Tinné. They slashed her with their sabers, cutting off her hand so that she could not use her revolver. The attackers fled, leaving her to bleed to death. She perished, alone, on the desert.

rugged terrain of mountains, swamps, waterfalls, and deserts made traveling tiresome and dangerous. Wild animals also posed a constant threat to their safety. Often their hired guides deserted them or led them the wrong way. There was also the threat of unfriendly tribes who practiced cannibalism. If they considered the white man their enemy, they would kill and eat him.

The biggest danger for the explorers, however, was disease. Many unknown tropical viruses and infections attacked the white man. Medical science learned much about these diseases and their treatment from the explorers, but many explorers suffered or died first. An ever-present problem was lack of food. Supplies often went bad, ran out, or were stolen. Game and fruit were not always plentiful. Despite these hardships, the explorers went on, many of them echoing Henry Stanley's words: "I can die, but I will not go back."

Results of Exploration

The explorers sent or brought home reports of their work. With each report, the map of Africa grew more detailed. Throughout the nineteenth century **cartographers** (map makers) slowly filled in the continent with rivers, mountains, plains, and deserts. In western Africa the explorers charted the course of the **Niger River** (NYE jur). In central Africa they found the source of the **Congo River.** In southern and eastern Africa they discovered the **Zambezi River** (zam BEE zee) with the magnificent **Victoria Falls** (named for Queen Victoria of Great Britain), **Lake Nyasa** (NYAH sah), and **Lake Tanganyika** (TAN gun YEE kuh). The search for the source of the Nile River was a most intriguing as well as time-consuming hunt.

Africa's Major Waterways

Suez Canal

Lake Nasser

Niger R.

Lake Chad

Blue Nile

White Nile

Congo R.

Stanley Falls

Lake Victoria

Lake Tanganyika

Lake Nyasa

Zambezi R.

Victoria Falls

Limpopo R.

In Africa's interior the explorers saw many strange plants and animals for the first time. Zebras, giraffes, and rhinoceroses (which had at one time been mistaken for unicorns) were just a few of the animals unfamiliar to the explorers. Often the explorers found unusual plants with fruits and nuts, which they ate when their food ran out. The continent contained a vast field of study for botanists (scientists who study plants) and zoologists (scientists who study animals). The explorers made detailed descriptions of plants and animals to send back to Europe. Even today Africa remains a favorite place of study for many scientists.

The explorers also met many different African tribes. Each tribe had its distinctive customs even though most had similar traditional cultures. The explorers recorded in writing and drawings tribal clothing, houses, ceremonies, and art. A constant fear to any explorer was whether a new tribe he met would be friendly or savage. Some chiefs welcomed the white men, while others attacked them.

The explorers brought valuable information to Africa as well as taking it from Africa. They brought their heritage of Western ideas and technology. The explorers exposed the Africans to Western politics, economics, education, science, and medicine. This exposure to Western culture came mostly through teaching the Africans to read and write. First, African languages had to be written out and then Western works translated into them. It was slow work but one that had a great impact on African culture.

The explorers also helped to end the slave trade. They saw the harsh treatment of the slave dealers, and their reports to home spurred on those who fought to abolish the trade. Many explorers believed the way to end the slave trade was to increase the trade in other goods. Most African traders desired European goods and sold slaves to get them. If African resources in gold, diamonds, tin, and agricultural products were developed, the explorers said, then these would replace slaves as the most desired product of Africa. European businessmen soon saw the truth of this observation and began to develop some of Africa's resources. When the slave trade was abolished, these resources were developed even more.

Section Review

1. List four reasons that explorers went to Africa.
2. List four discoveries about Africa made by the explorers.
3. What did the explorers fear most about meeting new tribes?
4. How did Western culture come to African tribes?
5. What did the explorers suggest could replace the slave trade?

How did the Industrial Revolution help make exploration possible?

"I just love exploring! Don't you?"

SETTINGS—Southern Africa

Location—This African region lies below the equator and includes Angola, Zambia, Malawi, Mozambique, Zimbabwe, Namibia, Botswana, Lesotho, Swaziland, and South Africa. The region is south of Tanzania and the Democratic Republic of Congo. The Atlantic and Indian Oceans form Southern Africa's western and eastern borders.

Climate—There are several climate areas in Southern Africa. Much of the northern portion of the region is savannah. Here great herds of animals migrate with the rainy season and the dry season. South of the savannah is a broad band of semiarid steppe climate, which along the west coast turns into desert. The harsh desert softens around Cape Town, South Africa, where a mediterranean climate takes over. Rains are much more consistent on the east side of South Africa, including Lesotho and Swaziland. This portion is the only humid area in the region.

Topography—There is a narrow coastal plain around this region. It averages about twenty miles wide with the exception of the large plain in Mozambique. From this plain the land rises sharply to the inland plateau. Because of this sharp rise, most rivers are navigable for only a few miles. The **Namib Desert** lies along the west coast of Namibia. Great fogs roll in off the ocean, bringing the only source of water to desert plants and animals. In the southern interior lies the **Kalahari Desert,** which, although it receives little rain, has many rivers running through it that support wildlife.

Natural Resources—Southern Africa is rich in mineral resources. It ranks among the top world producers of gold, chrome, antimony, manganese, bauxite, phosphate, asbestos, iron ore, and copper. Nearly all the world's diamonds are mined in Southern Africa.

Geography & Culture—For years climate and topography hindered inland exploration. In this region, only South Africa has a climate that Europeans found hospitable. As a result, this area was settled early and came under European domination. Europeans' ignorance of tribal boundary lines when dividing other Southern African countries caused much internal strife for those countries. In spite of the great resources of the region, many countries are trapped in poverty because of unstable governments. Many areas remain unsettled and underdeveloped even today.

Settings Review

1. What climate region is home to many animals?

2. What two deserts are located in Southern Africa?

3. How are the deserts different?

4. This region is almost the world's sole source of what gem?

Name one way that an unstable government would keep a land underdeveloped and poor. Explain your answer.

This South African woman's wealth is in her neck rings, while this farmer seeks prosperity in a good harvest. Modern South African cities, such as Johannesburg, are changing the traditional agrarian lifestyle of some African people.

Africa Evangelized

The most important gift brought to Africa by the explorers was the gospel. Many of the explorers were really missionaries who explored new territory in their work. Other missionaries followed the routes of the explorers to reach the tribes of interior Africa for Christ.

The Gospel to Africa

Many contributions made by westerners to Africa—written languages, abolition of slave trade, and better medical care—came from the work of missionaries. They set up schools and hospitals. They learned strange languages so that they could teach the people of God's love from the Bible in their own tongues. They saw many leave their worship of idols and evil spirits and come to a knowledge of salvation through the Lord Jesus Christ.

Robert Moffat

Robert Moffat was born in Scotland in 1795. His parents were diligent, thrifty, and religious. His mother would gather the children together on winter evenings to teach them to sew and knit—the boys too. While they were busy practicing, Moffat's mother would read stories from the church papers about missionaries to Greenland and Labrador. God used both these early sewing lessons and the inspirational stories in the life of Robert Moffat.

In 1816, when Robert was eighteen, he took a job as a gardener in London. Just as his parents had taught him, Robert continued to read his Bible faithfully. It was at this time that the Lord brought Robert into contact with a group of Methodists who had been saved under the preaching of John Wesley. After Robert attended several Methodist meetings, he began to wonder whether he was truly converted.

He asked a question that often confronts children born in a religious home. He wondered how he could have a conversion experience like the ones he read in the Bible when he had never been a great sinner. (He even considered doing great sins so that he could repent and be saved.)

This question burned in Moffat's heart and caused him to read the Bible even more. "One evening while poring over the Epistle to the Romans, I could not help wondering over a number of passages which I had read many times before. They appeared altogether different. I exclaimed with a heart nearly broken: 'Can it be possible that I have never understood what I have been reading?' turning from

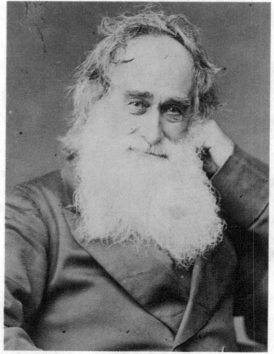

Robert Moffat

one passage to another, each sending a renovation of light into my darkened soul. The Book of God, the precious undying Bible, seemed to be laid open, and I saw what God had done for the sinner. I felt that, being justified by faith, I had peace with God through the Lord Jesus Christ."

Later that year after his conversion, Moffat was walking across a bridge and saw a sign posted that advertised a missionary meeting. As he stood and read, he "resolved to go to sea again and get landed on some island or foreign shore where [he] might teach poor heathen to know [the] Savior." In 1817 Robert Moffat landed on that shore, South Africa, to begin his ministry.

In the early years especially, life in Africa was difficult. Moffat often went without much food and drank brackish (salty) water. When he lived in one African village, he had to be careful at night because wandering village cows would come into his hut.

In spite of uncomfortable conditions, Moffat tried to keep himself neat. The sewing he had learned from his mother helped him keep his clothes in good repair. Another trick he learned from her did not help, however. He had watched his mother sometimes fold a shirt and slap it with a flat board to get the wrinkles out. Without a board available, Moffat used a smooth piece of granite. After slapping his shirt smooth, he picked it up and found that he had worn holes the size of his finger into it. At the end of his first year, Moffat came back to Capetown with all his shirt sleeves cut off.

Moffat's homestead shows his efforts at cultivating fruit trees and vegetables native to Europe.

Two years after Moffat came to South Africa, his sweetheart, Mary Smith, made the harrowing voyage from England to Capetown. After much prayer, she had decided to give up the comforts of England and home to join Moffat on the mission field. They were married on December 27, 1819.

During Moffat's fifty-three years in South Africa, he took the gospel to many tribes and established a mission that became a way station for later missionaries. He taught other missionaries to grow foods in the African soil and become self-sufficient in the harsh land. He established friendships with several tribal leaders and did much to bring peace to the area. Moffat also translated the Bible, *Pilgrim's Progress,* and a hymnal into one of the African dialects. Several of Moffat's sons and grandsons became leaders in South African politics. His daughter, Mary, married David Livingstone.

Fighting Malaria

Malaria sickened and killed many explorers and missionaries, as well as natives, in Africa during the 1800s. Even in modern times, as many as one million people die annually as a result of malarial infection.

In ancient Italy the people found that if they lived in a swampy area they sometimes developed fevers. They went so far as to name the fever diseases *mal aria*—"bad air." For centuries, people believed that the fever (and many other diseases) came from the air. Their belief seemed to be supported by the fact that when they drained swampy areas, the incidence of malaria decreased. It would be years before they would find the true cause.

In 1880 a French physician found the cause of malaria. Charles Laveran discovered a **parasite** (an organism that grows in or feeds on another organism without contributing anything to it) in the blood of someone infected with the disease. Dr. Laveran knew that the parasite was making the victim sick, but how did the parasite get into the bloodstream? In 1897 a British doctor, Ronald Ross, discovered the same parasite in mosquitoes. The connection had been made. Dr. Ross was sure that the malaria parasite was transmitted to humans by the bite of the mosquito.

If the mosquito is sucking blood out of your arm, how does a parasite get into you? Does it swim "upstream"? No. Before it sucks, the mosquito injects you with a fluid to deaden the area

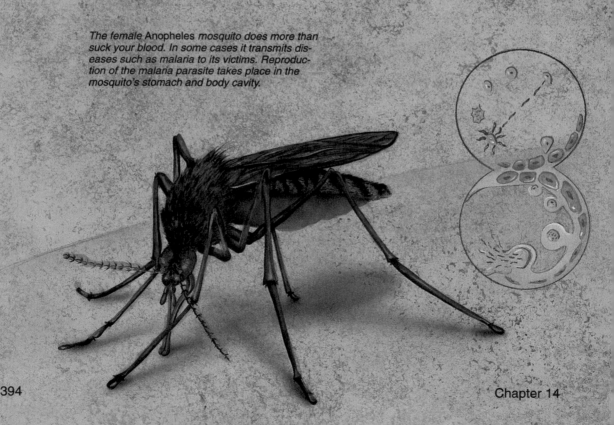

The female Anopheles *mosquito does more than suck your blood. In some cases it transmits diseases such as malaria to its victims. Reproduction of the malaria parasite takes place in the mosquito's stomach and body cavity.*

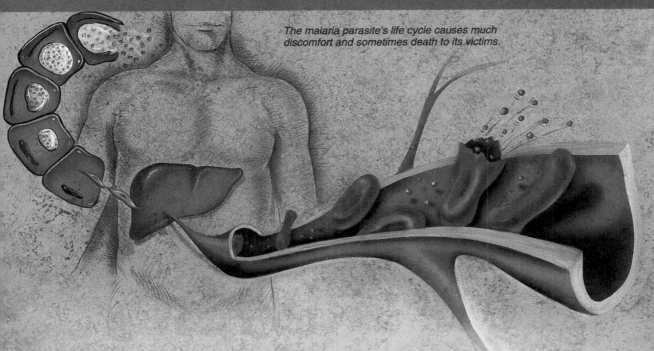

The malaria parasite's life cycle causes much discomfort and sometimes death to its victims.

to pain. Parasites are transmitted through this fluid. It is not until the mosquito has already begun sucking that your body's defenses react to the fluid and you feel the need to scratch. Then you see the fat, red-bellied thief on your arm. By that time, the microscopic parasites have flowed down the tubelike mouth of the mosquito into your blood.

Once in your bloodstream, the parasite continues its growth in stages. One stage develops inside your red blood cells. When mature, the parasites burst through the cells. The breaking of these cells (and your body's response to it) throws your body thermostat off, and you come down with chills and fevers.

Doctors can tell what kind of malaria parasite you have been infected with by timing the intervals between "attacks" of chills and fevers. If the attacks occur every 48 hours, then you have the *Plasmodium vivax, falciparum,* or *ovale* parasite.

If they occur every 72 hours, then you have the *Plasmodium malariae.* "So what?" you might be saying. But the timing of the intervals allows doctors to administer the drug that is most effective on the specific parasite. Identification could be a matter of life or death—yours or the parasite's.

Even though doctors did not know until after 1880 how malaria was caused or what transmitted it, they did have a treatment that helped the symptoms long before that. When the Spanish Jesuits came to South America, the natives shared with them a cure for the fevers. The Indians knew that when the bark of the cinchona (sin KONE nuh) tree was boiled, it produced a liquid that helped the fevers. The medicine that resulted is called **quinine.** Every well-prepared explorer or missionary of the 1800s had a stock of quinine with him. Today most malaria cases are treated with synthetic drugs.

David Livingstone

The most famous missionary to Africa in the nineteenth century was **David Livingstone** (1813-73) from Scotland. He arrived in South Africa in 1840 and served on the continent until his death in 1873. His few return trips to Great Britain allowed him to set before Europe the need for missionaries in Africa. His chief aim in life lay in telling Africans about Jesus Christ.

Livingstone was also one of the greatest explorers of Africa. Desiring to take the gospel to all men, he ventured far inland to places no white man had ever seen. He once wrote to his father, "I am a missionary, heart and soul. God had an only Son, and He was a missionary and a physician. A poor, poor imitation of Him I am, or wish to be. In this service I hope to live, in it I wish to die." Wherever Livingstone went, he preached Christ to the natives, in both word and deed. He followed the Zambezi River, discovered Victoria Falls, and later traveled around the great lakes of eastern Africa. It was on the shore of Lake Tanganyika that **Henry Stanley** found him and where he later died. His faithful native companions buried his heart in Africa, where it had always been. Then they embalmed his body and carried it to the coast. It

David Livingstone

was shipped to England and buried in Westminster Abbey.

In response to David Livingstone's plea for workers, many other missionaries took up the work in Africa. The missionary societies that sent men and women to India and China soon saw the need of Africa and sent missionaries there too. New societies began with the main object of reaching the lost of Africa. These men and women trusted God to keep them from hostile Africans, wild beasts, disease, harsh conditions, and loneliness while they worked for Him. These missionaries heard and responded to the message of Romans 10:13-15:

> "For whosoever shall call upon the name of the Lord shall be saved. How then shall they call on him in whom they have not believed? and how shall they believe in him of whom they have not heard? and how shall they hear without a preacher? And how shall they preach, except they be sent? as it is written, How beautiful are the feet of them that preach the gospel of peace, and bring glad tidings of good things!"

Many lives were changed by God's grace because of the willingness of these missionaries to go to Africa and their selflessness in staying there to tell of Christ Jesus.

This stone in Westminster Abbey marks David Livingstone's burial site.

Livingstone's faithful African friend, Susi, waits with Livingstone's body after the long trip from Africa.

Section Review

1. What was the most important gift the Africans received from the Europeans?
2. List four other contributions Europeans made to Africa.
3. Who was the most famous missionary to Africa in the 1800s?
4. Why did he explore as well as preach?
5. What was the attitude of missionaries going to Africa?

Someone once said, "A man's life is more than the measure of his days." In what way did Livingstone's life continue to affect the world after his death?

Africa Divided

In the second half of the nineteenth century, Europe turned its eyes toward Africa. As they had in India and the Far East, the land-hungry European nations carved up Africa and added the pieces to their growing empires. This rush for territory in Africa was known as **the Scramble.** Colonial expansion in Africa is one example (China was another) of European imperialism in the nineteenth century.

Europe's Big Appetite

The European imperialists needed colonies for trade and raw materials for their new factories built during the Industrial Revolution. They also needed new markets in which to sell their manufactured goods. Their crowded population needed new territory to overflow into. Africa, with its untouched mineral and agricultural resources, presented a valuable source of materials, offered opportunities for new markets, and provided new frontiers for adventurous colonists.

For years some European nations had maintained colonies in Africa, but in the mid-nineteenth century, other countries increased their involvement in Africa. France began taking over areas in northern Africa. Then Britain added to its territory by taking control of Egypt (which was having financial problems) to protect the **Suez Canal.** Most of these territories were on the coastline, but it was the actions of **King Leopold II** of Belgium and **Otto von Bismarck** of Germany that did much to cause the Scramble.

Belgium Takes a Colony

Leopold had tried using his family fortune to purchase existing, undeveloped colonies from Portugal, France, and Britain. He told the British ambassador, Saville Lumley, that Belgium needed "a safety valve for her surplus

King Leopold hid selfish plans under the guise of humanitarianism.

energies." Leopold's idea was rejected by his own cabinet. Each country he approached rejected his proposal.

But events were taking place that would help Leopold come up with another plan. David Livingstone's journal had been published. His plea had been "to heal the open sore of Africa" from its slave trade and spiritual darkness. Livingstone had suggested that honest trade would make up for lost profit of the slave trade. Verney Cameron, an explorer, had just returned from the Congo with reports of "unspeakable riches." But the governments that already had colonies were unwilling to pay for further exploration. Leopold decided to act.

He hosted a convention of explorers in 1876 and offered to help pay to "open to civilization the only part of our globe where it has yet to penetrate, to pierce the darkness which envelops whole populations." Leopold encouraged investment by other countries into what would be called the **International African Association** (IAA), but he retained control of the organization as president.

The world saw Leopold as the leader of the crusade against slavery. The fact that he used his own money was called "the greatest humanitarian work of his time." Leopold had finally gotten his "slice" of Africa. By 1882 Leopold owned the company that resulted from the IAA. The other European nations were becoming nervous.

What the investors in the IAA later found was that, far from humanitarian work, Leopold encouraged the harsh treatment and torture of African workers (slaves) on his plantations. Leopold's detestable actions caused an outcry that persuaded the Belgian government to take control of the territory themselves in 1884. The territory in the interior of Africa along the Congo River was called the **Belgian Congo.**

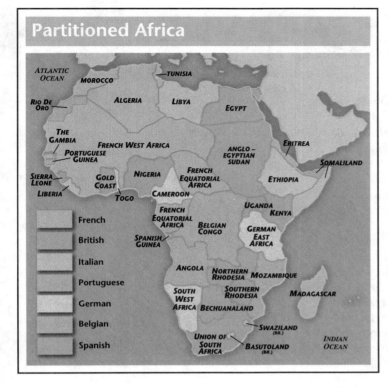

Partitioned Africa

French

British

Italian

Portuguese

German

Belgian

Spanish

could establish territory without actually occupying it.

The Scramble was well under way in 1884 when European leaders met at Berlin, Germany. The purpose of their meeting, the **Berlin Conference,** was to set down rules for claiming Africa. The result of the meeting was the **Berlin Act.** This act set the ground rules for claiming territory. Before any country could claim a territory, that country was required to inform the other European countries of its claim. If any other country had a claim to that territory, the countries must then negotiate boundaries. In this way the European powers hoped to avoid military conflict in Africa and Europe. The act also established the Niger River and the Congo River as free-navigation areas no matter who controlled the riverbanks.

With the rules set down, the race was on. Following Germany's lead of claiming land without occupying it, European nations began dividing up Africa on paper. If they had any claim to a region, they took a map of the area and drew in boundaries to their colony. This dividing process is called **partitioning.** Every European nation began taking more of Africa. Portugal, France, and Britain expanded existing colonies into the interior of Africa. They staked their territories based on treaties with African kings, but often the African leaders did not fully understand what the treaties meant. The division of land by these treaties caused many problems in the twentieth century when the African nations claimed their independence. By 1914 there was little of Africa that had not been claimed by a European empire.

Germany Joins In

In 1884 Germany, still a young nation, became interested in forming colonies. Otto von Bismarck, the German chancellor, chose colonies that would be politically beneficial. Bismarck made choices that would show preference to France by supporting its bids for territory in West Africa and Egypt. At the same time Germany's colonies greatly inconvenienced British commerce. In this way, Bismarck hoped to make Britain fall in line with German desires.

Germany made several claims in early 1884. It established protectorates over Togoland and Cameroon in West Africa. It then took Zanzibar in East Africa as a protectorate. Bismarck scared the rest of Europe by showing that any country with enough power to defend its claims

ANALYSIS

The Suez Canal

Since the days of the pharaohs, men had dreamed of a waterway connecting the Mediterranean Sea to the Gulf of Suez. Egyptian legend says that a canal that connected the Nile to the Bitter Seas was actually built in 1500 B.C. by the ruler Sesostris. At that time the Bitter Seas were connected to the Red Sea, so the shallow canal made travel between the Mediterranean and the Red Sea possible.

For the next two thousand years, the Canal of the Pharaohs was opened or closed according to the whim of the current ruler. One ruler would have the canal filled with sand, and another would have it re-excavated. During the Roman occupation of Egypt, the canal was reopened under the name Canal of Trajan (the Roman emperor). The canal helped Rome to trade with more nations, manage its empire, and transport exotic circus animals from Africa and Asia to Rome.

After explorers such as da Gama (1498) opened the route to India by sailing around Africa, other European traders began thinking about getting to the East faster so that they could better compete with Portugal. They realized that a canal from the Mediterranean to the Red Sea would shorten the trip to the Far East by thousands of

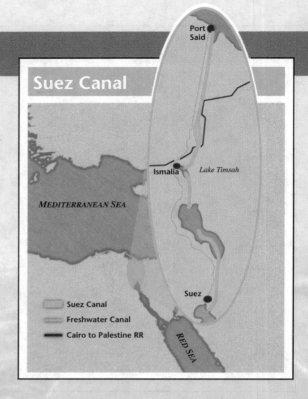

miles. But the Ottoman Empire effectively blocked any attempts by Europeans to reopen the Canal of the Pharaohs.

Napoleon was the first man in modern times to attempt to build a canal. He led an expedition into Egypt in 1798 and afterwards ordered a survey of the area. After a year, Napoleon's surveyor, Jacques-Marie Le Pere, came back with the report that the Red Sea was thirty-two feet higher than the Mediterranean. This difference he said would have to be fixed by building a series of locks (otherwise the Red Sea would flood Egypt).

It is a good thing that Napoleon never got a chance to build, because locks were unnecessary. Le Pere's calculations were wrong. The Red Sea and Mediterranean Sea are almost identical in height, with seasonal variations making the Mediterranean higher in the summer and the Red Sea higher in the winter. A canal could be

Suez Canal (map legend)
- Suez Canal
- Freshwater Canal
- Cairo to Palestine RR

Map labels: Port Said, Ismalia, Lake Timsah, MEDITERRANEAN SEA, Suez, RED SEA

built without the extra expense of locks. But it was still several years before anyone would begin construction.

Much wrangling went on among France, Austria, England, and three separate viceroys of Egypt before Viceroy Said Pasha (sah-EED PAH-sha) gave permission for **Ferdinand de Lesseps,** a former French diplomat, to build a canal. De Lesseps had formed a relationship with Said during his years of service in Egypt. On November 15, 1854, de Lesseps presented his plans to the viceroy and received the following response: "I am convinced; I accept your plan; we will concern ourselves during the rest of our expedition as to the means of carrying it out. You may regard the matter as settled, and trust to me."

Conflict and confusion continued within France, Austria, Egypt, and Britain even as a French construction company finally began work in 1859. Ten years later the Suez Canal opened for traffic. About one hundred miles long, the canal runs from Port Said (a man-made port) on the Mediter-ranean coast down to the city of Suez on the Gulf of Suez.

In 1875 the British bought out the Egyptian share of the canal and became partners with the French. The two managed the operation of the canal until 1956. In that year, the Egyptian government seized control and began collecting tolls from ships passing through the canal. From 1957 to 1967 Egypt collected as much as $227 million a year in tolls.

In 1967 Israel invaded Egypt, and the Suez Canal was closed. For the next seven years, all the ships that had once transported oil from Arabia through the canal had to make the long trip around Africa's tip as in da Gama's day. When the conflict was finally ended, the canal was out-of-date. During the war years, new oil tankers had been built that needed deeper channels. The old canal was too shallow. Egypt was faced with the daunting job of not only removing war debris from the canal but also digging to widen and deepen it. The improved Suez Canal was re-opened in 1979.

Covered wagons and oxen teams transported Boer families into Southern Africa's interior.

Conflicts

The desire for colonies inevitably led to conflict. One conflict occurred in South Africa. The Dutch, who were called **Boers,** had first settled on the Cape of Good Hope in the seventeenth century. When the British took over **Cape Colony** in the nineteenth century, the Boers decided to move northward. This movement is known as the **Great Trek.** The Boer Great Trek was much like the westward movement in the United States, as families packed their belongings into covered wagons and set out to find new lands. Later in the century, conflict broke out again when gold and diamonds were discovered in the Boer lands. The British wanted some of this wealth, but the Boers refused. In 1899 war broke out. The **Boer War** lasted for three years. Expert

Boer marksmen and horsemen defended their lands until the British defeated them in 1902. To bind up the wounds created by the fighting, the British gave the Boers an equal say in government. In 1909 the people of South Africa formed the **Union of South Africa.**

Jealousies grew between other European nations. The French, who controlled most of North Africa, resented Britain's control of Egypt. The British, who hoped to rule land stretching from Egypt to South Africa, were stopped when the Germans obtained land in central East Africa. The Italians struggled against all the other powers to obtain a small piece of the continent. Many of these problems in Africa and other regions touched by imperialism contributed to the outbreak of World War I in 1914.

Effect of Imperialism on Africa

Conflict also arose between the Europeans and the Africans. The Europeans usually obtained land by superior military force or by signing treaties with tribal chiefs. The Europeans ignored tribal identities and land ownership while carving out areas suitable to their own needs. Often enemy tribes were put in the same parcel, or a tribe was divided between two competing European rulers. Sometimes the Europeans treated their African subjects harshly. Rarely did the Africans have a voice in government.

Some Europeans hoped to help Africa and brought many gifts to them. We have already talked about these in the chapter: the gospel, written languages, new technology, trade, and Western learning. These gifts were often only side effects of European rule. The Europeans desired Africa mainly to help themselves in industrial development and political superiority. However, the Europeans also prepared Africa to enter the modern world one day.

European influence greatly changed African culture. The abundance of Western knowledge and technology encouraged Africa to become part of the world around it. But European ignorance of African history and traditions caused the Africans to resent European rule. By 1914 the Europeans had given Africa both the tools and the reasons for throwing off foreign rule. In the twentieth century, Africa would demand independence. Chapter 19 will address some of the conflicts Africa faced in the twentieth century.

Section Review

1. What was the rush for territory in Africa called?

2. What was the purpose of the Berlin Conference?

3. What term is used to describe the division of land?

4. What two nations desired land in Southern Africa? What conflict resulted from this desire? What new nation was born from the conflict?

5. How did the Europeans violate tribal organization?

6. What gifts did the Europeans bring to Africa? Why did the Africans resent the Europeans?

Could Europeans have established colonies in Africa while maintaining good relations with the African people? Explain your answer.

Summary

Europeans had their first contact with interior Africa in the seventeenth century. The explorers who sailed along the African coast traded goods for slaves brought from the interior. From these beginnings the slave trade grew until slaves became the most important African export. The slave trade was a horrible abuse of human beings that was finally made illegal in the late 1800s. The explorers and missionaries who traveled into interior Africa provided a major voice against the slave trade. Discovering much of the beauty and wealth of Africa, as well as the horrors of the slave trade, they encouraged Europeans to develop other African resources. The Europeans took their advice and began to develop Africa. The Europeans brought many gifts to the Africans, but they also began to claim land there. The Europeans' desires for land led to conflicts with the Africans and with each other. Eventually these conflicts led to African movements for independence in the twentieth century.

People, Places, and Things to Know

slave trade	Victoria Falls	David Livingstone	Berlin Conference
abolition	Lake Nyasa	Henry Stanley	Berlin Act
Liberia	Lake Tanganyika	the Scramble	partitioning
Lake Victoria	Namib Desert	Suez Canal	Ferdinand de Lesseps
Ruvironza River	Kalahari Desert	King Leopold II	Boers
cartographers	Robert Moffat	Otto von Bismarck	Cape Colony
Niger River	malaria	International African	Great Trek
Congo River	parasite	Association	Boer War
Zambezi River	quinine	Belgian Congo	Union of South Africa

Review Questions

Listing
Make lists for the following.

1. The explorers in Africa met many hardships. How many can you list?

2. The explorers in Africa found the sources of a number of rivers and discovered many lakes. Name three African rivers and three African lakes.

True/False
Identify each of these statements as either true or false.

3. Europeans were the first to enslave the Africans.

4. By 1780 about seventy thousand African people were taken into slavery each year.

5. Africans helped capture fellow Africans to sell as slaves.

6. Explorers and missionaries helped end slavery.

Matching
Match the following items.

7. Berlin Conference
8. Great Trek
9. abolition
10. imperialism
11. partitioning

(a) dividing land on paper

(b) did away with slavery

(c) rule of one nation over another

(d) the movement of Boers inland

(e) decided rules for dividing Africa

Fill in the Blank

Write the word or words that correctly complete the sentence.

12. The source of the Nile River is the _____ River.

13. Stanley found Livingstone on the shore of _____.

14. Diamonds and gold were found in _____.

15. King Leopold II of Belgium bought _____ as a personal colony.

16. The British took control of _____ because of Egypt's financial problems.

17. When Livingstone discovered these falls, he named them _____ in honor of the queen of Great Britain.

18. The Boers first settled in _____.

Think About It!

Compare the exploration and colonization that took place in Africa in the 1800s to the exploration and colonization that took place in the New World during the 1500s. (Think about factors that led up to each exploration and conditions that made exploration possible.)

Music and Art in History

Art and music are important mirrors that reveal how people are affected by and view the world around them. Many artists and composers with their various styles have already been discussed in previous chapters. Seeing those styles in the broader view of the panorama of history should help you understand them better and perhaps grasp the sequence of history more fully.

Virtually no music but some art from the years before Christ has survived to this day. Art pieces that remain are durable pieces, sculpted from or painted on stone or rock. Much of the art preserved from early civilizations records religious activities as in Mayan ruins or political figures as in Egyption ruins.

Rather than revealing the common people's preoccupation with these things, the art probably reveals that kings and temple leaders could afford to commission artists to create art for them.

The art also reveals the thoughts of the people. In Egypt, the art done on the interior walls of the pyramids looks strange to us with its half profile, half full front poses. But it was important to the Egyptians to show the whole person in the painting because they believed that only the things in the painting would be with the deceased person in the afterlife. If an arm was missing because it was hidden from view, then that person would be missing an arm after death.

Pre-Renaissance Art

An Egyptian officer directs slaves and soldiers as they prepare a chariot for battle.

In most early civilizations there is a general absence of art for pure enjoyment except in the form of decorated objects for everyday usage. Pottery bowls reveal the common person's desire to beautify his world with art, but the lack of permanent art by the common man suggests that life then revolved around functional activities. Not only was there less leisure time for creative endeavors, but there were fewer resources available for art.

Architectural remains from the late B.C. years and early A.D. years seem to indicate that the Greeks and Romans felt good about themselves. They saw themselves as having knowledge and worth. Their sculpture reveals that they studied the human form as well as the world around them. They also had money left over after buying staple goods so that they could decorate with artwork. The remains of many homes have floor mosaics and wall frescos (pictures painted in wet plaster). Archaeological records also reveal that the Romans surrounded themselves with finely painted and glazed pottery and kept their oils, wines, and perfumes in beautiful bottles of colored glass.

Meanwhile, art in China seemed to expand from stone religious and political images to delicately painted silk banners. These silk banners honored people and illustrated proverbs. In China the interest in painting continued for the next several hundred years and reached its height during the T'ang dynasty. Portraits of emperors and courtiers were mingled with masterful landscapes and still lifes. Later, paintings decorated the walls of most temples and many homes.

As the Roman Empire waned, the center of Western art shifted to the Byzantine Empire. With Constantine's declaration that Christianity be made the official religion of the empire, religious art flourished. Elaborate mosaics depicted saints from the Bible and from church tradition. Iconography came to its height during the Byzantine Empire (500-1500) when works of art served as tools for worship in the Orthodox Church (see pages 464-65). Byzantine icons look strangely flat when compared with the three-dimensional work of the Romans. Again, the art reveals the beliefs of the people. Icons represented celestial beings; these saints and Bible characters were not intended to look like regular people. Their eyes were often painted looking upward to draw the viewer to thoughts of heaven. Their physical features were unrealistic so that no viewer would mistake them for mere humans.

During the Byzantine Empire, Islam began to spread around the Mediterranean Sea. Islam prohibited the representation of people or animals because such representation was considered idolatry. Islamic decoration was very geometric and abstract with intertwining vines and flowers or repeated shapes.

Near the end of the Byzantine Empire, the Persians to the east came under the influence of the Mongols after years of Islamic control. The Mongol ruler Tamerlane brought Chinese influence to the art of Persia. Miniature paintings recorded historical events against highly stylized Asian backgrounds. Texts that recorded Persian history and told stories about the gods of the land were dotted with full-color illustrations.

While Europe wallowed in the Dark Ages, small groups of Irish monks kept the Scriptures safe by laboriously copying them by hand.

While they copied, they illustrated Bible stories in the margins. The *Book of Kells* is one of the most beautifully illustrated manuscripts from this time period. What the pictures lack in perspective and accuracy is made up in gold-leaf highlights.

During the Renaissance, rich patrons began to support individual artists instead of artist guilds. With this change, artists became very competitive. The rise in towns gave middle-class people extra money with which to commission family portraits and other works commemorating their success. Finally, with the invention of the printing press, artist's etchings, such as those Dürer produced, could be mass-produced for books.

Before continuing the history of art, let's look back at music history to see how the two came together in their growth and development.

An early Chinese landscape shows a peaceful dwelling nestled at the base of the mountains.

Pre-Renaissance Music

An older David receives inspiration for his psalms (King David Playing the Harp, *Vouet*, Bob Jones University Collection).

Music has been part of man's development for thousands of years. Genesis 4:21 proclaims that Cain's descendant Jubal "was the father of all such as handle the harp and organ." Every culture since that time has sung and played folk music. Unlike art, singing does not require extra money or equipment. Music, however, is not something that can be preserved in stone.

Until the beginning of musical notation, musical pieces were passed from person to person and from generation to generation. Sometimes the songs were poems set to music. They often recorded stirring historical or political events. A few of these "songs" live on through their words even though the tunes are lost forever.

The Bible records many songs in the book of Psalms. The word *psalm* means "song" or "hymn." These Bible songs record great vic-tories in battle, trials of sorrow, and praises to God. When God saved the children of Israel from death at the hands of pursuing Egyptians, the Bible records in Exodus 15:1 that "then sang Moses and the children of Israel this song unto the Lord, and spake, saying, I will sing unto the Lord, for he hath triumphed gloriously: the horse and his rider hath he thrown into the sea."

The music that the people of Israel sang would probably have sounded unusual to Western ears. The music that dominated the countries in the Middle East and across Asia featured rhythms and note patterns that were very different from European music. Even today, some Asian music sounds unusual to Western ears.

For over two thousand years, music has been performed by Chinese instrumental groups for religious and political events. Traditionally, Chinese musicians play a melody line with no harmony. In Japan, court music also flourished beginning in the 700s. Japanese theater productions were almost always accompanied by music in song or orchestra.

In other parts of Asia, musical form is dominated by religion. In India, note patterns called *ragas* are played according to the time of the day or the celestial significance of the notes. The musician uses the *raga* pattern as a starting point and then improvises the rest of the piece around the *raga*. In contrast, in the

Muslim countries of the Middle East, music is not allowed in religious worship at all, so it is used for entertainment only. The *muezzins* (criers) call Muslims to worship from the tops of minarets with a singsong call to prayer, but it is not normally considered "music."

Even the ancient Greeks emphasized music, saying it was the foundation of an ideal society. During great feasts, warrior chiefs hired men such as the famous Greek poet Homer to sing. Epic poems, such as *The Iliad* and *The Odyssey,* were divided into sections, which made it possible for the immense poems to be sung over a period of several days. In exchange for a meal or lodging, traveling singers brought information and entertainment to villages and towns. The tradition of the traveling minstrel, or *troubadour,* continued for centuries.

Music in Europe changed during the medieval years. The development of a musical notation system allowed music to be written and preserved for generations to come. But later innovations and philosophies caused the most dramatic change. Music and art started a journey which took them beyond the realm of religion and the wealthy into the homes and hearts of the common people.

Music and Art Since the Renaissance

The Renaissance revived Roman humanism. People considered themselves to be God's finest creation. Artists studied anatomy and reveled in the beauty of all that was man's to subdue. The backgrounds of paintings were now filled with mountains, trees, and rivers. By the end of the Renaissance, men had been to the ends of the earth. They were beginning to understand more fully the laws of science, and they had discovered more of the workings of the body. They no longer looked with such longing at eternity in heaven but looked for ways to make heaven on earth.

The Renaissance not only changed man's view of life but also brought new technology that changed the production of music and art forever. The invention of the printing press provided the written word for all to read in their own language. Soon the written word included verses of hymns and etchings of art. Reformers such as Luther used the printing press to put new hymnbooks into the hands of converts who were eager to sing God's praise. The effect of the Reformation on music continued through the baroque period (1600-1750) as great composers such as Bach and Handel set passages of Scripture to music.

Music in the 1700s continued its transformation with the development of orchestras, which delighted music enthusiasts. Court composers such as Haydn regularly wrote new music for kings and queens. The elegant upper class spent their evenings attending concerts and fancy balls.

In art, neoclassicism rejected the frills of the baroque style and went back to the ideals of Greek and Roman history to remind people of their noble heritage. As the nineteenth century approached, people saw that they knew many things that the Greeks and Romans never knew. They had seen more of the world than those other cultures ever imagined. Thus, romantic artists left the cold formalism of neoclassicism and showed exotic places and events such as Eugène Delacroix's *Lion Hunt.*

Reason, in the 1700s, taught people that they could know everything and did not need God to be involved in their daily lives; but without God, mankind fell into despair. Upheavals occurred as the agricultural revolution began to tear away at traditional farming society. People whose families had worked for generations as farmers were jobless. The Industrial Revolution of the 1800s further wore away the foundation of agricultural society. Displaced people crowded the cities. Discontented people overthrew governments.

Throughout the 1800s, romantic music masked social and political upheaval. Symphonic poems by Bedřich Smetana and Antonín Dvořák stirred nationalist pride as they wove their music around common folksongs.

In the 1800s the development and factory production of the piano allowed middle-class families to gather around the piano in the parlor and play popular tunes printed on sheet music. During this century people began to have more leisure time and more money to spend on art and music. From the middle class to royalty, many girls' education included art and music lessons.

In contrast to the consistent, romantic style of music during the 1800s, art went through a quick succession of styles as artists had more time to experiment. Artists began to paint for art's sake, not just to please an audience.

Romantic style art continued in the early 1800s with artists such as John Constable, but some painters were not content showing lovely landscapes or faraway places. Life was so much more than that. These painters were realists. They thought that the everyday events were significant enough to be depicted in art. Gustave Courbet painted the burial of an ordinary villager; Rosa Bonheur depicted a common horse fair in remarkable size and detail. In 1814 Francisco de Goya's painting *The Third of May* showed the reality of the Spanish revolution in stark colors and horrifying detail.

Toward the end of the 1800s, painters questioned their methods of painting. What was the purpose of doing sketches of nature and then bringing them indoors to a studio and painting in unnatural lighting? The newly invented camera showed the effects of light on a scene. That was what they wanted to paint! The impressionists were intrigued by light and color.

Starry Night, *a painting by post-impressionist Vincent Van Gogh, shows the transition from impressionism to fauvism.*

They tried to capture an impression of what the eye sees. The famous impressionist Claude Monet did several paintings of the same scene at different times of day and in different light just to see how the light affected color.

In America, painters continued in realism, ignoring the impressionists of Europe. These expressive realist painters such as Thomas Eakins, African American painter Henry Tanner, and self-taught Winslow Homer realistically recorded everyday events in America.

Their paintings told stories about life in the emerging nation.

The impressionist painters of Europe influenced young composer and pianist Claude Debussy. Debussy changed his style of composing to capture the impression of a moment through his music. He deliberately ignored some of the standard harmonic rules of the classics and chose chords for their beauty rather than for their "correctness." His efforts greatly affected the composers of the twentieth century.

Change in the Twentieth Century

The twentieth century has been a century of rapid change. Communication, through the telephone, radio, television, and recording technology, has made the world a smaller place. Rapid change has also occurred in the arts as the pendulum of style swings rapidly from strict form to rejection of form.

When science and liberal philosophy shook church doctrine in the early 1900s, artists began to question the rules of art even more. A group of artists that European critics called *Fauves* ("wild beasts") painted in a style that was wild and free. They used intense colors and stressed design over perspective. Henri Matisse was the leader of this group with his brightly colored paintings. His paper cut-out piece entitled "The Knife Thrower" gives the minimum of detail in the intense squiggle that represents the knife thrower and the calm female form that awaits the throw against a quiet wallpaper of leaves. This style opened the way for nonobjective art and cubism.

In 1909 Wassily Kandinsky initiated nonobjective art by painting to express mood without any recognizable shapes. He felt that color and line by themselves could represent the inner emotion of the painter. His nonobjective art freed artists from having to express themselves using objects from nature.

Around the same time, Pablo Picasso left his realistic style and pushed the boundaries of art with cubism. After all, if Albert Einstein's theory of relativity was true and the laws of nature could be questioned, perhaps the laws of art and music could also be questioned. Instead of portraying a picture of a moment, Picasso showed several views of an object or event at the same time.

Debussy's earlier push against classic rules inspired composer Arnold Schönberg in the early 1900s to experiment with twelve-note scales and strange mathematical combinations of notes. Similar in style to Schönberg's works, Igor Stravinsky's ballet *The Rite of Spring* sounded primitive and barbaric to listeners in 1913, but it proved that modern sounds had a place in acceptable music.

Even as society questioned absolute rules and chose instead to do whatever brought immediate happiness, some musicians of the mid-1900s felt that even the definition of music was too confining. Composer John Cage defined music as any collection of sounds. His composition *Imaginary Landscape* featured

Will Henry Stevens, 1881-1949, untitled ["Abstraction: Primordial Forms"], 1940, Greenville County Museum of Art, Greenville, SC, Gift of Janet S. McDowell

two performers changing the volume and station settings on twelve radios. In contrast, other musicians anchored their music in ethnic heritage by once again using folksongs in new pieces. Appeal to the common man helps make composer Aaron Copland's music, such as *Appalachian Spring,* easy to listen to.

In the art world, Dadaism and surrealism wanted to sweep away the pain and devastation of civilization. These two art forms not only rejected rules but also inserted fantasy into their art. Mérat Oppenheim's fur-covered cup and saucer, which obviously could not be used for beverages, and Salvador Dali's *Persistence of Memory,* which features melting watches, are examples of Dadaism and surrealism, respectively.

Rather than desiring to do away with modern civilization, the American regionalists Grant Wood and Edward Hopper painted very realistic pictures to capture feelings about America. Wood's painting *American Gothic* reminded people during the depression of their roots in family and farm. Hopper's *Night Cafe* showed the loneliness of a city despite thousands of people living there.

After World War II a new art movement gained immediate recognition. Abstract expressionism showed the feelings of the painter—not in the subject painted but by the way the paint was applied and by the colors that the artist used. Jackson Pollack's enormous splattered canvases are an example of this movement. Once again, this art revealed a continued push toward freedom from rules and constraint.

The history of music and art provides another record of man's experiences in life. It exposes man's emotions of optimism or pessimism. It uncovers man's spirit by showing the god he worships. It reveals his relationships to the authority placed over him. Be aware of the art and music around you. How does it reflect the feelings of the people of your world?

ACT FOUR

CONFLICTS

1900 TO Present

As Act Three closed, events set the stage for conflict. The first conflict of Act Four is described as a "war to end all wars." But its benefits are limited. An uneasy peace holds Europe together while the United States slowly builds a reputation for power and prosperity. Soon Europe is again at war, and all the world is drawn into the fray.

When World War II ends, two new giants, the United States and the Soviet Union, stand facing each other across an "iron curtain," waiting for any hint of aggression. Communism and capitalism war for the minds of new nations in Africa, Asia, and South America. Struggles result that change the balance of power. South American countries develop for themselves and not for European mother countries. African nations free themselves from the domination of Europe. Many of these countries find new oppression as powerful men and their ideas strive for control.

When the iron curtain collapses, glimpses of the Soviet Union show the weakened state of Communism in Europe. The inevitable breakup of the Soviet Union causes confusion, poverty, and more conflict in Europe. The ripples are felt around the world.

Japan and China become the first of several Asian countries to gain economic strength and, with it, political power. Europe moves toward unifying into one powerful economic and political bloc. The nations of Africa and Latin America cautiously embrace democratic government. Yet war and conflict do not cease. Violence is as natural to humanity as eating and drinking. There can be no peace on earth until the Prince of Peace reigns.

CHAPTER 15

At the conclusion of Sir Arthur Conan Doyle's story "His Last Bow," Sherlock Holmes and Dr. Watson are preparing to turn their prisoner, a captured German spy named Von Bork, over to Scotland Yard. It is August 2, 1914. Holmes looks eastward to the sea and says, "There's an east wind coming, Watson."

"I think not, Holmes," replies Watson. "It is very warm."

"Good old Watson!" cries Holmes. "You are the one fixed point in a changing age. There's an east wind coming all the same, such a wind as never blew on England yet. It will be cold and bitter, Watson, and a good many of us may wither before its blast. But it's God's own wind none the less, and a cleaner, better, stronger land will lie in the sunshine when the storm has cleared."

The storm Sherlock Holmes referred to was World War I. That conflict was indeed a cold and bitter wind upon all Europe. And it was God's own wind, for God controls the affairs of men and directs nations as He chooses. But Europe was not cleaner, better, and stronger for it. World War I brought the old order of Europe crashing down. From that wreckage came hope as democracy rose from the rubble. But also from that storm came a new and terrible challenge—cruel and bloody dictators. The twentieth century in Europe was to see the clash of democracy and dictatorship with the continent itself as the winner's prize.

A.D. 1900 - PRESENT

World W
1914-1

1900   1910   1

A New Political Order in Europe

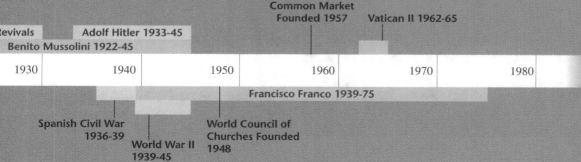

r Revivals

Adolf Hitler 1933-45

Benito Mussolini 1922-45

Common Market
Founded 1957

Vatican II 1962-65

| 1930 | 1940 | 1950 | 1960 | 1970 | 1980 |

Francisco Franco 1939-75

Spanish Civil War
1936-39

World War II
1939-45

World Council of
Churches Founded
1948

The Old Order Passes: World War I

Have you ever seen a fight about to break out? Two enemies approach each other, maybe in a vacant lot, each cautiously eyeing the other. Perhaps the friends of each fighter spread out behind their man, watching what the other side will do. When one fighter thinks he has the advantage, he lashes out, trying to win quickly. The other hits him back, his friends join in, and soon an all-out battle breaks loose.

Before World War I, Europe was like a group of wary fighters looking each other over. Germany was the strong man, with the best army in Europe. Its leader, Kaiser **Wilhelm II,** was ready to take on all comers to show the world that Germans were the most powerful people in Europe. Russia, under Czar Nicholas II, was huge but slow. It took a long time to get Russia going, but once it started—it fought like a bear. The Austro-Hungarian Empire had a big reputation, but the empire had stumbled in some smaller fights. Some European nations began to think the empire was not as tough as it used to be. Austria-Hungary depended on its ally Germany for help.

France was something like a kid who was always getting his nose bloodied (by Germany usually) and always coming back for more. But now the French had learned to get friends on their side. France had lined up Russia in particular. Italy went from one side to the other, depending on who it thought would offer the best deal for helping. Great Britain stood on the other side of the English Channel. With its powerful navy for protection, Britain claimed not did not care who was boss in Europe. But it watched closely to see who was becoming dangerously powerful.

The little countries of Europe varied in their attitudes. Belgium and the Netherlands just tried to stay out of everybody's way. But in the Balkans, some small nations were placing a chip on their shoulders and daring the big powers to knock it off. These little nations—Serbia, Bulgaria, Romania, Greece, and others—had recently become independent of the Turkish Ottoman Empire. Most of the Balkan people

Kaiser Wilhelm II

The *New York Times* *announces the assassination of Archduke Francis Ferdinand and his wife, the event that touched off World War I.*

were Slavs, and they wanted other Slavs to be free too. But many of their fellow Slavs lived in Austria-Hungary, and the Austro-Hungarians wanted to expand their empire into the territory where the Turks had moved out. The Austrians hesitated, though, because the Russians were also Slavs. The Russians made it clear that they did not want their "little brothers" in the Balkans being pushed around.

By 1914, all Europe was lined up into two camps. On one side were Germany and Austria-Hungary. Italy said it would go along with them, but when war came, it did not. On the other side were France, Russia, and eventually Great Britain. In the middle of them all were the Balkans, "the powder keg of Europe." The danger with a keg of gunpowder is that just a spark can set it off.

The spark came on June 28, 1914. A Serbian terrorist assassinated Archduke **Francis Ferdinand,** the heir to the Austro-Hungarian throne. Austria-Hungary declared war on Serbia. Russia declared war on Austria-Hungary to protect Serbia. Germany declared war on Russia to keep its promise to Austria-Hungary. France came to the aid of Russia and went to war with Germany. Germany invaded Belgium to find an easier path into France. Great Britain declared war on Germany to protect Belgium. Shortly thereafter, the Ottoman Empire and Bulgaria joined Germany and Austria-Hungary. They became known as the **Central Powers.** Italy eventually joined the other side, which became known as the **Allies.** The conflict known as **World War I** engulfed Europe.

A New Political Order

German troops in full battle regalia, including gas masks, strike a pose, and Allied troops march in silhouette against the sky.

At first, everyone thought it would be a brief war, although each side thought it would be the one to win. But it did not work that way. After some early German successes, both sides began to dig trenches. They strung barbed wire in front of their lines. Artillery and machine guns protected their positions. Between the two armies was a muddy, bloody "no man's land." Each side hurled its men forward in waves, trying to break through the enemy's lines. Neither succeeded; men just died. For over four years, the nations of Europe tore at each other.

But a change took place as the war went on. At first, it was hard to tell just whose side was right. But soon it became apparent that this was more than just a fight for who would dominate Europe. The Central Powers con-sisted of nations built on military power and ruled by leaders who said their authority was not to be questioned. On the other side were France and Great Britain, democratic nations. Russia was originally a militaristic empire too, but in the middle of the war the Russian people overthrew the czar and Russia became a republic—for a while. When the United States joined the Allies in April 1917, President **Woodrow Wilson** told the American Congress, "The world must be made safe for democracy."

Wilson's dream seemed to come true. In 1918 the Allies won. Kaiser Wilhelm II fled, and Germany established the Weimar Republic. The Allies broke Austria-Hungary into several smaller nations, each with a chance to rule itself. Parts of the old Russian Empire were freed too. Poland, for example, became an independent nation for the first time since 1795. In a thanksgiving sermon for the end of the war in Washington, D.C., African American pastor Francis Grimké said, "There are to be no more kaisers; no more czars; no more emperors with autocratic powers. The reign of the people has come—the reign of the common people. It is wonderful when you think of it!"

Section Review

1. What event sparked World War I?
2. What four countries made up the Central Powers?
3. Why did Woodrow Wilson say he wanted the United States to fight in World War I?
4. What was the name given to the government of Germany after the war?

How could a war make the world "safe for democracy"?

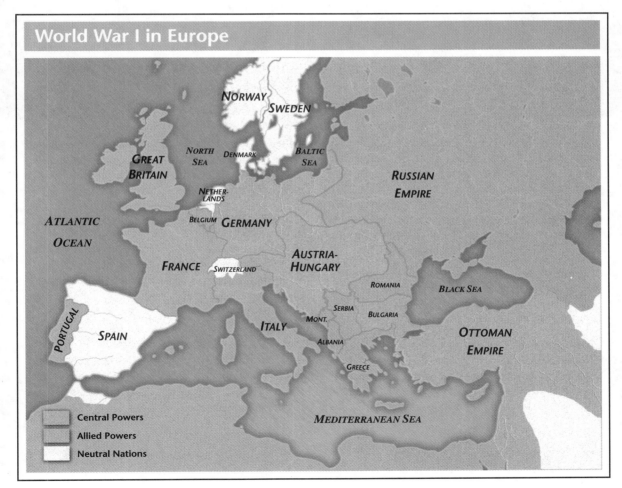

World War I in Europe

- Central Powers
- Allied Powers
- Neutral Nations

Location—The Balkan Peninsula is located in southeastern Europe. It lies south of the Danube and Sava Rivers. It is made up of Albania, Bosnia and Herzegovina, Bulgaria, Croatia, Greece, Macedonia, Romania, Slovenia, and Yugoslavia—as well as a small piece of Turkey. On the east are the Black and Aegean Seas. On the west and south are the Adriatic, Ionian, and Mediterranean Seas.

Climate—The climate is moderate; most of the region has a mediterranean climate. Temperatures range from 28°F to 70°F. Rainfall averages between 15 and 47 inches.

Topography—The word *Balkans* comes from a Turkish word meaning "forested mountain." This description fits the peninsula, which is mountainous. A few river valleys cut the mountains, and a narrow coastal plain meets the water.

Natural Resources—The area does not contain an abundance of natural resources. Some minerals, such as coal, uranium, and iron ore, are found. However, the most important resource is oil.

Geography & Culture—Because it is at the crossroads between Asia and Europe, the Balkan Peninsula has been invaded many times throughout history. As a result, its culture is a mixture of East and West. In the late Middle Ages the Balkans came under the control of the Ottoman Turks. It was not until the 1800s and early 1900s that these areas became free from the Turks. Then after World War II the Soviet Union imposed Communist governments on these nations. It was not until the late 1980s and early 1990s that the Balkans threw off this yoke. Most of the people in the Balkans belong to an ethnic group known as the Slavs.

Settings Review

1. What seas lie to the east of the Balkan Peninsula?

2. What is the origin of the name *Balkans?*

3. What is the most important natural resource of the region?

4. Who took control of the Balkans in the Middle Ages? Who took control after World War II?

Why would mountainous terrain like that in the Balkans tend to create disunity in a region? What other factors could cause disunity?

Scenes from the Balkans: a Muslim receives the gift of a Bible, a child suffers from the conflicts that tear the region apart, and a lovely restored section of Mostar Old Town in Yugoslavia.

Despair and Dictators: Between the Wars

The hopes of peace did not last. Four years of bloody fighting had tired out the democratic nations of Europe. Many men had died in the trenches; the war had snuffed out a whole generation of Europeans. Germany's struggling new Weimar Republic had to pay huge debts to the victorious Allies. Then in the late 1920s the **Great Depression** hit, one of the most terrible economic downturns in history. All around the world, large companies went out of business. Millions of people lost their jobs. Many governments could not pay their debts. Economic bad times created greater suffering and greater political instability.

Rise of the Dictators

As a result of these conditions, dictators arose. A **dictator** is a ruler something like the absolutist monarchs discussed in Chapter 9. But a dictator has even greater power. His word is law, and with a word he can sentence people to prison or death. In the 1920s and 1930s, with powerful armies and secret police to support them, the dictators became major leaders in Europe.

In Russia the Communists toppled the young republic and established a dictatorship. (This revolution is discussed in the next chapter.) In Italy in 1923 **Benito Mussolini** and his gang of followers, called Fascists, frightened the king into making Mussolini the Italian leader. Mussolini, in fact, took the title *Il Duce* (DOO chay)—"the Leader." Throughout Europe, struggling young republics gave way before military "strong men" who ruled with an iron hand. Most of these rulers were Fascists.

Fascists basically believed in glorifying the state. Although people might own property, they had to be willing to let the state use their property however the nation's leaders

Adolf Hitler of Germany (left) and Benito Mussolini of Italy (right) were the most prominent in a wave of dictators who took power in Europe between the two world wars.

wished. Because they stressed national power, Fascists tried to make their nations financially independent. Because they stressed national glory, Fascists tried to build strong armies and dreamed of military conquest. All the rights of the people—freedoms of speech, of religion, of the press—were subject to the whims of the state. Mussolini and his Italian Fascists were the first to gain power in Europe. But the worst of these Fascists were the Nazis of Germany. And the worst of the Nazis was their leader, **Adolf Hitler.**

Hitler was born in Austria in 1889. He dreamed of becoming a painter, but he lacked the talent. He stayed for a time in Vienna, hoping to profit from living in that great center of art and culture. But all he did was starve. He also learned to hate anyone more successful than he was because he thought they kept his talent from being discovered. Most of all he irrationally hated the Jews.

Hitler served as a courier in the German army in World War I. He was in a military hospital when the war ended, recovering from an attack by poison gas. With his eyes bandaged, Hitler heard the news that Germany had surrendered. He wept and blamed the "traitors" (Jews, Communists, and other "disloyal" Germans) who had stabbed Germany in the back. Hitler later wrote,

> The more I tried to achieve clarity on the monstrous event in this hour, the more the shame of indignation and disgrace burned my brow. What was all the pain in my eyes compared to this misery?
>
> There followed terrible days and even worse nights—I knew that all was lost. Only fools, liars and criminals could hope in the mercy of the enemy. In these nights hatred grew in me, hatred for those responsible for this deed.
>
> In the days that followed, my own fate became known to me. . . .
>
> I . . . decided to go into politics.

The face of evil: Adolf Hitler

Hitler joined a tiny political party called the National Socialist Workers' Party, or **Nazi Party** for short. Hitler practiced speaking until he could hold people spellbound with his words. Powerfully, Hitler preached hate and revenge.

Hitler and the Nazis got their chance when the depression hit in the late 1920s. Millions of Germans were out of work and were willing to listen to anyone who promised them help. Others feared the Communists and thought that the Nazis might help protect Germany. Many Germans thought their country had been wronged by the Allies and heeded this man who promised them revenge. Finally, in 1932 the Nazis became the largest party in the German legislature. The following year Hitler became chancellor of Germany and had the legislature pass a law making him dictator of Germany.

Adolf Hitler became *der Führer* (FYOOR ur; "the Leader"). He began to rebuild the army. This act created pride in the nation and put many workers back on the job building equipment for the army. He built a great highway system and sponsored colorful rallies and special holidays. Hitler encouraged Germans to look up to him, even to worship him. Children in Nazi orphanages offered blessings to him before they ate:

O Führer, my Führer, sent to me by God,
Protect and maintain my life,
Thou who has served Germany in its hour
of need.
I thank thee now for my daily bread.
Oh! Stay with me, Oh! Never leave me,
Führer, my Führer, my faith and my light.

A group called the **"German Christians"** arose. They claimed to serve Christ and Adolf Hitler at the same time. "The Swastika on our breasts, and the Cross in our hearts" was their motto. But Hitler would not settle for divided loyalties. As a Nazi prosecutor said, "Christianity and we National Socialists have one thing in common, and one thing only: we claim the whole man." The German Christians eventually found, as Jesus said, that they could not serve two masters (Matt. 6:24). Some followed Christ and paid the price. Others sold out their Lord as Judas did and embraced the Nazis.

Hopelessness in the Democracies: The Arts and Culture Between the Wars

While the Fascists were growing in power across Europe, the Communists in the Soviet Union to the east appeared as yet another threat. The democracies meanwhile seemed buried in hopelessness and helplessness. The Great Depression in the 1930s threw millions out of work. The leaders of the democratic nations seemed colorless, unheroic, and unable to confront the might of these foes. Even in countries such as Great Britain and France,

Hitler stands in the middle of his cheering followers after one of his speeches, dwarfed by the trappings of his militaristic Nazi regime.

some politicians began claiming that their nations should also follow the Fascist or Communist way.

This sense of hopelessness was reflected in the arts between the wars. No longer did men write, as Robert Browning had written in 1841, "God's in His heaven— / All's right with the world." Many writers, painters, and sculptors were not even sure there was a God, let alone whether He was in heaven. And they felt certain that all was not right with the world. The terrible destruction of World War I and the rise of dictatorships caused many Europeans to lose hope in the future.

One example of this sense of drift was a group of writers known as the **"Lost Generation."** Most of these were Americans living in Europe, usually in Paris. Their nickname came from an American living in Paris who wrote to novelist **Ernest Hemingway,** telling him and others who had fought in World War I, "You are a lost generation." Hemingway used the line at the beginning of his novel

Tools and Fruit of Production *by Strzeminski is an example of Surrealist art.*

The Sun Also Rises. He adopted a pessimistic view of the brutality of life. Other writers shared this outlook, such as novelist F. Scott Fitzgerald and poet E. E. Cummings. The "Lost Generation" also found sympathy among German writers such as **Erich Maria Remarque.** His popular novel *All Quiet on the Western Front* portrayed the senselessness the Lost Generation felt about the war.

Styles in painting began to emphasize man's inner turmoil and to focus less on outward reality. A style known as **expressionism** became popular. Expressionist painters concentrated on representing their feelings about the objects they painted and not the object itself. **Cubist** painters tried to capture objects by presenting several views of an object at once. **Pablo Picasso** of Spain was the best-known cubist painter. **Surrealist** painters were perhaps most extreme. They painted regular objects but placed them in bizarre, unrealistic settings or distorted them. In the paintings of **Salvador Dali,** for example, watches melted and dripped off the edges of tables and trees like chocolate bars left lying in the sun.

Music also reflected a sense of discontent with the past. Composers began to alter the traditional tonal or key system. (Traditional Western music has an eight-tone scale, or key,

Pablo Picasso, Guitar, 1919, *(Museum of Modern Art, New York)*

T. S. Eliot

called an octave.) **Igor Stravinsky** (struh VIN skee) wrote pieces using several keys at once. These works sound harsh and dissonant to our ears. **Arnold Schönberg** (SHURN burg) wrote music with no fixed key. His pieces also sound very harsh and strange to our ears.

But the era was not devoid of hope, as illustrated by the career of poet **T. S. Eliot.** Born in St. Louis, he moved to England when he was in his twenties and became a leading poet. At first, Eliot also was one of the Lost Generation who felt despair about the future. His early poems are full of doubt, fear, and hopelessness. In one of his most famous poems, "The Hollow Men," he likens modern man to dry scarecrows whose voices are like "rats' feet over broken glass / In our dry cellar." At the conclusion of that poem, he says despairingly, *"This is the way the world ends / Not with a bang but a whimper."*

But in the late 1920s, Eliot suddenly announced to the world that he was embracing Christianity. His poems began to breathe hope instead of despair. His "Journey of the Magi" is the narrative of one of the wise men who journeyed to discover the Christ child—and the salvation He would bring. Eliot also offered a Christian response to the dictatorships that were spreading across Europe. He wrote a play, *Murder in the Cathedral,* about English Archbishop Thomas à Becket, who died for opposing the policies of King Henry II. Those living in the days of Hitler and Mussolini, with their policies of iron and fear, must have pondered Becket's words at the climax of the play—

It is the just man who
Like a bold lion, should be without fear.
I am here.
No traitor to the King. I am a priest,
A Christian, saved by the blood of Christ,
Ready to suffer with my blood.

Dictators could not answer that kind of faith.

Section Review

1. Who was the leader of the Fascists in Italy?
2. What was the Fascist party called in Germany? Who was its leader?
3. What does *der Führer* mean?
4. Who popularized the phrase "the Lost Generation"? In what novel did he use the phrase?
5. What German novel portrayed the senselessness of war? Who wrote it?
6. What leading poet turned his back on hopelessness and embraced Christianity?

What was the motto of the German Christians? Why would following this motto be difficult for a true Christian?

Democracy vs. the Dictators: World War II

Some had called World War I "the war to end all wars." Yet only a little more than twenty years later, Europe was again plunged into war. Hitler's dreams of dominance turned into a nightmare for the peoples of Europe.

Prelude to War

Europe looked on and wondered as Hitler rebuilt Germany. He began a series of "bloodless conquests" that increased his prestige and Germany's power. After World War I, for example, the Allies had required Germany to keep all military forces out of the **Rhineland,** a section of Germany next to France. In 1936 Hitler sent his army into the Rhineland. France and Great Britain did nothing.

In 1938 Germany annexed the German-speaking nation of Austria. This act was also a violation of a treaty, but no one did anything. In 1938 at a conference in Munich, Germany, Hitler convinced France and Britain to let him have the **Sudetenland** (soo-DATE-en-land), a German-speaking section of Czechoslovakia. Then after he had that territory, Hitler went ahead and took all of Czechoslovakia. He had gained huge tracts of territory without firing a shot. Hitler held the French and British in contempt. "Our enemies are little worms," he said. "I saw them at Munich."

Meanwhile, a civil war had broken out in Spain in 1936. A Spanish general, **Francisco Franco,** led the Fascist side against the Loyalists (a mixture of anti-Fascists including the Communists). Hitler and Mussolini sent troops and equipment to help Franco. With the aid of German and Italian soldiers, tanks, and planes, the Spanish general won the war in 1939. Fascism seemed on the verge of taking over Europe. More than that, in the Spanish civil war Europe saw what would be called the "dress rehearsal" for World War II.

Adolf Hitler was not satisfied. He wanted more power. He surprised the world by making a treaty with the Communist Soviet Union, his hated enemy. A secret part of that treaty was that Germany and the Soviet Union would split Poland between them if war came. With no fear of Communist attack, Hitler had a green light to launch his war.

Francisco Franco, leader of the Spanish Fascists and dictator of Spain

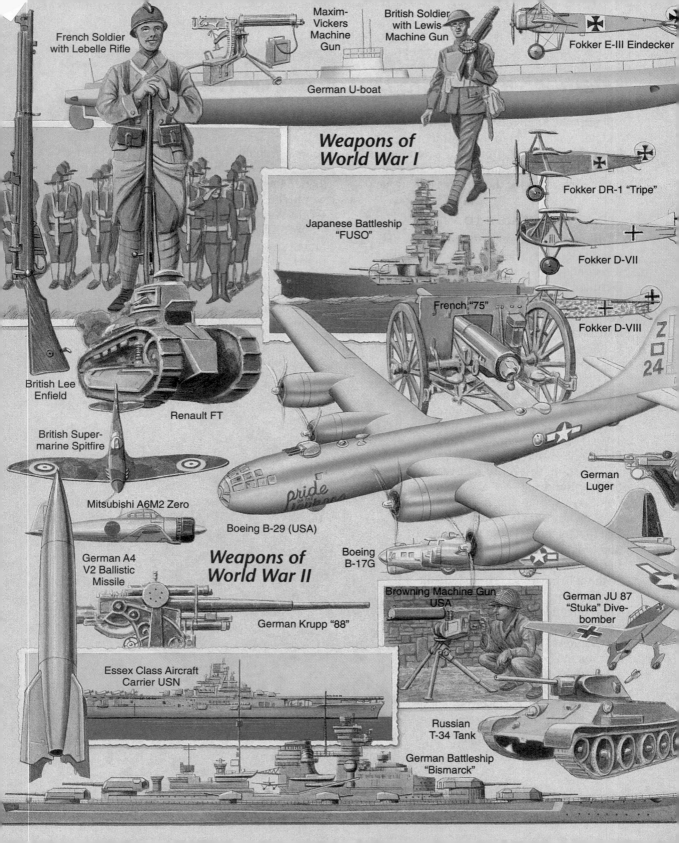

French Soldier with Lebelle Rifle

Maxim-Vickers Machine Gun

British Soldier with Lewis Machine Gun

Fokker E-III Eindecker

German U-boat

Weapons of World War I

Fokker DR-1 "Tripe"

Japanese Battleship "FUSO"

Fokker D-VII

French "75"

Fokker D-VIII

British Lee Enfield

Renault FT

British Super-marine Spitfire

German Luger

Mitsubishi A6M2 Zero

Boeing B-29 (USA)

Weapons of World War II

German A4 V2 Ballistic Missile

Boeing B-17G

German JU 87 "Stuka" Dive-bomber

German Krupp "88"

Browning Machine Gun USA

Essex Class Aircraft Carrier USN

Russian T-34 Tank

German Battleship "Bismarck"

The Coming of War

World War II began on September 1, 1939, when Hitler sent his forces crashing into Poland. This time the British and French did not back down. They came to the defense of Poland and declared war on Germany. But the help of France and Britain was not enough to save Poland. The German army developed a new type of warfare, **blitzkrieg** ("lightning war"). Using fighters and bombers, armored tanks and trucks, Hitler's forces overwhelmed opponents with dazzling speed and relentless pressure. Poland collapsed in less than five weeks.

Then Hitler turned west. His forces conquered Denmark effortlessly. Then a daring operation by sea and air brought Norway under Nazi rule. Finally, the armored divisions of Germany swept across the Low Countries, smashed the armies of France, and sent the British army reeling. France surrendered on June 22, 1940, only six weeks after Hitler's invasion. Mussolini brought Italy into the war on Germany's side. Germany, Italy, and Japan joined together as the **Axis Powers.** Adolf

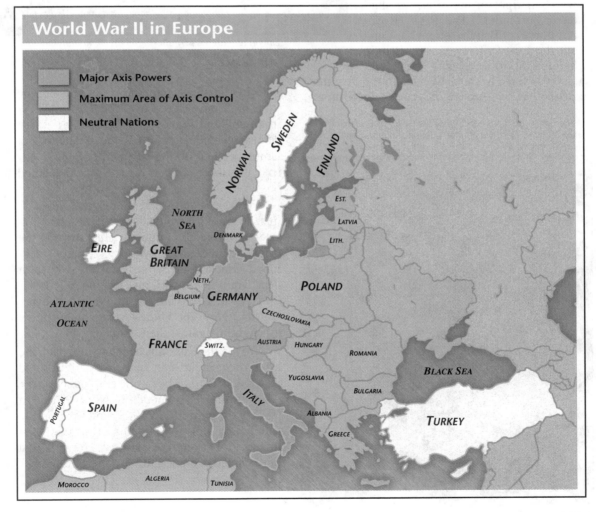

World War II in Europe

Major Axis Powers

Maximum Area of Axis Control

Neutral Nations

Hitler was the master of Europe. Or almost the master.

Still defiant was Great Britain. Between the Nazi forces in France and the British homeland lay the English Channel, protected by Britain's mighty navy. Hitler tried to bring down the British by sending his **Luftwaffe** (air force) to bomb the British into submission. British prime minister **Winston Churchill** vowed, "We shall fight on the landing grounds, we shall fight in the fields and in the streets, we shall fight in the hills; we shall never surrender." The **RAF** (Royal Air Force) of Britain fought back and cut the Luftwaffe to pieces. Britain had fought off the Nazis.

Frustrated because he could not defeat the British, Hitler turned on the Soviet Union,

Driven to extremes by shortages resulting from the war, French farm women pull the plow themselves to prepare their fields.

Hitler looks on the wreckage of his German Empire. He had said his Third Reich would last a thousand years. It lasted only twelve.

ignoring his treaty with the Communists. The invasion commenced on June 22, 1941. As in Poland and France, the German blitzkrieg devastated the surprised Soviets. The Soviet Union seemed on the verge of collapse. Hitler's dream of conquering the world seemed possible.

Then the tide turned against the Nazis. A freezing Russian winter stopped the Nazi blitzkrieg. Even the fuel in their tanks froze in the frigid weather. Meanwhile, Germany's ally Japan attacked the American naval base at Pearl Harbor, Hawaii, on December 7, 1941. (For Japan's role in World War II, see pp. 483-85.) Now the United States again threw its might in against the Germans.

Slowly the Russians began to turn back the Nazi forces in the east. In the west, the United States and Britain began to chip away at the Axis empire. They landed in North Africa in 1942, then in Sicily in 1943, and then on the mainland of Italy two months later. Finally, on June 6, 1944, known as **D-day,** a huge Allied force landed in France and shattered Germany's defenses. Like a vise, the Allied forces crushed the Axis nations between them. Italian rebels shot Mussolini and hung his body up in a gas station. Hitler shot himself in his bunker under the ruins of Berlin rather than surrender. On May 8, 1945, the war in Europe ended.

Peace came but at a great cost. Including the deaths in the fighting in Asia, over fifty million soldiers and civilians died in the war. But even these figures were not the end of the horror. As the Allied forces moved into Germany, they found death camps where the Nazis had slaughtered peoples they considered inferior—Slavs, the physically and mentally handicapped, and especially Jews. It is estimated that six million Jews died in the Nazi death camps. This horrendous slaughter has become known as the **Holocaust.**

Section Review

1. What country had to sacrifice territory as a result of the Munich Conference?

2. Who was the leader of the Fascists in the Spanish Civil War?

3. What country made a treaty with Hitler that gave him freedom to launch his war?

4. The invasion of what country sparked World War II?

5. What does *blitzkrieg* mean? Why was it a good description for how the Germans fought?

6. How did Mussolini and Hitler die?

7. What is the name we give to Hitler's slaughter of the Jews?

If you had been a political leader in Great Britain in the 1930s, what would you have advised the nation to do about Hitler's expansion? What arguments would you have used?

Two emaciated survivors from a German concentration camp gaze blankly at the camera. Millions did not survive.

Winston Churchill

Winston Churchill at times wanted to be a soldier, sometimes a writer, and sometimes a statesman. He eventually did all three, and did them very well.

Born in 1874, Churchill graduated from Britain's leading military school and joined the army. He soon found himself in exotic places. He fought against a Muslim uprising in Sudan in 1898. There he came under fire in one of the last great cavalry charges in history. Afterwards, he wrote a history of the campaign, *The River War,* one of the first of many books he was to write. Soon afterwards he was in South Africa covering the Boer War as a newspaper correspondent. During the fighting he was captured by the Boers. Churchill escaped and daringly made his way back to British lines. The dramatic account he wrote of his escape made him famous in Britain.

Churchill began a spectacular rise in politics. When World War I broke out, he was head of the British navy. But he risked his career supporting a dangerous attack on the Ottoman Empire. The British hoped the attack by the army and navy would knock the Turks out of the war. But the attack failed, and Churchill was blamed and forced to resign as head of the navy.

Churchill's rise turned suddenly into a devastating fall. He wrote an excellent history of World War I, *The World Crisis,* but his political career went up and down. He was even voted out of Parliament for a time. When a group of British politicians visited the Soviet Union in 1932, Soviet dictator Joseph Stalin asked about several leading British politicians. "What about Churchill?" he said.

"Churchill?" replied one visitor with a laugh. "Oh, he's *finished.*"

In the 1930s Churchill stood on the fringes of politics. As the dictators rose to power on the Continent, he sounded warnings. At first, he was ignored by those who feared another war. But as Hitler became more powerful, more people began to listen to Churchill. After the Munich agreement sacrificed Czechoslovakia to Germany, Churchill declared, "And do not suppose that this is the end. This is only the beginning of the reckoning. This is only the first sip, the first foretaste of a bitter cup."

When war broke out, the British government made Churchill the prime minister. He knew the difficult job that lay ahead and told the people, "I have nothing to offer but blood, toil, tears, and sweat." His eloquence became a rallying point for the British. U.S. president John F. Kennedy later said, "He mobilized the English language and sent it into battle." On one occasion, for example,

Churchill surveys the rubble from a German bombing raid on London.

Churchill treads the deck of a warship in preparation for a wartime meeting with President Franklin Roosevelt.

Churchill said, "We have not entered this war for profit or expansion, but only for honour and to do our duty in defending the right." In one of his most famous speeches, Churchill urged, "Let us therefore brace ourselves to our duties, and so bear ourselves that, if the British Empire and its Commonwealth last for a thousand years, men will say, 'This was their finest hour.'"

Just after the defeat of Nazi Germany, Churchill was surprisingly defeated for reelection. But he did not allow defeat to silence him. Before the war, he warned the world of Nazi tyranny. After the war, he warned of the equal danger of Communist tyranny. In a famous speech in Fulton, Missouri, in 1946 Churchill solemnly announced, "From Stettin in the Baltic to Trieste in the Adriatic, an iron curtain has descended across the Conti-

nent." Soon the phrase "iron curtain" was on everyone's lips. For millions of people Churchill had perfectly pictured the boundary between freedom and Communist slavery.

In 1951 Churchill returned to power as prime minister of Britain. He served until 1954 when poor health forced him to retire. Meanwhile, he had written a six-volume work, *The History of the Second World War,* which won him the Nobel prize for literature. The Queen of England knighted him, making him "Sir" Winston Churchill, and the United States made him an honorary American citizen. When he died in 1965, the British prime minister said, "The words and deeds of Winston Churchill will form part of the rich heritage of our nation and of our time for as long as history comes to be written and to be read."

Democracy Triumphant but Tried

The war was over, but there was enormous rebuilding to do. The United States helped Europe through the **Marshall Plan.** Named for the American secretary of state, the Marshall Plan poured $12 billion into Europe to help the continent rebuild. However, the great European powers, France and Great Britain, were no longer as mighty as in the past. They

King Juan Carlos of Spain reviews his troops. The king used his personal popularity to keep the army from toppling Spain's fragile young democracy.

lost their overseas empires and found themselves taking a back seat in world affairs to the United States and the Soviet Union.

Europe faced danger from the Communist Soviet Union. At the end of World War II, the Soviet armies stayed in the Eastern European countries they had invaded in order to attack Hitler. Countries such as Poland, Hungary, and Czechoslovakia fell under Communist dictatorships. Germany was split in two, and East Germany became a Communist state.

But **West Germany** was free. Aided by Western powers such as the United States, West Germany began to recover from the devastation of the war. Within ten years it had become a major economic power and a firm supporter of Western Europe against Communism.

Furthermore, Fascism began to die out in Europe. The last stronghold of Fascism was Spain under Francisco Franco. Franco himself had no desire to change, but he also knew he could not live forever. Instead, he decided to restore the Spanish monarchy. Franco declared that at his death Prince Juan Carlos, grandson of the last king of Spain, would become king.

When Franco died in 1975, King **Juan Carlos** declared that Spain would now become a democracy. But only with difficulty did he lead the nation away from dictatorship. Many of Franco's former followers resisted the move. The army, always Franco's main support, began plotting to overthrow the government.

On February 23, 1981, two hundred military policemen broke into a meeting of the Spanish legislature. One attacker fired his gun into the ceiling as the leader of the force declared that the army was taking control. The rebels held the legislators and other high

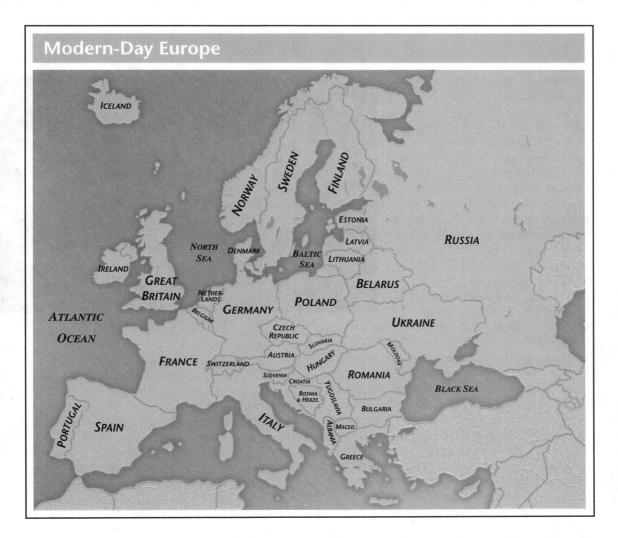

Modern-Day Europe

government officials hostage. The leader allegedly said that if the government forces tried to force their way in, he would block the doors with the bodies of the legislators.

Army officers began cautiously moving forward with their plot. One colonel declared a military emergency in the province of Valencia. In Madrid the army seized the television and radio stations. Spain teetered on the brink.

King Juan Carlos would have none of it. He told his advisers the plotters would have to shoot him if they wanted to seize power. He called leading generals on the phone and said

that he was throwing his authority against the plot. The king went on television while the rebels were still holding the legislature captive. There would be no revolution, he declared. "The crown, symbol of the nation's permanence and unity, cannot tolerate, under any form, the action or attitude of those who seek by force to interrupt the democratic process."

The revolt collapsed. The government arrested and tried thirty-two military officers who had been involved in the plot. It was a turning point for Spain. Rather than return to the dictatorship of Franco, Spain would move forward into the ranks of the Western democracies.

Spain symbolized the changes taking place in Europe. Those parts of the continent not under Communist rule began to put away conflicts of the past and try to work together. In 1957 the Western European powers established the European Economic Community, better known as the **Common Market.** The Common Market was an economic agreement. The nations involved eliminated many trade restrictions and worked together to enrich the member nations.

The Common Market's success caused some Europeans to dream of what Churchill had once called "a kind of United States of Europe." One step toward achieving this dream was the founding of the **European Union (EU)** in 1994 to draw Europe together not only economically but also politically. When Communism collapsed in Eastern Europe in the late 1980s (see the next chapter), Europe greeted its greatest opportunity in centuries to reshape the continent in peace and unity.

A house wrecked by fighting reflects the destructive forces unleashed in the Balkans at the end of the twentieth century.

But Europe was still plagued by disagreements. The European nations argued over basic questions, such as whether to have a single currency for the whole continent. Some matters were more significant. With the collapse of Communism in Eastern Europe, the Balkans again became a powder keg. Freed from Communism, some Balkan states simply replaced Communist dictatorships with other kinds of dictatorships. The Balkan nations fought wars and civil wars. People fled in fear from their homes, seeking refuge from the fighting. Many civilians were killed in the fighting or brutally murdered by enemy troops. Problems great and small still stand in the way of the dream of a "United States of Europe."

Canadian soldiers serve as peacekeepers in the war-torn country of Bosnia.

The United Nations

After World War I, the nations of the world formed the League of Nations. This organization was to provide a place where nations could talk through their differences in a civilized manner. Unfortunately, "uncivilized" aggressors such as Germany, Italy, and Japan simply ignored the League and launched brutal plans of conquest. Since members of the League of Nations were not willing to go to war to protect their members, the League collapsed.

During World War II, the Allied Powers often referred to themselves as "the United Nations," that is, united against the Axis Powers. After the war, the victorious powers formed a new organization dedicated to preserving world peace. Founded on April 25, 1945, in San Francisco, the organization took the name **United Nations (UN).**

Headquartered in New York, the UN has tried to preserve peace through discussion and debate. Virtually every nation in the world is represented in its General Assembly. On some occasions when discussion has failed, the UN, unlike the League of Nations, has even used military action. In the 1950s the United Nations defended South Korea from invasion by Communist North Korea, and in the 1990s the UN helped free Kuwait after it was invaded by neighboring Iraq. At other times,

the UN has created "peacekeeping" forces made up of soldiers from the armies of its members. UN peacekeepers travel to troubled areas of the world and try—with varying degrees of success—to maintain peace.

The United Nations has had its share of failures. Member nations are often more concerned (sometimes rightly) with their own good than what the UN considers the good of the whole. The most powerful nations can usually ignore the United Nations whenever they wish. Some dictatorships have used the UN to cover their cruelty; their UN ambassadors speak of freedom and human rights while the government back home practices oppression. The UN has accomplished some good, but it has not been the instrument of world peace that its founders dreamed it would be.

THE UNITED NATIONS FIGHT FOR FREEDOM

Section Review

1. Through what plan did the United States give Europe billions of dollars to rebuild after World War II?

2. Who transformed Spain from a dictatorship into a democracy?

3. What is the name for the agreement that broke down trade barriers in Western Europe?

4. What region of Europe was a center of revolution and warfare in the late twentieth century?

Do you think the idea of a United States of Europe is a good one? Why or why not?

Religion in Modern Europe

The victory of democracies over dictatorships in Europe has been a noble one. But not all trends in modern European history are positive. One dismaying characteristic has been the decline of religious faith in Europe. There has been a great falling away from the teachings of the Bible, even from simple matters such as church attendance. In England, for example, church attendance plummeted after World War I.

France is yet another example of religious decline. In 1900 some 97 percent of the population claimed to be adherents of the Roman Catholic Church. By the end of the twentieth century that percentage had shrunk to 68.5 percent. Even within this group, a large number

The Cathedral of Chartes reflects the past glories of French Catholicism but masks its contemporary decline.

(4.5 million) were "disaffiliated." They had been born and baptized into the Catholic Church, but they had repudiated that bond. One-third of French Catholics did not practice their faith at all. Only about one in five Frenchmen attended church at least once a week.

In European countries, the drop in Christian profession was not because Europeans were converting to Islam or some other religion. People simply ceased to regard religion as important. Europe was dominated by **secularism.** This means simply that people were concerned about the affairs of this life. They seldom bothered to think about heaven or God at all.

Some Christian leaders tried to rouse interest in the church by urging Christians to unite. They led an **ecumenical movement** to try to bring all the churches of the world together. (The word *ecumenical* means simply "worldwide." Today the term normally refers to efforts to bring all Christians together.) In 1948 many Protestant and Eastern Orthodox churches formed the **World Council of Churches** as a means of bringing churches together. In the 1960s the Catholic Church held a council called **Vatican II** to discuss reform. One major change was allowing Catholics to discuss possible union with other churches.

In trying to bring people together, the ecumenical leaders downplayed biblical doctrine because, they said, "doctrine divides." They failed to understand that the Scriptures' doctrines are the basis of the Christian faith. The apostle Paul stated that the Bible is a source for doctrine, which he said is necessary in order for Christians to "be throughly furnished unto all good works" (II Tim. 3:17). Paul also said that without the biblical teaching of the

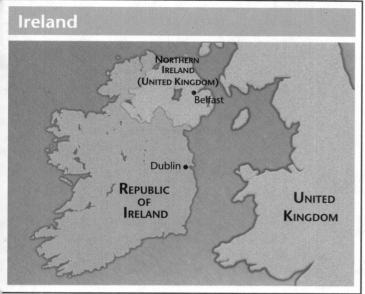

Ireland

NORTHERN
IRELAND
(UNITED KINGDOM)
• Belfast

Dublin •

REPUBLIC
OF
IRELAND

UNITED
KINGDOM

Evangelist W. P. Nicholson

resurrection "we are of all men most miserable" (I Cor. 15:19). The apostle John warned that anyone who did not hold proper doctrine about Jesus Christ could not be a Christian, and real Christians were to have nothing to do with such false teachers (II John 7-11). Christians cannot de-emphasize the Bible's teachings even to achieve unity.

Not all the history of Christianity in modern Europe is dark. In the 1920s, for example, the British province of Northern Ireland (also called Ulster) experienced a widespread revival. An Ulster evangelist named **W. P. Nicholson** preached with great power across the province. "Some fool wrote in the newspapers objecting to me talking about Christ as if He was my next door neighbour," Nicholson said in one meeting. "He is far nearer to me than my next door neighbour. He is in my heart." He preached as though Christ were in his heart, and he urged his hearers to open their hearts to Christ too. Thousands heard him, and numbers were converted under his blunt, direct preaching.

The Ulster revival is all the more remarkable because Northern Ireland was in the midst of major unrest over the separation of Ulster from the southern part of Ireland. (See p. 442.) Many times the crowds in Nicholson's services would hear gunfire outside.

The Irish Problem

The greed of a twelfth-century English king started more than eight hundred years of strife for England. King Henry II (1154-89) seized control of the neighboring island of Ireland and claimed it as an English possession. Understandably, the Irish did not appreciate this conquest, and they resisted. In the centuries that followed, numerous English kings sent forces into Ireland to put down rebellions and establish royal authority.

King James I (1603-25) tried to solve the Irish problem in a different manner. Just before James's reign, the divisions deepened between England and Ireland. England embraced the Protestant Reformation while Ireland remained steadfastly Roman Catholic. King James decided to settle thousands of Scottish and English Protestants in the northern part of Ireland. He thought that such settlements would make the population more loyal to the crown. Instead, the conflict worsened.

The new settlers were loyal, but the native Irish resisted the English even more.

The native people of southern Ireland wanted "home rule"—the right to rule themselves free of English control. Northern Ireland, however, remained loyal to Britain. In 1921 the twenty counties of southern Ireland won their independence and became the Irish Free State (later the Republic of Ireland). The six counties of northern Ireland, also known as Ulster, became the province of Northern Ireland within the British Commonwealth.

Today the Protestant majority of Northern Ireland still wishes to remain joined to Britain. However, a large Roman Catholic minority in Ulster and the Catholic majority in the Republic of Ireland desire a united Irish state independent of Britain. Violence often erupts between these groups—especially in Ulster. Fighting still goes on to determine the future of Ireland, over eight hundred years since the conflict began.

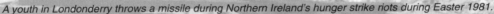

A youth in Londonderry throws a missile during Northern Ireland's hunger strike riots during Easter 1981.

Those who rode streetcars to the services would sometimes lie on the floor to avoid stray bullets that flew through the windows. Despite the danger, they came, and God's Spirit moved among them.

But revivals like that in Northern Ireland have become rarer in Europe over the years. Christian faith is by no means dead in Europe, but it is certainly embraced by fewer people than it was in the past. Perhaps Europe should heed the message that Christ gave to the church at Sardis:

> Be watchful, and strengthen the things which remain, that are ready to die: for I have not found thy works perfect before God. Remember therefore how thou hast received and heard, and hold fast, and repent. If therefore thou shalt not watch, I will come on thee as a thief, and thou shalt not know what hour I will come upon thee (Rev. 3:2-3).

Section Review

1. What is secularism?
2. What organization founded in 1948 claims to be dedicated to furthering Christian unity?
3. In what part of Europe was there a notable revival in the 1920s? What minister led this revival?

Read all of Christ's message to the church at Sardis (Rev. 3:1-6). In what ways would these be appropriate verses to apply to modern Europe?

Summary

At the beginning of the twentieth century, Europe was divided into rival camps. Conflict in and over the Balkan Peninsula eventually sparked World War I. That war did not solve Europe's problems, however. After the war, Communist dictators and Fascist dictators (notably Benito Mussolini and Adolf Hitler) threatened the free nations of Europe. Hitler eventually sparked a second world war, which ended in the destruction of Nazi Germany, Fascist Italy, and Japan. Europe rebuilt after the war, and the remaining Fascist and Communist states in Europe eventually collapsed. Europe achieved some economic unity and dreamed of political unity. Unfortunately, more troubles in the Balkans unsettled the continent. Also Europe turned its back on its rich spiritual heritage and became increasingly secular in its outlook.

CHAPTER REVIEW

People, Places, and Things to Know

Wilhelm II	*der Führer*	T. S. Eliot	Marshall Plan
Francis Ferdinand	"German Christians"	Rhineland	West Germany
Central Powers	"Lost Generation"	Sudetenland	Juan Carlos
Allies	Ernest Hemingway	Francisco Franco	Common Market
World War I	Erich Maria Remarque	World War II	European Union (EU)
Woodrow Wilson	expressionism	blitzkrieg	United Nations (UN)
Great Depression	cubism	Axis Powers	secularism
dictator	Pablo Picasso	Luftwaffe	ecumenical movement
Benito Mussolini	surrealism	Winston Churchill	World Council of
Fascists	Salvador Dali	RAF	Churches
Adolf Hitler	Igor Stravinsky	D-day	Vatican II
Nazi Party	Arnold Schönberg	Holocaust	W. P. Nicholson

Review Questions

Relations

Choose which of the items in the following lists are least related to the others and explain how the other three are related.

1. (a) Winston Churchill
   (b) Francisco Franco
   (c) Adolf Hitler
   (d) Benito Mussolini

2. (a) F. Scott Fitzgerald
   (b) Ernest Hemingway
   (c) W. P. Nicholson
   (d) Erich Maria Remarque

3. (a) cubism
   (b) expressionism
   (c) Nazism
   (d) surrealism

4. (a) Austria-Hungary
   (b) Germany
   (c) Ottoman Empire
   (d) United States

Matching

Match the following people to the quotation that best fits each.

Winston Churchill   Ernest Hemingway   Juan Carlos
T. S. Eliot   Adolf Hitler   Woodrow Wilson

5. "Only fools, liars and criminals could hope in the mercy of the enemy."

6. "I have nothing to offer but blood, toil, tears, and sweat."

7. "This is the way the world ends / Not with a bang but a whimper."

8. "The world must be made safe for democracy."

9. "The crown . . . cannot tolerate . . . the action or attitude of those who seek by force to interrupt the democratic process."

10. "You are a lost generation."

Identify

Name the country described by each of the following phrases.

11. World War II began when Germany invaded this country.

12. The king of this nation crushed a rebellion by appearing on television.

13. The Munich Conference took the Sudetenland from this country and gave it to Germany.

14. Most of the American writers of "the Lost Generation" lived in this country for a time.

15. After World War II, this country was split into two parts, one part under Communist rule and the other part under democratic rule.

16. This nation had the first Fascist government in Europe.

Think About It!

Think about Robert Browning's words "God's in His heaven— / All's right with the world." Do you agree or disagree with his statement? Why?

CHAPTER 16

John Reed, American reporter and Communist, walks along the streets of St. Petersburg, Russia, on November 7, 1917. The city, now going by its Russian name of "Petrograd," is in turmoil. The emperor, Czar Nicholas II, has been deposed and imprisoned somewhere. Russia's fragile new democratic "Provisional Government" fights for its life. World War I rages, but the German army to the west is only one problem facing Russia. Other factions are struggling to seize power. Later, Reed will set down his impressions of these momentous events in his book *Ten Days That Shook the World*.

On this day Reed tours the confused city. He goes to the Winter Palace, formerly the czar's home and now the headquarters of Aleksandr Kerensky, head of the Provisional Government. Reed walks in past the guards. Soldiers and sailors mill around, arguing with each other and ignoring their officers. One officer approaches Reed. "I am very anxious to go away from Russia," he says to the reporter. "I have made up my mind to join the American army. Would you please go to your Consul and make arrangements? I will give you my address."

It is rumored that the Communists, the most extreme political group, are going to seize power. Reed hears about a dramatic meeting of the Petrograd Soviet (a workers' organization). In that meeting the Communist leader, Lenin, has announced that the Provisional Government is doomed. As night falls, guns boom in the darkness. The revolutionaries occupy government offices, and Kerensky flees the city. Petrograd is in Communist hands. Eventually, all of Russia will be.

A.D. 1910 - PRESENT

World War I
1914-18

1910

1920

Vladimir Lenin
1917-24

Communist Revolution
1917

Red Menace in Russia

Cuban Missile Crisis 1962

Czech Uprising 1968

Invasion of Afghanistan 1979

1940　　1950　　1960　　1970　　1980　　1990

Joseph Stalin 1924-53

Nikita Khrushchev 1953-64

Leonid Brezhnev 1964-82

Mikhail Gorbachev 1985-91

World War II 1941-45

Hungarian Uprising 1956

Lenin and the Communist Revolution

Reed goes on to write, "So. Lenin and the Petrograd workers had decided on insurrection, the Petrograd Soviet had overthrown the Provisional Government. . . . Now there was all great Russia to win—and then the world! Would Russia follow and rise? And the world—what of it? Would the peoples answer and rise, a red world-tide?"

Three years later, John Reed died of typhus, and the revolutionary government buried him with great honors in Red Square in Moscow. Seventy years later, the "red world-tide" Reed described would ebb. The Soviet Union was born just after the turn of the twentieth century; it died just before the turn of the twenty-first.

Students are often confused that the Communist Revolution is sometimes called "the October Revolution" since it occurred on November 7, 1917. The cause of this confusion is calendars. The czars (emperors) of Russia had refused to join the nations of Europe in adopting the Gregorian calendar (devised by Pope Gregory XIII in 1582). They followed the old Julian calendar (devised by Julius Caesar), which ran eleven days behind the Gregorian. The Communists changed the country over to the Gregorian calendar. This change might have been hard for some people to get used to, but it was actually one of the mildest changes the Communists made.

Lenin addresses the masses, attempting to rally them to revolution. Joseph Stalin stands directly behind Lenin.

Building to a Revolution

The name of the leader of the Communist Revolution, **Vladimir Ilich Lenin,** was actually fake. He had been born Vladimir Ilich Ulyanov in 1870 but took the name Lenin to protect himself from the czar's secret police. He came from a well-to-do family but one with a streak of revolutionary fervor. His brother joined a plot against Czar Alexander III. Lenin's brother was then caught, arrested, and hanged.

Lenin became a revolutionary too, but he had little success. Eventually he was forced to leave Russia and live in Europe, where he might have lived for the rest of his life had it not been for World War I. Russia was not ready

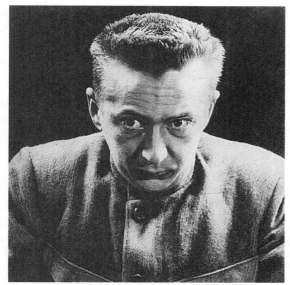

Aleksandr Kerensky

1917 the Russian people overthrew the czar. The new **Provisional Government,** led by **Aleksandr Kerensky,** promised freedom and relief.

Kerensky did not take Russia out of the war, however. Germany therefore smuggled Lenin back into the country, hoping that he would stir up trouble and weaken Russia even more. The war was not going any better for Kerensky than it had for Nicholas II. The Russian people began to listen to Lenin's slogan of "Peace, Land, Bread."

Lenin finally succeeded, and the Communist Revolution toppled the Provisional Government. Other factions fought for control of Russia too. For two years Russia fought a bloody civil war. The Communists finally defeated all their opponents and imposed their rule. In the mid-1920s Communist Russia officially took the name **Union of Soviet Socialist Republics (USSR),** or **Soviet Union** for short.

for war, and the Germans inflicted grave defeats on the Russians. The people were starving from shortages of food. The poorly equipped, poorly led Russian soldiers were dying for a cause they no longer cared about. Czar Nicholas II was incompetent. In March

After the Communist Revolution, outside powers intervened to help the anti-Communist forces. Here Japanese soldiers march beneath the flags of the nations that tried, in vain, to halt the revolution.

Nature of Soviet Communism

In Chapter 11 we studied about socialism, including the Marxist and Communist forms. You will recall that Karl Marx taught that the root of society's problems was the unequal distribution of wealth. The rich controlled the means of producing goods and kept the profits while the laborers who did all the work received little. Marx believed that eventually the workers would rise up against the rich. They would institute a government in which there would be no classes. All men would be equal. No one would actually own anything, but everybody would share with anyone who was in need.

Lenin added a twist to Marx's ideas. The Russian revolutionary did not think that revolution would arise naturally. Instead, revolu-

tionaries might use violence, as Lenin did, to spur the revolution along. Once his revolution had been brought to its bloody climax, Lenin was ready to impose his Communist state.

There was no room for individual freedom or private ownership of property. The people, in whose name the revolution had been made, actually had little power. The government ran the businesses and paid the workers. The people had to obey the government's orders and accept the Communist philosophy or risk punishment. The people became little better than slaves to their Communist leaders. Lenin promised "Peace, Land, Bread," but he gave the people little of these.

Lenin at first tried to establish pure Communism with what he called **"War Communism."** The Communists took over all

Union of Soviet Socialist Republics

Lenin's tomb in Moscow where the embalmed remains of Lenin are still on public display.

businesses, took control of all private property, and seized all the food for distribution. The nation nearly starved. Lenin then announced the **"New Economic Policy."** This was really old capitalism in disguise. Farmers could sell some of their produce, and merchants could make profits from their goods. The government invited foreign investment in Russian industry. Under this plan, the Soviet Union began to recover.

Lenin intended for the New Economic Policy to be only temporary, but he never had a chance to change it. He survived an assassination attempt in August 1918 but never fully recovered. His health steadily declined, especially after a series of strokes beginning in 1922. The last two years of his life Lenin spent as an invalid waited on by a huge team of doctors and nurses. He died on January 21, 1924. His body was laid in public view in a glass case in a mausoleum (MAW suh LEE um; a large building housing a tomb) in Moscow's Red Square. Lenin was gone, but his revolution went on.

Section Review

1. Who was the leader of the Provisional Government, which the Communists overthrew?

2. How did Lenin get back into Russia after World War I began?

3. What idea did Lenin add to the theories of Karl Marx?

4. What was Lenin's name for the pure form of Communism he first tried to impose? When it failed, what policy did he replace it with?

   Why would the slogan "Peace, Land, Bread" have appealed to the Russian people in 1917?

SETTINGS—Russia

NORTH SEA

NORWEGIAN SEA

BERING S

NORWAY

SWEDEN

FINLAND

BALTIC SEA

KALININGRAD (RUSS.)

POLAND

ESTONIA

LATVIA

LITHUANIA

BELARUS

MOLDOVA

UKRAINE

⊛ Moscow

Siberia

S i b e r i a

Ural Mountains

SEA OF OKHOTSK

RUSSIA

BLACK SEA

Caucasus Mts.

TURKEY

GEORGIA

ARMENIA

CASPIAN SEA

IRAQ

AZERBAIJAN

ARAL SEA

KAZAKHSTAN

MONGOLIA

CHINA

NORTH KOREA

SEA OF JAPAN

JAPAN

SOUTH KOREA

Location—Russia occupies the eastern part of Europe and all of the northern part of the Asian continent. It is bordered in the west by Norway, Finland, Estonia, Latvia, Lithuania, Belarus, and Ukraine. A piece of western Russia, Kaliningrad, is separated from the rest of the country and is wedged between Lithuania and Poland against the Baltic Sea. In the south are Georgia, Azerbaijan, Kazakhstan, China, Mongolia, and North Korea. The northern and eastern sides are bordered by water.

Climate—The climate of Russia varies from icy in the north to dry in the south. In the land between, the climate is mostly highland or snowy. The European section of Russia has mostly a humid continental climate, and the Asian section has mainly a subpolar climate. Along its northern border, Russia has a polar (tundra) climate, and along the southern border it has a semiarid (steppe) climate. Temperatures throughout Russia vary from between -33° and 10°F in the winter to between 30° and 80°F in the summer.

Topography—Most of Russia is on a plateau. Much of the plateau consists of steppes (grassy plains), thick forests, and high mountain ranges in the central and eastern parts. Many rivers flow through the land. The Ural Mountains cut through the country. They divide European Russia from Asian Russia. The Caucasus Mountains separate Russia from Georgia and Azerbaijan and have been a hiding place for rebellious factions throughout history.

Natural Resources—The abundant farmland of Russia has some of the richest soil in the world. Thick forests provide wood. The many rivers are a source, largely untapped, of hydroelectric power. Almost every mineral needed for industry is found in quantity. The only exception is tin.

Geography & Culture—Even though much of Russia is on the Asian continent, this nation's culture is mainly European. The European part of Russia was more favorable to settlement and development, and European Russia is far more heavily populated than the Asian part. The regions near the Baltic and Black Seas have become agricultural and industrial because the favorable climate and topography have made transportation possible. In contrast, the Asian section (Siberia) has a cold climate that is unfavorable for agriculture, industry, or stable transportation facilities.

The desire to escape the cold has shaped Russia's history. For many years, Russia had no warm-water ports; all of its seaports were frozen during the winter months. Therefore, Russia constantly pushed toward the Baltic Sea in the east and the Mediterranean Sea in the south. The Russians reached the Baltic finally but have never succeeded in getting a port on the Mediterranean.

Settings Review

1. What kind of climate is generally found in the European section of Russia? What kind of climate is generally found in the Asian section?

2. What mostly untapped source of electricity is abundant in Russia?

3. What is the only important mineral for industry that Russia does *not* possess in sufficient quantity?

Why would the cold climate of Siberia make it less suitable for settlement?

Scenes from modern Russia: a shopping mall in Moscow (top right), the Russian countryside (bottom right), and St. Basil's Cathedral in Moscow (left)

Stalin and the "Age of Terror"

Lenin's successor was **Joseph Stalin.** He was born Josef Dzhugashvili but, like Lenin, took a false name for safety. He chose Stalin because it means "man of steel." Stalin liked the tough sound of the name. He would prove, at any rate, that he had a heart of steel, for Joseph Stalin became one of the cruelest dictators in history.

Industrialization and Collectivization

Because the Soviet Union was far behind Europe in industry, Stalin began to build modern factories. Under his **Five-Year Plans** (beginning in 1928), Stalin directed factories to produce goods for industry, agriculture, and the military. Factories made few consumer goods. Many people went without household

Joseph Stalin

goods and new clothing as factories followed Stalin's, not the people's, desires. Not only did people miss owning luxuries; often they could not find decent shoes or clothing to buy.

The suffering caused by Stalin's plan of industrialization, however, was nothing compared to the suffering caused by his agricultural policies. Stalin sought to collectivize the farms of the USSR. **Collectivization** meant taking the land from owners of all farms and joining it into large farms run by the government. Communist officials then assigned farmers to work the new farms and ordered them to turn the harvest over to the government. The government paid the farmers low wages, with which they purchased food and goods in the government-run stores.

Many farmers fought collectivization. They slaughtered their animals and dumped out their milk rather than give it to the government. Some held huge feasts to wolf down their food before the Communists could get it. Stalin sent many farmers to the cold, harsh region of Siberia in the far northeast. These may have been the fortunate ones. Without enough food to go around, Stalin simply let many people starve.

People died of starvation, but courts gave death sentences to those who tried to steal food off the collective farms. Sometimes if someone showed no sign of starvation, officials assumed he was stealing food. They would beat him to find out where he was hiding it. In desperation, a few Soviets resorted to cannibalism but were put to death when the Communists discovered what they were doing. Hatred of Stalin was almost as great as fear of the Soviet dictator. An American visiting Soviet farms in the late 1930s saw a grave marked, "I love Stalin. Bury him here as soon as possible."

Two scenes reflecting the changes Stalin brought to the Soviet Union: peasants joining a collective farm and the Bereznikovsky chemical factory

The collectivized farms were a failure. Whatever farmers grew went to the state. With little reward for success, workers did not put out their best efforts. The most productive farming took place on tiny plots of land given to the peasants to grow what they wanted. On these plots, farmers could keep all they grew. In 1938 these private plots were 4 percent of Soviet farmland, but they provided 20 percent of its produce.

Purges

Stalin cruelly disposed of all opposition to his rule. To do this he used the secret police and fixed trials. The secret police watched the people and tortured those they arrested in order to get "confessions." In the schools and local meeting places, government officials taught the people to report any antigovernment attitudes or actions, such as hiding food. Neighbors turned in neighbors to the Communists. Even children, prodded by their teachers, accused their own parents.

Stalin trusted no one. In the 1930s he began a series of **purges** to eliminate anyone he thought might be disloyal. The secret police arrested loyal Communists. Special courts accused the astonished officials of all sorts of fictitious crimes against the state. In almost every case the verdict was guilty and the punishment either imprisonment or death. Stalin swept away political officials, military officers, and anyone else he thought could be a threat to his power, even writers, artists, and actors. Membership in the Communist Party could be more a danger than a protection. In 1934 nearly two thousand delegates attended a major Communist Party assembly. Within five years, over half of these had been shot on Stalin's orders.

A prosecutor reads the verdicts in a Stalinist trial.

World War II

Yet there was also a source of suffering for the Soviet people that was not Stalin's doing, at least directly. As we learned in the last chapter, Adolf Hitler desired to launch a war of conquest, and he made a treaty with Stalin in 1939. Germany and the Soviet Union agreed not to attack each other, and they agreed to split Poland between them when the war broke out.

Neither dictator intended to keep this bargain, but Hitler broke it first. In June 1941 Nazi Germany attacked the Soviet Union. At first, the Germans won devastating victories over the surprised Soviet army. Some citizens even welcomed the Nazis as liberators from the oppression of Stalin.

Hitler, however, hated the Russian people as an "inferior race." Therefore, German soldiers treated the people with great cruelty. The people rallied against the invaders. Many practiced a **"scorched-earth" policy.** As they retreated, the Soviet people burned food, crops, homes—anything that the Germans might be able to use.

The people suffered terribly from the fighting. The Germans surrounded Leningrad (formerly St. Petersburg). For 880 days, the Germans encircled the city. Inside, thousands of people died each day from starvation. Many just collapsed quietly and died at their jobs or in the streets. Starvation killed a million people. But the citizens of Leningrad held on. Despite the German siege, composer Dmitri Shostakovich worked on what would become his Seventh, or "Leningrad," Symphony. After writing the first two movements, the composer went on the radio to announce he had finished them. "Why do I tell you this?" he asked. "I tell you this so that those Leningraders who are now listening to me shall know that the life of our city is going on normally."

Finally, in the spring of 1944, the Soviets broke the siege of Leningrad.

The United States and Great Britain poured supplies into the Soviet Union to help the Soviets defeat Germany. The people, although they hated Stalin, rallied to defend their homeland. The turning point was the **Battle of Stalingrad,** fought from July 1942 to February 1943. Germans and Soviets fought ferociously for the city, reducing Stalingrad to a heap of rubble. The new factories Stalin had built for his Five-Year Plans became blood-drenched battlefields. The fighting was incredibly fierce. A German officer wrote,

> We have fought fifteen days for a single house, with mortars, grenades, machine guns, and bayonets. By the third day fifty-four German corpses lay strewn in the cellars, on the landings and the staircases. . . . There is a ceaseless struggle from noon to night. From story to story, faces black with sweat, we bombard each other with grenades in the middle of explosions, clouds of dust and smoke, [and] heaps of mortar. . . . Ask any soldier what half an hour of hand-to-hand struggle means in such a fight. And imagine

A Russian commander urges his troops forward against the invading Germans.

Soviet troops hug the ground in the middle of the rubble of Stalingrad.

Stalingrad: eighty days and eighty nights of hand-to-hand struggles. . . . Stalingrad is no longer a town. By day it is an enormous cloud of burning, blinding smoke; it is a vast furnace, lit by the reflections of the flames. And when the night arrives, one of those scorching, howling, bleeding nights, the dogs plunge into the Volga [River] and swim desperately to gain the other bank. The nights of Stalingrad are a terror for them. Animals flee this hell; the hardest stones cannot bear it for long; only men endure.

The battle ended with the death or surrender of over two hundred thousand German soldiers. After Stalingrad, the Soviet army slowly became stronger, and the German army gradually became weaker. Finally, in 1945, Soviet troops moved into Berlin itself, and Hitler committed suicide.

The Soviet Union had won a great victory but at great cost. Estimates are that seven million soldiers and seven million civilians died in the war. The war did not change Stalin's nature. He quickly moved to enslave Eastern Europe. He forced Poland, Czechoslovakia, East Germany, and other nations to accept Communist governments. Stalin did not even spare his own suffering people. When Soviet soldiers returned from German prison camps after World War II, Stalin feared that they might have picked up "dangerous ideas" during their imprisonment. So he sent them straight to Communist prison camps in Siberia.

How many people died under Stalin's reign of terror? In 1991 the Soviet secret police estimated that 42 million citizens died by execution or starvation or died in prison between 1928 and 1952. This huge number does not even count the millions of Soviet soldiers and civilians who died in World War II. Historians rightly consider Nazi dictator Adolf Hitler a monster. But even Hitler did not slaughter as many people as the bloody-handed Joseph Stalin. "A single death is a tragedy," Stalin once said coldly. "A million deaths is a statistic." If so, he was an expert in statistics.

Section Review

1. What does *Stalin* mean?
2. What was Stalin's name for his plans to improve Soviet industry?
3. What is meant by the "collectivization" of agriculture?
4. During World War II, what Soviet city was the site of a lengthy German siege?
5. What battle was the turning point of the war for the Soviet Union?
6. What did Stalin do in Eastern Europe after World War II?

Why were the private plots of Soviet citizens, which were only 4 percent of Soviet farmland, able to provide 20 percent of the nation's produce?

The Cold War and the Communist State

Before Stalin died in 1953, he began what has been called the **Cold War.** A "hot war" is one in which two sides fight openly against each other. World War II was a hot war. The phrase "Cold War" refers to a period of competition between the Communist world and the free world. Sometimes it broke out into a hot war, as in the Vietnam War. Usually, though, the two sides—led by the Soviet Union and the United States—competed behind the scenes. The Soviet Union sought to expand its power and spread Communism around the world. It sought to avoid an open war with the United States and other free nations. A Cold War seemed safer because by the 1950s both the U.S. and the USSR had nuclear weapons that could destroy each other. Indeed some people feared that at any time the tension between the free world and the Communist world might explode into a horrible nuclear war.

The leaders of the Soviet Union after Stalin, therefore, wanted to expand Communism's influence without provoking a war. The leaders of the free world sought to contain Communist growth, also without sparking a war. This tense Cold War continued from

Europe and the Cold War

NATO (Includes Canada and the U.S.)

Warsaw Pact Countries

Other Communist Countries

ICELAND

SWEDEN

FINLAND

NORWAY

Oslo

Stockholm

Helsinki

DENMARK
Copenhagen

BALTIC SEA

Moscow

Dublin

GREAT BRITAIN

NETH.

Berlin

POLAND

U.S.S.R.

IRELAND

Amsterdam

EAST GERMANY

Warsaw

London

Brussels

Bonn

Prague

BELG.

WEST GERMANY

CZECHOSLOVAKIA

ATLANTIC OCEAN

Paris

LUX.

Vienna

Budapest

Bern

AUSTRIA HUNGARY

FRANCE

SWITZ.

ROMANIA

Belgrade

Bucharest

YUGOSLAVIA

ITALY

Sofia

BLACK SEA

SPAIN

Rome

Tiranë

BULGARIA

Ankara

PORTUGAL

Madrid

GREECE

TURKEY

Lisbon

Athens

ALBANIA

MEDITERRANEAN SEA

shortly after the end of World War II until the collapse of the Soviet Union in the 1980s.

Khrushchev

Replacing Stalin as Soviet dictator was **Nikita Khrushchev** (KROOSH chef). He surprised the world by announcing a policy of **"de-Stalinization."** Stalin had gone too far, Khrushchev said, in his policies of terror and repression. He would allow more openness in Soviet society. Symbolically, Soviet officials took Stalin's body from its place next to Lenin's and buried it under tons of concrete. The government freed many prisoners from Stalin's prison camps. One prisoner was writer **Aleksandr Solzhenitsyn** (SOLE zhuh NEET sin). The Soviet government not only released him but allowed him to publish a novel, *One Day in the Life of Ivan Denisovich,* that was harshly

Nikita Khrushchev

A man burns a picture of Lenin during the 1956 uprising in Hungary. The Soviets ruthlessly crushed the Hungarians.

critical of the labor camps. The book won international acclaim and seemed to prove that a change was taking place in the USSR.

Khrushchev also announced a policy of **"peaceful coexistence"** with the nations of the free world. Instead of military competition, he said, the two sides would get along with each other and compete economically. The Soviet leader was so sure of the superiority of the Communist system that he told the West, "We will bury you."

But Khrushchev's reforms had their limits. When he took power, he quickly had the head of Stalin's secret police arrested and executed. Then Khrushchev made one of his own followers the leader of the secret police. He did make less use of prison camps than Stalin had, but under his leadership the Soviets began treating **dissidents** (people who criticized the Soviet government) as being mentally ill. Instead of being sent to Siberia, dissidents found themselves in mental hospitals where "psychiatric treatment" was the punishment instead of hard labor. Khrushchev may not have been as bad as Stalin—but then very few men in history have been as cruel as Joseph Stalin.

At the United Nations during the Cuban missile crisis, the Soviet ambassador (left) protests, saying, "I am not in an American courtroom, sir. Therefore, I do not wish to answer questions put to me in the fashion in which a prosecutor puts questions." American ambassador Adlai Stevenson (right) replies, "You are in the courtroom of world opinion right now."

Neither did Khrushchev lighten the Soviet rule in countries under his control. As mentioned before, at the end of World War II, Stalin had forced Communist governments on Eastern Europe. In 1956 the people of Hungary tried to throw off Soviet domination. Hungarian rebels broadcast radio messages to the West begging for help. No help came as Khrushchev sent in the army and crushed the uprising.

The Soviets also sought to expand their power under Khrushchev. They won an enormous victory in 1959 when the island of Cuba came under the rule of a Communist dictator, Fidel Castro. Now Communism was fewer than a hundred miles off the coast of the United States. But Cuba also turned out to be Khrushchev's undoing. In 1962 he decided to strengthen his position by placing nuclear missiles in Cuba. The United States, under President John F. Kennedy, would not tolerate this threat. The U.S. put a naval blockade around Cuba and demanded that the Soviets remove the missiles.

In this **Cuban missile crisis,** the world teetered on the brink of nuclear war. But Khrushchev knew his nuclear arsenal was not as big as Kennedy's, and he backed down.

The humiliation of the Cuban missile crisis angered many Communist leaders. They began plotting to get rid of Khrushchev. Finally, in 1964 the Communist Party announced that Khrushchev had "retired" for "health reasons." In reality, he was sent to live in exile until his death in 1971. Even then, he remained proud of the changes he claimed to have brought to the Soviet Union. After his fall he wrote, "They were able to get rid of me simply by voting. Stalin would have had them all arrested."

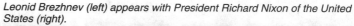

Leonid Brezhnev (left) appears with President Richard Nixon of the United States (right).

Fearful of democracy, the Soviet Union sent its forces into Czechoslovakia to crush a Czech reform movement in 1968.

Brezhnev

Eventually succeeding Khrushchev was his former assistant **Leonid Brezhnev** (BREZH nef). Like Khrushchev he said that the Soviet Union saw no reason to continue the Cold War. Instead of "peaceful coexistence," Brezhnev announced his support of a policy of **détente** (day TAHNT), from a French word referring to the relaxing of tensions. Many people in the West took him at his word.

Détente was not for regions under Soviet control, however. In 1968 Czechoslovakia, like Hungary in 1956, tried to reform the Communist system. And like Khrushchev, Brezhnev sent in the army to crush the movement. Under Brezhnev, the Communists promoted and supported revolutions in Asia, Africa, and Latin America. They helped the Communist forces in Vietnam (discussed in the next chapter). Some leaders in the West began to warn that détente was just a smokescreen to hide Soviet expansion.

Brezhnev was one of the Communist leaders who felt humiliated by the Cuban missile crisis. He was determined that nothing like that would happen again. He oversaw a great buildup of Soviet military forces and built an arsenal of nuclear weapons that could match that of the United States. The Soviet Union geared its whole economy toward supporting its military forces. The result was a powerful army.

The result was also a stagnant economy. Stores contained very few goods and only a poor quality of food. When goods were available, people would stand in line for hours to buy basic items such as flour or sugar. The state-run factories were inefficient and poorly

The Soviet Union maintained its military power by devoting much of its economy to building weaponry at the expense of the citizens' need for food and clothing.

Soviet troops in Afghanistan, which became to the Soviets a problem as great as Vietnam had been for the United States

managed. The products they turned out were often shoddy. Workers gave little effort to earn the nearly worthless Soviet money. One worker said, "We pretend to work, and they pretend to pay us."

Shortly before he died in 1982, Brezhnev launched the Soviet Union into one of its biggest disasters. In 1979 he invaded the neighboring nation of Afghanistan to prop up its Communist government. The Afghan people fought back. Brezhnev had spent billions on building the Soviet army. But this expensive army proved unable to crush the Afghans. Although few observers realized it, the Soviet empire was beginning to fall apart.

Section Review

1. What is the phrase describing the period of competition between the Communist world and the free world from the end of World War II to the 1980s?

2. What author did Khrushchev release from a Soviet labor camp? What book did that author write describing life in such camps?

3. In what Eastern European nation did Khrushchev crush a democratic uprising in the 1950s? In what Eastern European nation did Brezhnev crush a similar movement in the 1960s?

4. What island nearly became the cause of war between the United States and the USSR? What Soviet act on this island sparked this crisis?

5. What neighboring nation did the Soviet Union invade in 1979?

Why would Khrushchev be proud that his followers had voted him out and that he had not had them arrested as Stalin would have done?

Religion in the Soviet Union

The Communists were officially atheists. **Atheism** (from the Greek meaning "no God") is the belief that God does not exist. In 1913 Lenin wrote, "Every religious idea, every idea of God, even flirting with the idea of God, is unutterable vileness." The Communists thought that religion was a drug that leaders used to keep people quiet. Therefore, they sought to destroy religion. They closed most churches and persecuted Christians. Jews and Muslims also suffered under Communist rule.

General Persecution

The Soviet constitution promised citizens "the right to profess . . . any religion." But the government did everything it could to discourage religion. To oppose the churches, the Communists set up the League of the Militant Godless. This atheistic group claimed five million members at its height.

Even the **Russian Orthodox Church** was not spared. The Orthodox Church had been the state church of Russia for centuries. The czars had permitted almost no other groups to exist, and most Russians belonged to the Orthodox Church. The Communists, however, sought to control or crush it. They defaced **icons,** the pictures of Christ and saints used in worship in Orthodox churches. They stripped jewels and gold off the icons to pay for building factories. The wooden icons themselves were burned as firewood.

Leaders of the Orthodox Church were arrested for opposing the state.

The Communists forced over fifty thousand churches to close their doors. They turned some churches into museums or factories. Sometimes they were more subtle. In later years, the Soviet television network would broadcast its most popular programs on Easter Sunday to lure people away from attending church.

The Russian Orthodox Church built beautiful cathedrals, which the Soviets often turned into factories or museums.

BACKGROUNDS

The Orthodox Church

Christians in the Americas and Western Europe often think of Christianity in terms of Protestantism and Roman Catholicism. We have already seen, however, that there have been other churches within Christendom (the Christian world). We studied the Nestorian Church in Chapter 4 (pp. 95-96). We also mentioned the Coptic Church in Egypt (p. 114; see also p. 569) and the Ethiopian Church (p. 114; see also p. 569). Another important and influential section of Christendom is the Orthodox Church. It is still the most important Christian group in Eastern Europe and Russia.

The Orthodox Church is often called by other names. Sometimes it is called the Eastern Orthodox Church as opposed to the "Western" Roman Catholic Church. Sometimes it is called the Greek

Russian icon, Madonna and Child, *17th Century (Bob Jones University Collection)*

Orthodox Church because its headquarters for many centuries was in the Greek-speaking Byzantine (BIZ un TEEN) Empire. It also goes by the name of the different countries in which it is located. One of the largest segments of the Orthodox Church is the Russian Orthodox Church.

During the Middle Ages, the church in Western Europe and the church in Eastern Europe began to drift apart. The church in the West became known as the Roman Catholic Church. It used primarily Latin in its services and was led by the pope. The church in the East used primarily Greek. It had no single leader but a group of patriarchs. The most important of these patriarchs was the **patriarch of Constantinople,** the capital of the Byzantine Empire. The Western and Eastern churches often clashed. Finally in 1054 the pope and the patriarch of Constantinople declared each other "outside of the church." From that date the Roman Catholic Church and the Orthodox Church were considered officially separate.

Despite its arguments with the popes, the Orthodox Church did not differ greatly from the Roman Catholic Church. It stressed tradition and formal worship. Bishops and monks were the spiritual leaders of the church. The Orthodox Church is distinct in its use of icons to aid worship. Icons are pictures of God or Christ or the saints. Orthodox worshipers are supposed to focus their attention on these pictures to help them imagine the real person they represent. Some other Christians believe that this practice leads to idolatry as people begin to treat the picture as though it were an object to be worshiped.

The Orthodox Church never underwent a reform like the Protestant Reformation. One leader, Patriarch **Cyril Lucar** of Constantinople, tried to introduce Protestant reforms in the 1600s. His efforts failed, however, and the church rejected his teaching. Therefore, the Orthodox Church is still generally characterized by the formalism and traditionalism that Protestants reject in Roman Catholicism.

In 988 Grand Prince Vladimir of Kiev announced that he was converting to the Orthodox faith. This event is said to mark the conversion of Russia. Vladimir ordered mass baptisms of his subjects. Soon Orthodox priests and missionaries began to spread out all over Russia, and almost all Russians became members of the Orthodox Church. After Constantinople fell to the Ottoman Turks in 1453, Russia became the main center of Orthodoxy.

The Orthodox Church, however, has always suffered from the control of political leaders. The patriarch of Moscow was the leader of the church. But the famous Russian leader Czar Peter the Great did away with the office of patriarch of Moscow in the 1700s. In its place he created the **Holy Synod,** which made the Orthodox Church virtually a department of the Russian government.

When the Communists took power, they cut off government support of the Orthodox Church. The church in turn opposed the government. The ruling council of the Orthodox Church restored the office of patriarch of Moscow as the church's leader. The new patriarch, Tikhon, denounced the Communist government. He was finally arrested but was released after reversing himself and declaring himself loyal to the Communist state. From that time, most church leaders tried to work with the Communists. The fall of Commu-

Cyril Lucar, patriarch of Constantinople (1620-38)

nism in the Soviet Union brought new freedom to the Orthodox. However, Orthodox Church leaders have used their new influence with the government of Russia to try to keep Christian missionaries out of their land.

Stalin, who had once studied for the Russian Orthodox priesthood, was one of the worst persecutors. He killed or imprisoned countless religious leaders and lay Christians. Only during World War II did he become more tolerant. Because of the Nazi invasion, Stalin rallied Christians to his side by allowing them more freedom. Khrushchev, despite his policy of "de-Stalinization," was almost as bad as Stalin. In fact, some of the most concentrated persecution of Christians took place under his rule in the 1950s. Khrushchev routinely tore down churches for government building programs. This oppression took place while Khrushchev was announcing Soviet reforms to the rest of the world.

The Example of the Russian Baptists

The troubles of Christians in the Soviet Union are illustrated by the story of the Russian Baptists. In the 1800s the czars had allowed some German Mennonites to settle in Russia. These were descendants of the Anabaptists of the Reformation. To attract these farmers to his country, the czar allowed them to practice their own religion instead of Russian Orthodoxy. In the mid-1800s some of these Mennonites were influenced by the **Stundist revival.** The name of this revival comes from the German word *stunde,* meaning "hour." Much of the revival took the form of special hours of Bible study and prayer. Many people were converted and many Christians spiritually strengthened through these hours of study and prayer. The czar also allowed some German Baptist missionaries and English missionaries to work among the immigrants. These believers often considered themselves both Mennonites and Baptists because both groups practiced the baptism of adults by immersion.

After several years, the czar began to worry about the growth of the Russian Baptist movement, and he began to persecute its followers. The czar was especially angry that some native Russians were turning to the gospel from the deadness of Russian Orthodoxy. The Russian Revolution at first brought relief to these Christians. The Soviet government needed all the help it could get, and it allowed some freedom of religion. The Communists even allowed missionaries into the country. Once their control was firm, though, the Communists began to crack down on all Baptists and

A Russian Mennonite family poses in 1929 in China, where they had fled to escape Communist persecution.

other Protestants. Many Baptist leaders died in prison camps.

During World War II, when he was trying to win over the churches to his side, Stalin encouraged these different Protestant groups to form the **Union of Evangelical Christians—Baptists** (1944). Later Khrushchev's government demanded that this group follow certain guidelines. They were to limit evangelism, for example, and not to baptize anyone under the age of thirty.

Members of an unregistered church meet in the woods for worship.

These requirements split the Baptists. One portion wanted to go along with the government. The Communists recognized their organization, and they became known as the **"registered churches."**

Others would not sacrifice their beliefs in this way. They became known as the **"unregistered churches"** and began to meet illegally. The Communists treated the unregistered churches harshly. Their leaders were arrested and imprisoned. Ministers found themselves in jail cells with murderers and rapists. The registered churches did not suffer so harshly. Yet even they faced constant government regulation and interference with their churches.

The two groups opposed each other. The registered churches thought the unregistered churches were making trouble when they did not have to. The unregistered churches thought the registered churches were compromising the gospel.

The collapse of the Soviet Union brought relief to both the registered and the unregistered churches. Baptists now number somewhere between two and three million, although that is still a small portion of the population. The two groups nonetheless still suffer division over the bitterness of past conflicts.

Section Review

1. What is the official religious belief of Communism?

2. What was the state church of Russia?

3. Among what religious-ethnic group did the Russian Baptists originate?

4. What was the difference between the "registered" and the "unregistered" Baptist churches?

Which policy do you think was more biblical in its relationship to the Soviet government, that of the registered or the unregistered churches? (Consider Acts 5:29 and Romans 13:1 as you answer.)

Decline and Fall of the Soviet Empire

After Brezhnev died, the weaknesses in the Soviet Union began to appear. The two leaders who followed him were aged and died after brief terms in office. The war in Afghanistan was going badly. The Afghan people, supported by the United States, were fighting back against the Soviet army. The Soviet forces could hold the main Afghan cities but could not conquer the countryside. The Soviet people were sick of the war and tired of a Communist economy, which could not provide them with decent food and clothing.

Gorbachev

At this point, in 1985, the Communists chose a new leader. **Mikhail Gorbachev** (GOR buh CHAWF) was much younger than Brezhnev and his successors. He announced that he wanted better relations with the free world. More important, he seemed to have energy and a vision for reforming the Soviet system that earlier leaders had lacked.

Two Russian terms sum up Gorbachev's efforts at reform. First, he called for *perestroika* (PEHR ih STROY kuh), which means "restructuring." Gorbachev wanted to fix the Soviet economy. By improved technology and increased productivity, he would improve the quality and output of Soviet industry. He promised to reduce government interference and eliminate corruption. He even allowed some capitalistic practices, as Lenin had done with his New Economic Policy. These small changes, however, could not cover up the fact that the economy of the Soviet Union was a wreck.

The more important term associated with Gorbachev's reform was *glasnost* (GLAHS nust), which means "openness." He wanted to allow more freedom and give people more say in the government. The government relaxed some of the restrictions on churches and released many prisoners. Gorbachev pulled the troops out of Afghanistan and ended that unpopular war. However, Gorbachev said plainly that the nation would not abandon Communism. The Soviet Union remained a military dictatorship with power in the hands of the Communist Party.

Gorbachev found that *glasnost* was hard to control. Having tasted a little freedom, the people wanted more. The first break came in Eastern Europe in 1989. When Gorbachev began withdrawing Soviet troops from that region, the nations of Eastern Europe began throwing off their Communist governments. East Germany got rid of its Communist leaders and reunited with West Germany. Other nations, such as Poland, Hungary, and Czechoslovakia, became free for the first time in years.

Unrest spread to the Soviet Union itself. Some reformers were elected to the legislature while protesters called for more changes. Sections of the Soviet Union, such as Ukraine, declared their independence. Unable to maintain control of the country, Gorbachev resigned on Christmas Day 1991. A few days later, the Soviet Union officially broke into a confederation of independent states binding themselves loosely as the "Commonwealth of Independent States" (CIS). The Soviet Union was dead.

Mikhail Gorbachev

CHARACTERIZATIONS

Andrei Sakharov

In the Soviet Union, one of the most dangerous labels to wear was "dissident." The secret police watched and harassed dissidents. Some vanished, never to be seen again. One famous dissident was a man who had been one of the Soviet Union's heroes, Andrei Sakharov (uhn-DRAY SAHK-uh-rawf).

Sakharov was a brilliant scientist. He graduated from college during World War II but was kept out of the army to conduct scientific research for the government. Sakharov is best known for helping the Soviets develop the hydrogen bomb in the 1950s. But he also made several breakthroughs for peaceful uses of nuclear power.

The bomb he had helped create started Sakharov on the path to dissidence. He protested to Khrushchev against unnecessary nuclear tests. He feared these tests needlessly endangered people's lives and health. From this protest, he went to asking for greater freedom of speech. The government removed him from his top-secret work and revoked his special status as a scientist. Losing his special privileges made Sakharov realize what drab and dreary lives most Soviet citizens led.

Persecution only made him speak out more. He called for greater religious liberty and defended others who had spoken out and been imprisoned. The secret police began to watch him and to compile files of information that could be used against him. He enjoyed little protection. After Sakharov criticized activities of the USSR's Arab allies, Arab terrorists broke into his apartment. They held him, his wife, and his stepson hostage for over an hour. "Do you want to kill us?" Sakharov's wife asked. "We can do worse things than kill you," they replied. After the terrorists left without doing anything, the scientist re-

Andrei Sakharov with his granddaughter Anya

ported this incident to the police. They were not interested.

All that saved Sakharov was that he was well known outside the Soviet Union. The Communists feared that if something happened to him it would harm the USSR's image abroad. But when Sakharov criticized the Soviet invasion of Afghanistan in 1979, that was too much. He was exiled to the industrial city of Gorky. There he was constantly watched by secret police outside his apartment. He went on hunger strikes to protest government policies and his treatment. Fearing that he might die, the Communists put him in the hospital and force-fed him.

When demanding reform, Sakharov had called for *glasnost*, "openness." In 1986 Mikhail Gorbachev, an advocate of *glasnost*, allowed the dissident scientist to return from exile. Sakharov continued to call for reform. In 1989 he was chosen to serve in a new Soviet legislature. On December 12, 1989, he publicly demanded an end to Communist rule. Two days later he died of natural causes. But two years later his demand became reality as the Communist government dissolved. It was the bravery of men and women such as Andrei Sakharov that helped bring an end to the Communist dictatorship.

Aftermath

The events of 1991 did not solve the region's problems. The new states simply divided the Soviet Union's economic and political problems among themselves. Russia, the largest and strongest of these states by far, dominated the Commonwealth. Some extremists proclaimed that Russia should rebuild its empire and bring the new nations back under its control.

Still, there were certainly changes for the better. In 1993 Russia had its first free election since 1917. The Communist Party still existed, but it was now only one party among several. Russia and the other new states had imperfect democracies, but they were nonetheless democracies. This was more than Russia had enjoyed under either the czars or the Communists. Still it would take time to develop an informed and intelligent electorate. Until the people were ready to bear the responsibility of governing themselves, their democracy would be fragile.

The future of Russia and the other nations that made up the Soviet Union is unclear. They may fall back into dictatorships, perhaps even Communist ones. Communism, after all, continues to exist in China. But the "red world-tide" that John Reed had portrayed in *Ten Days That Shook the World* had not swept the world. Instead, it had been swept away.

Commonwealth of Independent States

Factory workers in the former Soviet Union symbolize the transition from a Communist to a capitalist economy.

Section Review

1. What Soviet leader took power in 1985?
2. What is the meaning of *perestroika?* of *glasnost?*
3. When the Soviet Union dissolved, what confederation took its place? What nation dominated this confederation?

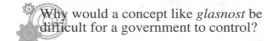 Why would a concept like *glasnost* be difficult for a government to control?

Summary

In *Russia and the Independent States,* Daniel C. Diller recounts a popular joke from the last days of the Soviet Union. A train is traveling across the USSR. Among the many passengers, in a special compartment, are Lenin, Stalin, Khrushchev, Brezhnev, and Gorbachev. Suddenly, the engine breaks down and the train comes to a halt. Lenin says he will take care of it, and he goes to the engine and lectures the engineer on the principles of Marxism and the importance of duty to the Soviet Union. The train still doesn't go, so Stalin goes to the engine and shoots the engineer. Still the train doesn't move, so Khrushchev says, "We must not hold the engineer's past mistakes against him." He proceeds to the engine and props up the engineer's body at the controls. When this doesn't help, Brezhnev suggests they close the blinds and pretend the train is moving. This they proceed to do, remarking about how quiet the ride is. Finally, Gorbachev gets out, climbs on top of the train, and announces, "Look, everybody, the train is not moving!" The passengers are delighted to have a leader so honest.

The train, however, still doesn't go anywhere.

CHAPTER REVIEW

People, Places, and Things to Know

Vladimir Ilich Lenin
Provisional
  Government
Aleksandr Kerensky
Union of Soviet
  Socialist Republics
  (USSR)
Soviet Union
War Communism
New Economic Policy
Joseph Stalin

Five-Year Plans
collectivization
purges
"scorched-earth" policy
Battle of Stalingrad
Cold War
Nikita Khrushchev
de-Stalinization
Aleksandr Solzhenitsyn
peaceful coexistence
dissidents

Cuban missile crisis
Leonid Brezhnev
détente
atheism
Russian Orthodox
  Church
icons
patriarch of
  Constantinople
Cyril Lucar

Holy Synod
Stundist revival
Union of Evangelical
  Christians—Baptists
"registered churches"
"unregistered
  churches"
Mikhail Gorbachev
perestroika
glasnost

Review Questions

Matching

Match the Soviet leader with the term most closely associated with him.
Answers may be used more than once.

1. collectivization
2. de-Stalinization
3. détente
4. Five-Year Plans
5. *glasnost*
6. New Economic Policy
7. peaceful coexistence
8. *perestroika*
9. treaty with Hitler
10. War Communism

(a) Lenin
(b) Stalin
(c) Khrushchev
(d) Brezhnev
(e) Gorbachev

Chronology

Put the following events in their proper chronological order from earliest to
latest.

11. The Battle of Stalingrad takes place.
12. Cuba turns Communist.
13. Czar Nicholas II is overthrown.

14. German Mennonites settle in Russia.
15. Gorbachev becomes the Soviet leader.
16. Hitler invades the USSR.
17. Khrushchev falls from power.
18. Lenin dies.
19. The Provisional Government is overthrown.
20. The Soviet Union invades Afghanistan.
21. The Soviet Union is dissolved.
22. The Cuban missile crisis takes place.
23. Uprising in Czechoslovakia is crushed.
24. Uprising in Hungary is crushed.
25. World War I begins.

True or False?

Which of these statements are true and which are false?

26. Communism teaches that society should have no classes.
27. Communism teaches that people should own their own property.
28. Communism teaches children to honor their parents more than their country.
29. Communism is officially atheistic in belief.
30. Communism is based on the teaching of Karl Marx.

Think About It!

Read the chapter summary on page 471. In a paragraph or two, describe how this story summarizes the history of the Soviet Union. Explain how its portrayal of the five leaders reflects the actions and character of each leader.

CHAPTER 17

Asia is huge. It is larger than any other continent (over seventeen million square miles). Over three billion people (more than half of the world's population) live there. Trying to study such an enormous region in a single chapter is rather like trying to stuff a tablecloth into a napkin holder. Because Asia has that much land and that many people, you can imagine the variety of cultures, and conflicts, the continent of Asia might have. For this reason, we study Russia and the Middle East individually even though they are part of Asia.

One way to approach Asia in the twentieth century is to look at the parallel history of two of its major countries, China and Japan. Those two nations have dominated events in the continent and have drastically affected their neighbors— including each other.

As important as China and Japan are to Asian history, there is much more involved than just those two nations. We will touch on other countries, notably India, and look at the history of Christianity in modern Asia. We will seek to understand the conditions of life in this land that is home to over half the people in the world.

A.D. 1910 - PRESENT

Overthrow of Manchu
Dynasty 1911

| 1910 | 1920 |

Divisions in Modern Asia

Ministry of
John Sung
1930-40

World War II
1940-45

Chiang Kai-shek 1926-49

Vietnam War 1946-73

Mao Zedong 1949-76

0   1940   1950   1960   1970   1980   1990

Japan's War
Against China
1937-45

Korean War 1950-53

Tiananmen Square 1989

The Long
arch 1934

Independence
of India 1947

anese Invade
nchuria 1931

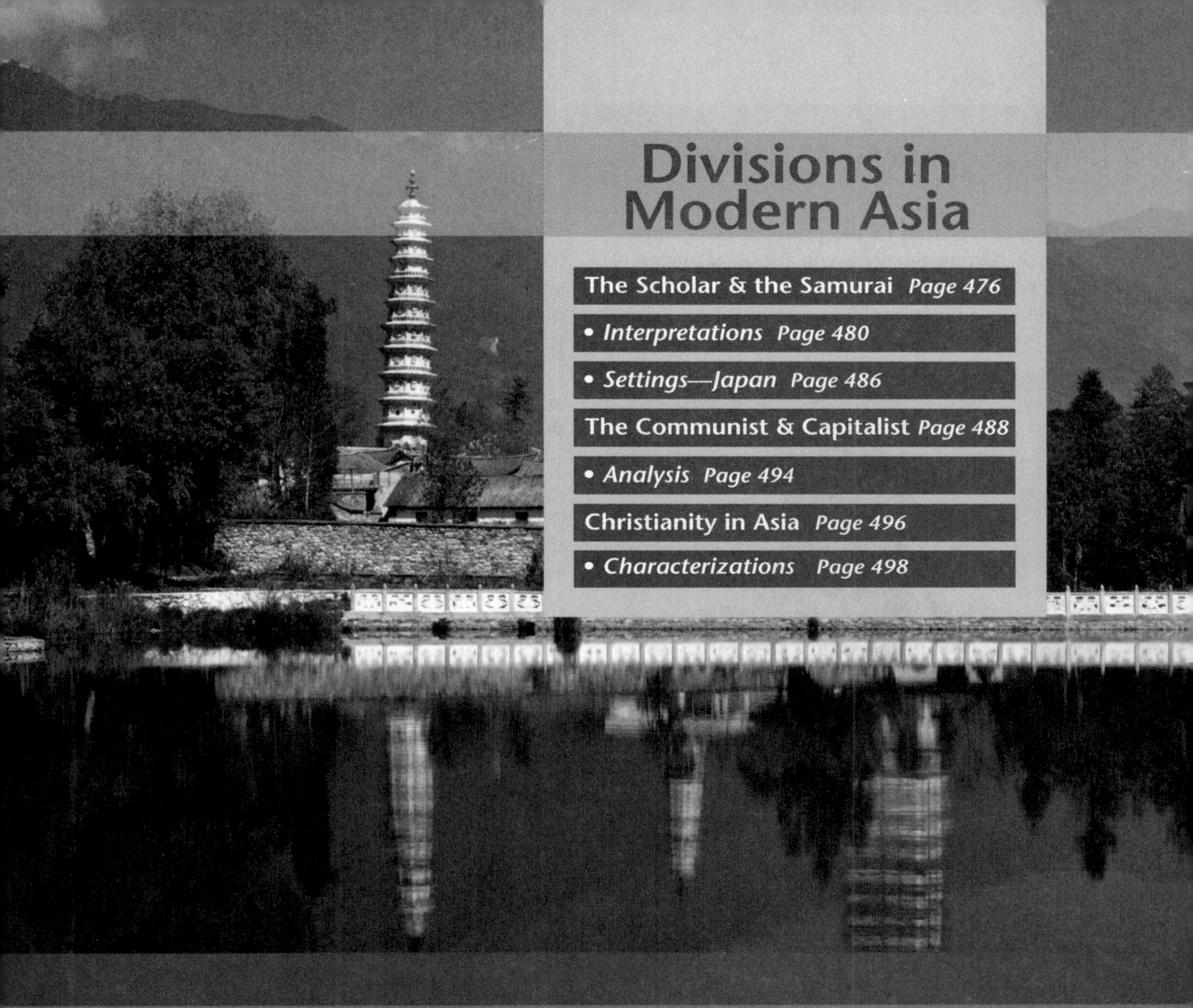

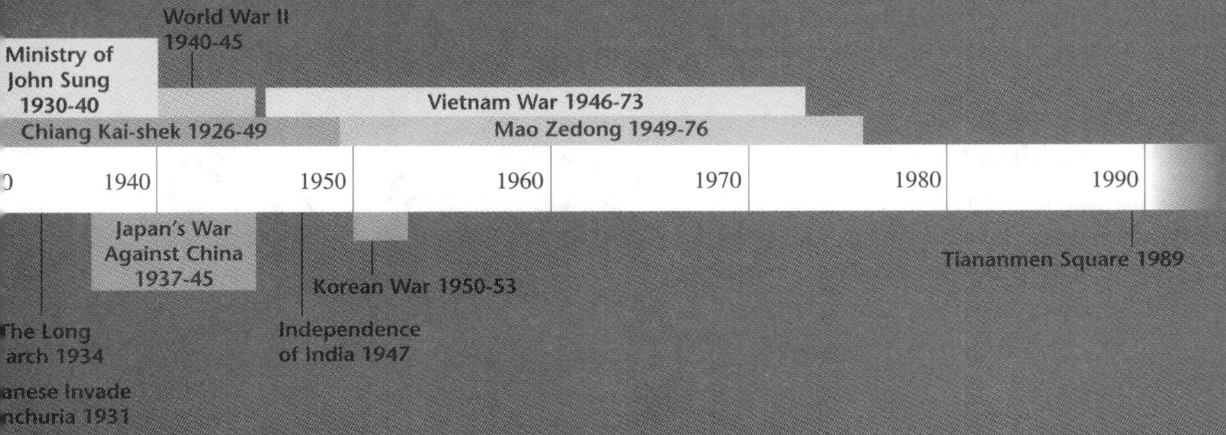

The Scholar and the Samurai

Since the time of the philosopher Confucius, the Chinese have given a special place of honor to scholars. It was the scholars who studied and preserved Chinese tradition. Chinese empires might rise and fall, but the scholar

Confucius

class endured. Japan, on the other hand, has honored its class of warriors, the samurai. Japan has had a long line of emperors, but from the Middle Ages until the 1800s, the real ruling power was the shogun. This "great general" (which is what *shogun* means) ruled the nation like a samurai chief. Of course, there were warriors in China and scholars in Japan. But the image of the Chinese scholar and the Japanese warrior helps us understand the history of Asia in the first half of the twentieth century.

China to 1949

As we noted in Chapter 13, in the early 1900s China faced several enormous problems. European countries wanting to trade with China had forced their way into the country. The snobbish manners of these foreigners angered the Chinese, and the foreigners forced their laws and customs on some parts of China. Because they had shunned the ideas of Europe, the Chinese lacked the weapons, machinery, and other technology that could have helped them defend their country.

The Chinese people hated not only Europeans but also their own rulers. The Chinese detested the Manchu leaders who controlled the country. Landlords and the government heavily taxed the poor peasants. The rich and powerful, both Chinese and foreign, lived in luxury while millions of poor Chinese suffered terrible hardships. This discontent finally exploded in revolution.

Sun Yat-sen

In 1911 the Chinese arose in revolt against the Manchu government. **Sun Yat-sen** led the

Sun Yat-sen

movement to form a Chinese republic. Although born in China, Sun had a Western education. As a teenager, he went to school in Hawaii. Later, he studied medicine and became a doctor. As a highly educated man, Sun represented in many ways the class of Chinese scholars.

Sun developed a plan for reforming China called the **Three Principles of the People.** The first principle was nationalism. Sun believed that the Chinese should rule themselves. This meant he opposed not only foreign power in China but also the Manchus because the Manchus were from Manchuria and not considered native Chinese. His second principle was democracy. Sun wanted China to have a constitutional government in which all Chinese were considered equal. His third principle was livelihood. Sun and his followers sought to provide every Chinese man with the means to support himself and his family. To further his ideas, Sun founded the **Kuomintang** (KWOH min TAHNG), or Nationalist Party.

The Manchu dynasty ended, but Sun's hopes for a Chinese government that would solve the country's problems were not fulfilled. Strife and rebellion in China grew. China suffered under a system similar to feudalism in Europe in the Middle Ages. Military leaders known as **warlords** ruled the different regions of China. These warlords raised and paid their own armies. Anyone who would lead China had to persuade at least some of the warlords to support him. The division of China among the warlords made some fear that the country would break apart.

Chiang Kai-shek

When Sun Yat-sen died, **Chiang Kai-shek** (CHANG KYE-SHEK) took over as leader of the Kuomintang. Chiang had been leader of Sun's military school. He followed Sun in seeking to establish a stable government in China, and he managed to become president. Chiang faced many obstacles to solving China's problems. One problem was the warlords, but an even greater problem was the Communists.

While Chiang tried to gain control of the large and unhappy country, Communists began to spread their teachings. These Communists

Chiang Kai-shek

Mao Zedong in 1937

munists with limited success. The Communists, led by **Mao Zedong** (MOU DZUH-DONG), made friends with the Chinese peasants by promising them a better life under Communism.

Fierce fighting took place between Chiang's Nationalist forces and Mao's Communist forces. Sometimes Chiang seemed on the verge of winning. In 1934, with the help of advisors from the German army, the Kuomintang nearly surrounded and destroyed the Communist army. However, Mao Zedong led his forces on a five-thousand-mile retreat into northern China. This retreat, known as the **Long March,** resulted in the death of eighty thousand Communist soldiers. But it preserved the nucleus of a Communist army to fight on.

Chiang's problems became worse in the 1930s when Japan attacked and conquered portions of China. (These attacks are discussed in the next section.) He tried to fight both the Communists and the Japanese but could stop

were inspired and supported by the Soviet Union, and they hoped to make China a Communist country. Chiang fought against the Com-

China relied heavily on the Allies for help against the Japanese. Here Chiang Kai-shek and his wife meet with Franklin Roosevelt and Winston Churchill in Cairo, Egypt (1943).

A Chinese sentry guards the "Flying Tigers," P-40 fighters with American pilots that provided the first American contribution to China's war against Japan.

neither. The Chinese people were in turmoil. Finally, Chiang and the Communists agreed to fight together against the Japanese.

With help from the United States, China held out against Japan. The hard fighting brought death and destruction to the land, and the Chinese were weary of the violence. When Japan was defeated at the end of World War II (1945), China regained her territory. But soon a civil war broke out as Communists sought to take over the country.

Chiang and his Nationalists fought for four more years to stop the Communists. During those years, more of the Chinese became convinced that the Communists would improve the bad conditions in their country. In 1949 Chiang and many of his followers fled to the island of Taiwan and set up the government of Nationalist China. Mao and his followers set up their rule over Communist China on the mainland. The end of Japanese oppression was about to bring a new oppression to the Chinese, this time by their own leaders.

Gandhi and Indian Nonviolence

In 1947 the greatest symbol of European imperialism, Raj India, came to an end: Great Britain granted India its independence. The main leader in India's drive for independence was an unusual man named **Mohandas Gandhi.** Slender, bald, and stooped, he hardly looked like a man who could topple the British Empire.

Gandhi, often called "Mahatma" ("great soul") by his admirers, was the son of a government official. After becoming a lawyer, he dedicated himself to working for Indian independence from Britain. Drawing on his Hindu background, Gandhi announced that he would pursue independence by a policy of nonviolence instead of relying on riots or terrorism. He supported "non-cooperation," for example. Gandhi simply urged Indians not to work with the British rulers. Teachers would refuse to teach. Government officials would refuse to perform their tasks or would resign their positions. Gandhi himself went on hunger strikes to attract notice to his cause.

Gandhi was famous for his policy of **civil disobedience.** He said that Indians should not obey laws they thought were unjust. By doing so, they would pressure the British to give up and leave India. The most famous example of Gandhi's civil disobedience was his protest of British salt laws. Indians had to buy government-approved salt on which they had already paid taxes. They could not gather their own salt from the seashore or salt marshes. In 1930 Gandhi led a two-hundred-mile march to the sea, where he and his followers illegally gathered salt. This simple act won Gandhi and his cause the attention of the world. Across the land Indians began to gather salt illegally in protest of British policies and British rule. The salt lump that Gandhi himself picked up from the seashore was later auctioned off for 1,600 rupees.

Mohandas Gandhi (center)

Gandhi actually wanted nonviolent protest to provoke a violent response from the British. Then British citizens would be revolted by the violence, he said, and the world would rally to the Indian cause. He wrote, "I want world sympathy in this battle of right against might." To a great extent, his plan worked. His success later inspired others to use his methods, such as Martin Luther King Jr. in the American civil rights movement.

Gandhi's policies worked, but they could work only against a government with some sense of morality. The British people and the British government could not bring themselves to practice the brutality needed to crush the Indian movement. Later Martin Luther King Jr. saw success with these methods by appealing to the conscience of the American people. But when a government is willing to put down any unrest with unrestrained force, the methods do not work. South Africans who tried to use Gandhi's methods experienced only repression, violence, and death. Gandhi himself was somewhat gullible about the depth of human sinfulness. He once wrote a letter to Adolf Hitler at the height of World War II to urge the Nazi dictator to embrace nonviolence.

Christians also object to these methods. The Bible teaches that Christians may disobey the law only when the law contradicts the commands of God. Even then, the Christian must stand ready to face the consequences. When the Jewish Sanhedrin told the apostles to stop preaching about Jesus Christ, Peter told them, "We ought to obey God rather than men" (Acts 5:29; see also 4:18-20). Gandhi broke laws that he did not have to break so that he could pressure the British government to change. Christians, however, must honor the law and the government except when the government demands what belongs to God (Rom. 13:1-7).

Gandhi saw his movement crowned with success when Britain gave India its independence. But the event was not as nonviolent as Gandhi had wished. Some of the Indian resistance to Britain was very violent. Also, Britain divided the area into two nations, Hindu India and Muslim Pakistan. With independence, Hindus and Muslims clashed in fighting that left as many as one million people dead. Gandhi himself was assassinated by a fellow Hindu. Since that time India has continued to suffer religious and civil conflict. Mohandas Gandhi's philosophy of nonviolence has not spared his land from bloodshed.

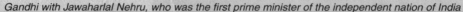

Gandhi with Jawaharlal Nehru, who was the first prime minister of the independent nation of India

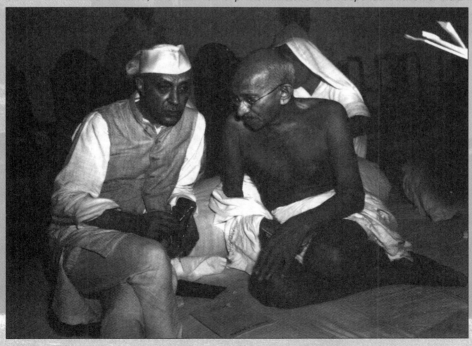

Japan to 1945

As we learned on page 368, over two hundred years of Japanese isolation ended in 1853. In that year Commodore Matthew Perry of the United States visited with his fleet and opened Japan to trade. In a later visit Perry brought with him several inventions that amazed the Japanese people. One was a telegraph system, which could send messages from one town to another. Another was a miniature train and railroad track. Japanese officials took turns riding around on the small train pulled by its own steam locomotive. The Japanese realized that they had much to learn if they were to catch up with the rest of the world.

Modernizing Japan

The Japanese began to trade not only with the United States but also with other countries. Soon the Japanese were **"westernizing"** their way of life (making it like that of the United States and Europe). They built factories to make new products. They sent some of their young men to the United States and Europe to learn more about new developments in industry. They began to build a large, powerful navy and army of their own.

In the midst of all this modernization, the rule of the shogun came to an end. In 1868 the emperor, Meiji (MAY jee), became the ruler of the land in reality as well as in name. He helped Japan accomplish many of the achievements listed above. At the same time, Japan developed a sort of "Dr. Jekyll and Mr. Hyde" personality. On the one side were Japanese who admired the democratic governments of the West and wanted Japan to be like them. On the other hand were militarists, warriors who wanted to use Japan's new industrial might to put all of eastern Asia under Japanese control. It soon became obvious that the samurai attitude was going to dominate Japan's future.

Militarizing Japan

When he was a student at Harvard in 1902, Franklin Roosevelt had a Japanese classmate. Roosevelt listened with interest as the young man described to him a hundred-year Japanese schedule of conquest. Starting in 1889, Roosevelt's classmate said, the Japanese were going to proceed by twelve steps to surpass China and Russia and first take over Korea; then parts of China, along with Australia and New Zealand; and finally all of the Pacific islands including Hawaii. This account impressed Roosevelt, especially when he became

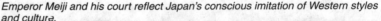
Emperor Meiji and his court reflect Japan's conscious imitation of Western styles and culture.

A Chinese child cries amid the wreckage resulting from Japan's brutal attack on the Chinese city of Shanghai.

starving. To supply more raw materials for their industries and to provide more land for the growing population, the Japanese set out to control all of eastern Asia.

Japan needed land and food, Japan's military leaders said, so Japan should just take them. Like Hitler's Germany, Japan began to think that "might made right." Anyone who opposed the growing power of the military was risking his life. Between 1912 and 1945, six prime ministers were assassinated for opposing the policies of the military. Many Japanese fanatically supported the military's goals. When a group of officers was tried for the assassination of one prime minister in 1932, some Japanese wrote letters of support—in blood. Nine citizens showed their support of the assassins by cutting off their little fingers and sending them in a jar to the government.

Warrior Japan

In 1931 the Japanese attacked the northeastern section of China called **Manchuria.** The Japanese military made this attack despite the orders of the civilian government. But the campaign was so successful that no one dared question it. Japan soon became virtually a military dictatorship like that of Nazi Germany or Fascist Italy. Japan, in fact, made an alliance with Germany and Italy (as we studied in Chapter 15). Supposedly the Japanese revered their emperor and believed he was a god. Yet the emperor told the American ambassador that even he would be murdered if he

president of the United States and he watched as Japan appeared to be following such a schedule of conquest.

Japan first humiliated China in a short war in 1895. As a result Japan captured the island of Formosa (Taiwan) and later took over Korea in 1910. In 1904-5, Japan took on Russia. Most countries expected Russia to crush the Japanese. Instead, Japan humiliated Russia. The Japanese navy trapped Russia's Pacific fleet in port. Russia then sent its fleet from the Baltic Sea on a ten-thousand-mile trip to the Pacific. When the Russian fleet arrived, the Japanese promptly sank it. Russia made peace on terms favorable to the Japanese. Later, in World War I, Japan sided with the Allies and seized all German colonies in the Pacific.

Japan was not driven by greed alone. The nation was suffering. Japan could not grow enough food for its people and had to import tons of rice. Even then, some Japanese were

The Japanese attack on Pearl Harbor caught the United States off-guard but also brought America into the war.

stood up to the military faction. In 1937, not satisfied with Manchuria, Japan launched a war against China. Although China was bigger, the superior Japanese army seized large chunks of Chinese territory. In 1940 Japan officially entered World War II on the side of the Axis, but it had already been fighting in China for almost ten years.

The United States criticized Japanese aggression and sought ways to stop it. To prevent American interference with their conquests, the Japanese launched a surprise attack. They bombed the American naval base at **Pearl Harbor,** Hawaii, in 1941. This attack destroyed or damaged a large part of the U.S. Navy in the Pacific. In response to this attack, America entered the war.

For six months after Pearl Harbor, the Japanese enjoyed spectacular success. They took American territories, such as the Philippines, and British territories, such as Burma. Their army and navy seemed unstoppable. Soon they controlled most of China, Southeast Asia, and many islands in the Pacific Ocean. The Japanese enforced their rule with fierce cruelty. They used prisoners of war for bayonet practice and used others as slave labor for their building projects. The peoples of Asia began to rally to the Allies against the Japanese.

It took time for the United States to recover from Pearl Harbor. But finally at the **Battle of Midway Island** in 1942, the Americans defeated the Japanese fleet. The tide of war turned. The United States began to take back, one by one, the islands controlled by Japan. After three and one-half years of fighting and

The atomic blast on Hiroshima left the city a ruined shell.

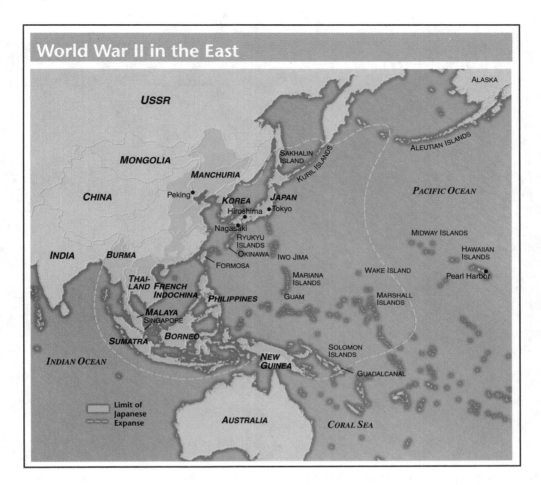

World War II in the East

USSR
ALASKA
MONGOLIA
MANCHURIA
SAKHALIN ISLAND
KURIL ISLANDS
ALEUTIAN ISLANDS
CHINA
Peking
KOREA
JAPAN
PACIFIC OCEAN
Hiroshima
Tokyo
Nagasaki
RYUKYU ISLANDS
MIDWAY ISLANDS
OKINAWA
IWO JIMA
HAWAIIAN ISLANDS
INDIA
BURMA
FORMOSA
WAKE ISLAND
Pearl Harbor
THAI-LAND
FRENCH INDOCHINA
MARIANA ISLANDS
PHILIPPINES
GUAM
MARSHALL ISLANDS
MALAYA
SINGAPORE
SUMATRA
BORNEO
SOLOMON ISLANDS
INDIAN OCEAN
NEW GUINEA
GUADALCANAL
Limit of Japanese Expanse
AUSTRALIA
CORAL SEA

hundreds of thousands of casualties, the United States ended the war by dropping two atomic bombs in 1945. One fell on the city of Hiro- shima and the other on the city of Nagasaki. Large portions of these Japanese cities were destroyed, and Japan surrendered.

Section Review

1. Name and describe each of Sun Yat- sen's Three Principles of the People.

2. Who became leader of the Kuomin- tang after Sun Yat-sen? Who was his main Communist opponent?

3. Where did the Nationalists establish their government after the Communist takeover in 1949?

4. What does it mean to say that a country, such as Japan, has been "westernized"?

5. What nation did Japan defeat in a war in 1895? in 1904-5?

6. What section of China did Japan attack in 1931?

7. On what two Japanese cities did the United States drop atomic bombs?

Explain why the samurai (warrior) image is a useful way to describe Japan up to the end of World War II.

Location—Japan is a chain of islands located in the Pacific Ocean east of Russia, Korea, and China. At its closest, Japan is less than 150 miles off the Asian mainland.

Climate—The southern half of Japan has a humid subtropical climate; the northern half has a humid continental climate. Japan's temperate climate varies from north to south, much as the climate varies along the eastern coast of the United States. Average temperatures range from winter lows of 21°F in the north to summer highs of 79°F in the south. Japan receives an annual average of fifty inches of precipitation.

Topography—Japan is made up of four main islands (Hokkaido, Honshu, Shikoku, and Kyushu) and thousands of smaller islands. The Japanese islands are really the peaks of submerged mountains, and thus much of the land is mountainous. The Japanese Alps on the island of Honshu include Mt. Fuji, Japan's highest mountain (12,388 ft.). Many of the mountains are volcanoes. Some volcanoes are still active, but most, such as Mt. Fuji, are dormant.

Natural Resources—Japan has few natural resources. Its mountainous terrain leaves less than 15 percent of the land available for farming. About two-thirds of Japan is covered with forests. Small deposits of coal, zinc, copper, lead, and gold occur. The many short, swift rivers are used to provide electricity and to irrigate rice paddies.

Geography and Culture—Living on islands encouraged the Japanese people to use the sea for transportation and food. Japan's closeness to China also led to a great deal of Chinese influence on Japan's arts and religion. Japan has always faced problems because of its small size, large population, and limited resources. Sometimes this situation has caused Japan to seek to expand through military conquest. At other times, the scarce resources and large population have encouraged the Japanese to be creative and efficient.

Settings Review

1. In what ocean is Japan located?
2. What are the four main islands of Japan?
3. What is Japan's tallest mountain?
4. What country greatly influenced Japan's arts and religion?

Why would Japan's small size, large population, and limited resources encourage the Japanese to be creative and efficient?

In the shadow of beautiful Mt. Fuji, the Japanese people learn to balance the old ways with the new.

The Communist and the Capitalist

Before World War II, the world rightly saw Japan as a dangerous aggressor and sympathized with China as the victim of outside aggression and inner disorder. After China fell to the Communists, that view changed. China became the aggressor who endangered peace and freedom in Asia. Japan, however, embraced democracy and capitalism. It became a wealthy and stable power for progress in Asia.

Chinese Communists worked diligently to bring the young into their party and indoctrinate them with Communist teachings.

Communist China

The Chinese Communists called their nation the **People's Republic of China.** It is also called Mainland China or Communist China to distinguish it from **Nationalist China** on the island of Taiwan. When the Communists took over, many Chinese rejoiced. They believed that prosperity would now come to their land. But they were dead wrong.

Living Under Communism

Many people had died during the Chinese civil war, but many more were to die under Communist rule. The Communists urged the Chinese to kill "rich" land owners and officials of the old Nationalist government. (The "rich" included those unlucky enough to own as little as thirty acres of property.) Probably two million people were killed or died in prison in the first years of Communist rule.

Those who lived suffered the loss of their freedoms. As in the Soviet Union and other Communist countries, the people could not write or speak as they thought. They could not travel to another city without permission. Of course, the atheistic Communists took away the freedom of the Chinese to worship as they wished.

The leaders of Communist China cared little for the people. Mao Zedong said he did not fear war, even nuclear war. "We may lose more than 300 million people," he said. "So what? War is war. The years will pass and we'll get to work producing more babies than ever before." In the late 1950s, Mao tried to reorganize Chinese agriculture and industry in what he called the **Great Leap Forward.** The result was a famine that killed nineteen million Chinese in 1960 alone.

Communist China's attempts at economic reform have spurred some industrialization in that nation.

When Mao died in 1976, many Chinese hoped conditions would get better. Eventually a new ruler emerged, **Deng Xiaoping** (DUNG SHYOU-PING). He promised to reform China's economy. Deng persuaded foreign companies to invest in Chinese businesses and industries. Soon American companies such as McDonald's fast-food restaurants sprang up in Chinese cities. The government also set quotas for family farms to meet and told the farmers they could keep any extra food they produced to eat or sell for a profit. Factory workers began receiving bonuses for good work. China seemed to be turning to a form of capitalism. Deng even said in 1986, "To get rich is not a sin."

China was still a dictatorship, however. The Communist leaders needed money to survive, but they would grant no political freedom. In April of 1989, a group of students took over **Tiananmen Square** in the capital of Beijing. They called for reform of corruption and greater political freedom. As a symbol of their movement, they built a thirty-foot replica of the Statue of Liberty. The Communist authorities cracked down. Tanks rolled into Tiananmen Square and routed the students out. Two thousand people died in the putting down of the protest. The heart of Chinese Communism had not changed.

China's Wars

After it fell to Communism, China sought to spread Communism throughout Southeast Asia just as the Soviet Union was doing elsewhere in the world. Noting Churchill's description of a Communist "iron curtain" in Europe, some observers spoke of a "bamboo curtain" between freedom and Communism in Asia. China's first major battleground was Korea.

In 1950 Communist North Korea invaded South Korea, a non-Communist state since 1948. To help South Korea, the United Nations sent troops, most of them American. When it

A brave student stands up to Communist tanks at Tiananmen Square. Just after this picture was taken, he was pulled to safety.

looked as though the UN forces would defeat North Korea, China poured two hundred thousand soldiers into Korea to help the Communist cause. The **Korean War** dragged on until 1953 as the Chinese kept sending in men to help North Korea. Finally, the two sides signed an armistice in which neither side was the winner. North and South Korea have remained separate countries, the North Communist and the South free. China suffered one million casualties in the war.

A Korean mother and her child flee the war as an American tank rumbles by.

The spread of Communism in Asia next shifted south to Indochina and the country of Vietnam, a former French colony. During World War II the Communists had grown strong in northern Vietnam. After the war, the French tried to retake control of Vietnam, but the Communists resisted them. War broke out, and the French were unable to defeat the Communists. In 1954 the French left, and the country of Vietnam was split into North (Communist) and South (free) Vietnam.

Other countries became interested in this **Vietnam War.** The Soviet Union and Communist China continued to support the Vietnamese Communists. Supplies for North Vietnam flowed across China's borders. The United States took up the cause of South Vietnam. In 1964 the U.S. Congress voted to send combat troops to help the South Vietnamese.

The fighting in the jungles of Vietnam was hard and bloody. Like the conflict in Korea, this war dragged on, but for even longer than in Korea. Many Americans began to protest the war. Some wanted peace, no matter what it cost, even if it left the South Vietnamese at the mercy of Communism. Finally in 1973 both sides reached an agreement for American forces to leave. The

French soldiers in Vietnam question a suspected Communist.

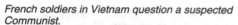

World War II left Japan devastated.

Cities were rebuilt after the destruction of warfare. Factories began to produce peacetime products. Before the war, for example, the Japanese had produced high quality lenses that were used in bombsights and other weapons. After the war, these lenses helped Japan build a profitable industry in manufacturing cameras. Trade with other nations was restored. After World War II China adopted Communism and became a harsh dictatorship. Japan adopted the capitalism of the West and became a prosperous, democratic nation.

Since World War II, Japan's economy has grown. This little island country produces everything from giant oil tanker ships to automobiles to tiny transistor radios and digital watches. Electronics has been a special strength of Japanese industry. The Japanese have produced high quality televisions, computers, stereo equipment, and other electronic items. In fact,

troops withdrew, leaving South Vietnam unsupported. Two years later the Communists attacked and took over all of Vietnam and also the neighboring countries of Laos and Cambodia. The fall of China to Communism in 1949 had led to Communist enslavement throughout Southeast Asia.

Capitalist Japan

When World War II ended in 1945, the United States began to supervise the government of Japan. The Emperor **Hirohito** stunned the nation by going on the radio and announcing that he was not a god and that it was not true "that the Japanese people are superior to other races and fated to rule the world." Japan established a new republican government. The constitution called for a parliament elected by the people and a prime minister to lead the country. It prohibited Japan from rebuilding its army.

A Japanese officer weeps as he hears Emperor Hirohito's surrender address.

Japanese industry, destroyed by the war, rebounded and has made Japan a major industrial power.

Japan has replaced the United States as the major manufacturer for many of these items. Because Japan lacks farmland and natural resources, it imports food and raw materials. In

The Japanese have become world leaders in producing consumer goods, such as electronics.

return, it exports its manufactured goods to other countries.

In addition to being well made, Japanese products often cost less than similar items made in America or Europe. The main reason is that Japanese workers usually make less money than Americans or Western Europeans. Since the labor to make Japanese products costs less, the price is lower. This does not mean, however, that Japanese workers are poorer. They also pay less for the goods they make. Most Japanese are able to buy the basic modern conveniences that Americans enjoy. They live in comfortable apartments and houses, and most families have a car.

Other nations have noted Japan's path to prosperity and have followed. After fleeing to Taiwan, Chiang Kai-shek molded that island's economy on the pattern of the West. Today, the wealth of Taiwan per person is five times greater than that of Communist China. After its destructive war with North Korea, South Korea rebuilt its economy as Japan did. Now South Korea generates twenty times more wealth each year than North Korea does. Singapore, a former British colony in Southeast Asia, also adopted a capitalist economy when it became independent in 1965. Today it has one of the highest rates of income per person in Asia. Not all of these states have been as democratic as Japan, but they do provide more liberty than Communist states. They have realized that Japan, not China, offers the better model for peace and prosperity.

Section Review

1. What was the name of Mao Zedong's plan to reorganize Chinese agriculture and industry? What was the result?

2. What Chinese leader after Mao introduced some capitalist practices to Communist China?

3. What two countries, both the sites of major wars, were split into northern (Communist) and southern (free) parts after World War II?

4. Name at least three products that Japan began to produce in the years after World War II.

5. What other countries in Asia followed Japan's pattern of economic development?

Why would the protesting students in China use the Statue of Liberty as their symbol?

The nation of Singapore symbolizes the western-style prosperity characterizing Asian nations that have embraced capitalist economies.

Nintendo: Power Through Playing

This is the story of a little card manufacturer that became one of the biggest businesses in Japan and then conquered the United States.

In 1889 the Yamauchi (yah mah OO chee) family of Kyoto, Japan, founded Nintendo Koppai as a maker of playing cards for a popular Japanese game called *hanafuda*. The company soon moved to making other kinds of cards and eventually became Japan's leading manufacturer of playing cards.

The name *Nintendo* can be translated, "Work hard, but in the end it is in heaven's hands." The story of Nintendo's success is one of hard work and good fortune. Nintendo was not hit as hard by World War II as other Japanese businesses. Part of the reason was that it was located in Kyoto, one of the few major Japanese cities not to be bombed by the Allies. When Japan's economy began to boom in the 1950s, Nintendo profited as well.

Hiroshi Yamauchi, the president of the company from 1949, realized that for his company to grow, he needed to make more than just playing cards. In 1970 Nintendo began to produce toys and games. Then in 1977 the company produced its first video game. This was the first step in carrying Nintendo to worldwide fame.

Since the Japanese were becoming world leaders in electronics, Nintendo had the idea of using a computer to drive its games. In 1983 the company introduced its first game system: "Famicom." This computer-driven system allowed the Japanese to play electronic games on their televisions.

The idea behind Famicom was to sell the system for a relatively cheap price in order to sell many games. Nintendo made this strategy work by producing popular games. Its first big hit was *Donkey Kong* in 1981. It was sold first as an "arcade game" (one set up in places like shopping malls) and later as a home video game. The creator of the game, Shigeru Miyamoto, intended the unusual name of the game to mean something like "goofy gorilla." At any rate, it was a success. The game also introduced Mario, the short, mustached hero who fought the gorilla. Mario became Nintendo's best-known symbol.

Nintendo decided that it should next launch its home game system in the United States. This would be a challenge. When Nintendo decided to sell its system in the United States in 1985, everyone said it couldn't be done. An American company, called Atari, had launched the video game craze in 1972 and had built a huge business. But poor planning—and dull games—caused Atari to collapse in 1984. Experts said the home video-game industry was dead.

Undaunted, Nintendo invaded the United States. By 1985 American kids and their parents were flocking to stores to buy an NES (Nintendo Entertainment System) and the games to go with it. When Nintendo launched its SNES (Super Nintendo Entertainment System) in 1991, the units sold at the rate of one every five seconds. In 1989 Nintendo released a hand-held video-game system called "Game Boy." It sold forty thousand units the first day it was released. Nintendo's profits soared to well over a half-billion dollars a year, and "Nintendo" became a household word. During the Gulf War against Iraq in 1991, the commanding general noted all the advanced electronic technology his army was using and said that the conflict was "the first Nintendo war."

The Gulf War aside, conflict was no stranger to Nintendo. Parents worried that their children spent too much time playing the games. Others pointed with dismay to the gruesome violence and occult elements in some of the games. Competitors claimed that Nintendo was using its dominant position to pressure stores to carry only Nintendo products. The U.S. government investigated and found at least some of these charges true. Nonetheless, the Nintendo story is a remarkable example of how Japanese industry has become a major force in modern commerce.

Christianity in Asia

Over 250 million people in Asia are considered "Christians." That number sounds impressive, until you realize that also in Asia are over 700 million Hindus, 625 million Muslims, over 300 million Buddhists, and over 150 million atheists. Christians are a minority in Asia, and probably only a minority of those 250 million are genuine Christians. In Asia only the Philippines claims a majority of its people are Christians. Over 80 percent of Filipinos are Roman Catholic, and about 10 percent are Protestant.

There are many different kinds of Christians in Asia. India, for example, is home to the Mar Thoma ("St. Thomas") Church. This group takes its name from the legend that the apostle Thomas was the first to preach the gospel in India. Although it probably does not go back to the days of the apostles, the church's roots go back far into India's history. It is a very small group, however. Roman Catholics are the largest single Christian group, with over 100 million members.

The amount of religious freedom that Christians enjoy varies from country to country. Some countries allow as much religious freedom as the United States does. Others are very repressive. Some nations became less repressive as the twentieth century went on. Before World War II Japan was very strict in its control of religious groups. Today, Japan has perhaps the greatest religious freedom in Asia.

An Armenian church built in the tenth century typifies the many "eastern churches" (neither Roman Catholic nor Orthodox) that spread eastward across Asia during Europe's Middle Ages.

Ni To-sheng, known in the West as Watchman Nee

Some countries have become more repressive. For example, China allowed great freedom of religion after the 1911 revolution. The Communists, however, wanted an atheistic nation and cracked down on not only Christians but also other religious groups. The difference between China before and after the Communist revolution is seen in the career of **Ni To-sheng,** better known in the West as Watchman Nee. He was an important Christian leader during the rule of Chiang Kai-shek. Ni planted independent churches across the land and wrote popular devotional books that sold well in the West as well as in Asia. In 1952, after the Communist takeover, the government arrested Ni. He spent the rest of his life in prison and died in a prison work camp in 1972.

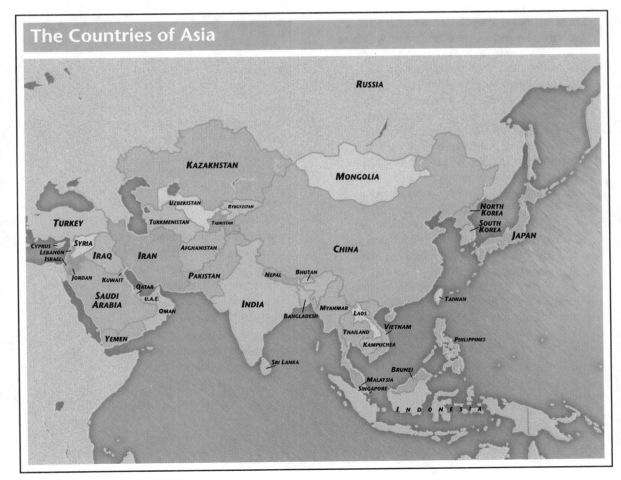

The Countries of Asia

CHARACTERIZATIONS

John Sung

Sung Shang-chieh was born in 1901 into the family of a Methodist pastor in Fukien Province in China. As a child, he claimed conversion during a revival that swept the region in which he lived. When he was eighteen, however, Sung went to the United States to study and underwent a terrible spiritual struggle.

Sung worked himself to the point of exhaustion and made a brilliant record in college. Incredibly, he finished a Ph.D. in chemistry in less than two years. But he was spiritually troubled. Sometimes Sung wondered if he were even a Christian. "The heavy burden of my soul became heavier day by day," he said, "until . . . I got to the point when I no longer had any desire to live." In the midst of this inner battle, God gave him assurance of his salvation and a conviction that he was to return to China and preach. After this, Sung took the name "John" after John the Baptist. Like John, Sung would proclaim, "Behold the Lamb of God, which taketh away the sin of the world" (John 1:29). Also like John, he would say of Christ, "He must increase, but I must decrease" (John 3:30).

Back in China, **John Sung** began an extraordinary preaching career. He preached first in his home region, then in other regions of China. A real turning point came when he preached in Nanchang in 1931. Before that meeting, Sung prayed earnestly for revival, and he saw a great awakening. At Nanchang he caught a vision for all of China, and it marked the beginning of his major evangelistic work.

Sung was a fiery, fervent preacher. An atheist once came "just to see that madman Sung jumping around the platform"; but when he heard the message, he was converted. Sung often preached for two hours at a time with breaks for the audience to sing gospel choruses. He fiercely denounced

Not even crutches could keep John Sung from preaching the gospel.

sin, especially the hypocrisy of professing Christians. His central theme was always forgiveness of sin through the cross of Jesus Christ and the shedding of His blood.

To catch people's attention and drive home his point, Sung used object lessons. A missionary once decorated the platform with plants. Seeing this, Sung preached on uprooting sin in the life and uprooted all the plants one by one as he dealt with each sin. Another time he took off his outer robe as he preached and stuffed it into his shirt to represent hidden sin. Then as he talked about confessing and forsaking sin, he slowly pulled the robe out.

Preaching in China in the 1930s, Sung could not help being affected by political events. He was preaching in Manchuria in 1931 when the

Japanese invaded. In fact, he preached with great effect in the city of Mukden just before the Japanese captured it. Although the Japanese allowed him to preach in areas they controlled, they would not let him go to the interior of China, which was under Nationalist control.

As the 1930s went on, Sung's crowds got bigger. Audiences numbering in the thousands crowded into auditoriums and stadiums. If nothing big enough was available, the people met in vacant lots and sat on mats to hear him. We do not know how many people found salvation in Jesus Christ through John Sung's preaching. One Christian who knew Sung studied his evangelistic campaigns from just 1933 to 1936 and estimated that one hundred thousand people professed conversion.

Because many Chinese had immigrated to Southeast Asia and the South Pacific, Sung eventually had an international impact. He made preaching tours among the 15 million Chinese living in the Philippines, Formosa (Taiwan), Thailand, Singapore, the Malay peninsula, the Dutch East Indies (modern Indonesia), Indochina, and Burma. The effects of the revivals in China, Thailand, and the Dutch East Indies helped sustain the churches through the harsh Japanese occupation of World War II.

John Sung's health was always weak. He suffered from tuberculosis and a heart condition. Finally, he developed cancer and underwent surgery late in 1940, the first of four operations. He never recovered his strength and died on August 18, 1944.

Once a liberal missionary suggested to Sung that the Chinese church could profit by the teachings of Hindu leader Mohandas Gandhi and liberal preacher Harry Emerson Fosdick. Sung replied, "China does not need the teaching of Fosdick or Gandhi. The teaching of Confucius is far better than theirs. What the Chinese need is Jesus Christ and His Cross."

Christians in a church in Singapore led by a convert from one of John Sung's campaigns are but a small part of the fruit of Sung's work in southeast Asia.

Christians meet in house churches in Communist China.

missionaries planted thriving churches in northern Korea. A remarkable revival broke out in 1907, called by one leader the "Korean Pentecost" after the revival on the Day of Pentecost in Acts 2. But suffering followed revival. The Japanese ruled Korea from 1910 to 1945. In the worst incident of persecution, the Japanese set fire to a church and shot those who fled. Usually the Japanese simply arrested those who refused to worship at the official Shinto shrines. Many Christians died from abuse in prison. When the Communists took over North Korea after World War II, they sought to eliminate Christianity. Today South Korea has religious freedom and a large Christian population. Communist North Korea, once the site of a tremendous revival, apparently has almost no Christians.

A more recent example of repression is the treatment of **house churches** in China. Believers began meeting in private homes and formed their own congregations. The Chinese government, however, required all churches to register and considered these house churches illegal. Often Chinese officials raided house churches and arrested leaders. Some of these Christians were tortured and killed. The body of one leader was found with rope burns around his ankles that showed he had been hung in the air and beaten. One Australian evangelist arrested by the police in China said that he was told, "Too many people believe in Jesus today in China."

Korea is another example of a nation in which believers have faced persecution. In the early 1900s American Presbyterian

As these incidents illustrate, God has used many different believers to spread His truth in Asia. From national Christians such as Ni To-sheng in China to the American missionaries in Korea, the heralds of the gospel came from different backgrounds. Today there are

many Christians in Asia, but there are many, many more people who need to hear the gospel of Jesus Christ. Christians around the world should pray for Asia, give to further the gospel there, and consider going themselves as missionaries. As Jesus said, "The harvest truly is great, but the labourers are few: pray ye therefore the Lord of the harvest, that he would send forth labourers into his harvest." (Luke 10:2)

Section Review

1. What is the only nation in Asia that claims a majority of its citizens are Christians?

2. According to legend, who was the first person to preach the gospel in India?

3. What is the largest Christian group in Asia?

4. By what name is Ni To-sheng better known in the West?

Why would Christians call a revival like the one in Korea in 1907 a "Pentecost"? (See Acts 2.)

Summary

Like all continents, Asia has seen triumphs and tragedies. The nation of India rejoiced in winning its independence from Great Britain in 1947. Yet the new nation suffered from poverty and violence. China established a republic in 1911. But the nation suffered from terrible civil wars until 1949 when the Communists imposed their tyranny on the land. Not satisfied with that conquest, the Communists attempted to make all of Korea Communist and succeeded in moving into Southeast Asia. Japan embraced the technology of the West and modernized their country. Then the Japanese used that technology to launch wars of conquest that ended only with the near destruction of the nation in World War II. At least in the case of Japan and a few other nations such as South Korea, the last half of the twentieth century saw a growth of democratic government and economic prosperity. Perhaps the greatest triumph for Asia was the success of both Asians and missionaries in spreading across the continent the good news of salvation through Christ.

CHAPTER REVIEW

People, Places, and Things to Know

Sun Yat-sen
Three Principles of the People
Kuomintang
warlords
Chiang Kai-shek
Mao Zedong

Long March
Mohandas Gandhi
civil disobedience
"westernizing"
Manchuria
Pearl Harbor
Battle of Midway Island

People's Republic of China
Nationalist China
Great Leap Forward
Deng Xiaoping
Tiananmen Square

Korean War
Vietnam War
Hirohito
Ni To-sheng
John Sung
house churches

Review Questions

Matching

Match the following terms to their definitions.

1. Kuomintang
2. westernizing
3. bamboo curtain
4. shogun
5. civil disobedience

(a) Becoming like the United States and Europe
(b) Disobeying laws that one thinks are unjust
(c) Nationalist Party in China
(d) "Great general"
(e) Imaginary line between free and Communist Asia

Matching

Match the following people to their contributions.

6. Hirohito
7. John Sung
8. Sigeru Miyamoto
9. Deng Xiaoping
10. Mohandas Gandhi
11. Chiang Kai-shek
12. Mao Zedong

(a) Led the drive for Indian independence
(b) Preached the gospel throughout China and across Southeast Asia and the South Pacific
(c) Attempted a Great Leap Forward in Chinese industry and agriculture
(d) Encouraged American companies to invest in Communist China
(e) Told the Japanese people that he was not a god
(f) Established a government on Taiwan
(g) Developed *Donkey Kong*

Chronology

Locate the following events in the chapter and put them in chronological order from the earliest to the latest.

13. South Vietnam falls to Communism.

14. Ni To-sheng is arrested by the government of Communist China.

15. India wins its independence from Great Britain.

16. Nintendo introduces its home game system to the United States.

17. China overthrows the Manchu dynasty.

18. Japan sinks Russia's Baltic fleet.

19. The United States drops atomic bombs on Hiroshima and Nagasaki.

20. Korean War begins.

21. Japan attacks Manchuria.

22. Students protest Communist tyranny in Tiananmen Square in Beijing.

Think About It!

How does the story of Japan in the twentieth century reveal the advantages and the dangers of modernization and westernization?

Canada

The year 1867 was the beginning of modern Canada. The British North America Act, passed in that year (see p. 215), united the different British colonies in North America into the single dominion of Canada in the British Empire. At that time, Canada began to take major steps toward filling out its borders and finally achieving full independence. Such a task was mammoth, for Canada is second only to Russia in the size of its territory.

One challenge Canada faced was uniting diverse cultures. The majority of Canadians are British Protestants. A very large and important minority are the French Catholics centered in Quebec. These two groups have often clashed over the direction Canada should go. Many Canadians, for example, served bravely in World War I and World War II. But the Canadians who supported the war most strongly were of British descent. Those of French descent preferred to stay isolated from what looked to them like two European fights.

Yet Canada's history is not one of conflict alone. Many Canadians have made contributions to both their own land and other nations. Canadian scientists Charles Best and Frederick Banting discovered insulin in 1921. Their work has aided the treatment of diabetes. Canadian author Lucy Maude Montgomery has entertained young people of many lands with her *Anne of Green Gables* and other works. Nationalities other than British and French have also enriched the land—Russian Mennonites, Germans, Ukrainians, Scandinavians, and Eastern Europeans as well as Inuits and Indians. In 1965 Canada symbolized its desire to unite these many peoples when it adopted a new flag displaying one uniquely Canadian symbol—the maple leaf.

The Challenge of the Land

One of the first tasks facing Canada in 1867 was subduing its wild and woolly wilderness. The frozen lands of the north and the undeveloped lands of the west posed both barriers and challenges. Tying the nation together was the great transcontinental railroad,

The maple leaf flag of Canada replaced the British Union Jack in 1965.

completed in 1869. Along the way, though, Indians and Métis (people of mixed Indian and French descent) resisted such settlement and development. They foresaw the destruction of their way of life of hunting and trapping, and they feared the dominance of the English-speaking Canadians. In 1885 the Métis and Indians actually rebelled, but the Canadian government put down the uprising and hanged the leader. The settlement went on. Eventually the western plains became known as one of the world's "breadbaskets," one of the largest wheat-growing regions on the planet.

A different sort of frontier struggle was the Klondike gold rush of the 1890s. In 1896 prospectors discovered gold in Bonanza Creek, near the Klondike River. Soon hordes of gold seekers flocked to the frozen north. The city of Dawson sprouted from nothing into a bustling town of over 20,000 in two years. Getting to Dawson was an adventure in itself. One route was known as the "Dead Horse Trail" for its murderous effect on animals—and it was considered the *good* trail. Food was often scarce in winter, and prospectors sometimes faced near starvation. The food that was available was expensive. The price of flour in Dawson, for instance, rose from six dollars to one hundred dollars a sack. The year 1898 was the peak for individual prospectors. After that, digging for gold was so difficult that big mining companies moved in with heavy equipment to reach the deeply buried gold.

One of the last frontiers of Canada was the Northwest Passage. Since the days of the first explorers, men had sought to sail around the top of North America to reach the Far East. By the 1800s there was no longer much profit to be made in such a trip; there were cheaper ways to the East. But men stubbornly kept trying. One disastrous effort was a British expedition led by Sir John Franklin in the 1840s. His ships became trapped in the ice, and all of the crew perished. The skeletons of some were found at a place discoverers named "Starvation Point." They chose this grim name because the crewmen had resorted to cannibalism. Finally, in a difficult trip lasting from 1903 to 1906, famed arctic explorer Roald Amundsen traveled through Arctic waters from the Atlantic Ocean to the Pacific. In 1969 the oil tanker USS *Manhattan* became the first commercial ship to make the trip.

A more recent battle against nature was the creation of the Saint Lawrence Seaway. The Saint Lawrence River links the Great Lakes with the Atlantic Ocean. However, several stretches of shallow water and rapids near Montreal made the river impossible to navigate there. Early canals built by the Canadians were too small to permit modern cargo ships to pass. Therefore, in 1954 Canada and the United

Pioneers sledding across the frozen Yukon trail in the 1890s

States began to build the Saint Lawrence Seaway. They enlarged the old canals and built new ones to bypass the treacherous water. When it opened in 1959, ocean-going ships were able to travel to the major cities on the Great Lakes. A resulting financial boom in shipping benefited both Canada and the United States.

Prime Ministers

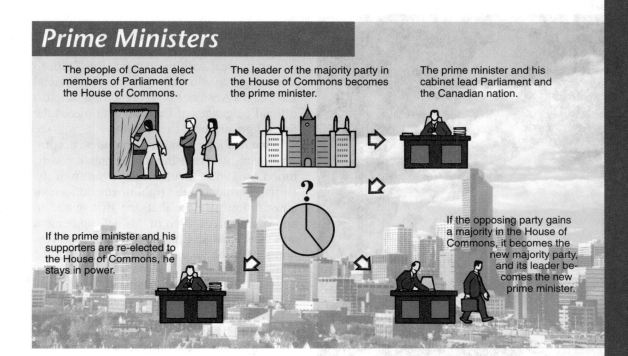

The people of Canada elect members of Parliament for the House of Commons.

The leader of the majority party in the House of Commons becomes the prime minister.

The prime minister and his cabinet lead Parliament and the Canadian nation.

If the prime minister and his supporters are re-elected to the House of Commons, he stays in power.

If the opposing party gains a majority in the House of Commons, it becomes the new majority party, and its leader becomes the new prime minister.

Canada has a parliamentary government, like that of Great Britain. The political party that wins the most seats in the legislature makes its leader the prime minister (the head of the government). Canada has had many prime ministers, but several have been especially notable.

The first prime minister of Canada was Sir John A. MacDonald, who served 1867-73 and 1878-91. A member of the Conservative Party (later renamed the Progressive Conservative Party), he sought to unify the new Canadian dominion. As prime minister, MacDonald pushed for the expansion of Canada and the settlement of its wilderness regions. Perhaps his greatest achievement was the construction of Canada's transcontinental railway.

Sir Wilfrid Laurier, leader of the Liberal Party, was prime minister for fifteen years (1896-1911). He was a part of Canada's French-speaking Catholic minority, but he sought to unite all Canadians. For example, a heated issue during the election of 1896 was a situation in the province of Manitoba. That province prohibited teaching in the French language in its schools. Neither could the schools offer religious instruction in Catholicism. Once in office, Laurier worked out a compromise so that French-speaking Manitobans could be taught in their own language and religion. The growth of wheat farming in the west and the Klondike gold rush helped make Laurier's term of office one of the most prosperous periods in Canadian history.

One of the most influential prime ministers in Canadian history was also a Liberal, W. L. Mackenzie King, who served a total of more than twenty years (1921-30, 1935-48). King was named for his grandfather, who had led a rebellion against the British in 1837. Like his grandfather, the prime minister promoted the idea of being Canadian instead of

Canadian prime minister Pierre Trudeau with American president Ronald Reagan

British. King helped push for the Statute of Westminster passed by the British Parliament in 1931. This legislation made Canada a completely independent nation within the British Commonwealth. Despite his desire to be independent of Europe, King threw Canada's support on the side of the Allies in World War II.

Perhaps the most important prime minister since World War II was Pierre Trudeau, who served from 1968 to 1979 and from 1980 to 1984. Like Laurier and King, he was a Liberal. A major challenge Trudeau faced was the discontent in French-speaking Quebec. Many French-speaking Canadians argued that they could defend their rights and culture only by taking Quebec out of Canada and making it an independent nation. In 1970 Quebec extremists kidnapped and murdered Pierre Laporte, Quebec's labor minister. Trudeau responded by giving the police and the army special powers to deal with the danger. But Trudeau also sought to win over Quebec. The Official Languages Act made both French and English official languages of Canada and ordered the federal government to use both.

One of Pierre Trudeau's proudest accomplishments was revising the Canadian constitution. In 1982 Canada finally won from the British Parliament the right to amend its own constitution. (Before that, the British had to approve changes.) Part of this new agreement was the Canadian Charter of Rights and Freedoms, similar to the Bill of Rights in the United States. Now the only tie remaining between Canada and Britain is that Canada recognizes the monarch of Great Britain as its official head of state.

In 1984 the Progressive Conservatives took power by winning the biggest electoral victory in Canadian history, 211 out of 282 seats in the Canadian legislature. Their leader, Brian Mulroney, became prime minister. Mulroney successfully promoted trade and cooperation with Canada's huge neighbor to the south, the United States. He failed, however, in calming Quebec. Mulroney offered a revision to the Canadian constitution that recognized Quebec as a "distinct society" with special privileges within Canada. The plan failed, though, when other provinces of Canada opposed it. They feared that the change would not protect the individual rights of English-speaking Canadians within Quebec.

Mulroney resigned in 1993. He was replaced by Kim Campbell, Canada's first female prime minister. But in 1993 the Progressive Conservatives suffered the worst defeat in Canadian history. Dismayed with the economic bad times and the failure of the constitutional reform, voters gave the Conservatives only two seats in the legislature.

Provinces

The Royal Canadian Mounted Police, or "Mounties," are one of the most familiar symbols of Canada.

As the failure of Mulroney's constitutional reform shows, provinces are extremely powerful in Canadian politics. Canada consists of ten provinces and three territories (the Yukon Territory, Nunavut, and the Northwest Territories). The federal government takes care of the three territories; the provinces take care of themselves. The provinces of Canada possess much more power over their own affairs than do the states of the United States.

Canadians group the provinces into several regions. The Maritime Provinces in the east (sometimes called the Atlantic Provinces) are New Brunswick, Nova Scotia, Prince Edward Island, and Newfoundland. The Central Provinces are Quebec and Ontario. The Western Provinces are Alberta, Saskatchewan, Manitoba, and British Columbia. (Sometimes Alberta, Saskatchewan, and Manitoba are referred to as the Plains Provinces.) The government of each province is like that of Canada as a whole. The party that controls the provincial legislature makes its leader the head of the provincial government. The chief executive of each province is known as a premier.

One of the longest serving premiers was E. C. Manning, who served as premier of Alberta from 1943 to 1968. Part of the reason for his popularity was Alberta's prosperity. The discovery of oil spurred an economic boom in the province. Hundreds of millions of dollars flowed into Alberta's treasury from oil leases and sales. Manning was able to reduce the province's debt, cut taxes, and pay dividends to citizens. Manning built roads, schools, and libraries. "When the day comes that our oil runs out," he said, "these benefits will remain."

Manning was also unashamedly a Christian. Although a layman, he often preached and broadcasted a popular religious radio program.

E. C. Manning

"I abhor the word *politician*," the premier said. "I would much rather concentrate on my Bible work." He told one visitor, "People may not agree with my beliefs, but it's amazing how many respect them. . . . I believe that a whole lot of Christians get themselves into trouble by sitting on the fence instead of making their stand clear."

The great independence of the provinces has created the problem of regionalism in Canada. Each province or region (such as the Plains Provinces) can pursue its own interests without regard for other regions. The obvious example is Quebec, where some citizens talk about leaving Canada entirely. But other provinces want to maintain their independence too. Alberta has clashed with the federal government over who controls the province's rich oil resources. Newfoundland is another good example of an independent-minded province. When the Dominion of Canada was formed in the 1800s, that province refused to join. In fact, Newfoundland did not join Canada until 1949, and even then it was by a narrow vote.

Religion

The rich decoration of the Notre Dame Basilica in Montreal illustrates the strong presence of Catholicism in Canada, especially in the province of Quebec.

The Roman Catholic Church is the largest religious group in Canada. The majority of Catholics are from the French-speaking minority, but there are many English-speaking Catholics too. Canada's British heritage has also had an influence on the nation's religion. About a tenth of the Canadian people belong to the Anglican Church of Canada, a descendant of the established church of Great Britain.

The second largest church in the nation is the United Church of Canada. This group formed in 1925 when Canadian Methodists, Presbyterians, and Congregationalists merged. To unite these different groups, the new church had to downplay doctrine. Therefore the United Church of Canada has tended to be liberal in its theology. A sizable minority of Presbyterians opposed the merger. They wanted to preserve their doctrine and heritage, so they stayed out of the merger and formed the Presbyterian Church in Canada.

Many evangelical Christian leaders have come from Canada. A. B. Simpson was born in Canada, where he was converted and then ordained to the ministry. He pastored churches in the United States until he formed the Christian and Missionary Alliance in 1887. This group organized churches in the United States and Canada and planted missionary churches around the world. Jonathan and Rosalind Goforth were Canadian missionaries to China who not only proclaimed the gospel in that land but also inspired others to missionary service. T. T. Shields of the Jarvis Street Baptist Church in Toronto was a leading Baptist Fundamentalist. Shields attacked growing religious liberalism in both Canada and the United States. These are but a few of the Canadian Christians who found opportunity to serve Christ at home and abroad.

Conclusion

A five-thousand-mile-long border separates Canada from the United States. Unlike national borders in many parts of the world, Canada and the United States have a large, unfortified border. Citizens of both countries may easily cross to the other side. Canada and the United States are alike in desiring peace and cooperation. Like members of the same family, these two nations share a common heritage, but Canada remains unique, "The True North, Strong and Free."

Cars line up to cross the border between Canada and the United States, symbolizing the peaceful and friendly relations that these two nations enjoy.

CHAPTER 18

The history of the Middle East in the twentieth century begins at Armageddon.

Most Christians recognize "Armageddon" as the site of the final battle between God and the forces of rebellious mankind (Rev. 16:16). But the site of Armageddon is probably a location in Palestine known as Megiddo. Some two hundred battles have taken place in that region since the days of the pharaohs and ancient Israel. (See Judg. 5:19.) In September of 1918 another fateful battle took place at Megiddo.

World War I did not just pit Germany against France and Great Britain. The Turkish Ottoman Empire sided with the Central Powers. Across the Middle East the Turks clashed with the British and Britain's Arab allies. The victorious Allies captured the ancient cities of the East: Baghdad, Mecca, and Jerusalem. General Edmund Allenby's British-Arab forces in Palestine launched the final blow on the Turks on September 18, 1918. Allied infantry cracked the Turkish front on the Mediterranean coast. Allied cavalry then swept up the Plain of Sharon, crossed behind enemy lines to Megiddo, and cut the Turks off. Shattered by the speed and strength of the blow, the Turkish forces collapsed and retreated. In less than a month, all Turkish resistance in the region was gone.

The Allied victory at Megiddo did not just end the campaign in Palestine. It also sealed the doom of the Ottoman Empire. Four hundred years of Turkish rule had ended. A new era had begun in the Middle East.

A.D. 1910 - PRESENT

World War I
1914-18

Ke▶

1910   1920

Realignment in the Middle East

ibn-Saud 1932-53

Suez War 1956

Six-Day War 1967

Yom Kippur War 1973

Gulf War 1991

1940   1950   1960   1970   1980   1990

Mohammed Reza Shah Pahlavi 1941-79

Iran-Iraq War 1980-88

Independence of Israel 1948

OPEC Founded 1960

The Rise of Turkey

Just how much did the Middle East change after World War I? To answer that question, we need only to look at **Anatolia** (Asia Minor). Before the war, the Anatolian Peninsula was the center of the decaying Ottoman Empire. After the war, it was the heart of the aggressively modern state of Turkey.

Collapse of the Ottoman Empire

Around 1300 the Ottoman Turks stormed out of a corner of northwestern Anatolia and began an incredible wave of conquest. The Ottomans swept east to Persia and south to Arabia. They subdued North Africa, all of Asia Minor, and eventually conquered the Byzantine Empire of the Greeks. By the 1500s the Ottoman Empire stretched all across the Middle East from Asia to Africa and into Europe.

But by the beginning of the twentieth century, the Ottoman Empire was tottering. Its government was corrupt, and its domains were restless under Ottoman rule. Some regions, such as the Balkans and Egypt, threw off Ottoman control. The Ottoman Empire became known as "the sick man of Europe." The leading nations of Europe looked greedily toward seizing Ottoman territory. Fortunately for the Turks, the European nations distrusted each other. They feared that if the Ottoman Empire fell apart, one nation, such as Russia,

Middle East Before WWI

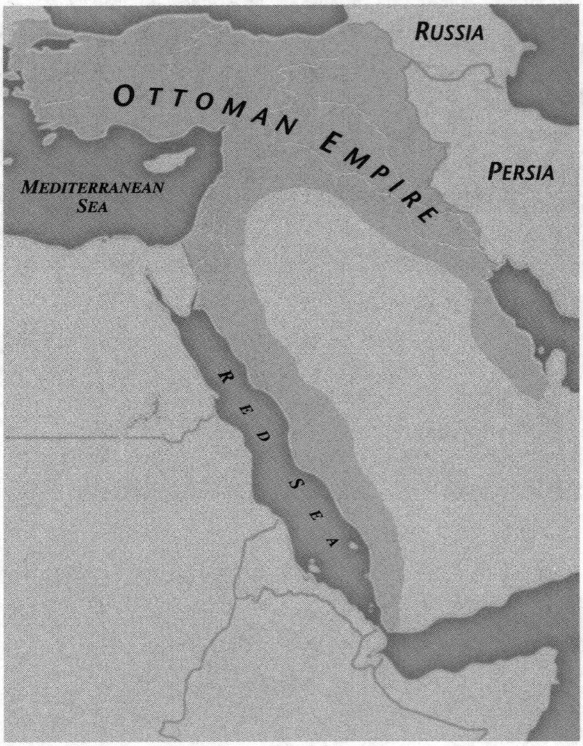

Middle East After WWI

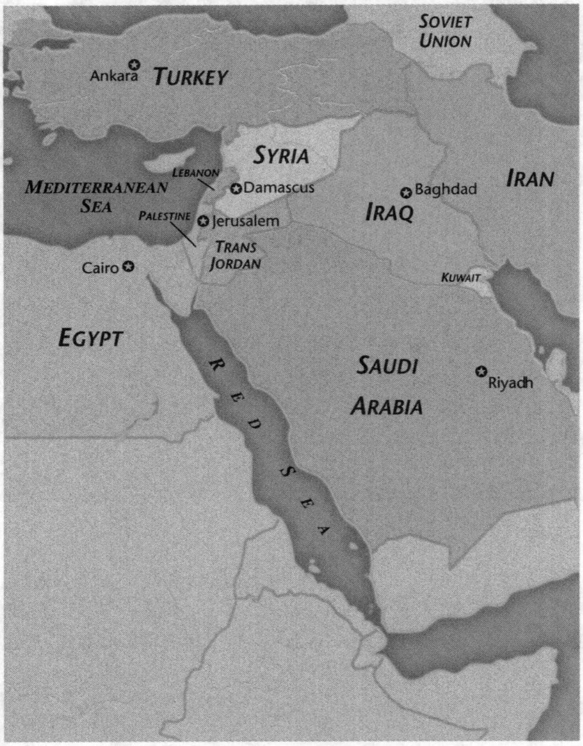

The mayor of Jerusalem prepares to surrender his city to the British during World War I as British, Arab, and Turkish troops look on.

World War I. At the end of the war, he opposed the peace settlement because he foresaw the destruction of the Turkish nation. The sultan (ruler) of the Ottoman Empire, however, was willing to go along with the Allies to try to save his throne. Mustafa Kemal began plotting to overthrow the sultan in order to save the nation. Because of riots in Asia Minor, the government gave Mustafa Kemal command of all soldiers in the interior along with broad powers to halt the violence. This was the chance he had been waiting for.

The Turkish leader launched a campaign to overthrow the sultan and halt Allied attempts to break up the Turkish homeland. His battle cry was "Independence or Death." He set up his capital in Ankara instead of Constantinople, and the Turkish people rallied to him. His main obstacle was Greece. The Allies had given Greece a section of Asia Minor surrounding the coastal

might snatch the pieces and become too powerful. Therefore, Europe helped prop up the empire.

Then World War I broke out. Since the Russians had been mortal enemies of the Turks for centuries, the Ottoman Empire sided with Germany. The decision proved disastrous. When the Allies defeated the Central Powers, the Ottoman Empire lay helpless before the Allied armies. Arabia, Palestine, and other territories were permanently lost. Even the Turkish homeland in Asia Minor was to be divided among the victorious Allies. The Ottoman Empire was destroyed; it appeared that Turkish rule in Anatolia would soon follow.

"Father of the Turks"

The Turkish homeland was saved through the efforts of **Mustafa Kemal** (moos-TAH-fuh kuh-MAHL). An officer in the Turkish army, Mustafa Kemal had been a hero during

Mustafa Kemal, later known as Kemal Atatürk

Many Muslim Turkish women still wear traditional head coverings and veils during their daily activities.

city of Smyrna, which had a large Greek population. When Mustafa Kemal began his uprising, the Allies relied on Greece to put him down. But the Turkish commander rallied his forces and defeated the Greek army. In 1922 Mustafa Kemal's forces captured Smyrna and drove the Greeks entirely out of Asia Minor.

Mustafa Kemal then proceeded to reorganize the state. He abolished the office of sultan, established a legislature, and became the nation's president. He introduced sweeping changes. The new nation became known as **Turkey.** Other names changed too: Constantinople became Istanbul, and Smyrna became Izmir. The legislature gave its ruler a new name as well—**Kemal Atatürk,** "father of the Turks."

Atatürk forced the Allies to recognize his new nation. He gave up all claim to non-Turkish Ottoman possessions such as Palestine and Arabia. He wanted his state to be *Turkish,* not *Muslim* as the Ottoman Empire had been. In other words, Turkey was to be a secular state. It would not be ruled by religious law with religious leaders holding power. All religions would supposedly be equal, and the government would be religiously neutral.

Atatürk had other changes in mind. He wanted to model Turkey after the powerful Western nations of Europe and North America. He began dressing in Western-style suits. He banned the **fez,** the traditional headgear of Turkish Muslims. The ban of the fez was one example of how he sought to build a secular state. Islamic law says that a man must not wear a hat which keeps him from touching the ground with his forehead as he prays. Atatürk, however, wore billed hats and made laws to force all other men to do so too.

Atatürk also raised the status of women. He did away with the Muslim requirement that a woman always wear a veil in public. He gave women the vote and allowed them to hold office. Dismayed that less than 20 percent of the people knew how to read and write, he reformed Turkish education. He closed the Muslim schools and opened secular ones in their places. He reformed the alphabet, changing from a complex Arabic script to a simpler Western Latin alphabet.

The Atatürk dam on the Tigris River symbolizes the modernization that Kemal Atatürk sought to bring to Turkey.

Although he was not a tyrant like Hitler, Atatürk was a dictator. He used his authority to force these changes on sometimes unwilling citizens. He had enemies tried and executed. But he tried to move his country toward peaceful development. "The arm that wields the sword tires," he said, "but the arm that guides the plow grows stronger every day." He also hoped to move Turkey toward a more democratic government, but he was unable to accomplish this goal in his lifetime.

Atatürk died in 1938, leaving behind a nation that bore little resemblance to the creaky empire from which it had emerged. Even in death, Atatürk pushed his westernization policies. He left orders that at his funeral there was to be no traditional Turkish music. He was laid to rest to the music of Frédéric Chopin.

Section Review

1. What place in Palestine is probably the site of the Battle of Armageddon?
2. The modern-day country of Turkey is located on what peninsula?
3. Which empire joined with the Central Powers and was destroyed at the end of World War I?
4. The old city of Constantinople was renamed by Mustafa Kemal. What was its new name?

5. List at least three other changes that resulted from Kemal Atatürk's leadership of Turkish government.

Consider Atatürk's statement "The arm that wields the sword tires, but the arm that guides the plow grows stronger every day." What does this mean? Do you agree with the statement? Why or why not?

The Armenian Massacres

"Who still speaks today of the extermination of the Armenians?" asked Adolf Hitler. The Nazi dictator expected to get away with his deeds because, after all, no one seemed to remember the Turkish massacres of the Armenians. Hitler was mistaken in thinking he would escape, but, truly, few people recall what the Turks did to the Armenians.

The Armenians lived in a region in eastern Anatolia in the Caucasus Mountains. Mount

Homeless Armenian refugees, the result of the Turkish massacres of the Armenian people

Ararat, where Noah and the ark landed, is located there. Most of the Armenians came under control of the Ottoman Empire in the 1400s. When the empire began to decay in the 1800s, the Turks started to view the Armenians as a threat. The Armenians were Christian, whereas the Turks were Muslim. Also, many Armenians lived in nearby Russia. The Russians hoped to use the Armenians in the Ottoman Empire as a lever to pry more territory away from the Turks. When the Armenian people began asking for more self-rule, the Turks responded violently. Over one hundred thousand Armenians died in the first round of killing in the 1890s. Another round of repression in 1909 saw the deaths of over thirty thousand more. But this was nothing compared to what happened during World War I.

When the war broke out, some Turkish leaders feared the Armenians might side with the enemy. Others saw an opportunity to settle "the Armenian question"—permanently. At first, there was the harassment, torture (such as nailing horseshoes to the feet of victims and making them dance), and killing of individuals. Then the Turks began rounding up and imprisoning or killing the Armenian leadership in Constantinople. Armenian soldiers in the Ottoman army were moved to "labor units." The Turks used these soldiers much as Hitler would later use slave labor in the Third Reich; members of the labor units did backbreaking jobs until they died of exhaustion. Other Armenian soldiers were simply gunned down.

Then in 1915, the real horror came. A high Turkish official wrote to one of his subordinates that "the Government has decided to exterminate entirely all the

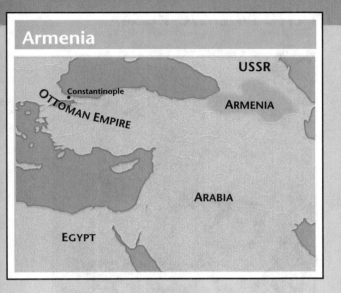

Armenia

USSR

Constantinople

OTTOMAN EMPIRE

ARMENIA

ARABIA

EGYPT

Mount Ararat, in the heart of the traditional Armenian homeland

Armenians living in Turkey. . . . Without pity for women, children and invalids, . . . their existence must be terminated."

Soldiers killed Armenians freely. They shot them, bayoneted them, burned them to death in their houses. Then the Turks decided to march them two to three hundred miles to Syria and Palestine, where they would not be a "threat." In the heat of the blistering summer of 1915, the Armenians began their death march. Guards killed some on the march in order to steal their goods. Many others died of heat, exhaustion, hunger, abuse, and disease. One group that started with 18,000 finished with only 150 surviving. Those who made it to the camps were often no better off. One Turkish official kept five hundred Armenians in an outdoor pen in the summer heat without food and water until they went insane.

The U.S. ambassador complained strongly to the Turks that innocent women and children were suffering. Surely, he argued, they posed no threat. A Turkish official replied, "Those who are innocent today might be guilty tomorrow." The killing went on.

After the war, a famine killed even more Armenians. Mustafa Kemal did not continue the policy of wiping out the Armenians. But his forces did kill many Armenians in the battles against Greece and his struggle to unite the country under his rule.

Estimates vary, but apparently 1.5 million Armenians died between 1915 and 1923. Another half-million were forced to live in exile. Not more than one hundred thousand Armenians remain in Turkey today. Most Armenians are either in the Republic of Armenia in the former Soviet Union or have moved to countries such as the United States. The nation of Turkey denies that the slaughter ever took place.

"Who still speaks today of the extermination of the Armenians?" said Hitler. The world has not forgotten Hitler's slaughter of the Jews, but, sadly, it seems to have forgotten the suffering of the Armenians.

Progress and Tradition in the Middle East

Turkey was not the only nation to emerge from the wreckage of the Ottoman Empire. Eventually, Syria, Lebanon, Iraq, and other countries became independent states in the Middle East. These nations, although similar in background, followed many paths of development. These different paths are illustrated by the history of two important Middle Eastern countries: Iran and Saudi Arabia.

Iran: Embracing Progress

When World War I began, there was only one other major independent power in the Middle East besides the Ottoman Empire: the ancient kingdom of Persia. After World War I, Persia's leaders imitated Kemal Atatürk in trying to build a modern, Western state.

In 1921 a cavalry officer, Reza Khan, toppled the government. He took power and in 1925 became ruler as **Reza Shah Pahlavi** (pah LAHV ee). (The word *shah* is Persian for "king.") He decided to modernize his country as Atatürk had done. Muslim custom required women to cover themselves completely except for the face or just the eyes. The shah did away with these restrictions on women's dress; in fact, the shah made it a law that women had to dress in Western styles. He expanded the nation's roads and railroads. He founded the University of Teheran to promote education. The shah even changed the name of the country. He stopped using the European *Persia* and began to use the native name, *Iran.*

However, the shah ruled by force. Crossing his will could be dangerous. Once he took an official who displeased him and literally threw him out a window. Iranians quickly learned to obey. Once at an exhibition, the shah sampled a glass of beer and said, "This beer is not bad." A government official stand-

Mohammed Reza Shah Pahlavi

ing nearby quickly agreed. The shah looked at him and said, "You don't drink. How do you know it's good?" The official replied, "Your Majesty, I am not the servant of the beer, I am Your Majesty's servant. If you say it is good, then I too say it is good; if you deny it, I too shall deny it."

The shah fell from power by making the same mistake the Ottoman Empire had made in World War I. He threw Iran's support to Germany in World War II because he feared the Soviet Union. As a result, the British, Americans, and Soviets virtually occupied his country to keep it from helping the Axis Powers. The shah resigned, and in 1941 his son **Mohammed Reza Shah Pahlavi** became the new shah of Iran.

The new shah followed his father's path. Because the shah staunchly opposed the Communist Soviet Union to his north, Western powers such as the United States supported him. The United States sold him millions of dollars worth of military equipment and modern technology. But the shah, like his father, ruled through terror. Relying on his secret police, the shah used torture, exile, and execution to keep his opponents in line.

Although himself a Muslim, the shah offended devout followers of Islam. Like his father, he reduced the political power of Muslim clergy. The shah shifted responsibility for education from the clergy to the state. He allowed women to divorce their husbands in violation of Islamic law. The shah even changed the Iranian calendar. Muslims number the years from the time of the prophet Muhammad. The shah, wanting to stress Persia's ancient glories, changed the basis to Cyrus the Great's founding of the Persian Empire. Thus the year 1975 (according to the Western calendar, based on the birth of Christ) became 2535 instead of the Islamic 1355.

The shah's most serious effort to transform Iran was a series of reforms he called the **"White Revolution"** in the 1960s and the 1970s. Some of the reforms he proposed were good, such as giving women the vote and improving education. Much of his reform involved difficult and expensive development of agriculture and industry. He built highways, railroads, and dams. He expanded the mining of Iran's natural resources, built new factories, and planned to construct nuclear reactors. The billions of dollars needed to finance this revolution came from Iran's enormous profits from selling oil.

But there was a harsh side to the White Revolution. The shah tried Stalin's plan to collectivize agriculture. (See p. 454.) He established huge government-run farms on which the peasants worked. In the interest of efficiency, the shah ordered over sixty thousand small rural villages combined into thirty thousand larger villages. Bulldozers leveled villages as the government forced villagers into the new settlements. In doing so, the shah shattered local ties and stirred resentment.

The shah's palace displays the luxury that caused resentment among his subjects.

Iranian revolutionaries man a bunker in front of Iran's parliament building, awaiting an attack by the shah's forces.

The shah managed to offend everyone. His outrageous spending created inflation, and the middle class turned against him as prices soared. The rural villagers resented the destruction and relocation of villages. The strict Muslims hated his casual attitude toward the teachings of Islam. The upper class had never liked either him or his father because of their "lower-class" origins. Only the army and the secret police kept him in power.

In 1978 riots broke out in protest of the shah's rule. In the violence perhaps as many as ten thousand people died. With no base of support, the shah could not reestablish order. Finally, he fled Iran in 1979, and a group of strict Muslims under the leadership of the Ayatollah Khomeini established an Islamic state. (See p. 539.) Ironically, a nation that had sought to become modern was now trying to lead the Middle East back toward tradition.

Saudi Arabia: Embracing Tradition

While Iran was trying to follow the model of Turkey and become a modern, Western nation, another major Middle Eastern nation dedicated itself to preserving tradition. The nation of Saudi Arabia was solidly traditional, even backward, in its outlook. Yet, unexpectedly, it became one of the richest, most powerful nations in the Middle East.

At the beginning of World War I, the Arabian Peninsula was divided. The Ottoman Empire controlled the northern and western sections. Several smaller Arab kingdoms existed along the seacoast and in the interior. A few regions were under European control, such as British-controlled Aden in the south. Many of the Arabian people, however, felt loyalty only to their local tribes. These were **Bedouins,** herders of sheep and goats who lived in tents and wandered from oasis to oasis to graze their flocks.

With a picture of Khomeini pinned to her dress, a child poses with a toy gun in front of the American embassy in Iran.

King Faud of Saudi Arabia (above) and a platform in the Persian Gulf for loading oil tankers (right)

Among the smaller kingdoms was the kingdom of the Nejd ("highland") in eastern Arabia, ruled by **Abdul Aziz ibn-Saud** (SAH ood). He was the descendant of a family that had fought the Ottoman Turks for over a hundred years. The Saud family were followers of the **Wahhabi** (wah HAHB ee) **movement.** This was a very strict form of Islam that arose in Arabia in the 1700s. The Wahhabis wanted to cleanse Islam of all forms of paganism and rule entirely by the Koran. They condemned dancing, music, and smoking. Part of their faith is that a Wahhabi may not leave someone alone who believes differently; the Wahhabi must make others believe as he does.

Born around 1880, ibn-Saud spent part of his childhood in exile with his family. Then in 1902 he and a band of forty handpicked men captured Riyadh, the capital of the Nejd. Slowly, he expanded his power. He first brought all of the Nejd under his control. During World War I, he captured territories controlled by the

Ottoman Empire. After the war, in 1924, he captured Mecca, Islam's holy city. Finally, in 1932 he established the independent kingdom of **Saudi Arabia.** Ibn-Saud's rule was based on power. "Draw a sword in their face," he said of those he ruled, "and they will obey."

The new kingdom covered about three-fourths of the Arabian Peninsula, but its power did not lie in its physical size. In the eastern sections, near the Persian Gulf, oil was discovered in 1938. After World War II, nations needed oil to run their industries, fuel their automobiles, and warm their homes. Saudi Arabia's oil reserves became an enormous source of wealth. Saudi Arabia was earning $4 billion a year from its oil sales in 1973. That figure skyrocketed to over $100 billion by 1981. Although profits dropped after that year, the nation still enjoyed enormous wealth. During this financial boom, bankers sometimes opened their doors each morning to people lined up

Under Arabia's barren sands lies untold wealth in petroleum deposits.

without connection to the Saud family rightly saw this as unfair.

Saudi Arabia was a repressive state. A Saudi prince admitted in 1961, "In our country there is no law that upholds the freedom and rights of the citizen." Slavery was not abolished until 1962. The government held public beheadings for crimes such as murder and drug dealing. For a more minor crime such as stealing, authorities cut off the hand of a thief. Women chafed under the highly restrictive Islamic law. In 1990 forty-seven women drove cars into Riyadh to protest the Islamic prohibition that women not drive. The result was a near-riot. Devout Muslims held protest marches, and the government fired many of the women from their jobs for their act.

Yet there is an irony in Saudi Arabia's history. The Sauds followed one of the strictest forms of Islam. But the great wealth brought in by oil has also brought in corrupting influences. Drug abuse, for example, has become a terrible problem. A new group, called Islamic Awakening, arose to oppose the Sauds and call for a return to a purer form of Islam. The Sauds, who had sought to purify both Islam and Arabia, had become symbols of corruption in a nation increasingly marked by corruption.

waiting to deposit suitcases and garbage bags full of money.

None was more wealthy than the ruling Saud family. The family controlled the government and reaped its wealth. Because the family was so large, not all of the Sauds could be rulers. Some members of the family went into private business. Even then, the government made sure that the best business contracts went to family members. Businessmen

Section Review

1. Give the modern name of Persia.
2. List at least three reforms of the "White Revolution."
3. How did the Ayatollah Khomeini rise to power in Iran?
4. Which one of the countries of Iran or Saudi Arabia tried to be aggressively modern? traditional?
5. What are Bedouins?

6. Describe the Wahhabi movement.
7. Describe law and punishment in Saudi Arabia.

People have clashed violently over both traditions and modernization in the Middle East as well as many other places in the world. What might make one of these more desirable than the other? What are the pros and cons of each? How would you balance them?

The Rise of Israel

Among the Arab and Muslim nations of the Middle East, the Jewish nation of Israel stands out in bold contrast. Its Jewish character and its democratic form of government make Israel distinct. The unusual nature of Israel is the result of its unique heritage.

Zionism and the Founding of Israel

The beginnings of the Israeli state lie in a movement known as **Zionism.** (Zion is one of the hills on which Jerusalem is built. The word *Zion* is often used to refer to Jerusalem or to the whole Jewish nation.) **Theodor Herzl,** a German Jew, had originally dreamed of seeing the Jewish people blended into European culture. But he witnessed cruel examples in "civilized" Europe of unreasoning hatred of the Jews. The last straw for Herzl was France's

Theodor Herzl

court-martial of a Jewish army officer on false charges. Some French newspapers and politicians used this incident as an excuse to denounce all Jews. Herzl decided that the answer was for Jews to have their own nation. He launched an international movement to form a homeland for the Jews. This desire for the formation of a Jewish homeland became known as "Zionism."

Originally, Herzl did not care where the Jews established their homeland. He even considered British offers of land in East Africa. But most of the Jews who embraced Zionism would accept no other site than Palestine, the Promised Land of Jewish history. Herzl himself finally concluded, "Palestine is the only land where our people can come to rest." Around the world, Jewish interest in the Zionist cause grew tremendously.

Until World War I, the Turks controlled Palestine and allowed only a few Jews to settle there. After the war, Great Britain controlled the region. During the war, Britain had tried to win Jewish support by issuing the **Balfour Declaration.** In this document, the British promised to support the formation of a Jewish homeland in Palestine. But it was not to be that easy. The Arabs who lived in Palestine did not want their land made into a Jewish homeland. The British wavered, wanting to please the Arabs. When Jews tried to enter Palestine, the British sent them back.

The Zionists did not give up. The Nazi Holocaust swayed world sympathy to the Jews. Zionist groups in Palestine began working toward a Jewish state. Unfortunately, some of the Jewish independence groups used violence. In what was perhaps the worst incident, Jewish terrorists blew up the King David Hotel in Jerusalem in 1946. Ninety-one people died, including seventeen Jews. Fighting continued among Jews, Arabs, and British soldiers.

The British finally handed the whole Palestine question over to the United Nations. The UN in turn divided Palestine into Arab and Jewish sections. The Arabs refused to accept this decision; they wanted all of Palestine to be an independent Arab nation. The Israelis declared the independence of their section on May 14, 1948. The Arabs went to war, but the Jewish forces won a hard-fought victory. The modern state of Israel was born.

The Arab-Israeli Wars

The fortified hill of Masada has a special place of honor in Jewish history. A towering plateau near the Dead Sea, Masada was the site of fortifications built by Herod the Great. For seven months in A.D. 72-73, an army of Jewish Zealots had held out against a much larger Roman army. When the Romans were on the verge of finally breaking through the walls, nearly the entire garrison—960 men, women, and children—chose to commit suicide rather than surrender. Today the Israeli army brings new recruits to Masada. In the midst of the ruins and memories of Masada, with the Israeli flag snapping in the wind, the recruits vow in the words of the Hebrew poet Lamdan, "Masada shall not fall again!"

The Israeli **War of Independence** in 1948 was only the first of several Arab-Israeli wars that Israel had to fight for its existence. Arab states denied Israel's right to exist. One Arab leader said before the War of Independence, "This will be a war of extermination and a momentous massacre." In that conflict alone, five countries sent troops against Israel: Egypt, Jordan, Syria, Lebanon, and Iraq. Arab sympathy with the Arabs in Palestine and Muslim opposition to the Jewish presence there set the entire Middle East against Israel.

Thanks to support from countries such as the United States, Israel survived. The Israelis built an efficient military force. In 1956 Israel and Egypt fought a brief war in the Sinai Peninsula. There the Israelis dazzled the Egyptian forces with their speed and daring and captured the peninsula in one hundred hours. As part of the settlement after that war, however, Israel withdrew from Sinai.

Even more impressive was Israel's performance in the **Six-Day War** (1967).

Masada, the site of Jewish resistance to the Romans in the first century, symbolizes Israel's determination to endure against the opposition of its enemies.

Moshe Dayan, the Israeli commander who planned the spectacularly successful campaigns in the Sinai Peninsula and the Six-Day War

mined enemies, the Israelis faced the danger of defeat. Knowing they could not fight on two fronts at the same time, the Israelis turned on the Syrians first. They mauled the Syrian forces and drove them back. Then the United States began to pour arms and equipment into Israel. The Israelis fought across the Suez Canal and surrounded and trapped a portion of the Egyptian army. Both sides were exhausted, and the United Nations negotiated a cease-fire.

The **Yom Kippur War** had been a close call. But out of the war came a move for peace. Tired of unprofitable conflict, Anwar el-Sadat, the president of Egypt, astounded the world with an offer of peace between his country and Israel. With the help of the United States, Israel and Egypt made peace. Israel returned the Sinai Peninsula (which it had captured in 1967) to Egypt. Egypt in return ended the state of war and recognized Israel's right to exist. In 1994 Jordan became the second Arab nation to make peace with Israel.

Palestinian Conflict

But peace with Egypt did not solve all of Israel's problems. Other nations in the Middle East, notably Syria, remained deadly enemies of Israel. The greatest challenge facing Israel was the "Palestinian problem." In the 1967 Six-Day War, Israel had taken the **West Bank** (territory on the western side of the Jordan River, including the eastern section of Jerusalem) from Jordanian control and the Gaza Strip (territory along the Mediterranean coast) from Egyptian control. These conquests placed a large number of Arab Palestinians under Israeli rule.

The United Nations, as mentioned earlier, had originally intended to divide Palestine into Jewish and Arab sections. The Jewish state of Israel was obviously one part of that

Just before the war, President Gamal Nasser of Egypt said the goal would be "to exterminate the State of Israel for all time." Realizing that Egypt, Syria, and Jordan were about to attack, Israel struck first. The Israeli air force destroyed the opposing air forces while they were still on the ground. Israeli armor and infantry overwhelmed the enemy.

But in 1973 Egypt struck first. Launching an attack on Yom Kippur (October 6, the Day of Atonement, a major Jewish holiday), the Egyptians surprised the Israelis. Syria also attacked in the north. Pressed by two deter-

plan. What about the Arabs? Were they to be under the control of Egypt and Jordan—as they had been until 1967? Or were they too to have their own independent state in Palestine? The idea of an independent Arab state became the goal of Arabs in Israeli-occupied Palestine.

Nearly all Arabs in the occupied areas wanted their own government, free of Israeli control. A minority resorted to violence to achieve that goal. Terrorists, notably the **Palestine Liberation Organization (PLO),** used riots, bombings, and guerrilla attacks to force the Israelis to give in to their demands.

Israel, however, feared that a new Arab state would be just one more enemy to face. Furthermore, many Israelis wanted to hold on to the occupied territories, especially the West Bank. For some, this territory would help make Israel more secure. Others, especially devout Jews, treasured the West Bank as part of God's gift of the Promised Land to the Jews. And almost no one in Israel wanted to surrender eastern Jerusalem.

At first, Israel stood firm against terrorists. In 1976 Arab terrorists hijacked a French jetliner with eighty-nine Israelis aboard. They flew to Entebbe, Uganda, and demanded the Israelis release fifty-three terrorists imprisoned in Israel. Otherwise, the hijackers would kill the passengers. The Israelis mounted a brilliant rescue operation. They landed at the airport at night, attacked the terrorists, and freed nearly all of the hostages.

But fighting back became more and more difficult. When some Palestinian terrorists began using bases in Lebanon, Israel invaded that country in 1982. World opinion condemned the act. To make matters worse, Lebanese troops working under Israeli officers went into Palestinian refugee camps and butchered over two thousand men, women, and children. Even Israeli citizens were revolted as pictures of the victims' bodies appeared on television. Incidents such as this convinced many Israeli leaders that the country must find a peaceful solution to its problems.

An Arab refugee camp on the West Bank of the Jordan River

So Israel moved slowly toward meeting Arab demands. Despite more years of unrest and violence, the Israeli government and the PLO surprised the world in 1993 by announcing an agreement. It was not so much a final settlement as an agreement to work out difficulties. But under the agreement, Israel gave the Arabs some self-rule in the Gaza Strip and in selected cities and villages of the West Bank. It also left the door open for future discussions.

The government of Israel has been far from perfect. Sometimes it has mistreated Arab minorities, and its military actions, such as that in Lebanon, have caused suffering. Yet Israel remains the strongest democracy in the Middle East. With all of its flaws, Israel has remained committed to democratic ideals. The rule of law, reliance on the ballot box instead of bullets, and a commitment to justice all characterize the Jewish state. This example is very much needed in the Middle East.

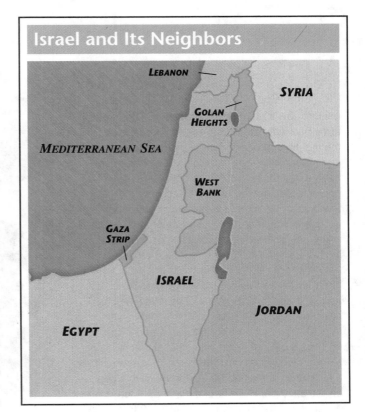

Israel and Its Neighbors

Section Review

1. Who was the founder of the Zionist movement?

2. In what area was the nation of Israel reborn? In what year did Israel become an independent nation?

3. In what war did Israel destroy its enemies' planes before they could even get off the ground?

4. Where is the West Bank? the Gaza Strip?

5. What group of terrorists has attempted to regain Palestine for the Arabs by using violence against the Israelis?

Why have the Arabs been so intent on keeping Israel out of the Middle East? Look up Genesis 16 to see what the Bible has to say about the relationship between the Israelites and the Arabs; describe what you find.

Golda Meir

On June 9, 1967, Golda Meir (MYE ur) stood before the Wailing Wall, all that remained of the ancient Jewish temple in Jerusalem. The Israeli army had just recaptured eastern Jerusalem. For the first time in nearly twenty years, Jews could again approach the wall. Golda Meir had never been a devout Jew, but the sight of Israeli soldiers pressing against the wall touched her. "Only a few hours earlier," she wrote, "they had fought furiously for the liberation of Jerusalem and had seen their comrades fall for its sake. Now, standing before the Wall, they wrapped themselves in prayer shawls and wept, and I, too, took a sheet of paper, wrote the word *'shalom'* (peace) on it and pushed it into a cranny of the Wall, as I had seen the Jews do so long ago." A soldier walked over, put his head on her shoulder, and wept. "I felt greatly blessed," she said, "that at that moment a young lad whom I did not know chose me to be a mother to him when he felt the need to weep on the shoulder of someone close and dear."

Golda Mabovitch was born in 1898 to a Jewish family in Russia. The family fled Russia because of persecution and settled in Milwaukee, Wisconsin, in 1906. At an early age, Golda showed talents of organization and persuasion. When she was eleven years old, she found that some students in her school in Milwaukee needed money for their textbooks. She rented a hall and sent out invitations. Golda spoke to those who came about how students needed money for their texts. For the first time, Golda raised money for her cause and got her name into the newspapers.

Even while living in Russia, Golda had heard of Zionism, the desire for a Jewish homeland in Palestine. This idea became her dream too. In America she met and married Morris Meyerson in 1917. Together they moved to Palestine in 1921.

Golda Meir

Golda began working for Zionist organizations and became a leader in the movement for a Jewish homeland. The British tried to halt this movement to please the Arabs. In fact, when the British arrested many Zionist leaders in the 1940s, Golda was mildly insulted not to be arrested too.

When Israel declared its independence, Golda was one of the signers of the Israeli declaration of independence. During the War for Independence she visited the United States and raised $50 million from American Jews to help Israel. The next year she went back and raised $150 million more. She had certainly come a long way from raising money for textbooks in Milwaukee.

Golda became an important official in the Israeli government. She served as ambassador to the Soviet Union (1948-49), minister of labor (1949-56), and foreign minister (1956-65). As minister of labor she faced special challenges brought on by the Law of the Return (1950). This law gave automatic citizenship to any Jew who came to live in Israel. As hundreds of thousands of Jews poured into the tiny country, she had to find housing and jobs for them. Also at this time, she, like many Israelis, took a Hebrew name. "Meyerson" became "Meir," from the Hebrew for "illuminate."

In 1969 Golda Meir became prime minister of Israel. She led Israel through some of its darkest days during the Yom Kippur War of 1973. She admitted later that the Egyptian attack caught her off guard. The prime minister realized that to lose the war would mean the destruction of the nation. She inspired and encouraged her people through the nerve-wracking days when Israel's fate hung in the balance. And she saw the nation through to final victory.

Golda Meir in 1970 described her hopes for her grandchildren: "I don't want them to live in an Israel that will always be complimented as the only democratic state here, the only developed state. I want Israel to be part of a highly developed, culturally advanced Middle East with much cooperation between its peoples. . . . Above all, I hope that Israel will become the ideal, just society of which we dreamed." She died in 1978 in Jerusalem.

Golda Meir with American civil rights leader Roy Wilkins

Religion in the Middle East

Islam, Judaism, Christianity—all of these religions were born in the Middle East. The history of the region makes no sense to someone who does not understand the importance of religion there. In the drama of twentieth-century Middle Eastern history, Judaism and Islam have played leading roles.

Judaism

Judaism began when God called Abraham from Ur of the Chaldees. God promised him the land of Palestine (Gen. 12:1-7). From that time Abraham's descendants lived in that land, but not without interruption. From the time of Joseph (1876 B.C.) to Moses (1446 B.C.), the Hebrew people lived in Egypt. During the Babylonian captivity (586-539 B.C.), most of the Jews lived in exile. Then in A.D. 66 and again in A.D. 132 the Jews rebelled against the Roman Empire. The Romans destroyed Jerusalem and scattered the Jews all around the world. Not until the twentieth century was there a major movement of Jews back to Palestine.

During the many centuries after the Romans scattered the Jews, different forms of Judaism developed. Some of these forms are cultural and geographic. Two major groups of this kind are the **Sephardim** and the **Ashkenazim.** Sephardic Jews are those who have their roots in medieval Spain and Portugal; their traditions go back to the Jews who lived in Babylon after the exile in 586 B.C. Ashkenazic Jews have their roots in medieval northern and eastern Europe; their

traditions go back to the Jews who lived in Palestine. The Ashkenazim developed the language known as **Yiddish,** a mixture of Hebrew and German. There are also other, smaller groups. Earlier we also mentioned Ethiopian Jews (p. 115). They have lived in Africa since the Middle Ages. Many of these groups are represented in modern Israel, but the Ashkenazic Jews have generally provided the leadership in that nation.

There are also different theological varieties of Judaism. The most liberal is **Reform Judaism.** It teaches that Judaism is basically

Orthodox Jews in Jerusalem

Jews gather to pray at the Wailing Wall, the only surviving section of the Jewish temple of Jesus' day. The Dome of the Rock, a Muslim mosque built on the site of the temple, is clearly visible above the wall.

concerned with principles of right and wrong. Therefore, Jews may adapt their forms of worship and manner of living to the age in which they live. Reform Jewish temples often look little different from Christian churches. Their services are conducted in the native language instead of Hebrew. Reform Jews are less concerned with traditional Jewish dietary laws, such as the ban on eating pork. They even ordain women as rabbis—a practice strongly denounced by traditional Jews.

Next is **Conservative Judaism.** This branch is similar to Reform Judaism in that it holds that Jews may adapt their manner of life to the times in which they live. Conservative Jews, however, place much more value on Jewish tradition. Congregations vary in practice; some may follow dietary laws, for example, while others do not.

Finally there is **Orthodox Judaism.** This is the general term for the strictest form of Judaism. The Orthodox believe that the Old Testament and Jewish tradition were given directly by God. Therefore, they insist on strict adherence to the law. Followers of Orthodox Judaism carefully follow all the Jewish laws concerning diet, the Sabbath, and Jewish holy days. They forbid marriage with non-Jews and wear traditional clothing. Men, for example, always wear a hat or skullcap (a *yarmulke*) to show their respect to God.

There are different forms of Orthodox Judaism. One influential group is the **Hasidim.** These are strict Jews with roots in Eastern Europe. Hasidic Jews are traditional, but much of their tradition traces back to Eastern Europe in the 1700s. They speak the language, Yiddish, that developed there. Their clothes are the style of that era: long black coats, broad-brimmed hats, and long-sleeved white shirts. The men often wear long curls of hair from their temples, their way of obeying

Leviticus 19:27, "Ye shall not round the corners of your heads."

Many Jews today are "nonobservant," or "secular." They do not practice any religion but think of themselves as an ethnic group. The majority of Jews in Israel are secular Jews. But the Israeli government recognizes only Orthodox Judaism as the official form of Judaism. Only the Orthodox may serve as chaplains in the Israeli armed forces, and only Orthodox rabbis may perform weddings. The Orthodox in Israel also control small political parties that hold the balance of power in the Israeli **Knesset** (legislature). Orthodox Judaism exerts more influence in modern Israel than its numbers might indicate.

A Jewish boy celebrates his bar mitzvah at the Wailing Wall.

Islam

Muslims believe in only one God, Allah, but there is more than one form of Islam. Most Muslims (90 percent of the world's Muslim population) are **Sunnite Muslims.** The Sunnis viewed the **caliphs** as the legitimate successors to Muhammad. (*Caliph* means "successor.") Starting with the first caliph, Abu-Bakr, the son-in-law of Muhammad, the caliph was the main religious leader of the Muslims. The caliph, it was believed, guarded the traditions handed down by the prophet. The Sunnis followed the caliphs of Islam until 1924, when Kemal Atatürk abolished the office. Over the years, however, the Sunnis developed a system of Islamic law called the **shari'a.** As long as Muslim governments follow the shari'a, Sunnis say today, the caliph is no longer needed.

Shiite Muslims consider the caliphs to be illegitimate successors to Muhammad. They

A gilded Muslim minaret

believe that only direct descendants of Muhammad should be leaders of Islam. The Shiites give special honor to a line of **imams** ("leaders"). Whereas the caliph was supposed to preserve tradition, the Shiite imam had special teaching authority from Allah. The twelfth imam disappeared as a child around 878. With him the office stopped, and Shiites now await the return of the twelfth imam to bring about a golden age. Scholars have always had a large role in Shiite

Devout Muslims regularly bow in the direction of Mecca to pray.

Islam. An example of the influence of these scholars is the Ayatollah Khomeini's leadership in Iran (discussed in the next section).

The Sunnites and Shiites are often bitterly opposed to each other. Only two major countries have Shiite majorities. In Iran Shiites compose 95 percent of the population, and they make up two-thirds of the population of Iraq. (The tiny nation of Bahrain also has a Shiite majority.) Elsewhere, Sunnites are in the overwhelming majority. There are varieties even within these two groups. The Wahhabis in Saudi Arabia practice a very strict form of

Sunnite Islam. (See p. 523.) The Druze are a splinter group from Shiite Islam living in Syria and Lebanon. Because the Druze do not consider Muhammad the true prophet of Allah, most Muslims consider them heretics.

In the 1970s, the strictest Islamic groups began grabbing headlines around the world. The most extreme of these groups even rebelled against governments that they thought were not purely enough Islamic. The story of the Iranian Revolution in the next section provides a chilling example of Islamic extremism in action.

Section Review

1. What language did the Ashkenazim develop?

2. List the three theological varieties of Judaism and briefly describe each.

3. Describe the Hasidic form of Orthodox Judaism.

4. Name and briefly describe the origins of the two major forms of Islam in the Middle East today.

5. What is the title of the "successor" to Muhammad that Sunnite Muslims followed? Who put an end to this office?

Compare and contrast Judaism and Islam. Is either comparable to Christianity? How? How are they different?

Hasidic Jews represent the most conservative branch of Judaism. Their strongly traditionalist Jewish faith is sometimes mistakenly labeled "fundamentalist."

Religious "Fundamentalisms"

A group of Muslim extremists force their way into a worship service at the Holy Mosque in Mecca on November 20, 1979. For two weeks they hold this site. Finally, troops of the Saudi government force their way into the mosque and engage the rebels. Over a hundred rebels die, and another hundred are captured. The leader of the group is publicly beheaded less than a month later. Newspapers announce that the Muslim "fundamentalists" have been routed.

On April 26, 1984, Israeli officials arrest twenty-seven members of a Jewish extremist group. They had been caught wiring explosives to five buses scheduled to carry Arabs. While questioning the prisoners, the Israelis discover a plot even more shocking. This group has been planning to attack the Dome of the Rock, a Muslim holy site in Jerusalem located where the Jewish temple once stood. Members of the group armed with automatic weapons are to kill the guards, plant twenty-seven bombs, and blow the Dome to pieces. Television reports that the government has foiled this plot of these Jewish "fundamentalists."

The media and some scholars have popularized the term fundamentalist as a label for extremist religious groups. They use the term to describe certain kinds of Muslims, Jews, Buddhists, and other religious groups. Not all those labeled "fundamentalist" are as extreme as the ones described above. Even so, this use of the term *fundamentalist* is incorrect.

The term *Fundamentalist* originated in America. In the early 1900s, many Protestants in the United States opposed the growth of liberal theology. Liberals denied biblical truths such as Christ's deity, virgin birth, and resurrection. They said they wanted to make Christianity more "modern." (One form of liberalism is often called "Modernism.") In response, conservatives published a series of pamphlets called *The Fundamentals*. Articles in these pamphlets defended the teachings of God's Word against liberal attack. Then in 1920 a Baptist newspaper editor wrote, "We suggest that those who still cling to the great fundamentals and who mean to do battle royal for the fundamentals shall be called 'Fundamentalists.' "

The Fundamentalists battled the Modernists for control of the major American denominations in the 1920s. When they lost those battles, the Fundamentalists organized their own schools, denominations, and mission boards. Because these Fundamentalists sought to defend historic Christianity, some have argued that any group that strives to maintain its traditional religious beliefs should be called "fundamentalist."

There are problems with this definition, however. Although Protestant Fundamentalists "fought for the faith," their battling was not violent. They published magazines and books, preached sermons to persuade audiences, and voted democratically in church elections as their way of standing for their faith. Non-Christian "fundamentalists," however, are commonly associated with violence. Even the many who do not commit acts of violence often support the overthrow of governments. Protestant Fundamentalists say every man should have the freedom to think and believe as he wishes. These other groups usually hold that they must force nonbelievers to accept their group's teachings.

Fundamentalism is not about *how* a person behaves but *what* he believes. Some who use the label "fundamentalist" argue that traditional Jews, Muslims, and others practice their faith in the same way as Christian Fundamentalists. But Protestant Fundamentalism is about defending the beliefs of the Christian faith. A "fundamentalist" Muslim or Jew would never accept the Bible's teaching that Jesus is God, but a Fundamentalist insists that there is no salvation apart from that belief. Historically, a Fundamentalist is not someone who holds to the "fundamentals" of just any religion; he is one who upholds the essential truths of Christianity.

The Dome of the Rock is a Muslim mosque built on the site of Solomon's temple and the rock from which Muhammad allegedly ascended to heaven. It is a point of conflict between traditionalist Jews and Muslims.

Oil, Revolution, and War

Jesus warned, "Take heed, and beware of covetousness: for a man's life consisteth not in the abundance of the things which he possesseth" (Luke 12:15). Sections of the Middle East enjoy great wealth through their rich resources in oil. But wealth has not brought peace to the region. Instead, it has brought competition and conflict. Some nations have used the need for the oil itself as a weapon to bend other nations to their demands. Oil has driven some nations to attack their neighbors in a frenzy of greed. Religion complicates the situation. Many of the nations fighting over oil also fight over who follows the purest form of Islam. Oil and religion are an explosive mix.

Oil

The modern world runs on oil. Anyone who drives a car or just mows his lawn relies on an oil product, gasoline. Industries use oil for fuel or for lubrication. Many homes are

Supertankers load oil at the Sea Island, one of Saudi Arabia's huge seacost terminals.

heated by oil or by electricity produced by oil-driven generators. Petroleum (oil and natural gas) is also an important ingredient in producing asphalt and insecticides, as well as paint, plastic, rubber, fibers, and much more.

Two-thirds of the world's known oil deposits lie underground in the Middle East. Before World War I, only Persia (Iran) produced much oil for sale. Today, the Middle East is the center of the world's oil production. By the 1990s the Middle East produced a third of the world's oil supply; Saudi Arabia alone produced nearly half of that.

To increase their profits and power, the oil-producing nations of the Middle East formed **OPEC** in 1960. *OPEC* stands for "Organization of Petroleum-Exporting Countries." It became OPEC's goal to push oil prices as high as possible. OPEC was formed as a **cartel.** A cartel exists when the producers of an item get together to control the price of the item they produce. In this case, the members of OPEC would agree to limit how much oil they produced so that they could push the price up.

For the first few years OPEC had little success. Then when Egypt and Syria went to war against Israel in 1973, the Arab nations of OPEC refused to sell to nations that supported Israel, including the United States. They also raised the price for other countries. Oil prices shot up. A barrel of oil sold for $3 before the Arab-Israeli war began. By 1981 oil was selling for $35 a barrel.

For a few years, the OPEC nations were gorged with profits. But the oil boom did not last. As prices for oil products rose, people found ways to avoid buying Arab oil. They bought cars that used less gasoline, sought out new deposits of oil, or even turned to different

The Ayatollah Khomeini greets a crowd of his adoring followers.

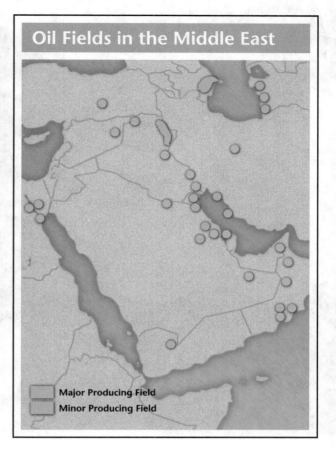

Oil Fields in the Middle East

Major Producing Field

Minor Producing Field

sources of fuel such as coal. As demand slackened, prices fell. Also some members of OPEC needed money and cheated the cartel by producing more oil then they said they would. This extra oil on the market helped keep prices down. The oil producers ignored a basic law of economics: the demand for an item is always related to its cost. If a producer tries to ask for too much money for his goods, he will find that demand falls as his prices rise.

Conflict in the Middle East

While oil prices were rising and falling in the 1970s and 1980s, the Middle East suffered some jolts. The first came in 1979 in Iran. As mentioned earlier, a popular uprising overthrew the shah. In his place arose a frightening figure, the **Ayatollah Ruholla Khomeini** (EYE-uh-TOH-luh roo-OH-luh koh-MAY-nee). An *ayatollah* is a respected teacher and leader among Shiite Muslims. Khomeini proceeded to establish in Iran a Muslim state of the

strictest kind. He began by executing hundreds of officials from the shah's government.

Khomeini's "Islamic republic" in Iran was in many ways the exact opposite of Atatürk's secular state in Turkey. Atatürk wanted a nation in which no religion could force its will on everyone. Khomeini insisted on a state in which everyone lived according to Islamic law. Atatürk opened the door to Western ideas. Khomeini considered Western ideas corrupt and devilish. Under the Ayatollah, Iran again required women to wear the heavy veils of Islamic custom. Those who defied the law risked arrest and beatings from the Revolutionary Guards. Khomeini's fervor did not stop with Iran. He promised "to export our revolution to the four corners of the world."

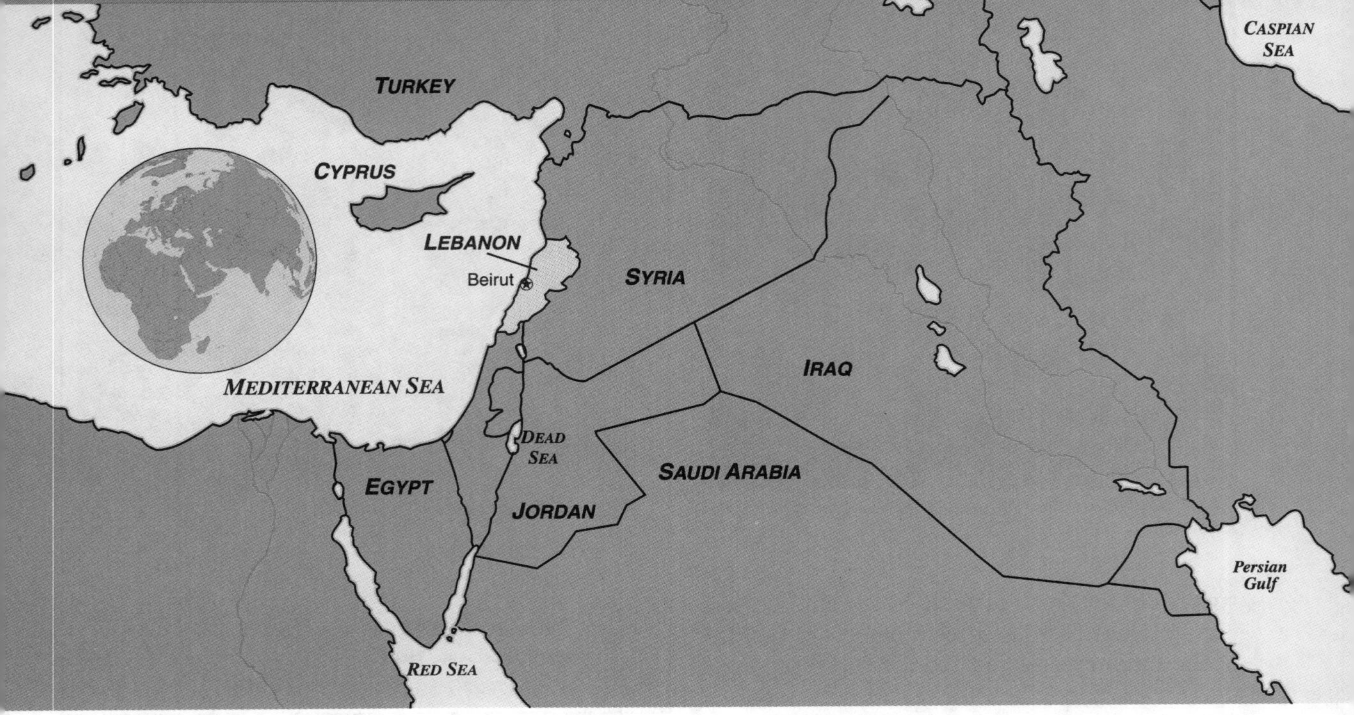

Location—Lebanon is located in the Middle East. It is bordered in the north and east by Syria and in the south by Israel. Its western border is the Mediterranean Sea.

Climate—Lebanon has a mediterranean climate with warm, dry summers and mild, wet winters. Temperatures tend to be highest along the coast while rainfall is most plentiful in the western Lebanon Mountains.

Topography—Lebanon's topography lies in four parallel strips. Along the Mediterranean Sea runs a narrow coastal plain. The backbone of the country, running north to south, is the Lebanon Mountains. To the east of the mountains lies the rich Bekaa Valley. Beyond this valley stands the Anti-Lebanon Range along the border with Syria.

Natural Resources—In ancient times Lebanon was known for the beautiful wood of its magnificent cedar trees. (See II Sam. 5:11; I Kings 5:1-12; Ezek. 27:5.) Overcutting reduced these great forests, however. Today only a limited number of cedars are available for commercial use. Instead the nation's limestone deposits make Lebanon an important producer of cement and gravel. Lebanon exports citrus fruits, apples, and tobacco. However, banking, not natural resources, is the nation's largest source of income.

Geography & Culture—Lebanon sits at a crossroads of the Middle East. Both sea trade and overland trade have enriched the region. In ancient times Lebanon was part of Phoenicia, dominated by the major trading cities of Tyre and Sidon. The richness of the region later attracted Greek and then Roman conquerors. Islamic empires dominated the area from the 600s to the breakup of the Ottoman Empire after World War I. Lebanon became a nation under French oversight in the 1920s and in 1943 became completely independent.

Lebanon is also a religious crossroads. The nation is 60 to 70 percent Muslim and 30 to 40 percent Christian. An important minority of the Muslims are the Druze. (See p. 535.) Lebanon has the highest percentage of Christian citizens of any Arab country. The largest Christian group in Lebanon are the Maronites. This group is part of the Roman Catholic Church, but it maintains its own practices and customs. Unfortunately, these religious groups sometimes clash. Not only do Christians and Muslims fight each other but sometimes the Muslims fight among themselves. Lebanon is a small land, but it suffers from many conflicts.

Settings Review

1. What country lies on Lebanon's eastern border?
2. What type of climate does Lebanon have?
3. What type of wood is Lebanon known for?
4. Modern-day Lebanon was part of what kingdom in Old Testament times?

Read I Kings 5:1-12. What kind of goods did Solomon purchase from Hiram of Tyre? Why would Solomon get workers from Hiram? How might these business relationships have promoted the peace between Solomon and Hiram described in verse 12?

Scenes from Lebanon: a war-scarred building in Beirut showing the ravages of the nation's civil war (left) and an aerial view showing the cities, mountains, and famous cedars of Lebanon

Saddam Hussein

The revolution in Iran certainly caught the attention of its next-door neighbor. Dictator **Saddam Hussein** (suh-DAHM hoo-SAYN) of Iraq saw the revolution as both a danger and an opportunity. On the one hand, he feared that his own Shiite population might get revolutionary ideas from Iran. On the other, he saw the disorder in Iran as an opportunity to seize an important waterway between the two countries.

Saddam attacked Iran on September 22, 1980. Eight years of warfare followed. The two sides blasted and bombed each other. The Iranians sent waves of fervent revolutionary soldiers streaming against Iraqi lines. Iraq in turn loosed poison gas on the Iranians. Iraqi planes bombed Iranian cities, and Iranian missiles rained down on Iraqi cities. After eight years of fighting, the two exhausted sides agreed to peace, but hatred burned on. Khomeini wished that Iran could continue until Saddam Hussein was destroyed. He said that accepting peace was "more deadly than taking poison."

Having failed in Iran, Saddam then looked for an easier victim. He found one in the small but oil-rich country of Kuwait to his south. He invaded Kuwait on August 2, 1990. If the war against Iran had been a mistake for Iraq, then the invasion of Kuwait was a disaster. The world frowned as Iraq attacked a neighbor without cause. Then the world worried as Saddam Hussein put massive forces on the border of Saudi Arabia. He threatened to seize control of a huge portion of the world's oil supply.

The United States provided the bulk of the troops used to drive Iraq out of Kuwait in the Gulf War of 1991.

Chapter 18

Other nations saw the danger that Saddam posed. Led by the United States, the United Nations authorized military action against Iraq. The United States, European nations such as Great Britain, and Arab nations such as Saudi Arabia and Egypt sent over 250,000 troops to drive Iraq back. The **Gulf War** began on January 17, 1991, with five weeks of heavy bombing of targets in Iraq. On February 24, the anti-Iraq coalition struck. In just one hundred hours, the U.S.-led forces destroyed much of the Iraqi army and surrounded most of what was left. Kuwait had been freed and Iraq humiliated.

War rarely settles problems, however. The competition for oil wealth continued. Islamic extremism still promoted violence in the region and tried to export violence worldwide. Friction between differing ethnic groups heated into even more violence. The Middle East was the birthplace of the Prince of Peace, Jesus Christ. But the region itself is far from enjoying peace.

Section Review

1. What does OPEC stand for and what was its goal?

2. What is an *ayatollah?*

3. Iran fought what country for control of an important waterway?

4. The Gulf War resulted from Iraq's invasion of which Middle Eastern country?

Why did Khomeini say that accepting peace was "more deadly than taking poison"? Do you agree? Why or why not?

Summary

The collapse of the Ottoman Empire at the end of World War I ushered in a new era of Middle Eastern history. Turkey, the heart of the old Ottoman Empire, became a modern secular state under the rule of Kemal Atatürk. Iran, under the Pahlavis, also tried to become a modern state but eventually fell under the control of Muslim extremists led by the Ayatollah Khomeini. Saudi Arabia, with its immense oil wealth, tried to be a traditionalist Muslim nation, but it found that its wealth attracted corrupting influences. Only the nation of Israel has maintained a stable democracy in the Middle East. But it has done so only in the face of Arab hostility. Religion has also been a source of conflict. Jews and Muslims have clashed not only with each other but also among themselves. Enormous wealth has not been able to forestall violence, as shown by two wars involving the nation of Iraq. Peace is not among the riches of the Middle East.

People, Places, and Things to Know

Anatolia	Abdul Aziz ibn-Saud	Palestine Liberation	caliph
Mustafa Kemal	Wahhabi movement	Organization (PLO)	shari'a
Turkey	Saudi Arabia	Sephardim	Shiite Muslim
Kemal Atatürk	Zionism	Ashkenazim	imam
fez	Theodor Herzl	Yiddish	OPEC
Reza Shah Pahlavi	Balfour Declaration	Reform Judaism	cartel
Iran	War of Independence	Conservative Judaism	Ayatollah Ruholla
Mohammed Reza	Six-Day War	Orthodox Judaism	Khomeini
Shah Pahlavi	Yom Kippur War	Hasidim	Saddam Hussein
"White Revolution"	West Bank	Knesset	Gulf War
Bedouins		Sunnite Muslim	

Review Questions

Identify

Give the term for each definition.

1. strict form of Islam based in Arabia which wishes to make others believe as it believes

2. the movement to form an Israeli state

3. Jews whose roots are in Spain and Portugal

4. Jews whose roots are in northern and eastern Europe

5. strict Orthodox Jews with traditions from the 1700s

Matching

Match each form of religion to its definition.

(a) Conservative Judaism (d) Shiite Muslims

(b) Orthodox Judaism (e) Sunnite Muslims

(c) Reform Judaism

6. believe in Muhammad's descendants as the only proper leaders of Islam

7. believe in caliphs as legitimate successors to Muhammad

8. strictest form of Judaism

9. form of Judaism which stresses conformity to the age in which one lives

10. form of Judaism which conforms to the age but keeps tradition

Association

Name the country with which each of the following is associated.

11. Ayatollah Ruholla Khomeini
12. ibn-Saud
13. Kemal Atatürk
14. Mohammed Reza Shah Pahlavi
15. Mustafa Kemal
16. Reza Shah Pahlavi
17. Golda Meir

Think About It!

With your knowledge of the world today, predict the relationship of Middle Eastern countries to each other as well as to the rest of the world, especially in relation to oil and religion.

CHAPTER 19

Africa is not a country; it is a continent. Africa is a land of deserts, jungles, and savannahs. A visitor to Africa can shiver in the snows of Mount Kilimanjaro or swelter in the humidity along the banks of the Congo River or roast in the heat of the Sahara Desert. The people of Africa are as diverse as the land—from the Muslim Berbers in North Africa to the tall Tutsi people of East Africa to the small Pygmy peoples of West Central Africa.

When we study African culture and history, it is important that we take into account this diversity. One way of studying the African continent is to study it by regions. In this chapter, we will look at four main regions: North or Saharan Africa, West (or West Central) Africa, Southern Africa, and East Africa.

But this is a history book, after all. As we look at each region, we need to understand the events that have shaped that region—and all of Africa—in the twentieth century. To accomplish this goal, we will focus on one country in each region. Then we will examine one theme of modern African history that is reflected in the history of that nation. Let us travel, then, to Algeria, Ghana, South Africa, and Rwanda to catch a glimpse of modern Africa.

A.D. 1900 - PRESENT

Boer War
1899-1902

First Pan-Afric
Conference 19

| 1900 | 1910 | 192 |

African National Congres
Founded 1912

Africa Redrawn

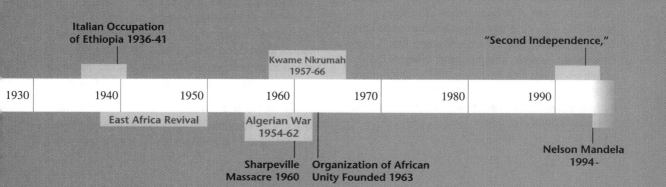

Italian Occupation
of Ethiopia 1936-41

"Second Independence,"

Kwame Nkrumah
1957-66

1930	1940	1950	1960	1970	1980	1990

East Africa Revival

Algerian War
1954-62

Sharpeville
Massacre 1960

Organization of African
Unity Founded 1963

Nelson Mandela
1994-

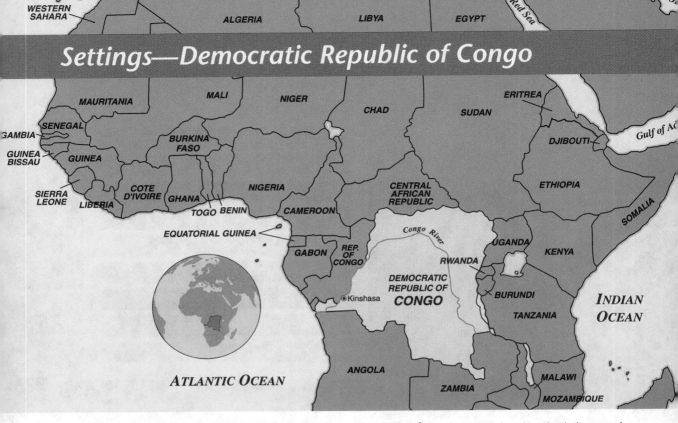

Location—The Democratic Republic of Congo is located in West Central Africa. It is mostly land-locked, with a small strip touching the Atlantic Ocean in the west. Bordering the nation are the Republic of Congo on the west (whose name is confusingly similar); the Central African Republic and Sudan to the north; Uganda, Rwanda, Burundi, and Tanzania to the east; and Angola and Zambia to the south.

Climate—Most of the northern portion of the country has a tropical wet (rain forest) climate. Most of the southern half has a tropical wet and dry (savanna) climate. Rainfall and temperatures vary with the region. The rain forest along the Congo River basin receives about seventy to eighty inches of rain each year with an average daily temperature of 90°. The savanna region receives less than 40 inches of rain each year and daily temperatures average around 75°.

Topography—At over nine hundred thousand square miles, Congo is the third largest country in Africa (after Sudan and Algeria). A major feature of the topography is the Congo River, second only to the Nile as the longest river in Africa. Above the Congo River region rise high plateaus and, in the far east, mountains.

Natural Resources—Congo has many natural resources that are thus far little developed. The country is one of the largest copper producers in the world, and it also enjoys large deposits of cobalt (nearly two-thirds of the world reserves) and diamonds. Most Congolese farmers grow crops such as bananas for their own families. But the country also exports coffee, cocoa, cotton, tea, and rubber.

Geography & Culture—The people of the Democratic Republic of Congo belong to many different tribal, or ethnic, groups. There are so many local languages that the government uses French as the official language since it is more commonly understood. About three-fourths of the Congolese claim to be Christian. The majority of these are Catholic, but about 10 percent of the population belong to the Kimbanguist Church. (See p. 572.)

Several early African kingdoms flourished in this area. The most important of these was probably the Kongo kingdom, which in the 1400s covered much of what is today Congo and Angola. Europeans took control of the region when Belgium's King Leopold established the Congo Free State in 1885 as his own personal colony. Leopold's rule was so cruel that the Belgian government took control in 1908 and renamed the colony the Belgian Congo.

In 1960 the region became the independent nation of Congo. (The country went by the name *Zaire* from 1971 to 1997). The southeastern section of the country, called the Katanga Province, tried to become independent in 1960. It was brought back in 1963 with help from troops from the United Nations. During most of its history since independence, Congo has been ruled by military dictatorship.

Settings Review

1. Describe the two types of climates in Congo.
2. What is the second longest river in Africa?
3. List five natural resources of Congo that are commonly used today.

4. What is the official language of Congo?
5. Who established this area as his personal colony in 1885?

Why might a person or nation want territory in a land such as Africa? Discuss the resources available and the prestige of obtaining land.

Dominated by the Congo River and lush jungles, the Democratic Republic of Congo lies in the heart of Africa.

Saharan Africa: Algeria and Decolonization

Imagine a place almost as large as the United States (including Alaska). Imagine that in this place there are fewer than one hundred villages and no cities. Imagine that between those villages lie hundreds of miles of sand and rock. Imagine temperatures climbing above 100°F in the day and then falling to near freezing at night. Years may pass in parts of this land before a drop of rain falls. When rain does come to this parched place, the water rolls quickly over the sand and rock. Soon, however, the scorching heat licks up the moisture, and the land is hot and dry once more.

The place you have just imagined is the largest desert in the world, the **Sahara.** It stretches for three thousand miles across northern Africa from the Atlantic Ocean to the Red Sea. It reaches southward from the Mediterranean coast or nearby mountains for over one thousand miles. So vast is the Sahara Desert that writers often divide the continent into Saharan Africa (the northern section dominated by the desert) and sub-Saharan Africa (that part that lies south of the Sahara).

Decolonization and Assimilation

We learned in Chapter 14 that the European nations in the late 1800s began dividing up Africa among themselves. France, Great Britain, and even Spain, Portugal, and tiny Belgium began to build enormous empires for themselves in Africa. Arab North Africa was likewise divided up by the European powers.

After World War II, these European empires in Africa began to break up. We sometimes call this process the **decolonization** of Africa. In 1960 alone fourteen former colonies became independent nations. Sometimes the transition to independence was peaceful. Tanganyika (later called Tanzania) in East Africa won its independence peacefully from Britain in 1961. Sometimes the coming of independence was violent. In no country was decolonization any bloodier or more destructive than in the North African nation of Algeria.

France took control of the major coastal city of Algiers in 1830 and by degrees extended its control over all of Algeria. France pursued a policy of the **assimilation** of Algeria.

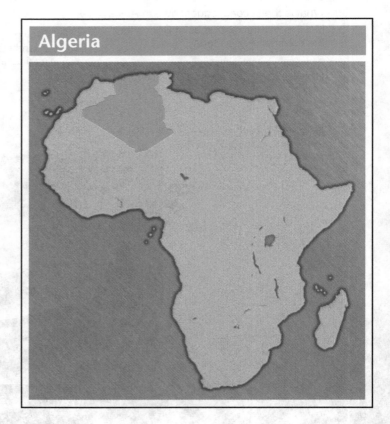

Algeria

Charles de Gaulle greets Muslim soldiers in Algeria. He took power in France in part to find a solution to the Algerian crisis.

In other words, the French hoped to make Algeria a province of France—a real part of the French nation.

The French, however, were slow to grant full political rights to all Algerians until they thought the people ready for such rights. Instead they gave full rights to the many Europeans who settled there and to a small number of Algerian Muslims who embraced French culture. Most Algerians, however, received none of these benefits and furthermore had no desire to be French.

War in Algeria

In 1954 war broke out in Algeria. The **Front for National Liberation** (*Front de libération nationale,* or FLN) was a native Muslim Algerian group that dedicated itself to winning Algerian independence. Eight years of warfare followed. The FLN used terror to advance its cause, and the French responded with fierce repression.

The FLN at first killed only Muslims who cooperated with the French. "Take their children and kill them," said one leader of how to treat the pro-French Algerians. "Kill all those who pay taxes and those who collect them." Then the FLN decided to spread the terror further by slaughtering European civilians. They sought international attention for their cause, and as one Algerian terrorist said, "One corpse in a suit is always worth more than twenty in uniform." In an attack on Philippeville in 1955, FLN terrorists murdered over one hundred people—men, women, and children, Algerian and European.

The French responded firmly, even harshly. As many as 500,000 French troops came to Algeria to restore order. When some rebels began setting up bases in neighboring Tunisia and Morocco, the French closed the borders. They did so by an elaborate system of defenses, including an electric fence two hundred miles long. To get information and frighten the FLN, the French began to torture prisoners.

The French found themselves forced to hold on to Algeria by a military occupation almost as harsh as that the Nazis had imposed on France during World War II. The government began to lose control of the army. The French army bombed a village in Tunisia to get at rebel bases, without even bothering to get government approval. Army officers threatened to bring down the whole French government if France tried to abandon Algeria.

The Italo-Ethiopian War

To Africans, perhaps no state has been as symbolically important as Ethiopia. At the beginning of World War I, Ethiopia (sometimes called Abyssinia) was the only major area of Africa not under European control. (The tiny nation of Liberia in West Africa was also independent.) The nation's history of independence went back all the way to the days of the Roman Empire. The area had embraced Christianity in the 300s, and an independent Ethiopian Orthodox Church had existed from that time. During the Middle Ages, Ethiopia's highlands and mountains had enabled the nation to defend itself against Muslim conquest. Later these same features had helped Ethiopia resist European dominance.

Ethiopia's independence was not the result of being ignored by Europe. In 1896 Italy invaded Ethiopia to make the nation part of the growing Italian empire in Africa. The Ethiopians stunned the world by defeating the Italians at the Battle of Adowa. Ethiopia was safe, but Italy burned for revenge.

In the 1930s the Fascist dictator Benito Mussolini determined to avenge Adowa as a step in building a new Roman Empire. Italy controlled colonies bordering on Ethiopia (Eritrea and Italian Somaliland) and had been arguing with Ethiopia over the boundary. On December 5, 1934, the two sides clashed at Walwal, an oasis in the desert just inside the Ethiopian border. This clash gave Mussolini the excuse he needed for war.

It took months for the Italians to prepare for the campaign, and the invasion began on October 10, 1935. The Ethiopians knew the land well, and in small clashes their troops fought with brave ferocity. But technology favored the Italians. Ethiopia did not have enough guns for every man to have one, and its air force had only twelve planes. The Italians had hundreds of planes, heavy artillery, tanks, and poison gas. Italian engineers skillfully built roads and bridges over the rough Ethiopian countryside.

Air power was probably the Italians' main advantage. Their bombing of Ethiopia was a foretaste of what Europe would experience in World War II a few years later. Mussolini's son was one of the pilots in the Ethiopian campaign, and he described what he called the "beauty" of dropping bombs on tribesmen and seeing them spread out "just like a flowering rose."

During a visit to Italy's African colonies, Mussolini waves a "sword of Islam" given to him by his Muslim subjects.

As the Italians advanced, foreigners and Ethiopian leaders prepared to flee. A group of Swedish officers who had been advising the Ethiopian army were met by the cadets they had been training. The young Ethiopians wept and said, "This is the end of Ethiopia. . . . Go, God bless you. Save yourselves." The Italians occupied Addis Ababa, the capital, on May 5, 1936.

The emperor of Ethiopia, **Haile Selassie** (HYE-lee seh-LAS-ee), managed to get out of the country. He went to Geneva to appeal to the League of Nations (an international organization much like today's United Nations). Before representatives of the nations of the world he said, "I assert that the problem submitted to the Assembly today . . . is not merely a settlement of Italian aggression. . . . In a word, it is international morality that is at stake. . . . It is us today. It will be you tomorrow."

At the conclusion of his speech, Haile Selassie said, "What reply shall I have to take back to my people?" The reply was silence. The nations of Europe were not willing to go to war over Ethiopia. Mussolini announced that "civilization has triumphed over barbarism" and established a new colony, Italian East Africa. At times, however, Italian rule looked more barbaric than civilized. After an attempt to assassinate the colonial governor, vengeful Italian troops killed over three thousand Ethiopians and executed many Ethiopian nobles. The Italians even attacked a monastery accused of being disloyal to Mussolini and killed over three hundred monks

When World War II broke out, however, Italian forces in Africa found themselves cut off. A force led by British and African troops liberated Ethiopia, and Emperor Haile Selassie reentered Addis Ababa May 5, 1941, exactly five years after the Italians had captured it. The leading free state in Africa was free once more.

Emperor Haile Selassie of Ethiopia vainly entreats the League of Nations to intervene on behalf of his nation against the Italians.

Africa Redrawn

Veiled Muslim women converse in the Casbah section of Algiers, Algeria.

DeGaulle Seeks Peace

Under pressure from the armed forces, the government reorganized. **Charles de Gaulle,** a former general and World War II hero, became the new president of France. But de Gaulle quickly realized that France could not hold Algeria. To the anger of the generals, President de Gaulle dedicated himself to decolonizing Algeria.

The furious soldiers reacted violently. They attempted to assassinate de Gaulle. Then in 1961 the army and European settlers in Algeria arose in rebellion against the French government. When that uprising was crushed, a small secret organization of former French army officers launched a terrorist campaign as bloody as that of the FLN.

But de Gaulle persevered. In 1962 Algeria became an independent nation. Virtually all settlers of European descent fled Algeria at independence. Their numbers went from over a million to only about 30,000 by the end of 1962. A Muslim official told de Gaulle that the pro-French Algerians would suffer when the French pulled out. De Gaulle replied, "Oh, well, you will suffer." Many Muslims who had cooperated with the French were slaughtered by the new government.

But independence did not bring peace to Algeria. Within three years the Algerian army had toppled the government and set up a military dictatorship. By the 1990s Algeria experienced a new wave of terrorism from Muslim extremists inspired by the revolution in Iran. (See p. 522.) The FLN still held power long after Algeria had won independence from France. But it held on against terrorist attacks as fierce as those it had launched against the French. And the FLN maintained power by means as harsh as those France had used in ruling the region. In some ways, independence had not changed the situation in Algeria.

Section Review

1. List the four main regions of Africa.
2. What is the largest desert in the world?
3. What country wanted to assimilate Algeria into its nation?
4. What group fought against the French for independence?
5. Which French president tried to decolonize Algeria?

How could the decolonization of the African empires have been done more easily? Why would a nation have wanted to be assimilated or decolonized during this period? Explain your answer.

West Africa: Ghana and Dictatorship

When many non-Africans try to picture Africa, they often imagine steaming jungles and hordes of wild animals. West (sometimes called West Central) Africa probably comes as close to this image as any section of the continent. Although the Sahara Desert lies only a few hundred miles to the north, most of West Africa receives abundant rainfall. Rain forests and thick jungles dominate the landscape. Meandering through this lush undergrowth are the Niger and Congo Rivers. Wild animals such as hippopotamuses, crocodiles, pythons, and colorful tropical birds roam the region.

West Africa is the home of many nations, large and small, that gained independence after World War II. But many African peoples had little experience in self-government, except on a local level. As a result, many African nations began as democracies with several political parties but soon became dictatorships ruled by one party which was led by one powerful leader. There are several examples of cruel dictatorships in Africa, such as the bloody rule of Idi Amin Dada in Uganda in the 1970s. But rulers such as Amin were never anything but thugs. What is even sadder is the story of well-intentioned, idealistic rulers who nonetheless took their nations into dictatorship. Such is the story of Kwame Nkrumah (uhn KROO muh) of Ghana.

The lush jungle vegetation of Ghana

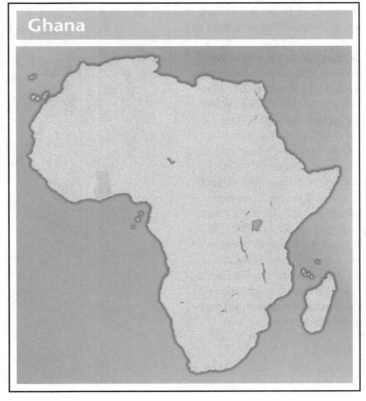

Ghana

Pan-Africanism

At the dawn of the twentieth century, most of Africa lay under European rule. Despite that fact—or perhaps because of it—African hopes for the future found expression in a new movement. **"Pan-Africanism,"** as it became known, is not an easy term to define. Originally, the movement was a call for fair treatment of all people of black African descent regardless of where they lived. It presented Africa as the fatherland to all blacks, who would look to the continent for inspiration and who would offer it their help in its struggles. Many early spokesmen for Pan-Africanism were African Americans who were as concerned with the situation of blacks in the United States as with those in Africa. An idea dear to all Pan-Africanists, though, was the liberation of Africa from colonial control.

American **W. E. B. Du Bois** was a major leader. In 1919, while the powers of Europe were holding the Versailles Peace Conference at the end of World War I, Du Bois held a Pan-African Congress in Paris. Du Bois and the other leaders sought to give a united voice for blacks around the world. They urged the victorious Allies to grant equality to the land of Africa and to all people of African descent. The congress saw few victories. It did at least, however, persuade the European powers not to divide Germany's African colonies among the victors of World War I. Instead, the colonies became mandates supervised by European nations under the guidance of the League of Nations. The supervising nations would theoretically prepare these mandates for independence.

Future Pan-African Congresses did not accomplish even this much. Some black African leaders opposed what they saw as overly harsh criticism of colonialism by Du Bois. Blaise Diagne of Senegal argued that black Africans must work with the colonial powers. "To isolate the black race and to let it work out its own evolution is ridiculous," he said. "The evolution of our race . . . requires the cooperation of everybody." Discouraged, Du Bois eventually moved to Ghana in 1961 shortly before his death. There, at least, he could live under the rule of a leader, Kwame Nkrumah, who was a Pan-African Marxist like himself.

W. E. B. Du Bois

The fighting and suffering caused by Nigeria's Biafran War severely tested the Organization of African Unity and its attempts to deal with Africa's problems.

As new nations in Africa emerged after World War II, the Pan-African spirit showed new vigor. Along with Nkrumah of Ghana, other new African leaders such as Kenneth Kaunda of Zambia embraced the idea. They asserted the unity of all the peoples of Africa and said how they must all work together to solve the problems of the continent. There was some shift in the meaning of Pan-Africanism. It became less racial ("black") and more geographical ("African") as Arab North African states became part of the Pan-African movement.

The most visible expression of Pan-Africanism was the founding of the Organization of African Unity (OAU) in 1963. The OAU sought to defend Africa from exploitation and to promote cooperation. Still existing today, it is a forum for nations to discuss their problems, much like the United Nations. Like the UN, the OAU has enjoyed some successes and many failures. The organization settled border disputes between Somalia and Kenya and between Somalia and Ethiopia. But it proved unable to stop the bloody Biafran civil war in Nigeria in the late 1960s.

The problem for the OAU and the whole Pan-African movement is that neither Africa nor Africans have one set of problems or one set of enemies. Instead, different groups with conflicting goals usually compete to accomplish their own individual goals. Only as a movement succeeds in creating a common purpose can it achieve unity.

From Gold Coast to Ghana

The nation of Ghana on the western coast of Africa was originally the British colony of Gold Coast. As its colonial name suggests, the land was rich in gold. In addition, the region has supplies of diamonds, and it is a large supplier of cocoa, the main ingredient in producing chocolate. Gold Coast was in fact one of the most prosperous colonies in Africa.

But the people of Gold Coast desired to be free of British rule. One of the leaders of the drive for independence was **Kwame Nkrumah.** Born in Gold Coast in 1909, Nkrumah went to study in the United States and Great Britain. There he adopted the views of Karl Marx, joined the Communist Party, and became a leading opponent of British imperialism in Africa. In 1947 he returned to Gold Coast as secretary for a group seeking independence from Britain.

Kwame Nkrumah (in center on dais) is sworn in as the first prime minister of Ghana.

Ghana possessed rich resources that seemed to promise future prosperity for the nation after it gained independence.

Nkrumah soon seized control of the independence movement by his spellbinding personality and political shrewdness. The British first imprisoned him. Then, when Nkrumah still proved popular, the British made him prime minister of the colony. He ruled well and helped convince the British that Gold Coast, with him as the leader, could make the transition from colony to nation.

A new nation was born in 1957 with Nkrumah as its prime minister. It took the name *Ghana* after the African empire that had covered western Africa in the Middle Ages. Nkrumah embraced the idea of Pan-Africanism (see pp. 558-59) and dreamed that Ghana would become the leader of an independent African continent. "Our independence is meaningless," he said, "unless it is linked with the total liberation of the African continent."

From Democracy to Dictatorship

Circumstances looked promising for the young nation. Its parting from Great Britain had been friendly. Its economic resources gave the nation great potential for prosperity. And its new leader was idealistic and full of hope.

But things did not go well in Ghana. Nkrumah's government began to spend the nation's wealth on wasteful building projects. He built a major highway from the capital to the seacoast, although there were few vehicles to use it. He built huge silos to store cocoa, but they were so poorly constructed that they proved

useless. While Nkrumah built, the standard of living for unskilled workers fell to its lowest level since before World War II.

Nkrumah began to crack down on his opponents as he ruled by terror. He outlawed all political parties but his own and had himself declared president for life. He had some of his former associates tried for treason. When the judge declared them innocent, Nkrumah over-turned the verdict. He had the men retried and convicted this time. He not only fired the judge but threw him into jail, where he died two years later.

Nkrumah began to organize special security forces to enforce his rule and to protect him from assassination. He portrayed himself to the people of Ghana as a sort of messiah. A loyal newspaper said, "When our history is recorded, the man Kwame Nkrumah will be written of as the liberator, the Messiah, the Christ of our day." Groups of young people paraded through the streets carrying signs that said "Nkrumah never dies" and "Nkrumah is the new Messiah." Nkrumah took all of this praise seriously. He said in 1961, "All Africans know that I represent Africa and that I speak in her name. Therefore no African can have an opinion that differs from mine."

His government became increasingly corrupt as his officials enriched themselves by

Farmers in Ghana split the cocoa pods (right) and spread the seeds out to dry (left). Cocoa has long been one of Ghana's main sources of wealth.

The African coast near Accra, Ghana

In the 1990s, however, the continent of Africa went through what some writers have called a **"second independence."** Some fifteen nations, in varying degrees, turned their backs on one-party dictatorship. Some adopted new constitutions, and nearly all held new elections in which several parties could participate. Two entirely new nations won their independence (Namibia in 1990 and Eritrea in 1993). Ghana shared in this new birth of freedom. The nation approved a new constitution in 1992 that allowed for multiparty politics.

taking bribes. Finally, in 1966, while Nkrumah was visiting Communist China, the army overthrew him. Nkrumah died six years later in exile. But the end of Nkrumah's rule brought no peace to Ghana. The nation went through alternating periods of multiparty democracy and military rule. Ghana experienced four uprisings between 1972 and 1981.

The future for these struggling democracies is still uncertain. The road to stable democracy in Africa has not been an easy one. But at least there are signs that the dreams of independence that followed World War II might yet become a reality.

Section Review

1. What was Ghana originally named by the British and why?

2. Who led the drive for independence in Ghana?

3. Explain one result of Nkrumah's belief in himself as a kind of messiah.

4. In the "second independence" of the African continent in the 1990s, what two new nations gained independence?

Why do you think Kwame Nkrumah became a dictator after his original attraction to Marxism? Do you know of other examples of those who promoted Communism and then turned toward dictatorship?

Southern Africa: South Africa & Racial Conflict

Southern Africa is roughly the area explored by the famous British missionary David Livingstone. It is an area rich in diamonds and gold and somewhat drier and cooler than the rest of Africa (although not as dry, of course, as the Sahara Desert). Much of the land consists of plateaus and highlands. Pleasant savannas (grasslands) also cover much of the region. Along rivers such as the Zambezi you can also find jungles like those in West Africa (although smaller).

Southern Africa was the first part of sub-Saharan Africa to be settled by white Europeans in large numbers. (See Chapter 14.)

Historically, it has been the site of the fiercest racial conflict between blacks and whites. Racial conflict in Africa is not always black vs. white. Jews have often suffered persecution from African governments, particularly those with Muslim rulers. Israel helped resettle within its borders many Jews from Ethiopia to protect them from oppression. Uganda in the 1970s expelled nearly all of its Asian citizens and seized their wealth. Still, the black-white conflict, especially that in South Africa, has been the most prominent racial clash on the continent.

Afrikaners and Apartheid

As we noted in Chapter 14, after the Boer War (1899-1902) the sections of Southern Africa settled by the Dutch (called Boers and later **Afrikaners**) were joined to the sections settled by the English in the Union of South Africa. At that time, whites made up only a

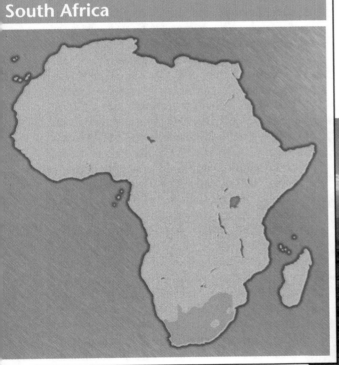

South Africa

Africa Redrawn

The breathtaking landscape of South Africa

The South African policy of apartheid called for almost total separation of the races, even to the point of separate entrances to buildings.

South Africans march to call for an end to discrimination in their land.

little under a third of the population, but the white minority—both Dutch and English—refused to share power with the black majority.

Until World War II the English-speaking whites led the government. After the war the Afrikaners took power. The English had already established a pattern of legal racial separation, but the Afrikaners made the distinction firmer. They instituted a policy called **apartheid** (from an Afrikaans word meaning "separate"). In theory, apartheid provided for the separate development of the ethnic groups in South Africa. In addition to blacks and whites, South Africa is home to Asians and **"coloureds"**—those of mixed racial heritage. In practice, apartheid preserved white economic and political dominance.

Apartheid laws rigidly separated the races. The government marked areas in which each race could live and forcibly moved those who did not conform. Invariably it was the blacks or coloureds who were moved, not whites. The Afrikaner government mandated complete racial segregation in education, marriage, and even churches. The government took control of all education and effectively shut down schools run by missionaries. The government even determined the kinds of jobs blacks could hold (reserving certain occupations for whites) and how much they could be paid. The South African government ruthlessly crushed dissent.

But there was dissent nonetheless. Black resentment of apartheid led to protests and riots. The leading opposition group was the **African National Congress (ANC)**, founded in 1912. Its early leaders supported peaceful demonstrations and boycotts. The situation changed drastically on February 3, 1960. On that day, in what became known as the **Sharpeville massacre,** the police opened fire on a group of unarmed demonstrators, killing sixty-nine and wounding eighty-six. Thereafter, many protest leaders rejected peaceful means of change. One leader, **Nelson Mandela,** formed a radical branch of the ANC called *Umkonto we Sizwe* ("Spear of the Nation").

Mandela advocated violence and called for the overthrow of the white government. This fact, along with Mandela's ties to Com-

Nelson Mandela

Finally, the opposing sides agreed on a transition from minority rule to majority rule. In a 1994 election Mandela and the African National Congress won handily. Mandela himself received over 60 percent of the vote for president against several candidates, while de Klerk was a distant second with 20 percent. The two candidates also shared a great honor. They both received the Nobel Peace Prize for their work in trying to heal the divisions in South Africa.

South Africa had finally moved from minority to majority rule, but violence did not end. White and black extremists opposed the agreement. Even some of Mandela's supporters argued among themselves. Yet the evil of apartheid had ended, and all South Africans held their future in their hands through the ballot. They could hope only in the vision that Nelson Mandela had offered twice—once at his trial in 1964 and again during his election

munism, led to his arrest in 1962 and his imprisonment for twenty-seven years. But even in prison he proved to be a powerful symbol of resistance.

Winds of Change

Other nations inside and outside Africa began pressuring South Africa to reform and allow majority rule. The white minority dug in and tried to hold on to power. Rich resources in diamonds, gold, chromium, and other materials at first gave the nation the economic strength to resist this pressure. But a growing economic boycott by other nations and internal violence weakened the minority's resolve. Finally, an Afrikaner prime minister, **F. W. de Klerk,** began to reform the state. He led the repeal of apartheid laws and released Mandela from prison. In a special vote, two-thirds of the whites in South Africa approved of his efforts to draft a new constitution.

The cell in Robben Island Prison in which South African authorities imprisoned Mandela for eighteen years

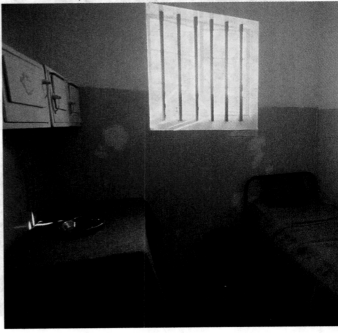

Africa Redrawn

campaign in 1994. He said, "I have fought against white domination, I have fought against black domination. I have cherished the ideal of a democratic and free society in which all people live together in harmony and with equal opportunities." If the leaders of South Africa can attain that vision, then perhaps all races in the region can live together peaceably. But any leader who would rule well must always acknowledge the problem of man's natural sinfulness. There is no true and lasting harmony apart from Jesus Christ.

Section Review

1. Name at least two sets of conflicting groups in Southern Africa.

2. List two other names for the Dutch-descended people of Southern Africa.

3. What does apartheid mean?

4. What group led the protest against apartheid?

5. What powerful leader of the ANC was jailed but later became president?

6. Who was the prime minister of South Africa who worked for reform and won the Nobel Peace Prize with Nelson Mandela?

What causes one person to think of another as inferior to himself? What steps would be needed to correct the problem in thinking? Use Bible verses to support your reasons. Possible verses include I Samuel 16:7, I Corinthians 12:1-27, and James 2:1-9.

Nelson Mandela receives an award in Philadelphia as F. W. de Klerk and President Clinton of the United States congratulate him.

East Africa: Rwanda and Tribal Conflict

The landscape of East Africa is incredibly diverse. From low coastal plains, the land soars to plateaus and mountains. **Mount Kilimanjaro,** the highest mountain in Africa, lies in this region. Scorching deserts lie in areas bordering the Red Sea. Running through East Africa is a deep valley, the massive **Great Rift Valley.** Africa's largest lakes—**Lake Victoria, Lake Tanganyika,** and **Lake Nyasa**—lie in the region.

Many people in East Africa speak Swahili, a language whose roots date back to the Middle Ages. But the widespread use of this language partially masks a division common among African societies. Racial conflict, as in South Africa, is not the only conflict in Africa. Even older is the historic African conflict between tribes. A tribe, you will recall from Chapter 5, is a group of people who share a common language, beliefs, and customs. When the European nations divided Africa and later allowed their colonies to become nations, they often drew national boundaries without caring where the different tribes lived. As a result, some peoples were divided by artificial boundaries. In other cases, tribes that had been enemies for years became citizens of the same country.

This conflict between African peoples is called **tribalism** or sometimes regionalism. There are many painful examples of such conflict in Africa. From 1967 to 1970 Nigeria underwent a bloody civil war between the Ibo people on the one side and the Yoruba and Hausa on the other. Estimates are that as many as one million people died in the Nigerian war. Likewise the racial conflict in South Africa was complicated by strife between the Xhosa and Zulu tribes.

Tutsi vs. Hutu

Small African nations are not immune to this sort of conflict. The tiny nation of Rwanda is an example. Long before Europe colonized Africa, this area in East Africa had seen conflict between the remarkably tall **Tutsi** people and the more numerous **Hutu** people. The Tutsi had maintained control by ruling as an aristocracy, like that which existed in

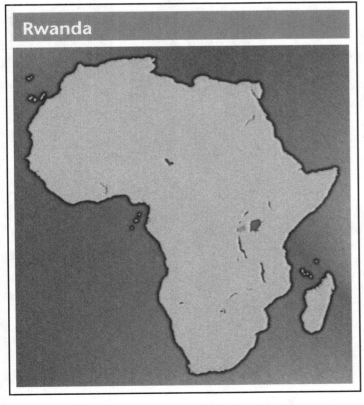

Rwanda

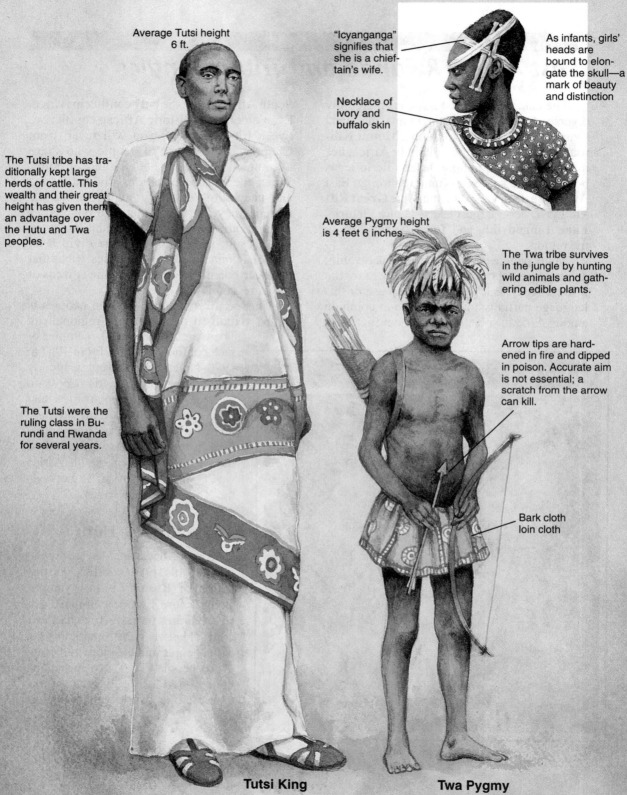

Tutsi Noblewoman

"Icyanganga" signifies that she is a chieftain's wife.

As infants, girls' heads are bound to elongate the skull—a mark of beauty and distinction

Necklace of ivory and buffalo skin

Average Tutsi height 6 ft.

The Tutsi tribe has traditionally kept large herds of cattle. This wealth and their great height has given them an advantage over the Hutu and Twa peoples.

The Tutsi were the ruling class in Burundi and Rwanda for several years.

Average Pygmy height is 4 feet 6 inches.

The Twa tribe survives in the jungle by hunting wild animals and gathering edible plants.

Arrow tips are hardened in fire and dipped in poison. Accurate aim is not essential; a scratch from the arrow can kill.

Bark cloth loin cloth

Tutsi King

Twa Pygmy

Tutsi refugees, young and old, flee Hutu massacres in Rwanda.

nents, invaded Rwanda several times after independence. Each time the invaders were driven out with great bloodshed on both sides. Inside Rwanda's borders were constant clashes between the tribes.

Other factors worsened the tribal conflict. The economy of the tiny, overcrowded country was weak, depending chiefly on a few exports such as coffee and tin. Rwanda is completely landlocked and must ship its goods through other countries. But conflicts with those countries, notably Uganda, sometimes closed the borders. Economic suffering resulted as Rwanda could not get its goods out to markets. Also the government of Rwanda was dictatorial and corrupt. Therefore, even some Hutus sided with the Tutsis working for reform.

Rwandan Patriotic Front

Refugees in Uganda eventually formed the **Rwandan Patriotic Front (RPF)** to overthrow the government. Led mainly by the Tutsis, the RPF called for political and economic reform. On October 1, 1990, the RPF invaded Rwanda from Uganda. The rebels

France before the French Revolution. When first the Germans and then the Belgians controlled the region, they worked through the Tutsi leaders.

But the Hutus saw no reason that they should serve the less numerous Tutsis. Just before independence, the Hutus of Rwanda threw off the Tutsis. About 150,000 Rwandans died in this fighting. When the Republic of Rwanda was born in 1962, it was under Hutu control. Many Tutsis became **refugees** (people fleeing war, persecution, or other dangers) and lived across Rwanda's borders in Congo, Uganda, Tanzania, and Burundi. There they built refugee camps that became centers of opposition to the Hutus.

The Tutsis did not give up without a fight. From their bases in neighboring countries, Tutsi forces sometimes attacked Rwanda. Tutsi invaders, called "cockroaches" by their oppo-

won a number of victories but could not take the whole country. Finally, in August of 1993, the two sides agreed to a peace treaty. President Juvénal Habyamira, although himself a Hutu, promised to rule in a manner fair to all sides.

But the peace was shattered in April 1994. Hutu extremists, angered at Habyamira's compromise with the Tutsis, shot down his plane and killed him. Civil war broke out again as the RPF renewed its campaign. The RPF took control of the country in July 1994. But before they did so, Hutu forces began slaughtering Tutsis. Probably five hundred thousand died in this attempt at **genocide** (the destruction of a whole racial, ethnic, or political group).

The Tutsi-led Rwandan Patriotic Front fought the Hutu-led government of Rwanda and eventually won control of the nation.

The RPF now had power but still had trouble. The country was devastated by the fighting. The economy was ruined. It now became the Hutus' turn to be refugees as some two million fled the country. The refugee camps became centers of death by disease as well as bases for raids by Hutu forces on Rwanda. The new government began trying to bring the mass murderers of the Tutsis to justice. But it found that the court system was so ravaged by violence that it had ceased to function. The United Nations had to step in to restore order.

There are no easy answers to such tribal conflict. Years of hatred and conflict cannot be solved by a small dose of goodwill on the part of a few. The Christian realizes that only as men's natures are changed by Christ can they really make peace with one another (II Cor. 5:17-21).

Section Review

1. Name Africa's highest mountain. Name its three largest lakes.
2. Give two examples of tribal conflict in Africa.
3. Name the two major tribes in Rwanda and describe each.
4. What is genocide?

Why is tribalism such a problem in Africa? Compare this tribalism to tribes in the Americas.

Christianity in Modern Africa

Christianity has existed in Africa for centuries. The Bible records the conversion of the "Ethiopian eunuch" (Acts 8:26-40) in the first century. Some churches in Africa have a history tracing back to the era of the Roman Empire. Members of the **Coptic Church** in Egypt number around five million. The Copts,

The Church of St. Barbara in Cairo is part of Egypt's Coptic Church, one of the oldest Christian groups in Africa.

however, often suffer severe persecution and even violence from the Muslim majority. The **Ethiopian Orthodox Church** in Ethiopia is almost as old as the Coptic. It is in fact very close to the Coptic Church in teaching and practice. Until 1959 the *abuna* (head of the Ethiopian Church) was appointed by the Coptic Church. Today, the Ethiopian Church is independent. Roman Catholics have been present in Africa since the 1400s. The largest numbers of Catholics in Africa today are in those countries that were once colonies of Catholic nations, such as Belgium and France.

Some of the most notable Christian growth in Africa in the twentieth century has come among Protestant and independent groups. Often these churches are connected to denominations in Europe and North America. Many of these churches resulted from the work of American and European missionaries. Today, national pastors (pastors native to Africa) are taking more and more of the burden from missionaries—but there are still great needs.

African Independent Churches

The growing importance of African Christian workers is also seen in what are known as the **African Independent Churches.** These are churches, denominations, and other groups that are controlled entirely by Africans. According to estimates, there are over five thousand different groups that can be classified as independent. There are two major kinds of African Independent Churches: Ethiopian churches and Zionist churches.

Members of the Ethiopian Orthodox Church join in a Christmas celebration at the rock-hewn Bet Marian Church.

CHARACTERIZATIONS

Janani Luwum

Three hundred thousand Ugandans died under the rule of cruel dictator Idi Amin Dada of Uganda. But no death was more publicized than that of Janani Luwum. The future martyr was born in 1922 in northern Uganda. Although reared in a Christian home, Luwum was not converted until 1948. At that time he became one of the *balokole* ("saved ones") as a result of the East Africa Revival. In his first public testimony he said, "Today I have become a leader in Christ's army. I am prepared to die in the army of Jesus. As Jesus shed His blood for the people, if it is God's will, I will do the same."

Luwum eventually decided to become a minister of the Anglican Church in Uganda. He studied in both his own country and England. He pastored small scattered churches across rugged northern Uganda, and he also worked with a college. His church made him bishop of northern Uganda in 1969.

Luwum was made an archbishop in 1974. On his election, he said, "Many people have learned about Christ as an academic exercise. The church must help such people to transfer Christ from their heads into their hearts. I had Christ in my head and not my heart before I was converted. In 1948 I was 'born again' and Christ became the controller of my life. My sense of direction and values changed. Even now I am still growing in Him."

Archbishop Janani Luwum was human and had his failings. In some ways he was undiscerning. Despite his knowledge of the need for conversion, he tended to accept everyone as "Christian" who claimed the term, no matter what a person might teach or how he might live. But the archbishop showed great courage in the face of evil.

From 1971 to 1979 Uganda suffered under the rule of General Idi Amin Dada. To call Amin

Janani Luwum

cruel would be an understatement. He ruthlessly slaughtered not only opponents but also friends and family members. His security forces delighted in torture. A man accused of theft, for example, was taken to a stadium and tied down. Then soldiers drove motorcycles over his body until he was dead. Amin himself was said to practice cannibalism. A Muslim, the dictator hoped to change Uganda from a predominantly Christian country to an Islamic one.

The archbishop tried vainly to work with Amin and cooperate with the government. The violence only got worse. Finally, in August 1976 Luwum held a meeting of religious leaders of Uganda. They asked for an end to the killings and illegal arrests. Amin was furious and was especially angry at Luwum, who had called the meeting and whose signature was first on the protest. A few months later Luwum said, "I live as though there will be no tomorrow. I face daily being picked up by the soldiers. While the opportunity is there, I preach the gospel with all my might, and my conscience is clear before God. . . . Whenever I have the opportunity I have told the President the things the churches disapprove of. God is my witness."

On February 16, 1977, Amin called a number of religious leaders to a meeting. There an official read charges accusing the archbishop of plotting to overthrow the government. As this was being read, Luwum whispered to a bishop standing by him, "They are going to kill me. I am not afraid." The officials dismissed the group but held Luwum back because Amin wanted to see him. As his friends left, the archbishop said, "I can see the hand of the Lord in this."

It is not known exactly what happened next. Some accounts say that Amin tried to force Luwum into signing a confession that he had committed treason. When Luwum began to pray,

Amin told his guards to shut him up, and they shot him in the mouth, then twice in the chest. The government refused to release the body and announced that the archbishop was killed in a car accident.

Luwum's death took place on the one hundredth anniversary of the coming of Christianity to Uganda. At a service following the archbishop's martyrdom, the congregation sang a hymn originally sung by the first Ugandan martyrs nearly a century before:

> Grant, O Lord, our eyes be open
> Here to see our Saviour King,
> And our hearts be ever eager
> Him to hear, His praise to sing.

Two years later, the Amin regime ended, but the church of Jesus Christ continues forward.

Ugandan dictator Idi Amin Dada, persecutor of Christians and slayer of Janani Luwum

An African church service

Zionist groups will borrow ceremonies from traditional pagan African religions or incorporate elements of witchcraft. Zionist churches also usually look to one outstanding leader who is treated as a kind of prophet.

The Kimbanguist Church, centered in Congo, is a good example of a Zionist church. The founder was Simon Kimbangu (1889-1951), a popular Baptist preacher and healer. Such large crowds began to gather to hear him that authorities in the Belgian Congo (today the Democratic Republic of Congo) arrested him in 1921 and sentenced him to death. The sentence was changed to life imprisonment, and he remained jailed until his death. Even with Kimbangu in prison, the church grew. After his death, Kimbanguists sang hymns claiming that Kimbangu had been raised from the dead in some manner and continued to work among men. The importance of Kimbangu to the church as a prophet is reflected by its official name, "The Church of Jesus Christ on Earth Through the Prophet Simon Kimbangu."

Ethiopian churches take their name from Psalm 68:31—"Ethiopia shall soon stretch out her hands unto God." Because Ethiopia never came under European control, Africans see that land as a symbol of independence. Psalm 68:31 also expresses the hope of many African Christians that the entire continent will come under the influence of the gospel of Christ. Ethiopian churches are often much like European or North American churches in practice and doctrine. Their main distinguishing characteristic is their total independence from non-African control. Many of these Ethiopian churches are also involved in politics as a way to solve Africa's problems.

Zionist churches are also independent of non-African control, but they are even more independent in their teaching and practice. The Zionist churches often blend Christianity with traditional African culture. Zionist churches, for example, may permit polygamy (the marriage of a man to more than one wife) despite the Bible's teaching against it. Often

East Africa Revival

One of the most dramatic events in modern African church history was the **East Africa Revival,** which centered in Tanzania, Uganda, and Kenya. It began among Anglican evangelicals in the 1930s and profoundly affected the Protestant churches of the region. Its effects continued through at least the 1950s, and many major religious leaders of Africa were converted in the revival, such as Archbishop Janani Luwum of Uganda (see pp. 570-71).

The revival stressed the confession of sin and the need to preach the gospel to the unsaved. The importance of Christ's atonement for sin through the shedding of His blood became an important theme. A favorite gospel song of the revival was "What can wash away my sin? Nothing but the blood of Jesus." One Christian converted in the revival described the effects of the awakening:

> Conviction of sin came upon people. The Word of God became real and alive. The church was packed and the atmosphere was charged with the power of the Spirit. . . . People were rejoicing and talking from experience and singing praises to God. Jesus was so close, they talked about him while shopping. They talked about him when they drew water. People were even converted at the watering places for cattle—cattlemen speaking to cattlemen. It was wonderful! This was like what happened in the New Testament.

In short, the religious life of African Christians is probably as diverse as it is in any continent. But events such as the East Africa Revival reveal that God is working among Africans as He is among all peoples of the world. As the apostle Peter said, "Of a truth I perceive that God is no respecter of persons: but in every nation he that feareth him, and worketh righteousness, is accepted with him" (Acts 10:34-35).

Section Review

1. In what country is the Coptic Church found? the Ethiopian Orthodox Church?
2. Name the two major kinds of African Independent Churches.

3. Describe the East Africa Revival.

How did European and American religions spread to Africa? Describe the effects that those cultures had on Africans.

Summary

African history and culture in the twentieth century has been just as diverse as the continent's landscape. The modern age has presented Africa with many challenges: decolonization (as illustrated by Algeria), dictatorships (as illustrated by Ghana), racial conflict (as illustrated by South Africa), and tribal conflict (as illustrated by Rwanda). But in addition there has been hope on the continent, especially the hope of the gospel found in Christianity. God moves among the Africans as He moves among all the peoples of the world.

People, Places, and Things to Know

Sahara
decolonization
assimilation
Front for National
  Liberation (FLN)
Haile Selassie
Charles de Gaulle
"Pan-Africanism"
W. E. B. Du Bois

Kwame Nkrumah
"second
  independence"
Afrikaners
apartheid
"coloureds"
African National
  Congress (ANC)
Sharpeville massacre
Nelson Mandela

F. W. de Klerk
Mount Kilimanjaro
Great Rift Valley
tribalism
Tutsi
Hutu
refugees
Rwandan Patriotic
  Front (RPF)

genocide
Coptic Church
Ethiopian Orthodox
  Church
African Independent
  Churches
Ethiopian churches
Zionist churches
East Africa Revival

Review Questions

Matching

Match each section of Africa with the country used to characterize it.

1. Saharan Africa
2. West Africa
3. Southern Africa
4. East Africa

(a) Algeria
(b) Ghana
(c) Rwanda
(d) South Africa

Fill-in-the-Blank

5. Egypt has about five million members in the _____ Church.

6. The _____ Church in Ethiopia is led by the *abuna*.

7. Churches that are similar to non-African churches but are distinguished by their independence from outside control are known as _____ churches.

8. The _____ churches combine Christianity with traditional African culture.

Connections

Write a sentence describing the relationship between the following pairs of terms.

9. decolonization / assimilation
10. Nelson Mandela / F. W. de Klerk
11. "Pan-Africanism" / W. E. B. Du Bois

Matching

Match each term with the country it represents.

12. Front for National Liberation (FLN)
13. Tutsi
14. Gold Coast
15. apartheid
16. tribalism
17. Belgian Congo
18. African National Congress
19. Afrikaners
20. Hutu
21. Charles de Gaulle
22. Haile Selassie
23. Kwame Nkrumah
24. King Leopold
25. Mussolini

(a) Algeria
(b) Ethiopia
(c) Ghana
(d) Rwanda
(e) South Africa
(f) Democratic Republic of Congo

Think About It!

What are some other examples of planned or practiced genocide? What might man's reasoning be to use genocide? Can genocide ever be justified?

CHAPTER 20

Even at this point in the school year, you probably remember that Chapters 6 and 7 discussed the early history of Latin America. We saw there how the Spanish moved first into Central America and the Caribbean and how they shared the settlement of South America with Portugal. Today over five hundred million people live in Latin America. These millions of inhabitants represent several cultural heritages—Spanish, Portuguese, Indian, African, and other nationalities. How can anyone survey the history of a people so numerous and so diverse in just a single chapter?

Actually, we can learn the basic themes of Latin American history by studying selected countries in the region. By looking at Mexico, Argentina, and Costa Rica, we can get some idea of the course of Latin American history. In addition, the Characterizations, Settings, and other special features in the chapter allow us to take a few "detours" to sample Latin American history—just as you might sample Latin American food at a feast by tasting a little bit of everything. Of course, you will not learn *everything* about Latin American history in just a few pages. But you will discover some of the forces and personalities that have shaped the region.

A.D. 1910 - PRESENT

	Mexican Revolution 1910-20	
1910		1920

The Changing Face of Latin America

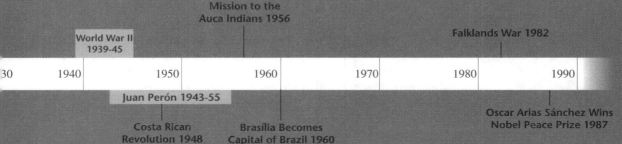

Mission to the
Auca Indians 1956

World War II
1939-45

Falklands War 1982

| 30 | 1940 | 1950 | 1960 | 1970 | 1980 | 1990 |

Juan Perón 1943-55

Costa Rican
Revolution 1948

Brasília Becomes
Capital of Brazil 1960

Oscar Arias Sánchez Wins
Nobel Peace Prize 1987

Mexico: Preserving a Revolution

Mexico is one of the largest Latin American countries. Originally home to the Mayan and Aztec civilizations, Mexico fell under Spanish control. From the conquest of the Aztecs by Cortés in the 1500s, Mexico was a colony of Spain until it gained independence in the 1820s.

In the 1800s, after independence, Mexico went through periods in which it was an empire, a republic, and a dictatorship. A disastrous war with the United States (1846-48) cost the nation half of its territory. The Mexicans also suffered through a period in which Emperor Napoleon III of France tried to force an Austrian nobleman on the nation as its emperor.

Mexico

Mexico achieved some stability in 1877 when General **Porfirio Díaz** (por-FEER-ee-oh DEE-ahs) became dictator. He encouraged foreign investment and reorganized the Mexican government. By stern rule, Díaz kept order in the country.

Porfirio Díaz

Revolution

But after more than thirty years of Díaz's rule, many leaders were tiring of his sometimes harsh control. They wondered who would succeed the aging dictator. In 1910 Francisco Madero challenged Díaz in a presidential election. The dictator tried to fix the election and at first declared himself the winner. But there was such an uproar of protest and rebellion that Díaz's dictatorship collapsed.

But the end of Díaz did not mean relief for the Mexican people. The nation was soon suf-

Pancho Villa on horseback

In northern Mexico, Francisco **"Pancho" Villa** (VEE-uh) was a bandit who supported Madero. A skilled soldier, he helped the revolutionary forces win major victories in the north. Villa at first supported Carranza but soon broke with him and joined forces with Zapata. When the United States supported Carranza, the angry Villa murdered sixteen American engineers working in Santa Isabel and then crossed the U.S. border to attack Columbus, New Mexico. Angered by these actions, President Wilson sent a U.S. Army force under General **John Pershing** into Mexico to track down Villa. But American soldiers could never pin down the wily Villa, and they eventually withdrew.

Emiliano Zapata

suffering through a bloody period that has become known as the **Mexican Revolution.** Madero tried to rule, but he was quickly overthrown and executed by General **Victoriano Huerta** (WHER ta), who became dictator.

But Huerta could not establish order either. Other revolts flared up across the country, and the United States opposed Huerta. President Woodrow Wilson called him "that scoundrel" and a "desperate brute." Huerta's government fell, and rival armies began contending for control of Mexico.

In southern Mexico, **Emiliano Zapata** led an uprising of peasants who wanted to break up the large estates and provide land for the small farmers. They took the slogan "Land and Liberty!" Zapata was able to gather as many as twenty-five thousand men into his forces. He virtually ruled the south of the country.

In central Mexico, **Venustiano Carranza** had been a supporter of the slain Madero. Carranza rallied the opposition to Huerta but was unable to hold his forces together after Huerta was gone. He eventually presented himself as the legitimate leader of Mexico and won the support of the United States.

The Changing Face of Latin America

All three revolutionary leaders died violently. Zapata was killed in 1919 in an ambush by Carranza's forces. Villa retired to his ranch in 1920 but was gunned down in 1923 under mysterious circumstances. Carranza seemed to be the victor when he became president of Mexico in 1917. Moreover, he presided over the adopting of the Constitution of 1917, the constitution by which Mexico is still governed today. But in 1920 he tried to arrange for one of his supporters to succeed him as president. The army rebelled, and Carranza was killed as he attempted to flee Mexico City.

Search for Stability

This violence, bloodshed, and unrest convinced Mexico's leaders that they must find a better way to rule the country. Violence continued in the 1920s, but Mexico began to build a stable system. They finally decided that the solution was to move away from personal rule. In other words, the government would no longer be centered on the popularity of a single leader. The cry of politics became "No reelection." With reelection forbidden, Mexican presidents would find it harder to increase their power by winning (or sometimes stealing) election after election. After one six-year term, the president had to step down.

Mexican leaders decided to preserve the revolution by replacing personal rule with party rule. In 1928 what became known as the **Institutional Revolutionary Party** *(Partido Revolucionario Institucional,* or **PRI**) was established. The PRI virtually became the government of Mexico. The president and most of the high officials belonged to the party. Under the PRI's guidance, Mexico escaped revolutionary violence. Although still a poor nation in many ways, Mexico began to industrialize and change itself into a more urban country. Under the rule of the PRI, Mexico found stability.

As its name indicates, one of the goals of the PRI was to "institutionalize" the revolution. The party's leaders wanted to preserve all the gains of the Mexican Revolution and carry forward its principles of reform and democracy. The government demonstrated this concern in many ways. One of the most visible ways (literally) was Mexico's support of the **muralists.** Painters such as **Diego Rivera** and José Clemente Orozco painted great murals on the walls of public buildings. In a deceptively simple style, these murals celebrate Mexico's history and feature the common

Distribution of Arms, a mural by Diego Rivera celebrating the Mexican Revolution

people, not the rich elites that the muralists despised. Rivera said, "For the first time in the history of art, Mexican mural painting made the masses the hero of monumental art."

But there was a cost to stability. The PRI allowed Mexicans to participate in the rule of their country—but they usually had to do so through the PRI. The party manipulated elections so that it won most of them. Although other parties could usually win a few offices, power remained in the hands of the PRI. Not until 1997 did the Mexican legislature start a session without a majority of its members belonging to the PRI. As a result, Mexico has a government that is sensitive to the people's wishes but that also devotes its energies to maintaining power. A Mexican poet described government under the PRI as a "philanthropic ogre." In other words, the government of Mexico is well-meaning in its attempt to rule justly and provide for the needs of its people. But it is an "ogre," a monster, in that it is controlled by just one faction that will use even corrupt means to stay in power.

A scenic view of Monterrey, Mexico, illustrates how far the nation has come since the revolution in the early twentieth century.

The one-party rule of Mexico has served the country better than the multiple governments and revolutions of the 1800s. Also, thanks to the nation's natural resources—notably oil—the nation has even enjoyed some prosperity. But Mexico still suffers from debt and economic depression, especially when oil prices drop. The corruption sometimes characterizing the PRI's rule has led other parties to seek an end to PRI domination. A few radical groups have even taken up arms against the government. Mexico has enjoyed some peace and prosperity, but it has yet to enjoy a truly open democracy.

Section Review

1. To whom did Mexico lose half of its territory in the middle of the 1800s?

2. Whom did Victoriano Huerta overthrow to become president of Mexico?

3. Name the three leaders of Mexico who vied for control in the 1910s and tell from which section each came.

4. What is the major political party in Mexican politics?

5. Name two well-known muralists from this time period.

Give other examples of government being a "philanthropic ogre." What evidences do we see in the Mexican government to support this? How would one balance philanthropy and big government?

Location—The largest country in South America, Brazil dominates the continent. On its eastern side are thousands of miles of coastline along the shore of the Atlantic Ocean. On its western side, Brazil touches at some point every other Southern American country, except Chile and Ecuador. The equator falls across the northern part of the country.

Climate—The northern part of Brazil, along the Amazon River Basin, has a tropical wet (rain forest) climate. This region receives over eighty inches of rain per year. The climate of the southern plateau and the highlands is chiefly tropical wet and dry (savanna). Rainfall here is only forty to sixty inches per year.

Topography—Dominating the northern half of the country is the Amazon River Basin. The future of the rain forest along this river has become a source of international concern. Brazil has been clearing away the rain forest to provide land for farming and industry. Some scientists worry that this policy will harm the ecology of not just Brazil but also the rest of the world. The rest of the nation outside the Amazon region is mostly plateau and highlands.

Natural Resources—Brazil enjoys some mineral wealth. Its most profitable mineral products are iron and manganese, although Brazil lacks the coal it needs to turn the iron to steel. Brazil, like many Latin American countries, has tended to rely on one major crop for export. Originally, sugar was Brazil's main cash crop and later rubber was an important export. Today, Brazil's main crop is coffee, and the country is the world's largest coffee grower. The problem with one-crop economies is that national prosperity goes up and down as the crop's value goes up and down. Brazil has learned this fact to its sorrow and now tries to diversify its exports.

Geography & Culture—Brazil differs from the rest of Latin America in that its culture is Portuguese instead of Spanish. Its major cities include Rio de Janeiro (day zhuh-NEHR-oh; the original capital) on the Atlantic coast and São Paolo (its largest city).

Brazil's capital, **Brasília,** has an unusual history. Most of Brazil's major cities are on the coast. To encourage development of the interior, in 1957 the Brazilian government began building a new capital city some five hundred miles inland. Starting from virtual wilderness, the thoroughly modern city of Brasilia rose above that wilderness and was dedicated as the capital in 1960. Today the former wilderness is home to over a million inhabitants.

After winning independence from Portugal, Brazil was an empire for many years. (See pp. 182-83.) The country was a republic from 1889 to 1930. Since that time Brazil has alternated between military dictatorships and democratic governments. In 1985 military rule finally gave way to a democratic civilian government.

Settings Review

1. What is another name for tropical wet climate? tropical wet and dry?
2. What area of Brazil is a source of international ecological concern?
3. What is Brazil's major export today?
4. What is the main language in Brazil?
5. Name two major cities in Brazil.

What are the pros and cons of ecological conservation? Should we do anything to take care of God's creation, or should we allow nature to take care of itself?

Three faces of Brazil (left to right): the modernizing nation, the rain forest, and an immigrant to a newly settled area

Argentina: From Dictatorship to Democracy

At the beginning of the twentieth century, Argentina was one of the richest nations in Latin America. Its exports of grain and beef built a strong trading relationship with other nations, especially Great Britain. Argentina prided itself on being European in its culture and tastes.

Argentina

This situation began to change from the time of World War I to the beginning of the Great Depression in 1929. Argentina found that its farm exports no longer brought in enough money to maintain prosperity. Although Argentina was not harmed by the Great De-pression as much as some other Latin American countries, the economic downturn led to changes.

One distinct change throughout Latin America and in Argentina was the end of the hacienda as a major economic force. In the 1800s the haciendas dominated the economic life of the region. Much of life outside the cities centered on the hacienda. (See p. 178.) But when the profits began to fall, the system began to fall apart. Many hacienda workers went to the cities to find better-paying jobs in factories. The hacienda owners exercised less and less influence on the government.

Dictatorship

A more drastic change in Argentina was in government. The earlier period of prosperity brought stable democracy to Argentina. But democracy was one of the first victims of hard times. In 1930 the military toppled the government and dominated Argentine politics in the 1930s and 1940s. Many Western democracies were worried by Argentina's open sympathy with the Fascist states of Germany and Italy. Argentina, in fact, remained neutral in World War II until it was obvious that the Axis powers would lose.

In 1943 the army again brought down the government, but a leader in this rebellion would soon transform Argentine politics. **Juan Perón** (puh ROHN) was a leading military officer. Like many in the army, he was sympathetic to Germany under the Nazis. He also spent time as a representative for the Argentine government in Italy in the 1930s, where he developed an admiration for Mussolini's Fascist state.

When the army installed a new government in 1943, Perón became secretary of the army and secretary of labor. By winning the

Juan Perón and his wife Eva wave to cheering crowds of Argentine workers.

support of both the army and the workers, Perón built a base of support unlike the previous governments. The army gave him military support; the workers gave him widespread popular support.

One worker said of Perón, "He had the virtue of leaving his audience satisfied without promising them anything." But Perón did keep some of his promises. He supported the large meatpackers' union in its conflicts with management. As secretary of labor, he gave the workers a minimum wage and paid holidays. His wife, former actress **Eva Duarte Perón** (known as "Evita"), increased his appeal. Evita was beautiful and at least as magnetic in personality as her husband. She had risen from poverty herself and sympathized with the poor. The Peróns identified themselves with the *descamisados* (DAYS-kah-mee-SAH-thohs; "shirtless ones"), the poor factory workers who crowded into Argentina's cities.

The support of the *descamisados* paid off for Perón. The army, fearing his labor reforms, forced him out of office and arrested him. But on October 17, 1945, the workers marched on the capital chanting, "There is no work with-

The tomb of Eva Perón in Buenos Aires is still honored by her admirers years after her death.

out Perón." Frightened by the unity of the workers, the government freed Perón. In February of 1946, Perón was easily elected president of Argentina.

President Perón continued his program of social reform. His wife led the Eva Perón Foundation, which distributed money, food, and medicines to the poor. (She raised the money by telling businesses that they might find the government more cooperative if they gave to her foundation.) Income began to rise, and Perón gave women the vote in 1947. A

The plaza of modern Buenos Aires, Argentina

popular slogan was *"Perón cumple"* ("Perón delivers"). He was easily elected to a second term in 1952. At a huge rally that year, Evita thrilled the crowds with her oratory:

> It is the working people, the little people of the nation, who here and throughout the country are on their feet, ready to follow Perón, the Leader of the people, the Leader of humanity, because he has raised high the banner of salvation and justice for the masses; ready to follow him against the oppression of traitors within and without, traitors who in the darkness of the night would like to inject their snake venom into the soul and body of Perón, which is the soul and body of the Nation. But they won't succeed, any more than toads in their jealousy can succeed in silencing the nightingale's song or snakes succeed in halting the flight of the condor. They won't succeed, my General, because we—the men and women of the People—we are here to guard your dreams and watch over your life . . . and we would

never forgive ourselves if we hadn't protected a man as fine as General Perón, who nurtured the dreams of all Argentines, particularly the dreams of the working people.

But after his reelection, Perón's regime began to fall apart. Shortly after giving this speech, Evita—so enormously popular among the poor—died of cancer. More harmful to Perón was the downturn of the economy. By remaining neutral for most of World War II, Argentina had traded with both sides and built a huge financial surplus. Perón, however, spent this surplus to keep his followers happy, and by the early 1950s, the surplus was gone. As an admirer of Fascism, Perón had never much respected basic freedoms such as freedom of the press. When discontent began to grow, he became even harsher in his rule. The dictator became increasingly unpopular. Finally, in 1955, the military ended his rule just as Perón himself had helped topple the government in 1943. He fled the country.

From Disorder to Democracy

But the exile of Perón brought no peace to Argentina. In the nearly twenty years that followed his departure, not a single president of the nation finished out his term of office. Each time, the armed forces forced the president out of office. Finally Perón himself returned to Argentina and was elected president in 1973. His next wife, Isabel, was elected vice president. The aged dictator died less than a year after taking office. Isabel Perón tried to rule for two years after her husband's death, but the military eventually toppled her as it had her husband and so many other presidents.

Argentina became an undisguised military dictatorship. The military began to crack down on all opponents. In what became known as the **"dirty war"** against opposition, the government began arresting citizens suspected of treasonous views. Those arrested simply vanished, never to be seen again by their friends and family. Economically, Argentina suffered from staggering inflation. Prices rose as much as 600 percent a year.

Increasingly unpopular, the military rulers tried a desperate gamble to increase their support among the people. Argentina and Great Britain had for years been arguing over who should control the **Falkland Islands** in the south Atlantic. (See pp. 588-89.) Argentina's rulers stunned the British by sending troops to seize the Falklands in April of 1982. The Argentine rulers hoped that the British would do nothing. Instead, Great Britain recaptured the islands and humiliated the Argentine armed forces. The discredited dictators were forced out of power.

In 1983 free elections were again held in Argentina—and this time the president was allowed to finish out his term. The new government brought members of the old dictatorship to trial and punished them for their abuses of power. In 1989 Argentina elected a member of the Perónist party as president, and reelected him in 1995. Now even the Perónists were committed to democratic government. Many obstacles lie ahead, but Argentina appears to be on its way to establishing stable democracy.

Section Review

1. What were two major changes in Argentina after the Great Depression?

2. Who was sympathetic to Nazism and Fascism while he served as secretary of labor and later became president?

3. Who were the *descamisados?*

4. Describe government in Argentina after Perón was ousted from power.

5. Whom did Argentina fight for control of the Falkland Islands?

Why might such a popular leader as Perón have been ousted from office? Explain the influence his wife had on his success in government. Why was he allowed back?

The Falklands War

The Falklands are a group of islands in the south Atlantic, about three hundred miles off the coast of Argentina. There are two main islands—East Falkland and West Falkland—and many smaller ones. The islands have few natural resources, an average temperature range of 35° in winter to 49° in summer, sparse vegetation, and only around two thousand inhabitants—although there are about five million penguins. Yet the Falklands have been a point of contention between Europe and Latin America.

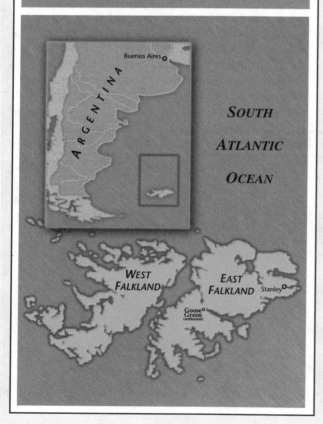

Falkland Islands

Buenos Aires

ARGENTINA

SOUTH

ATLANTIC

OCEAN

WEST FALKLAND

EAST FALKLAND   Stanley

Goose Green (settlement)

Beginning in the mid-1700s, Britain, France, and Spain all tried to settle the then-uninhabited Falklands. Each of these early settlements failed, but the British finally established a permanent colony there in 1833. The settlers all came from Britain and were fiercely loyal to their native country. The Falklands became a British colony, and the colonists devoted themselves to making a living on the islands. They concentrated on farming, especially the raising of sheep. (There are over three hundred sheep for every human being on the Falklands.) The small seaport of Stanley (population about one thousand) became the capital.

However, Argentina also claimed the Falklands, which it called the Islas Malvinas. The Argentines said that the early Spanish claims on the islands—which Argentina said it inherited—and the closeness of the Falklands to their nation made them part of Argentina. They demanded that Britain leave. Great Britain refused to surrender the Falklands, especially since the people of the Falklands wished to remain British.

Years of negotiation over the islands seemed to accomplish nothing, so in 1982 Argentina invaded the Falklands. The Argentine forces easily overwhelmed the small garrison of British marines and claimed the islands. Angrily, Great Britain sent a fleet of warships to retake the Falklands. The war lasted less than three months, but it drew worldwide attention.

Britain's armed forces proved superior to those of Argentina. British bombers destroyed the airstrip near Stanley so that the Argentines could not use it. A British submarine sank the cruiser *General Belgrano,* causing Argentina to pull back its warships for fear of losing even more. (Ironically, Argentina had bought the *General Belgrano* from the United States, where the ship had survived the Japanese attack on Pearl Harbor in 1941.) Argentina's air force then took on the burden of the fighting and did very well,

The Falklands War: The British warship HMS Fearless *patrols the Falklands coast with an Argentine Mirage III-E fighter just visible between its masts (above), and the HMS* Sheffield *burns after being struck by a missile fired by an Argentine aircraft (left).*

sinking some British ships and downing several enemy planes.

In the end the superior discipline of the British army won out. Landing on the west side of East Falkland, the British troops spread out rapidly and pushed back the inexperienced Argentines. In the battle for the town of Goose Green, for example, fewer than five hundred British paratroopers defeated and captured over fifteen hundred Argentine soldiers. Eventually the Argentines surrendered and left the island. The war did not settle the question, however, for Argentina still claimed the islands, and the British had to commit forces to the Falklands to protect them from further attack.

The Changing Face of Latin America

Costa Rica: Latin American Success Story

A Chinese curse says, "May you always live in interesting times." The reason that this bland statement is a curse is that wars, floods, and famines are what makes an era "interesting." By comparison, peace and prosperity seem dull.

Sometimes it is easy to focus on the "interesting" in Latin American history and miss the less dramatic success stories. The Central American republic of Costa Rica is rarely in newspaper headlines. Although located between the troubled nations of Nicaragua and Panama, the nation is never involved in wars. It does not even have an army. The story of Costa Rica is a quiet story of successful democracy.

A Moderate History

Costa Rica is Spanish for "rich coast." It was discovered in 1502 and named by Christopher Columbus, who thought it might be a land rich with gold. However, Costa Rica has no great mineral wealth. It does have rich soil and a moderate climate, though. Other Latin American nations suffered exploitation from outside the region. Some nations developed societies split by class conflict between rich and poor. But Costa Rica developed an agricultural economy made up of numerous small farmers. There was not great wealth, but what there was was spread evenly.

Costa Rica continued its unusual development after it separated from Spain in 1821. It was the first Latin American country to abolish

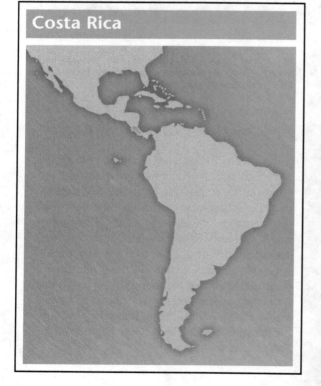

Costa Rica

The volcanic activity in Costa Rica is in sharp contrast to the relative peace of that nation's history.

Jose Maria Figueres Ferrer

slavery. In 1869 Costa Rica established a free public school system. (Its first president, in fact, was a schoolteacher.) In 1889 the little nation held what is considered to be the first free election in Latin America.

Conditions were not perfect, of course. In the 1930s, for example, the nation had a leader with pro-Nazi sympathies. Political corruption also troubled the land on occasion. A stolen election, in fact, sparked a remarkable revolution and reform that were uniquely Costa Rican.

In 1948 the government, after losing an election, tried to hold on to power illegally. A Costa Rican coffee planter, **Jose Maria Figueres Ferrer** (fee GAYR ays; fondly called "Don Pepe"), put together an army to challenge the corrupt government. Figueres's small army defeated the government forces, losing only sixty men to the two thousand of his opponents. But Figueres did not establish a dictatorship. After reorganizing the government, he peacefully handed over power to the winner of the 1948 election. Figueres said, "The health of democracy in Latin America demands that men who have seized power by force go home when normalcy is restored. We restored normalcy and went home." Grateful Costa Ricans later elected Figueres to full terms as president in 1953 and 1970.

Perched near a Costa Rican river, an egret surveys the scene.

The Changing Face of Latin America

Oscar Arias Sánchez

Safeguards for Democracy

The new government under Figueres enacted several reforms to protect Costa Rican democracy. As in Mexico, the president could no longer succeed himself. This reform made it impossible for a leader to entrench himself by holding on to power for a long time. To guarantee free and honest elections, the **Supreme Electoral Tribunal** became a separate branch of government, like the legislature and the courts. This independent body watches over the election process to guard against abuses. The tribunal even takes control of the police during elections to make sure that no other government department uses the police to influence the outcome of the election.

The most important reform of Figueres was to abolish the army. Since 1948 only a police force of over ten thousand men exists to maintain order. Costa Rica relies on international organizations such as the Organization of American States to protect itself against foreign threats. Twice, in 1948 and 1955, the OAS helped Costa Rica against invasions from Nicaragua. The absence of an army is certainly unusual and has even attracted settlers. The lack of an army, for example, drew a group of North American Quakers (who do not believe in fighting in wars) to Costa Rica. There they developed a profitable cheese-manufacturing business.

Costa Rica's heritage of democracy has enabled it to play a leading role in the affairs of Central America. In the 1980s, for example, the region was torn by conflicts in Nicaragua, El Salvador, and elsewhere. In 1987 Costa Rica's President **Oscar Arias Sánchez** put forth a plan to bring peace to the region. The Arias plan called for a cease-fire in all Central American conflicts between governments and rebels. It also demanded an end to the flow of military supplies from outside the region and free elections in all nations. Under the Arias plan, all the conflicting sides would sit down and discuss their differences.

Eventually, the Central American nations agreed to the proposals. Although peace did not suddenly come to the region, the Arias plan was a first step toward solving some of the area's problems. In recognition of his peace plan, Arias was awarded the Nobel Peace Prize for 1987. When asked whether the award had made a difference in his life, Arias replied, "Yes, people no longer introduce me as the president of Puerto Rico."

There are still problems in Costa Rica. Its economy, based on the export of coffee and bananas, is subject to ups and downs according to how well those products are selling around the world. Costa Rica has also sometimes found itself in the crossfire of the ugly drug trade that thrives in some parts of Latin America. Some drug smugglers have used the country as a secret supply point for the drug trade. But on the whole, Costa Rica endures as a model of how democracy can work in the region of Latin America.

Section Review

1. *Costa Rica* is the Spanish term for what?

2. What type of economy did Costa Rica have that was able to spread wealth more easily than in other Latin American countries?

3. What is Jose Maria Figueres Ferrer known for?

4. What organization has helped Costa Rica against Nicaraguan threats?

5. Name two problems that exist in Costa Rica.

Why has Costa Rica been able to establish a democratic government? What factors in its government enable it to stay democratic? What other groups of people might be expected to move to an army-free nation? Explain your answer.

Although a small land, Costa Rica is blessed with beautiful scenery.

CHARACTERIZATIONS

Heitor Villa-Lobos

Heitor Villa-Lobos (VEE-luh-LOH-bohs) was born in Rio de Janeiro in 1887; he died in Rio de Janeiro in 1959. Although his life began and ended in the same city, in between he traveled the world and built a reputation far beyond the city limits of Rio. He became not simply Brazil's greatest musician but one of the world's leading composers.

Heitor Villa-Lobos

Villa-Lobos had little formal musical training and was really self-taught. He mastered the cello (with lessons from his father, a librarian and amateur musician) and guitar. As a young man, Villa-Lobos listened to the popular musicians of Brazil and played along with them. He traveled to the Brazilian interior and even to Barbados to study native music. (He later spun a tale of how he was once captured by cannibals and persuaded them

to spare him because of his talents as a musician.) He began to write music based on what he heard.

In 1919 Villa-Lobos met the famed pianist Arthur Rubinstein, who was touring Brazil, and showed the pianist samples of his compositions. Deeply impressed by the young man's work, Rubinstein successfully urged the Brazilian government to support Villa-Lobos.

With this government help, Villa-Lobos was able to study in Paris from 1923 to 1930. The composer, however, claimed he was more interested in making Brazilian music known than in learning French styles. He told a French interviewer, "Did you think I came here to absorb your ideas? I came here to show you what I've done. If you don't like what I do, I'm going away."

He returned to Brazil in 1930, where the government made him Director of Music Education. Villa-Lobos promoted the teaching of music in Rio de Janeiro's public schools and established a conservatory for Brazilian musicians. In 1945 he founded the Brazilian Academy of Music. The composer also found time to tour the United States and become popular there through his concerts.

Villa-Lobos wrote perhaps two thousand works in his lifetime. (He would often leave the manuscripts of his works lying around the house, and souvenir hunters would carry them off.) Like other classical composers, he wrote symphonies, concertos, and string quartets. But he also wrote classical pieces based on Brazilian folk music. For example, as a young man he heard street musicians play a *choro,* a kind of dance music. Inspired by this music, Villa-Lobos wrote fourteen *Chôros* (1920-29).

There was always a strong Brazilian flavor to his music. Since drums were so dominant in Brazilian folk music, he used a lot of percussion in his compositions. Villa-Lobos incorporated the sound of the bird calls of the jungles in pieces such as *Cancão da Terra* ("Song of the Earth"). He even used some lyrics written in the native tongues of Indians of Brazil and used Indian myths as his themes.

Perhaps the best example of the composer's blending of styles was his *Bachianas brasileiras*. As the name suggests, these nine suites combined elements of the music of both Johann Sebastian Bach and Brazil. Villa-Lobos noticed some similarities between Bach's style and that of some Brazilian folk music. He then composed the *Bachianas brasileiras*, which are perhaps more inspired by Bach than an actual copy of Bach's music. Villa-Lobos even named the segments of the suites with both classical terminology (e.g., Aria, Toccata) and Brazilian terms (e.g., *Picapao,* after a woodpecker-like bird whose sound the music suggests). These suites are among his finest works.

The music of Heitor Villa-Lobos embodies the spirit of Brazil. The composer himself said, "I study the history, the country, the speech, the customs, the background of the people. I have always done this, and it is from these sources, spiritual as well as practical, that I have drawn my art."

Villa-Lobos was a prolific composer, writing numerous classical pieces of astonishing variety.

Christianity in Latin America

Ever since the colonization of Latin America by Spain and Portugal, Roman Catholicism has been Latin America's main religion. About four hundred million Latin Americans (over 80 percent of the population) are Catholics.

A Catholic church in Hermosillo, Mexico

Catholicism

The Catholic Church has long exercised great political and economic power in the region. Since the church often used that power on behalf of sometimes repressive governments, many Latin American reformers sought to curb the church's power. Beginning in the 1800s, many Latin American nations began taking away Catholicism's official government support. These reformers believed that only as Catholicism was limited could democracy flourish. During the debates over the Mexican Constitution of 1917, Francisco Múgica said,

> I am an enemy of the clergy because I consider it the most baleful and perverse enemy of our country. . . . What ideas can the clergy bring to the soul of the Mexican masses, or to the middle class, or to the wealthy? Only the most absurd ideas—tremendous hate for democratic institutions, the deepest hate for the principles of equity, equality and fraternity.

By the 1960s, however, some Catholic priests and theologians had become reformers themselves. But these Catholic reformers, known as **liberation theologians,** did not address the root of man's problems: sin. (See Matt. 12:35; Mark 7:21; James 4:1.) Instead, they borrowed concepts from Karl Marx. They saw the struggle between rich and poor as the root of society's problems, not as a symptom of human sinfulness. Some even preached liberation through violence.

The great majority of Catholics, though, follow traditional Catholic teaching. They heed the teaching of the church and obey their priests. When Pope John Paul II visited Latin America in the 1980s, crowds of traditionalist Catholics warmly greeted him.

Center Stage

Mission to the Aucas

"He is no fool who gives what he cannot keep to gain what he cannot lose." This was the testimony of Jim Elliot, a missionary who literally gave his life for Jesus Christ. In 1956 Elliot and four other men—Nate Saint, Roger Youderian, Ed McCully, and Pete Fleming—became twentieth-century martyrs for Christ.

These men believed that God wanted them to go to the mission field and to preach to a people who had never before heard the gospel, the **Auca Indians** of Ecuador. The Aucas were a fierce, primitive people. Every other contact between the Aucas and whites had ended in violence. In the 1800s the Aucas had clashed with rubber hunters in the Amazon. Only a little more than ten years before the missionaries arrived, the Aucas had killed eleven employees of Shell Oil who were working in Ecuador. When Elliot's wife mentioned the danger, he replied, "Well, if that's the way God wants it to be, I'm ready to die for the salvation of the Aucas."

The missionaries began planning their effort. They worked first among a group of friendly Indians to become familiar with the land and the work. They talked with one Auca woman who had fled the tribe. She helped them learn a little of the Auca language, but warned of the Aucas: "Never, never trust them. They may appear friendly and then they will turn around and kill."

In January 1956 the missionaries began their outreach by flying over an Auca village. As Nate Saint, the pilot, flew the plane over the village, they dropped presents to attract the Indians to the base. They called out in Auca, "I like you" and "I want to be your friend." They set up a base on a riverbank near the village. After a few days, three Aucas visited the missionaries. The missionaries talked to them in the Auca language and tried to

Three of the "Ecuadorian martyrs," missionaries who gave their lives in carrying the gospel to the Auca Indians: Ed McCully, Pete Fleming, and Jim Elliot

win their friendship. The Indians left after a few hours, but the next day Saint flew over the village and saw a group of Aucas moving toward the base. He radioed to his wife, "Pray for us. This is the day! Will contact you next at four-thirty."

The four-thirty call never came.

When no word came from the base by the next morning, the missionaries' wives notified the authorities. A group of missionaries and Ecuadorian soldiers journeyed through the jungles to the base. There they found that the Aucas had attacked and killed all five missionaries. The would-be rescuers buried the bodies near the landing strip that the five missionaries had used as their base.

Their deaths, however, did not end the story of the Auca mission. Inspired by the Ecuadorian martyrs, others dedicated themselves to missionary service to Ecuador and other nations. The widows of the martyrs continued to work among the Aucas. Even some of the Indians who had killed the missionaries came to Christ through this work. Out of the deaths of Jim Elliot, Nate Saint, Roger Youderian, Ed McCully, and Pete Fleming, God brought triumph.

A Protestant church service in Latin America

Protestantism

One surprising characteristic of religious life in Latin America has been the growth of Protestantism since World War II. Violence has sometimes greeted such growth. In the 1950s, for example, Catholic mobs in Colombia killed over a hundred Protestants and destroyed over fifty churches.

Although their numbers are not nearly as large as those of the Roman Catholics, Protestants have grown from only a tiny fraction of the population in the 1800s to perhaps a tenth today. Some ethnic minorities have been even quicker to embrace Protestantism. The Quichua (KEE-choo-ah) Indians in Ecuador and the Miskito Indians in Central America are examples of groups that turned to Protestantism in large numbers. Some experts estimate that by early in the twenty-first century a nation such as Guatemala may become the first predominantly Catholic country to become predominantly Protestant.

Most of these converts to Protestantism are known as **Pentecostals** or Charismatics.

These two groups actually overlap. The name Pentecostal derives from the biblical Day of Pentecost. On the Day of Pentecost the apostles "began to speak with other tongues, as the Spirit gave them utterance" (Acts 2:4). Pentecostals believe that when a Christian is baptized by the Holy Spirit, he will speak in tongues as a sign of the Holy Spirit's presence. Pentecostals also believe in the practice of other miraculous gifts such as healing the sick and exorcising demons.

The **Charismatics** are closely related to Pentecostals. In fact, many Pentecostals would claim to be Charismatics. The name *Charismatic* comes from the Greek word for "gift" *(charisma)* because Charismatics also claim to practice spiritual gifts such as tongues-speaking. One difference between Pentecostals and Charismatics is their denominational association. Pentecostals usually belong to groups that have the word "Pentecostal" in their name (such as the Pentecostal Missionary Church) or that describe themselves as Pentecostal in teaching (such as the Assemblies of God). Charismatics, on the other hand, can belong to nearly any denomination—Baptist, Presbyterian, Episcopalian. Even some Roman Catholics claim to be Charismatic.

The Pentecostals and Charismatics have grown in influence as their numbers have grown. Guatemala even had a dictator (1982-83), Mario Enrique Ríos Montt, who belonged to a leading Charismatic church in that country. Many Pentecostal and Charismatic leaders, however, warn their followers against becoming so involved in politics that they neglect spiritual concerns.

In evaluating any group, the Christian should not look just at outward signs—large numbers of followers or apparent miracles. A person or group that is truly Christian will also display "the fruit of the Spirit" (Gal. 5:22-23). This fruit, the apostle Paul says, includes "love, joy, peace, longsuffering, gentleness, goodness, faith, meekness, temperance." Where this fruit is present, a Christian has reason to believe that the Holy Spirit is truly present.

Section Review

1. What percentage of Latin Americans are Roman Catholic?
2. What problem do liberation theologians not address?
3. Compare and contrast Pentecostals and Charismatics.

Why might Protestantism be gaining ground in Latin America? What effects might Pentecostalism or Charismaticism have on formerly dominantly Roman Catholic nations? Would you support these groups based on what you know about them and Roman Catholicism?

Summary

Modern historian Edwin Williamson has noted of Latin America that "in the mid-1970s only Colombia, Venezuela and Costa Rica had elected governments." Yet, by the 1990s, he pointed out, only a handful of Latin American nations did *not* have elected governments. With all of the challenges the region has faced, democracy has grown. Sometimes that growth stopped short of full democracy (as in Mexico). Sometimes that growth has been through violence and unrest (as in Argentina). And sometimes that growth has been so quiet as to be almost unobserved (as in Costa Rica). We can only hope that the trend toward stable, honest, peaceful democracy at the close of the twentieth century will continue to be the trend of the future in Latin America.

CHAPTER REVIEW

People, Places, and Things to Know

Porfirio Díaz
Mexican Revolution
Victoriano Huerta
Emiliano Zapata
Venustiano Carranza
"Pancho" Villa
John Pershing

Institutional Revolu-
    tionary Party (PRI)
muralists
Diego Rivera
Brasília
Juan Perón
Eva Duarte Perón

descamisados
"dirty war"
Falkland Islands
Jose Maria Figueres
    Ferrer
Supreme Electoral
    Tribunal

Oscar Arias Sánchez
Heitor Villa-Lobos
liberation theologians
Auca Indians
Pentecostals
Charismatics

Review Questions

Completion

Argentina
Costa Rica

Brazil
Mexico

1. General Porfirio Diaz became dictator of _____ and reorganized government.

2. _____ set up the Supreme Electoral Tribunal to oversee elections.

3. Juan and Evita Perón were extremely popular leaders of _____ .

4. Brasilia is the capital of _____ .

5. A group of Quakers moved to _____ because it has no army.

6. The old capital of _____ was Rio de Janeiro.

7. John Pershing was sent to find Pancho Villa, a bandit in _____ .

8. _____ fought the British for control of the Falkland Islands.

9. Villa-Lobos was a famous composer from _____ .

Matching

(a) liberation theologians

(b) Pentecostals

(c) Charismatics

10. believe in speaking in tongues

11. generally Catholic

12. belong to many denominations

13. concentrate on the struggle between rich and poor

14. take their name from Acts 2:4

15. comes from a word meaning "gift"

Multiple Choice

Choose the letter of the answer that correctly finishes the statement.

16. When the United States gave support to another Mexican revolutionary, _____ crossed the border into New Mexico and murdered sixteen U.S. citizens.
    - (a) Victoriano Huerta
    - (b) Emiliano Zapata
    - (c) Venustiano Carranza
    - (d) "Pancho" Villa

17. Diego Rivera and José Clemente Orozco were _____ who represented the concerns of the common people.
    - (a) priests
    - (b) muralists
    - (c) politicians
    - (d) military leaders

18. The control of the Falkland Islands was at the center of an international fight between _____ and Great Britain.
    - (a) Argentina
    - (b) Mexico
    - (c) Brazil
    - (d) Chile

Think About It!

Based on our study of Latin America, what causes the government of a nation to succeed or to experience problems? Give examples in Latin America of both a successful government and a government that experienced problems.

"Proving what is acceptable unto the Lord." (Eph. 5:10)

We have traveled a long way this year in World Studies. We have toured distant lands, met unfamiliar people, and seen thousands of events. And now we are at the end. Or are we? In many ways the end of this book is only a beginning. Yes, history will continue until the decree of God ends it. But more than that, this is a beginning for you. You have studied many things this year, and now you must answer the question, "What will I do with what I have learned?"

By now you are very familiar with the three elements of world studies: geography, history, and culture. In studying *geography,* we have learned about the place that God provided for man to live in, the earth. We have seen that where one lives affects how he acts and thinks. For example, the ancient Chinese believed that they were at the center of the world because so many natural barriers surrounded them. Medieval towns were built near rivers for transportation. Because geography does affect people's ways of life, a knowledge of geography is important to help you understand people around the world.

The *history* we have studied has given us a framework in which to see the working of God in time. It has also given us many examples for living, both positive and negative. In many cases we have learned good and bad from the same people. In the life of Genghis Khan, we may admire his leadership abilities but must reject his brutality and wickedness. The key to judging between a good and a bad example in history is discernment learned from the truth of God's Word. The Lord promises that the Holy Spirit will guide the Christian into truth (John 16:13) so that he can discern good from evil in all he does.

However, while geography tells us where people lived and history tells us when people lived, the focus in World Studies has been on *how* people have lived, that is, their *culture*. We have divided culture into six elements: government, economics, thought and learning, arts and crafts, society, and religion. Each of these elements characterizes not only the lives of people living in the past or in different places, but also your own life.

At the beginning of this book, you were asked to look at your own culture, or way of life. As you have read this book, you have learned more about your culture by comparing it with other cultures. You have also had many opportunities to compare your way of life with what the Bible says about living. In these last few paragraphs, apply that information to these six areas in your own life. It is now up to you to decide what to do with the truth.

Government All your life you have had people in authority over you. Your parents, teachers, pastors, coaches—each of these people contributes to the governing of your life. They have a responsibility to make and enforce rules that will help you become a godly person. Your response to their rule will carry over to your eventual response to governmental authority. In reacting to any authority you should follow the guidelines set down in Scripture. "Let every soul be subject unto the higher powers. For there is no power but of God: the powers that be are ordained of God" (Rom. 13:1). However, the Christian's highest authority is God. Our obedience to Him and His Word comes before obedience to any person on earth. As Peter said in Acts 5:29, "We ought to obey God rather than men."

Economics Although you do not have a full-time job yet, you may have some work responsibilities—babysitting, delivering papers, or doing odd jobs. Each of us works for different reasons, but nearly everyone who works does so to support himself or his family. Even now you need to be developing principles to determine how you earn and spend money. In studying World Studies this year, you have met many industrious traders, merchants, manufacturers, and businessmen who were successful— at least in the world's eyes—because they gained great wealth. You have also learned about many pastors, missionaries, and other godly men and women who attained great spiritual success without much financial gain. A Christian should make sure that his first priority is spiritual wealth, not earthly wealth. "Lay not up for yourselves treasures upon earth, where moth and rust doth corrupt, and where thieves break through and steal: but lay up for yourselves treasures in heaven, where neither moth nor rust doth corrupt, and where thieves do not break through nor steal: for where your treasure is, there will your heart be also" (Matt. 6:19-21). All we have comes from God and should be returned to Him with grateful hearts and sincere service.

Thoughts and Learning Right now you are probably thinking more about your vacation and summer plans than about schoolwork. And yet, learning does not stop—not even in the summertime. God has given each of us a brain with the ability to think and to learn. With that gift comes the responsibility to use it to glorify Him. One way to do that is by using your mind wisely and diligently in learning all that you can about God's Word and then applying that knowledge to all other areas of learning. As God gave Daniel, Shadrach, Meshach, and Abednego "knowledge and skill in all learning and wisdom" (Dan. 1:17), He can give you the ability to master the subjects you will encounter. God desires for us to learn as much as we can so that we will be well equipped to reach others with the gospel.

Arts and Crafts You may or may not have any artistic talent. Perhaps you can play the piano, the flute, or the trombone. Perhaps you can paint or draw. These talents are special gifts from God. He desires for you to use them to honor and glorify Him. That means you must be diligent in developing them. It also means that you must follow scriptural principles in your use of them. For example, the music you play or the pictures you draw must not offend His holiness. We usually judge a work of art by its beauty; and, although individuals may have different opinions about what is beautiful, it is interesting to note the use of beauty in Scripture. Several times in the Old Testament we read the phrase "the beauty of holiness," which tells us that God often measures beauty in spiritual terms. If as Christians we desire to create or appreciate true beauty, then our standard must be God's Word, which reveals the nature of His holiness.

Society We all have families and friends. Beyond our families and friends we each have neighbors, live in communities, and are citizens of a nation. The relationships we have with others in these groups are the social part of our lives. God created us to enjoy fellowship, first with Him and then with others; the people we know or will someday know are a part of His plan for our lives. From your own experience you know that they influence you and that you influence them through your words and actions. Scripture has much to say about our social relationships and our testimony before others. Galatians 6:10 gives us clear guidance for a Christian's behavior toward others: "As we have therefore opportunity, let us do good unto all men, especially unto them who are of the household of faith." In doing good to others, we show God's love to them and influence them for the gospel. In the same way, if we do evil to others, we will turn them away from the gospel and the message of God's love. Sometimes a Christian's actions and attitudes are all that others will know of God's message. What a great responsibility we have to make every part of our relationships with others pleasing to God!

Religion The most important relationship you will ever have is your relationship with Jesus Christ. Your human relationships, your abilities, your knowledge—all will be worthless unless you have eternal life by accepting Christ as your Savior. Throughout this study of the world, we have talked about man's religions. The word *religion* comes from the same Latin root as the word *rely.* Whatever a person relies on for the safety of his eternal soul is his religion. Some people rely on idols made of stone or wood, and some rely on their ancestors. Others rely on evil spirits or rituals, while others trust in their own intellectual understanding. These "religions" are all false religions that cannot give their followers peace in this life or in the next. The only true religion is complete reliance on the Lord Jesus Christ for salvation through His blood.

If you do not know that you are relying on God for your salvation, examine your life to see whether you have confessed your sins to God and asked Christ to save you. God has promised us that "whosoever believeth in him should not perish, but have everlasting life" (John 3:16). This is the most important decision you will ever make and one that no one else can make for you.

If you are trusting in Christ for salvation, are you relying on Him each day for guidance and strength? The familiar verses Proverbs 3:5-6 tell us how we should live: "Trust in the Lord with all thine heart; and lean not unto thine own understanding. In all thy ways acknowledge him, and he shall direct thy paths." At this point of beginning, the rest of your life stretches before you: *What will you do with what you have learned?*

"Be ye doers of the word, and not hearers only." (James 1:22)

ARCTIC OCEAN

BEAUFORT SEA

Baffin Bay

GREENLAND

ICELAND

BERING SEA

Gulf of Alaska

Hudson Bay

LABRADOR SEA

S

IRE

CANADA

NORTH ATLANTIC OCEAN

NORTH PACIFIC OCEAN

U. S. A.

PORTU

MOR

CANARY ISLANDS

MEXICO

Gulf of Mexico

THE BAHAMAS

WESTERN
SAHARA

CUBA

MAURI

JAMAICA

DOM. REP.

BELIZE

HAITI

SENEGAL

HONDURAS

GAMBIA

GUATEMALA

CARIBBEAN SEA

GUINEA BISSAU

GUIN

EL SALVADOR

NICARAGUA

SIERRA LEONE

COSTA RICA

VENEZUELA

GUYANA

LIB

PANAMA

SURINAME

COLOMBIA

FRENCH GUIANA

ECUADOR

PERU

BRAZIL

BOLIVIA

SOUTH PACIFIC OCEAN

CHILE

PARAGUAY

ARGENTINA

URUGUAY

FALKLAND ISLANDS

SOUTH GEORGIA ISLAND

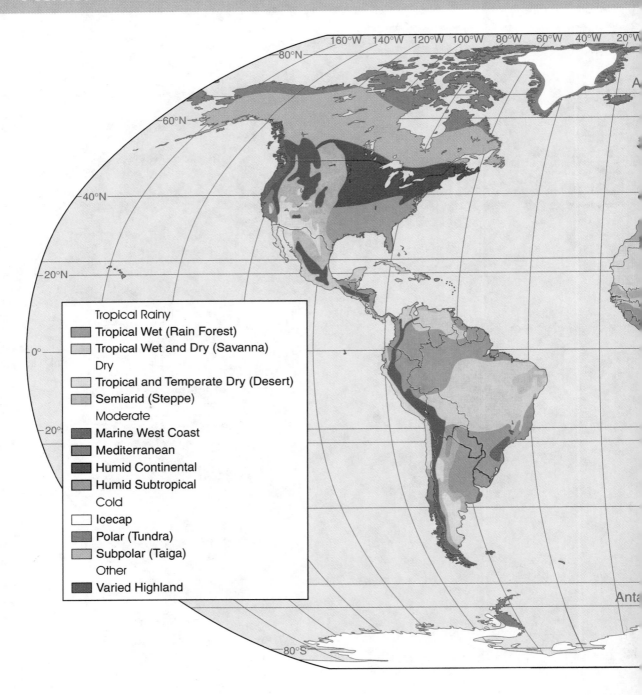

160°W 140°W 120°W 100°W 80°W 60°W 40°W 20°W

80°N

60°N

40°N

20°N

0°

20°

20°

80°S

A

Anta

Antarctica

Tropical Rainy
- Tropical Wet (Rain Forest)
- Tropical Wet and Dry (Savanna)

Dry
- Tropical and Temperate Dry (Desert)
- Semiarid (Steppe)

Moderate
- Marine West Coast
- Mediterranean
- Humid Continental
- Humid Subtropical

Cold
- Icecap
- Polar (Tundra)
- Subpolar (Taiga)

Other
- Varied Highland

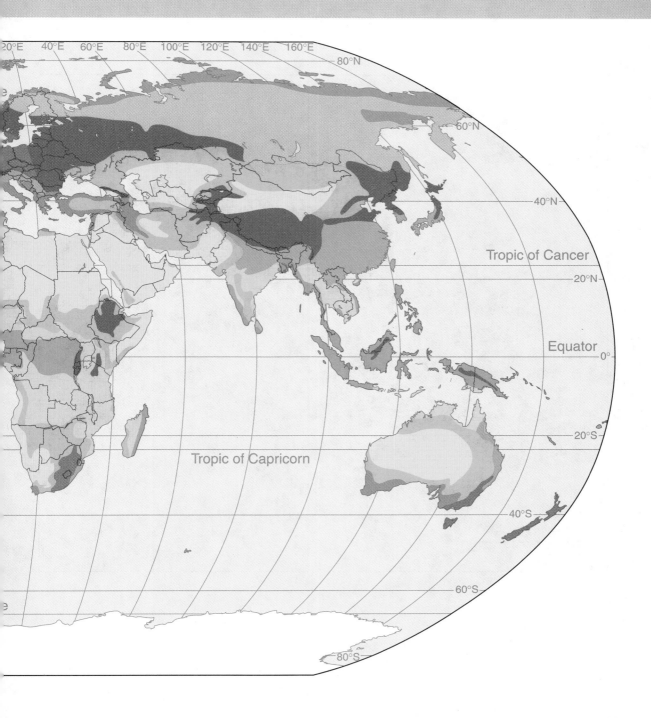

80°N

60°N

40°N

Tropic of Cancer

20°N

Equator 0°

20°S

Tropic of Capricorn

40°S

60°S

80°S

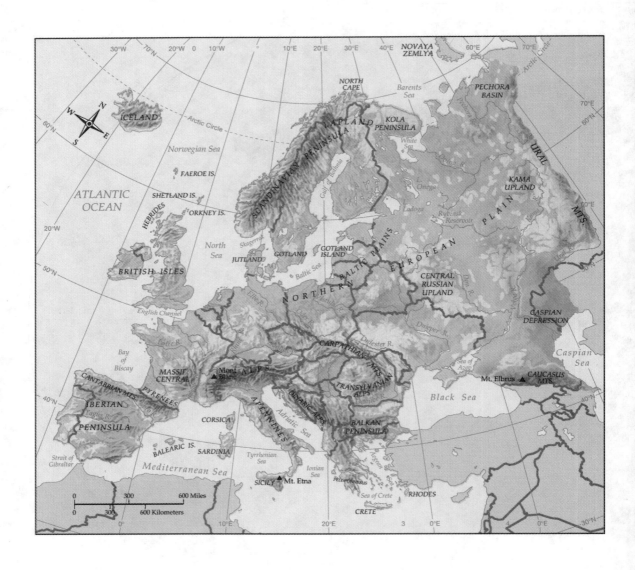

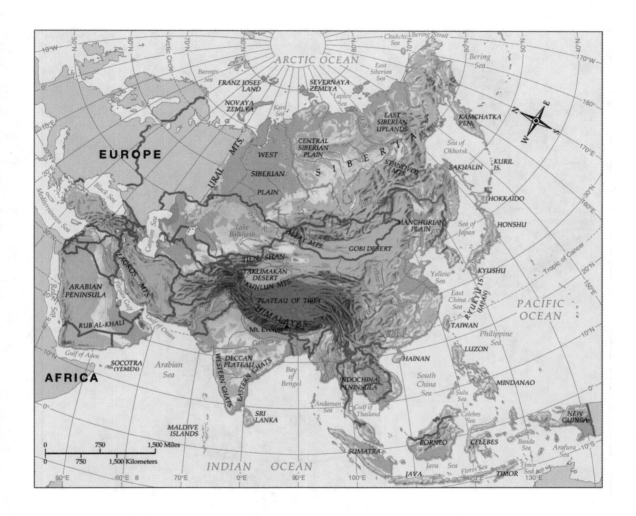

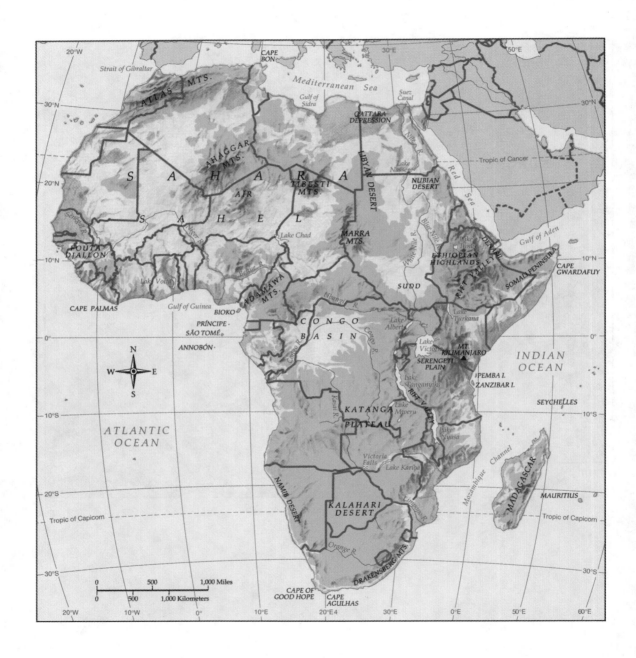

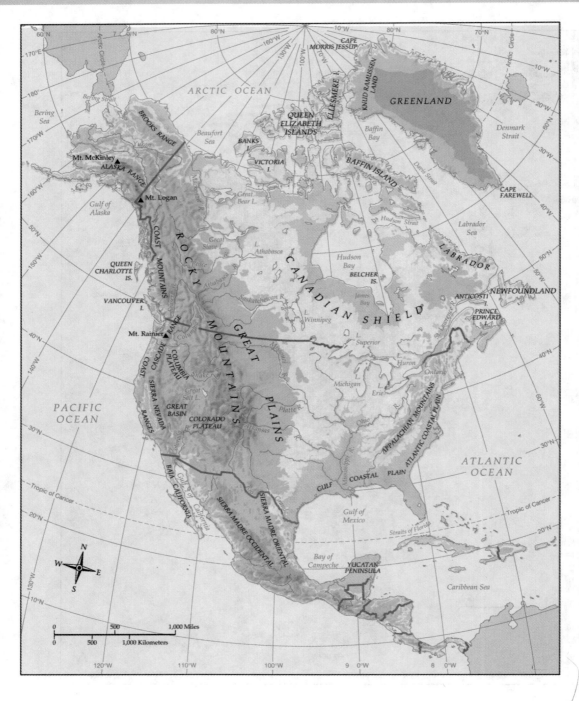

ARCTIC OCEAN

CAPE
MORRIS JESSUP

GREENLAND

Bering
Sea

Bering Strait

Beaufort
Sea

QUEEN
ELIZABETH
ISLANDS

ELLESMERE I.

KNUD RASMUSSEN
LAND

Baffin
Bay

Denmark
Strait

BROOKS RANGE

Yukon

BANKS
I.

VICTORIA
I.

BAFFIN ISLAND

Davis Strait

CAPE
FAREWELL

Mt. McKinley
ALASKA RANGE

Mt. Logan

Great
Bear L.

Hudson Strait

Labrador
Sea

Gulf of
Alaska

COAST

Great
Slave L.

Hudson
Bay

LABRADOR

MOUNTAINS

Peace

L.
Athabasca

QUEEN
CHARLOTTE
IS.

Athabasca

BELCHER
IS.

NEWFOUNDLAND

ANTICOSTI
I.

CANADIAN SHIELD

VANCOUVER
I.

Saskatchewan R.

James
Bay

PRINCE
EDWARD
I.

R O C K Y

M O U N T A I N S

L.
Winnipeg

St. Lawrence

L.
Superior

Mt. Rainier

Columbia

G R E A T

CASCADE RANGE

COLUMBIA
PLATEAU

L.
Huron

L.
Ontario

Snake R.

Michigan

COAST

SIERRA NEVADA

GREAT
SALT L.

Great
Salt L.

P L A I N S

Platte R.

L.
Erie

APPALACHIAN MOUNTAINS

PACIFIC
OCEAN

RANGES

GREAT
BASIN

COLORADO
PLATEAU

Ohio

Arkansas R.

ATLANTIC COASTAL PLAIN

Tropic of Cancer

BAJA CALIFORNIA

Gulf of
California

SIERRA MADRE ORIENTAL

SIERRA MADRE OCCIDENTAL

Grande

GULF

COASTAL

Mississippi R.

ATLANTIC
OCEAN

PLAIN

Gulf of
Mexico

Straits of Florida

Tropic of Cancer

N
W   E
S

Bay of
Campeche

YUCATAN
PENINSULA

Caribbean Sea

0   500   1,000 Miles

0   500   1,000 Kilometers

Index

A

Abraham, 532
absolutism, 225-26, 229, 238, 246
Afghanistan, 462, 468-69
Africa, 132, 135, 138, 144, 151
Age of Reason, 233, 236-37, 239, 241, 246
Akbar, 100
Aksum, 114
Alberta, 509
Alexander III, 448
Allenby, Edmund, 512
Allies, 419-20, 424-25, 429
Amundsen, Roald, 506
Anabaptists, 466
Anatolia, 514-15, 518
Anglican Church
    See Church of England
Anglican Church of Canada, 510
apprentice, 13
architecture, 67
    baroque, 67, 69
    Gothic, 17
    neoclassical, 236-37
    Romanesque, 17
Armageddon, 512
Armenia, 519
Ashkenazim, 532
Asia Minor, 514-15
Austria-Hungary, 418-20
Axis Powers, 431, 439
Aztecs, 146-49, 152

B

Bach, Johann Sebastian, 69, 410
Balfour Declaration, 525
Balkans, 418, 438, 443, 514
banks, 11
Banting, Frederick, 504
Baptist Missionary Society, 344
barter, 10
Battle of Midway Island, 484
Battle of Stalingrad, 456
Becket, Thomas à, 428
Beethoven, Ludwig van, 316
Belgian Congo, 398
Belgium, 304, 418-19
Bell, Alexander Graham, 308
Berlin Conference, 399
Best, Charles, 504
Bill of Rights, 229
Bismarck, Otto von, 398

Bitterman, Chet, 256
Black Death, 15
blitzkrieg, 431-32
Bolívar, Simón, 179-80, 182
Bonaparte, Napoleon, 302
Boniface, 252
Boxer Rebellion, 256, 351, 371, 373-74
Bradford, William, 204, 207
Brahms, Johannes, 316
Brezhnev, Leonid, 461, 468, 471
British Commonwealth of Nations, 215
British Empire, 327, 331, 333, 339, 345
British North America Act, 215, 504
Bulgaria, 418-19, 422
Burma, 255
Burton, Richard, 384-85

C

Caesar, Julius, 448
Calvin, John, 55, 71
Cambodia, 491
Campbell, Kim, 508
Canada, 186, 189, 200, 206, 208, 210-11, 215-17, 219, 504, 506-11
Canadian Charter of Rights, 508
Canterbury Tales, 28
capitalism, 310-11
Carey, William, 254-55, 341, 344
Cartier, Jacques, 198-99
Castro, Fidel, 460
cathedrals, 17
Central Kingdom, 352-53, 356
Central Powers, 419
Champlain, Samuel de, 199-200
Chaucer, Geoffrey, 28
Chiang Kai-shek, 477, 492, 497
China, 82, 86-87, 94-95, 97-98, 253, 256, 407, 474, 476-77, 479, 482-83, 486, 488-92, 497-501
China Inland Mission, 365
Chopin, Frédéric, 316
Christian and Missionary Alliance, 511
Church of England, 56
Churchill, Winston, 432, 434, 438
Clive, Robert, 324
Cold War, 458, 461
Columba, 252

Columbus, Christopher, 137, 139, 142, 146
Common Market, 438
Commonwealth of Independent States, 468
Communism, 311-12, 436, 438, 446, 448-50, 454, 457-60, 462-63, 465-66, 468-70, 478, 488-91
Congress of Vienna, 303
Conservative Judaism, 533
Constantinople, 515-16, 518
Constitution, 214
Copernicus, Nicolaus, 62
Coptic Church, 119
cordillera, 180, 360
Cortés, Hernando, 146-47, 152
Council of the Indies, 164
Council of Trent, 57
Crusades, 252
Cuba, 460
Cuban missile crisis, 460-61
Cubism, 427
Cummings, E. E., 427
Cyril, 252
Cyrus the Great, 521
Czechoslovakia, 429, 434, 436, 457, 461, 468

D

da Gama, Vasco, 138, 142, 322
Dali, Salvador, 413, 427
Dante Alighieri, 28
Darwin, Charles, 313-14
D-day, 432
de Avilés, Pedro Menéndez, 194
Debussy, Claude, 318, 412
Deism, 239
de Lesseps, Ferdinand, 401
Deng Xiaoping, 489
de Nobili, Robert, 253
de Soto, Hernando, 193-94
de Souza, Thomé, 163
de Vaca, Cabeza, 192-93
Dias, Bartolomeu, 138
Dickens, Charles, 316-17
Diet of Worms, 50, 69
Divine Comedy, The, 28
Dome of the Rock, 536
Dominicans
    See friars
Drake, Francis, 142-43
Druze, 535, 541

E

Eastern Orthodox Church, 252, 408, 440
East India Company, 255, 324-25, 340-41, 345
Egypt, 514, 526-27, 532, 538, 543
Eliot, John, 253
Eliot, T. S., 428
Elizabeth I, queen of England, 324
England, 188, 196, 200-201, 206, 210-11, 381, 385, 396, 401
Enlightenment, 238
Ethiopia, 110, 114, 119
Ethiopian Orthodox Church, 115
European Union, 438
excommunication, 50
expressionism, 427

F

fairs, 10
Fascists, 424-26, 429
Ferdinand, Francis, 419
Ferdinand, king of Spain, 139
Fitzgerald, F. Scott, 427
Five-Year Plans, 454, 456
flying buttresses, 18
France, 8, 186, 196, 198, 206, 210-13, 381, 398-99, 401, 418-19, 426, 429, 431-32, 436, 440
Franciscans
   See friars
Franco, Francisco, 429, 436-37
Franklin, John, 506
Frederick the Great, 229
French Revolution, 246
friars, 15
   Dominicans, 15
   Franciscans, 15
Frumentius, 114

G

Galileo Galilei, 62
Gandhi, Mohandas, 480, 499
Gaza Strip, 527, 529
Genghis Khan, 82-83, 85, 87, 94, 96-98
Germany, 46, 48-49, 52-54, 69, 304, 398-99, 449, 456-57, 483, 512, 515, 520
Ghana, 110, 112, 123
Goforth, Jonathan, 256, 371-72, 511
Goforth, Rosalind, 511
Gorbachev, Mikhail, 468-69, 471
Gordon, Charles, 367

Great Britain, 354, 418-19, 426, 429, 432-33, 436, 507-8, 510, 512, 525, 543
Great Depression, 424, 426
Great Exhibition, 294, 296, 307, 313
Great Leap Forward, 488
Great Schism
   See Papal Schism
Great Trek, 402
Greece, 304, 418, 422, 515, 519
Gregory XIII, 448
Gregory the Illuminator, 252
guilds, 12
Gutenberg, Johannes, 35

H

Handel, George Frederick, 69, 410
Harvey, William, 63-64
Hasidim, 533
Haydn, Franz Joseph, 236, 250, 410
Hemingway, Ernest, 427
Henry II, 428, 442
Henry, prince of Portugal, 132
heretics, 34
Herzl, Theodor, 525
Hirohito, 491
Hiroshima, 485
Hitler, Adolf, 425, 428-29, 431, 433-34, 436, 443, 456-57, 481, 483, 517-19
Holocaust, 433, 525
Hong Kong, 359, 362
Huguenots, 56
humanism, 25, 29, 43
humanities, 27
Hungary, 460-61, 468
Hung Hsiu-chuan, 366
Hussein, Saddam, 542

I

ibn-Saud, 523
imperialism, 397, 402
impressionism, 316, 318, 321
India, 253-56, 409, 474, 480-81, 496, 501
indulgences, 48
Industrial Revolution, 242-43, 411
Inquisition, 34
International African Association, 398
Iona, 252
Iran, 520, 522, 535, 538-39, 543
Ireland, 252, 442
Isabella, queen of Spain, 139

Islam, 252, 516, 521-24, 532, 534-35, 538-39, 543
Islamic Awakening, 524
Israel, 512, 525-28, 530, 532, 534, 538, 540, 543
Italy, 304, 418-19, 424, 431-32, 439, 443, 483

J

James I, 442
Jamestown, 201, 204
Japan, 145-46, 368-69, 409, 474, 478-79, 482-84, 486, 488, 491-92, 494, 496, 501
Jerusalem, 251, 512, 525, 527-28, 530-32, 536
Jesuits, 171, 253
Jordan, 526-27
journeyman, 13
Juan Carlos, 436-37
Judaism, 532
Judson, Adoniram, 255

K

Kemal Atatürk, 516, 520, 534, 539, 543
Kemal, Mustafa, 515, 519
Kennedy, John F., 434, 460
Kerensky, Aleksandr, 446, 449
Khomeini, Ayatollah Ruholla, 522, 535, 539, 543
Khrushchev, Nikita, 459, 461, 466-67, 469, 471
King, Martin Luther Jr., 480
King, W. L. Mackenzie, 507
Kipling, Rudyard, 339-40
Klondike gold rush, 505, 507
Knesset, 534
Knox, John, 55, 71
Korea, 482, 486, 489-90, 492, 500-501
Korean War, 490
Kuomintang, 477

L

Lalibela, 115, 119
Laos, 491
Las Casas, Bartolomé de, 171
Laurier, Wilfrid, 507
Law of the Return, 531
League of Nations, 439
Lebanon, 520, 526, 528, 535, 40-541
Lenin, Vladimir Ilich, 446, 448-50, 454, 459, 463, 468, 471
Leonardo da Vinci, 39